SUPREME BUT NOT INFALLIBLE

These essays, published to commemorate the fiftieth anniversary of
the Supreme Court of India, by leading Indian and foreign scholars,
eminent judges, senior advocates, and a distinguished journalist,
cover many different aspects of the Court's working since its
inauguration in 1950. The notable contributions examine a range of
issues that the Court has dealt with and present a wide-angle view
of its contribution to the development of contemporary law in
India.

The doctrine regarding the basic structure of the Indian
Constitution, its emergency provisions, the concept of the due
process of law, human rights and social justice, environment
protection, gender justice, preventive detention, freedom of the
press and media are among the subjects of the essays. The book
also presents fascinating glimpses into the early days of the court
and the personalities connected with it.

This volume will be useful not only for those connected with the
study and practice of law, but also for all citizens concerned about
the rule of law and constitutional liberties.

SUPREME BUT NOT INFALLIBLE

Essays in Honour of
the Supreme Court of India

edited by
B.N. KIRPAL
ASHOK H. DESAI
GOPAL SUBRAMANIUM
RAJEEV DHAVAN
RAJU RAMACHANDRAN

OXFORD
UNIVERSITY PRESS

OXFORD

UNIVERSITY PRESS

Oxford University Press is a department of the University of Oxford.
It furthers the University's objective of excellence in research, scholarship,
and education by publishing worldwide. Oxford is a registered trademark of
Oxford University Press in the UK and in certain other countries

Published in India by
Oxford University Press
22 Workspace, 2nd Floor, 1/22 Asaf Ali Road, New Delhi 110 002, India

First published 2000
Oxford India Paperbacks 2004
32nd impression 2025

ISBN-13: 978-0-19-567226-8
ISBN-10: 0-19-567226-7

Typeset in Garamond
by Sheel Arts, New Delhi
Printed in India by Repro India Pvt. Ltd.

Contents

Preface

Coinciding as they did with the beginning of a new century, the golden jubilee celebrations of the Supreme Court of India provided an opportunity for the Supreme Court to invite both a celebration and a critique of its work.

No one was better placed to participate in this celebration and critique than the lawyers and others who had been associated with the Court's work—including those who were present at the inaugural session on 28 January 1950 and continue to contribute towards the development of law.

These essays recall some of the events that have gone by, describe the development of public law in the hands of the Supreme Court, and remonstrate when the writers feel that the Court is wrong or has gone astray. Over this span of time, the Court has had 142 judges and witnessed a complex nation transform from 362 million in 1951 to a billion people in the year 2000. The Court has been privileged to witness this transformation and be associated with the many issues that have arisen from day to day. Many a time, the Court has changed its mind and adapted the law and Constitution to suit India's need. If its work has been appreciated, it has not always escaped criticism.

The essays in this volume are concerned with the work of the Court in areas relating to public law and the Constitution. Appreciative in their tone and, often, powerfully unsparing in their criticism, these essays, hopefully, constitute the beginning of a process to evaluate the on-going work of the Court in all areas of its many jurisdictions. It is through such efforts that the Court learns about itself.

The title of the volume 'Supreme but not Infallible'—is taken from an oft quoted self-reflection of an American judge: 'We are not final because we are infallible, we are infallible only because we are final.'[1] We would like to believe that the Supreme Court has gone about its task less conscious of its supremacy and more warily with the intuition that the Court, though final, is fallible. These essays are a reminder of what the Court is and does.

I thank the contributors, the members of the publication committee who have co-edited this volume and the publishers for bringing this anthology of essays together within so short a space of time.

B.N. Kirpal,
Judge, Supreme Court of India,
Chairman, Publication Committee.

---

[1] Justice Robert Jackson in *Brown v Allen* (1953) 344 US 443 at 540.

Notes on Contributors

Tehmtan R. Andhyarujina is a Senior Advocate of the Supreme Court of India, who specialises in constitutional and administrative law. A former Solicitor-General of India and Advocate-General of Maharashtra, he has appeared in several leading constitutional and other cases and is the author of *Judicial Activism and Constitutional Democracy in India* (1992).

Granville Austin is an independent historian and a leading authority on the Indian Constitution. He was formerly Fellow of St. Antony's College, Oxford, staff member of the US Senate and Founding Director of the Committee for Arab-Israeli Peace. His publications inlude *The Indian Constitution: Cornerstone of a Nation* (1996) and - *Working a Democratic Constitution: The Indian Experience* (1999).

Lord Cooke of Thorndon; K.B.E., was educated in Wellington and Cambridge. Called to the Bar in 1954 and designated a Queens Counsel in 1964, he has been judge of the Supreme Court of New Zealand, Judge of the Supreme Court of Fiji (1981-2), President of the Court of Appeal of Western Samoa (1982) and of the Cook Islands (1994), the Hong Kong Court of Appeal, and a member of the Judicial Committee of the Privy Council, a court of appeal in the House of Lords. A member of the International Commission of Jurists his writing includes the Hamlyn Lectures on *Turning Points in the Common Law* (1997).

J.B. Dadachanji is one of India's leading lawyers who has practised in the Supreme Court almost since its inception. As the head of one of the leading Solicitor Firms in the Country—J.B. Dadachanji and Co., he is known for his expertise in diverse fields of law, has appeared in innumerable courts and tribunals all over the country and is known for his deep interest in matters relating to law and justice.

Gobind Das is a Senior Advocate of the Supreme Court of India. He was Advocate-General of Orissa twice, once in 1980's and again in 1998. He is the author of *Justice in India* (1967) and *Supreme Court in Quest of Identity* (1987).

Ashok H. Desai isa Senior Advocate practising in the Supreme Court of India. Between 1996 and 1998, he was Attorney-General for India and in 1989–90 the Solicitor-General of India. He was educated in Pune, Bombay and London and called to the Bar in England. Among other positions he has held are: legal correspondent, *Times of India*; Professor, Law College, Bombay and Bombay College of Journalism. He has contributed to *The Constitutional Law of India*, to *International Libel Hand-book*, to *India Fast Forward* and to *Democracy, Human Rights and the Rule of Law*.

Rajeev Dhavan was called to the Bar in India and England, and is now a Senior Counsel practising in the Supreme Court of India. Educated at Allahabad, Cambridge and London Universities, he has taught at Queen's University (Belfast) and at the University of West London, with visiting and other assignments at the Universities of London, Austin, Madison and Delhi. An Honorary Professor of the Indian Law Institute, the Director of Public Interest Legal Support and Research Centre (PILSARC) and a member of the International Commission of Jurists, he is the author of many books and articles on constitutional law, policy and public affairs.

Anil B. Divan is a Senior Advocate of the Supreme Court of India and Vice-President of the Bar Association of India. He has argued a number of landmark cases, some of them as *amicus curiae*. A former President of the Law Association of the Asia and Pacific (LAWASIA), Mr Divan is associated with several international professional bodies.

Marc Galanter is John and Rylla Bosshard Professor of Law and South Asia Studies at the University of Wisconsin-Madison. A leading figure in the empirical study of the legal system, he has conducted extensive research on litigation, lawyers and courts in India and in the United States. He has served as editor of the Law and Society Review and President of the Law and Society Association. His major works on India are *Competing Equalities: Law and the Backward Classes* (1984) and *Law and Society in Modern India* (1989). During 2000, he will serve as Centennial Visiting Professor at the London School of Economics.

Indira Jaising is a Senior Advocate of the Supreme Court of India. She has been a fellow of the Institute of Advanced Legal Studies London and a visiting scholar at Columbia University. She is the Secretary of the Lawyers Collective, an organization of lawyers, and students which deals with socio-legal issues of public interest, and is the editor of a monthly magazine 'The Lawyer' which deals with issues connected with law and social justice.

Ram Jethmalani, formerly the Law Minister of India. Called to the Bar in 1941 and having practised in the Supreme Court of India and other courts, he has taught law in Bombay, Michigan and at the National Law School, Bangalore. A former President of the Bar Council of India, he has been elected to the Lok Sabha in 1977 and 1984; and for two successive terms in the Rajya Sabha in 1994 and the year 2000. He has written widely on law and public affairs.

Claire L'Heureux-Dube is a Judge of the Supreme Court of Canada. She received her LL.L from Laval University (1951) before being called to the Quebec Bar (1952). She practiced law in Quebec City, before being appointed to the bench in 1973. She is the President of the International Commission of Jurists and actively involved in projects on judicial education.

Michael D. Kirby is a Justice of the High Court of Australia. Previously, he served as President of the Court of Appeal of New South Wales and of the Solomon Islands, a Judge of the Federal Court of Australia, Deputy President of the Australian Conciliation and Arbitration Commission and Chairman of the Law Reform Commission. He serves on the Ethics Committee of the Human Genome Organization and the International Bioethics Committee of UNESCO. Other recent posts include President of the International Commission of Jurists and Special Representative of the UN Secretary-General for Human Rights in Cambodia. In 1998 he was named Laureate of the UNESCO Prize for Human Rights Education.

B.N. Kirpal, who is a Judge of the Supreme Court of India since 1995 was a Judge of the High Court of Delhi (1979–93), the Chief Justice of Gujarat (1993–95) and inquired into the air crash of the Air India plane, the 'Kanishka', off the coast of Ireland in 1985. His writings include papers and contributions to meetings and colloquia in India and abroad on taxation, intellectual property, the environment and various aspects of private and public law.

Inder Malhotra is a veteran journalist and author who also appears regularly on radio and television. During a career spanning half a century, he has been chief political commentator, later deputy editor, of *The Statesman*, the correspondent in India of *The Guardian* and editor of *The Times of India*, New Delhi. He is now a syndicated columnist. He is both a Nehru Fellow and a Woodrow Wilson Fellow. His publications include *Indira Gandhi: A Personal & Political Biography* (1989); and *India: Trapped in Unvertainty* (1991). He is working on a book on *Indian Security, Past, Present and Future*.

S. Murlidhar was enrolled as an Advocate in 1984 in Chennai and has been practising in the Supreme Court of India since 1987. Designated as *amicus curiae* by the Supreme Court in several public interest litigations, he has recently been nominated a member of the Supreme Court Legal Services Committee and writes widely on various legal and public matters including a well known *Annual Survey of Public Interest Law*.

Fali S. Nariman is a Senior Advocate, practising at the Supreme Court of India. The President of the Bar Association of India, he has held, or continues to hold, positions in various organizations including: the International Council for Commercial Arbitration, the International Court of Arbitration, International Commission of Jurists, and the Law Association for Asia and the Pacific (LAWASIA). A former Additional Solicitor-General of India, he was honoured by the country's President with a Padma Bhushan for distinguished service in the field of jurisprudence. In November 1999, he was nominated to the Rajya Sabha, the Upper House of the Indian Parliament.

Ranjit S. Narula is a Senior Advocate who practised before the Federal Court of India from 1943–50; and, thereafter, in the Supreme Court from 1950. He has been a Judge and, later, Chief Justice of the Punjab High Court. A human rights activist, and the author of several books, articles and papers, he has taught at several universities and colleges and was conferred the distinction of being a 'Living Legend of the Law' by the International Bar Association.

Raju Ramachandran is a Senior Advocate of the Supreme Court of India, who specialises in public law, has appeared in several landmark cases before the Supreme Court of India, is a member of the General Council of the National Law India University, Bhopal and the Governing Body of the Consumer Education and Research Centre, Ahmedabad and has written frequently in India's leading newspapers.

M. Jagannadha Rao is Judge of the Supreme Court of India. He practised as a lawyer in the Andhra Pradesh High Court from 1960. He has been a Judge of the Andhra Pradesh High Court (1982–1991), Chief Justice of the High Court of Kerala (1991–1994) and Chief Justice of the High Court of Delhi (1994–1997) before being appointed as Judge of the Supreme Court of India in 1997.

P.P. Rao is a Senior Advocate of the Supreme Court of India whose areas of interest are constitutional law and administrative law. He has appeared in several leading cases involving the interpretation of the Indian Constitution on behalf of state governments. Co-author of 'Emergency and Law' and the chapter on 'Union Judiciary' in the authoritative 'Constitutional Law of India' published by the Bar Council of India Trust he writes widely on law and justice. Before joining the Bar, he was a law teacher in the University of Delhi.

Harish N. Salve is a Senior Advocate of the Supreme Court. He is currently the Solicitor-General of India. He has appeared in several leading constitutional cases in the Supreme Court and was privileged to be appointed *amicus curiae* to the Supreme Court in several matters relating to the environment.

B. Sen was called to the Bar in 1946, practised before the Privy Council and Federal Court and now in the Supreme Court of India. Designated a Senior Advocate in 1956; he served as Legal Adviser to the Ministry of External Affairs 1956 to 1966 and later as Secretary-General of an inter-governmental organization from 1980 to 1987. He is a Visiting Fellow at the University of Cambridge Research Centre for International Law and a Member of the Council of UNIDROIT. His publications include *A Diplomats Handbook on International Law and Practice.* He was decorated with the Order of the Rising Sun, Gold and Silver Star.

Atul M. Setalvad is a Senior Advocate, practising principally in the Bombay High Court since 1958. He specialises in constitutional and administrative law as also the law of indirect taxes and company law. He has written extensively and has edited, jointly with his father M.C. Setalvad, Mulla's *Transfer of Property Act, 1882.* He also extensively appears in public interest litigation in the fields of human rights and the environment.

Soli Sorabjee is a Senior Advocate of the Supreme Court of India and Attorney-General for India, who has appeared in many landmark constitutional cases since the 1960s. An ardent champion of human rights, Mr Sorabjee was, until 1999, the United Nations' Special Rapporteur on Nigeria, and is currently a member of that organization's Sub-Commission for the Prevention of Discrimination and the Protection of Minorities. He has served on the boards of several international non-governmental organizations, including Article XIX, Interights, the Commonwealth Human Rights Initiative, and the Commonwealth Lawyers' Association. A prolific writer, Mr Sorabjee contributes frequently to leading Indian newspapers, and is the author of *The Law of Press Censorship in India* (1976).

Gopal Subramanium is a Senior Advocate of the Supreme Court, was educated in the Delhi University, called to the bar in 1980 and designated a Senior Advocate in 1993. He has appeared in a large number of courts and tribunals throughout India on diverse areas of law and has been invited by the Supreme Court as *amicus curiae* in various matters of national importance. Counsel to the Verma Commission (1991), which dealt with the security lapses relating to the assassination of Prime Minister Rajiv Gandhi and the Wadhwa Commission (1999), which inquired into the murder of the Australian missionary Reverend Staines, he takes a sustained interest in matters relating to law, justice and the Constitution.

Lord Templeman was educated at Cambridge University, served in the Indian army (1941–6), called to Bar in 1947, designated a Queens Counsel in 1964, Attorney-General of the Duchy of Lancaster, a Judge of the Chancery Division of the High Court (1972–1978), and a Member of Court of Appeal (1978–82) before he became a Lord of Appeal in Ordinary in the House of Lords (1982–1994). He has served as a member of various commissions and tribunals, has been the President of the Senate of the Inns of Court and is an Honorary Member of the American and Canadian Bar Associations.

One

The Supreme Court and the Struggle for Custody of the Constitution

Granville Austin

Difficulty and controversy in the interpretation of any great document are as inevitable as the changing seasons.[1] The institution entrusted with interpreting a constitution has that constitution in its custody. The institution, the judiciary or parliament, is in a position to protect, damage, or destroy it. Within months of the Indian Constitution's inauguration, a struggle over custody began between the judiciary, headed by the Supreme Court, and Parliament led by Jawaharlal Nehru. These first struggles over interpretation especially concerned pursuit of the social revolution as embodied in the Directive Principles of State Policy, in the Fundamental Rights, and in the provisions for special consideration for minorities and the disadvantaged members of society. Social revolutionary goals, and within them property relations, would continue to be the genuine or spurious justification for the most significant amendments to the Constitution. The response–counter-response pattern that developed between the Court and Parliament when Nehru was Prime Minister, which may be described as shared custody, would change greatly under his daughter. Her counter-response, as leader of Parliament, consisted entirely of attacks on the judiciary: either to deny it judicial custody of the Constitution or to subvert its independence.

As Nehru and his government began working the new Constitution, it became clear to them that reconciling judicial independence and Parliament's custody of the Constitution, when legislating for social revolution, would not be easy. How were both ends to be served? As Chief Justice of India Harilal Kania said at the Supreme Court's inauguration, the Court must be 'quite untouchable by the legislature or the executive authority in the performance of its duties.'[2] Beyond this, judges should be, and be perceived to be, unmoved by the 'extraneous considerations' feared likely to influence them. Credibility of intention would be vital to whoever had custody of the Constitution, whether whole or partial. For the Court this would demand that its members be able jurists, that its processes be effective, and its decisions rational and clear. The Court's authority would have to flow principally from the respect its performance would gain.

The first tests over custody, although important for the social revolution (having to do with personal liberty, assisting backward sections of society, zamindari abolition, and taking over private property), were more important for the constitutional philosophies they revealed. In response to citizens' petitions, several high courts and the Supreme Court read Article 31 and interpreted the word 'compensation' there in the classical manner to mean a fair equivalent value for the property taken. They read Article 19(1)(a) and (g) as protecting free expression and the right to carry on a trade or business. When the government intruded on these (and sometimes defended its action with flawed data), the courts objected. The Supreme Court also read Articles 14 and 15, found them in conflict, and ruled the Madras General Order unconstitutional because it denied equality under the law.

When, to remedy these situations, the government brought the First Amendment to Parliament, Nehru defended both an independent judiciary and limiting its custody of the Constitution in favour of Parliament. The judiciary has no role where great schemes and big social changes are involved, he told the Lok Sabha. We should see if the Constitution was rightly framed and whether 'it is desirable to change it ... to give effect to what really was intended *or should be intended*' (emphasis added).[3] Expanding this argument at a later date, Nehru said that the Supreme Court's interpretations of the Constitution were to be respected, but even a powerful and independent judiciary should 'not decide about high political, social or economic or other questions. It is for Parliament to decide the laws we have.'[4]

Far more radically, the First Amendment contained the Ninth Schedule which apparently developed from a letter to Law Secretary K.V.K. Sundaram from K.T. Chari, the advocate general of Madras. Chari proposed that land tenure laws that were to be exempted from judicial reach be included in a separate schedule to the Constitution.[5] With the schedule, Nehru, the genuine democrat and firm supporter of judicial independence, had created a hierarchy of laws. Those included in the schedule were beyond, indeed above, the Constitution because not subject to judicial review to determine whether or not they were constitutional. In the new hierarchy, the Constitution came next, followed by ordinary legislation. Moreover, Nehru's government was the first to place laws other than land laws in the schedule, contrary to the popular view that his daughter's government was the first to do this. (The Fourth Amendment added The Railway Companies Act and portions of two others.)

To jump ahead of our narrative, it was not until 1964 and the Seventeenth Amendment that the schedule's abuse drew wide attention. Then, the government proposed to place 124 state land laws in the schedule. A joint parliamentary committee deleted 88 of these—after widespread criticism of the amending bill and the confession of law ministry officials that they had not read many of the laws proposed for inclusion. An even darker side of the schedule was revealed by one of its supporters, G.S. Pathak. He justified putting laws there 'because there may be some provisions which are of doubtful validity or which may be open to attack. We want to immunize all these acts.'[6]

Justice Mehr Chand Mahajan thought the Ninth Schedule a 'lamentable departure' from Nehru's usual trust in the judiciary, and he was not the only critic at the time.[7] President Rajendra Prasad thought elements of the amendment unconstitutional, and he doubted that its speedy enactment was desirable. He cautioned Nehru in this vein, and gave his assent to the bill only after being informed that he was constitutionally bound to do so. No thought was given to the schedule's potential for abuse, senior civil servants and elected officials of the time have told the author.

We may interject here that the Constitution, itself, had bestowed on Parliament custody of the Constitution concerning a broad area of personal liberty. Article 22 authorized Parliament to legislate preventive detentions for periods of unspecified length without involvement of any other body (Clause 7) and permitted the detaining authority to withhold details of the case—even from the courts—whose disclosure would not be in the public interest (Clause 6).

When Chief Justice Patanjali Sastri in the Shankari Prasad case upheld the First Amendment as constitutional, notably *without* excluding judicial review of amendments, it seemed that the Court had ceded to Parliament a significant degree of custody over the Constitution. But not necessarily. In the Kameshwar Singh case the Patna High Court declared a law unconstitutional despite its having been placed in the Ninth Schedule, and the government lost in several major property cases, among them Bela Banerjee and Sholapur Mills. Shaken, fearing that Parliament's custody was not secure and that the Constitution did not meet the nation's social revolutionary needs, the Congress Working Committee in 1954 established a subcommittee to reassess the Constitution. At the time, Nehru told the chief ministers that party members think 'we are not moving fast enough and are too cautious and conservative'.[8]

In its report, the subcommittee bitterly attacked the judiciary's continuing custody of the Fundamental Rights and recommended that the courts' powers to issue directions and prerogative writs for the enforcement of the Rights should be restricted to failures of justice and that the high courts should lose their authority to issue the writs 'for any other purpose' as provided for in Article 226. In the Cabinet, Nehru successfully fought against the worst anti-judiciary sentiment, by saying that a socialist programme could be pursued without 'striking at the judiciary's roots'. Nevertheless, as we know, the Fourth Amendment diminished the Supreme Court's custody over the Fundamental Rights by providing that a variety of government actions concerning property could not be challenged on the ground that they abridged the rights in Aritcles 14, 19, and 31. The presence of the right to property in the Rights would progressively attract broader attacks on the Rights as a whole.

The Golak Nath decision, and Chief Justice K. Subba Rao's political 'argument of fear' in support of it, escalated the struggle for custody into a decade-long battle. Within five weeks came the initial counter escalation. Samyukta Socialist Party member of Parliament Nath Pai introduced his private member's bill to assure 'the supremacy of Parliament' in amending the Constitution. To its supporters this merely restored the framers' intentions for Article 368. Its most ardent opponents were Rammanohar Lohia and Madhu Limaye, Nath Pai's fellow party members. Lohia, who had received his doctorate in Berlin in 1933, damned the measure, likening it to the 'Enabling Law' that Hitler used as the legal basis for his dictatorship.[9] Picking up the concept employed by Golak Nath's lawyers, Limaye said Parliament had no right 'to change the basic principles of the country' and it 'cannot snatch away the rights of the common people'. Both Lohia and Limaye advocated taking 'property' out of the Fundamental Rights as a means of protecting the other rights from damage. The bill died in the Lok Sabha two years later because Mrs Indira Gandhi's government lacked the votes to pass it.

But with the 350 parliamentary seats she had won in the 1971 elections and stung by Court decisions, particularly in the Bank Nationalization and Privy Purses cases, Mrs Gandhi set about acting on the Congress election manifesto's promise to enact 'such amendments of the Constitution as may be necessary' to establish a just social order.[10] Discussions in the Cabinet all boiled down to parliamentary custodianship in some form: Parliament should have absolute supremacy along the lines advocated by Nath Pai; the courts should be excluded from subjects like property and compensation; the Directive Principles should be given precedence over the Rights.

With the Young Turks and the members of the Congress Forum for Socialist Action vociferously calling for strong socialist measures, events took an ominous turn. Gaining 'custody' of the Constitution for many in Parliament indicated an unwary willingness to erode the Constitution the better to pursue social revolution. In others, it revealed a preference for authoritarianism. The Tweny-fourth Amendment gave Parliament full constituent power over the Constitution for 'addition, variation or repeal'. The Twenty-fifth Amendment denied the courts jurisdiction over government acquisition and requisition of property and compensation for it, and gave the two most classically socialist provisions in the Directive Principles—Article 39, Clauses (b) and (c)—precedence over the fundamental right to equality before and equal protection of the law (Article 14), the 'freedoms' of Article 19, and Article 31 dealing with property. Furthermore, this amendment contained in Article 31-C what the author has termed the 'escape clause', which provided that a law declared as giving effect to this policy could not be questioned in court because it did not further the policy.

The Prime Minister told the Lok Sabha that the government did not wish to weaken the judiciary, but 'there is no decision in the world that is not political'.[11] Law Minister Gokhale asserted that the worst danger would be to enable judges 'to infuse their own political philosophy in their judgements ...'[12] Mohan Kumaramangalam's explanation of the Twenty-fifth Amendment was the most telling: 'The clear object of this amendment is to subordinate the rights of individuals to the urgent needs of society.'[13] The bad joke in all this was that the failure to implement social revolutionary measures came far less from court decisions than from the Congress central and state governments' lack of enthusiasm for reform.

The Law Commission, led by former Chief Justice P.B. Gajendragadkar, a consistent believer in Parliament's unrestricted power of constitutional amendment, and with the support of members V.R. Krishna Iyer and P.K. Tripathi, issued a special report recommending that the 'escape clause' in Article 31-C be eliminated. The commission saw 'no justification for excluding judicial enquiry ... as to whether there is any rational nexus ... between the law passed ... and the objective to be achieved'.[14] Gajendragadkar had such 'serious misgivings' about the provision that he expressed them to the Prime Minister personally and in a letter.[15] As with the Ninth Schedule, few at the time foresaw the dangers lurking in the amendments. Recalled Mohan Dharia, 'The members had no intentions against freedom, liberty and the democratic structure'.[16] The magic mantra of socialism had mesmerized the Lok Sabha, recalled Vasant Sathe. 'Anything socialist was great; we thought property and capitalism absolutely bad.'[17]

Among those who did foresee the amendments' dangers was Nani Palkhivala. When J.B. Dadachanji told him about a petition he had received from a Kerala advocate on behalf of one Swami Kesavananda Bharati (an individual neither had met nor ever would meet) concerning the property of a mutt in the state, Palkhivala seized upon it as a vehicle for challenging the two amendments.[18] In the well-known Kesavananda Bharati decision, the thirteen judges performed an act of judicial statesmanship. They upheld the constitutionality of the amendments, while striking down the language that Gajendragadkar had opposed, but strengthened the Court's power of judicial review by enunciating the basic structure doctrine—thereby reasserting the Court's custody of the Constitution. As Upendra Baxi wrote at the time, the judgement 'is, in some sense, the Indian Constitution of the future'.[19]

Yet, the Court's manner of reaching that decision did nothing to bolster the knowledgeable public's confidence in its ability to fulfil its custodial function responsibly. There were bickerings among the judges on the bench and recriminations among them about unprofessional conduct. There were allegations of susceptibility to the direct and indirect pressures government was exerting to gain a ruling in its favour, according to judges on the bench and senior advocates involved. 'Excitement and unusual happenings' marked the case, Justice Y.V. Chandrachud recalled. Justice Jagan Mohan Reddy referred in his opinion to 'the threat of dire consequences which the Court would have to face if the judgement went against the government'.[20] In addition, the opinions on the various points of law from eleven of the thirteen judges provoked controversy about what truly had been decided—despite, or perhaps because of, the opinions' great length.

The government then attempted to subvert the Court's custody with a 'grievous blow to the independence of the judiciary', as Justice H.R. Khanna put it.[21] Mrs Gandhi's supersession of three senior judges to appoint A.N. Ray as Chief Justice of India is often attributed to the government's 'pique' at the Kesavananda decision. This may be accurate in part, for the government apparently knew of the bench's inclination weeks before its decision. There is however persuasive evidence that supersession had been brewing for months. For example, Mohan Kumaramangalam had spoken to R.C. Dutt in 1972 of a supersession and placing on the Court judges committed to 'basic principles'.[22] To such sentiment, the Prime Minister added her own purpose. She 'was bent on getting rid of [Justice K.S.] Hedge [for his prior involvement in her election case]. She was the moving force behind it', according to her secretary, N.K. Seshan.[23] Justice Gajendragadkar opposed this tampering with the Court's independence as 'constitutionally unsound and politically unwise'.[24]

The Supreme Court Bar Association condemned the supersession, and an All-India Convention of Lawyers on Independence of the Judiciary, returning to a theme in the Law Commission's Fourteenth Report, resolved that, to protect the Supreme Court's independence, its justices be appointed by a committee of its five senior judges and two members of the bar. Jayaprakash Narayan warned the Prime Minister that leaving the appointment of chief justices in the hands of prime ministers meant that 'the highest judicial institution of this country cannot but become a creature of the government of the day'.[25] Mrs Gandhi replied that there had been no question of the executive subordinating the judiciary.

The emergency proclaimed in June 1975 represented not an aberration but a culmination of trends regarding the judiciary and in the nation's politics more broadly, particularly those since the late sixties. The Prime Minister's intentions, in S.L. Shakdher's view, were that her personal political position not be detrimentally affected, that Parliament be unable to overturn her decisions, and that the executive be able to function without judicial interference.[26] She and her tame Parliament were to have unrestrained custody of the Constitution, and the judiciary was to be enfeebled.

The evidence was plain to see. The spurious justifications of the Emergency as necessary to save democracy from chaos and to pursue the social revolution effectively, were followed in July by the Thirty-eighth and Thirty-ninth Amendments. The former retroactively barred judicial review of presidential and gubernatorial ordinances, proclamations of emergency and of President's Rule, and it allowed laws contravening the Fundamental Rights to be made during emergencies. The latter amendment placed in Parliament's hands adjudication of election disputes involving the President, the Vice President, the Prime Minister, and the Speaker of the Lok Sabha. It provided that a petition against the election of a person later appointed prime minister should 'abate'. Also, in a masterpiece of dense wording, the amendment made not illegal the offences with which Mrs Gandhi had been charged in Raj Narain's 1971 election petition. The amendment also placed in the Ninth Schedule changes made earlier in the Representation of the People Act and other election laws enacted to assure Mrs Gandhi's tenure in office.

With Mrs Gandhi's tenure secure, the government could turn to taking custody of the Constitution. It first sought to overturn the basic structure doctrine by having the Court review the Kesavananda Bharati decision. When this attempt failed with the disintegration of the Kesavananda Review Bench, the Constitution and the Court had survived their most critical moment since the original Kesavananda ruling. Mrs Gandhi was however determined to take control of the Constitution from the Court. This cloud over 'the supremacy of Parliament acting in its constituent capacity' should be removed, said a Congress Party resolution. Subsequently a mixed Congress government committee headed by Sardar Swaran Singh recommended that amendments to the Constitution be placed beyond judicial review.[27] Parliament was also, in effect, to take custody of the Fundamental Rights, for the Swaran Singh Committee also recommended that all the Directive Principles take precedence over all the Rights.[28] In the Supreme Court the constitutionality of laws was to be decided by benches of seven and by two-thirds majorities. Justice Gajendragadkar thought the Swaran Singh Committee's endeavours shallow. He wrote to the Prime Minister agreeing that amendments to expedite the 'socio-economic revolution' were necessary, but urged her to appoint a high-powered committee to deliberate carefully.[29]

These proposals did not go far enough for Mrs Gandhi and several of those around her. Several months before the Singh Committee published its first report a small group began secretly to draft what would become the Forty-second Amendment. Bhupesh Gupta sensed this, and at the amending bill's introduction in the Rajya Sabha he commented that officials in the Secretariat and others had tampered with the report 'to smuggle in things ... absolutely unnecessary ... from the point of view of socio-economic changes'.[30]

In essence, these 'things' were to enable the Prime Minister and her tame Parliament to reign supreme. Accepting most of the Swaran Singh report's proposals (as above), the amendment went beyond them. It retroactively barred judicial review of amendments. It removed from the judiciary and bestowed on tribunals, which the amendment established, jurisdiction over land revenue and other sensitive matters. It abolished the constitutional requirement that a legislature's quorum must be one-tenth of its members. Therefore, as was pointed out, a single member of Parliament in an otherwise empty house could legislate for the nation. Also, laws against 'anti-national' activities could not be challenged under Article 19, and high courts were prohibited from issuing stay orders relating to 'any work or project of public utility'. These are only some of the provisions that turned the Constitution on its head.

Meanwhile, having already detained thousands of persons, the government placed civil liberty even further beyond the courts' reach with its increasingly harsh preventive detention measures. Mrs Gandhi transferred several high court judges (out of a total of sixteen transferees) who had upheld detenus' habeas corpus petitions even while the Supreme Court was deliberating in the Habeas Corpus case. At the Court, 'apprehensions were real and tangible', according to Upendra Baxi. Had the Court acted in certain ways, it 'might have imperilled the Court's existence', Baxi wrote.[31] Jayaprakash Narayan's reaction to the Court's Habeas Corpus decision was that 'Mrs Gandhi's dictatorship both in its personalized and institutionalized forms is now almost complete'.[32] Dr Lohia's ghost must have been murmuring, 'I warned you'.

Fortunately for constitutional government, Indira Gandhi had the President call elections. When Janata had won them, Acting President B.D. Jatti announced the new government's policy: to enact a 'comprehensive measure ... to amend the Constitution to restore the balance between the people and Parliament, Parliament and the Judiciary, the Judiciary and the Executive, the states and the Centre, the citizen and the government'.[33] In considerable measure, Morarji Desai, Shanti Bhushan, his Law Minister, and others in government kept its promises. The government and Parliament not only restored much of the judiciary's lost authority and repaired most of the damage to the Constitution done by the Emergency amendments, it added further safeguards against abuses—for example to the Emergency Provisions.

However, considerably due to a miscalculation by Bhushan, the Janata party failed to return to the Court that vital dimension of constitutional custody, judicial review of amendments. The story began with Law Minister Shanti Bhushan's view that defining the Constitution's basic structure should not be left entirely to the Supreme Court. Arguing to the Lok Sabha that government should not operate 'behind their [the people's] backs', he also thought that the Court, 'under the guise of protecting the basic structure, could prevent a much needed amendment'.[34] The remedy, he suggested, would be to add a referendum to the pre-Emergency version of Article 368. This would be invoked if an amending bill would affect certain of the Constitution's basic features: which, according to the amending bill's Statement of Objects and Reasons, included the Constitution's secular and democratic character, free and fair elections, the Fundamental Rights, and compromising the judiciary's independence.

This provision passed in the Lok Sabha, but, disliking the referendum especially, the Congress defeated it in the Rajya Sabha, exacting its price for supporting nearly all the amending bill's other provisions. Bhushan's strategic miscalculation left intact Article 368 as it had been amended by the Forty-second Amendment, that is, Parliament's unlimited constituent power and no judicial review of amendments. This condition lasted until the Supreme Court in 1980 in the Minerva Mills case struck down these portions of Article 368, thus reducing Parliament's power of amendment to that in the Twenty-fourth Amendment as interpreted in Kesavananda. The Minerva bench also returned to the Court nearly complete custody over the Fundamental Rights by striking down the Forty-second Amendment's provision that all the Directive Principles took precedence over Rights Articles 14 and 19. As it had with Article 368, Janata had failed to achieve this against Congress opposition in the Rajya Sabha.

Led by Morarji Desai, the government also acted to protect judicial independence. The judges transferred during the Emergency were offered return transfers to their 'home' high courts. However, to protect judicial independence, Desai twice had to hold the line against his own colleagues. When Ram Jethmalani and K.S. Hedge, among others, pressed Desai to ask M.H. Beg to step down from the Chief Justiceship in favour of H.R. Khanna, who Mrs Gandhi had superseded for the post just before leaving office, both Desai and Khanna rejected the idea. When it came Beg's turn to retire, Desai, with the help of Shanti Bhushan, withstood pressure from Janata notables like Jayaprakash Narayan and from others, like M.C. Chagla, to supersede Justices Y.V. Chandrachud and P.N. Bhagwati on the ground that they had proved themselves 'committed judges' when on the bench in the Habeas Corpus case. Had this scheme succeeded, V.R. Krishna Iyer would have become the Chief Justice of India.

Towards the end of the Janata party period, the Supreme Court made what may be interpreted as its own assertion of independence. By granting standing to third parties in civil rights and other disputes, by employing the concept of public interest litigation, and by acting without waiting for government to present it with complaints of rights violations, it carved out a potentially expansive role for itself as protector of citizens' rights. The Court had gone from its 'conservative' fifties to 'judicial activism'.

The nation might have expected that after all this constitutional activity, quiet would descend, but with Mrs Gandhi's return as Prime Minister in 1980, the struggle for custody of the Constitution re-emerged. She has been accused of attempting to overturn the basic structure doctrine in the Minerva Mills case. This is not however correct, for the case came to the Court under the Janata party, and the Court's deliberations, leading to upholding the doctrine, were under way by the time Mrs Gandhi resumed office. Moreover, her Law Minister never seriously pursued his petition for review. On the other hand, several dangerous security situations contributed to the enactment of harsher and harsher preventive detention measures, which curbed the courts' custody over the freedoms in Article 19.

The struggle resumed, in the eyes of the government's antagonists, principally over judicial independence. Rumours that the Prime Minister favoured changing to a presidential system of government, and firm evidence that many around her did so, inflamed suspicions that she had designs on the judiciary. Justice Khanna, for example, feared changing systems when Congress spokesmen 'have made no secret of their aversion to ... judicial review and their desire to clip the courts of their powers'.[35] Into this already mistrustful atmosphere re-emerged the perennial issue of the transfer and appointment of Judges.

It became apparent late in the spring of 1980 that the government was considering adopting a policy that high court chief justices and one-third of the puisne judges whould be from the state. Justice R.C. Srivastava in July resigned from the Allahabad High Court charging that the transfer policy was 'aimed at creating fear and a sense of instability' in the minds of judges.[36] The following January began an affair whose several elements confirmed the suspicions of many that the government was bent on undermining judicial independence. Several high court justices were transferred amidst disagreement between the Chief Justice and Law Minister Shiv Shankar. A circular letter from Shankar to chief ministers was interpreted as executive interference in judicial appointments because it requested these politicians to obtain from additional judges their consent to be appointed permanent judges in another high court. Also, the renewal or non-renewal of the tenures of several additional high court judges was understood to involve political considerations. Petitions concerning these matters came to the Supreme Court grouped as S.P. Gupta, or Judges, case. Relations between the Law Ministry and the Court and within the Court, itself, grew bitter—although some could see advantages in judges from out of the state.

The decision of the four-judge majority in the S.P. Gupta case that a judge's consent was not necessary for his transfer, but that transfers were not to be punitive, and that the Chief Justice of India's advice about transfers did not bind the President—'consultation' did not mean 'concurrence'—resulted in a reluctant truce on the issue that lasted a decade. Yet at the time the goings-on within the bench nearly overshadowed the ruling. Neither the image nor the stature of the Court or of the judiciary as a whole had been improved by the decision, wrote S. Sahay in the *Journal of the Bar Council of India*. The journal's editorial added that the case 'ended up with ... a sadly divided court embroiled in personal rivalries'.[37]

Fears about the executive's intentions toward judicial independence ruptured this truce in the early nineties. In the 'Second Judges Case', a special bench of nine held that the Chief Justice of India did have 'primacy' in the appointment of Supreme Court and high court judges and in the transfers of the latter. At a meeting two months later of the Chief Justice and the chief justices of the high courts, chaired by Prime Minister Narasimha Rao, it was agreed that one-sixth of high court chief justices and one-third of justices should come from the state. Chief Justice M.N. Venkatachaliah thereupon set up a 'peer committee' to finalize norms of transfers.

However, the Court and the judicial institution were not yet home and dry. They now may be, thanks to Attorney General Soli Sorabjee's assurance in 1998 that the government would accept as binding the Supreme Court's answers to a Presidential Reference. At the heart of these answers was that the primacy of the Chief Justice means the primacy of a process in which four senior judges of the Court would be consulted and the opinions of all five sent to the government in writing. One may hope that this mature arrangement will survive.

Because of its intrinsic merit and its centrality to custody, controversies about judicial independence predictably will be with India always, as with other democracies. Disputes are inevitable over a potential judge's character, personal connections, juristic capabilities, and ideological predispositions. Nor, of course, is the issue of custody ever finally settled. The contestants for it are the most powerful institutions of government, and the balance in a system of checks and balances is never firmly horizontal. What does the Constitution mean for the context of today? One man's reasoned response is another's error.

Yet a written constitution as a nation's foundation document is not only law but also a 'law above the law', for other laws should be consonant with it. Therefore, it seems that a judicial body, the supreme court of the land, is the logical, primary custodian for that constitution; its interpreter and guardian. The Supreme Court in India seems admirably suited for this role. Despite occasional self-inflicted wounds, the Court has been the bastion of the Constitution. Parliament enjoys the authority to amend the Constitution. The Court has the authority to measure amendments against the basic structure doctrine.

As custodian, the Court's work never will be done, nor will its performance, as an institution of human beings, be above reproach. Reduction of its overburdened agenda and reforms in its glacial processes have been called for over the years during Law Day and other speeches by judges and members of the bar, whose own conduct has rarely speeded up settlement of cases. In a society given to suspicions of nefarious influences in legal matters, the Court, and the entire judicial community, will have to labour to maintain its credibility. Substantively, it seems to this writer, the Court's most awesome task will be to help to fulfil the promise of Article 14. As we know, this Rights article enjoins 'the State' not to deny persons equality before, and equal protection of, the law. Yet action or inaction by government daily denies this equality to hundreds of millions of citizens. For example, their civil liberties are violated or denied by the police—to whom prudent women dare not take their claims at all. Poor men are jailed; the better off go free. Upper caste members violate the rights of lower caste citizens. The initiative for reform lies first with the executive branches at the Centre and in the states and secondarily with legislatures. The Supreme Court is however custodian of the equality under the law that lies at the heart of the country's constitutional democracy. Unless the Court strives in every possible way to assure that the Constitution, the law, applies farily to *all* citizens, the Court cannot be said to have fulfilled its custodial responsibility.

Notes

[1] This essay draws heavily on the author's book, *Working a Democratic Constitution: The Indian Experience*, Oxford University Press, New Delhi, 2000.

[2] (1950) SCR 1 at 7.

[3] *Parliamentary Debates*, Vol. 12, Part 2, Col. 8832, 16 May 1951.

[4] *Lok Sabha Debates*, 1955, Vol. 3, No. 16, Cols. 1948, 1953 and 1956. Nehru was speaking in favour of the Fourth Amendment.

[5] Letter dated 14 March 1951. (Law Ministry File No. F34/51-C, National Archives of India.)

[6] *Parliamentary Debates Rajya Sabha*, Vol. 48, No. 6, Col. 808.

[7] For Mahajan, see his 'A Pillar of Justice' in Rafiq Zacharia, *A Study of Nehru*, Times of India Publications, Bombay, 1960, p. 386.

[8] Nehru letter dated 15 March 1954. (*Jawaharlal Nehru Letters to Chief Ministers*, Oxford University Press, New Delhi, Vol. 3, p. 501.)

[9] *Lok Sabha Debates*, Fourth Series, Vol. 7, No. 45, Col. 13795.

[10] The Congress Party was not alone. Eight of ten party manifestos advocated changes in the Constitution.

[11] *Lok Sabha Debates*, Fifth Series, Vol. 9, No. 13, Cols. 337–46.

[12] Ibid., No. 12, Col. 230.

[13] S. Mohan Kumaramangalam, *Constitution Amendments: The Reasons Why*, AICC, New Delhi, November 1971.

[14] Law Commission of India, *Forty-sixth Report on the Constitution (Twenty-fifth Amendment)* Bill, 1971, p. 10.

[15] Gajendragadkar–Indira Gandhi letter dated 18 October 1971. (Gajendragadkar Papers, Subject File 1, Nehru Memorial Museum and Library.)

[16] Mohan-Dharia in n interview with the author.

[17] Vasant Sathe in an interview with the author.

[18] J.B. Dadachanji in an interview with the author.

[19] Upendra Baxi, 'The Constitutional Quicksands of Kesavananda', in Malik, Surendra (ed.), *The Fundamental Rights Case: The Critics Speak*, Eastern Book Company, Lucknow, 1975, p. 130.

[20] Jagan Mohan Reddy, *We Have a Republic: Can We Keep It?*, Sri Venkateswara University, Tirupati, 1984, p. 99.

[21] H.R. Khanna, *Judiciary in India and Judicial Practice*, S.C. Sarkar and Sons, Calcutta, 1985, p. 22.

[22] R.C. Dutt in an interview with the author.

[23] N.K. Seshan in an interview with the author.

[24] Told of the impending action by H.R. Gokhale the day before the supersession, Gajendragadkar asked Gokhale to convey his advice to the Prime Minister. He reminded her of this in a letter dated 24 August 1977. (Gajendragadkar Papers, Nehru Memorial Museum and Library.)

[25] Jayaprakash Narayan, 'Appointment of Chief Justice' in Kuldip Nayar (ed.), *Supersession of Judges*, Indian Book Company, New Delhi, 1973, pp. 69–72.

[26] S.L. Shakdher in an interview with the author.

[27] The quotation is from the political resolution adopted at the Congress's annual session at Kamagata Maru in December 1975.

[28] *Proposed Amendments to the Constitution of India by the Committee Appointed by the Congress President Shri D.K. Borooah on February 26, 1976*, All India Congress Committee, New Delhi, 1976, p. 5.

[29] Letter dated 13 August 1976. (Gajendragadkar Papers, Nehru Memorial Museum and Library.)

[30] *Parliamentary Debates Rajya Sabha*, Vol. 98, No. 5, Col. 47.

[31] Upendra Baxi, *The Indian Supreme Court and Politics*, Eastern Book Company, Lucknow, 1980, p. 40.

[32] Statement issued on 15 May 1976. (Narayan Papers, Third Instalment, Subject File 323, Nehru Memorial Museum and Library.)

[33] In his speech inaugurating Parliament on 26 March 1977. (*Asian Recorder*, 23–9 April 1977, p. 13709.)

[34] Shanti Bhushan in an interview with the author.

[35] H.R. Khanna, 'Shall We Toss for a President' in *Times of India*, 19 April 1981.

[36] Quotation from Srivastava's resignation letter to the President. (*Hindustan Times*, 26 July 1980.)

[37] *Journal of the Bar Council of India*, Vol. 9, No. 2.

Two

The Supreme Court: An Overview

Gobind Das

Introduction

The modern Indian world was restructured by the British between the end of the eighteenth century and middle of the twentieth. Various branches of Indian law, apart from modern contitutional law, were developed and defined on the basis of the British model. This transformation of the traditional normative system emerges as one of the most remarkable achievements of the history of inter-cultural relations, comparable to the revolutionary legal structures devised by the Romans to administer the regions they had conquered.

Adapting the British system of law to one suitable for India presented several intrinsic difficulties. The cultural traditions were different, the modes of thought were different, the Indian was primarily member of a particular caste or religion and could therefore be scarcely regarded as an autonomous being, while the British legal system was generally premised on the individual. Added to this problem was India's size, which often led to difficulties of various kinds, for this was not conducive to a unified, inflexible legal structure.

In spite of these and several similar problems, it is remarkable how the Indian legal elite have not only succeeded in preserving a very admirable judicial system, the most Europeanized of Indian institutions, but at the same time advanced and revitalized it to play a crucial role in the developing social and political life of the country. Several judges who served the Court contributed immeasurably to its achievements.

The judicial journey that commenced from the Federal Court of India, supervised by the Privy Council, continued till 1950, when legal administration at the apex level was assumed by the Supreme Court of India after India adopted its constitution. The Supreme Court in the

United States of America and the House of Lords in the UK served as models for the Supreme Court. English emigrants to different parts of America were profoundly influenced by English Common Law in the regulation of their rights and liberties *vis-à-vis* the State, and this ensured an underlying compatibility between the legal systems of those two countries.

Various principles and concepts that had been developed in the English and American Courts served as a reference point for the Indian Supreme Court and furnished the jurisprudential basis for ruling on cases in India, necessarily tempered to the conditions prevalent here.

After Independence, India was intensely political, with economic development high on the national agenda, and awash with diverse ideas on the direction and form that developments could take. The Constitution has conferred on the Supreme Court vital responsibility to act as the apex arbitrator of disputes and the fountain-head of jurisprudence. In the judicial sphere it was accountable to none, barring the limitations it imposed on itself.

The current political mood of the country, the prevailing economic situation, the dominant ideas prevalent in the society at a particular time have governed the activities of the Court. The values that the Court seeks to uphold during any particular period are determined by such ideas and the Court's own appreciation of the needs of society. Assessment of such needs and requirements is often moulded by the philosophy and beliefs of individual judges.

The Court has throughout sought to be a defender of the rights of the people against excesses of the executive. Faced with a liberal and enlightened executive it sought to cooperate with it, confronted with an aggressive and bellicose one the courts stepped aside, and when the executive was weak or negligent the courts were obliged to step in to ensure that the needs of the people were met. Vicissitudes in the fortunes of successive executives perpetually required the court to readjust its position, and often the Court's approach was dependent on the leadership of the Court.

The Court during the period from January 1950 till August 1999 has decided almost 20,491 cases covering nearly 97,240 printed pages of Indian law reports.

There are two ways of looking at an institution. One through the perspective of history and the other by ignoring it. The institution we are looking at is the Supreme Court of India, the most revered, the most adulated, and the least studied of Indian judicial bodies.

The court gazers had noticed distinct phases of judicial activities linked with the political mood of the country, prevailing economic situation, and the dominant idea amongst people during the last fifty years. Any overview of the Supreme Court must in my view be based on its history, as evident from the judgements delivered—there is no other way of recording the history of a Court.

The First Period, 1950–60

During its first decade from 1950–60, in a Nehruvian era of economic progress, political stability, and nascent optimism in the country, the Court, led by four erudite Chief Justices, Sastri, Mahajan, Mukherjee, and S.R. Das, functioned with commendable prescience. While apparently maintaining a balance of power among the three wings of the State, the Court gradually and cautiously expanded its own authority. This laid the foundation for the future activities of the Court. The Court moved forward and backward, eventually drawing a line, combining the orthodox judicial function with policy making. It sought particularly to protect the rights of the rural landowning class from legislation that threatened them.

The judicial power in the hands of these judges did not foreclose the future. They often closed the doors but left them unbolted. The majority and the minority were moving round the centre and it was invariably a brilliant, disciplined, and learned debate. There was a great dissenter like Justice Vivian Bose who spoke for the future. The cases of Gopalan (1950),[1] Kameswar (1952),[2] Shankari Prasad (1952),[3] Purushottam Lal (1958),[4] V.G. Row (1952)[5] set the direction along which the subsequent journeys were made, built the foundation for the larger debates in subsequent times. They asked the questions to which subsequent Courts attempted to find answers, set the tone and delineated the parameters. The Court also used and defined a range of concepts and principles such as eminent domain, police power, due process of law, concepts of delegated legislation when deciding cases during this period. The voice with which they spoke reverberates through the corridors of time, distinguished by its high sense of seriousness, certitude, sense of right, and dignity born of the authority, assurances, and power the Court wielded.

In the *Gopalan* case the Preventive Detention Act 1950 was challenged. The Court, rejecting the American doctrine of due process of law, refused judicial review, but struck down section 14 of the Act which prohibited communication of the grounds of detention. It is on the basis of this right to have the grounds of detention communicated to the person concerned that judicial review of the orders of detention was possible in the future. The cases pertaining to freedom of the press, which was held to be implicit in freedom of speech and expression, were upheld in the *Romesh Thapar*[6] and *Brij Bhushan* cases.[7] In *Kameswar Singh's* case the provisions of section 4(b) of the Bihar Land Reforms Act was struck down on the ground that the power of eminent domain did not justify the acquistion of 'choses in action'. Similarly, section 23(f) of the Bihar Land Reforms Act was struck down on the ground that it was a piece of colourable legislation. The Court was indignant that the landlords were being unjustly deprived of the compensation due to them because of the abolition of their zamindaris. The Court was sympathetic to the claim for compensation and the provisions of the various statutes connected with compensation were struck down because of inadequate provisions made for giving compensation.

The Second Period, 1960–70

During the second decade (1960–70) the economic situation was depressing. The Third Five Year Plan had proved a dismal failure. Jawaharlal Nehru died in 1964. The political climate was vitiated by uncertainty and corruption. Political instability, economic decline, and lack of political morality were the challenges before the Court. The government resorted to populist measures, which it saw as progressive, like nationalization of the banks and abolition of privy purses.

In these circumstances the Court decided to take corrective measures to establish a just economic, political and moral order in the interest of the country. Subba Rao, the Chief Justice, led this new trend, disturbed by the constitutional amendments that frustrated the power and scope of judicial review.

The Golak Nath Case

The opportunity presented itself in the *Golak Nath Case*[8] of 1967. In view of the earlier judgements, a Bench of eleven Judges was constituted to consider the power of Parliament to amend the fundamental rights, and more specifically in relation to the 1st, 4th, and 17th Amendments. The amendments were effected by Parliament acting under its amending power provided by Article 368 of the Constitution. There was Article 13 which prevented the state from making any law that takes away or abridges the fundamental rights and which states that any law so made shall be void. In February 1967, by a majority of 6:5 the Court held that Article 368 could not override the specific provision of Article 13(2) and that Parliament was not competent to amend the chapter on fundamental rights in the Constitution so as to take away or abridge those rights. Since the consequence would have led to complete chaos, the Court, basing itself on American decisions, held that the decision would not govern amendments that had been made in the past but would only be prospective, based on the doctrine 'of prospective over-ruling'.

This case was a landmark in the history of the Supreme Court where the Court for the first time based its judgement on political philosophy.

The Bank Nationalization Case

The Congress government passed the Bank Nationalization Act of 1970 whose validity was questioned before the Supreme Court. The majority held that the Act was within legislative competence but that it discriminated against the named banks who were debarred from carrying on banking business while others, Indian and foreign, were permitted to continue such banking business. The Act also, the Court held, violated the guarantee of compensation under Article 31(2), in that the quantum had been determined in accordance with principles that were not relevant in the determination of compensation and that therefore the amounts so arrived at could not be regarded as compensation. The Court thus took the lead in the determination of an important aspect of the economic policy of the nation. The right to property was the cornerstone of all freedoms. Eventually in the *Bank Nationalization* case[9] the Banking Compensation (Acquisition and Transfer of Undertaking) Act, 1969 was declared unconstitutional. In this judgement the *Gopalan* case was overruled in relation to the salience of each of the fundamental rights. It left wide scope for the future and added a new dimension to law.

The Privy Purse Case

There was strong demand for the abolition of the privy purses granted to erstwhile rulers of the princely states because those and other amenities provided by the Constitution enabled them to become a political force to reckon with. Since the constitutional amendment had failed by a fraction of vote to secure a two-thirds majority in the Rajya Sabha, the President passsed an order withdrawing constitutional recognition of the rulers. Since monetary benefits and immunities flowed from such recognition the erstwhile rulers, challenged the Presidential order. The majority of the Court held that rulership is not a privilege that the President was entitled in his discretion to bestow or withdraw, and declared it illegal and unconstitutional. The order was held to be violative of the fundamental rights enshrined in Articles 19(1)(f), 21, and 31(1) of the Constitution. Destroying the institution of rulership was contrary to the concept of Rule of Law. It was held that the claim to receive a privy purse was right to property which had been illegally violated.

These three judgements, namely in the *Golak Nath, Bank Nationalization,* and *Privy Purse*[10] cases, hammered nails in the coffin of political sovereignty. The Prime Minister dissolved Parliament and the President declared fresh elections. The power of Parliament to amend was one of the electoral issues. The Congress sought a mandate for constitutional amendments necessary 'to overcome the impediments in the path of social justice'.

The Third Period, 1971–6

Elections to the Lok Sabha were held in 1971 and the Congress party secured a two-thirds majority. Parliament thereupon passed the Constitution 24th Amendment, amending Articles 368 and 13(2), to nullify the effect of the *Golak Nath* case, the Constitution 25th Amendment bill amending Article 31 and adding Article 31(c), thereby seeking to nullify the judgement in the *Bank Nationalization* case, and the Constitution 26th Amendment Act abolishing privy purses and the privileges extended to the erstwhile rulers of the princely states, to nullify the judgements in the *Privy Purse* case. In addition, the Constitution 29th Amendment Act came into force placing the Kerala Land Reforms Act in the Ninth Schedule of the Constitution. By 1971 and 1972 Parliament thus dismantled the edifice that the Court had raised.

The Kesavananda Bharati Case

In a Kerala case under Article 32 of the Constitution the petitioner sought enforcement of his fundamental rights. Since it entailed a review of the *Golak Nath* case decided by eleven Judges, a Bench of thirteen Judges was constituted. All the constitutional amendments were to be reviewed in this case. It is known as the *Kesavananda Bharati*[11] case. The debate before the Court was widened to cover broad fundamental issues relating to the kind of polity the country was destined to have, the basic framework of the republic, the extent and desirability of abrogation of fundamental rights, the relationship between directive principles and fundamental rights, the concept of sovereignty and whether it lay in Parliament or the people of India, to decide the future course of the Constitution without any inherent limitation, the scope of judicial review and other similar issues. The Court heard the argument for sixty-nine days spread over five months. The largest Bench sat for the longest time to decide on issues that were important not merely for the future of this country but the future of democracy itself. The judgement covered 700 closely printed pages in the official report but nothing was decided in this case. Six Judges decided the case in favour of the citizen and six in favour of the State. Justice Khanna agreed with none of the twelve judges and took a position midway between the two conflicting views. He held that the power of amendment was limited and did not enable Parliament to alter the basic structure or framework of the Constitution.

The Indira Gandhi Election Case

In the meantime Indira Gandhi's election was set aside by the Allahabad High Court and through an interim order of 24 June 1975 the Vacation Judge, Krishna Iyer, directed that the Prime Minister Indira Gandhi was not to function as a member of Parliament but could exercise the powers and perform the functions of Prime Minister. The order did not satisfy Indira Gandhi and on the following day a state of internal emergency was proclaimed in India.

To protect Indira Gandhi's election, the election laws were amended pending appeal. The Constitution 39th Amendment inserted Article 329(A) making special provisions regarding election disputes *vis-à-vis* the Prime Minister and Speaker. Article 329(A)(4) cancelled out not merely the judgement of the Allahabad High Court but also the election petition and the law relating to it. It deprived the defeated candidate of the opportunity to question the validity of his election. A legislative judgement was passed in exercise of the constituent power validating the election. The validity of this amendment was challenged before the Court and the majority struck it down. This did not however affect the result of the election, since the statute had already been amended.

In pursuance of the declaration of emergency, a large number of persons in the various states were detained and the detenus challenged their arrest in habeas corpus petitions before their respective high courts. The high courts had held in several cases that the petitions were maintainable. The state and central governments preferred appeals in what is known as the *Shukla* case[12]. Chief Justice Ray led the majority and held that liberty was a gift of law and may by law be forfeited. He relied upon Article 359 of the Constitution which prescribed suspension of the enforcement of fundamental rights during a period of emergency. However Justice Khanna dissented, and to him what was at stake was the rule of law. He also held that life and liberty are basic assumptions of the rule of law, and that such rights exist even in the absence of Article 21. Judgements of the high courts upholding the maintainability of the petitions were set aside by the majority, but Justice Khanna upheld them.

There was an election in 1977. People were by and large convinced that the judgements of the Supreme Court in various cases, including *Shukla*'s case, were unjust. The verdict of the people swept away the very foundations of the judgements of the Supreme Court, leaving the institution to groan under self-inflicted wounds. In January 1977 Justice H.L. Khanna was superseded and Justice M.H. Beg was appointed Chief Justice of India. The *Kesavananda Bharati* judgement was delivered on 24 April 1973, Chief Justice Sikri's last day in office. On 25 April 1973 Justice Ray was appointed Chief Justice of India succeeding Chief Justice Sikri and superseding senior judges Shelat, Hegde, and Grover who resigned thereafter. Justice Ray had dissented from the majority in the *Bank Nationalization* and *Privy Purse* cases.

After the *Kesavananda Bharati* case, the Congress party passed a resolution in 1976 proposing to curtail the powers of the highest judiciary and to reduce the scope of judicial review. This was incorporated in the 42nd Amendment. Thereafter Parliament was dissolved and the country went for election.

The Fourth Period, 1977–80

In 1977 the Janata party came to power with overwhelming support, defeating the Congress almost to extinction. The Janata party dismantled the constitutional amendments brought into law by the Congress party. In the relaxed atmosphere that followed Mrs Gandhi's devastating defeat, the Court sought a revival of the pre-eminent position it had lost during the Emergency. The Court delivered a momentous decision in the *Maneka Gandhi* case[13] in 1978 which reintroduced due process in Indian jurisprudence. It was followed by the *International Airport Authority* case[14] in 1979. Judicial power over administrative action became virtually limitless. A new judicial culture emerged during this period, the chief innovators of which were Justices Bhagwati and Krishna Iyer. The Court did not interfere with political questions and gave way to the executive in the belief that its actions reflected the new aggressive public temper. In the *Maneka Gandhi* case, which related to the issue of a passport, the Court under the leadership of Justice Bhagwati held that the procedure established by law in Article 21 must satisfy the test of 'just, fair and reasonable' in Article 14. Such wider meaning of Article 14 was dovetailed with Article 21 with its expansive connotations marking it out as a momentous case, with the Court assuming a wide power of judicial review. In the *International Airport Authority* case the issue was that the tender of a respondent who was not qualified had been accepted, and the acceptance of this by the airport authority was challenged by the petitioner as discriminatory. It was contended that it was the discretion of the airport authority to accept or to reject the tender but the petitioners the Court held that wealth was changing its traditional character and was taking a new form of leases, licences, contracts, and privileges. When government jobs formed part of the contract, government quota, licences, and other forms of largesse, its action must conform to a fixed standard or norm and could not be arbitrary, irrational or irrelevant. The State was acting through instrumentalities or agencies of different kinds, and the actions of such corporations had to be in conformity with rules and regulations, steering clear of arbitrary action.

The last battle for property and for the controversy relating to the validity of Article 31(C) was faught in the *Minerva Mills* case.[15] The majority held that Article 31(C) violated the basic structure of the Constitution and was therefore void.

Thus ended the short and significant period from 1977 to 1980. Due to internal dissension, the Janata party government collapsed. In 1980 another election was held and Indira Gandhi and the Congress party returned to power.

The Fifth Period, 1980–4

The year 1980 brought Mrs Gandhi back to power. Her victory at the polls was decisive, with a large majority in Parliament. The Supreme Court had always been uncomfortable with Mrs Gandhi's governance; during the late sixties her economic and political policies were struck down in the *Bank Nationalization* and *Privy Purse* cases; in the early seventies the Court was locked in the *Kesavananda* battle and again in her election cases; when the court supported her emergency in the *Shukla* and *Detenu* cases[16] it was execrated by public opinion; and during the Janata rule the Court was confirming legal attempts for her political extinction in the *Special Courts Bill* [17] and *Assembly Dissolution* cases.[18] Whenever the Court opposed her policies it had to pay the penalty in the form of supersession of judges and constitutional amendments. When it supported her policies, it was denigrated by critical public opinion. The Court would neither accommodate her nor reject her. Now the Court decided to keep out of the way of major confrontation with her new government.

It opened up new fields of interest and different areas of judicial activities; it chose the poor, the helpless, the oppressed in the name of socialism, constitutional conscience, and the rule of law. Public Interest Litigation

(PIL) was born, though not all judges were equally enthusiastic about it. Five judges, Justices Krishna Iyer, Bhagwati, Desai, Chinnappa Reddy, and later Justice Thakar, constituted a fraternity. They apparently had a mission to perform through the instrumentality of Court, finding their way through gaps in the wall. Bhagwati J chose PIL, Desai J and Thakar J the area of tenants, employees, and workmen, Chinnappa Reddy J the realm of socialism, Krishna Iyer J the broader fields of egalitarianism and the cause of prisoners. The scene was thus set for the inauguration of new and progressive socialist judicial area. In contrast to other judges, with these judges compassion had the aggressive flavour of crusaders.

Since 1980 India made a mini-leap forward. The agricultural economy was faring well, and in the areas of oil production and industrial growth progress was satisfactory. In brief, there was a spurt of economic growth in the post-1980 period.

As mentioned earlier, the Court did not interfere with the major political and economic decisions of the government. The *Judges Appointment and Transfer* case, known as the *S.P. Gupta* case (1981)[19] allowed the supremacy of the executive in the appointment of judges. The National Security Ordinance was challenged in the *A.K. Roy* case (1982),[20] where the majority approved the ordinance and held that it was established within the meaning of Article 21. The question of judicial review of Presidential satisfaction was hesitantly reserved for the future. Similarly, the Special Bearer Bonds (Immunities & Exemption Act, 1981),[21] the object of which was to canalize black money and enable it to be invested in Special Bonds was approved. In the *Sanjeev Coke*[22] case it was held that the scheme of nationalization of coking coal was essentially a matter of State policy which was an inherently inappropriate subject for judicial review. The Coking Coal Mines (Nationalization Act, 1972) was approved.

As has been noted, Public Interest Litigation (PIL) was born and it became the philosophy of a new judicial movement. Several benefits were conferred through PIL. The doctrine of *locus standi* was liberated from Anglo-Saxon fetters and a new strategy evolved for the benefit of the poor and lowly. Access to justice was simplified and appropriate jurisprudence was evolved for the benefit of the poor and illiterate. In the process many of the age-old precedents, procedures, and technical rules were jettisoned by some judges.

Due to differing perspectives, the judges disagreed amongst themselves. Emphasis differs, shades of meaning vary, even the processes of reasoning may lead to some other destination, said Krishna Iyer J. 'Special reasons' are bound to differ from judge to judge depending upon his value system, and social philosophy. Judicial activism in favour of the weaker class in fulfilment of the Directive Principles were promoted. Empathy with lowly individuals became constitutional culture. Law was sought to be interpreted keeping in view the word 'Socialist' in the preamble of the Constitution and the Directive Principles echoed the familiar language of the philosophy of socialism.

In Industrial law all termination of services, whatever the reasons, was to be treated as retrenchment under the Industrial Disputes Act. Treating daily wage employees of many years standing was contrary to constitutional philosophy and socio-economic justice and was highly unethical, said Desai J. Rule 10 of the certified Standing Orders provided that the retiring gratuity would be payable at the discretion of the Company. Desai J said that Rule 10 appeared to have been framed in the heyday of laissez faire and was not consistent with modern notions of social justice and the Directive Principles. He added that the concept of the managerial function was slowly withering away and the Constitution had ushered in a socio-economic revolution through law. The law of landlord and tenant was interpreted in favour of the tenants on the ground of the rule of law. He said that the rent control statute should not be so interpreted as to enable landlords to evict tenants.[23] During this period, judicial review of *Preventive Detentions*[24] was expanded and had to satisfy the test of reasonableness and fariness evolved in *Maneka Gandhi* case.

During this period there was a litigation explosion that created utter chaos, said Krishna Iyer J. He added, however, that the Court is not a hotel or airlines that could turn away people for non-availability of accommodation.

The Sixth Period, 1985–7

During 1985 there was a new government at the Centre, a new Chief Justice in the Supreme Court, and a new perception of the Indian economy. With surplus wheat in the granaries and a promise to eradicate corruption, the country was relaxed, and optimistic. A fresh youthful breeze blew across India in what was akin to an Indian version of the Kennedy era in America.

The Supreme Court was concerned. Bhagwati J, as the new head of the national judiciary expressed serious concern about the need for judicial reforms for, according to him, the judicial system was in peril. Several proposals were mooted. The Supreme Court proposed a holistic approach to participatory management with the executive.

The Administrative Tribunal Act, 1985 was passed and enforced. There are several obnoxious features of the Act but the Court did not decide the issues; did not strike down the Act but directed the correction of its defects, which was effected and the Act as altered was approved. Similar directions were issued in other cases.

In the *Tulsiram Patel* case[25] the doctrine of pleasure so far as civil servants are concerned was revived. No Act or rule can be framed to affect the doctrine of pleasure, said Madon J. Private interest of personal livelihood must yield to its denial in public interest. Public policy requires, public interest needs, public good demands tha there should be a doctrine of pleasure.

In the *Water Transport Corporation* case,[26] there were some employees whose services were terminated under Rule 9 which provided that all the services of permanent employees would be terminated on intimation of three months' notice from either side or payment of three months' pay. These orders of termination were challenged. The matter was eventually decided by the Supreme Court. The rule was declared void as it militated against public policy under section 23 of the Contract Act and was violative of Articles 14, 39A, and 41 of the Constitution. The Court would strike down unconscionable terms of any contract resulting from unequal bargaining power, said Madon J. The Court should by interpretation adopt law to suit the needs of the society. The doctrine of unequal bargaining power had arrived in India and was consistent with the 'temper of the times', updating law relating to the instrumentality of the State.

In the *National Anthem* case (1986)[27] students of a Kerala school, followers of the Jehovah's Witnesses sect, a worldwide Christian denomination, refused to sing the national anthem on the grounds that it was against their religious faith and were therefore expelled. There was also a circular from the school authorities to that effect. They filed writ petitions before the Kerala High Court against their expulsion. The Supreme Court allowed the appeal of these children. Chinnappa Reddy J, on behalf of the Bench, held that refusal to sing the national anthem did not violate the provisions of the Prevention of Insults to National Honour Act, 1971. The circular of the Director of Public Instruction obliging the children to sing the national anthem was a violation of Article 25 of the Constitution guaranteeing the freedom of conscience. The right to remain silent was upheld by the Court as part of the fundamental right to freedom of speech and expression.

Several significant judgements were delivered during the last few days of Bhagwati J's court. In the *DCM* case,[28] the liability to pay compensation to persons injured by accident due to hazardous or inherently dangerous activities of a business enterprise was held to be strict and absolute, and the quantum of compensation would depend upon the magnitude and capacity of the enterprise concerned. The limitations and exceptions to the rules in *Rylands v Fletcher*[29] were held not to be applicable in India.

In the *Wadhwa* case,[30] the large-scale promulgation of ordinances by the Governor of Bihar successively without bringing them before the legislature was held to be beyond the scope of Article 213, and as such the ordinances were improper and invalid. Such practice of issuing ordinances was held to be a colourable exercise of power and a fraud on constitutional provisions.

Bhagwati CJ will be remembered for giving a wider connotation to the doctrine of promissory estoppel, to social action litigation, to expansive connotation of Articles 14 and 21, and lastly for the revolution in the law of Tort in the *DCM* case. Bhagwati CJ is however to be criticized for upholding laws capable of annihilating individual liberty. The judgement in the *Shukla* case (1976) and upholding the validity of the National Security Act in the *A.K. Ray* cse (1982), where he could have but did not apply the test of the *Maneka* case (1978) will be pointed out as grey areas in his otherwise brilliant and progressive judicial career.

Justice Pathak became the Chief Justice of India after the retirement of Bhagwati J in 1986.

The Last Decade, 1987–98

During the period 1987–99 India saw twelve Chief Justices. K.N. Singh J was the Chief Justice for the shortest period of eighteen days, Pathak J and Ahmadi J for the longest, of a little over two years each. During the same period there were eight Prime Ministers. There was instability in the governance of the country. Political parties lost their credibility and capacity to rule. Bureaucracy became a powerful and significant lever of power. Corruption became rampant. The people suffered acutely as a consequence of the nexus between politicians and bureaucrats on the one hand and criminals on the other.

The downward drift in economic growth in India, which began in 1985, continued its downward spiral till it reached its nadir in 1991. The period began with doses of liberalization and globalization, the prospect of which was viewed by many with trepidation. Industrial production slowed down considerably and there was no significant expansion of agriculture. Public sector undertakings became merely mismanaged departments of the government and the country seethed with corruption.

The recent experience of South-East Asian countries was very depressing. Lenin's statue being pulled down and the collapse of the Berlin Wall symbolized the demise of Russia as also of socialism as State policy, and the only alternative appeared to be liberalization and market economy. The five activist judges had retired by 1987. The number of judges of the Supreme Court increased from six (1950) to the present strength of twenty-five.

The period from Pathak to Punchhi, 1987–92, was an unprecedented era in many ways. There were a number of scams, the gas disaster in Bhopal, Ayodhya, large-scale caste violence following the implementation of the Mandal reports, the demolition of the Babri Masjid and the nationwide communal riots that followed, allegations of corruption against a sitting judge, and several other momentous and explosive public issues which all appeared before the Court as legal questions.

The charges of corruption in high places involving the Prime Minister, Chief Ministers, Governors, members of Parliament, bureaucrats, private sector managers and operators causing loss of thousands of crores of rupees convulsed the country and eventually the apex Court during the later part of the decade.

Environmental pollution engaged the attention of the Court. The rivers, the beaches, the lakes, the streets, and the skies of metropolises were polluted, the forest was denuded. The Court had to indicate and initiate ameliorative corrective measures with appropriate expedition, vigour, and authority.

The Court did not have any particular doctrine nor any particular direction. It had no recognized leader but it functioned collectively and effectively, responding to all the challenges during the first half of the decade, going, as Black J said, for 'the jugular'.

The Union Carbide Case

Soon after Pathak joined as Chief Justice several issues arising out of the *Union Carbide* case reached the Court. The case went through several twists and turns and the disaster of Bhopal had a noble victim in Delhi in no less a person than the Chief Justice himself. Cases narrated thereafter met similar turbulence in the then prevailing political climate of the country. (The relevant cases will reveal the circumstances in greater detail than has been possible within the compass of this article.)

The leak and escape of poisonous fumes from the chemical plants of the multinational corporation called Union Carbide caused the death of nearly 4000 people and tens of thousands of citizens of Bhopal were affected by the long-term and short-term effect of the disaster. There was clamour and demand for compensation from the victims and other organizations representing the dead and maimed. After an initial battle in the American courts, the legal activities shifted to India and eventually ended up before the Supreme Court. The Court succeeded in persuading the government and the company, ignoring the victims, to arrive at a settlement. The settlement was brief: three paragraphs. There was a hue and cry condemning the settlement because the compensation was grossly inadequate; and provided immunities from criminal action against both Union Carbide and the government because it passed a statute assuming total responsibility for compensation; and against the Chief Justice, in particular, as he was the star performer. Pathak CJ's Court yielded to the public clamour and referred the question of validity of the Act to a Constitution Bench and the question of compensation was referred to another Bench. The Court explained why it had accepted the settlement and had not considered the legal questions involved. Two judgements were delivered, one upholding the constitutional validity of the Bhopal Act and the other upholding the settlement and quantum of compensation awarded. On the morning of 19 June 1989, before the delivery of these judgements and amidst the engulfing chaos Pathak CJ resigned from the Supreme Court on appointment to the International Court of Justice.

The Bhopal Gas leak Disaster (Processing of Claims) Act, 1985 empowered the Union of India to take over the conduct of all litigation in this regard. The validity of the Act was upheld in *Charanlal v Union of India*[31] substantially on the doctrine *parens patriae* or analogous to the doctrine, applied in Indian context. It literally meant 'parent of the country' and was invoked by the State in exercise of its sovereign power to protect and take into custody the rights and privileges of the citizens in discharge of its obligation. In the second case in *Union Carbide v UOI*[32] the issue was the validity of settlement. The settlement was upheld basing on its own power under Article 142; however the Court struck down the clause of the settlement quashing the criminal proceeding either pending or in prospect.

The Antulay Case

In the *Antulay* case,[33] a seven-judge Bench overruled its earlier direction of the Constitution Bench directing the transfer of the case from a special judge to the high court. This direction was contrary to the statute, namely the provisions of Criminal Law Amendment Act, 1952. The five-judge majority judgement in the *Seven Judges Bench* case wiped Antulay's slate clean. It was said that it would be a negation of the rule of law and a violation of the procedure established by law. The earlier order was said to be *per incuriam* as it was not conscious of having violated the statute.

The Ramaswamy Case[34]

Ramaswamy was functioning as the Chief Justice of the Punjab and Haryana High Court and was later elevated to the Supreme Court. While functioning as Chief Justice, it was alleged by the Comptroller and Auditor General of the state that he had committed several financial irregularities. The Court, the bar, and the media took notice of the allegations. Notice was served by 108 members of the Ninth Lok Sabha for his impeachment. The Speaker admitted the motion and constituted a committee of inquiry. Minutes after the admission of the motion and the constitution of the committee by the speaker, the Lok Sabha was dissolved. The Congress party came to power and treated the motion admitted by the Speaker as having lapsed after the dissolution of Parliament, and deemed the inquiry committee to have ceased with it. It was believed that Ramaswamy had the support and confidence of the Congress party.

A section of the Supreme Court Bar took up the cause against Ramaswamy J and demanded that the inquiry committee complete its inquiry. Before the Constitution Bench several questions relating to the power, jurisdiction, propriety, and bona fides of the Speaker in passing the order in the circumstances and its validity after the dissolution of the House were raised. Further questions relating to the *locus standi* of the petitioners and interpretation of Judges Enquiry Act, 1966 and its validity were the subject matter for decision before the Court.

The majority held that the doctrine that dissolution of the House passes sponge over the Parliamentary State, nor the doctrine of lapse apply in these cases. Judicial review lies against the first part of the proceedings from initiation of investigation ending in proof of the Speaker's action which is statutory and not in relation to the second part of the proceedings which is a parliamentary process. The purview of judicial review is in relation to the first part of the processing from initiation of the investigation ending in proof of the Speaker's action which is statutory and not in relation to the second part of the proceedings which is a parliamentary process. The judge concerned is not entitled to any notice of hearing. The doctrine of necessity protects the Speaker from any allegations of acting mala fide. The petitioners had a *locus standi*, the judgement was merely declaratory. The dissenting judge held the entire process to have been parliamentary and that therefore the matter was not justiciable.

After the judgement, further writ petitions were filed to correct the earlier judgement in another case that was held to be unmaintainable. The dissenting judge held that the committee be directed to expunge the evidence of outsiders like Fernandes from the Janata Dal and Jaswant Singh from the BJP as they should not have been permitted to intervene in the proceedings in which they had no *locus standi*.

Ramaswamy J's wife had filed a writ petition seeking that a copy of the inquiry report of the committee be furnished to her husband before it was forwarded to the Speaker. It was held by the majority that judicial review is not available against the findings of the committee. The same cannot be cannot be made available before its submission to the Speaker but that the Speaker is obliged to supply a copy of the report to the judge concerned when causing it to be laid before Parliament under section 4(3) of the Act for consideration of the motion against the judge. Parliament's decision to adopt the motion or reject it has to be on merits on the basis of the entire material, including the dissenting opinion of any member of the committee, if any, as well as the comments of the judge concerned. Prior to the decision the judge should be afforded an opportunity to show cause. The motion to impeach V. Ramaswamy J was defeated in Parliament because the Congress and AIADMK members abstained from voting. What began as a political move was dissolved by an opposite political counter political move.

The Veeraswamy Case[35]

K. Veeraswamy was Chief Justice of the Madras High Court. The Central Bureau of Investigation (CBI) had registered a case against him alleging possession of assets disproportionate to his known sources of income and of his having committed an offence under the Prevention of Corruption Act. After investigation, a charge sheet was filed. The special judge issued notice for his appearance. Having failed to appear before the Madras High Court, the judge challenged the trial as wholly without jurisdiction, therefore illegal and void. His contention was that he was not a public servant and that the Prevention of Corruption Act did not apply to judges of high courts and the Supreme Court. Dismissing the appeal the majority held that high court judges and those of the Supreme Court are public servants. The President of India is the sanctioning and removing authority but in the interests of the independence of the judiciary the sanctioning authority must act in accordance with the advice of the Chief Justice of India. There is no law protecting the judges from criminal prosecution.

The Mandal Case[36]

The Union of India issued an Office Memorandum on 13 August 1990 on the basis of the report of the Mandal Commission purporting to extend reservation to socially and educationally backward classes in its service. That Memorandum reserved 27 per cent of the vacancies to other backward classes in addition to the 22.5 per cent already reserved for the scheduled tribes and castes. This reservation was to apply to vacancies in public sector undertakings and public institutions such as banks, etc.

The decision was explosive. An orgy of violence followed the clash of two groups of youths, one buoyed up with new-found hope and the other driven by extremes of despair. The controversy reached the Supreme Court. In the meantime a new government had taken power at the Centre and issued another Office Memorandum adding another 10 per cent for other backward sections of the higher castes and other religious and deprived sections of society in the 27 per cent quota.

A nine-judge Bench was constituted to consider conflicting judgement by earlier Benches. Eventually, the earlier Office Memorandum was constitutionally upheld with certain modifications, alterations, and deletions by a majority of 6:3. The modified Office Memorandum drawn up by the new government was struck down.

The majority held that reservation can be provided for other classes under Article 16(1) and Article 16(4) was not an exception to the former. It also held that caste in India can be and quite often is a social class. Economic criteria cannot therefore be the sole basis for determining a backward class. There can be no reservation for the poor even under Article 16(1). Reservation could not normally exceed 50 per cent unless a special case was made out. The backward could include the more backward, and the creamy layer excluded. It further held that the executive could provide reservation and there was no special standard of judicial scrutiny in matters arising under Article 16(4). Reservations could only be for the initial appointment and not for promotion but the existing provision should continue for five more years.

As recently as on 10 August 1999[37] it was held that reservation will not apply to super specialities and that merit alone can be the basis of selection of candidates for such courses as medicine and engineering. No special provisions are permissible for admission into medical and engineering colleges on the basis of reservations, that being contrary to the national interest. The Court struck down on 12 August 1999 the UP Post Graduate Medical Education Act, 1997 reducing the minimum qualifying marks from 35 to 20 per cent for the reserve category candidates to postgraduate medical classes. Similarly, the Court struck down the order by the state of Madhya Pradesh prescribing lower qualifying marks for scheduled caste and scheduled tribe candidates and other backward classes. Non-identification of the creamy layer will result in violation of Article 14 and will also infringe upon the basic structure of the Constitution.

Article 16(4-A) was introduced by the 77th (Amendment) Act, 1995, stating that nothing in the Article shall prevent the state from making any provision for reservation in the matters of promotion to any class or classes or posts in favour of scheduled castes and tribes, which in the opinion of the state are not adequately represented in the services under the state.

In the second *Indira Sawhney* case,[38] it was held that Article 16(4-A) is only an enabling provision and it does not confer any fundamental right.

It was held in *Ajit Singh*'s case[39] that Articles 16(4) and 16(4-A) confer a discretion but do not create any duty or obligation which could be enforced by issuing a writ of mandamus to provide reservation or relaxation.

Jawaharlal Nehru had described reservation at the cost of efficiency as a disaster. The judgement will, however, be prospective. Palkhivala voiced the view that 1992 was one of the saddest years in the history of our jurisprudence as the Supreme Court continued the scourge of casteism rather than ruling in favour of an effective, cohesive, unified classless society.

The Ram Janmabhumi–Babri Masjid Case[40]

A movement by extremist Hindu organizations supported by the BJP government in UP was launched to construct a Ram temple at the Ram Janmabhumi–Babri Masjid complex. A large number of *kar sevaks* converged on Ayodhya for the purpose. Writ petitions were filed to direct the UP government to put a stop to these activities. The Supreme Court from time to time issued orders to arrest the massive waves of inspired religious individuals from proceeding to Ayodhya and committing the threatened act. The Court took note of the alarming situation, sometimes requested, took a solemn undertaking from the UP government, issued directions to it, and appointed officers to monitor the situation. The Court believed that its writ would run and nothing untoward would occur. As it happened, a massive crowd gathered on the outskirts of Ayodhya, was addressed by senior leaders, descended on Ayodhya, stormed Babri Masjid and with lightning speed and skill razed the mosque to the ground. Violence and destruction of property followed.

It was an act that shamed the nation, and shameful too that the UP government was unable to or unwilling to discharge its obligations.

The President, under Article 356, dissolved the UP Assembly and banned communal organizations. An ordinance was promulgated followed by an Act to acquire certain tracts of lands at Ayodhya involved in the disturbances there. A reference was made to the Supreme Court under Article 143(1) of the Constitution. The validity of the Act to acquire the land and the President's order were challenged before the Supreme Court. Serious challenges were made against the provisions for abetment of suits and legal proceedings in respect of right, title and interest relating to the properties vested in the central government, as provided in section 4 of the Act, since the statute did not provide effective alternative dispute mechanism in substitution of the pending suits. The Court accepted the submission, as did the central government, and section 4(3) of the Act was declared invalid and void. The majority however held it was severable from the rest.

The majority held that the Act was not anti-secular and was relatable to entry 42 List III and therefore Parliament had the competence to enact the legislation. Regarding the larger question whether a mosque could be acquired, the majority held that precedents and textual authorities supported such a proposition.

The next question was the validity of the reference. The Court, after many hearings over a long period, eventually held that the reference, namely whether a Hindu temple or religious structure existed prior to the construction of the Babri Masjid on the area on which the structure stood, was superfluous and unnecessary and did not require to be answered. The majority held that the Court respectfully declined to answer the reference and returned it. Consequently, the suits were revived.

The Court was in no mood to forgive the UP government or its Chief Minister for their breach of their undertaking to the Court. Contempt proceedings were initiated by the Court and in the course of these it was held that the state and its chief minister were punishable for their failure to obey the judicial orders. The chief minister was convicted and was imprisoned for a day and fined Rs 2000.

The Court did not resolve the dispute entrusted to it by the government, but while not doing anything it did achieve something significant. It gained time; it gained time for the government and this the government desperately needed. The volcano that erupted at Ayodhya on 6 December 1992 was allowed to cool down during the following two years and by 24 October 1994, when the Court delivered the judgement in the case, Ayodhya remained only a wound which, though once deep, had by then largely healed.

The Bommai Case[41]

President's rule was promulgated under Article 356 in different states at different times. All such orders were challenged before a nine-judge Bench. Four basic features were involved in these cases, namely federalism, democracy, secularism, and the power of judicial review.

The facts varied from state to state, as in Karnataka, Meghalaya, and Nagaland. In Madhya Pradesh, Himachal Pradesh, and Rajasthan President's rule was imposed after demolition of Babri Masjid on 6 December 1992. So far as Karnataka was concerned, it was held that the proclamation smacked of mala fide and was held to be invalid. In Meghalaya the governor's unnecessary anxiety to dismiss the ministry was apparent and it was also testimony to failure to give effect to the Court's order. In Nagaland the governor should have allowed the new leaders to prove their strength on the floor of the assembly. Since this was not done the proclamation was held to be unconstitutional. In Madhya Pradesh, Himachal Pradesh, and Rajasthan, where BJP goverments ruled, action counter to the tenets of secularism was prima facie proof of conduct in defiance of the Constitution, and therefore the President had acted on the basis of this in these states. It cannot be argued that there was no material before the President, and on the basis of this he came to the conclusion that government in these three states could not be carried on in accordance with the provisions of the Constitution. There had been a violation of the secular features of the Constitution which is a ground to hold that conditions of Article 356 are fulfilled. It was held that the expression 'cannot be carried' in Article 356(1) does not mean impossible to conduct the government of the state.

Article 365 is merely an illustration. Satisfaction in Article 356 is merely subjective satisfaction based on objective materials warranting legitimate inference. As much as federalism forms a basic structure of the Constitution, so does positive secularism implying the equality of all religions.

This was a landmark case relating to the concept of judicial review. The objective part was justiciable, the subjective part might not be. The sufficiency of the material may not be questioned but the legitimacy of the inference is open to judicial review. The Court often faces difficult decisions due to lack of judicially manageable standards. The wall of separation between the State and religion was breached justifying the Presidential rule.

The V.C. Misra Case[42]

The conduct of V.C. Misra, a senior advocate, before an Allahabad judge was reported to the Supreme Court. The Supreme Court's prima facie view was that contempt had been committed by Misra. The jurisdiction of the Supreme Court to take cognizance of contempt of the high court flows from Article 129 in view of the expression 'including'. It was held that the power of the Supreme Court to punish for contempt was not limited by any statute. The Court held Misra guilty of the offence of criminal contempt of the Court for having interfered with and obstructed the cause of justice by attempting to threaten, overcome and overbear by using insulting, disrespectful, and threatening language. Since the contemner was a senior member of the Bar, and held the high office of Chairman of the Bar Council of India, President, UP High Court Bar Association, Allahabad and other, his conduct was bound to infect the members of the bar all over the country. Therefore the Court was of the view that exemplary punishment should be meted out to him:

The facts and circumstances of the present case justify our invoking the power under Article 129 read with Article 142 of the Constitution, to award to the contemner a suspended sentence of imprisonment together with the suspension of his practice as an advocate as directed herein. The contemner shall stand suspended for practising as an advocate for three years.

The Supreme Court Bar Association filed a petition under Article 32 of the Constitution seeking for a declaration that the disciplinary committee of the Bar Council alone has the jurisdiction to enquire into and suspend an advocate from practising law for professional or other misconduct, and for a declaration further that the Supreme Court or high court had no such jurisdiction. The Constitution Bench of the Court heard the matter and held *inter alia*,

we are conscious of the fact that the conduct of the contemner in V.C. Misra's case was highly contumacious and even atrocious. It was unpardonable. The contemner therein had abused his professional privileges while practising as an advocate. He is holding very senior position in Bar Council of India and was expected to act in a more reasonable way. He did not. These factors appear to have influenced the Bench in that case, to itself punish him by suspending his licence to practise also while imposing a suspended sentence of imprisonment for committing contempt of Court but while doing so this court vested itself with a jurisdiction where none exists.

The Court concluded:

We cannot persuade ourselves to agree with that approach. It must be remembered that wider the amplitude of its power under Article 142, greater is the need of care for this Court that power is used with restraint without pushing back the limits of the Constitution so as to function within the bounds of its own jurisdiction. To the extent this Court makes statutory authorities and other organs of the state perform their duties in accordance with law, its role is unexceptionable but it is not permissible for the Court to 'take over' the role of the statutory bodies or other organs of the State and 'perform' their functions.

The judgement was delivered by Anand J on behalf of the Court. Unprecedented litigation, unpredictable causes, contentious issues, inconceivable allegations, highly controversial questions came up before the Court and the dance of wolves in its premises shook the Court and country during the first part of the last decade.

1993–8

The second part of the last decade witnessed a new significant phenomenon, momentous in its dimensions and disturbing in its impact, i.e. the persistent, continual exposure of sordid events in both the print and electronic media. Hitherto unknown facts were exposed regarding the participation of the powerful and persons in high positions in scams and scandals of vast dimensions which shocked and scandalized the nation. The movement for the right to information, call for transparent governance, and the accountability of public functionaries together with a lure for the sensational, aggravated the situation and brought the issue of corruption into intense focus. The media *inter alia* had a direct impact on the judiciary and, more significantly, on democracy itself. During the past, it was the law that provided the source of authority for democracy, which today appears to have been replaced by public opinion with the media serving as it arbiter.

Similarly, gross environmental pollution in all spheres has been a source of widespread concern.

Public Interest Litigation

The judicial movement towards socialism was virtually eclipsed during the first part of the last decade. The 'cause' was half abandoned: a mission was half fulfilled before losing steam. Public Interest Litigation (PIL) however resurfaced with greater vigour and enthusiasm in a different sphere. Now not so much in the interest of the underprivileged but against corruption, pollution and other social evils during the second part of the last decade. PIL became an instrument in the hands of the conscientious middle-class citizen inspired by the media to correct the inadequacies and slothfulness of the authorities and the establishment.

There was an acute sense in Indian society, particularly urban society that the overall quality of life was in terminal decline, a kind of civilizational malaise gripped the nation. A feeling that a deep gulf had developed between those in power and the people; that the former were wholly out of touch with the spirit of the times.

The Supreme Court chose not to remain silent in this crisis of confidence, speaking in its own way. It responded to the evidence uncovered by the media, and collected evidence from the street. 'The great problems', said Nietzche, 'are in the street'.

The Court, having remained unfulfilled by its superficial engagement with hollow concepts and shallow causes so far, sought to engage with the basic questions of human existence, of the everyday life of the people. It had interpreted the legal world in sundry ways; it sought to change it by combating the indifference and negligence of the legislatures and executive who had lost all credibility. In this crusade there were some individual judges who had the requisite judicial courage to take this task in hand, and respond to the call of the times. Two leaders of the judiciary performed their role admirably, although some aver that they exceeded their brief. These were the courageous Justice Verma, who later became the Chief Justice of India, and the irrepressible Justice Kuldip Singh. One focused on corruption, the other on pollution, and rather than view the problem in its overall ramifications, dealt with the 'here and now' of questions of sanitation, corruption, and social inequity. They sought to promote a new judicial culture by playing an enforcement role, which constituted a new form of judicial activity.

The Court resorted to an identifiable procedure in PIL for remedy of social and political abuses of power brought to their notice. Articles 14 and 21 were expanded to suit the situation. Articles 141 and 142 were invoked when necessary. Encouraged by the Court's responses and wide coverage of such judicial activities in the media and applause from outside, those involved in such causes pressed the Court to broaden the scope of its activities in those spheres. The Court was consequently caught up in an image trap. Its empire expanded. 'Little sincerity is a dangerous thing and a great deal of it is absolutely fatal', said Oscar Wilde on one occasion.

In these matters, the Court adopted a particular pattern. When the matters were brought before it and there were large numbers of these, it issued simple notices to respondents, compelled appearance, pursued the matters, saw to it that returns were filed, first with a little pursuasion and thereafter with threat of appropriate inquiry or investigation. It followed up the cases with vigour and zeal and ensured that charge sheets were filed where issues of corruption were concerned and that there was compliance with the numerous directions in cases relating to the environment. It utilized the CBI as its own exclusive agency for its purpose. It is not possible within the scope of this essay to enumerate in detail the steps taken by the Court but some reported cases have been referred to that will partially reveal the nature of the Court's intervention. The cases relating to corruption were *Hawala, Narasimha Rao, Chandraswami, Allotment of Petrol Pumps* and *Allotment of Houses, Skippers,* the *Vohra Committee Report, Donations to Political Parties,* amongst others.

Fifty-four significant politicians across different political parties, and several officials were involved in the Rs 40 crore bribery cases revealed in the personal diary of one Jain, seized by the CBI. The authorities were ambivalent and were dragging their feet in the investigation of the offences. PIL goaded the Court, and Justice Verma took it up with great zest for nearly four years. Three reported orders indicate the nature of the Court's initiative. It issued directions and orders to government authorities like the CBI and the Revenue Department to complete the investigation expeditiously. Copies of final reports, submitted, were to be supplied to the Court for its perusal and satisfaction. No settlement was to be made without the Court's permission. In *Vineet Narain v Union of India,*[43] charge sheets were filed in compliance with the Court's order, and the Court directed that in the *Anukul Pradhan* case[44] the trial was to be completed most expeditiously. In the *Hawala* case the inertia or inaction on the part of the CBI to initiate investigation against the politicians and bureaucrats named in the Jain diary were commented upon and steps were taken to insulate the CBI from extraneous influences.

The Court was concerned with the adverse impact of the lack of probity in public life leading to high degree of corruption. This also had an adverse effect on foreign investment and funding from the IMF and the World Bank, who have warned that future aid to developing countries may be subjected to requisite steps being taken to eradicate corruption, which prevents aid from reaching those for whom it is meant. Increasing corruption has led to investigative journalism, which is of value to a free society. The need to highlight corruption in public life through the medium of PIL invoking judicial review may be frequent in India but is not unknown in other countries.

The Court held that the powers conferred on it under Article 32 read with Articles 141, 142, and 144 empower it to issue directions to fill in the vacuum till such time as the legislature steps in to fill the lacuna and the executive discharges its responsibilities.

In 1998 however, in the *Hawala*[45] case it was held that the file containing loose sheets of paper was not a book of account and hence entries in the Jain diaries were not admissible under section 34 of Evidence Act; that the statements made on them did not alone constitute sufficient evidence to charge any person with liability. In the facts of the case, the entries made in the Hawala diaries, though admissible under section 34 did not constitute sufficient proof because they were not supported by independent evidence. Shukla and others were acquitted in the judgement that was delivered by a Bench comprising Justices Mukherjee, Kurdukar, and Thomas in *V.C. Shukla v Union of India*.[46]

A certain Lakhubhai Pathak of the United Kingdom filed a complaint that led to a case under section 120-B read with section 420 IPC being registered against Chandraswami and another. It was alleged that Chandraswami and another came into contact with Lakhubhai Pathak and led him to believe that they had sufficient influence in India to secure a lucrative contract in India for him. It was further alleged that the appellant Chandraswami induced him to pay US$ 100,000 to procure the contract for him. The money was alleged to have been paid to Chandraswami by two cheques. There was a dragging of feet but under the direction of the Supreme Court eventually charge sheets were filed.

Similarly, there was the *St Kitts forgery* case[47] involving Chandraswami relating to the fabrication of documents in which a charge sheet was filed by the CBI against him at the direction of the Court. Further directions were given by the Court that the trial be proceeded with and completed with the utmost expedition. This was necessary to meet the ends of justice and to maintain the credibility of the judicial process. This was true for all trials involving public men and preferably they should be completed within three months of commencement. The trials are at present continuing and the petitioner is on bail.

Again there was the case against Narasimha Rao in the *JMM Bribery* case[48] where the allegations were that JMM members were bribed during P.V. Narasimha Rao's Prime Ministership. Investigations were undertaken in which the Court intervened on many occasions. The trial continues.

Pursuant to a news item, the Director of Common Cause filed a PIL challenging the allotment of retail outlets for petroleum products (petrol pumps)[49] by the then Minister of State for Petroleum and Natural Gas Satish Sharma in favour of fifteen persons on the ground of poverty or unemployment. The allottees were related either to politicians or Oil Selection Boards or various officials within the Ministry. There were no fixed criteria or guidelines for making the allotments and no advertisement was issued. The allotments were held to be wholly arbitrary and discriminatory, having been made on wholly extraneous grounds, and were therefore mala fide and were struck down.

Pursuant to this order, after the above judgement was delivered, a show cause notice was issued to the Minister, Satish Sharma, as to why directions should not be issued to the police authorities to register a case and initiate criminal prosecution against him for breach of trust. Since the concept of absolute liability of a public servant for misfeasance has been of recent origin in India, even while awarding exemplary damages, it was felt that leniency should be shown. Bearing in view the facts and circumstances of the case, the Minister was directed to pay a sum of 50 lakh rupees as exemplary damages to the government exchequer within nine months. The CBI was further directed to complete investigation within three months of the receipt of the order. The Court expressed the view that this was a case fit for exemplary damages since the action of the public servant had been oppressive, arbitrary or unconstitutional. This case is reported as *Common Cause v Union of India*.[50]

However, in a review petition it was held that the State itself cannot have the right of being compensated for damages by its officers on the ground that they had contravened or violated the fundamental rights of a citizen.

In this case, where there was no identifiable plaintiff, even though the actions of the minister were arbitrary, it was short of misfeasance. The Court also held that the mere right to allot is not property capable of being misappropriated. Therefore, no case had been made out for registration of the case and investigation. Being a minister does not make one a trustee.[51]

In *Shiv Sagar Tiwari v Union of India*[52] the allotment of shops/stalls by Sheila Kaul, the then Minister for Housing and Urban Development to her own relatives/employees/domestic servants from a discretionary quota without following any policy criteria was held to be wholly arbitrary, mala fide, and unconstitutional. Following Satish Sharma's case, in which it was held that the minister was liable to pay Rs 60 lakh as exemplary damages to the government failing which it would be recovered from him, it was decreed that the CBI would inquire whether a prima facie case had been made out or not. Notice was issued to the allottees as to why their allotment should not be cancelled. Various facts were considered. The Committee's report regarding alternative accommodation was also raised. Several conclusions were arrived at and some palliative measures were suggested.

The question of subletting and recovery of licence fees was considered in another case between the same parties, *Shiv Sagar Tiwari v Union of India.*[53]

As an anticlimax, the entire exercise of the Supreme Court to curb discretionary power by enunciating a doctrine of trusteeship, and the principle of exemplary damages applicable to the arbitrary action of a minister was nullified when the President on a Sunday promulgated an ordinance to regulate the out-of-turn allotment of government houses to about 1800 government employees, nullifying the Supreme Court's order to evict them.

In the *Skipper* case,[54] a construction company invited the public to book flats in a multi-storeyed building constructed by it. Advances were paid and flats were booked, but the builders refused to allot the flats nor were they willing to return the advances to the investors. On a PIL the Court took notice of the impropriety. The Court took the government officer concerned to task, and directed the builders to allot flats, or to return the deposit. They failed. The Court auctioned the private properties of the builders, and directed that they be imprisoned. Rs 16 crore realized from auction by the Court was set aside to reimburse the investors. The various cases of *DDA v Skipper* illustrate the facts.

There was the Vohra Committee Report[55] kept under wraps by the government, which referred to the nexus amongst politicians, bureaucracy, and criminals. The Court in 1997 directed a nodal agency with the necessary powers, comprising high-level independent members, to be set up and be assisted by the investigating agencies. This body was to be appointed by the President, on the advice of the Prime Minister in consultation with the Speaker of the Lok Sabha to investigate matters such as those referred in the Vohra Committee Report. The judgement was delivered in 1997 on a PIL.

In order to curb money power in elections, the Court in response to a PIL[56] issued notice to all political parties to disclose the contributions they had received and whether they were maintaining proper receipts and expenditure accounts in line with the provisions of the Income Tax Act. The Court ruled that if the parties did not provide satisfactory responses, the substantive expenditure shown in the election return should be added to the candidates' own expenditure. This was intended as a means of substantially curbing the generation and consumption of black money. The political parties admitted that they had not filed returns and the government that it had not enforced the mandatory provisions for filing returns. Both were directed to comply with the legal provisions.

There were several other cases of corruption that were brought to the notice of the Court to which it attended.

There were cases of pollution of water due to discharge of toxic effluents by industries situated on the banks of rivers.[57] The Court sought to remedy this by issuing various directions. The discharge of polluting effluents harmful to the environment was sought to be controlled by issuing necessary directions. To halt the denudation of forests, activities associated with wood products like saw mills were directed to cease their activities.[58] Illegal mining operations, when brought to the notice of the Court, were directed to stop forthwith.[59] Hazardous industries from Delhi were sought to be shifted outside the municipal limits,[60] through a series of orders. Alternative sites were identified to enable such a shift. The Court issued notices to tanneries[61] which were polluting water sources, directing them to move to alternative locations. Various directions were issued for the installation of pollution control system to minimize air pollution by industires.[62] Shrimp farms[63] were polluting water sources. Various directions were issued by the Court and eventually shrimp farms were directed to close down. The problem of Traffic pollution[64] was looked into and remedies provided for. The Court was seriously concerned with garbage disposal[65] in Delhi city. For three years in succession, orders and directions were issued periodically by the Court for enforcement of the prescribed remedies.[66] It involved the public trust doctrine relating to preservation of natural resources, the doctrine of precautionary principles and sustainable development theories to arm itself with the right to intervene in the event of pollution and to provide sundry remedies.

Conclusion

In virtually all the significant cases there have been differences of opinion amongst the judges with regard to the ultimate decision. In reality, the decisions of the Court are the choices of the particular elderly persons chosen from time to time, and appear to be mere preferences. In construing statutes, rules, executive orders or the Constitution, the Court inevitably weighs competing arguments, interests, and philosophies to arrive at decisions. Every judicial decision rewards a particular interest or viewpoint and deprives another. 'Decisions are therefore allocative of societies' scarce resources making them by definition, political.' Someone said, 'Legal reasoning is bunk, law is politics and its agencies and agents are part of the push and pull of political process.' 'The so-called objective legal values can be manipulated to justify an almost infinite spectrum of possible outcomes. There is no middle ground. If law is politics it is little else. All is indeed preference: the policy choice of those in a position to make or influence legal decisions.' As has been noted earlier, the pulls and pressures of contemporary political forces, the prevalent economic realities and social events have influenced the functioning of the Court, and though it remains unaltered in form, new voices, new emphases, new sounds emerge, perhaps, as they say, like the constant 'ringing in the sun'.[67]

It would be immensely disturbing to acknowledge that law is nothing but politics. To call judicial decisions reasoned, means little, because they are merely tools and not an end. We are currently in a situation in which one or a group of select few hold supreme authority to impose their preferences periodically over society as a whole. People would, however, like to believe that the decisions reached by the Court are neutral, perfect, and almost divine. This gap between such illusions and the actual reality is occupied by what Mac Iver would call 'myths' which play a specific role in sustaining 'social unities and social continuities'.

Society in India today in the interests of the judiciary, for its unity, existence, and authority, has evolved some myths and symbols. 'Justice' is the greatest of them all. 'We are a Government of Law and not of men' is another. 'Similarly, however high you be, law is above you.' These myths operate to create a situation of acceptance of things as they are; of the status quo. These and most others 'conjure up the notion of a higher divine, impersonal law'. The accompanying symbols like robe, elevated Benches, the special language and the courtroom help to sustain the myth of an impersonal law. Due to these myths, the judiciary is believed to be a source of divine decisions based on some objective truth encapsulated in the Constitution and knowable only to a select few.

One notices that the decisions are often inconsistent, the pendulum of the court sometimes swinging from one side to the other. Its orders are likened by some to a throw of dice, yet people abide by their judgements, obey their decisions, regard the Court as if it were a secular deity and the judges Gods in secular form.

Notes

[1] *A.K. Gopalan v State of Madras* AIR 1950 SC 27.
[2] *State of Bihar v Maharajadhiraja Kameswar Singh & Others* (1952) SCR 889.
[3] *Sri Sankari Prasad Singh Deo v Union of India & State of Bihar* (1952) SCR 89.
[4] *Parshotam Lal Dhingra v Union of India* (1958) SCR 828.

[5] *State of Madras v V.G. Row* 1952 SCR 597.

[6] *Romesh Thapar v State of Madras* (1950) SCR 594.

[7] *Brij Bhusan* case. *Brij Bhushan v State of Delhi* (1950) SCR 605.

[8] *I.C. Golak Nath v The State of Punjab* (1967) 2 SCR 762.

[9] *Rustom Cowasjee Cooper v Union of India* [UOI] (1970) 3 SCR 530.

[10] *H.H. Maharajadhiraja Madhav Rao Jiwaji Rao v UOI* (1971) 3 SCR 9.

[11] *His Holiness Kesavananda Bharati Sripadagalvaru v State of Kerala* (1973) Supp SCR 1.

[12] *A.D.M. Jabalpur v S.S. Shukla* (1976) Supp SCR 172.

[13] *Maneka Gandhi v UOI* (1978) 2 SCR 621.

[14] *Ramana Dayaram Shetty v The International Airport Authority of India* (1979) 3 SCR 1014.

[15] *Minerva Mills Limited v UOI* (1981) 1 SCR 206.

[16] *Union of India v Bhanu Das* (1977) 2 SCR 719.

[17] *In re The Special Courts Bill,* (*1978*) 1979 2 SCR 476.

[18] *State of Rajasthan v UOI* (1978) 1 SCR 1.

[19] *S.P. Gupta v UOI* (1982) 2 SCR 365.

[20] *A.K. Roy v UOI* (1982) 2 SCR 272.

[21] *R.K. Garg v UOI* (1982) 1 SCR 947.

[22] *Sanjeev Coke Manufacturing Co. v Bharat Coking Coal Ltd. & Another* (1983) 1 SCR 1000.

[23] *Pravakar Production v Rajendra Kumar Tondon* 1998 *Rahabar Productions Pvt. Ltd. v Rajendra Kumar Tandon* (1998) 4 SCC 49; *Malpe Viswanath Acharaya & Ors v State of Maharastra & Others* (1998) 2 SCC 1.

[24] *Karimahen K. Bagad v State of Gujarat* (1998) 6 SCC 264; *Smt. Sultan Abdul Kader v Jt. Secy. to Government of India* (1998) 8 SCC 343; *Premalata Sharma v District Magistrate, Mathura* (1998) 4 SCC 260; *Union of India v Parasmal Rampuria* (1998) 8 SCC 402.

[25] *Union of India v Tulasiram Patel* (1985) Supp 2 SCR 131.

[26] *Central Inland Water Transport Corpn v Brojonath Ganguly* (1986) 3 SCC 156.

[27] *Bijoe Emmamuel v State of Kerala* (1986) 3 SCC 615.

[28] *M.C. Mehta v UOI* (1986) 2 SCC 176.

[29] *Rylands v Fletcher* (1868) LR 3 HL 330.

[30] *Dr D.C. Wadhwa v State of Bihar* 1987 1 SCC 378.

[31] *Charan Lal Sahu v UOI* (1990) 1 SCC 613.

[32] *Union Carbide v UOI* (1991) 4 SCC 584.

[33] *A.R. Antulay v R.S. Nayak* (1988) 2 SCC 602.

[34] *Subcommittee of Judicial Accountability v UOI* (1991) 4 SCC 699; *Sarojini Ramaswami v UOI* (1992) 4 SCC 506.

[35] *K. Veeraswami v UOI* (1991) 3 SCC 655.

[36] *Indra Sawhney v UOI* 1992 Supp 3 SCC 217.

[37] *Dr Preeti Srivastava & Anr v State of MP IT* 1999(5) SC 498.

[38] *Indira Sawhney v UOI IT* 1999 (5) SC 557.

[39] *Ajit Singh & Ors v State of Punjab* (1999) 7 SCC 209.

[40] *Dr M. Ismail Faruqui v UOI* (1994) 6 SCC 360; *Achhan Rizvi v State of UP* (1994) 6 SCC 751–62; (1994) 6 SCC 751–62.

[41] *S.R. Bommai v UOI* (1994) 3 SCC 1.

[42] *In Re V.C. Misra* (1995) 2 SCC 584; *SC Bar Association v UOI* (1998) 4 SCC 409.

[43] *Vineet Narain v UOI* (1996) 2 SCC 199.

[44] *Anukul Chandra Pradhan v UOI* (1996) 6 SCC 354.

[45] *Vineet Narayan v UOI* (1998) 1 SCC 226.

[46] *CBI v Shukla* (1998) 3 SCC 410.

[47] *Chandraswami v CBI* (1996) 6 SCC 751; *Chandraswami v CBI* (1998) 9 SCC 380; *CBI v Chandraswami* (1997) 3 SCC 214; *CBI v Chandraswami* JT (1998) SC 2 667.

[48] *Commissioner of Police, Delhi v Registrar Delhi High Court.* 1996 6 SCC 323; *P.V. Narasimha Rao v State* (CBI/SPE) JMM (1998) 4 SCC 626.

[49] *Centre for Public Interest Litigation v UOI* (1995) Supp 3 SCC 382; *Common Cause, A Regd Society v UOI* (1996) 6 SCC 530.

[50] *Common Cause, A Regd. Society v UOI* (1996) 6 SCC 593.

[51] *Common Cause, A Regd. Society v UOI* (1999) 6 SCC 667.

[52] *Shiv Sagar Tiwari v UOI* (1996) 6 SCC 599; *Shiv Sagar Tiwari v UOI* (1997) 1 SCC 444.

[53] *Shiv Sagar Tiwari v UOI* (1997) 10 SCC 211.

[54] *DDA v Skipper* (1995) 3 SCC 507; *DDA v Skipper* (1995) Supp (2) SCC 160; *DDA v Skipper* (1996) 1 SCC 272; *DDA v Skipper* (1996) 4 SCC 622; *DDA v Skipper* (1997) 11 SCC 430.

[55] *Dinesh Trivedi MD v UOI* (1997) 4 SCC 306.

[56] *Common Cause, A Regd Society v UOI* (1996) 2 SCC 752.

[57] *Vineet Kumar Mathur v UOI* (1996) 1 SCC 119; *In Re Bhavani River* (1998) 2 SCC 601.

[58] *Banwasi Seva Ashram v State of UP* (1993) 2 SCC 612; *T.N. Godavarman Thirumulkpad v UOI* (1997) 2 SCC 267; *Supreme Court Monitoring Committee v Mussoorie–Dehradun Devp. Authority* (1997) 11 SCC 605; *T.N. Godavarman Thirumulkpad v UOI* (1998) 9 SCC 632 & 672.

[59] *M/s ARC Cement Ltd v State of UP* (1993) Supp 1 SCC 426; *M.C. Mehta v UOI* (1996) 8 SCC 462.

[60] *M.C. Mehta v UOI* (1996) 4 SCC 351; *M.C. Mehta v UOI* (1997) 11 SCC 327.

[61] *Vellore Citizen's Welfare Forum v UOI* (1996) 5 SCC 647; *M.C. Mehta v UOI* (1997) 2 SCC 411; *M.C. Mehta v UOI* (1998) 9 SCC 448.

[62] *M.C. Mehta v UOI* (1994) Supp 3 SCC 717.

[63] *S. Jagannath v UOI* (1997) 2 SCC 87; *Gopi Aqua Farms v UOI* (1997) 6 SCC 577; *Animal Environment Legal v UOI* (1997) 3 SCC 549.

[64] *M.C. Mehta v UOI* (1999) 1 SCC 413; *M.C. Mehta v UOI* (1998) 8 SCC 648; *M.C. Mehta v UOI* (1998) 8 SCC 206.

[65] *Virendra Gaur v State of Haryana* (1995) 2 SCC 577; *Dr B.L. Wadehra v UOI* (1996) 2 SCC 594; *M.C. Mehta v UOI* (1996) 4 SCC 750; *Research Foundation for Science v UOI* (1999) 1 SCC 223.

[66] *Public Trust Doctrine of 'precautionary principles' and 'substainable development'.* *Indian Council for Enviro–legal Action v UOI* 1(1996) 3 SCC 212; *M.C. Mehta v Kamal Nath* (1997) 1 SCC 388; *Suo Motu Proceedings in the Delhi Transport Deptt* (1998) 9 SCC 250.

[67] Harry P. Stumpf, *American Judicial Politics,* San Diego: Harcourt Brace Jovanovich, 1988.

Three

The Supreme Court and the Constitution

Lord Templeman

The Constitution

On 9 December 1946 there met for the first time a Constituent Assembly whose members had been chosen by the Provincial Assemblies elected under the Government of India Act, 1935. The task of the Constituent Assembly was to draft a constitution for free India. By the Indian Independence Act, 1947 the Constituent Assembly was authorized to promulgate the Constitution which was passed on 26 Novermber 1949 and came into force on 26 January 1950.

In the course of their deliberations the members of the Constituent Assembly rejected the Presidential form of government exemplified by the United States of America and, with some reluctance, the devolved form of village government dear to the heart of Mahatma Gandhi and chose a federal parliamentary form of government based on adult suffrage.

India was declared to be a Union of States. Legislative powers were divided between the Parliament of the Union and the Legislative Assemblies of each state. The executive powers of the Union were vested in the President acting in accordance with the advice of the Council of Ministers headed by the Prime Minister and accountable to the lower house of Parliament, the House of the People or the Lok Sabha. The executive powers of each state were vested in the Governor acting on the advice of the Council of Ministers headed by the Chief Minister accountable to the Legislative Assembly.

Article 124 of the Constitution established the Supreme Court of India consisting of the Chief Justice of India and seven, now twenty-five, judges. High Courts for each state and subordinate Courts were established and authorized.

The Powers and Duties of the Supreme Court

By Article 131 the Supreme Court was given original and exclusive jurisdiction in any dispute between the Government of India and state or between states involving any question of law or fact on which the existence of the extent of a legal right depends.

By Article 132, an appeal to the Supreme Court from a high court lies in any civil, criminal, or other proceedings if a high court certifies that a substantial question of law as to the interpretation of the Constitution is involved. By Article 133(1), civil and criminal appeals lie from any decision of the high court on a question of law, and with leave. In addition, by Article 136 the Supreme Court may grant special leave to appeal from any decision 'in any cause or matter passed or made by any court or tribunal in the territory of India'. By Article 144, all authorities, civil and judicial in the territory of India shall act in aid of the Supreme Court. Thus, the Supreme Court was given extensive powers to interfere in any proceedings to secure justice.

In a federal Constitution it falls to the judiciary to interpret and enforce the powers, right, and limitations conferred and imposed on institutions and individuals. Thus, as early as 1803, Chief Justice Marshall in *Marbury v Madison*,[1] speaking of the constitution of the United States, said: 'It is emphatically the power and duty of the judiciary to say what the law is'. In *Kaul's* case[2] the Supreme Court of India observed that

In a written Constitution the powers of the various organs of the State are limited by the Constitution. The extent of those limitations has to be determined on the interpretation of the relevant provisions of the Constitution ... the task of interpreting the provisions of the Constitution is entrusted to the judiciary which is vested with the power to test the validity of the actions of any authority functioning under the Constitution ... in order to ensure that the authority exercising the power conferred by the Constitution does not transgress the limitations imposed by the Constitution on the exercise of that power. This power of judicial review is therefore implicit in a written Constitution and unless expressly excluded by the provisions of the Constitution, the power of judicial review is available in respect of the exercise of powers under any provision of the Constitution.

The Supreme Court and the Preamble

The Preamble to the Constitution as amended in 1976, affirms the resolve of the people of India to constitute India into a Sovereign, Socialist, Secular, Democratic Republic and to secure to all its citizens Justice, social economic and political, Liberty of thought, expression, belief, faith and worship, and Equality of status and opportunity.

In *Berubari's* case[3] the Supreme Court said that the Preamble set forth the general principles for which the Constituent Assembly made the several provisions of the Constitution but is not any part of the Constitution. In *Ragunathrao's* case[4] the Preamble was said not to be the source of any substantive law or the source of any prohibitions or limitations. In *Bommai's* case[5] the Court said that the Preamble indicates the basic structure of the Constitution. In practice, the Preamble has assisted the Court in the construction of the various provisions of the Constitution and in the determination of those features of the Constitution that are basic and inviolable.

In *The Synthetics* case[6] the Court said that 'Sovereignty' meant that the state has power to legislate on any subject to promote the health, moral standards, education, and good order of the people subject only to the due process of legislation and to the limitations imposed by the Constitution.

The word 'Socialist' added to the Preamble in 1976 has been productive of some misunderstanding and generated some hostility towards India, particularly in the United States. The form of democracy embodied in the Constitution is inconsistent with the discredited system of communism found in the constitution of the USSR. In *Nakara's* case[7] the Supreme Court of India rejected the argument that socialism involves collectivism or nationalization and opined that the principal aim of a socialist state is to eliminate inequality in income and status and standards of life. In practice, that aim is seen by governments to involve less interference and greater economic freedom.

The word 'Secularism' does not, said the Court in *Bommai's* case impinge on the freedom of religion granted by the Constitution to individuals, but that freedom only permits the free pursuit of the spiritual life as distinct from the secular life, which remains the exclusive domain of the affairs of state; therefore no political party can base itself on a religious aim.

The Supreme Court and the Fundamental Rights

In the forefront of the Constitution designed to give effect to the Preamble, Part III of the Constitution defines and guarantees to the citizens of India certain Fundamental Rights. Those Rights include those which the declarations of the United Nations, the European Union, the United States, and other national Constitutions perceive to be essential, including equality before the law, prohibition of discrimination on grounds of religion, race, caste, sex, or place of birth, freedom of expression, freedom of religion, and the protection of life and liberty.

The Rights asserted by the Constitution would be of no avail if there were no means of enforcement. By Article 13 of the Constitution, all laws inconsistent with the Fundamental Rights are void, and it is of course the province of the Courts to identify and strike down any infringing laws. The Supreme Court is the ultimate Court of appeal from the high courts. In addition and uniquely, with some safeguards to prevent abuse, appeals to the Supreme Court lie from any court or tribunal in the territory of India. Finally, Article 32 of the Constitution confers on every citizen the right to move the Supreme Court for the enforcement of the Fundamental Rights. The Court is given power to issue directions or orders or writs for the enforcement of the Fundamental Rights. Thus, the Supreme Court may act as a first or last Court of resort to protect Fundamental Rights for any of the citizens of India who now number 930 million. This enormous jurisdiction is only kept under control by the Court selecting cases of great importance or gravity, and even so the workload of the Court and the inevitable delay in many cases are onerous and taxing. The Supreme Court has exercised its powers without adherence to procedures which would prevent the ignorant or illiterate from claiming their rights. The Court demands responses from any authority, public or private, and grants the widest forms of relief including injunctions and orders for payment of compensation. The Court has said that 'Where a letter is addressed by an aggrieved person or a public spirited individual, or a social action group for enforcement of constitutional rights of a person or class or group of persons who by reason of poverty, disability or social or economic disadvantage find it difficult to approach the Court, the Supreme Court is bound to treat the letter as a writ petition for relief (*State of H.P. v Parent of a Student*[8]). Fundamental rights are not to be stultified by rules of procedure; *Nakara's* case. In one instance a journalist wrote to the Court drawing attention to the plight of a number of youths awaiting trial for a period exceeding the possible punishment for the alleged offences and overlooked in prison. The letter was treated as a formal application for relief by the prisoners and inquiries and orders were made resulting in the speedy release of the accused.

The Supreme Court has also been innovative in the construction of the ambit of the Fundamental Rights. Article 21 of the Constitution, which protects life and liberty 'except according to procedures established by law' was held to confer the right to legal aid which the Court ordered the States to provide (*Khatri's* case).[9]

The Court pioneered the concept of public interest litigation; see *Ratlam Municipality v Vardichand.*[10] In the protection of fundamental rights to equality and life the Court has outlawed arbitrary or unreasonable actions of all kinds. Protection has been extended to pavement dwellers, destitute women, bonded labourers, victims of pollution, and other disadvantaged groups and individuals. In *Randhir Singh v Union*[11] the principle of equal pay for equal work was accepted by the Court.

The Supreme Court and the Executive

Democracy cannot survive without an independent judiciary assisted by an independent legal profession. There are inevitable conflicts of view between an executive taking action which ministers deem to be in the public interest and an independent judiciary charged with ensuring that executive action does not exceed the powers conferred by the Constitution or infringe the rule of law.

The Supreme Court has been robust in maintaining its independence. In 1973 three senior Supreme Court judges who had delivered judgements unpalatable to the government were passed over when the office of Chief Justice became vacant. The three judges resigned and great disquiet was voiced by the legal profession and commentators. Now in practice the next senior judge is appointed Chief Justice of India when a vacancy occurs. Whatever the theoretical disadvantages of this convention, it has produced a number of distinguished leaders of the Supreme Court who have not only been responsible for illuminating the law but have also been active in reforming practice and procedure, and introducing new methods of making the law accessible and less costly and time consuming. The flood of litigation in India shows no signs of subsiding, and that flood is largely a reflection of the desirable spread of knowledge of the rights conferred by the Constitution on all citizens.

In 1976 the government proposed to transfer some fifty-six state and other judges against their will, a procedure calculated to make judges careful not to offend the executive. This procedure was successfully challenged by one of the threatened judges.

Article 124 of the Constitution empowers the President (acting on the advice of the Prime Minister and Cabinet) to appoint the judges of the Supreme Court. The President is given a discretion about consulting judges of the Supreme Court and High Courts but 'in the case of appointment of a Judge other than the Chief Justice, the Chief Justice of India shall always be consulted'. Similarly, Article 217 requires the Chief Justice of India to be consulted concerning the appointment of a judge of the High Court of a state. In 1993 in the *Supreme Court Advocates on Record Association* case[12] the Supreme Court by a majority held that, having regard to the independence of the judiciary and the separation of powers which the Court held to be implicit in the Constitution, the views of the Chief Justice of India expressed when he was consulted must be supreme. The Court also laid down guidelines governing the appointment and duration of office of temporary acting judges. The majority decision has been criticized as an extension of the meaning of the word 'consultation'. However, having regard to the earlier experience in India of attempts by the executive to influence the personalities and attitudes of members of the judiciary, and having regard to the successful attempts made in Pakistan to control the judiciary, and having regard to the unfortunate results of the appointment of Supreme Court judges of the United States by the President subject to approval by Congress, the majority decision of the Supreme Court of India in the *Advocates on Record* case marks a welcome assertion of the independence of the judiciary and is the best method of obtaining appointments of integrity and quality, a precedent method which the British could follow with advantage.

In *Bommai's* case the Supreme Court struck down a Proclamation made by the President of India under section 356 whereby the Union government may suspend a state government where that government has effectively broken down and may substitute, temporarily, government by the Union. The Court asserted the right to judicial review of the Proclamation and declared the Proclamation in respect of the State of Karnataka invalid because there was no material on which the President could have based a conclusion that state government had broken down. A Proclamation against Uttar Pradesh was however upheld because there was evidence that the state government was pursuing anti-secular policies notwithstanding that secularism was part of the basic structure of the Constitution.

The Supreme Court and the Legislature

The Supreme Court has also been vigilant to protect the integrity of the Constitution from an impatient Parliament asserting total supremacy through the operation of the express power contained in the Constitution for the amendment of the Constitution. Article 368 authorizes Parliament to amend the Constitution by a Bill passed by a majority of the total membership of each House and a majority of not less than two-thirds of the members of that House present and voting. Certain amendments require ratification by the legislatures of not less than one half of the states. The authors of the Constitution would have been surprised to discover that upwards of seventy-five amendments were passed in the first fifty years.

In 1971, the Twenty-fourth and Twenty-fifth Amendments to the Constitution sought, *inter alia,* to prevent any challenge in the Courts to the validity of amendments under Article 368 and sought also to remove certain legislation from challenge on the grounds that the legislation involved a breach of fundamental rights. In *Kesavananda's* case[13] the Supreme Court held that Article 368 did not permit amendments to the Constitution which were inconsistent with the basic structure of the Constitution; that basic structure requires adherence to the principles of democracy and the rule of law. The Supreme Court decided that Article 368 gave Parliament a wide but not untrammelled power to amend the Constitution. The power did not extend to any amendment that infringed the basic structure of the Constitution which enshrined democracy and the rule of law. The rule of law requires that an independent judiciary should have the right and duty to consider in all cases whether Parliament or any other institution has exceeded the bounds prescribed by the Constitution. It was the task of the Supreme Court to determine whether any amendment and any statute infringed the basic structure of the Constitution. The offending parts of the 24th and 25th Amendments were held to be invalid. *Kesavananda's* case and subsequent authorities have established that it is for the Supreme Court to determine the basic structure of the Constitution and to rule on infringements, and that the power of judicial review and the independence of the judiciary form part of the basic structure.

In 1975 the Thirty-ninth Amendment purported to free the election of a prime minister from challenge in the Courts and purported to reserve the decision of the High Court of Allahabad which had set aside the election of Mrs Indira Gandhi on her conviction for electoral malpractice. The offending parts of the Thirty-ninth Amendment were struck down in *Indira Gandhi v Raj Narain*[14] on the grounds that they were inconsistent with the doctrine of the separation of powers, which was a basic feature of the Constitution. The Supreme Court has held on more than one occasion that basic structure includes the rule of law and precludes the legislature from interfering with the right and duty of the judiciary to hear and determine causes lawfully before the courts and precludes the legislature from placing any individual above the law.

By the Forty-second Amendment (1976) Parliament purported to restrict the exercise of the fundamental freedoms affirmed by Articles 14 and 19, namely, equality before the law and freedom of speech. Parliament also purported to exclude certain enactments from judicial review. These restrictions and exclusions were held to be void in the *Minerva Mills* case[15] because, the Court held, Articles 14 and 19 confer the most elementary freedoms without which a free democracy is impossible. The Amendment infringed the basic structure of the Constitution in respect of two essential features, namely, the limited extent of the power of amendment conferred on Parliament and the power of judicial review for the purpose of examining whether any authority under the Constitution has been exceeded; both these features form part of the basic structure of the Constitution which cannot be abrogated. See also *Wamanrao's* case[16] and *Gupta's* case[17] where the independence of the judiciary was emphasized to be part of the basic structure of the Constitution. The history of the twentieth century would have been different if the judiciary of the Weimar Republic had publicly asserted the independence of the judiciary, the power of judicial review, and the rule of law when these principles were first threatened.

Conclusion

The Supreme Court has proved to be a steady and consistent upholder of the intentions of the Constituent Assembly expressing the ideals and beliefs of Jawaharlal Nehru and the other founders of independent India. The Court has been tireless in upholding fundamental rights which are the hallmark of a civilized society and in interpreting and enforcing those provisions of the Constitution which preserve a democratic society.

In 1947 India was torn apart and now the Republic of India is faced with the enmity of Pakistan, the malice of China, and the hostility of other countries where democracy and the rule of law has had no place. Federations throughout the world have been or are being broken up by groups and individuals preaching violence and exploiting ignorance. India with the burden of an expanding population, has inherited problems of poverty and illiteracy. The work of the Government of India for the improvement of economic and social standards and for the preservation of a democratic society deserves recognition and support by other democratic countries. The work of the Supreme Court of India in protecting the people of India from oppression and in upholding the rule of law demands respect and admiration.

Notes

[1] (1803) 1 Cranch 137.

[2] *A.K. Kaul v UOI* (1995) 4 SCC 73.

[3] *The President of India under Article 143(1) v of the Constitution of India implementation* (Berubari's case) (1960) 3 SCR 250.

[4] *Raghunathrao Ganpatrao v UOI* (1993) 1 SCR 480.

[5] *S.R. Bommai v UOI* (1994) 2 SCR 644.

[6] *Synthetics & Chemicals Ltd. v State of UP* (1989) Supp 1 SCR 623.

[7] *D.S. Nakara v UOI* (1983) 2 SCR 165.

[8] *State of HP v Student's Parent Medical College, Shimla* (1985) 3 SCR 676.

[9] *Khatri v State of Bihar* (1981) 3 SCR 145.

[10] *Municipal Council Ratlam v Vardhichand & Ors* (1981) 1 SCR 97.

[11] *Randhir Singh v UOI* (1982) 3 SCR 298.

[12] *Supreme Court Advocates on Record Association v UOI* (1993) Supp 2 SCR 659.

[13] *Holiness Kesavananda Bharati Sripadagalvaru v State of Kerala* (1973) Supp SCR 1.

[14] *Indira Nehru Gandhi v Raj Narain* (1976) 2 SCR 347.

[15] *Minerva Mills Ltd v UOI* (1981) 1 SCR 206.

[16] *Waman Rao v UOI* (1981) 2 SCR 1.

[17] *S.P. Gupta & Ors. v Union of India & Ors.* (1982) 2 SCR 365.

Four

Fifty Years on

Marc Galanter

The Supreme Court's fiftieth anniversary is a fitting occasion to survey the achievements of the judiciary of a reborn India. As someone who has spent much of my life working on Indian law, I have always been saddened by the apathy toward India that is so prevalent in the legal world ouside the country. India has pulled off the astonishing feat of sustaining a regime of constitutional liberty with vigorous judicial pro- tection of human rights in a very large, very poor and very diverse soci- ety. In the face of daunting obstacles, the Indian courts have succeeded in sustaining a regime of constitutional order and legal regularity. With scant material resources, they have managed to adapt the structure of colonial law to the vastly different conditions of independent, demo- cratic India and to protect and extend constitutional liberty. For all its flaws and imperfections, this is surely one of the epic legal accomplish- ments of this century, yet it has gone largely unappreciated by support- ers of democracy and the rule of law.

For a legal order to flourish requires not only the leadership of judges and the mediation of lawyers, but the responsive participation of the citizenry. For the law to infuse the practices of institutions and inform the dispositions of citizens, those citizens need access to the law's protec- tions and remedies. Since courts are passive institutions, they have to be moved by citizens. One of the glories of the Indian legal system is that citizens have direct access to the higher judiciary to effectuate one vital set of protections. However, for most citizens and most matters, the site at which they could use the system is the lower courts. At the very time that the higher reaches of the judicial system have proved extraordinar- ily responsive and resilient, its lower reaches appear to be locked into a spiral of escalating gridlock and ineffectiveness.

One sign of this infirmity is public disdain for and avoidance of these lower courts. Since British times, it has been widely believed that the Indian population is extremely litigious.[1] This piece of received wisdom is however far from the mark. Indeed the rate of utilization or invocation of these courts by the citizens of India is very low. Reliable data are scarce and the state of record-keeping makes collecting them a daunting task, but there are sufficient bits to suggest that India is among the lowest in the world per capita use of courts. Before his untimely death, the late Professor Christian Wollschlager, the trailblazer of comparative judicial statistics, presented a comparison of the per capita rate of filing of civil cases in some 35 jurisdictions for the ten-year period 1987–96. Rates of filing in courts of first instance per 1000 persons ranged from 123 in Germany and 111 in Sweden at the high end to 2.6 in Nepal and 1.7 in Ethiopia at the bottom.[2] Since no national figures are available for India, Professor Wollschlager included in his comparison figures on Maharashtra, which ranked thirty-second of the thirty-five jurisdictions with an annual per capita rate of 3.5 filings per 1000 persons. There is no reason to believe that Maharashtra has less litigation than India as a whole, since the data point to a general correlation of court use with economic development. A few qualifications are however necessary to frame the comparison. First a smaller proportion of the population of Maharashtra are adults than is the case in the developed countries at the top of the list. Second, societies differ in what matters they assign to courts or to alternative institutions. Third, the nomenclature and record-keeping of these alternatives may defeat any attempt to include them. Thus, in Maharashtra the count was of courts and did not include the many matters brought to tribunals of various kinds. Finally, in India, civil courts' delays and court fees may induce some claimants to divert their efforts to criminal courts. These qualifications, notwithstanding the Wollschlager study, suggest that the received wisdom is quite unrelated to actual patterns of use of Indian courts.

The suspicions aroused by the Wollschlager study gain some confirmation from an earlier study by Robert Moog, who examined litigation rates in Uttar Pradesh from 1951 to 1976; a stopping point dictated by the fact that the state stopped issuing these statistics then.[3] He found that per capita civil filings in all district level courts in UP had fallen dramatically from the early days of Independence, when there were 1.63 per thousand persons in 1951 to 1976 when there were only 0.88 per thousand. Again, such a fall might reflect the decrease in adults as a portion of the total population and diversion into tribunals, as well as the effect of land reforms. However, once again we find the data contravene the dominant perception of India as increasingly litigious.

How can it be that few and perhaps fewer Indians invoke the courts while there is a widespread perception that the courts are inundated with cases, that frivolous litigation is rife, and that there is an abundance of hungry lawyers? Is there a connection between the relative scarcity of litigation and the impression that there is so much of it?

Certainly the Indian courts are desperately congested, even though the number of cases filed is small on a per capita basis. They appear to be heavily used because there are relatively few courts (in comparison to other common law countries). These courts are poorly equipped and inefficient. Delay is endemic. Outmoded procedural laws provide abundant scope for delaying tactics. Judges, fearful of the Bar, lack leverage to discipline lawyers or use the available tools to expedite proceedings. Cases linger interminably and arrears mount.

The public has low (and generally realistic) expectations of law, lawyers, and courts.[4] Potential users forgo the lower courts or avoid them wherever possible; many from ignorance and many from calculation. The basic problem of low use of the courts and lawyers is that they are able to deliver so little by way of remedy, protection, and vindication. The courts provide a useful facility for those who wish to postpone payment of taxes or debts and those who wish to forestall eviction or other legal action. Generally, they serve those who benefit from delay and non-implementation of legal norms, that is, parties who are already in possession or satisfied with the status quo. For those who require vindication and prompt implementation of remedies and protections against dominant parties—women from husbands or relatives, labourers from landowners, citizens from government—the system works only haltingly, partially, and occasionaly. Since so many of the potential meritorious claims are absent from the courts, it is not surprising that the claims that are present there include a significant proportion that are 'frivolous' in the sense of being brought for purposes of harassment and delay.

Given the long delay (and high interest rates at which future value must be discounted), mounting expenses and meagre damage awards, the present value of most suits for money damages is probably close to zero if not negative. Indeed, much litigation in India can be described as a 'sunk cost auction'[5] in which the competitors invest ever-higher amounts in the hope of staving off larger losses. Widespread popular intuition of this produces avoidance of the civil courts and the diversion of potential money damages cases into criminal cases and claims for injunctive relief.

For large sectors of society and large areas of conduct, courts afford no remedies or protections. When pressure builds up to provide remedies, the solution is typically not to reform the lower courts but to bypass them. In a way, the writ jurisdiction is the prototype for this bypassing strategy, which has been applied to motor vehicle accidents and consumer grievances. The forums created by these measures are court-like: they weigh competing proofs and arguments within a framework of authoritative rules. The notion is that they will do a superior or at least more efficient job of adjudication than the regular courts.

Recently, would-be reformers have embraced another strategy of reform which we might label informalism; an approach that abandons or dilutes the idea of adjudication. In most or all societies with flourishing legal systems, most regulation takes place and most disputes are resolved through informal processes of deference, reciprocity, and bargaining rather than through the formal legal process; and of those disputes taken to formal legal processes a great many or most are resolved by informal bargaining that leads to settlement. The fact that informal appendages of the formal legal system are the location of the resolution of so many disputes gives rise to the impression that informal devices produce results independently of the formal legal system. Their independent functioning however is at least partly illusory.

So long as recourse to the courts is a viable alternative, the outcomes in informal bargaining reflect to some degree the bargaining endowments conferred by the law, as registered in the commonplace 'bargaining in the shadow of the law'.[6] The parties' endowments reflect not only the entitlements conferred by substantive legal rules, but also the rules (or procedure, evidence, and so forth) that enable those entitlements to be vindicated. Rules are however only one part of the endowment conferred by the legal forum: the delay, cost and uncertainty of eliciting a favourable determination factors that reflect rules but are heavily influenced by such non-rule factors as the number and organization or courts and lawyers—also confer bargaining counters on the disputants.[7]

The present enthusiasm for Lok Adalats presents a striking instance of this illusion of informal remedies as a realm independent of the law. The Lok Adalats' achievement, it appears, is to provide an official process for claimants to secure a portion of their entitlements without the aggravation, extortionate expense, inordinate delay, and tormenting uncertainty of the court process. To secure this, they yield up discounts. Assume, for example, a motor accident claimant who would secure

Rs 50,000 compensation after an expensive ten-year struggle in the courts. Imagine that this same claimant might be able to get half that amount at a Lok Adalat in just a few months. This is clearly a preferable outcome for the claimant, given the legal costs avoided and given the appropriate discount for the futurity and uncertainty of the court recovery. Thus, the establishment of the Lok Adalat is viewed as providing a significant benefit for a claimant in this situation.

Of course, this claimant is actually entitled not to the discounted 2010 value of his claim, but to the full 2000 value. What makes the delivery of the discounted amount a 'benefit' is simply that the full entitlement can be vindicated only by recourse to a disastrously flawed system that can at best deliver it in 2010. Thus the 'benefit' is a benefit only by virtue of the enormous transaction costs imposed by that system.[8] Besides, these transaction costs impact differentially on different kinds of parties. Those who are risk-averse and unable to finance protracted litigation are the ones who have to give the discounts in order to escape these costs; those who occupy the strategic heights in the litigation battle are able to command steep discounts. Since the sums ordinarily awarded by the courts fall far short of fully compensating the injured, the injured are triply under-compensated: first, by the inadequate level of compensation; second, by the high transaction costs; and finally by the discounts they must yield to avoid the infliction of these costs. As the injured are under-compensated, injurers are under-assessed for the costs they impose on society for their risk-creating behaviour and under-deterred from persisting in injurious conduct.

The establishment of Lok Adalats represents the use of scarce reform energies to create alternatives that are 'better' than the lower courts. It is not however necessary to be very good to be better than that. The flaws of the system serve not as a stimulus to reform it, but as a reason for setting up institutions to bypass it. Lok Adalat proponents take pride in delivering needed compensation expeditiously to a large number of claimants. It is telling that the bulk of the caseload at many Lok Adalats is not made up of cases diverted from the rigidities of ordinary unreformed civil proceedings. Instead, they are cases diverted from a 'reformed' and 'streamlined' sector of the court system, the Motor Accident Claims tribunals, themselves established to provide expeditious proceedings with no court fees and some compensation available without a showing of fault. This accentuates the point that Lok Adalats do *not* provide additional access to justice: they do *not* provide new facilities for the vast number of potential claims that are discouraged—by court fees, the cost of lawyers, the prospects of delay, and paltry recoveries—from using the courts at all. Instead, they provide a truncated process for some of the few who *do* attempt to utilize the courts. What is remarkable is how modest are the aspirations their promoters have for them. The post-Independence proponents of *nyaya* panchayats, in contrast, sought to provide a convenient, accessible, understandable forum that would encourage popular participation, express popular norms, and promote harmonious interaction. They were unable to deliver on this, but the aim was to provide a system of justice superior to that of India's British-style courts. In contrast, the virtues claimed for Lok Adalats are their expeditiousness and lower processing cost. No one claims that they deliver a form of justice superior to that promised (though frequently not delivered) by law.

Lok Adalats are then an instance of a debased informalism—debased because it is commended not by the virtues of the forum it provides but by avoidance of the torments of the formal institutional process. Lok Adalats are only the most visible manifestation of this debased informalism, premised on the irredeemability of the formal legal process. A most dramatic and striking instance of this was the February 1989 settlement of the Bhopal case. The Government and many observers, including some in the judiciary, justified the settlement as beneficial to the victims by comparing it with the results of further litigation that would have lasted 'anywhere from 15 to 25 more years'.[9] This was not a claim that the settlement represented the victims' true entitlements; rather it was an assertion that whatever the magnitude of those entitlements, the unalterable character of the Indian legal system made it inevitable that they could not be obtained before passage of so long a period that the discounted present value of these claims was less than the amount to be delivered under the settlement. The features of the system that insured protracted delay were treated as given and unchangeable.

Lok Adalats and other manifestations of 'banyan tree justice' are reflections of 'failing faith'[10] in the efficacy and virtue of the formal legal process—at least in the lower courts. Abandoning all hope of reform, what is offered instead is a programme of palliation which is virtually a photographic negative of the animating idea of Public Interest Litigation (PIL) that the Supreme Court pioneered in the 1980s. PIL sought to be 'strategic'; it sought to empower organizable constituencies of the disadvantaged. In contrast, the new informalism addresses isolated individual victims. Where PIL sought to marshal facts by extensive investigation and to develop the law by trailblazing cases, the new informalism seeks compromises that obviate both factual and legal definition. Where PIL encouraged the development of new specialized expertise and wide dissemination of new knowledge, the new informalism demands no expertise and generates no new knowledge. Where PIL sought to use the wider, radiating effects of legal action to bring large-scale movement toward constitutional ideals, the new informalism eliminates consideration of these wider aggregate effects and confines its concern to specific cases.

Law Commissions and other observers have been decrying the conditions of the lower courts for a century. It is curious that the current surge of defeatism should appear just as expanded understanding of the dynamics of courts and new technologies supply would-be reformers greater insight and more options than were available earlier. Although energizing the broad base of the judicial system to make it responsive to public needs requires legislative enactments, many initiatives could be pursued by the higher judiciary in its role as overseer and guide of the lower courts. For example, the Supreme Court could set a model for the courts by curtailing unlimited oral argument; it could propose ways to free lower court judges from recording evidence and to modify the evaluation of those judges to reward resistance to delay; it could give priority on court dockets to cases involving claims of excessive delay in the lower courts, so that powerful interests who wanted their cases heard promptly would be enlisted to support measures to assure that lower courts were functioning adequately.

In addition to these institutional and procedural changes, the higher courts have some scope to provide the lower courts with the substantive tools they need to make justice accessible to ordinary citizens. Perhaps the single greatest opportunity is the development of tort law, a field that legislative neglect has left to the judiciary for incremental common law development.[11] The rationale of tort law is that in addition to dramatizing public standards of care, it secures compensation that makes an injured party 'whole', shifting cost of injuries to injurers and inducing potential injurers to invest in preventive efforts that reduce the incidence of future injury. Experience elsewhere has shown that tort is a rather spotty and uneven way of providing compensation for injuries and that the preventive effects it generates are often less than optimal. However, in a setting of no remedies for negligent injury and no pressure for prevention from the law, the net incremental benefits of a vivified tort law would be substantial.[12]

In addition to being viable because it is already 'there' in theory, tort law has a further advantage: it does not depend on continuing inputs from government or external actors, but would generate strong incentives among lawyers and parties for its continuing use and development.

Besides, it can operate without the extensive *ex ante* investment that it takes to put into place safety regulations or administrative controls and the continuing investment in updating and enforcing them. The major function of government would be to resist pressures from discomfited parties to dismantle or cripple the system.

The need for the legal system to adapt to international capital flows and new productive technologies is widely understood. However, the changes incident to modernization of the economy also impact on the workers, consumers, and neighbours; machinery, transport, and chemicals bring unprecedented benefits, but they also bring injuries and risks of greater magnitude, typically caused by remote entities over whom there is no control through the ordinary reciprocities of life. The development of the kinds of remedy and accountability that may be afforded by tort law is particularly needful in an industrializing society in which neither social insurance nor effective administrative regulation is present.

In the coming decades the Supreme Court will be challenged by many difficult and momentous legal questions. It will also face difficult problems of restructuring itself as an institution to meet the new demands that will engulf it. In addition, the Court will encounter the daunting task of building a strong and effective system of lower courts in which ordinary Indians can find expeditious remedies for everyday harms. Those remedies cannot be found in informalism detached from a flourishing system of efficacious courts. The road to useful informalism is through vigorous reform of formal legal institutions, not through resigned surrender to the unalterability of their defects.

Notes

[1] References to many expressions of this view among British adminstrators are found in Marc Galanter, *Law and Society in Modern India*, Oxford University Press, Delhi, 1989, 38–9.

[2] Christian Wollschlager, 'Exploring Global Landscapes of Litigation Rates', in Jurgen Brand and Dieter Strempel (eds), *Soziologie des Rechts: Festschrift fur Erhard Blankenburg zum 60. Geburtsag* Nomos Verlagsgesellschaft, Baden-Baden, 1998, 577, 582.

[3] Robert Moog, 'Indian Litigiousness and the Litigation Explosion', *Asian Survey*, Vol. 33, No. 12 (1993) 1136, 1138.

[4] Velcheru Narayana Rao, 'Courts and Lawyers in India: Images from Literature and Folklore', in Y.K. Malik and D.K. Vajpeyi (eds), *Boeings and Bullock-Carts: Studies in Change and Continuity in Indian Civilization*, Chanakya Publications, Delhi, 1990, Vol. 3, p. 196.

[5] A sunk cost auction is a game, often used as a business school exercise, in which some good (say a lakh of rupees) is awarded to the highest bidder, but the person who bids the second-highest amount also must pay the amount he bid. Thus, even if the opponent's

last bid exceeds one lakh, there is an incentive to bid just a little more in order to reduce one's loss by the value of the prize, but then the opponent is presented with a similar incentive, ad infinitum. In practice, the game ends when one party runs out of money or grows indifferent to the possibility of reducing the loss by the prize amount.

[6] Robert Mnookin and Lewis Kornhauser, 'Bargaining in the Shadow of the Law: the Case of Divorce', 88 *Yale Law Journal* 950 (1979).

[7] Galanter, 'Justice in Many Rooms: Courts, Private Ordering and Indigenous Law', 19 *Journal of Legal Pluralism* 1 (1981).

[8] For purposes of the argument here, transaction costs include lawyers' fees, court fees, bribe, and other litigation expenses, lost time, uncertainty of outcome and uncertainty of execution if a favourable outcome is obtained.

[9] The Government of India's anonymous justificatory statement noted that '[e]minent lawyers have argued that this case, which has already been four years in various courts in the pretrial stage, would in the most optimistic circumstances need anywhere from 15 to 25 more years for an ultimate decision'. 'Bhopal Gas Settlement: Govt. justifies Amount', *Hindustan Times*, 3 March 1989.

[10] Cf. Judith Resnik, 'Failing Faith: Adjudicatory Procedure in Decline', 53 *University of Chicago Law Review* 494 (1986).

[11] In the discussion that follows, the possible development of tort law is assessed in regard to personal injury (due to negligence or related notions of strict liability) and cases of misuse of authority. I put aside the question of whether a new regime for tort cases should include other intentional torts (defamation, malicious prosecution, etc.), which have a history in the subcontinent of employment in the course of personal feuds, etc.

[12] It is easy to imagine schemes of social insurance and administrative regulation that might perform these functions in a superior fashion. Choices among institutions however turn not only on images of their optimal performance, but also on the probability of their being enacted and sustaining themselves. See Neil K. Komesar, *Imperfect Alternatives: Choosing Institutions in Law, Economics and Public Policy*, University of Chicago Press, Chicago, 1994. Is there any likelihood that other institutions that would produce more ample compensation or more efficacious prevention might be put in place in its stead? It seems evident that neither comprehensive social insurance against negligent injury nor effective governmental regulation of risks are at all likely in the near future. The choice is not between these and tort law; it is between tort law and the present no-remedy no-accountability system for dealing with personal injuries.

Five

The Supreme Court of India and Australian Law

Michael Kirby*

A Time of Anniversaries

The Constitution of India was adopted by the Constituent Assembly on 26 November 1949. It came into force on 26 January 1950. The first sitting of the Supreme Court of India, created by the Constitution, took place on 29 January 1950. It is therefore timely to pause and reflect upon the achievements of the Supreme Court of India as it celebrates its Golden Jubilee.

The establishment of complete political independence and the creation of a democratic and constitutional republic was a mighty achievement of the Indian people. They were blessed by leaders of rare ability. India shares with Australia the same National Day, 26 January. Australians celebrate that day as the anniversary of the arrival of the First Fleet under Governor Arthur Phillip RN. The landing of that enlightened viceroy began the process that would eventually result in British rule over the entire Australian continent. 26 January 1950 saw the final severance of India's governmental links with the British Crown which, over a period longer than its rule in Australia, had gradually extended its sovereignty or suzerainty over the entire Indian subcontinent.

Now, in Australia, we are approaching the celebration of the centenary of our federal Constitution. It came into force on 1 January 1901. In November 1999, a referendum of the Australian people was held to determine whether the Commonwealth of Australia is to remain a constitutional monarchy under the Crown of the United Kingdom or to

*The author acknowledges the assistance of Mr Ben Wickham, Legal Research Officer of the High Court of Australia, in the preparation of this paper.

become a republic. Both India and Australia, independent states, are members of the Commonwealth of Nations which accepts the Queen as its Head. We do this out of recognition of the history that inescapably binds us together with so many other lands and peoples in every corner of the world. That history, and the English language, law, sports, and customs provide links between us which are indissoluble. As we celebrate our respective anniversaries, reflect upon the strengths and weaknesses of our constitutional arrangements and on the rich legacies of our ultimate courts, we should look beyond our own countries to the nations with which we share so much in common. The relationship between India and Australia has been a neglected one. In times of jubilee we should consider where we have come from, where we are and how, in the future, we can strengthen the bonds between us.

The Constitution of India which established the Supreme Court drew, as did the Australian Constitution fifty years earlier, upon lessons and examples from the Constitution of the United States of America. The Indian Constitution, like that of Australia, adopted the federal arrangement and the creation of a judicial branch wholly independent of the other branches of government. Judicial review, to keep all donees of pubic power within the Constitution and other applicable laws, was faithfully imitated. The Indian Constitution however went further. It adopted (as some suggest the Australian Constitution should now do) the republican principle.[1] It also incorporated a Bill of Rights which, until very recently, has been regarded as a notion alien to the sovereignty of Parliament so central to the constitutional governance of the United Kingdom.[2] Yet, despite these important features that distinguish the Indian Constitution from that of Australia, overwhelmingly their governmental and legal systems are similar. Whereas the Indian Head of State is called President, he acts, like the sovereign of the United Kingdom and the Queen and her representatives in Australia, on the advice of Ministers who are accountable to the lower house of Parliament. In this sense, the President's functions are similar to those of the Governor-General of Australia, although the President is not the representative of the monarch.[3] As Mr Seervai remarks:[4]

To remove a common misconception, it ought to be stated that the machinery of Govt. set up by our Constitution follows in essentials the British, and not the American model. The doctrine of the separation of powers and the doctrine that legislatures of the delegates of the people which are basic doctrines of the US Constitution do not form part of the Constitution of Great Britain or the Constitution of India. Our Constitution has rejected the Presidential form of Govt., that is of an Executive independent of and not responsible to, the legislature and adopted the British Executive responsible to, and removable by the legislature.

Similarly, with respect to the functions and powers of the Supreme Court, Mr Seervai notes:[5]

The position occupied by our Sup Ct more closely resembles that of the Sup Ct of Australia than of the US Sup Ct. The US Sup Ct is not the final Court of Appeal in Civil and Criminal cases throughout the United States. It has appellate jurisdiction to control inferior Courts, but its principal work is as a Constitutional Court. Our Sup Ct is a final Court of Appeal in all matters from all courts in India and not merely on Constitutional matters. It has a limited original jurisdiction ... and an exclusive original jurisdiction in disputes between the Union and the States. The Sup Ct of Australia is a final Court of Appeal in Australia in all matters, Civil, Criminal and Constitutional.[6]

There is no doubt as Mr Seervai discerns (citing his kindred spirit, Dr Wynes of Australia) that the fact that the Supreme Court of India, like the High Court of Australia, is a general court of appeal, profoundly influences its image of itself, its methodology, and its work. Although, in deciding constitutional and other cases, the supreme court of any nation, India and Australia included, is inescapably involved in the resolution of political questions, the performance of the responsibilites of a general court of appeal has a tendency to tame the larger ambitions, to control the kinds of people who are appointed and to encourage a methodology that promotes consistency and diminishes the more unrestrained flights of judicial fancy.

Yet for all the similarities, which even reach down to matters of titles, courtroom courtesies, curial organization, hours of work, and the like there are inescapable differences. The Indian judiciary, led by the Supreme Court of India, is the 'guardian angel'[7] of the Constitution which brings the rule of law to one of the most populous, diverse, and challenging societies of the world. The crippling case loads of the courts of India far exceed those of Australia, heavy though these seem. Poverty and ancient prejudices and disadvantages have imposed on the Indian judiciary, led by the Supreme Court, pressing obligations to adapt constitutional and other laws to secure and uphold an essential social revolution. These are obligations that judges in Australia do not have to face, at least to anything like the same degree. In part, this phenomenon explains the jurisprudence of the Supreme Court of India, enlarging the *locus standi* of those who would engage the courts[8] in a way that has not yet been copied in the ultimate court of Australia[9] or, indeed, in most other countries of the common law.

In the past we in Australia have learned much of law and wisdom from the Supreme Court of India and we are likely to do so increasingly in the future as our links expand. The Supreme Court of India has also used the jurisprudence of the High Court of Australia in developing its own thinking, both on the Indian Constitution and on other areas of the law. The Internet, direct contacts, and a growing realization of the things we have in common will make it likely that this use will increase in the years ahead. Whereas in the past, many countries of the Commonwealth of Nations tended to look only to England for comparative law materials relevant to shared problems, in the future we will venture upon the greater treasure-house now made available to us from the leading courts of the common law world. Of these, the Supreme Court of India is a mighty exemplar. Lit by a golden glow of fifty years of achievement, it can be assured of the high opinion in which it is held throughout the world and not least in Australia.

Indian Use of Australian Law

The similarities of constitutional texts, together with the common legal tradition and shared judicial assumptions made it natural, in the earliest days of the Supreme Court of India, that its judges would look to decisions of other federal supreme courts for guidance, including those of the High Court of Australia. By that time, the latter had fifty years of judicial elaboration of the Australian federal Constitution. The early decisions of the Supreme Court of India drew substantially on this.

In 1954, in *Commissioner, Hindu Religious Endowments, Madras v Sri Lakshmindra Thirtha Swamiar of Sri Shirur Mutt*[10] Mukherjea J, in relation to a case concerning the protection of religious freedom as guaranteed by the Indian Constitution, called in aid the decision of Latham CJ in *Adelaide Company of Jehovah's Witnesses v The Commonwealth*.[11] Mukherjea J held that Latham CJ's 'observations apply fully to the protection of religion as guaranteed by the Indian Constitution'. The exercise of religion is not unfettered. The provision for its protection exists in a constitutional context. It is to be interpreted in conjunction with the other provisions of the Constitution. For example, restrictions may lawfully apply to the free exercise of religion on the basis of public order, morality, and health, and the regulation of economic, financial, political and secular activities of the religion.[12]

In *Ratilal Panachand Gandhi v State of Bombay*,[13] Mukherjea J said:

The distinction between matters of religion and those of secular administration of religious properties may, at times, appear to be a thin one. But in cases of doubt, as Chief Justice Latham pointed out ... the court should take a common sense view and be actuated by considerations of practical necessity.

Mukherjea J was one of India's great judges. He was foremost in the early days in asserting the judiciary's independence from the executive. When in 1953 Prime Minister Nehru proposed to supersede Mahajan J (then the senior judge) for appointment as Chief Justice and to appoint Mukherjea J as Chief Justice, the latter told him that he would rather resign than become Chief Justice of India out of turn. Ultimately, Mahajan J was appointed Chief Justice of India in January 1954. On his retirement in December that year, Mukherjea J, next in line, became Chief Justice. Mukherjea CJ's portrait deservedly hangs in Court Room 1 of the Supreme Court of India. He is honoured and remembered in Australia.

In the same realm of discourse, another great judge, Khanna J, in *St Xavier's College v Gujarat*[14] also drew on Latham CJ's opinion in the *Jehovah's Witnesses Case*. He cited Latham CJ's warning:

It should not be forgotten that such a provision as s 116 [of the Australian Constitution], is not required for the protection of the religion of the majority. The religion of a majority can look after itself. Section 116 is required to protect the religion (or absence of religion) of minorities, and, in particular, of unpopular minorities.[15]

Another area of jurisprudence which was called in aid in the earliest days of the Supreme Court of India concerned the constitutional guarantee of just terms for any law providing for federal acquisition of property.[16] In *Chiranjital chowdhuri v Union of India,*[17] the Supreme Court of India first noticed the expansive view adopted of the Australian constitutional guarantee as expressed in the decision of the High Court of Australia in *Minister of State for the Army v Daiziel.*[18] This is still good law in Australia and has been applied recently.[19] In *R.C. Cooper v Union of India*[20] Ray J drew on the Australian decision. So did Sastri CJ in *State of West Bengal v Subodh Gopal Bose.*[21]

The broad view adopted in the Australian decisions concerning the meaning of 'property' for the purpose of constitutional provisions relating to compulsory acquistion of property undoubtedly influenced many early decisions of the Indian Court. In *Dwarkadas Shrinivas v Sholapur Spinning and Weaving Co.,*[22] Mahajan J expressed the opinion that 'the true concept of the expression "acquistion" in our Constitution ... is the one enunciated by Rich J and the majority of the court in *Dalziel's* case'.[23] Care must of course be taken in adopting words used in relation to a different constitutional text, expressed in different terms and applicable to utterly different social circumstances and needs. Special care must be taken in the case of India because of the successive amendments to the provisions of the Constitution relating to the compulsory acquisition of property.[24] However, the use of the jurisprudence of the High Court of Australia indicates the particular open-mindedness of the early judges of the Supreme Court of India and their willingness to look beyond the traditional source of the English judiciary and the rich home resource of India itself, to the court decisions of Australia, given in another federation sharing the same general legal tradition.

One of the most vexed areas of Australian constitutional law has concerned the guarantee in section 92 of the Australian Constitution of absolute freedom of interstate trade, commerce, and intercourse. The adoption of a counterpart provision in the Indian Constitution (Article 301) made it natural enough that attempts would be made, in the early days, to borrow from the meandering course of Australian case law for the guidance which it could give to the Supreme Court of India. In *Automobile Transport (Rajasthan) Ltd v State of Rajasthan*,[25] Das J referred to the need to read the Indian provision in a constitutional context which acknowledged the need and legitimacy of a measure of regulatory control, whether by the Union governemnt or by the governments of the States. In this, Das J relied upon the observations of Australia's first Chief Justice, Griffith CJ, in *Duncan v State of Queensland*.[26] That fine jurist had said: 'The word "free" does not mean *extra legem*, any more than freedom means anarchy. We boast of being an absolutely free people, but that does not mean that we are not subject to law.' Thus the Supreme Court of India, like the High Court of Australia, adopted the view that the notion of freedom employed in the guarantee of free internal trade and commerce is to be understood in the context of 'the working of an orderly society'. As such, it is necessary 'to add certain qualifications subject to which alone that freedom may be exercised'.[27]

Subba Rao J, in his opinion in the *Automobile Transport Case,* undertook an extensive review of the Australian case of law on freedom of trade, commerce, and intercourse. He noted that 'some of the leading Australian decisions contain an interesting and instructive exposition of the conflict of jurisdiction and useful suggestions for resolving it'.[28] Perceptively, he noted.[29]

Paradoxically the Courts of Australia ... evolved the power to restrict the said freedom by the States from the concept of absolute freedom itself. This was necessitated because there were no statutory provisions limiting the absolute freedom and, as uncontrolled freedom may lead to chaos, limitations on the freedom were evolved to save the said freedom. The scope of the limitations so evolved would be useful to construe the relevant provisions of our Constitution.

Hidayatullah J, whilst relying on the Australian decisions, was careful to predicate his own consideration of the article with the qualification:[30]

Nothing is more dangerous [than] to suppose that the Indian Constitution wished to secure freedom of trade, commerce and intercourse in the same way as did the Australian Commonwealth.

However, like the Australian decisions, Hidayatullah J concluded that a law which targeted interstate trade and commerce *as such* would be invalid.[31] This is still the law in the Australian Commonwealth. However, since the early borrowings from our jurisprudence a new enlightenment has been reached in Australia.[32] As this is a difficult and controversial area, littered with legal tombstones, I hesitate to suggest that it will provide great assistance to Indian lawyers. The words of Das CJ in *The State of Bombay v RMD Chamarbaugwala*[33] in this area, as in all others, must resonate in our minds. Australian cases, he said, should:[34]

be used with caution and circumspection ... The scheme of the Australian Constitution ... is different from that of ours, for in the Australian Constitution there is no such provision as we have in Art 19(6) or Arts 302–304 of our Constitution. The provision of s 92 of the Australian Constitution being in terms unlimited and unqualified the judicial authorities interpreting the same had to import certain restrictions and limitations dictated by common sense and the exigencies of modern society.

There are two particular areas of constitutional jurisprudence in which the decisions of the Australian High Court have proved useful to the Supreme Court of India. The first of them concerns the approach to constitutional interpretation. In this, we are all children of the great Chief Justice of the United States Supreme Court, Marshall CJ. His seminal decision in *McCulloch v Maryland*[35] put a stamp on the approaches to judicial review and constitutional construction that have been adopted ever since by the ultimate courts of federations which must fulfil the role of the constitutional arbiter.

In the elaboration of Marshall CJ's basic approach, judges in India and Australia have adopted a generally similar view. In *Goodyear v State of Haryana*,[36] Mukharji J relied upon the decision of the High Court of Australia in *Attorney-General (NSW) v The Brewery Employees Union of New South Wales*[37] as authority for the proposition:

That the words of the Constitution must be interpreted on the same principles as any ordinary law, and these principles compel us to consider the nature and scope of the Act, and to remember that the Constitution is a mechanism under which laws are to be made, and not a mere Act which declares what the law is to be. Hence, such mechanism should be interpreted broadly, bearing in mind, in appropriate cases, that the Supreme Court like ours is a nice balance of jurisdictions.

The same judge in *India Cement Ltd v State of Tamil Nadu*[38] drew once again on that early decision of the Australian court, written in the days when the Justices were entering, for the first time, upon the elaboration of the Australian Constitution, needing always to remind themselves that a somewhat different approach was required for that task than for that traditionally taken in the construction of ordinary legislation.

There have been other cases where the Supreme Court of India has drawn upon the approach adopted by the Australian High Court to constitutional elaboration.[39] Judges whose days are often spent in construing ordinary legislation need constantly to remind themselves of the shift of mental gears necessary to properly perform the judicial function of constitutional elaboration.

Perhaps the area of constitutional law in which Australian decisions have been most frequently and consistently utilized by the Supreme Court of India concerns inconsistency or repugnancy of state and federal (or central) laws. The provision of the Indian Constitution in this regard (Article 254) is similar to that of section 109 of the Australian Constitution. The analysis of section 109 offered by Dixon J seventy years ago in *Ex parte McLean*[40] has proved as powerful an influence upon the minds of successive generations of Indian judges as it has upon those of Australia. Take for example the decision in *V .K. Sharma v State of Karnataka*.[41] There, K. Ramaswamy J, in dissent as to the outcome, closely examined the history of Australian jurisprudence on the subject of constitutional inconsistency of laws. The need to approach inconsistency and repugnancy in the constitutional sense in the context of a federal polity which is expected to work harmoniously as between the several parts, has been emphasized both in Australian and in Indian jurisprudence.[42]

In *Ch Tika Ramji v State of Uttar Pradesh*,[43] Justice N.H. Bhagwati drew on the Australian constitutional decisions, and in particular *Ex parte McLean*, in concluding:[44]

If it appeared that the Federal law was intended to be supplementary to or cumulative upon State law, then no inconsistency would be exhibited in imposing the same duties or in inflicting different penalties. The inconsistency does not lie in the mere coexistence of two laws which are susceptible of simultaneous obedience. It depends upon the intention of the paramount

Legislature to express by its enactment, completely, exhaustively, or exclusively, what shall be the law governing the particular conduct or matter to which its attention is directed.

The metaphor used in *Ex parte McLean*, by which the federal or central law will expel its state competitor if its clear purpose was to 'cover the field', has entered Indian jurisprudence on this subject, just as, for seventy years, it has influenced countless Australian decisions in like problem areas.

There are many areas of the law outside constitutional law, where decisions of the High Court of Australia have proved useful to the Supreme Court of India. One area is in the vexed distinction between capital and revenue in the field of taxation law. In *Alembic Chemical v Commissioner of Income Tax*,[45] the Supreme Court of India was faced with the delineation between capital and revenue expenditure. Venkatachaliah J referred to the reasons advanced by Dixon J in *Sun Newspapers Ltd and Associated News Papers Ltd v Federal Commissioner of Taxation*,[46] Specifically, he drew upon the elaboration of the consideration mentioned by Dixon J in seeking to stamp a measure of consistency and predicability upon this vexed area of decision-making.

In the earlier case of *Assam Bengal Cement Co v Commissioner of Income Tax*,[47] the distinction between capital and income was explored by Justice N.H. Bhagwati.[48] He too drew on the opinion of Dixon J in the *Sun Newspapers* case. In *Empire Jute Co. v Commissioner of Income Tax*,[49] Justice N.H. Bhagwati, in the same area of disputation, also called upon and applied the test expounded by Dixon J in the High Court of Australia in *Hallstroms Pty Ltd v Federal Commissioner of Taxation*,[50] The difficulty of reaching entirely satisfactory distinctions in this area, whether with the aid of Australian or other court decisions was accepted by Pathak J in *Commissioner of Income Tax v Damodaran*.[51] In a very recent decision of the Australian High Court,[52] I pointed out that this area of the law has bedevilled courts in many countries for over a century.

The general similarity between parts of Indian and Australian tax laws has resulted in borrowings in revenue law beyond the field of income tax. Thus, in the field of estate duty,[53] in *Controller of Estate Duty v Godavari Bai*[54] the Supreme Court of India enlisted the aid of the opinion of Isaacs J of the High Court of Australia in *Lang v Webb*.[55] In the field of statutory sale of goods and sales tax, the Indian Supreme Court in *Vishnu Agneices v Commercial Tax Officer*,[56] followed in *Coffee Board v Commissioner of Commercial Taxes*,[57] considered and relied upon a number of decisions of the High Court of Australia.[58] Reaching for such assistance depends very largely upon the knowledge, skills, and resources of the advocates who appear before the courts. In areas such as revenue law, where a highly specialized cadre of advocates is commonly developed, it is not at all unusual for a commercial transaction under study to have an international aspect. This takes today's lawyers, more than in the past, into the field of comparative law and to knowledge of the legal systems and decisions of other countries. In these circumstances it seems likely that more opinions, helpful to local decision-making in specialized areas, will help build bridges between courts such as the Supreme Court of India and the High Court of Australia and the lawyers who practise before them.

Another area of discourse where there are links across national borders is in the field of administrative law, labour law, and human rights law. These are spheres in which there is much dialogue between lawyers throughout the Commonwealth of Nations. Administrative law in particular has seen enormous developments in recent decades in the hands of the judiciary, and nowhere more so than in India. Yet even in this field occasional assistance has been derived by the Supreme Court referring to decisions of the High Court of Australia.[59] Similarly, in the field of labour law, the Supreme Court, in a decision which remains good law, *Bangalore Water Supply v A. Rajappa*,[60] followed decisions of the High Court of Australia.[61]

Australian Use of Indian Law

The utilization of judicial opinions is usually a two-way street. Sometimes it comes about by reason of the advocacy of diligent lawyers who have researched their subject beyond the familiar fields of local law. Sometimes, however, it comes about almost accidentally. So it was, when I was President of the New South Wales Court of Appeal, that I found support for my reasoning from decisions of the Indian Supreme Court in a case that concerned the common law obligations of officials to give reasons for their decisions.

By chance, Justice P.N. Bhagwati, an intrepid traveller, was on a visit to Sydney in 1984. I told him in conversation about a case which had just been argued before me in the Court of Appeal. It concerned the right to reasons from a government official. Australian courts had held that a judicial officer was obliged to provide reasons for an adverse decision.[62] However, the legal obligations of administrators were much less certain. In England, Lord Denning MR had concluded that sometimes administrators were legally obliged to state their reasons.[63] However, the majority judicial opinion in that country suggested that there was no such obligation unless Parliament had specifically provided it.[64]

Within Australia, the position was complicated by the enactment of specific federal legislation affording persons affected by adverse decisions of federal administrators a right to obtain reasons for such decisions.[65] Such legislation did not extend to the decisions of New South Wales State officials under consideration in my court.

Justice P.N. Bhagwati drew to my attention two leading cases of the Supreme Court of India: *Siemens Engineering and Manufacturing Co. of India Ltd v Union of India*[66] and *Maneka Gandhi v Union of India*.[67] In the course of giving my reasons for decision in the case before me, to the effect that the state official was obliged to give reasons to a person adversely affected by his decision, I called to notice the decisions of the Indian Supreme Court:[68]

In *Siemens* Bhagwati J said that the rule requiring reasons to be given was 'like the principle of audi alteram partem, a basic principle of natural justice' ... The case is complicated by the reference to the India Constitution [sic] and various statutory provisions. However the basis for the obligation to provide reasons would appear to have been expressed to lie in the duties or akin to those imposed in this country by the rules of natural justice.

Although a majority in the Court of Appeal favoured this approach, the decision was taken on appeal to the High Court of Australia where it was unanimously reversed.[69] In rejecting the assistance of the decisions of the Supreme Court of India, Gibbs CJ remarked:[70]

These decisions appear to state the common law of India, although without a detailed knowledge of the course of decisions in that country it would be hazardous to assume that they have not been influenced by the provisions of the Constitution of India or by Indian statutes.

The Australian common law retreated. It is heartening to me to see that the Supreme Court of India has, since 1984, continued to insist upon standards of legal accountability. Thus in *S.N. Mukherjee v Union of India*[71] the appellant, a major in the army, was charged with misconduct and dismissed. The question before the Supreme Court of India was whether the Chief of the Army Staff was bound in law to record the reasons for the dismissal. The Supreme Court held that the requirement that reasons be recorded should govern the decisions of an administrative authority exercising quasi judicial functions regardless of whether the decision was subject to judicial review, appeal, or revision. The content of the duty would fluctuate according to the particular facts and circumstances. The essential duty was to indicate that due consideration had been given to the points in controversy.

In the course of elaborating these principles reference was made by the Supreme Court to the divergent position of the common law in other countries.[72] Agarwal J cited the majority position of myself and Priestley JA in the New South Wales Court of Appeal in *Osmond v Public Service Board of New South Wales*.[73] He noted that our decision had later been overruled by the High Court of Australia. However, he observed that, even in the High Court's decision, the duties cast on judicial decision-makers was affirmed. Agrawal J did not read the opinions in the High Court of Australia as wholly excluding the expansion of the common law duty to provide reasons to various administrators according to the common law. Perhaps future decisions in Australia will demonstrate that his opinion was prescient.

There are many areas where the Justices of the High Court of Australia have called upon decisions of the Supreme Court of India in explaining their reasons. Thus in *Bropho v Western Australia*,[74] the Court had to consider the application of the principle of statutory interpretation that general words in a statute will ordinarily be construed as inapplicable to the Crown (i.e. the State). The majority of the High Court, comprising Mason CJ, Deane, Dawson, Toohey, and McHugh JJ pointed to the fact that 'there has been a growing tendency to question the appropriateness of the old rule of immunity to modern circumstances'.[75] In doing so, they referred to the decision of the Supreme Court of India in *State of West Bengal v Corporation of Calcutta*.[76]

In the *Tasmanian Dam Case*,[77] Murphy J referred to the developed jurisprudence in a number of countries, including India, by which the constitutionality of legislation is presumed unless the contrary is demonstrated. Murphy J referred, amongst other decisions, to *Chiranjit Lal Chowdhuri v Union of India*,[78] *State of Bombay v F.N. Balsara*,[79] *V.M. Syed Mohammad and Co. v Andhra*[80] and *Krishnan v Tamil Nadu*.[81] With reference to further Indian decisions, Murphy J made the same point in *Attorney-General (Western Australia) v Australian National Airlines Commission*.[82]

In the context of equality before the law, a number of decisions of the Australian High Court have drawn upon opinions in the Supreme Court of India. Thus, in the important case of *Dietrich v The Queen*,[83] Deane J noted that reasoning similar to that in the United States which upheld the right of indigent prisoners to state-funded legal representation had 'prevailed in India'. He referred to *Hoskot v Maharashtra*[84] and *Hussainara Khatoon v Home Secretary, State of Bihar*.[85]

Deane J also drew upon the decision of the Supreme Court of India in *Maneka Gandhi v Union of India*[86] in support of the principle that a constitutional guarantee, such as that contained in section 117 of the Australian Constitution, should be interpreted broadly and not confined to 'narrow technicality or legalism'.[87] In the same case, Gaudron J[88] referred to the jurisprudence of the Supreme Court of India on the notion of equality before the law. Specifically, she cited the remarks of Das J in *State of West Bengal v Anwar Ali*.[89]

All persons are not, by nature, attainment or circumstances, equal and the varying needs of different classes of persons often require separate treatment and, therefore, the protecting clause has been construed as a guarantee against discrimination against equals only and not as taking away from the State the power to classify persons for the purpose of legislation.

In another case, *Mabo v Queensland*,[90] Wilson J in the High Court of Australia referred to the decisions of the Supreme Court of India concerning equality before the law. Applying a passage in the reasoning of Mathew J in *Kerala v Thomas*,[91] Wilson J observed 'that 'formal equality before the law does not always achieve effective and genuine equality ... The extension of formal equality in law to a disadvantaged group may have the effect of entrenching inequality in fact'.[92] This same point was made by Brennan J in the Australian High Court in his decision in *Gerhardy v Brown*[93] where he referred to the 'pithily observed' remarks of Ray CJ that '[e]quality of opportunity for unequals can only mean aggravation of inequality'.[94] Brennan J remarked that '[t]he validity of these observations is manifest'.[95]

In many recent decisions I have myself drawn attention to developments of the law in India which are of relevance to us in Australia. In *IW v City of Perth*,[96] I referred to the trend throughout the common law world towards recognition of the right of the citizen to challenge decisions of public authorities and governmental agencies. In particular, I drew on *S.P. Gupta v President of India*[97] and *Bandhua Mukti Morcha v Union of India*.[98] In *Newcrest Mining (WA) Ltd v The Commonwealth*[99] I mentioned the jurisprudence of the Supreme Court of India on due process for deprivation of property.[100] I observed:

The [constitutional] provision required that no person should be deprived of that person's property save by authority of law and such law had to provide for compensation for the property so acquired or requisitioned.[101] The Supreme Court of India, while that test stood, insisted that provisions for compensation were a necessary condition for the making of a valid law providing for the acquisition or requisition of property by the state.[102]

In *Re Residential Tenancies Tribunal (NSW); Ex parte Defence Housing Authority*[103] I cited the links in the jurisprudence on inconsistency and repugnancy in India and in Australia. As I have already explained, in each country the courts have applied tests to uphold, where constitutionally required, the legislative supremacy of the federal (or Central) laws.

Conclusion

From the start, the Supreme Court of India was the undoubted apex of the judiciary of India, completely free of colonial ties to the Privy Council. It was the ultimate court of a new, confident, sovereign federal republic. In Australia, for most of this century, the High Court of Australia was not quite in the same position. Although in constitutional cases involving the powers *inter se* of the Commonwealth and the States of Australia a certificate was required before an appeal could be taken to the Privy Council, and although such a certificate was only once granted[104] and never repeated, the existence of an external court in London, as monitor and competitor, undoubtedly affected the jurisprudence of the High Court of Australia during the first seventy years. In a practical way, and intellectually, it bound the Australian courts into a necessarily harmonious relationship with the imperial court of the Privy Council. That link continued well after Empire. The casebooks of the Privy Council and House of Lords decisions remained on the shelves of Australian judges and lawyers. This had the effect of dicouraging a larger curiosity about the rich jurisprudence of other common law countries. When comparative law was needed, Australian jurists had a vast array close at hand, but so blinded did they become by the penumbra of English law that they commonly felt little need to look to other sources.

In the past two decades, since the demise of the Privy Council's last source of appeals from Australia in non-federal matters from the State courts[105] there has been a readjustment in the thinking of the High Court of Australia and of Australian courts and lawyers more generally. There has, for example, been a revival in the use of the decisions of the United States courts which were frequently used in the early decades of the Australian federation. There has also been an increase in the use of academic and non-legal materials. More significantly, there has been a growing willingness to encourage the citation of apposite decisions of the courts of other common law countries, particularly of New Zealand and Canada (whose societies are so similar) and more recently of South Africa, Zimbabwe, Singapore, and Hong Kong (whose economies are somewhat similar), and in the last decade the decisions of the courts of Malaysia, Sri Lanka, and India (which share our legal history and tradition).

I do not doubt that the utilization of all these rich sources of legal ideas will continue and grow apace. It will be stimulated by the capacity, especially of younger judges and advocates, to efficiently use the Internet and other sources of legal analogies to stimulate useful reasoning in the development of common law principle, statutory construction, and constitutional interpretation.

In late December 1998, on the eve of the opening of the year in which the fiftieth anniversary of the Indian Constitution was to be celebrated, I attended a conference of judges and lawyers in Bangalore. It was organized by Interrights (The International Centre for the Legal Protection of Human Rights) and the Commonwealth Secretariat, both in London. It was inaugurated by the Chief Justice of India. In his remarks,[106] Anand CJ drew to notice the growing impact on the domestic laws of India of the jurisprudence of international human rights norms.[107] He referred to the movement that is gathering pace throughout the Commonwealth of Nations through the time-honoured techniques of judicial elaboration and analogous reasoning. The Chief Justice of India referred to decisions in many countries, including Australia, which illustrated a similar movement.[108] As I sat there, surrounded by distinguished judges from Pakistan, Bangladesh, Sri Lanka, India, and countries far away, the Chief Justice's remarks brought home to me the privilege which we, brothers and sisters of the common law, share. It is as if we are linked by our own special Internet. Ideas are received. Some are rejected, but there is no force so powerful as an idea whose time has come. The shared willingness of courts in India and Australia to develop their municipal law in general harmony with developments in international law is one that was inevitably bound to accompany the revolutions of air travel, telecommunications, and personal contacts symbolized by the Bangalore meeting itself.

Another idea whose time has come is that two common law federations governed as parliamentary democracies sharing links of language, legal tradition, and constitutional stability, as India and Australia do, should come to know more of each other. In the future, building upon the many commonalities and the tentative efforts of our forebears, the justices of the Supreme Court of India and of the High Court of Australia should come to better know each other's work. Once we do, we will find much richness which we can share, richness of an intellectual and also of a personal dimension.

From a golden autumn day in Canberra, Australia, where I have written this paper, I send greetings and felicitations to the Supreme Court of India on its Golden Anniversary. It is a court which symbolizes the hope that the rule of law will spread its powerful message to the four corners of the world, bringing independent justice and the protection of basic rights to all peoples, not just those of the rich and the powerful states. When in fifty years the centenary of the Supreme Court of India is celebrated, may it be said that the bonds of friendship and intellectual association between the judiciaries of India and Australia have been deepened and broadened beyond our current imaginings.

Notes

[1] Indian Constitution, Preamble, first line Note *Constitution (Forty-second Amendment) Act 1976*, section 2; cf H.M. Seervai, *Constitutional Law of India* (4th edn, 1991), vol 1, p. 158.

[2] H.M Seervai, ibid., p. 159; cf M. Kachwaha, *The Judiciary in India*, Leiden, 1998, p. 15.

[3] Australian Constitution, section 61: 'The executive power of the Commonwealth is vested in the Queen and is exercisable by the Governor-General as the Queen's representative, and extends to the execution and maintenance of this Constitution, and of the laws of the Commonwealth'.

[4] H.M. Seervai, *Constitutional Law of India*, op. cit. p. 159, referring to *Shamsher Singh v Punjab* (1975) 1 SCR 814; (74)' ASC 2192.

[5] Ibid., p. 263.

[6] He refers to the theoretical exception of an appeal by certificate of the High Court of Australia to the Judicial Committee of the Privy Council in accordance with the Australian Constitution, section 74. That possiblity is now a dead letter. See *State of Western Australia v Hammersley Iron Pty Ltd [No 2]* (1969) 120 CLR 74. See also *Kirmanni v Captain Cook Cruises Pty Ltd [No 2]*; *Ex parte Attorney-General (Qld)* (1985) 159 CLR 461 at 463–5.

[7] M. Kachwaha, op. cit. The Judiciary in India n. 2, p. 5.

[8] *Fertilizer Corporation Kamagar Union v Union of India* [1981] 1 SCC 568; *S.P. Gupta v President of India and Ors* 1981 Supp SCC 87 at 186; cf V. Sripati, 'Human Rights in Inda—Fifty Years After Independence' (1997) 26 *Denver J. Intl. L. and Policy*, p. 93 at 119.

[9] For a recent Australian decision, see *Oshlack v Richmond River Council* (1998) 193 CLR 72; cf *Levy v Victoria* (1997) 189 CLR 579 and *Attorney-General for the Commonwealth v Breckler* [1999] HCA 28 at 102–9 where the light of intervention before the High Court of Australia is considered.

[10] (1954) SCR 1005 at 1024.

[11] (1943) 67 CLR 116 at 127.

[12] (1954) SCR 1005 at 1024, citing cl 2(a) and (b) of Article 25 of the Constitution.

[13] (1954) SCR 1055 at 1066.

[14] (1975) 1 SCR 173.

[15] (1975) 1 SCR 173 at 224–5 citing 1943 67 CLR 116 at 124.

[16] Australian Constitution, section 51 (xxxi).

[17] (1950) SCR 869 at 921.

[18] (1944) 68 CLR 261 at 285.

[19] For recent cases see *Newcrest Mining (WA) Ltd v The Commonwealth* (1997) 190 CLR 513; *The Commonwealth v WMC Resources Ltd* (1998) 72 ALJR 280; *Western Australia v The Commonwealth* 199 HCA 5.

[20] (1970) 3 SCR 530 at 635.

[21] (1954) SCR 587 at 610.

[22] (1954) SCR 674.

[23] 1954 ACR 674 at 704. See also *State of Karnataka v Ranganatha* (1978) 1 SCR 641.

[24] A point noted by the author in *Newcrest Mining (WA) Ltd v The Commonwealth* (1997) 190 CLR 513 at 659–60. In India, there has been a significant amendment to the Constitution with respect to property. The right to property, formerly protected in Article 19(f), has been deleted by the 44th Amendment. Article 300A was then incorporated, stating that no person shall be deprived of their property save by authority of law.

[25] (1963) SCR 491.

[26] (1916) 22 CLR 556 at 573.

[27] (1963) SCR 491 at 521 per Das J.

[28] (1963) SCR 491 at 545.

[29] (1963) SCR 491 at 544.

[30] (1963) SCR 491 at 575.

[31] Cf *Australian National Airways Pty Ltd v The Commonwealth* (1945) 71 CLR 29. For the comparable position in the European Union see P.J. Smith, 'Movement of Goods Within the EC and s 92 of the Australian Constitution'. (1998) 72 *ALJ* 465.

[32] *Cole v Whitfield* (1998) 165 CLR 360.

[33] (1957) SCR 874 at 906–7.

[34] (1957) SCR 874 at 918.

[35] (1819) 17 IS (4 Wheat) 316.

[36] (1989) 1 Supp SCR 510 at 533–4.

[37] (1908) 6 CLR 469.

[38] (1989) 1 Supp SCR 692.

[39] See, for example, *Supreme Court Advocates-on-Record Association v Union of India* (1993) Supp 2 SCR 659. Kuldip Singh J referred to *Ryder v Foley* (1906) 4 CLR 422 and *Copyright Owners Reproduction Society Ltd v EMI (Aust) Pty Ltd* (1958) 100 CLR 597.

[40] (1930) 43 CLR 472 at 483.

[41] (1990) 1 SCR 614.

[42] See, for example, Thakkar J in *Ram Chandra Mawa Lal v State of Uttar Pradesh* (1984) 2 SCR 348. For a closely divided recent Australian case, see *Gould v Brown* (1998) 72 ALJR 375.

[43] (1956) SCR 393.

[44] (1956) SCR 393 at 425.

[45] (1989) 2 SCR 302.

[46] (1938) 61 CLR 337.

[47] (1955) 1 SCR 972.

[48] (1955) 1 SCR 972 at 983–4.

[49] (1980) 3 SCR 1370.

[50] (1946) 72 CLR 634.

[51] (1980) 1 SCR 944.

[52] *Steele v Deputy Commissiner of Taxation* 199 HCA 7.

[53] Legislation relating to estate duty has been repealed and replace by a *Wealth Tax Act*, tax payable not contingent upon death.

[54] (1986) 1 SCR 349.

[55] (1912) 13 CLR 503.

[56] (1978) 1 SCC 520.

[57] (1988) 3 SCC 263.

[58] *Broken Hill South Ltd v Commissioner of Taxation (NSW)* (1937) 56 CLR 337; *Morgan v Deputy Federal Commissioner of Land Tax NSW* (1912) 15 CLR 661; *Peanut Board v Rockhamption Harbour Board* (1993) 48 CLR 266; *James v The Commonwealth* (1936) 55 CLR 1; *Milk Board (NSW) v Metropolitan Cream Pty Ltd* (1939) 62 CLR 116.

[59] See e.g., *S.R. Bommai v Union of Inda* (1994) 2 SCR 644 where B.P. Jeevan Reddy J applied Stephen J's opinion in *The Queen v Toohey, Ex parte Northem Land Council* (1981) 151 CLR 170 at 215–16. See also *Vishaka v State of Rajasthan* (1977) 6 SCC 241 at 251 where Verma CJ cited *Minister for Immigration and Ethnic Affaris v Teoh* (1995) 183 CLR 273 'as recognizing the concept of a contrary legislative provisions even in the absence of a Bill of Rights in the Constitution of Australia'.

[60] (1978) 2 SCC 213.

[61] *Federated Engine Drivers and Firemen's Association of Australasia v Broken Hill Proprietary Co Ltd* (1913) 16 CLR 245; *Federated State School Teachers' Association of Australia v State of Victoria* (1929) 41 CLR 569.

[62] *Pettitt v Dunkley* (1971) 1 NSWLR 376 CA at 388.

[63] *Breen v amalgamated Engineering Union* (1971) 2 QB 175 CA at 190–1.

[64] *Reg v Gaming Board for Great Britain, Ex parte Benaim and Khaida* (1970) 2 QB 417 CA at 430–1.

[65] *Administrative Decisions (Judicial Review) Act 1977* Aust., section 13; cf. *Administrative Law Act* 1978 Vic, section 8; *Tribunals and Inquiries Act* 1992 UK, secion 10.

[66] (1976) 2 SCC 981.

[67] (1978) 1 SCC 248.

[68] *Osmond v Public Service Board of NSW* (1984) 3 NSWLR 447 CA at 461 per Kriby P.

[69] *Public Service Board of NSW v Osmond* (1986) 159 CLR 656.

[70] *Public Service Board of NSW v Osmond* (1986) 159 CLR 656 at 668.

[71] (1990) Supp 1 SCR 44. See also the very recent decision of the Judicial Committee of the Privy Council in *Stefan v General Medical Council*, unreported, 8 March 1999.

[72] (1990) Supp 1 SCR 44.

[73] (1985) 3 NSWLR 447.

[74] (1990) 171 CLR 1.

[75] (1990) 171 CLR 1 at 20.

[76] (1967) 2 SCR 110.

[77] *Commonwealth v Tasmania* (1983) 158 CLR 1 at 165.

[78] (1950) 1 SCR 869 at 879.

[79] (1951) SCR 682.

[80] (1954) SCR 1117 at 1120.

[81] (1975) 2 SCR 715 at 729.

[82] (1977) 138 CLR 492.

[83] (1992) 177 CLR 292 at 334.

[84] (1979) 1 SCR 192 at 204–8.

[85] (1979) 3 SCR 760 at 765. The United State's decisions include *Betts v Brady* (1942) 316 US 455 at 476 per Black J and *Gideon v Wainwrith* (1963) 372 US 344–5 per Black J.

[86] AIR 1978 SC 597.

[87] *Street v Queensland Bar Association* (1989) 168 CLR 461 at 527.

[88] (1989) 168 CLR 461 at 571–2.

[89] (1952) SCR 284.

[90] (1988) 166 CLR 186 at 206.

[91] (1976) 1 SCR 906 at 951.

[92] (1985) 159 CLR 70 at 128–9.

[93] (1988) 166 CLR 186 at 206.

[94] (1976) 1 CLR 906 at 933.

[95] (1985) 159 CLR 70 at 129.

[96] (1997) 191 CLR 1 at 80.

[97] (1981) Supp SCC 87.

[98] (1984) 3 SCC 161.

[99] (1997) 190 CLR 513 at 659–60.

[100] Indian Constitution, Article 31.

[101] Citing *West Bengal v Subodh Gopal Bose* (1954) SCR 587; *State of West Bengal v Banerjee* (1954) SCR 558; *Madras v D. Namasivaya Mudaliar* (1964) 6 SCR 936.

[102] Citing *Vajravelu Mudaliar v Special Deputy Collector for Land Acquisition, West Madras* (1965) 1 SCR 614.

[103] (1997) 190 CLR 410 at 497.

[104] *Colonial Sugar Refining Co Ltd v Attorney-General for the Commonwealth* (1912) 15 CLR 182. In *Whitehouse v Queensland* (1961) 104 CLR 635 at 637–8 the Court held: '[I]t is only those who dwell under a Federal Constitution who can become adequately qualified to interpret and apply its provisions.'

[105] *Australia Act* 1986 (UK and Cth), section 11. See also *Privy Council (Limitation of Appeals) Act* 1968 (Cth); *Privy Council (Appeals from the High Court) Act* 1975 (Cth).

[106] A.S. Anand, 'The Domestic Application of International Human Rights Norms', unpublished address, Bangalore, 27 December 1998.

[107] He referred to *Jollly George Varghese v Bank of Cochi* (1980) 2 SCC 360; *Nilabati Behera v State of Orissa* (1993) 2 SCC 746; *Mackinnon Mackenzie and Co v Audrey D'Costa* (1987) 2 SCC 469.

[108] For example, he cited *Minister for Immigration and Ethnic Affaris v Teoh* (1995) 183 CLR 273 at 288–9 per Mason CJ and Deane J. See also *Mabo v Queensland [No 2]* (1992) 175 CLR 1 at 42 per Brennan J; *Kartinyeri v The Commonwealth* (1998) 72 ALJR 722 at 765 par 166 per Kriby J.

Six

The Goddess of Justice: The Constitution and the Supreme Court

M. Jagannadha Rao*

Between the two entrances from the Judge's wing, as one enters the Chief Justice's Court, there is a beautiful mural of coloured porcelain tiles, with the Goddess of Justice and Mahatma Gandhi, one on each side of the wheel of dharma. The eyes of the goddess are not blind-folded. Why?

The Goddess not Blindfolded

The beautiful mural between the two entrances is pregnant with mean-ing. Let us first examine the figures there. On the wall between these two doors, there is in the centre a rectangle in marble tiles with its length vertical, with six small lotuses on the smaller horizontal top and six on the corresponding horizontal bottom side. There are sixteen small tiles of peacocks on each of the two longer vertical sides. Between the Mahatma on the left and the Goddess on the right we have the rect-angle. At the centre of the rectangle there is a dharma *chakra* (wheel of justice) with twenty-four spokes and with an inscription below in San-skrit which reads 'Satyamevoddharamyaham' which means 'Truth alone I uphold'. The Goddess of Justice is on the right side of the rectangle in white robes and wearing a crown, holding a balance with scales in one hand and a book in the other. Her eyes are not blindfolded. On the left side of the rectangle, Mahatma Gandhi appears and below his figure are two *charkhas* (small spinning wheels).

*I acknowledge with gratitude the suggestions made by Justice M.N. Venkatachaliah, former Chief Justice of India and the suggestion for inclusion and translation of Sanskrit verses given by Justice M. Srinivasan, Judge, Supreme Court of India.

The idea of a deity representing justice was part of the ancient tradition of India, as was also the case in Greece, Rome, and elsewhere. According to the Vedic sutras, the deity of justice *does not close its eyes* but allows the graceful rays flowing from its eyes to illumine the administration of justice. The deity is seated in *padmasana* (crossed legs) on a throne, and has four arms like other deities in the Hindu tradition. On the right, one hand lifts a sword while the other holds a whip. On the left, one hand holds the book of *dharmasastra* while the palm of the other faces downwards which signifies the offer of total knowledge of dharma to one and all. The upper garment worn is a white shawl which exemplifies peace and purity and the reddish-yellow clothing *(kashaya)* up to the waist denotes renunciation. Among other ornaments, the deity wears a crown which destroys *adharma*. Behind the head, rays of light are visible which signify the name and fame of the deity whose pleasing expression is intended to inspire pleasant thoughts. The deity's long ears can hear the woes of the people. It is to be noticed that dharma in the Indian tradition is broader than the concept of justice and lays greater emphasis on duties prescribed by the Vedas rather than rights.

While this description of *dharma devata*[1] is to be found in various books, two other descriptions are found in two *slokas** in the ancient *Veda Bhashya* of Sri Narasimha:[2]

1. The holy Deity who initially acts as per Dharma is considered as embodiment of Dharma and is known as Yama.

The said Deity along with His divine Consort Shakti or Power, incarnates as the embodiment of Dharma.

The sparkling Deity shines with four faces, the face on the East is peace-loving reciting Vedas, the face on the West ensures good conduct and morals while the one on the South imposes Rules and the northern face imposes the conditions of Dharma.

2. Dharma Moorthi is seated on the hide of a tiger on a throne *(simhasana)* in *padmasana* posture [sitting with folded and crossed legs] with a vertical mark [on the forehead] and large eyes wearing a white robe and a snake as sacred thread, having three eyes and four hands; on the right side, one hand symbolically showing the right course *(neethi)* and the other hand holding a book symbolizing teaching; on the left side one hand holds a noose and the other hand holds a sword to enforce the commands; thus with the four hands the deity is glowing with brilliance and its eyes forever open.

Thus the deity in the Indian tradition has its eyes open *unmilya nethraschya*.

---

*See the Sanskrit quotation given at the end of this article.

In Greece, the concept of justice as a goddess originated with the mythical Greek figure Themis, the daughter of Uranus (heaven) and Gaia (earth). Homer described Themis as the personification of law, custom, and equity. Themis was Zeus's counsellor and consort. Her duties included convening the Agora, the Court of oral law. She held a pair of scales symbolizing the equilibrium of good and evil and impartiality. Her eyes *were not covered*. She did not need a blindfold because she had the gift of an inner eye signifying prophecy. She could see what was fair, just, and right. During the Renaissance in Italy, she remained without a veil over her eyes for being blindfolded could imply an absence of judgement, as in the case of Cupid, Fortune, and Ignorance.[3]

Mr Andrew Simmonds tells us that the goddess of justice was initially not blindfolded.[4] He says that in Rolfe's *The Attic Nights of Aulas Gellius*, it was shown that the goddess of justice of the Greeks and Romans had

a maidenly form and bearing, with a stern and fearsome countenance, a *keen glance of an eye*, and a dignity and solemnity which was ... awe-inspiring.[5]

In antiquity, the Goddess of Justice was noted for her 'clear-sightedness'. Simmonds believes that the blindfold was a misplaced symbol of impartiality:

The blindfold is misplaced as a symbol of impartiality. Justice blindfold cannot see the sword and scales in her hands to cut with the one and weigh with the other. The inconsistency of the blindfold with the sword and scales increases the allegoric mockery. As a symbol of impartiality, the blindfold is redundant.

He explains that even without the blindfold, the maiden's white robes themselves symbolize her purity and impartiality. He says:

Justice's impartiality is symbolized by her maidenly form. In the words of the Greek philosopher Chrysippus, 'she has the title of virgin as a symbol of her purity and an indication that she has never yielded to soothing words, the prayers and entreaties, to flattery, nor to anything of that kind'. Finally, the blindfold hides the expression on Justice's face, does not serve her venerable purpose of inspiring fear in the wicked and courage in the good.[6]

Judges, lawyers and litigants were also bound by the command 'Ne Vile Fano' meaning 'Do not defile the Temple of Justice'.

During the sixteenth century, the goddess of justice in Europe, particularly, in the North, was depicted as being blindfolded. This was the form of the earliest description of God by Albrecht Dürer in a woodcut of 1494.[7] A jester put the blindfold over her eyes; the idea being that she could perceive justice through the blindfold. Sometimes there were openings in the blindfold and sometimes not. Elsewhere, the eyes of the goddess were shaded by her upraised arm. In northern Europe it all began as ridicule of justice by placing the blindfold in a contemptuous way. Some intended it to imply an absence of judgement, ignorance, and the injustice in courts. In the *Bambergenesis*, in 1510, a woodcut showed a tribunal of five judges wearing jesters' hats and blindfolds. The accompanying legend suggested that 'out of bad habit, all that these blind fools do is to give sentence contrary to what is right'.[8] The Church too encouraged criticism of the secular courts which had replaced the church courts.[9]

In the sixteenth century, though the blindfold remained, it began to be given a new interpretation, namely, that it signified that the deity was governed by reason alone, clear of the misleading evidence of her senses.

The most beautiful description of the blindfolded goddess of justice is to be found in Cesare Ripa's *Iconologia* of the sixteenth century. It reads:

The personification of Justice is a blindfolded woman robed in white and wearing a crown. She supports a pair of *scales* in her lap with one hand. Her other hand holds a bared upright sword; and rests on a bundle of lectors' rods (fasces), from around which a serpent is unwinding. A dog lies at her feet. On the table are a sceptre, some *books* and a skull.

She is robed in white, for the Judge must be without moral blemish which might impair his judgement and obstruct true justice. She is *blindfolded, for nothing but reason, not the misleading evidence of the senses*, should be used in making judgements. She is regally dressed, for justice is the noblest and most splendid of concepts. The *scale*, used to measure quantities of material things, is a metaphor *for justice*, which sees that each man receives that which is due to him, no more and no less. The sword represents the rigour of Justice, which does not hesitate to punish. The same meaning is embodied by the lectors' rods, the Roman symbol of the Judges' power to punish and even to execute. The snake and the dog represent hatred and friendship, neither of which must be allowed to influence true justice. The sceptre is a symbol of authority; *the books, of written law*, and the skull of human mortality, which justice does not suffer, for it is eternal.[10]

Coming back to our mural, we have on the left side of the central rectangle, the picture of Mahatma Gandhi, the Father of the Nation, who won freedom for our country through his abiding faith in truth, non-violence, and peace. The two *charkhas* below his figure (wheels which are used to spin cotton at home) symbolize our spirit of self-reliance. Significantly, over the past fifty years, the philosophy of the goddess and of the Mahatma have permeated the judgements of the Supreme Court. The Court has developed a vast body of jurisprudence and also developed new and simple means of making justice accessible to the very poorest. Our goddess and the Mahatma have inspired the judges to deliver justice free from the shackles of rigid procedure. Today, in specific situations, grievances sent to the Supreme Court even in the form of letters, by the underprivileged are redressed, treating them as petitions for justice.

The *dharma chakra* in the mural is at the centre of the rectangle and has twenty-four spokes. Its design is reproduced from the wheel that appears on the abacus of the Sarnath Lion capital of Ashoka. The inscription in Sanskrit below that means 'Truth alone I uphold'. The dharma *chakra,* also referred to as the wheel of dharma, symbolizes Justice in a broader sense, encompassing truth, goodness, and equity. The Indian view is that dharma is the law that provides the greatest good to the greatest number, the term also signifying good and noble conduct. The wheel also signifies the cosmic concept of motion and progress, and the negation of static existence.[11]

The lotuses depicted in the border of the mural remind us of the flower that rises from mud and dust. It symbolizes, according to Dr S. Radhakrishnan, philosopher and India's former President, the nations that are oppressed today by political, economic or racial bondage, thriving to blossom into perfection.[12] The 'peacocks' signify the need for reverence of nature and the environment and the beauty of creation.

The main block of our Supreme Court building was built in a triangular plot in the fifties. According to Old Court Records of 1956, the Chief Architect was S.K. Joglekar. The broad decision taken at the highest level in 1956 was that the 'Supreme Court Building should be constructed in the triangular plot on Hardinge Avenue opposite Hardinge Bridge, in conformity with wishes of the Prime Minister, the Home Minister, Minister of Works, Housing and Supply and the Chief Justice of India, and that the Supreme Court of India should be housed

in a building distinctive in appearance, having grace and dignity befitting the country, at the same time being convenient and functional ...[13]

The building itself is in the form of a balance with two scales of justice. The central beam, from the ends of which the scales hang, comprises the Chief Justice's Court at the centre with two court-halls on either side. The right wing of the structure (as one looks at it from the front) consists of the Bar room, the offices of the Attorney-General and other Law Officers, and the Library of the Court. The left wing consists of

offices of the court. There have been two extensions, one in 1979 and
another in 1994, when buildings with more court-halls, office accommodation, and a medical unit were constructed at the rear in a semi-
elliptical form. There is a beautiful fountain at the centre at the back of
the building.

Such imagery as we have in our Court is not uncommon in courts
elsewhere. For example, the present building of the US Supreme Court
is in a square plot. In front two huge marble blocks flank the stairway,
and support large sculptures by James E. Fraser. On the right a seated
male figure representing the 'Authority of Law' holds a tablet inscribed
'Lex' in his left hand, while a sheathed sword at his side indicates the
power of government to execute the laws. The corresponding sculpture
on the left is entitled 'Contemplation of Justice' and features a classically draped female figure embodying the spirit of equity, as opposed to
strict law. In her right hand she holds a small statue of 'Justice' balancing the scales, while a book of law rests near the left hand. Like guardian
sculptures outside some ancient tomb, Fraser's giant creations evoke
the sense of apprehension and awe that laymen tend to associate with
the expounders of black letter law. At the top of the steps, a double row
of Corinthian columns supports a triangular pediment designed by
Robert Aitken. Aitken's frieze combines allegorical symbols and figures
from American history to celebrate the concept of ordered liberty; or as
the legend immediately below the group panel proclaims, 'Equal Justice under Law'. At the centre the Goddess of Liberty sits enthroned,
with the scales of justice on her lap; on either side a Roman soldier,
representing 'order' and 'authority', respectively, is in a protective stance.
Two other figures on each side represent 'Council' while a recumbent
figure, 'Research' fills out each end of the triangle. The toga-clad coun-
cillors on the right bear a marked resemblance to Charles Evans Hughes,
who succeeded Taft as Chief Justice in 1930, and Aitken himself. Those
on the left are likenesses of Cass Gilbert (who designed the edifice) and
lawyer-statesman Elihu Root. For his Research figures, Aitken chose to
portray John Marshall and William Howard Taft as young students.
The complementary pediment on the east side of the building bears an
inscription devised by Chief Justice Hughes, 'Justice, the guardian of
Liberty'. In his frieze, sculptor Herman A. MacNeil pays tribute to the
civilizing effects of legal authority. A trio of ancient law-givers—Moses,
flanked by Confucius and Salon—occupies the centre of the panel, which
otherwise features allegorical figures that are intended to symbolize the
beneficial aspects of judicial dispute resolution.

The Constitution—likened to a Gothic Cathedral and also to a Floating Dock

We now come to the Constitution, which has been likened to a Cathedral and a floating dock. J.M. Beck, in his *Constitution of the United States* provides one of the most beautiful metaphors[14] about the Constitution:

I have elsewhere likened the *Constitution* to a *Gothic Cathedral*, like that of Rheims. Its foundations seem secure, even though some of its buttresses may be weakened and its statuary mutilated. Nevertheless it remains a noble and serviceable temple of liberty and justice. Let us hope that, with the present indifference of the masses to the Constitution and the spirit of innovation of this restless and impatient age, that the time will not come that the Constitution will be as the Cathedral of Rheims when the author saw it in the summer of 1916. Rheims was a noble but pitiful ruin. Its high altar had been overthrown, and its glorious rose windows hopelessly shattered.

He says that the high altar of the Constitution is a self-restraint the people have imposed upon themselves and the rose windows, the traditions:

The high altar of the Constitution is the self-restraint which the American people of 1787 were wise enough to impose upon themselves, and their posterity, and the rose windows are those great traditions of Liberty which we have gained at an infinite sacrifice of treasure and life from our English speaking ancestry.

Beck also says[15] that the Constitution resists the ceaseless washing of time and circumstances and is very dissimilar to a sandy beach that is liable to be gradually eroded and destroyed. It is like a floating dock which is firmly attached to its moorings but yet rises and falls with the tide of time and circumstances. He says:

The Constitution is neither, on the one hand, a Gibraltar Rock, which wholly resists the ceaseless washing of time and circumstances, nor is it, on the other hand, a sandy beach, which is slowly destroyed by erosion of the waves. It is rather to be likened to a *floating dock*, which, while firmly attached to its moorings, and not therefore at the caprice of the waves, yet rises and falls with the tide of time and circumstances.

The Supreme Court a Lighthouse and a Lamp of the Constitution

Beck then describes the Supreme Court as a 'balance wheel',[16] as the 'lamp' of the Constitution. It is a lighthouse whose benignant rays of liberty and justice illumine the troubled surface of the water. He says:[17]

But always the Supreme Court stands as a great *lighthouse*, and even when the waves beat upon it with terrific violence (as in the civil wars, when it was shaken to its very foundation), yet after they have spent their fury, the *great lamp of the Constitution*—as that of another Pharos—illumines the troubled surface of the waters with the benignant rays of those immutable principles of liberty and justice, which alone can make a nation free as well as strong.

What is true of the American Constitution and the American Supreme Court is equally true of our Constitution and our Supreme Court. The Indian Constitution has, in spite of several amendments, been well protected by the Supreme Court so as to ensure that its basic structure remains intact.[18]

Way back in 1952, Chief Justice Patanjali Sastri wrote about the powers of the Supreme Court:

The Constitution of India contains express provisions for Judicial review of legislation as to its conformity with the Constitution, unlike in America where the Supreme Court has assumed extensive power of reviewing legislative acts under cover of the widely interpreted 'due process' clause in the Fifth and Fourteenth Amendments. If, then, the Courts of India face up to such important and none too easy task, it is not out of any desire to tilt at legislative authority in a crusaders' spirit, but in *discharge of a duty plainly laid* upon them by the Constitution. This is especially true as regards the *'fundamental rights'*, as to which the Supreme Court has been assigned *the role of a sentinel on the 'qui vive'*. While the Court naturally attaches great weight to a legislative judgement, it cannot desert its own duty to determine finally the constitutionality of an impugned statute.[19]

The Judicial Process

The Constitution is a living organism, and is interpreted as such by Indian judges. It was Chief Justice Marshall who said that we have to remember that it is the Constitution we are expounding. He said that the Constitution was intended to endure for ages to come, and consequently had to be adapted to the various *crises* of human affairs.[20]

Holmes said that the life of the law has not been logic but experience. The felt necessities of the time, the prevalent moral and political theories, intuitions of public policy, avowed or unconscious, even the prejudices which judges share with their fellow men, have had a good deal more to do than the syllogism in determining the rule by which man should be governed.[21] Chief Justice Rehnquist said a 'living' constitution was better than a dead one. Earlier he delivered a lecture entitled 'The Notion of a Living Constitution'.[22]

According to Professor T.R. Powell,[23] the accepted theory of 'Judicial Process' has been that the judge is like the oracle of Jupiter at Dodona who, upon being presented with the problem that called for decision, stupefied himself with vapours and listened to the dim voices that came to him. In other words, the judge brought ancient lights to illumine modern instances. The judge brought to bear his current outlook to manipulate the ancient rules.

In conclusion, let us sing in chorus a final tribute to our Constitution and our Supreme Court in words similar to those of the New York lawyer Henry Eastbrook eulogizing the American Constitution and its Supreme Court:[24]

Our great and sacred *Constitution*, serene and inviolable, stretches its benefi-cent powers over our land ... like the outstretched arm of God himself ... the people of the United States ... ordained and established one *Supreme court*— the most rational, considerate discerning, veracious, impersonal power—the most candid, unaffected, conscientious, incorruptible power ... O Marvellous Constitution! Magic Parchment! Transforming Word! Maker, Monitor, Guard-ian of Mankind.

Notes

[1] See C.M. Raghavendra Sharma, 'Dharma Devata' in C.M. Appaih Sharma (ed) *Principles of Veda and our Nation's Laws*, 1999, (Vol. I) p. 8.

[2] The sloka on Dharma Devata from the Veda Bhashya of Sri Narasimha (in Sanskrit) whose translation has been given in the body of the article. The sloka gives two other descriptions of the deity in Sanskrit:

[1] Dharmā Dharma Vidhischaiva
   Virāt Dharma Moorthi Bhihi;
   Yāmene Yamini Yama Dharmascha Sa
   Rudrena Rudro Dharma Moōrthihi;
   Poorve Santhi Kāmukā Vedamukha
   Prathichyām Neethi Niyama Dharmamukha;
   Yameyonudeechayām Niyama Dharma Mukha
   Yethāni Chaturumukhāni Dharma Rājo Prakāsithavān.

[2] Chathur Hasto Padmāsane
   Oordhva Pundra Visālakshaha;
   Dakshine Neethi Mudrascha Bodha Mudrasthu Pusthakaha
   Vāmecha Pāsatho Yuktho Khadgam Sāsana Pālakaha;
   Ethāni Chathur Hastāni Deepya Mānena Tejasā
   Simhāsana Mupāseena Swethambaradhara Sthithā;
   Nāgayagnopa-Veethancha Thrinethro Vyāghrāsanaha
   Sadā Unmilya Nethraschа Thishthantho Dharma Moorthihi.

(Sloka furnished from Narasimha Bhashaya by Sri Sadguru Pratapa Dakshina Moorthi Deekshitulugaru Omkaranagar (Kohir), Medak District, AP)

[3] See Alice I. Youmauns et al., 'Questions and Answers' *Law Library Journal*, 1990 (82), p. 197.

See also Michael E. Gehringer: 'Questions and Answers: Scales of Justice' (1980) 73, *Law Library Journal*, 740 at 744, 1980, on the history of the 'Scales of Justice'.

[4] Andrew Simmonds: 'Personal viewpoint' (1977) 68 *American Bar Association Journal* 1164.

[5] Ibid. at 1164 (emphasis added).

[6] Ibid. at 1164.

[7] Albrecht Dürer's woodcut, which illustrated Sebastian Brant's *Ship of Fools* (1494) is reproduced in Dennis E. Curtis and Judith Resnik: 'Images of Justice' (1987) 96 *Yale Law Journal* 1727–72.

[8] See Andrew Simmonds (*supra* n. 4) at 1164.

[9] For a comprehensive and fascinating account of the history of the depiction of the goddess of justice see Dennis E. Curtis and Judith Resnik (*supra* n. 7).

[10] As quoted in Dennis E. Curtis and Judith Resnik (*supra* n. 7) at 1748–9, which states that Cesare Ripa's *Iconologia* (Rome, 1593) is anthologised in E. Maser's edition of C. Ripa: *Baroque and Rococo Imagery* (1971) at 120.

[11] See R.S. Nathan, *Symbolism in Hinduism* by Central Chinmaya Mission Trust, Bombay, pp. 79–80.

[12] See Dr S. Radhakrishan, *Occasional Speeches and Writings*, Publications Division, Government of India.

[13] Maxwell (ed.), 'Architecture of the Supreme Court Building', *The Oxford Companion to the Supreme Court of the United States*, Oxford University Press, Oxford, 1992, p. 43–6.

[14] J.M. Beck, *Constitution of the United States: Yesterday, Today and Tomorrow?*, Oxford University Press, London, 1924, Introduction, p. xi.

[15] Ibid., p. 202.

[16] Ibid., pp. 218–31 at p. 226.

[17] Ibid., p. 231.

[18] *Kesavananda Bharati v State of Kerala* (1973) Supp SCR 1.

[19] *State of Madras v V.G. Row.* (1951) SCR 284.

[20] *McCulloch v Maryland* (1819) 4 Wheel 17 US 316.

[21] Oliver Wendell Holmes Jnr, *The Common Law and other Writings* (Birmingham, Ala; The Legal Classics Library 1982—originally published in 1881).

[22] See Justice William H. Rehnquist: 'The Notion of the Living Constitution' (1976) 54 *Texas Law Review* 693.

[23] See T.R. Powell, 'The Logic and Rhetoric of Constitutional Law', (1918) 15, *Journal of Philosophy, Psychology and Scientific Method*, quoted in Max Lerner 'The Supreme Court and American Capitalism', (1933) 42 *Yale Law Journal* 668 at 699.

[24] Song by Henry R. Eastbrook of the New York Bar, 1913 as reproduced in Alexander M. Bickel, *The Supreme Court and the Idea of Progress.* (New Haven, Conn; Yale University Press, at 185, and in the Notes)

Seven

Where Angels Fear to Tread*

Lord Cooke of Thorndon

In 1994 the persuasive representations of the then Attorney-General for India, Milon Banerji, Senior Advocate, and the present holder of that office, Soli Sorabjee, Senior Advocate, although evidently not jointly conceived, were concurrent causes of my writing for the inaugural issue of the journal *Law and Justice* an article entitled *Making the Angles Weep*. The title reflected another influence; that of a passage in the judgment of J.S. Verma J in *Supreme Court Advocates-on-Record-Association v Union of India*[1] (hereinafter called the *Judges* case) in which he quoted from *Measure for Measure*. Verma J was giving judgment on behalf of a majority of five judges in a court of nine holding *inter alia* that, under the Constitution of India, no appointment of any judge to the Supreme Court or any high court can be made unless it is in conformity with the opinion of the Chief Justice of India. The majority judgment further held that the opinion of the Chief Justice of India 'has not mere primacy but is determinative' in the matter of transfers of high court judges and chief justices, and that the consent of the transferee is not required.

Verma J (who himself later became Chief Justice) and his colleagues were anxious to emphasize that, no matter where legal power in these matters may ultimately reside and notwithstanding the primacy or conclusiveness conferred by the majority judgement on the opinion of the Chief Justice of India, a process of consultation with a view to a consensus between the executive and the judiciary and within the judiciary (or at least the higher echelons of the judiciary) is desirable. Such was the

*A revised version of a paper delivered to the Institute of Company Secretaries of India in New Delhi on 13 December 1998. The author records his gratitude to the International Centre for Alternative Dispute Resolution, New Delhi (Chairman, Dr H.R. Bhardwaj MP) for arranging the visit to India during which this paper was one of those delivered.

context in which Verma J aptly quoted from Isabella's plea to Angelo for her brother's life:[2]

> O, it is excellent
> To have a giant's strength, but it is tyrannous
> To use it like a giant.

It seemed to me, however—as I believe it has seemed to many other lawyers both inside and outside India—that the majority judgement, admirably motivated though it was by devotion to the rule of law, made free with the actual provisions of the Constitution. A layman might have felt bewildered by something like a sleight of hand. At the same time it might have been thought intrusive and cheeky for an outsider to say as much directly. It was therefore expedient to clothe the thought in Shakespearian language by a reminder that later in the same speech Isabella had added:[3]

> But man, proud man,
> Dressed in a little brief authority,
> ...
> Plays such fantastic tricks before high heaven
> As makes the angels weep ...

While recognizing that the decision in the second *Judges* case was a blow struck for judicial independence and a dramatic event in the international history of jurisprudence, 'Making the Angles Weep' thus responded with surprise rather than enthusiasm to the reasoning of the majority. The article represented a position and an audacity which Soli Sorabjee and Milon Banerji may not have expected. Now, in October 1998, has come the opinion of the Supreme Court in the third *Judges* case;[4] an opinion given upon a reference by the President under Article 143 of the Constitution. In some respects it takes the decision in the second *Judges* case further. In other respects it frankly amends that decision. If anything, it is even more debatable. If anything, my criticism of it will be even more presumptuous. Accordingly, an appropriate title continues the angles theme but reflects this time, *pace* E.M. Forster, the well-known observation of Alexander Pope: 'For fools rush in where angels fear to tread.' The excuse for rushing in can only be that the issues are of profound constitutional significance, going far beyond ordinary questions of law.

On their face, the immediately relevant articles of the Constitution, as amended, might seem straightforward:

74. **Council of Ministers to aid and advise President**—(1) There shall be a Council of Ministers with the Prime Minister at the head to aid and advise the

president who shall, in the exercise of his functions, act in accordance with such advice: ...

124. Establishment and Constitution of Supreme Court ...
(2) Every judge of the Supreme Court shall be appointed by the President by warrant under his hand and seal after consultation with such of the Judges of the Supreme Court and of the High Courts in the States as the President may deem necessary for the purpose and shall hold office until he attains the age of sixty-five years:
Provided that in the case of appointment of a Judge other than the Chief Justice, the Chief Justice of India shall always be consulted:

222. Transfer of a Judge from one High Court to another—(1) The President may, after consultation with the Chief Justice of India, transfer a Judge from one High Court to any other High Court.

The scheme of these provisions seems reasonably clear on first study. The appointment of any Supreme Court judge (including the Chief Justice) and the transfer of any high court judge is a function of the President acting in accordance with the advice of the Council of Ministers, commonly known as the Cabinet. There must however be prior consultation by the President (so advised, of course: in what follows I will not repeat this whenever the President is mentioned). As regards the appointment of a Chief Justice, the consultation is to be with such of the Supreme Court and high court judges as the President deems necessary for the purpose. Apparently, consultation with the outgoing Chief Justice is not constitutionally essential. As regards the appointment of Supreme Court judges other than the Chief Justice, the Chief Justice must always be consulted, and also such other Supreme Court and high court judges as the President deems necessary. As regards the transfer of a high court judge, the only consultation that is constitutionally required is with the Chief Justice of India: the Constitution does not require consultation with any other Supreme Court or high court judge, although it does not preclude such further consultation (nor, for that matter, consultation beyond the judiciary as widely as the President deems helpful).

For completeness it may be noted that by Article 217 the constitutional consultees for high court appointments are the Chief Justice of India, the Governor of the state, and, in the case of appointment of a judge other than the Chief Justice, the Chief Justice of the high court. For simplicity the present discussion concentrates on Supreme Court appointments, but similar reasoning would apply to high court appointments.

The consultation required by the Constitution must of course be in good faith, full and frank, with disclosure on both or all sides of any material information. That point is developed in 'Making the Angels Weep' and need not be elaborated here but, provided that the constitutionally required consultation has taken place, the ultimate responsibility under Article 124(2), Article 222(1), and Article 217(1) falls on the President, that is to say in effect the Cabinet.

The foregoing analysis must however be seen as superficial and incorrect—or at least seriously inadequate—according to the majority decision in the second *Judges* case and the unanimous opinion in the third *Judges* case. The analysis is substantially in accord with the earlier majority decision of four judges to three in *S.P. Gupta v Union of India*[5] (the first *Judges* case). Taking the view that in the appointment of Supreme Court and high court judges the Chief Justice of India did not enjoy primacy, Bhagwati J, later Chief Justice, said there in the principal judgement: 'It would therefore be open to the Central Government to override the opinion given by the constitutional functionaries required to be consulted and to arrive at its own decision in regard to the appointment of a Judge of the High Court or the Supreme Court, so long as such decision is based on relevant considerations and is not otherwise *malafide*.' There was a majority consensus in that case that the constitutional duty to consult did not imply a duty to obtain the concurrence of the person consulted. In short, consultation does not mean concurrence. Amongst the seven judges, Bhagwati J alone was prepared to read into Article 222(1) a requirement of consent on the part of the judge to be transferred.[6] Otherwise, zealous supporter of the rule of law though he is internationally known to be, he was not prepared to put any gloss on the constitutional requirements.

Disquiet developed quite widely about the effect of the first *Judges* case. It was seen by many within and outside the judiciary to lend too much power to the executive arm of the Union of India in relation to the judicial arm. The independence of the judiciary was understandably seen as an essential pillar of the Constitution. Recent Indian political history was thought to give ground for fear. In his judgement in the second *Judges* case Pandian J was to say that the judiciary were suffering suffocation caused by the excessive dominance of the executive in the matter of the appointment of judges to the superior judiciary as well as in the formation of its structural composition. The last words appear to be a reference to judge-strength in the high courts, a subject also considered in this line of cases but is one that is outside the scope of the present discussion.

Such was part of the background against which, following an order of a bench of three Supreme Court judges, two writ petitions in certain public interest litigation were placed before a bench of nine in the second *Judges* case, for the purpose, *inter alia*, of a review of the first *Judges* case. The result, after full arguments by leading counsel of the day, was a set of judgements of much learning, length, and complexity. The gradations and nuances of opinion make a satisfactory summary virtually impossible; but in broad outline it can be said that the concepts of the primacy of the Chief Justice of India in appointments and of concurrence rather than mere consultation prevailed. As already mentioned, Verma J delivered to that effect what emerged as the principal judgement, on behalf also of Dayal, Ray, Anand (the present Chief Justice), and Bharucha JJ. In separate judgements Pandian J, whose was the first and longest judgement, substantially concurred; Kuldip Singh J substantially concurred on the main points; Punchhi J (later Chief Justice), disagreeing with the view of the majority that the Chief Justice is bound to consult at least his two most senior colleagues, went furthest in the direction of allowing control to the Chief Justice; whereas Ahmadi J (who was to precede Verma J and Punchhi J as Chief Justice) dissented, adopting largely the position of the majority in the first *Judges* case and holding that in the appointments the Chief Justice does not enjoy a veto in the sense that the President and the Cabinet are bound to act according to his views.

In spite, or perhaps, of the copiousness of its language, the majority judgement in the second *Judges* case has an undeniable opaqueness in various respects. For instance, the distinction between having primacy and being determinative is elusive. To what extent does the judgement prescribe what it calls 'healthy convention' rather than binding law? What is to be done if the Chief Justice of India and his two seniormost colleagues cannot agree or if it is apparent that a majority of the existing Supreme Court Judges are opposed to the Chief Justice's recommendation? During the eight months of Punchhi CJ's tenure of the office a considerable number of his recommendations for appointments and transfers proved controversial. The Law Ministry alleged that the Chief Justice had not consulted with colleagues as required by the second *Judges* case. The Chief Justice denied this but is reported to have maintained that the Law Minister was not entitled to inquire into the extent of the Chief Justice's consultations. Not only was there acrimony at that level, but unconcealed dissatisfaction on the part of various members of high courts received much media publicity. Whether the judges of the Supreme Court, which now numbers twenty-five in addition to the Chief Justice, were content is doubtful.

In these circumstances the Union government resorted in July 1998 to Article 143(1) of the Constitution, which empowers the President to refer to the Supreme Court for consideration and report any question of law or fact appearing to the President to be of such a nature and of such public importance as to make this course expedient. Nine questions were formulated for the stated purpose of resolving doubts as to the interpretation of the law laid down in the second *Judges* case. Most of the questions related to the extent, if any, of the Chief Justice's duty to consult other judges on appointments or transfers. The last question was whether any recommendation made by the Chief Justice without complying with the norms and consultation process is binding on the government.

The Supreme Court is not bound to answer questions under Article 143(1). It has discretion. The government in turn has a discretion, not being bound to act on a report. Here again I must mention Soli Sorabjee. In no way is he associated with any views that I am expressing, but as Attorney-General for India he had a major influence on the third *Judges* case, for the opinion records that he had made to the Court, two statements of great importance. First, he said that the Union of India was not seeking a review or reconsideration of the judgement in the second *Judges* case. Secondly, he said that the Union would accept and treat as binding the answers of the Supreme Court to the questions set out in the reference. The first of these statements has the tendency of legitimizing any arguable usurpation by the judiciary in the second *Judges* case of constitutional power regarding judicial appointments and transfers. As to the rules actually enunciated in that case, however, the statement did not have any evident inhibiting effect. The Supreme Court did proceed to review and reconsider the second *Judges* case on some key points. The Attorney-General's second statement may eventually be of doubtful efficacy. As a matter of honour at least, it will no doubt be complied with by the present Government of India. Whether it would restrict any future government is more questionable. The argument will be available that one executive cannot bind its successors, and, further, that the Supreme Court would not have reported as it has but for a consensual submission to its jurisdiction.

Be that as it may, the Supreme Court certainly seized the opportunity presented to it. The opinion in the third *Judges* case is remarkable for several features. In contrast with the first and second *Judges* cases, it is unanimous, there being a single opinion given for the Court by Bharucha J. In added contrast, it is brief; a mere forty-three pages taken up mainly by reciting the terms of the reference and extensive passages from the majority judgement in the second *Judges* case. The composition of the bench of nine is striking to an outside commentator, in that there is a particularly strong contingent of judges from Bombay and Gujarat, and the judge of the Supreme Court whose appointment as the next Chief Justice had been announced before the substantive hearing began, Dr A.S. Anand, did not sit. Although the latter was scrupulously following the precedents set by the Chief Justices in office at the times of the first and second *Judges* cases, the balance of the court was thus not ideal.

As for the substance of the opinion, three points stand out. First, it reads more like a promulgation of policy than an exercise in juridical reasoning drawing inferences from the provisions of the Constitution. The reasoning is indeed noticeably limited. It is as if, in pursuance of the constitutional powers held to be vested in it by the second *Judges* case and accepted by the Attorney-General for India, and all other powers enabling it, the Court proclaims a set of rules to be followed in future in the making of appointments to high judicial office and transfers of high court judges.

Secondly, it disposes to a considerable extent, though not entirely, of the issue between convention and strict law by concluding in express terms: 'Recommendations made by the Chief Justice of India without complying with the norms and requirements of the consultation process, as aforestated, are not binding upon the Government of India.' The position in that event is not fully dealt with in the opinion, but the tenor of the opinion appears to be that the government must defer making a decision until the prescribed consultation process has been carried out. What is to happen if the process is exhausted without agreement involves considering the third outstanding element in the opinion, which is, in terms, the creation of a collegium larger than that favoured in the second *Judges* case.

What is now laid down in the third *Judges* case is that the opinion of the Chief Justice, which has primacy in the matter of recommendations for appointment to the Supreme Court, has to be formed in consultation with a collegium of judges. 'Presently, and for a long time now, the collegium consists of the two most senior Judges of the Supreme Court.' There follows recognition that the opinions of other judges, and indeed members of the Bar, may be taken into account, but it is said expressly that the members of the collegium *decide* on recommendations 'along with the Chief Justice of India'.[7] As to the composition of the collegium, the opinion goes on to amend the majority decision in the second *Judges* case as follows:

With this in mind, what has to be considered is whether the size of the collegium that makes the recommendation should be increased. Having regard to the terms of Article 124(2), as analysed in the majority judgment in the second Judges case, as also the precedent set by the then Chief Justice of India, as set out earlier, and having regard to the objective aforestated, we think it is desirable that the collegium should consist of the Chief Justice of India and the four seniormost puisne Judges of the Supreme Court.[8]

Regarding appointments and transfers of high court judges somewhat different rules are laid down; the details need not be examined here apart from mentioning that for appointments the collegium remains at three: the Chief Justice and his two most senior colleagues. It is necessary to note that in any case where a collegium is required to function, whether in relation to the Supreme Court or a high court, the views of all members of the collegium are to be in writing and must be conveyed by the Chief Justice of India to the Government of India together with the recommendation. On the issue of differences of view the opinion contains the following passage:

It is, we think, reasonable to expect that the collegium would make its recommendations based on a consensus. Should that not happen, it must be remembered that no one can be appointed to the Supreme Court unless his appointment is in conformity with the opinion of the Chief Justice of India. The question that remains is: what is the position when the Chief Justice of India is in a minority and the majority of the collegium disfavour the appointment of a particular person? The majority judgement in the second Judges case has said that if 'the final opinion of the Chief Justice of India is contrary to the opinion of the senior Judges consulted by the Chief Justice of India and the senior Judges are of the view that the recommendee is unsuitable for stated reason(s), which are accepted by the President, then the non-appointment of the candidate recommended by the Chief Justice of India would be permissible'. This is delicately put, having regard to the high status of the President, and implies that if the majority of the collegium is against the appointment of a particular person, that person shall not be appointed, and we think that this is what must invariably happen. We hasten to add that we cannot easily visualize a contingency of this nature; we have little doubt that even if two of the Judges forming the collegium express strong views, for good reasons, that are adverse to the appointment of a particular person, the Chief Justice of India would not press for such appointment.[9]

The sentence suggests prediction or convention only.

Rather than underlining the primacy of the Chief Justice, the opinion thus appears to have shifted power, to a significant extent, to a small number of Supreme Court judges other than the Chief Justice. This may be a far cry from anything envisaged by the framers of the Constitution of 1949. Nevertheless, it may work satisfactorily; only time will tell; more judges cases may come. There may be some risk of dominance by a particular school of thought. A Denning or a Murphy might have little prospect of appointment. On the other hand, there will be the advantage that overtly political appointments or transfers are unlikely. Moreover, if the interpretation about to be offered is correct, the risks just mentioned will be diminished.

If I may venture a suggestion, a close reading of the opinion also brings out that there are significant limits to its rigour. The crucial passage last quoted, containing the words 'we think that this is what must invariably happen', deals with a candidate or recommendee who is unsuitable for a stated and good reason. The emphasis is on the individual. The manifest aim is the exclusion from the Supreme Court of persons unsuitable to serve there. Neither that passage nor the opinion as a whole appears to go so far as to entitle the majority of a collegium to block the appointment of a person merely on the ground that they have a preferred candidate. They must be able to identify some reason—normally, one would suppose, something apparent from the history or characteristics of the candidate—which may fairly be regarded as, on personal grounds, disqualifying him or her for appointment. Of course, I speak of disqualification in the sense, not of a formal ground of ineligibility, but of a lack of the judicial qualities expected in a judge of the apex court.

The opinion does not specify the course to be followed in the event that an objection by a majority of a collegium is not based on grounds of the seriousness just outlined. Perhaps the position then would even be that which the Constitution appears to provide: namely, that the President on the advice of the Council of Ministers would be free to make the decision. In that area at least the distinction between consultation and concurrence may not yet be obliterated.

All in all, the opinion of the Supreme Court in the third *Judges* case must be one of the most remarkable rulings ever issued by a supreme national appellate court in the common law world. Since, in some respects, I have had to voice respectful doubts about the soundness of the constitutional foundations of that opinion, let me end on the happier note by saying that my admiration for the Supreme Court in its ordinary work, particularly in the field of human rights, is no whit abated.

Such expositions as that of Anand J, as he then was, in *Basu v State of West Bengal*,[10] where on behalf of Kuldip Singh J and himself he took a stand against torture, foreshadowing in a sense the speeches of Lord Nicholls of Birkenhead and Lord Steyn in the first *Pinochet*[11] case, are steps in the very slow but, I believe, very sure march towards a common law of the world. I am proud of the interaction between Indian and New Zealand jurisprudence which assisted us in New Zealand to recognize that there must be a remedy against the state for violations by state officers of human rights declared by the national legislature,[12] whether or not the statute contains an express remedies clause. Any eccentricities exhibited by the second and third *Judges* cases are Homeric nods by comparison with the whole corpus of the work of the Supreme Court of India. It was an honour to have the opportunity of sitting on the bench of the Chief Justice's Court during a hearing in December 1998 and it is a privilege now to join in honouring the Supreme Court as one of the most powerful and most interesting courts in the world.

Notes

[1] AIR 1994 SC 268.

[2] *Measure for Measure* 2, ii, 109.

[3] Ibid., 2, ii, 120.

[4] *In re* Special Reference 1 of 1998: (1998) 7 SCC 739.

[5] AIR 1982 SC 149.

[6] Paradoxically, the majority in the second *Judges* case rejected that implication and held that any transfer made on the recommendation of the Chief Justice of India is not justiciable on any ground.

[7] It had been stated earlier in the opinion that, at the time of the latest selection of judges appointed to the Supreme Court, the then Chief Justice of India (Verma CJ) had constituted a panel of himself and five of the then seniormost puisne Judges. Nothing that I am saying questions the right of a Chief Justice to constitute his own collegium as a matter of discretion.

[8] *In re* Special Reference 1 of 1998: (1998) 7 SCC 739 at pr. 16, p. 764.

[9] Ibid., pr. 24, p. 765.

[10] (1997) 1 SCC 416.

[11] *R v Bow Street Metropolitan Stipendiary Magistrate, ex parte Pinochet Ugarte* (1998) 4 All E.R. 897. The decision of the House of Lords on the rehearing is not available at the time of writing.

[12] See *Basu*, cit. sup. at 442–3, and *Simpson v Attorney-General (Baigent's* case) (1994) 3 NZLR 667.

Eight

The Supreme Court and
the Basic Structure Doctrine

Raju Ramachandran

When the framers of the Constitution provided the 'procedure' for its amendment in Article 368, no one could have anticipated that the extent of the amending power would become a source of continuing conflict between Parliament and the Supreme Court. They could not have foreseen that they would have to make changes in its text to overturn judicial decisions on agrarian reforms, free speech, and compensatory discrimination within a year of the Constitution being promulgated. Nehru's evocative indictment that lawyers had 'purloined' the Constitution,[1] did not stop the tussle. It went on. Over the past fifty years, the Constitution has been amended seventy-nine times. Some of the amendments simply tidied up matters to meet the exigent situation. The more controversial amendments, with which we are concerned in this essay, sought to overturn judicial decisions which the regime in power claimed obstructed social justice and the nation's progress.

Initially, the response of the Supreme Court to the rewriting of the Constitution was cautious—rejecting, in 1951 unreservedly, and in 1964, with reservations the challenge that the plenary power to amend the Constitution was subject to substantive restrictions. In 1967, in *I.C. Golak Nath v State of Punjab*,[2] a stronger counter-attack invalidated some of the amendments prospectively by testing them against the very fundamental rights that these amendments sought to amend. The executive and the judiciary were clearly at loggerheads—on the path to a collision. The legislature responded by seeking to get over *Golak Nath* by further amendments to the Constitution. A crisis was clearly in the offing. Would the judiciary break down? Alternatively, would it assert and claim the 'supreme' right to be the custodian of the Constitution?

In a watershed decision in the case of *Kesavananda Bharati v State of Kerala*,[3] the Supreme Court responded with the answer that the powerfully sovereign legislature, who were possessed of otherwise plenary power to amend the Constitution, could not alter the 'basic structure' of the Constitution. *Kesavananda*, with its concomitant basic structure doctrine, is one of the most remarkable cases of the century. It represents the high point of judicial innovation and alters the very basis on which the constitutional power is divided between the plenary amendatory bodies and the judiciary. The 'basic structure' doctrine alters the emphasis of democratic constitutionalism and had an immediate effect on the thinking of many Constitution makers and judiciaries throughout the world. Some Constitutions built the 'basic structure' doctrine into the text of the Constitution, others did not. Some judges, in other jurisdictions accepted the 'basic structure' doctrine, others did not. The Indian judiciary has used the 'basic structure' doctrine mostly to protect judicial power.

In *Kesavananda*, the Court assured for itself, a new and impregnable role in the constitutional politics of India. In enunciating the 'basic structure' doctrine and placing judicially created impediments on the plenary power to amend the Constitution, the Court made it clear that whatever the intention of the Constitution makers to evolve a democratic system of checks and balances, the final say belonged to the judges. The Court seemed to think that it was elementary that the Constitution was supreme, knowing all along that the Constitution is what the judges say it is.

This essay proceeds from the standpoint that the 'basic structure' doctrine is anti-democratic and counter-majoritarian in character, and that unelected judges have assumed vast political power not given to them by the Constitution. It puts the evolution and the consolidation of the doctrine in the context of the politics, and equally, the political personalities of the times we have passed through. It argues that a weakened political class, anxious to show adherence to the rule of law has quietly acquiesced in judicial primacy, and the court, armed with the ultimate power to annul amendments to the Constitution, has used it, and lesser powers flowing from it, extensively in the second half of its existence. This proactive role of the Court has helped it to live down its role during the Emergency of 1975–7. However, the writer shall argue, that the doctrine can now stand in the way of political and economic changes which may be felt necessary.

The Unlimited Amending Power Phase: 1951–67

It would be useful to begin with a brief history of how the Court has viewed its power to examine the validity of amendments to the Constitution over the years. Laws for agrarian reform, known popularly as Zamindari Abolition Acts, were passed in Bihar, Uttar Pradesh, and Madhya Pradesh. The laws were challenged in different high courts by owners of estates on the ground of violation of fundamental rights: mainly on the ground that differential treatment was accorded to landowners in the matter of payment of compensation, and that the right to equality under Article 14 was violated. The Bihar law was struck down, but the Uttar Pradesh and Madhya Pradesh laws were upheld by the respective high courts.[4] When appeals were pending in the Supreme Court, the Provisional Parliament passed the Constitution (First Amendment) Act, 1951. The First Amendment introduced Articles 31-A and 31-B, and inserted the Ninth Schedule into the Constitution. Article 31-A protected 'estate' laws from challenges based on violation of Fundamental Rights. Article 31-B provided that, without prejudice to the generality of the provisions of Article 31-A, any law placed in the Ninth Schedule would be immune from any attack based on the violation of Fundamental Rights. The Bihar Land Reforms Act, 1950 was placed in the said schedule along with twelve other Acts.

In *Sankari Prasad v Union of India*,[5] the Supreme Court considered a challenge to the First Amendment at the instance of aggrieved landowners. Apart from arguments based on the powers of the Provisional Parliament to pass the amendment and certain other objections relating to procedure, the main attack on the amendment was based on Article 13(2) which prohibited the state from making any 'law' in derogation of Fundamental Rights. The argument was that 'law' must also include an amendment to the Constitution. The Court dealt with this argument in precisely one paragraph, holding that there was a clear distinction between ordinary law made in exercise of legislative power and constitutional law made in exercise of constituent power, that the terms of Article 368 were perfectly general and empowered Parliament to amend the Constitution without any exception whatsoever, and that on a harmonious interpretation of Articles 13(2) and 368, the former did not affect amendments to the Constitution. When *Sankari Prasad* was decided, there were no doubts about constitutionalism taking root in the country. Despite Nehru's despair with the judiciary about the manner in which the right to property was being interpreted, his credentials as a democrat and as a respecter of institutions were never in doubt.

Three decisions of the Supreme Court in 1954[6] interpreted 'compensation' to mean fair and adequate compensation. Parliament responded by passing the Constitution (Fourth Amendment) Act in 1955. This amendment made changes in Article 31(2), to clearly draw a distinction between compulsory acquisition and requisitioning of private property, and deprivation of property by the operation of prohibitory or regulatory laws. It made it clear that compensation was payable only in the former case, but the amount of compensation payable was non-justiciable. The protection of Article 31-A, which was originally applicable to the zamindari abolition laws, was extended to other types of social welfare and regulatory legislation. It also inserted seven Acts in the Ninth Schedule. It is necessary to mention that the Fourth Amendment was not challenged in Court, and the question of its validity was raised only twelve years later, in the *Golak Nath* case. This, the writer submits, is a major problem in giving the Court the power to annul an amendment of the Constitution: the fate of a Constitution depends on a petitioner getting the right legal advice at the right time.

The Constitution (Seventeenth Amendment) Act, 1964 inserted as many as forty-four Acts in the Ninth Schedule, and came to be challenged in the *Sajjan Singh* case.[7] The majority affirmed *Sankari Prasad*, Significantly, in dealing with the plea of the petitioners that the said decision needed reconsideration, the Court observed,

... if the arguments urged by the petitioners were to prevail, it would lead to the inevitable consequence that the amendment made in the Constitution both in 1951 and 1955 would be rendered invalid and a large number of decisions dealing with the validity of the Acts included in the Ninth Schedule which have been pronounced by different High Courts ever since the decision of this Court in *Sankari Prasad's* case was declared, would also be exposed to serious jeopardy. These are considerations which are both relevant and material in dealing with the plea urged by the petitioners before us in the present proceedings that *Sankari Prasad's* case should be reconsidered.[8]

There were however two voices of dissent by Justice Hidayatullah and Justice Mudholkar, who otherwise agreed that the Seventeenth Amendment was valid. Justice Hidayatullah found some difficulty in accepting the reasoning of *Sankari Prasad* with regard to the meaning of 'law' in Article 13(2), saying that if amendments to the Constitution were to be excluded, the easiest and most obvious way was to say that the word 'law' in Article 13 did not include an amendment of the Constitution. Justice Hidayatullah felt that restricting fundamental rights by resort to clauses 2 to 6 of Article 19 was one thing, but removing them from the Constitution or debilitating them by an amendment was quite another. He said ominously, 'It is true that such things would never be, but one is concerned to know whether such a doing would be possible.'[9]

Justice Mudholkar, while agreeing that the Seventeenth Amendment was valid also indicated that *Sankari Prasad* was not the last word. He laid the foundation for the Basic Structure Doctrine in these words:

We may also have to bear in mind the fact that ours is a written constitution. The Constituent Assembly which was the repository of sovereignty could well have created a sovereign Parliament on the British model. But instead it enacted a written constitution, created three organs of state, made the union executive responsible to Parliament and the State executives to the State Legislature; erected a federal structure and distributed legislative power between Parliament and State Legislatures; recognized certain rights as fundamental and provided for their enforcement; prescribed forms of oaths of office or affirmations which require those who subscribe to them to owe true allegiance to the Constitution and further require the members of the Union Judiciary and of the higher judiciary in the States, to uphold the Constitution. Above all, it formulated a solemn and dignified preamble which appears to be an epitome of the basic features of the Constitution. Can it not be said that these are indicia of the intention of the Constituent Assembly to give a permanency to the basic features of the Constitution?[10]

Sajjan Singh was decided on 30 October 1964. Nehru had died just a few months earlier. The question 'After Nehru, who?' had been answered, but 'After Nehru, what', was not yet clear.

The Limited Amending Power Phase: 1967 and After

Just two years later, in *Golak Nath*, the Court again considered the validity of the same Seventeenth Amendment, and therefore necessarily the First and Fourth Amendments. By a thin majority of six to five, the Court held these amendments to be invalid. Conscious of the chaos that would have otherwise resulted, the Court invoked the doctrine of 'prospective overruling' (Justice Hidayatullah, concurring, resorted to the theory of acquiescence) in order to hold that the Court's decision would operate only in the future. The Court held that Article 368 did not contain the power to amend the Constitution but only its procedure, that an amendment was a legislative process and that an amendment was a 'law' within the meaning of Article 13 and therefore would be void if it took away or abridged Fundamental Rights.

Chief Justice Subba Rao was acutely conscious of the implications of the Court's decision, and observed:

It was said that if the provisions of the Constitution could not be amended it would lead to revolution ... What we cannot understand is how the enforcement of the provisions of the Constitution can bring about a revolution. History shows that revolutions are brought about not by the majorities but by the minorities and sometimes by military coups. The existence of an all comprehensive amending power cannot prevent revolutions, if there is chaos in the country brought about by misrule or abuse of power. On the other hand, such a restrictive power gives stability to the country and prevents it from passing under a totalitarian or dictatorial regime. We cannot obviously base our decision on such hypothetical or extraordinary situations which may be brought about with or without amendments. Indeed, a Constitution is only permanent and not eternal. There is nothing to choose between destruction by amendment or by revolution. The former is brought about by totalitarian rule, which cannot brook constitutional checks and the other by discontentment brought about by misrule. If either happens, the Constitution will be a scrap of paper. Such considerations are out of place in construing the provisions of the Constitution by a court of law.[11]

The judgements in *Golak Nath* were delivered on 27 February 1967. Indira Gandhi had already been installed as Prime Minister after the sudden demise of Lal Bahadur Shastri. While she had not displayed any authoritarian streak so far and had been preferred by the 'bosses' of the Congress party over the seemingly more independent Morarji Desai, the fact that she was Nehru's daughter and that there was a dynasty in the making must have indeed troubled the liberal democratic spirit in all sections of society, including the judiciary.

'The majority decision clearly appears to be a political decision not based on the true interpretation of the Constitution, but on the apprehension that Parliament, left free to exercise its powers, would, in course of time, take away the citizen's fundamental rights, including his freedom', wrote M.C. Setalvad, a distinguished jurist and India's first Attorney-General. Soon after *Golak Nath*, Chief Justice Subba Rao agreed, while still in office, to be the candidate of the opposition parties for the election to the office of the President of India, and resigned his office. The propriety of this decision was questioned by Setalvad, among others.

But *Golak Nath* kept a safety valve open. Without expressing a final opinion on whether a new Constituent Assembly could be called, Chief Justice Subba Rao observed that the residuary power of Parliament could be resorted to in order to call such an Assembly. Justice Hidayatullah was clear that this could be done.

Soon Indira Gandhi came into her own by breaking free from the 'syndicate' of the Congress party. She nationalized banks and abolished the privy purses of the rulers of the erstwhile princely states. In the *Bank Nationalization* case,[12] the Court struck down the nationalization of banks for failure to pay just compensation, while in the *Privy Purses* case,[13] the Court struck down the abolition of privy purses on the ground that it violated the right to property.

India's victory in the 1971 war with Pakistan, which resulted in the creation of Bangladesh, caused Mrs Gandhi to win the elections with a huge majority. The election manifesto of the Congress party had promised that impediments placed by the judiciary in the way of socio-economic reforms would be removed. The Constitution (Twenty-fourth Amendment) Act, 1971 brought about changes in both Articles 13 and 368. The newly introduced Article 13(4) made it clear that amendments to the Constitution were not 'law' for the purpose of Article 13(2). The marginal note to Article 368, which earlier said 'Procedure for amendment of the Constitution' was amended to read 'Power of Parliament to amend the Constitution and procedure thereof'. Article 368(1) now provided that 'Notwithstanding anything in this Constitution, Parliament may in exercise of its constituent power amend by way of addition, variation or repeal any provision of this Constitution in accordance with the procedure laid down in this article.' This was clearly the answer to *Golak Nath*. The Constitution (Tweny-fifth) Amendment Act, 1972 *inter alia* substituted the word 'amount' for 'compensation' in Article 31 and clarified that the right to hold, acquire, and dispose of property under Article 19(1)(f) would not apply to laws concerning acquisition under Article 31(2). It introduced Article 31C which gave primacy to the Directive Principles in Article 39(b) and (c) over the Fundamental Rights contained in Articles 14, 19, and 31. It also provided that no law containing a declaration that it was enacted to give effect to the Directive Principles under Article 39(b) and (c) could be called in question in any court on the ground that it did not give effect to such principles. The Constitution (Twenty-ninth Amendment) Act, 1972 included the Kerala Land Reforms (Amendment) Act, 1969 and the Kerala Land Reforms (Amendment) Act, 1971 in the Ninth Schedule.

Kesavananda dealt with a challenge to these three amendments. It is outside the scope of this essay to undertake a detailed analysis of the eleven individual judgements delivered by the Bench of thirteen judges or to reconcile the views of Justice Khanna, who tilted the balance, with the views of Chief Justice Sikri and Justices Shelat, Hegde, Grover, Jaganmohan Reddy, and Mukherjea in order to deduce the majority view. The following summary, though signed by only nine out of thirteen judges, has ever since been accepted as the Court's view:

[1] *Golak Nath's* case is overruled;

[2] Article 368 does not enable Parliament to alter the basic structure or framework of the Constitution;

[3] The Constitution (Twenty-fourth Amendment) Act, 1971 is valid;

[4] Sections 2(a) and 2(b) of the Constitution (Twenty-fifth Amendment) Act, 1971 are valid;

[5] The first part of section 3 of the Constitution (Twenty-fifth Amendment) Act, 1971 is valid. The second part, namely, 'and no law containing a declaration that it is for giving effect to such policy shall be called in question in any court on the ground that it does not give effect to such policy' is invalid;

[6] The Constitution (Twenty-ninth Amendment) Act, 1971 is valid.[14]

Thus, while overruling *Golak Nath*, the Court in fact went several steps ahead in asserting its power of judicial review. *Golak Nath* had confined itself to the taking away of Fundamental Rights, but *Kesavananda* gave the Court the power to scrutinize any amendment to see if it violated the basic structure, which it did not define, except illustratively. Even the referendum option would no longer be open, because what was part of the basic structure became immutable.

Indira Gandhi reacted by superseding three senior judges, Justices Shelat, Hegde, and Grover, who were part of the 'basic structure' majority and appointed Justice A.N. Ray as the Chief Justice of India after the retirement of Chief Justice Sikri. An unambiguous defence of the supersession, based on the social philosophy of judges, was offered by Mohan Kumaramangalam, a Cabinet Minister who did not hold the portfolio of law, but was one of Mrs Gandhi's closest advisers.

The differing perceptions of what would constitute the basic structure are best illustrated by what is set out in the different judgements of the majority. Sikri CJ observed:

The basic structure may be said to consist of the following features: (i) Supremacy of the Constitution, (ii) Republican and democratic form of government, (iii) Secular character of the Constitution, (iv) Separation of powers between the legislature, the executive and the judiciary, (v) Federal character of the Constitution. The above structure is built on the basic foundation, i.e. the dignity and freedom of the individual. This is of supreme importance. This cannot by any form of amendment be destroyed.[15]

It is necessary to point out that Sikri CJ did not enter a caveat that his list was 'illustrative'. Justices Shelat and Grover, however, while terming their list as illustrative, added to the features set out by Sikri CJ some additional features, namely sovereignty of the country, the unity and integrity of the nation, the dignity of the individual secured by the various basic rights in Part III, and the mandate to form a welfare State contained in Part IV.[16] Thus, while Sikri CJ laid stress only on Fundamental Rights, Justices Shelat and Grover gave importance to the Directive Principles as well. Justices Hegde and Mukherjea observed, 'Unlike in most of the other Constitutions, it is comparatively easy in the case of our Constitution to discern and determine the basic elements or the fundamental features of our Constitution: for doing so, one has only to look to the Preamble.'[17] Their illustrative list corresponds to the features set out by Justice Shelat and Grover. These observations from their judgement are pertinent:

Every Constitution is expected to endure for a long time. Therefore it must necessarily be elastic. It is not possible to place society in a strait-jacket. The society grows, its requirements change. The Constitution and the laws may have to be changed to suit those needs. No single generation can bind the course of generations to come.[18]

Justice Jaganmohan Reddy said, 'A sovereign democratic republic, Parliamentary democracy, the three organs of the State, certainly, in my view, constitute the basic structure.'[19] Justice Khanna's judgement, which tilted the balance, took the view that the democratic form of government, the secular character of the State and possibly judicial review were part of the basic character of the Constitution.[20]

Justice Khanna's concept of 'basic structure' was clearly different from the 'basic features' view of the six other judges. While the latter viewed certain features as unamendable, Justice Khanna's standpoint was different. It was that the power to amend the Constitution did not include the power to abrogate it and replace it with an entirely new one. It is from this perspective that he observed that the basic structure or framework of the Constitution could not be destroyed. Justice Khanna stressed, incidentally, that no generation had a monopoly on wisdom.

The Emergency and the Relevance of Kesavananda

The apprehension that the elected representatives of the people could not be trusted to act responsibly, which appeared ridiculous at the time when *Kesavananda* was decided, came true very soon and all too dramatically. Mrs Gandhi's election to the Lok Sabha was set aside by the Allahabad High Court on 12 June 1975 on the ground of committing a 'corrupt practice'. To quell the turmoil that followed, an internal Emergency was imposed on 25 June 1975. She filed an appeal in the Supreme Court. Before the appeal was taken up for hearing, the electoral law was amended retrospectively to take away the basis on which the finding of 'corrupt practice' was arrived at by the high court. In addition, an amendment to the Constitution, namely, the Constitution (Thirty-ninth) Amendment Act, 1975 was rushed through.

The amendment had three principal features. First, it substituted the existing Article 71 with a new article which stated that Parliament may by law regulate any matter relating to or connected with the election of the President or Vice-President including the grounds on which such election may be questioned. Secondly, it inserted Article 329A, which purported to apply to the Prime Minister and Speaker, but was clearly intended to apply to Mrs Gandhi, and had the effect of wiping out all judicial proceedings concerning her election. The third feature of the amendment was that the Representation of People Act, 1951, the Representation of People (Amendment) Act, 1974 which had been enacted in order to get over the judgement of the Court in *Amarnath Chawla v Kanwar Lal Gupta*[21] (where it was held that the expenditure incurred by a political party on his behalf would be included in the expenditure incurred by a candidate) and the Election Laws (Amendment) Act, 1975 were inserted in the Ninth Schedule. The most offensive feature of Article 329A was clause 4, which provided that no law made by Parliament before the commencement of the Thirty-ninth Amendment Act, in so far as it related to election petitions and matters connected therewith, shall apply or shall be deemed to have ever applied to or in relation to the election of the Prime Minister or the Speaker to either House of Parliament. The said amendment further provided that such election shall not be deemed to be void or ever to have become void on any ground on which such election could be declared to be void under any such law and notwithstanding any order made by any court before such commencement declaring such election to be void, such election shall continue to be valid in all respects and any such order and any finding on which such order is based shall be deemed always to have been void and of no effect.

In *Smt. Indira Nehru Gandhi v Raj Narain*,[22] a five-judge bench applied the basic structure doctrine to invalidate Article 329(A), though the Prime Minister's election was upheld on the basis of the retrospective amendment to the electoral law. Out of the five judges, four, namely, Chief Justice Ray and Justices Mathew, Beg, and Chandrachud had decided in favour of an unlimited amending power in *Kesavananda*, and only Justice Khanna was a 'basic structure' judge. More important, Chief Justice Ray and Justices Mathew and Beg had not even signed the summary. Nevertheless, all took the 'basic structure' doctrine as the law laid down in *Kesavananda*, and four judges invalidated the amendment on various grounds such as free and fair elections, democracy, equality, and the rule of law being parts of the basic structure of the Constitution.

The *Indira Nehru Gandhi* case showed the futility of theories of parliamentary supremacy in the face of hard reality. While courts normally refuse to be cowed down by arguments *in terrorem* and hold that the possibility of abuse of power is not the test of its existence, here was naked abuse of power manifesting itself in the form of an amendment to the Constitution solely to keep one individual in office passed by a pliant majority while members of the opposition were in jail. An anti-democratic doctrine had to be used to prevent the murder of democracy by a grotesque mutilation of the Constitution. At the same time, however, it must be remembered that the election of the Prime Minister was saved because the retrospective amendment to the electoral law passed the well-recognized judicial tests regarding validation.

In the midst of the Emergency, two further developments took place. The first was an unsuccessful attempt on the part of the government to get *Kesavananda* reconsidered, with Chief Justice Ray willingly constituting a bench for the purpose. However, with Palkhivala's impassioned address and resistance from some members of the bench themselves, the Chief Justice was forced to dissolve the bench after two days. The second was the enactment of the Constitution (Forty-second) Amendment Act, 1976 which *inter alia*, (i) amended Article 31C by protecting all laws that purported to implement *any* of the Directive Principles, as against the earlier Article 31C which referred only to the Directive Principles contained in Articles 39(b) and (c), (ii) amended Article 368 by completely shutting out judicial review over amendments to the Constitution, and (iii) inserted the words 'secular' and 'socialist' in the Preamble in its description of the nature of the state.

Though several other features of the Forty-second amendment were removed by the Forty-third and Forty-fourth amendments passed by the Janata government, which came to power after Mrs Gandhi's defeat, the Forty-fifth amendment which had proposed to amend Article 368 with provision for a referendum and with an enumeration of basic features in the article itself fell through as the Janata Party did not have the requisite majority in the Upper House.

The Consolidation of the Basic Structure Doctrine in the Post-Emergency Phase

The surviving provisions of the Forty-second amendment, which amended Article 31C and Article 368 were challenged before the

Supreme Court in *Minerva Mills v Union of India*.[23] It is necessary to set out the facts of the case in some detail, in order to appreciate what really arose for determination, and how the Court went further to consolidate the basic structure doctrine. The principal petitioner was a limited company owning a textile undertaking in Karnataka, and the other petitioners were its shareholders. On 20 August 1970, the central government appointed a committee under section 15 of the Industries (Development and Regulation) Act, 1951 to undertake full and complete investigation into the affairs of the mills, as it was of the opinion that there had been or was likely to be a substantial fall in the volume of production. The committee submitted a report to the central government, on the basis of which the latter passed an order dated 15 October 1971 under section 18-A of the said Act of 1951, authorizing the National Textile Corporation to take over the management of the mills on the ground that its affairs were being managed in a manner highly detrimental to public interest. Thereafter, the undertaking was nationalized, and taken over by the central government under the Sick Textiles Undertakings (Nationalization) Act, 1974. By the Constitution (Thirty-ninth) Amendment, the said Nationalization Act was included in the Ninth Schedule. The petitioners challenged the validity of the order dated 19 October 1971 and certain provisions of the Sick Textiles Undertakings (Nationalization) Act, 1974. Since the said Act had been included in the Ninth Schedule, it became necessary for them to challenge the Thiry-ninth amendment, because it was only then that they could get the Act out of the protective cover of Article 31B. At the time when the writ petitions were filed, Articles 368(4) and 368(5) were already in force as a result of the Forty-second amendment, and since they barred judicial review of any amendment to the Constitution, it became necessary for the petitioners to challenge section 55 of the Forty-second Amendment Act which inserted the said provisions. The petitioners also challenged section 4 of the Forty-second Amendment Act which amended Article 31C. The petitioners conceded the validity of the unamended Article 31C as it stood after the decision in *Kesavananda*. The declaration in the Nationalization Act referred only to Article 39(b) and not any other Directive Principle, and therefore it was the unamended Article 31C which protected it. Accordingly, a preliminary objection was raised by the Attorney-General with regard to the Court considering the validity of the amended Article 31C.

At this stage it is important to note the point of time when arguments took place in the *Minerva Mills* case. The hearings commenced on 22 October 1979 and concluded on 16 November. The government in power was that of Charan Singh, who had already resigned in July 1979. Elections had been ordered, but had not yet taken place: they were held in January 1980. Charan Singh, having had to resign as a result of withdrawal of support by Mrs Gandhi could not have been enthusiastic about defending an amendment passed by her during the Emergency. The writer submits that the stand of the Government before the Court could have only been finalized by two distinguished lawyers: S.N. Kacker, the former Solicitor-General, who was the Law Minister in Charan Singh's government, and Lal Narayan Sinha, the Attorney-General who was Mrs Gandhi's Solicitor-General when *Kesavananda* was argued.

With regard to Articles 368(4) and (5), the stand of the government was not that the Articles made *Kesavananda* irrelevant, which is what they plainly intended to do, but that they should be read down in accordance with the basic structure doctrine. This plea was rightly rejected by the Court, saying 'Provisions of this nature cannot be saved by reading into them words and intendment of a diametrically opposite meaning and content.' The Court found the question of the validity of Article 368(4) and (5) a comparatively 'easier question'. Here was an amendment obviously intended to make *Kesavananda* irrelevant, but the Court got over this by holding, 'Its avowed purpose is the "removal of doubts", but after the decision of this Court in *Kesavananda*, there could be no doubt as regards the existence of limitations on the Parliament's power to amend the Constitution'. A limited amending power, which had to be deduced from the thin judicial majorities in *Golak Nath* and *Kesavananda*, now came to be held as part of the basic structure of the Constitution.

As far as the preliminary objection to the consideration of the validity of the amended Article 31C was concerned, the Court gave it short shrift. It was conscious of the well-settled position that in constitutional matters it would not decide anything which did not directly arise for decision, but said that the Forty-second amendment was 'there for anyone to see'. It also held,

Besides, there are two other relevant considerations which must be taken into account while dealing with the preliminary objection. There is no constitutional or statutory inhibition against the decision of questions before they actually arise for consideration. In view of the importance of the question raised and in view of the fact that the question has been raised in many a petition, it is expedient in the interests of justice to settle the true position. Secondly, what we are dealing with is not an ordinary law which may or may not be passed so that it could be said that our jurisdiction is being invoked on the hypothetical consideration that a law may be passed in the future which will injure the rights of the petitioners. We are dealing with a constitutional amendment which has been brought into operation and which of its own force, permits the violation of certain freedoms through laws passed for certain purpose.[24]

The Court proceeded to strike down the amended Article 31C on the ground that it subordinated fundamental rights conferred by Articles 14 and 19 to the Directive Principles, that the Constitution was founded on the bedrock of the balance between Fundamental Rights and Directive Principles; that to give absolute primacy to one over the other was to disturb the harmony of the Constitution and that this harmony between Fundamental Rights and Directive Principles was an 'essential feature' of the 'basic structure of the Constitution'.

Minerva Mills represents the assertion of judicial supremacy without contest. The Mrs Gandhi who returned to power in 1980 was a different person. After having been chastened by her defeat in the 1977 elections and having had to live down her image as a destroyer of institutions, she could not have risked being seen again as tinkering with the Constitution or confronting the judiciary. Her son Sanjay Gandhi had died in June 1981. The Punjab problem was on her hands. Her tragic assassination in October 1984 brought Rajiv Gandhi to power. Rajiv Gandhi did not see the Constitution as an impediment. His focus was on technological modernization, not on constitutional change, and reassertion of parliamentary sovereignty was not high on the agenda of any subsequent government.

It is, however, necessary to point out that a subsequent Constitution Bench in *Sanjeev Coke Manufacturing Company v Bharat Coking Coal Limited* [25] expressed serious misgivings about the decision in *Minerva Mills*, observing: '... we confess that the case has left us perplexed',[26] and further,

We have serious reservations on the question whether it is open to a Court to answer academic or hypothetical questions on such considerations, particularly so when serious constitutional issues are involved. We [judges] are not authorized to make disembodied pronouncements on serious and cloudy issues of constitutional policy without the battle lines properly drawn. Judicial pronouncements cannot be immaculate legal conceptions. It is but right that no important point of law should be decided without a proper list between parties properly ranged on either side and crossing of swords. We think it is inexpedient for the Supreme Court to delve into problems which do not arise and express opinion thereon.[27]

Waman Rao v Union of India,[28] following close on the heels of *Minerva Mills*, is noteworthy for two reasons. First, as a logical extension of the basic structure doctrine, it held that any amendment of the Constitution after 24 April 1973 (when *Kesavananda* was decided), which included laws in the Ninth Schedule would have to be tested by reference to the basic structure doctrine. (The Court did not disturb the pre-*Kesavananda* insertions in the Ninth Schedule.)[29] This was also necessary to prevent a fraud on the Constitution, because laws which had nothing to do with agrarian reform or Directive Principles were included in the Ninth Schedule merely to protect them from constitutional challenge.

Secondly, *Waman Rao* applied the basic structure doctrine to uphold the validity of Article 31A and 31C instead of holding them valid on the basis of *stare decisis*. The majority took the view that in none of the earlier decisions, namely *Sankari Prasad, Sajjan Singh, Golak Nath*, and *Kesavananda* was the validity of the First Amendment put in issue and that it could only be said that the validity of Article 31A was recognized in those decisions. It then proceeded to hold that the Directive Principles contained in Article 39(b) and (c) were part of the Constitution as originally enacted, and that it was in order to effectuate the purpose of these Directive Principles that the First and Fourth Amendments were passed. It held that the First and Fourth Amendments strengthened, rather than weakened the basic structure of the Constitution. Article 31 had already been upheld in *Kesavananda*, apart from the second part of it. The amendment to Article 31C by the Forty-second Amendment had been struck down in *Minerva Mills*. The unamended portion of Article 31C, though already upheld in *Kesavananda*, was again upheld by applying the basic structure test, holding that laws passed truly and bona fide for giving effect to Directive Principles contained in Article 39(b) and (c) would, far from damaging the basic structure, fortify it.

Following *Waman Rao*, the Court invalidated section 27(1) of the Urban Land (Ceiling and Regulation) Act, 1976 (in so far as it imposed a restriction on transfer of any urban or urbanizable land with a building or of a portion of such a building which was within the ceiling area), though the Act had been inserted in the Ninth Schedule by the Constitution (Fortieth Amendment) Act, 1976.[30]

Minerva Mills and *Waman Rao* gave the Court the opportunity to regain the role of 'sentinel' which had suffered significant erosion during the Emergency. Though it had in the *Indira Nehru Gandhi* case struck down a constitutional perversion, it had failed to protect the citizen's liberty. In *ADM Jabalpur v Shivakant Shukla*,[31] it held that the suspension of Article 21 during the Emergency would deprive a detenu of the right to move for a writ of habeas corpus, holding that Article 21 was the sole repository of the right to life and personal liberty. The judgements were not merely legal, interpreting the letter of the law, but contained statements that ranged from the outrageous to the gratuitous. Ray CJ, for example, said, 'Liberty is the gift of the law and may by the law be forfeited or abridged.'[32] Beg J volunteered the view, '... we understand that the care and concern bestowed by the State authorities upon the welfare of detenus who are well-housed, well-fed and well-treated, is almost maternal',[33] and Chandrachud J added, 'Counsel after counsel expressed the fear that during the Emergency, the Executive may whip and strip and starve the detenu and if this be our judgment, even shoot him down. Such misdeeds have not tarnished the record of Free India and I have a diamond-bright, diamond-hard hope that such things will never come to pass.'[34] The public dismay with the Court's judgement, reversing the views taken by several high courts, is a matter of history. The recently born basic structure doctrine gave the Court an opportunity to show in *Minerva Mills* and *Waman Rao* that it was willing to stand up against Parliamentary might, and public opinion, happy and relieved that the Court was standing up again, preferred not to worry about the sovereignty of Parliament.

Basic Structure and Judicial Policy Making

The cases that followed dealt mainly with judicial review and judicial power. Ten years separate *S.P. Sampath Kumar v Union of India*[35] and *L. Chandra Kumar v Union of India*.[36] These cases give an insight into the Court's own policy-making considerations which have played a role in its use of the basic structure doctrine. The Forty-second Amendment inserted Article 323A which enabled the setting up of Administrative Tribunals and enabled the ouster of the jurisdiction of high courts. However, no steps were taken to set up such Tribunals. In *K.K. Dutta v Union of India*,[37] a Constitution Bench of the Court observed:

There are few other litigative areas than disputes between members of various services *inter se*, where the principle that public policy requires that all litigation must have an end can apply with greater force. Public servants ought not to be driven or required to dissipate their time and energy in courtroom battles. Thereby their attention is diverted from public to private affairs and their *inter se* disputes affect their sense of oneness, without which no institution can function effectively. The constitution of Service Tribunals by the State Governments with an apex Tribunal at the Centre, which in the generality of cases, should be the final arbiter of controversies relating to conditions of service, including the vexed question of seniority, may save the courts from the avalanche of writ petitions and appeals in service matters. The proceedings of such

Tribunals can have the merit of informality and if they will not be tied down to strict rules of evidence, they might be able to produce situations which will satisfy many ....[38]

In 1985, the Administrative Tribunals Act was enacted. The Act was challenged *inter alia* on the ground that it took away judicial review which was a basic feature of the Constitution. Logically, the challenge had to start with a challenge to Aricle 323A itself which enabled such an ouster of judicial review. The challenge to the Act was only consequential. However, the Court preferred not to deal with the challenge to Article 323A and suggested changes in the Act to make the Tribunals an effective alternative institution to the high courts. Ten years after *Sampath Kumar*, when the Supreme Court was flooded with special leave petitions against decisions of the Tribunals, it found an occasion in *Chandra Kumar* to examine the validity of Article 323A, and held that the ouster of the jurisdiction of the high courts violated the principle of judicial review which was a basic feature of the Constitution and directed that the decisions of the Tribunals shall henceforth be subject to the writ jurisdiction of the high courts. In *P. Sambamurthy v State of AP*,[39] the Court applied the basic structure doctrine to invalidate the proviso to Article 371(D)(5) which gave power to the state governments to modify or annul the orders of the Administrative Tribunal. This, along with the *Indira Nehru Gandhi* case, represents a less controversial instance of the application of the basic structure doctrine.

Other Application of the Basic Structure Doctrine

The *Indira Nehru Gandhi* case also dealt with the question whether the basic structure doctrine could be used to invalidate ordinary legislation. Three judges clearly held that the doctrine could be applied only to amendments to the Constitution. This appears to be self-evident. An ordinary legislation would be unconstitutional either if it violates a fundamental right or if it is passed without legislative competence over the subject or offends a specific article of the Constitution. This position was reiterated in *V.C. Shukla v Delhi Administration*,[40] and *Minerva Mills II v Union of India*,[41] but in *Ismail Faruqui v Union of India*,[42] the basic structure doctrine was resorted to in order to invalidate an ordinary legislation dealing with the demolished Babri Masjid, namely the Ayodhya (Acquisition of Certain Areas) Act, 1993. Similarly, in *G.C. Kanungo v State of Orissa*,[43] the Court resorted to the doctrine to invalidate an arbitration law from Orissa.[44] These two cases illustrate the danger of an easy resort to the basic structure mantra when the Court could have invalidated the concerned legislation on other well-recognized grounds. It is noteworthy that neither of these two decisions even attempted to distinguish the authoritative view laid down in *Indira Nehru Gandhi* case, that ordinary legislation could not be challenged on the ground of violation of the basic structure.

In *Ismail Faruqui,* the Court was *inter alia* considering a challenge to the validity of provisions which abated suits and other legal proceedings in relation to the disputed site, i.e. the site where the Babri Masjid stood, and did not provide an alternative mechanism for resolution of the dispute. The majority held this to be unconstitutional, as amounting to a negation of the 'rule of law', a basic feature. However, surely the extinction of a judicial proceeding was itself so arbitrary and unreasonable as to violate Article 14, and also the singling out of one dispute for extinction of the judicial remedy was discriminatory and therefore violative of Article 14. The minority took the view that the relevant provisions were slanted in favour of one religious community and that the core provisions were violative of the basic feature of secularism. Surely, however, secularism is also a facet of the right to equality, and the relevant provisions could have been invalidated on that ground alone.

In *G.C. Kanungo,* the Court struck down the Arbitration (Orissa Second Amendment) Act, 1991 which nullified awards of special arbitral tribunals, on the ground that it violated the Rule of Law, a basic feature of the Constitution. Over the years, however, the Court has laid down in the context of validating legislation that a judicial decision cannot be nullified and that only the underlying basis of a decision can be changed by a change in the law or the factual basis of the decision. The impugned provisions could therefore have been struck down on the ground that they interfered with judicial decisions. Moreover, the sheer unreasonableness and arbitrariness involved in nullifying arbitration awards could have resulted in the provisions being struck down as violative of Article 14.

S.R. Bommai v Union of India,[45] brought out an entirely new dimension of the doctrine. Governors of three states reported that the governments concerned were subverting secularism. This was in the context of the demolition of the Babri Masjid at Ayodhya on 6 December 1992. The BJP government in Uttar Pradesh resigned, virtually accepting responsibility. The mosque was demolished with the active cooperation of the state government, which had given a solemn undertaking in the Supreme Court to protect the structure. However, the governments of other BJP-ruled states, namely Rajasthan, Madhya Pradesh, and Himachal Pradesh were dismissed, and President's Rule was imposed. Various factors were cited in support of the decision. For example, the

BJP manifesto, on the basis of which the ministers in these three states had come to power, was committed to erection of the Ram Temple at the disputed site; some of the chief ministers and ministers belonged to the RSS—a banned organization; the ministers in the government concerned had exhorted people to join the *kar seva* at Ayodhya, had given a public send-off to those joining the *kar seva* and had welcomed them on their return; and that in Madhya Pradesh and Rajasthan there had been instances of atrocities against Muslims and loss of lives and destruction of properties.

The Court held that secularism was a basic feature of the Constitution and that if any political party in power in a state supported or encouraged acts that subverted, sabotaged, or eroded secularism, it could be said the government of the state could not be run in accordance with the Constitution. While there cannot be two views that secularism is a basic feature of the Constitution, there are serious difficulties in invoking it to justify resort to Article 356. The fact that the anti-secular stance of a government has resulted in loss of life and property, failure of law and order, and failure to guarantee safety to a minority community would certainly mean that the governance of the state cannot be carried on in accordance with the provisions of the Constitution, warranting resort to Article 356. If, however, the anti-secular posture of a government can itself lead to invoking Article 356, strange results can follow. The Forty-second Amendment also inserted 'socialist' in the Preamble, and the *Minerva Mills* bench took the view that this particular part of the amendment, along with the insertion of 'secular' in the Preamble, only strengthened the basic structure. If a government of a state, driven by the compulsions or the ideology of the market, pursues capitalist policies, it would by the *Bommai* logic, lend itself to dismissal for failure to follow socialism.

Since the basic structure doctrine took birth, it has been invoked on five occasions to strike down amendments to the Constitution: (i) the last part of Article 31C as inserted by the Twenty-fifth Amendment, (ii) the last part of clause (4) of Article 329A inserted by the Thirty-ninth Amendment, (iii) Articles 368(4) and 368(5) inserted by the Forty-second Amendment, and Article 31C as amended by the Forty-second Amendment, (iv) Clause (5) of Article 371D inserted by the Thirty-second Amendment, and (v) sub-clause (d) of Clause (2) of Article 323A inserted by the Forty-second Amendment. This is viewed by some as proof of judicial restraint in the matter of examining the validity of amendments to the Constitution. While it is nobody's contention that the Court has been running amok in its use of the doctrine, the use of restraint does not satisfactorily answer the question whether the power exists in the first place, and it is tempting to view all facets of judicial power as bricks of the basic structure. Thus, while there can be no quarrel with the Court treating independence of the judiciary as part of the basic structure,[46] it is doubtful whether there is justification for treating every aspect of the jurisdiction conferred on the Court by the Constitution as part of the basic structure of the Constitution. In *Delhi Judicial Service Association v State of Gujarat*,[47] which dealt with the power of the Supreme Court under Article 129 to punish for contempt of subordinate or inferior courts as well, the Supreme Court observed that:

Under the Constitutional scheme this Court has a special role in the administration of justice and the power conferred on it under Articles 32, 136, 141 and 142 form part of the basic structure of the Constitution.[48]

It is difficult to appreciate how Article 142, which gives the Court the power to pass any order in order to do 'complete justice' can be a part of the basic structure or how again the power of the Supreme Court under Article 136 to grant special leave can form part of it.

The Doctrine in South Asia

The basic structure doctrine has no doubt been the major contribution of the Supreme Court not only to the constitutional law of India but of South Asia. The Eighth Amendment to the Bangladesh Constitution amended Article 100 to curtail the jurisdiction of the High Court Division. The amendment was challenged on the ground that the plenary judicial power of the High Court Division of the Supreme Court over the entire Republic was part of the basic structure of the Constitution, which could not be altered or damaged. In *Anwar Hossain Chowdhury v Bangladesh*,[49] a majority of 3:1 of the Appellate Division of the Bangladesh Supreme Court struck down the amendment, applying the doctrine, and expressly relying on *Kesavananda*.

It is, however, interesting to note that in an early Pakistan case, originating from the erstwhile Dacca High Court,[50] the Pakistan Supreme Court has used the concept of 'fundamentals of the Constitution' in order to hold that the President's power to remove difficulties and adapt could not extend to a change in the essential features of the Constitution and such a change could be brought about only by an amendment to the Constitution. However, in later years, the Lahore and the Baluchistan High Courts have expressly applied the basic structure doctrine, while the Supreme Court has impliedly accepted it. Thus, in *Darwesh Arbey v Federation of Pakistan*,[51] which dealt with the validity of the Martial Law proclaimed by the government of Z.A. Bhutto, acting under Article 245, the Lahore High Court held that the Seventh Amendment which had amended Article 245 in 1977 was invalid because it affected the basic structure of the Constitution. In *Suleman v President, Special Military Court*,[52] the Baluchistan High Court struck down a Constitution amendment inserted by a Presidential Order at the time of President Zia's Martial Law, namely Article 212-A, which empowered the Chief Martial Law Administrator to establish military courts and barred the ordinary courts from interfering in all matters falling within the jurisdiction of such military courts. The Court held that the interim government was not entitled to make 'basic changes' in the Constitution so as to alter the 'fundamental structure of the Constitution'. In *Al-Jehad Trust v Federation of Pakistan*,[53] the Pakistan Supreme Court invalidated a portion of the Martial Law amendment establishing the Federal Shariyat Court by Article 203-C, which provided for the appointment and tenure of its judges in a manner which was wholly in conflict with the security of tenure and judicial independence guaranteed in Article 209. Notwithstanding a *non obstante* clause contained at the beginning of the chapter in Article 203-A, the Court resorted to the 'interpretation' based on 'basic features of the Constitution', and the 'intent and spirit of the Constitution' to hold that the original article would prevail over Article 203-C.

In Sri Lanka, the doctrine was invoked to test the Thirteenth Amendment, but a majority of the Full Bench of the Supreme Court in *In re The Thirteenth Amendment to the Constitution*,[54] held that the basic structure doctrine had no application to the Sri Lankan Constitution. Sharvananda CJ distinguished *Kesavananda* by pointing out that while Article 368 of the Indian Constitution did not define 'amendment' and did not indicate the scope of the term, in Sri Lanka Section 51 of the 1972 Constitution and Article 82 of the 1978 Constitution permitted the repeal of the Constitution itself, and as such there could be no unalterable basic structure.

In Nepal, the 1990 Constitution itself incorporates the theory of basic structure. Thus Article 116(1) provides:

A Bill to amend or repeal any Article of this Constitution, *without prejudicing the spirit of the Preamble of this Constitution,* may be introduced in either House of Parliament:

Provided that this Article shall not be subject to amendment. (emphasis supplied)

The objectives of the Constitution as recited in the Preamble are:

... to guarantee basic human rights to every citizen of Nepal: and also to consolidate Adult Franchise, Parliamentary System of Government, Constitutional Monarchy, and Multi-party Democracy by promoting amongst the people of Nepal the spirit of fraternity and the bond of Unity on the basis of liberty and equality:

And also to establish an independent and competent system of Justice with a view of transforming the concept of Rule of Law into living reality.

Perils of the Doctrine

Once the power to annul amendments to the Constitution, which is the highest form of activism, is conceded to the Court, the exercise of lesser powers is logical, and ultimately judicial restraint based on the Court's own view of its area of competence and effectiveness becomes the only check on the exercise of judicial power. Through the eighties and the nineties, the Court has interfered in diverse areas through public interest litigation, leading to criticism of its 'activism' and to pleas that the executive should be allowed to run the government. In all these situations however the Court is not transgressing its jurisdiction. It is merely, through new strategies, enforcing rights that traditionally were not believed to possess 'adjudicative disposition'. Armed, as it were, with the ultimate power, the Court has over the past two decades made its presence felt by its frequent interventions in public interest litigation. Thin parliamentary majorities and consequently weak executives have enabled the Court to occupy a space that it might not have otherwise.

Today the basic structure doctrine stands in the way of constitutional reform. The experience of short-lived coalitions and minority governments, and the consequent political instability, has led to a renewed debate on switching over to a presidential form of government. One of the essential features of the Constitution, according to the petitioners in *Kesavananda*, was a parliamentary form of government as distinct from a presidential one. At least one judge, Justice Jaganmohan Reddy, held that parliamentary democracy was part of the basic structure. If there is a serious move to switch over to a presidential form of government, a careful government will seek the advisory opinion of the Supreme Court under Article 143 of the Constitution. On the other hand, a determined government with the requisite majority would go ahead with an amendment to the Constitution, whose validity will then be tested in Court after the system of government has changed. Either situation is fraught with frightening possibilities which could not have been possibly envisaged when the basic structure doctrine was adopted in the context of litigation arising out of property rights.

If the basic structure test is to be rigorously applied to the question whether a switch-over to the presidential form of government is permissible, the answer has to be in the negative.

When he introduced the Draft Constitution for the consideration of the Constituent Assembly, Dr B.R. Ambedkar offered a detailed analysis of the presidential and parliamentary forms of government, and gave reasons why the Drafting Committee had preferred the latter.[55] Sir Alladi Krishnawami Ayyar pointed out that while the presidential system had worked splendidly in the US due to historical reasons, in India it was necessary to have a union between the executive and the legislature, and that the object of choosing the parliamentary form was to prevent a conflict between the executive and the legislature and to promote harmony between the different parts of the system.[56] Though both systems are forms of democracy, they differ in one basic principle: that of separation of powers. While the presidential form is based on a clear separation of powers between the legislature and the executive, the parliamentary form is based on a clear link between the two. The reversal of such a fundamental choice made by the Constituent Assembly cannot but fall foul of the basic structure theory.

A few more instances may be considered. If India decides to join a regional economic union which necessarily involves submission to the jurisdiction of supranational institutions, 'sovereignty', a basic feature is violated. Would the Court annul India's joining such a union? If India were to subject itself to the jurisdiction of an international human rights tribunal, it would again be surrendering a more 'basic' feature than which would be hard to find. If the nature of the Indian federation is to change from the present 'federation with a strong unitary bias' to a classical federation where the Centre retains only defence, currency, and foreign affairs, the basic structure would be damaged. If the present economic policies are continued by future governments and it is honestly decided to delete the word 'socialist' from the Preamble, the basic structure would be violated.

If the power to amend the Constitution cannot be exercised to amend its basic features, the power gets reduced to the status of a 'removal of difficulties' clause. Surely, high constituent power ought to mean something more. The basic structure doctrine rests on the unsure foundations of judicial perceptions and judicial majorities. It emerged for the first time in 1973 by a majority of one, twenty-three years after the working of the Constitution. Yet in 1980, in the *Minerva Mills* case, the Court found a limited amending power to be a basic feature of the

Constitution—when right from *Sankari Prasad* to *Sajjan Singh* the view was that there were no limitations on the amending power.

The basic structure doctrine proceeds upon a distrust of the democratic process, which itself must surely be part of the basic structure. In limiting the amending power, the basic structure doctrine in fact stifles democracy, a basic feature. The limitations of the basic structure doctrine were brought out by the Court's decision in *ADM Jabalpur*. The Presidential proclamation suspending Article 21 did not, according to the Court, leave the citizen with the right to protect his liberty. Thus a right which, applying the basic structure test, could not be taken away even by amending the Constitution, could be taken away by an executive proclamation. Also, eventually, the strengthening of the right to life and liberty was done by Parliament itself, by providing in the Forty-fourth amendment that the rights conferred by Articles 20 and 21 could not be suspended even during an emergency.

Fifty tumultuous years of the Republic have seen democracy and a culture of constitutionalism take firm roots in the country. The spectre of dictatorship loomed large but once. The Emergency was an aberration which was corrected through the political process itself. The basic structure doctrine has served a certain purpose: it has warned a fledgeling democracy of the perils of brute majoritarianism. Those days are however gone. Coalitions can only bring about major changes through consensus. The doctrine must now be buried. The nation must be given an opportunity to put half a century's experience of politics and economics into the Constitution.

Notes

[1] XII–XIII Parliamentary Debates (PD) (Pt II) Col 8832 (17 May 1951).

[2] AIR 1967 SC 1643: (1967) 2 SCR 762.

[3] (1973) 4 SCC 225.

[4] *Kameshwar Singh v State of Bihar* AIR 1951 Pat 91; *Surya Pal v U.P. Government*, AIR 1951 All 674; *Ram Dubey v Government of the State of Madhya Pradesh* AIR 1952 MB 57.

[5] (1952) SCR 89.

[6] *State of West Bengal v Bela Banerjee* (1954) SCR 558; *State of West Bengal v Subodh Gopal* (1954) SCR 587 and *Dwarkadas Srinivasa v Sholapur Spinning Company* AIR 1954 SC 119.

[7] *Sajjan Singh v State of Rajasthan* (1965) 1 SCR 933.

[8] Ibid. at pr. 23, p. 948–9.

[9] Ibid. at pr. 45, p. 962.

[10] Ibid. at pr. 57, p. 966.

[11] Ibid. at pr. 54, p. 815.

[12] *R.C. Cooper v Union of India* (1970) 1 SCC 248.
[13] *Madhavrao Scindia v Union of India* (1971) 1 SCC 85.
[14] Ibid. at pr. 1007.
[15] Ibid. at pr. 292–3, p. 366.
[16] Ibid. at pr. 582, p. 454.
[17] Ibid. at pr. 661, p. 484.
[18] Ibid. at pr. 634, p. 473.
[19] Ibid. at pr. 1159, p. 637.
[20] Ibid. at pr. 1426, p. 767 and pr. 1531, p. 819.
[21] (1975) 3 SCC 646.
[22] (1975) Supp SCC 1.
[23] (1980) 3 SCC 625.
[24] Ibid. at pr. 39, p. 649.
[25] (1983) 1 SCC 147.
[26] Ibid. at pr. 11, p. 160.
[27] Ibid.
[28] (1981) 2 SCC 362.
[29] Two reasons were given by the Court for drawing the line at *Kesavananda*. First, it did not want to upset settled claims and titles. Second, it found that with a few exceptions, the first sixty-six items which were inserted in the Ninth Schedule prior to *Kesavananda* pertained to agrarian reforms and would fall within the purview of Article 31A (1) (a) of the Constitution. Thus, they would be entitled to the protection. (See para 49, 50, p. 397).
[30] *Bhim Singhji v Union of India* (1981) 1 SCC 166. By an order dated 14 September 1999 in *IR Coelho(Dead) by LRs v State of Tamil Nadu* (1999) 7 SCC 570 and other connected matters, a five judge Constitution Bench referred the cases before it to a larger Bench, 'preferably of nine learned judges' finding that there were 'apparent inconsistencies' in *Waman Rao* which required to be reconciled. The Bench also felt that the decision in *Bhim Singhji* would have to be considered by the larger Bench for the purposes of arriving at the conclusion reached by Krishna Iyer J in the aforesaid case: 'What is a betrayal of the basic structure is not mere violation of Article 14 but a shocking, unconscionable or unscrupulous travesty of the quintessence of equal justice.'
[31] (1976) 2 SCC 521.
[32] Ibid. at pr. 35, p. 572.
[33] Ibid. at pr. 324A, p. 643.
[34] Ibid. at pr. 421, p. 679.
[35] (1987) 1 SCC 124.
[36] (1997) 3 SCC 261.
[37] (1980) 4 SCC 38.
[38] Ibid. at pr. 1, p. 39.
[39] (1987) 1 SCC 362.
[40] (1980) 2 SCC 665.
[41] (1986) 4 SCC 222.
[42] (1994) 6 SCC 360.
[43] (1995) 5 SCC 96.
[44] Arbitration (Orissa Second Amendment) Act, 1991.
[45] (1994) 3 SCC 1.
[46] *Supreme Court Advocates on Record Association v Union of India* (1993) 4 SCC 441.
[47] (1991) 4 SCC 406.

[48] Ibid. at pr. 36, p. 452.

[49] 1989 Bangladesh Law Documents (Spl) 1.

[50] *Fazlul Quader Chowdhry v Mohd. Abdul Haque* All Pakistan Law Decisions (1963) Supreme Court 486.

[51] All Pakistan Law Decisions (1908) Lahore 206.

[52] NLR 1980 civ. Quetta 873.

[53] All Pakistan Law Decisions (1996) Supreme Court 367.

[54] (1987) 2 Sri Lanka Law Reports 312.

[55] VII Constituent Assembly Debates (CAD), pp. 32–3 (4 November 1948).

[56] VII Constituent Assembly Debates (CAD), pp. 985–6 (10 December 1948).

Select Bibliography

Articles

Baxi, Upendra (1974), 'The Constitutional Quicksands of *Kesavananda Bharati* and the Twenty Fifth Amendment', *Supreme Court Cases (Journal Section Vol.1)*, 45–67.

Conrad, D. (1970), 'Limitation of Amendment Procedures and the Constituent Power', 15–16 *Indian Year Book of International Law*, 375–430.

Conrad, D. (1977–8), 'Constituent Power, Amendment and Basic Structure of the Constitution: A Critical Reconsideration', *Delhi Law Review*, 1–23.

Conrad, D. (1996), 'Basic Structure of the Constitution and Constitutional Principles', 3, *Law and Justice*, 99–114.

Dhavan, Rajeev (1977), 'Justice Ethnology of *Kesavananda* case', 19 *Journal of Indian Law Institute*, 489–97.

Dhavan, Rajeev (1978), 'Amending the Amendment: The Constitution (Forty-Fourth Amendment) Bill, 1978', 20 *Journal of Indian Law Institute*, 249–72.

Garg, Ramesh D. (1974), 'Phantom of Basic Structure of the Constitution', 16 *Journal of Indian Law Institute*, 243–69.

Raghavan, Vikram (1999), 'The Brooding Omnipresence of *Kesavananda*: The Doctrine of Basic Structure and the Indian Supreme Court', submitted to the National Law School of India for the H.M. Seervai Gold Medal.

Rao, P.P. (1999), 'Basic Features of the Constitution', Dr Alladi Krishnaswami Ayyar Memorial Lecture, 1999, delivered at Hyderabad in June 1999.

Sathe, S.P. (July–Sept 1998), 'Judicial Activism', 10, *Journal of Indian School of Political Economy*, 399–439.

Sunder Raman, 'Parliament's Power to Amend the Constitution: A Critique', 16, *Journal of Constitutional and Parliamentary Studies*, 78–90.

Books

Andhyarujina, T.R. (1992), *Judicial Activism and Constitutional Democracy in India*, Tripathi, Mumbai.

Baxi, Upendra (1978), 'Some Reflections on the Nature of the Constituent Power', in Rajeev Dhavan and Alice Jacob (eds.), *Indian Constitution: Trends and Issues*, Indian Law Institute, New Delhi.

Baxi, Upendra (1980), *The Indian Supreme Court and Politics*, Lucknow, Eastern Book House.

Dhavan, Rajeev (1976), *The Supreme Court and Parliamentary Sovereignty*, Sterling Publishers, Delhi.

Setalvad, M.C. (1971), *My Life: Law and Other Things*, Tripathi, Mumbai.

Nine

Emergency Provisions Under the Indian Constitution

Gopal Subramanium

While every Constitution strives to be imaginative and provides for measures to tackle extraordinary situations of an emergent nature, a state of emergency is clearly definable and distinct, making available an enormous reservoir of prerogative and discretionary power.

An emergency is a state of affairs unexpectedly arising and urgently demanding immediate action.[1] An emergency power is ordinarily equated with war power. The 'War Power' in the US Constitution,[2] and the 'Peace, Order and Good Government' (usually referred to as POGG) power in section 91[3] of the British North America Act, 1867 and section 51 of the Commonwealth of Australian Constitution Act, 1900[4] are all similarly constructed. In the UK too the discretionary power of the sovereign expands in emergencies.

In the US, Australian, and Canadian constitutions, there is no specific treatment of emergencies and emergent conditions. Oblique inferences have to be made from the delineation of the federal power to make inroads into the turf of units. Such inroads can even be made in ordinary times, as is the case with the 'concurrent list' in the Constitution of India.

In a unitary state like the UK, emergency powers flow out of the prerogative of the Crown. In emergencies, the Crown is responsible for defence of the realm and is the only judge of the existence of threats from external enemies.[5] The requisitioning of ships at short notice during the 1982 Falklands conflict is illustrative of royal prerogative during emergencies.

In Canada, the POGG clause in section 91 of the British North America Act, 1867 has been invoked in three types of contingencies: (i) as a 'gap' measure, i.e. whatever is not clearly defined as falling into the ambit of either the federal or the states' powers being relegated to that of the federal legislature, (ii) as a matter measuring up to one of 'national concern', and (iii) as an 'emergency measure'.

The War Measures Act (Canada), enacted during the First World War (1914), was invoked during the First and Second World Wars, and once subsequently in October 1970 in the wake of the challenge of insurrection posed by the Front de Liberation du Quebec. Despite substantial suspension of civil liberties, the constitutionality of the War Measures Act was never reviewed by the courts. An interesting area of extension of the POGG clause in section 91 to an emergency was in the Anti-inflation Reference 1976,[6] when the Supreme Court of Canada upheld the Federal Anti-Inflation Act as an emergency measure and legitimized the federal regulations for control on wages, prices, profits, and dividends. The then prevalent double-digit inflation and high rate of unemployment were considered to be a situation that could legitimately be characterized as an emergency.

The War Measures Act was in vogue till 1988 when it was repealed in favour of the Emergencies Act, 1988. This provides for four types of emergencies: (i) Public welfare emergencies (national disaster, disease, accident, pollution), (ii) Public order emergencies (the Quebec crisis of 1970), (iii) International emergencies (sanctions, embargoes, oil crises, etc.), and (iv) War emergencies.

The normal pattern in emergencies is for the executive power to be expanded and exercised in its discretion with a view to cope with the abnormal situation arising in a war situation. Section 45 of the Government of India Act, 1935[7] stated exactly this, providing for the assumption of powers by the Governor General to be exercised in his descretion. Winston Churchill, while intervening on the 1935 Constitutional proposals before they were adopted, had even described the sweeping character of the Governor General's powers as likely to arouse Mussolini's envy.[8] The occurrences following the enactment of the 1935 Act provided the backdrop against which the Constitution-makers considered the discretionary powers to be given to the President and the Governors. They naturally decided in favour of all functions of the President, including those under emergencies being exercised only on the advice of the Council of Ministers.[9] They were also reluctant to allow the Governor to declare an emergency at will and instead agreed to empower him only to report to the President the existence (or threat) of an emergency.[10]

II

The discussion on the discretionary powers of the Governor led to a debate on situations in which constitutional governance of states broke down, resulting in Article 356 empowering the President to supersede the normal structures in states even when there was no proclamation of emergency. Pious hopes were expressed during the debate that this provision would 'never be called into operation' and 'would remain a dead letter.'[11] Additional provisions were provided to cope with emergencies of a financial nature (Article 360).[12]

This resulted in the introduction of Part XVIII of the Constitution dealing with three types of emergencies:
   i) National Emergency (Articles 352, 353, 354, 358, and 359);
  ii) Emergency in states due to failure of the constitutional machinery there (Articles 356, and 357);
 iii) Financial Emergency (Article 360).

A National Emergency, as in (i), has been invoked three times, twice in conditions of war and external aggression, in 1962 (Chinese aggression) and in 1971[13] (Indo–Pak conflict), and once on grounds of 'internal disturbance' (since deleted by the Constitution (Forty-fourth Amendment) Act, 1978) in 1975.[14] Contrary to the expectations of Constitution-makers, Article 356 has been invoked over a hundred times. Article 360 (Financial Emergency) has never been invoked.

The Emergency provisions assume significance in the following:
  (i)   the modification of the federal structure;
 (ii)   the reconciliation of the inherent conflict between the fundamental rights of citizens and the power of the state in emergent conditions.

Before proceeding to analyse these, it appears necessary to examine whether the provisions throw light on themselves.

Article 352 deals with the proclamation of emergency. This article underwent substantial alteration through the Forty-second Amendment, 1976 and Forty-fourth Amendment, 1978. The Forty-second Amendment came in the wake of the June 1975 emergency declared to meet 'Internal Disturbance' by the government of Indira Gandhi. The Forty-fourth Amendment was at the initiative of the Janata government which was installed after the 1977 elections. The original article provided for a presidential proclamation in circumstances of grave emergency threatening the security of India or any part of its territory, due to (1) war, (2) external aggression, and (3) internal disturbance or imminent danger of this. The third prerequisite of 'internal disturbance' was deleted and replaced with the words 'armed rebellion' by the Forty-fourth Amendment.

Curiously, the words 'internal disturbance' were retained undisturbed in Article 355 which declares that it is the duty of the Union to protect every state against external aggression and internal disturbance. In order to fulfil this obligation, the Union can resort to a proclamation of emergency in the event of external aggression, but to contain an internal disturbance, it can only resort to its non-emergency powers. A proclamation of emergency may cover the whole of the Union of India or part of its territory. As the June 1975 proclamation of emergency on account of 'internal disturbance' had to be imposed even while the 1971 emergency, on account of external aggression, was still operative, the Forty-second Amendment permitted the overlap of different proclamations issued on various grounds.[15] The June 1975 emergency was declared on the recommendation of the Prime Minister (Indira Gandhi); the Forty-fourth Amendment inserted a clause (clause 3 in Article 352) that the President shall not issue such a proclamation in the absence of a specific recommendation to the effect by the Union Cabinet. The elaborate wording makes it even appear obligatory that such a recommendation has to be unanimous.[16]

The Forty-second Amendment had placed the action taken under Article 352 beyond the purview of judicial review. By deleting this provision, the Forty-fourth Amendment has subjected the promulgation of emergency to both legislative and judicial scrutinies. The proclamation has to be approved in both Houses of Parliament by a clear majority of total membership and a two-thirds majority of those present and voting within a period of one month. If the Lok Sabha has been dissolved in the interim, ratification has to be effected within a month of the newly elected House being convened after the elections. The Forty-fourth Amendment also provided that a special sitting of the Lok Sabha be convened if a notice in writing of disapproval has been given by not less than one-tenth of the members of the Lok Sabha. The proclamation can be reviewed and approved afresh at intervals of six months.

The major restructuring of Article 352 was a sequel to an unprecedented series of repressive measures introduced by the Congress government in 1975, ushering in emergency as a system of governance rather than invocation of constitutional emergency powers. By deleting 'internal disturbance' and introducing elaborate checks and balances, the prospect of the misuse of power has undoubtedly been sought to be curtailed. It is however worth pondering whether over-reaction to a situation (the June 1975 proclamation of emergency) has not led to a self-inflicted emasculation, impairing the capacity of the Union to quell internal disturbance without resort to emergency provisions and to discharge the duty cast upon it under Article 355 to protect every state against internal disturbance.

This observation assumes relevance when one reflects on it against the backdrop of the Constitution (Fifty-ninth) Amendment Act, 1988 and the Constitution (Sixty-third) Amendment Act, 1989. The Fifty-ninth Amendment inserted a new Article 359-A[17] in the Constitution. The piquant situation resulting from the deletion of the words 'internal disturbance' by the Forty-fourth Amendment, by depriving the government of resort to emergency powers, emasculated its ability to take effective measures in the wake of the widespread terrorism in Punjab. The statement of objects and reasons to the Fifty-ninth Amendment mentioned that

it may be necessary to invoke the provisions of Article 352 of the Constitution to declare a partial Emergency either in the whole of the State of Punjab or in particular districts of the State. If such a situation arises, the expression 'armed rebellion' included in that Article as one of the grounds for declaration of Emergency (which alone could be resorted to in the case of an internal Emergency) may not be appropriate in the prevailing situation in Punjab to declare a Proclamation in the State. It is, therefore, felt that Article 352 may be suitably amended in its application to the State of Punjab to include 'internal disturbance' in any part on the grounds that the integrity of India is threatened by internal disturbance in any part of the territory of India so as to facilitate the taking of action under that article if it becomes necessary at a future date. The expression 'internal disturbance' was one of the grounds included in that Article from the commencement of the Constitution till it was amended by the Constitution (44th Amendment) Act, 1978. Consequentially, Article 358 and 359 are also proposed to be amended so as to provide for the suspension of Article 19 of the Constitution and the issuing of an order by the President suspending the operation of any provisions of the Constitution and the other provisions contained in Part III (except Article 20) under Article 359, if and when a Proclamation of Emergency on the ground of internal disturbance is issued in relation to the whole or any part of the State of Punjab.

The newly introduced Article 359-A had a very short life, being withdrawn after barely a year by the Constitution (63rd Amendment) Act, 1989. Both these Acts of Amendment could have been avoided had the Forty-fourth Amendment not deleted 'internal disturbance' and substituted it with 'armed rebellion'.

There is yet another lapse. The proviso to Article 83(2) enables the extension of the life of the Lok Sabha during the operation of an emergency by a period not exceeding one year at a time and not beyond six months after the cessation of the emergency. While this has been done, the Constitution is silent on the extension of the period of six months between two consecutive sessions of Parliament, as in Article 85. What happens if an emergency arises during the period when one Lok Sabha has been dissolved and the subsequent one has yet to be constituted? The emergency may be such that the conduct of elections to the Lok Sabha may itself become difficult, making it necessary to extend the obligatory six-month period between two sessions of Parliament.[18]

Besides Article 83(2) there is another article outside Part XVIII which concerns emergency. Article 250 empowers Parliament to legislate on the State List during an emergency, which together with Articles 353 and 354, impact on the federal structure during its pendency. Article 353 enables the executive power of the Union to make inroads into state turf. The Forty-second Amendment introduces a proviso to this article through which the executive powers of the Union and the legislative powers of Parliament are extended even to territories other than those in which the emergency may be in operation. To some extent it may be necessary to go beyond geographic boundaries for effective enforcement, but this opens up scope for misuse of this special provision. It is a matter of surprise that the far-reaching nature of this proviso escaped the attention of the Fourty-fourth Amendment. Article 354 provides for modifications of the scheme of distribution of revenues delineated in Articles 268 to 279 during an emergency.

III

An emergency also impinges upon the fundamental rights of citizens. The earliest landmark case under the Emergency provisions was the *Makhan Singh* case.[19] In this the Presidential Order under Article 359 provided that the right of any person to move any court for the enforcement of a right conferred by Articles 14, 21, and 22 of the Constitution would remain suspended if such person had been deprived of any such right under the Defence of India Act, 1962 or any Rule or Order promulgated under it. Two judgements were delivered in the *Makhan Singh* case, one by Justice Gajendragadkar for himself, A.K. Sarkar, K.N. Wanchoo, M. Hidayatullah, K.C. Das Gupta, and J.C. Shah JJ. Subba Rao J delivered a partially concurring and partially dissenting opinion. Gajendragadkar J in an extremely learned judgement, traced the history of the right to move for a writ of habeas corpus and held that the rights under Articles 32 and 226, and that under section 491(1)(b) of the Code of Criminal Procedure, were distinct remedies but the right claimed was the same and both remedies stood suspended during the subsistence of the Presidential Order. In a brilliant statement, Gajendragadkar J, rightly excluded malafide actions and excessive delegation from such immunity. Yet Mr Setalvad's prophetic argument that during the operation of the Presidential Order, the executive may abuse its powers and citizens would have no remedy was strangely termed as 'essentially political' and its impact on the constitutional question was at best indirect!

Gajendragadkar J hastened to add that 'it may be permissible to observe that in a democratic State, the effective safeguard against abuse of executive powers whether in peace or in emergency, is ultimately to be found in the existence of enlightened, vigilant and vocal public opinion'.

After the *Makhan Singh* case, the next important judgement was in the *Habeas Corpus* case.[20] The *Habeas Corpus* case was one of great expectation in judicial history. A large number of people were being detained primarily on the basis of their political association after the emergency was declared on 25 June 1975 on the ground of internal disturbance. Many of these detention orders were passed under the provisions of the Maintenance of Internal Security Act, 1951 (MISA). Writ petitions were filed in the various high courts. The high courts of Allahabad, Bombay, Delhi, Karnataka, Madhya Pradesh, Punjab, and Rajasthan held in favour of the detenus and took the view that notwithstanding the very wide wording of the Presidential Order dated 27 June 1975 read with the proclamation of emergency of 25 June 1975 the high courts had the power of judicial review under Article 226 of the Constitution of India to examine the detention orders in order to verify whether they had been passed in accordance with the provisions of the MISA or were mala fide or had been issued on the basis of relevant material.

In an appeal by the State, the Supreme Court framed two issues for consideration:

(a) Whether, in view of the Presidential Orders dated 27 June 1975 and 8 January 1976 under Clause (1) of Article 359 of the Constitution, any writ petition under Article 226 before a high court for habeas corpus to enforce the right to personal liberty of a person detained under the Act, on the ground that the order of detention or the continued detention is for any reason not under or in compliance with the Act, is maintainable?

(b) If such a petition is maintainable, what is the scope of extent of judicial scrutiny?

The majority decision (Ray, CJ, Beg, Chandrachud and Bhagwati, JJ) appears to have been simplistically based upon the open-ended nature of the words in the Presidential Order of 27 June 1975. Ray CJ extracted the 1962 Presidential Order which was considered in the

Makhan Singh case and the 1975 Presidential Order which came up for consideration in the *ADM, Jabalpur* case. The 1962 Presidential Order declared that:

... the right of any person to move any court for the enforcement of the right conferred by Article 21 and Article 22 should remain suspended for the period during which the proclamation of emergency issued under Clause (1) of Article 352 on 26 October 1962 is in force, if such a person has been deprived of any right under the Defence of India Ordinance, 1962 or any Rule or Order made thereunder.

The 1975 Presidential Order did not carry the words 'if such a person has been deprived of any such rights under the Defence of India Ordinance, 1962 or any Rules of Order made thereunder'. The majority held that it was confined and limited by the condition of deprivation of rights under the Defence of India Ordinance or any Rule or Order made thereunder, whereas in the 1975 Presidential Order no statute was mentioned.

It is respectfully submitted that the majority judgement violates the rigour of reasoning in *Makhan Singh* and lacked the strength of spirit of a zealous sentinel safeguarding the rights of the citizen. The distinction sought to be drawn by the majority is no distinction at all, and further that the majority judgement in the *ADM, Jabalpur* case does not do justice to the enunciation in the *Makhan Singh* case that the validity of a detention order based on any right other than those mentioned in the Presidential Order would be challenged. Even otherwise, the ratio in the *Makhan Singh* case (Bench of seven judges) was binding on the Bench of the learned judges in the *Jabalpur* case.

Khanna J, in what must be considered to be a brave, courageous, conscientious dissent, took the view that even in the absence of Article 21 of the Constitution the State has no power to deprive a person of his life or liberty without the authority of law. The discussion on the rule of law in Khanna J's opinion is far more exacting and elaborate than in the opinion of the majority. It is submitted that Khanna J, while dealing with the question of rule of law, rightly took the view that even in the absence of Article 21 the State has no power to deprive a person of his life and liberty without the authority of law. This, he rightly said, is the essential postulate and basic assumption of the rule of law. The rule of law was meant to flow out of this very concept and was meant to be the benchmark of balancing individual liberty and public order which again was to be ensured by independent courts. Without the sanctity of life and liberty, the distinction between a lawless society and one governed by laws would cease to have any meaning. Life and liberty were described as priceless possessions, and the mere mention of Article 21 in the Presidential Order could not lead automatically to a suggestion that a person could be deprived of these without the authority of law. Khanna J's opinion looks at the practical effect of the Presidential Order upon the rights of the citizen; the opinions of the majority evades even examining, far from appreciating, the direct impact on the individual rights of a citizen while such an immunity favoured the executive. The majority legalistically examined the interpretation of the 1975 Presidential Order while failing to appreciate that any guarantee of right is matched by enforceability. After all, what is a right unless it is enforceable and capable of being subject to redress? Khanna J quoted the felicitous words of Lord Mansfield in *James Sommersett*:[21] 'It is so odious that nothing can be suffered to support it but positive law: whatever inconvenience may follow from this decision, I cannot say this case is allowed or approved by the law of England, and therefore the black must be discharged....'

He also quoted the words of Lord Mansfield in *Fabrigas v Mostyn*:[22] 'To lay down in an English court of justice that a Governor acting by virtue of Letters Patent, under the Great Seal, is accountable only to God and his own conscience; that he is absolutely despotic, and can spoil, plunder, and affect His majesty's subjects both in their liberty and property, with impunity, is a doctrine that cannot be maintained....'

Khanna J also referred to Articles 8 and 9 of the Universal Declaration of Human Rights[23] and held that the Presidential Order must be capable of being construed as authorizing only bona fide executive action, thus, 'the Presidential order, therefore, should be so construed not to warrant arbitrary arrest or to bar right to an effective remedy by competent national tribunals for acts violating basic right or personal liberty granted by law'. According to the law in India before the Constitution came into force, no one could be deprived of his life and personal liberty without the authority of law, and in view of Article 372, this continued to be the law even after the Constitution was adopted. The judgement of the majority evoked justifiable disappointment both in the legal profession and public opinion.

Before analysing the situation post the Forty-fourth Amendment, it would be relevant to recall the grim happenings during the 1975 emergency. The torture in police custody leading to the death of Rajan, an engineering student in Kerala, during the emergency is a classic example of the extent to which Article 359 could be misused. Rajan's detention, torture, and untimely death were not acknowledged by the Kerala government for a long time and their disclosure at a late hour led to the resignation of Karunakaran as Chief Minister. Some observations of the majority appear to be plainly out of place.[24] The consequences of this judgement were of such magnitude that the censors prevented its disclosure at that time.[25] It was the lone voice of Justice Khanna, who quoted Hughes CJ: 'a dissent in a court of last resort is an appeal to the brooding spirit of the law, to the intelligence of a future day, when a later decision may possibly correct the error into which the dissenting judge believes the court to have been betrayed'. This sentence was indeed prophetic, as was witnessed soon thereafter by the Forty-fourth Amendment.

Sub-article (5) of Article 352 introduced by the Forty-second Amendment made the President's satisfaction in a proclamation of emergency as final and conclusive, and stipulated that such satisfaction shall not be questioned in any court on any ground. It further barred the jurisdiction of any court to adjudge the validity of a proclamation made by the President and also the continued operation of such proclamation. Article 352(5) thus exluded judicial scrutiny and review of proclamations of emergency. This sub-article (5) has since been totally deleted by the Forty-fourth Amendment.

Article 358 provides that Article 19 can remain suspended during an emergency imposed on grounds of (i) external aggression and, (ii) war, but not on grounds of armed rebellion. Law can be enacted and executive powers exercised inconsistent with Article 19 and their validity cannot be challenged during the pendency of the emergency or even thereafter. There is, however, a proviso that the protection to legislative and executive acts modifying rights under Article 19 will be available only when there is a specific recital to the effect that such law is in relation to the proclamation of emergency and the executive action is only under a law encapsulating such a recital.

Article 359 empowers the President to suspend the right to seek legal redress for enforcement of rights conferred by Part III of the Constitution except Article 20[26] and 21[27] (Forty-fourth Amendment). The protection of Article 21 nullifies the majority decision in *ADM v Shukla* (1976 Supp SCR 172). There are two differences between Article 358 as modified by the Forty-fourth Amendment and Article 359 similarly modified. The amendment Article 358 is operative only in the context of an emergency declared in the wake of (i) war and (ii) external aggression but not (iii) armed rebellion. The suspension under Article 359 of the right of resort to law courts is in the context of all the three types of emergencies. Article 358 is for the entire duration of emergency while

Presidential Orders under Article 359 can even be for short periods as may be specified in the order. The point of convergence between Articles 358 and 359 is that the laws impacted by both these articles should have a specific recital to the effect that these laws have been made in the context of the emergency. Under Article 359, the rights would revive on the cessation of emergency and can be enforced even in relation to the period of emergency.

IV

While emergency, as in Article 352 has been imposed only three times so far, Article 356 has been invoked more than a hundred times, making one wonder whether such a frequent recourse would not disqualify this provision being included in a chapter on 'emergencies'. Indeed, sections 45 and 93 of the Government of India Act, 1935 were not styled emergency provisions. A chronicle of the actual experience of the use of Article 356 reveals a yawning chasm between precept and practice, especially when one recalls the pious hope expressed by Dr B.R. Ambedkar that this provision would never be called into operation and would thus remain a dead letter.

Article 356 derives its origin from section 93 of the Government of India Act, 1935 which, along with section 45 of the Act, provided for situations arising out of a failure of the constitutional machinery in the federal government and the provinces. Under these sections, the Governor General (in relation to a federation) and the Governor (in relation to a province) were enabled to exercise their powers in their discretion and to assume to themselves the powers of the federal and provincial legislature respectively. Section 93 of the Government of India Act, 1935 empowered the Governor himself to issue a proclamation and assume to himself the necessary powers in conditions of a failure of the constitutional machinery in the state. The original draft Article 278 also followed the same pattern, since the earlier proposal was to make the office of the Governor an elective one, but when that provision was altered in favour of the Governor being appointed by the President the section 93 (Government of India Act, 1935) pattern had to be abandoned in favour of vesting the Governor with only a recommendatory role.

The power under Article 356 flows from the responsibility enumerated in Article 355, casting a duty on the Union to protect every state against external aggression and internal disturbance and to ensure that the government of every state is carried on in accordance with the provisions of the Constitution. The spirit of Article 355 is the same as that of Article 4, section 4 of the United States Constitution which requires the United States to guarantee to every state a republican form of government. It also further elaborates the obligation of the United States to protect each state from foreign invasion; and on application by the legislature or the executive of a state, against domestic violence. A similar provision is available in Section 1.19 of the Australian Constitution.[28]

After enunciating in Article 355 the duty of ensuring that every state government is carried on in accordance with the provisions of the Constitution, Article 356 proceeds to elaborate on the remedial measures to be adopted in situations when the government of a state cannot be carried on in accordance with the provisions of the Constitution. Is the intention of Article 356 analogous to the POGG clause in the Canadian and Australian Constitutions? The answer is clearly in the negative.[29] Article 356 provides that if the President, on receipt of a report from the Governor or otherwise, is satisfied that the government of the state cannot be carried on in accordance with the provisions of the Constitution, the President may, by proclamation, (a) assume to himself the executive powers of the state, and (b) declare that the powers of the legislature of the state shall be exercisable by or under the authority of Parliament. Significantly, the proviso to Article 356(1) rules out the assumption of the powers of the high court. The report from the Governor would appear to fall within the ambit of his discretionary power, as in Article 163(2) of the Constitution.[30] The Governor's power obviously cannot be limited to acting on the advice of his ministry, for it may indeed be necessary for him to report to the President that his council of ministers was conducting the affairs of the state in a way that was indicative of a failure of constitutional machinery.

The proclamation has to be ratified within two months by both Houses of Parliament. If the Lok Sabha stands dissolved, the proclamation ceases to operate at the end of thirty days after the reconstitution of the Lok Sabha, unless it is ratified by the reconstituted body.

A proclamation, unless revoked, will cease to operate on the expiration of a period of six months from the date of issue of the proclamation. Six-monthly extensions are permitted with the caveat however that extensions beyond one year up to a total of three years, are permissible provided the two criteria mentioned in Article 356(5), namely, (i) a proclamation of emergency is in operation in the whole of India, or, as the case may be, in the whole or in any part of the state at the time when the resolution for extension is passed, and (ii) the Election Commission certifies that the extension is necessary on account of the difficulties in holding general elections to the state legislative assembly concerned.

Reference was made earlier to the situation arising out of the Forty-fourth Amendment dropping 'internal disturbance' as one of the circumstances for proclamation of emergency. The reference was in the context of the continued terrorism in the state of Punjab. The elaborate enumeration of preconditions for extension of the duration of the Proclamation under Article 356 also led to a messy situation, necessitating as many as five constitutional Amendments for the continuance of President's rule in Punjab. The Fifty-ninth Amendment (30 March 1988) introduced the proviso for extension to Article 356(5). The Sixty-third Amendment (6 January 1989) deleted it. The proviso was reintroduced by the Sixty-fourth Amendment (16 April 1990). This Sixty-fourth Amendment also introduced a second proviso to Article 356(4) permitting the extension of President's rule to a total of 'three years six months'. The Sixty-seventh Amendment (4 October 1990) amended this further to read 'four years'. The Sixty-eighth Amendment (12 March 1991) amended this still further to extend it to 'five years'. This plethora of constitutional amendments would have made Dr Ambedkar (who had prophesied that Article 356 would remain a dead letter) turn in his grave!

The earliest use of Article 356 related to Punjab as long ago as 20 June 1954. Kerala and Punjab have been placed under President's rule nine times each. Uttar Pradesh comes a close second. The longest spells of President's rule have been in Jammu and Kashmir and Punjab.

The background to the invocation of Article 356 varies from causes such as a no-confidence motion against the council of ministers (defeat of the government on the floor of the House), resignation of the Chief Minister, break-up of coalitions and defections, to public agitation, and reasons such as the emergence at the centre of a party other than that in power in the state.[31]

The proclamation issued on 30 April 1977 in relation to nine states introduced a new precedent. The 1977 elections to the Lok Sabha witnessed a rout of the Congress party at the Centre. The Union government took the view that the electorate had expressed a complete lack of confidence in the party that was in power in these nine states based on an earlier verdict of the electorate. Consequently, these governments were dismissed and the legislatures dissolved. The Supreme Court by its order of 29 April 1977 refused to intervene.[32] Following the mid-term Lok Sabha elections in January 1980, a similar proclamation was promulgated in relation to nine states on a similar ground that the ruling party in these states no longer represented the people.

Another interesting precedent was the proclamation of 15 December 1992 dismissing the three BJP governments in Rajasthan, Madhya Pradesh, and Himachal Pradesh, consequent to a similar proclamation in relation to Uttar Pradesh on 6 December 1992 issued in the wake of the demolition of a disputed (Babri Masjid) structure in Ayodhya.

The Constitution (Thirty-eighth Amendment) Act, 1975 sought to bar judicial review of a proclamation under Article 356 'on any ground'.[33] This clause was dropped by the Forty-fourth Amendment (1978). A landmark judgement on Article 356 emerged in *S.R. Bommai & Ors v Union of India & Ors*,[34] in which a bench of nine judges undertook a fairly exhaustive analysis of the amplitude and dimensions of the article. The Bommai judgement is an interesting amalgam of observations in six pronouncements and the legal position has to be carefully and skilfully determined.[35]

Prior to the *Bommai* judgement, the case which occupied centre stage in regard to Article 356 was that in *Rajasthan*, a case which curiously was heard when Article 356 contained a sub-article (5), inserted by the Thirty-eighth Amendment (since deleted by the Forty-fourth Amendment), which made the satisfaction of the President in accordance with Article 356(1) final and conclusive, which satisfaction was not to be questioned by any court on any ground. The decision in the case came dangerously close to the doctrine of 'the political question' adopted by the US Supreme Court, which has been discussed extensively in *Calgrove v Green*[36] and *Baker v Carr*.[37]

There is some controversy about whether the Court can adjudicate on a political question or whether it should confine itself to the determination of a legal right under Article 131 of the Constitution. *State of Rajasthan* conceded the competence of the Union to dissolve a state assembly under Article 356. Notwithstanding the then Clause (5) of Article 356, the Supreme Court held that the Court could legitimately examine the question whether the President had issued the proclamation on mala fide or irrelevant considerations. The Forty-fourth Amendment, by deleting all the provisos in the various emergency provisions restraining judicial review, had given a clear indication that the Court could institute a proper enquiry into the grounds of any proclamation of Article 356.

The *Bommai* decision concurred with *State of Rajasthan* to the extent that the Court cannot abandon a judicial review on the ground that the issue raises a political question. However, the minimal area of judicial review adopted in *State of Rajasthan* was abandoned in *Bommai* in favour of a wider scope and extent of judicial review. It may be recalled that in *State of Rajasthan* it was held that the satisfaction of the President is a subjective matter and cannot be put to objective tests. It is not a decision which can be based on what the US Supreme Court has described as 'judicially discoverable and manageable standards'. It would largely be a political judgement based on an assessment of diverse and varied factors. If the satisfaction is mala fide or is based on wholly extraneous and irrelevant grounds, the Court would have the jurisdiction to examine it. This is the narrow minimal area in which the exercise of power under Article 356(1) is subject to judicial review.[38]

The *Bommai* judgement addressed the core issue in Article 356 as one of determining whether the assessment was one where the governance of the state *cannot* be carried on in accordance with the provisions of the Constitution. 'Cannot' implies an unresolvable impasse.

In other words, if the situation is one in which a solution other than imposition of President's rule can be worked out, then such a solution should be explored. It follows, therefore, that departure from one or other article of the Constitution cannot be ground enough; the totality of the situation should be such that in the absence of President's rule the governance of the state cannot be carried on in accordance with the Constitution.

On justiciability, the *Bommai* decision has come to the conclusion that the Court should look into whether there was any material leading to the President's satisfaction: 'even if part of the material is irrelevant, the court cannot interfere so long as there is some material which is relevant to the action taken.' (Per Jeevan Reddy J and Agarwal J, agreed to by Pandian J, and dissented to by Sawant J and Kuldip Singh J). The Court can also verify that the satisfaction of the President was not 'absurd, mala fide or perverse or based on extraneous and irrelevant grounds'.

A ticklish issue that arises in this context is whether the Court is not debarred from looking into the advice of the council of ministers, in view of Article 74(2) of the Constitution. Article 74(2) states that 'the question whether any, and if so what advice was tendered by ministers to the President shall not be inquired into in any court'. The *Bommai* judgement distinguished between the material based on which the President was advised and the advice itself. 'Material is not advice.'

The words 'or otherwise' in Article 356 do not debar the courts from asking for material other than the report of the Governor, and if such information is not disclosed, the Court can refuse to recognize such information even if the proclamation states mechanically that the President was satisfied on the basis of other information received by him.

On the circumstances that led to the satisfaction of the President, is included the stipulation in Article 365 of the Constitution that

where any state has failed to comply with, or to give effect to, any directions given in exercise of the executive power of the Union under any provisions of this Constitution, it shall be lawful for the President to hold that a situation has arisen in which the Government of the state cannot be carried on in accordance with the provisions of this Constitution.

Lest this article provide a wide turf for the Centre, the *Bommai* judgement has annotated Article 365 to mean that the directions given must be lawful and their disobedience should give rise to a situation contemplated in Article 356(1).

Elaborating on governance in accordance with the Constitution, the *Bommai* judgement dwelt on the basic structure of the Constitution. The Court's view here appears somewhat sweeping. The matter before them was the rationale or the decision to dismiss the Rajasthan, Madhya Pradesh and Himachal Pradesh governments, on the basis of the earlier dismissal of the Uttar Pradesh government in the wake of the demolition of the disputed structure at Ayodhya. While secularism is a basic feature of the Constitution, Sawant J and Kuldip Singh J held that any professions and actions which go counter to the creed of secularism are prima facie proof of conduct in defiance of the Constitution. Jeevan Reddy J and Agarwal J, interestingly, held that any party which seeks to fight elections on the basis of a plank that has the proximate effect of eroding the secular philosophy of the Constitution would be guilty of following an unconstitutional course of action. The central question, it is submitted, ought to be: Did the government in power act in any manner violative of the basic structure of the Constitution; and not, whether the party in power espoused one ideology or the other. After all, Ministers take the oath of allegiance to the Constitution and actions relevant to Article 356 should be judged on the touchstone of whether they subsequently acted in any manner repugnant to this oath and not whether their utterances or actions prior to taking the oath were contrary to the basic structure of the Constitution.

The substantial areas in which the *Bommai* judgement has provided clear illumination for the future are, (i) the insistence on the floor test and (ii) the non-dissolution of the Assembly prior to ratification by Parliament. History is replete with instances where the Governor applied his mind and discretion to determine who and how many retained the confidence of the House. The *Bommai* judgement, therefore, clearly laid down that except in extraordinary situations where, because of pervasive violence, a free vote is not possible in the House, the floor test alone is the constitutionally proper method for testing the strength and confidence that the government has in the House. *Bommai*, is therefore a landmark contribution to facilitate upholding of democratic values.

It has often happened that despite much erudition, courts have not been able to dispense final relief in accordance with their findings. The reason is that irreversible steps had been taken before the court concerned began adjudicating the issue. With a view to providing relief that does not become infructuous, the Court held that the dissolution of the Assembly should not be undertaken prior to the ratification of the proclamation by Parliament. Pending parliamentary approval, the Assembly can be placed in suspended animation.

In the event that Parliament disapproves promulgation, the proclamation lapses at the end of the two-month period. In such a case, a government that was dismissed, revives, and the legislative assembly kept in suspended animation gets reactivated. Since the proclamation lapses, and is not retrospectively invalidated, the acts done, orders made, and laws passed during the period of two months do not become illegal or void.

If the court strikes down the proclamation, it will be open to it to restore the dismissed government to office, and revive and reactivate the legislative assembly wherever it may have been dissolved or kept under suspension. The court will also have the power to declare that acts done, orders passed, and laws made during the period the proclamation was in force shall remain unaffected and be treated as valid.

V

Besides Article 352 and 356 type of emergencies, the Constitution also provides for a financial emergency to be declared under Article 360 in a situation in which the financial stability or credit of India or of any part of the territory is threatened.[39] During such an emergency the executive authority of the Union can extend to giving suitable directions to the state. The finances of the states and Union are interwoven through the structures of the Finance Commission and the Planning Commission. The state of finances of the states is most frequently a consequence of certain actions of the central government; for example the pay and dearness relief revisions by the central government result in similar revisions by state governments. Most of the state debts are owed to or based on guarantees provided by the central government. The mounting debts and increasing fiscal deficits (currently 4.3 per cent of GDP) of the states are already a matter of concern. With globalization of financial management and monitoring, the financial health of both the Union and the states will come under active scrutiny in future, and increasingly form part of the new international financial architecture. It is expected that the emerging framework will itself provide checks and balances, and the necessity of declaring financial emergencies and devising surgical solutions may not be necessary in the future.

Moreover, in the three types of emergencies, there is an implicit connecting thread of faith in the infallibility of the structures and institutions of the Union in contrast to those of the states. However, the same body politic governs the panchayats, local bodies, the states and the Union. Seen in this context, the real efficacy of all emergency provisions would appear to be of minimal value.

VI

Perhaps disparate situations, emergencies and non-emergencies, have been brought together in a chapter of the Constitution that deals with emergencies. It may be possible to regroup the articles into those that are concerned with infractions of fundamental rights and those that are departures from the division of legislative powers.

Indeed, the detailed enunciation and elaborate amendment made in Part XVII of the Constitution stand in striking contrast to the brevity that shrouds emergencies in Constitutions, written and unwritten, elsewhere in the world. One is sometimes led to feel that the overkill in elaborate delineation of checks and balances is likely to make governance during real emergencies complex and difficult, if not ineffective and impossible. A real crisis or emergency situation needs expert and firm handling. It can be argued that this will be possible only if one of the three arms of governance, usually the executive, expands and those of the others, namely the legislature and judiciary remain static or are curtailed. However, the Forty-fourth Amendment has virtually expanded the scope and amplitude of all three arms of the state. Whether this will lead to chaos during real emergencies is yet to be seen. The plethora of constitutional amendments against the backdrop of Punjab terrorism could not have been possible had the ruling party not had a substantial majority in Parliament. We have fast moved into a situation where governance in the country has moved into the hands of makeshift coalitions, not of national parties alone but also of regional ones. It is one thing that after 1975 there has been no proclamation of national emergency, but should such a situation develop, there can be fresh challenges to effective governance.

To conclude, the efficacy of the arrangements will be shown by the outcome. Emergent situations need effective governance. It is a moot point whether such a result flows from the detailed enunciation of checks and balances (which would indeed lead to lapses and omissions) or whether it would be preferable to leave much unsaid and relegate the situation to statesmanly handling and the sane judgement of the nation. In the ultimate analysis, nations speak and act with one voice during crises and emergencies.

Notes

[1] *The Oxford English Dictionary*, 2nd edn, Vol. V, Clarendon Press, Oxford, p. 176 defines 'emergency' as a political term, to describe a condition approximating that of war; *occas* as a synonym or euphemism for War; also *state of emergency*, wherein normal Constitution is suspended.

[2] Article (4) of the US Constitution states that 'The United States shall guarantee to every State in this Union a republican form of Government, and shall protect each of them against invasion; and on application of the Legislature, or of the Executive (when the Legislature cannot be convened) against domestic violence'.

[3] Section 91 of the British North America Act 1867 (the Canadian Constitution) confers on the federal Parliament, the power 'to make laws for the peace, order and good Government of Canada, in relation to all matters not coming within the classes of subjects by this Act assigned exclusively to the Legislatures of the Provinces'.

[4] Section 51 of the Commonwealth of Australia Constitution Act, 1900 states that 'The Parliament shall, subject to this Constitution, have power to make laws for the peace, order and good Government of the Commonwealth, with respect to ...'.

[5] *R v Hampden* (1637) 3 State Tr 826.

[6] *Anti Inflaction Act* 1976 2 SCR 373.

[7] Section 45 of the Government of India Act, 1935.

S.45 *Power of Governor General to Issue Proclamations*

If at any time the Governor General is satisfied that a situation has arisen in which Government of the Federation cannot be carried on in accordance with the provisions of this Act, he may, by Proclamation—(a) declare that his functions shall to such extent as may be specified in the Proclamation be exercised by him in his discretion; (b) assume to himself all or any of the persons vested in or exercisable by any Federal body or authority; and any such Proclamation may contain such incidental and consequential provisions as may appear to him to be necessary or desirable for giving effect to the objects of the Proclamation, including provisions for suspending in whole or in part the operation of any provisions of this Act relating to any Federal body or authority.

Section 93 of the Government of India Act, 1935 was, *mutatis mutandis*, the same except that the Governors of Provinces were substituted for the Governor General, and the Government of the Province was substituted for the Government of the Federation.

[8] B. Shiva Rao (ed.), *The Framing of India's Constitution*, A Study, N.M. Tripathi, Bombay, 1968, p. 803.

[9] Minutes: Meeting of the Union Constitution Committee on 8 June 1947, item 8; *Select Documents, supra* n. 8, Vol. II, p. 555.

[10] The points contained in the Secretary's note dated 7 June 1947 were taken up seriatim.

Point (a) (1)—The Provincial Constitution Committee has decided that the Governor of a Province shall have the authority in his discretion to issue Ordinances for the purpose of preventing any grave menace to the peace and tranquillity of the Province or any part thereof. A suggestion was made that in view of the all-India repercussions of serious disturbances in any Province, such an Ordinance shall only be issued in consultation with the President of the Union.

It was decided that where a Governor thought that there was grave menace to the peace and tranquillity of his Province or any part thereof, he might report to the President of the Union and the latter would, thereupon, take appropriate action under the Emergency Powers listed in the Union by the Constitution.

(Minutes of the Joint Meeting of the Union and Provincial Constitution Committee, 10 June 1947, in *supra* n. 8, *Select Documents*, Vol. II, pp. 610–11.)

[11] Dr Ambedkar expressed the hope that the draft Article 278 (now Article 356) would be a dead letter, and added, 'I hope the first thing [the President] will do would be to issue a mere warning to a province that has erred that things were not appearing in the way in which they were intended to happen in the Constitution. If that warning fails, the second thing for him to do will be to order an election allowing the people to settle matters by themselves. It is only when these two remedies fail, that he would resort to this Article' (*Constituent Assembly Debates*, Vol. 9, p. 177).

[12] Could an emergency be declared by the President if a grave threat was posed to the country's financial stability or credit? A last-minute proposal to enable the Union government to deal with a financial emergency was introduced by Ambedkar on 16 October 1949. The view of the Finance Minister was that, as an economic crisis was analogous to war, it would be difficult to decide when the President would declare a situation as one which threatened the financial stability or credit of the country. It would be better if the centre were placed in a position to issue directions to the states in financial matters, at any time when it felt that any action taken by a state was at variance with the economic and financial policy of the centre.

Moving the article in the Constituent Assembly on 16 October 1949, Dr Ambedkar explained that it was drawn up more or less on the lines of the National Recovery Act of 1930 passed in the USA which gave powers to the President to make similar provisions in order to remedy the economic and financial difficulties that had overtaken the American people as a result of the great depression. (Ambedkar was presumably referring to the National Industrial Recovery Act, 1933, which was declared unconstitutional in 1935.)

(*Supra* n. 8, pp. 820–1.)

[13] Presidential Proclamation, 3 December 1971.

[14] Presidential Proclamation, 25 June 1975.

[15] Clause (4) as inserted by the Forty-second Amendment has been renumbered clause (9) by the Forty-fourth Amendment Act 1978 and reads as follows:

... The power conferred on the President by this Article shall include the power to issue different Proclamations of different grounds, being war or external aggression or armed rebellion or imminent danger of war or external aggression or armed rebellion, whether or not there is a Proclamation already issued by the President under Clause (1) and such Proclamation is in operation....

[16] Article 352(3) inserted by the Forty-fourth amendment reads as follows: The President shall not issue a Proclamation under clause (1) or a Proclamation varying such Proclamation unless the decision of the Union Cabinet (that is to say, the Council consisting of the Prime Minister and other Ministers of Cabinet rank appointed under Ar-

ticle 75) that such a Proclamation may be issued has been communicated to him in writing....

[17] ...*359-A. Application to this Part to the State of Punjab*—Notwithstanding anything in this Constitution, this Part shall, in relation to the State of Punjab, be subject to the following modifications, namely:

   (a) in Article 352,

   (i) in clause (1),

      (A) for the opening portion, the following shall be substituted, namely: 'If the President is satisfied that a grave emergency exists whereby:

      (a) the security of India or of any part of the territory thereof is threatened, whether by war of external aggression or armed rebellion, or

      (b) the integrity of India is threatened by internal disturbance in the whole or any part of the territory of Punjab,

      he may, by Proclamation, make a declaration to that effect in respect of the whole of Punjab or of such part of the territory thereof as may be specified in the Proclamation...'

      (B) in the Explanation:

      (1) after the words 'armed rebellion', the words 'or that the integrity of India is threatened by internal disturbance in the whole or any part of the territory of Punjab', shall be inserted;

   (ii) in clause (9), after the words 'armed rebellion' at both the places where they occur, the words 'or internal disturbance' shall be inserted;

   (b) In Article 358, in clause (1), after the words 'or by external aggression', the words 'or by armed rebellion, or that the integrity of India is threatened by internal disturbance in the whole or any part of the territory of Punjab', shall be inserted;

   (c) In Article 359, for the words and figures 'Articles 20 and 21', at both the places where they occur, the word and figures 'Article 20' shall be substituted.

   (2) The amendment made to the Constitution by sub-section (1) shall cease to operate on the expiry of a period of two years from the commencement of this Act, except as respects things done or omitted to be done before such cesser.

[18] During the Kargil cirsis (1999) there was an apprehension that had it escalated further, a proclamation of emergency might have to be invoked, the Lok Sabha having been dissolved prior to the crisis and the Lok Sabha elections being held just prior to the expiry of the six-month period. Had the Kargil crisis deepened, the conduct of elections itself might have become difficult due to the operational difficulties caused by a paucity of paramilitary forces. The Constitution contains no flexibility about the six-month period.

[19] *Makhan Singh v State of Punjab* (1964) 4 SCR 797.

[20] *Additional District Magistrate, Jabalpur v S.S. Shukla* (1976) Supp SCR 172.

[21] (1772) 16 Cri. Pract. 289.

[22] 1 Crown 161.

[23] Universal Declaration of Human Rights, Articles 8 and 9:

Article 8: Everyone has the right to an effective remedy by the competent national tribunals for acts violating the fundamental rights granted him by the Constitution or by law.

Article 9: No one shall be subjected to arbitrary arrest, detention or exile.

[24] (i) 'Furthermore, we understand that the care and concern bestowed by the State authorities upon the welfare of detenus who are well housed, well fed and well treated, is almost maternal' (Per Beg, J in *ADM Jabalpur v Shivkant Shukla* (1976 Supp SCR 172 at pp. 370–1).

(ii) 'People who have faith in themselves and in their country will not permit pictures of diabolic distortion and mendacious malignment of the governance of the country' (Per Ray CJ in *ADM Jabalpur v Shivkant Shukla*).

(iii) 'It seems to me that the Emergency Provisions could themselves be regarded as part of the basic structure of the Constitution. At any rate, they are meant to safeguard the basis of all orderly government, according to law' (Per Beg, J, (1976) Supp SCR 172 at p. 366).

[25] White Paper on the issue of mass media during the internal Emergency (August 1977), App. 13; Sept.: Serial No. 11.

[26] Article 20 of the Constitution of India:

> 20. *Protection in respect of conviction for offences:* (1) No person shall be convicted of any offence except for violation of the law in force at the time of the commission of the act charged as an offence, nor be subjected to a penalty greater than that which might have been inflicted under the law in force at the time of the commission of the offence.
>
> (2) No person shall be prosecuted and punished for the same offence more than once.
>
> (3) No person accused of any offence shall be compelled to be a witness against himself....

[27] Article 21 of Constitution of India

> 21. *Protection of life and personal liberty:* No person shall be deprived of his life or personal liberty except according to procedure established by law.

[28] Article 1.19 of the Commonwealth of Australia Act states: 'The Commonwealth shall protect every state against the invasion and on the application of the executive government of the State, against domestic violence.'

[29] Pandit H.N. Kunzru: Is it the purpose of Article 278 and 278A to enable the Central Government to intervene in provincial affairs for the State of good government in the provinces?

Dr Ambedkar: No, no. The centre is not given that authority ... Whether there is good Government or not in the Province is not for the centre to determine. I am quite clear on the point.

Pandit H.N. Kunzru: The House is entitled to know from the Hon'ble Member what is his idea of the meaning of the phrase 'in accordance with the provisions of the Constitution'?

Dr Ambedkar: The expression 'failure of machinery', I find, has been used in the Government of India Act, 1935. Everybody must be quite familiar therefore with its de facto and de jure meaning.

(*Constituent Assembly Debates*, Vol 9, pp. 176–7.)

[30] Article 163 of the Constitution

> 163. *Council of Ministers to aid and advise Governor:* (1) There shall be a Council of Ministers with the Chief Minister at the head to aid and advise the Governor in the exercise of his functions, except in so far as he is by or under this Constitution required to exercise his functions or any of them in his discretion.
>
> (2) If any question arises whether any matter is or is not a matter as respects which the Governor is by or under this Constitution required to act in his discretion, the decision of the Governor in his discretion shall be final, and the validity of anything done by the Governor shall not be called in question on the ground that he ought or ought not to have acted in his discretion.
>
> (3) The question whether any, and if so what, advice was tendered by Ministers to the Governor shall not be inquired into in any court....

[31] The first instance of defections leading to President's Rule took place as far back as in November 1954, when T. Prakasam's Ministry in Andhra was brought down by the ruling party members voting with the opposition in the no-confidence motion. Defections became more frequent after the 1967 general elections. In Haryana (1967 November) defections had become endemic. These had made a mockery of the Constitution and had brought democracy to ridicule (*President's Rule in the States and Union Territories*, Lok Sabha Secretariat, New Delhi, 1996).

President's Rule had to be imposed, consequent to break-up of ruling coalitions in Kerala (1979, 1981, 1982), Manipur (1992), Orissa (1961 and 1971), Punjab (1968), Tripura (1979), and Uttar Pradesh (1970).

Resignation of the Chief Minister led to President's Rule in Kerala (1970, 1979), Gujarat (1976), Punjab (1951), Sikkim (1979), Uttar Pradesh (1968, 1975) and West Bengal (1970).

Public agitations leading to President's Rule took place in Andhra Pradesh (1973), Assam (1979), Gujarat (1974), Kerala (1959), Punjab (1983 and 1987).

The rout of the Congress Party in the March 1977 Lok Sabha elections led to the imposition of President's Rule in the nine states of Bihar, Haryana, Himachal Pradesh, Madhya Pradesh, Orissa, Punjab, Rajasthan, Uttar Pradesh and West Bengal. A repeat of this occurred in February 1980 following the resurgence of the Congress party in the January 1980 Lok Sabha elections. The states involved were Bihar, Gujarat, Madhya Pradesh, Maharashtra, Orissa, Punjab, Rajasthan, Tamil Nadu, and Uttar Pradesh.

[32] The Supreme Court cannot ... interdict use of powers under Article 356(1) unless and until resort to the provision, in a particular situation, is shown to be so grossly perverse and unreasonable as to constitute patent misuse of this provision or an excess of power on admitted facts. The most that one could say is that a dissolution against the wishes of the majority in a State Assembly is a grave and serious matter. Perhaps, it could be observed that it should be resorted to under Article 356(1) of the Constitution only when 'a critical situation' has arisen. But the question is whether the State Assembly and the State Government for the time being have been so totally and emphatically rejected by the people that a 'critical situation' has arisen or is bound to arise unless the 'political sovereign' is given an opportunity of giving a fresh verdict. A decision on such a question undoubtedly lies in the Executive realm. (*State of Rajasthan v Union of India* (1977) 3 SCC 592.)

[33] In Article 356 of the Constitution, after clause (4) the following clause shall be inserted, and shall be deemed always to have been inserted, viz '(5) Notwithstanding anything in this Constitution, the satisfaction of the President mentioned in Clause (1) shall be final and conclusive and shall not be questioned in any Court on any ground'. (Constitution 38th Amendment Act, 1975.)

[34] (1994) 3 SCC 1.

[35] The main points of the above (Bommai) judgement are as follows:

(1) Article 356 of the Constitution confers a power upon the President to be exercised only where he is satisfied that a situation has arisen where the Government of a State cannot be carried on in accordance with the provisions of the Constitution. Under our Constitution, the power is really that of the Union Council of Ministers with the Prime Minister as its head. The satisfaction contemplated by the article is subjective in nature.

(2) The power conferred by Article 356 upon the President is a conditional power. It is not an absolute power. The existence of material—which may comprise or include the report(s) of the Governor—is a precondition. The satisfaction must be formed on relevant material. The recommendations of the Sarkaria Commission with respect to the exercise of power under Article 356 do merit serious consideration at the hands of all concerned.

(3) Though the power of dissolving the Legislative Assembly can be said to be implicit in clause (1) of Article 356, it must be held, having regard to the overall constitutional scheme, that the President shall exercise it only after the proclamation is approved by both Houses of Parliament under clause (3) and not before. Until such approval, the President can only suspend the Legislative Assembly under sub-clause (c) of Clause (1). The dissolution of the Legislative Assembly is not a matter of course. It should be resorted to only where it is found necessary for achieving the purposes of the Proclamation.

(4) The Proclamation under clause (1) can be issued only where the situation contemplated by the clause arises. In such a situation, the Government has to go. There is no room for holding that the President can take over some of the functions and powers of the State Government while keeping the State Government in office. There cannot be two Governments in one sphere.

(5) (a) clause (3) of Article 356 is conceived as a check on the power of the President and also as a safeguard against abuse. In case both Houses of Parliament disapprove or do not approve the Proclamation, the Proclamation lapses at the end of the two-month period. In such a case, Government, which was dismissed, revives. The Legislative Assembly, which may have been kept in suspended animation gets reactivated. Since the Proclamation lapses—and is not retrospectively invalidated—the acts done, orders made and laws passed during the period of two months do not become illegal or void. They are, however, subject to review, repeal or modification by the Government/Legislative Assembly or other competent authority.

(b) However, if the Proclamation is approved by both the Houses within two months, the Government (which was dismissed) does not revive on the expiry of the period of Proclamation or on its revocation. Similarly, if the Legislative Assembly has been dissolved after the approval under clause (3), the Legislative Assembly does not revive on the expiry of the period of Proclamation or on its revocation.

(6) Article 74(2) merely bars an inquiry into the question whether any, and if so, what advice was tendered by the ministers to the President. It does not bar the Court from calling upon the Union Council of Ministers (Union of India) to disclose to the Court the material upon which the President had formed the requisite satisfaction. The material on the basis of which advice was tendered does not become part of the advice. Even if the material is looked at by or shown to the President, it does not partake the character of advice. Article 74(2) and section 123 of the Evidence Act cover different fields. It may happen that while defending the Proclamation, the minister or the official concerned may claim the privilege under section 123. If and when such privilege is claimed, it will be decided on its own merits in accordance with the provisions of section 123.

(7) The Proclamation under Article 356(1) is not immune from judicial review. The Supreme Court or the High Court can strike down the Proclamation if it is found to be mala fide or based on wholly irrelevant or extraneous grounds.

The deletion of clause (5) (which was introduced by the Thirty-eighth (Amendment) Act)—by the Forty-fourth (Amendment) Act, removes the cloud on the reviewability of the action. When called upon, the Union of India has to produce the material on the basis of which action was taken. It cannot refuse to do so, if it seeks to defend the action. The Court will not go into the correctness of the material or its adequacy. Its inquiry is limited to see whether the material was relevant to the action. Even if part of the material is irrelevant, the Court cannot interfere so long as there is some material which is relevant to the action taken.

(8) If the Court strikes down the Proclamation, it has the power to restore the dismissed Government to office and revive and reactivate the Legislative Assembly wherever it may

have been dissolved or kept under suspension. In such a case, the Court has the power to declare that acts done, orders passed and laws made during the period the Proclamation was in force shall remain unaffected and be treated as valid. Such declaration, however, shall not preclude the Government/Legislative Assembly or other competent authority to review, repeal or modify such acts, orders and laws.

(9) The Constitution of India has created a federation but with a bias in favour of the Centre. Within the sphere allotted to the states, they are supreme.

(10) Secularism is one of the basic features of the Constitution. While freedom of religion is guaranteed to all persons in India, from the point of view of the State, the religion, faith or belief of a person is immaterial. To the State, all are equal and are entitled to be treated equally. In matters of State, religion has no place. No political party can simultaneously be a religious party. Politics and religion cannot be mixed. Any state government which pursues unsecular policies or unsecular course of action acts contrary to the constitutional mandate and renders itself amenable to action under Article 356. (*President's Rule in the States and Union Territories*, Lok Sabha Secretariat, New Delhi, 1996, Introduction, pp. ix, x.)

[36] (1945) 328 US 549.

[37] (1962) 369 US 186.

[38] ... The satisfaction of the President is a subjective one and cannot be tested by reference to any objective tests. It is deliberately and advisedly subjective because the matter in respect to which he is to be satisfied is of such a nature that its decision must necessarily be left to the executive branch of government. There may be a wide range of situations which may arise and their political implications and consequences may have to be evaluated in order to decide whether the situation is such that the government of the state cannot be carried on in accordance with the provisions of the Constitution. It is not a decision which can be based on what the Supreme Court of United States has described as 'judicially discoverable and manageable standards'. It would largely be a political judgement based on assessment of diverse and varied factors, fast changing situations, potential consequences, public reaction, motivations and response of different classes of people and their anticipated future behaviour and a host of other considerations, in the light of experience of public affairs and pragmatic management of complex and often curious adjustments that go to make up the highly sophisticated mechanism of a modern democratic government. It cannot therefore, by its very nature be a fit subject matter for judicial determination and hence it is left to the subjective satisfaction of the central government which is best in a position to decide it. The Court cannot in the circumstances, go into the question of correctness or adequacy of the facts and circumstances on which the satisfaction of the central government is based. That would be a dangerous exercise for the Court, both because it is not a fit instrument for the determining a question of this kind and also because the Court would thereby usurp the function of the central government and in doing so, enter the 'political thicket', which it must avoid if it is to retain its legitimacy with the people... (Per Bhagwati J in *State of Rajasthan v Union of India* (1977) 3 SCC 592.)

[39] Supra note 12.

Ten

Public Interest Litigation: Potential and Problems

Ashok H. Desai and S. Muralidhar

Introduction

Public Interest Litigation (PIL) as it has developed in recent years marks a significant departure from traditional judicial proceedings. PIL was not a sudden phenomenon. It was an idea that was in the making for some time before its vigorous growth in the early eighties. It now dominates the public perception of the Supreme Court. The Court is now seen as an institution not only reaching out to provide relief to citizens but even venturing into formulating policy which the State must follow.

At the time of Independence, court procedure was drawn from the Anglo-Saxon system of jurisprudence.[1] The bulk of citizens were unaware of their legal rights, and much less in a position to assert them. The guarantees of fundamental rights and the assurances of directive principles, described as the 'conscience of the Constitution',[2] would have remained empty promises for the majority of illiterate and indigent citizens under adversarial proceedings. PIL has been a conscious attempt to transform the promise into reality.

Background

A number of disparate factors, legal and political, led to the development of PIL.

Judicial Review as Basic Structure
In the early years, the Supreme Court interpreted the role of the judiciary merely as determining the *lis* before it in accordance with narrow

procedural rules. In *A.K. Gopalan v State of Madras*,[3] the Supreme Court remarked,

In India the position of the judiciary is somewhere in between the Courts in England and the United States. ... But our Constitution, unlike the American Constitution, does not recognise the absolute supremacy of the Court over the legislative authority in all respects, for outside the restricted field of constitutional limitations our Parliament and the State Legislatures are supreme in their respective legislative fields and in that wider field there is no scope for the Court in India to play the role of the Supreme Court of the United States.

This perception changed by the time of *Golak Nath* case,[4] where the Supreme Court declared that fundamental rights could not be derogated from even by an amendment to the Constitution. Six years later, in *Kesavananda Bharati's* case,[5] while overruling *Golak Nath*, the Court evolved another far-reaching doctrine under which Parliament was denied the power to amend the Constitution in a manner that violated its 'basic structure'. The Supreme Court also identified the power of judicial review as being part of such basic structure. Thus the legislature could not deny judicial review even by a constitutional amendment.

Introducing the Notion of 'Due Process'

The broadening of the contents of Fundamental Rights had to await the period following the Emergency of 1975–7. Initially the Court took a narrow view of the wording of Article 21[6] to mean that as long as there was some statute made by the legislature taking away a person's liberty, it could not be challenged as being violative of fundamental rights.[7] In a significant reversal, in *Maneka Gandhi v Union of India*,[8] decided soon after the emergency, the Court asserted the doctrine of substantive due process as being integral to fundamental rights on the ground that it emanated from the scheme underlying Articles 14, 19 and 21. The Court's power to strike down legislation was now expanded to include a critical examination of a statute, even on the basis of the substantive element of due process.

The Emergency

The deferential role of the Supreme Court during the emergency[9] contributed significantly to an opposite swing in the judiciary's view of its own role after the 1977 elections. The emergency witnessed large-scale violations of basic rights of life and liberty. These were facilitated by the enactment of a draconian statute, the Maintenance of Internal Security Act (MISA) and suspension of basic fundamental rights. An overwhelming number of high courts ensured that the state scrupulously followed the terms of the detention law. This obvious approach was however reversed by the Supreme Court in *A.D.M. Jabalpur v Shivkant Shukla*[10] which granted virtual immunity to any action of the executive affecting the life and liberty of the citizen. The judgement can best be described, in the words of Professor C.K. Allen,[11] as the contribution of the Supreme Court to the emergency. The judgement brought into question the role of the Supreme Court as the guardian of citizens' liberties. The vigorous growth of PIL was in some measure a reaction to this criticism.

Executive Interference in Judicial Appointments

Another development during the post-*Kesavananda* phase was the increase in executive interference with judicial appointments to the higher courts. The independence of the judiciary was seriously jeopardized when the executive of the day used the weapon of supersession twice in the appointment of the Chief Justice of India. The first was in 1973 when Justice A.N. Ray was appointed Chief Justice superseding Justices Shelat, Grover, and Hegde, each of whom had concurred with the majority view in *Kesavananda*. In 1976, Justice Khanna, who had dissented in *A.D.M. Jabalpur* was superseded and Justice Beg took over as the Chief Justice.

Reports on Legal Aid

In the meantime there were developments relating to legal aid to provide easier access to justice. In a report on legal aid in 1971, Justice Bhagwati[12] observed 'even while retaining the adversary system, some changes may be effected whereby the judge is given greater participatory role in the trial so as to place the poor, as far as possible, on a footing of equality with the rich in administration of justice'.[13]

Similarly, the report of the Committee on Legal Aid presided by Justice Krishna Iyer[14] in 1973 dealt with the nexus between law and poverty, and spoke of PIL in this context. It emphasized the need for an active and widespread legal aid system that enabled law to reach the people, rather than requiring people to reach the law.[15]

The two judges joined forces as a two-member committee on juridicare, which released its final report in August 1977. The report, while emphasizing the need for a new philosophy of legal services programme, cautioned that it 'must be framed in the light of the socio-economic conditions prevailing in our country'.[16] It further noted that 'the traditional legal services programme which is essentially court or litigation oriented, cannot meet the specific needs and the peculiar problems of the poor in our country'.[17] The report also included a draft legislation for legal services and referred to Social Action Litigation, a synonym for PIL. PIL was seen as a strategic arm of the legal aid movement intended to bring justice within the reach of those who, on account of their indigency, illiteracy, and lack of resources, were unable to reach the courts.

Post-Emergency Period

It is discernible that the strength of a judiciary is proportionate to the weakness of the executive. The Janata Party which came to power in 1977 and subsisted till 1979, was a weak government at a point in time when the judiciary consciously began to develop PIL. How the Court viewed its transformation during this phase is enunciated in a decision given a decade later, where it said:

Article 32 does not merely confer power on this Court to issue a direction, order or writ for enforcement of the fundamental rights but also lays down a constitutional obligation on this Court to protect the fundamental rights of the people and for that purpose this Court has all incidental and ancillary powers including the power to forge new remedies and fashion new strategies designed to enforce the fundamental rights. It is in realization of this constitutional obligation that this Court has in the past innovated new methods and strategies for the purpose of securing enforcement of the fundamental rights, particularly in the case of the poor and disadvantaged who are denied their basic human rights and to whom freedom and liberty have no meaning.[18]

Facets of PIL

Access and Standing

In a developing country, the legal process tends to intimidate the litigant, who feels alienated from the system. A poor person who enters the legal stream, whether as a claimant, a witness or a party, may well find the experience traumatic.[19] Lawyers have not done much to alleviate this. The way the Bar has developed gives issues of legal aid and legal awareness a low priority, thus ensuring that the lawyer is the only route of access to the legal system. The traditional rules of procedure in the adversarial system of law permit only a person whose rights are directly affected to approach the Court. Under the Common Law, a person claiming the writ of mandamus had to show that he was enforcing his own personal right.[20] In *Municipal Council, Ratlam v Shri Vardichan*[21] the Court reacted to this approach and observed:

The truth is that a few profound issues of processual jurisprudence of great strategic significance to our legal system face us and we must zero in on them as they involve problems of access to justice for the people beyond the blinkered rules of 'standing' of British-Indian vintage. If the centre of gravity of justice is to shift, as the preamble of our Constitution mandates, from the traditional individualism of *locus standi* to the community orientation of public interest litigation, these issues must be considered.

Seervai refers to the development of the expanded concept of *locus standi* in the context of one of the earliest PIL cases. He notes:[22]

The most striking illustration is furnished by the unreported judgement of Gandhi J, of the Bombay High Court, in a writ filed by a public spirited citizen—Mr. Piloo Mody. In *Piloo Mody v Maharashtra,* Gandhi J adopted the view of *locus standi* which was later laid down by Bhagwati J in the *Judges'* case. Piloo Mody complained that the Government—through three Ministers—had leased out valuable plots of land at a gross undervalue. Gandhi J rejected the respondents' contention that the petitioner had no *locus standi.* He upheld the petitioner's contention that the leases were granted mala fide at a gross undervalue. Having regard to the equities of the case, Gandhi J directed that if the lessees wanted to obtain the grant of a lease they should pay $33\frac{1}{3}$% increased rent or return the land to government.

The two originally separate rationales for a representative standing and citizen standing have now merged. The Supreme Court in the Judges' case,[23] said:

Where a legal wrong or a legal injury is caused to a person or to a determinate class of persons by reason of violation of any constitutional or legal right or any burden is imposed in contravention of any constitutional or legal provision or without authority of law or any such legal wrong or legal injury or legal burden is threatened and such person or determinate class of persons is by reasons of poverty, helplessness or disability or socially or economically disadvantaged position, unable to approach the Court for any relief, any member of the public can maintain an application for an appropriate direction, order or writ in the High Court under Article 226 and in case of breach of any fundamental right of such person or class of persons, in this Court under Article 32 seeking judicial redress for the legal wrong or injury caused to such person or determinate class of persons.

In such case the Court will allow any member of the public acting in a bona fide manner to espouse the cause of such person or class of persons.[24] Representative non-political, non-profit, and voluntary organizations who have a sufficient interest can maintain an action for judicial redress for public injury arising out of breach of public duty or violation of some provision of the Constitution. Lawyers,[25] medical practitioners,[26] and journalists[27] have brought such representative actions.

The Court has however been careful not to liberalize the concept of standing in criminal and service matters. In the *Janata Dal* case,[28] it held that the lawyer petitioner was concerned with the private interest of the accused and therefore lacked *locus standi* to pursue the case as a public interest litigation. It observed:

Even if a million questions of law were to be deeply gone into and examined in a criminal case of this nature registered against specified accused persons, it is for them and them alone to raise all such questions and challenge the proceedings initiated against them at the appropriate time before the proper forum and not for third parties under the garb of public interest litigants.[29]

In *Panchhi v State of UP*,[30] the Court refused permission even to the National Commission for Women to intervene in a case of a death sentence awarded to a woman. This, the Court said, was 'for the obvious reason that under the Code of Criminal Procedure, the National Commission for Women or any other organization cannot have *locus standi* in this murder case'.[31] Similarly, in service matters the Court has held that a third party cannot challenge the appointment of a person.[32] Although the Courts have permitted easier access in matters of PIL, they have been careful to note that PIL cannot be maintained by a meddlesome interloper or busybody,[33] wayfarers,[34] or officious intervenors having no public interest except for personal gain either for themselves or for the glare of publicity.[35]

Relaxation of Procedural Requirements

In order to permit fuller access to Courts, PIL has been marked by a departure from procedural rules extending to the form and manner of filing a writ petition, appointment of commissions for carrying out investigation, and giving a report to Court, and the appointment of lawyers as amicus curiae to assist the Court.

The flexibility of PIL procedure can best be illustrated by what is termed as 'epistolary jurisdiction'. Taking a cue from the American Supreme Court's decision in *Gideon v Wainwright*,[36] where a postcard from a prisoner was treated as a petition, the Supreme Court said in the *Judges'* case,[37] that a public-spirited person could move the Court even by writing a letter. The Court has accepted letters[38] and telegrams[39] as petitions. The danger of such ease of access leading to the apprehension that a litigant could indulge in forum-shopping and address a particular judge was expressed by Pathak J, in the *Bandhua Mukti Morcha* case:

When the jurisdiction of the Court is invoked, it is the jurisdiction of the entire Court. ... No such communication can be properly addressed to a particular judge. ...Which judge or judges will hear the case is exclusively a matter concerning the internal regulation of the business of the Court, interference with which by a litigant or a member of the public constitutes the grossest impropriety.[40]

Many of the early PILs, including *Sunil Batra (II) v Delhi Administration*,[41] *Dr Upendra Baxi v State of UP*,[42] *Veena Sethi v State of Bihar*,[43] and *People's Union for Democratic Rights v Union of India*[44] commenced with the petitioners sending letters to the Supreme Court.

On 1 December 1988, the Supreme Court, on its administrative side, issued a notification on what matters could be entertained as PIL.[45] Under this notification, letter petitions falling under certain categories alone would be ordinarily entertained. These included matters concerning bonded labour, neglected children, petitions from prisoners, petitions against the police, petitions against atrocities on women, children, and scheduled castes and scheduled tribes. Petitions pertaining to environmental matters, adulteration of drugs and food, maintenance of heritage and culture, and other matters of public importance could also be entertained. The notification set out matters that ordinarily were not to be entertained as PIL, such as landlord–tenant disputes, service matters, and admission to medical and other educational institutions. The notification also laid down the procedure: the petition would be first screened in the PIL Cell and thereafter it would be placed before a judge to be nominated by the Hon'ble Chief Justice of India for directions.

Appointment of Commission(er)s

A difficulty often faced by a genuine PIL petitioner is lack of access to information even where he has a genuine grievance.[46] One method by which the Court gathers facts is by the appointment of commissioners. The Court has appointed district judges,[47] journalists,[48] lawyers,[49] mental health professionals,[50] bureaucrats,[51] and expert bodies[52] as commissioners. In environmental matters, the Court has relied upon expert bodies like the CPCB[53] and the NEERI[54] to study the situation and submit a report to the Court. While the power to appoint commissioners in matters of civil nature is found in Order XXVI Civil Procedure Code (CPC) and Order XLVI Supreme Court Rules, the powers under Article 32 read with Article 142 are wide enough to permit such a course of action in any matter before the Supreme Court. Commissions have also been appointed to propose remedial relief and monitor its implementation. The Court in *Indian Council for Enviro-Legal Action v Union of India*,[55] appointed NEERI as an expert body to study the situation of ground water and soil pollution.

The Court has also drawn upon empirical data and expert studies to decide whether pavement dwellers' right to life and livelihood would be affected by their eviction.[56] Likewise, the Court relied upon the opinions of experts to dismiss a PIL challenging dairy imports from Ireland on the ground that they were radioactively contaminated by the leak from the Chernobyl nuclear plant.[57] However, in cases where there are rival contentions of expert bodies the Court will not intervene. Where the question concerned the seismic potential of the Tehri dam site, the Court stated that it did not have the expertise to give a final opinion on the matter.[58] The Court could only investigate and adjudicate if the government was not conscious of the inherent dangers.

The use of commissions has enabled the Court to check the facts alleged by the petitioner as well as the State after a proper scrutiny without affecting its role as an adjudicator. This has, however, had to be done with circumspection lest it appear that in its desire to redress the grievance, the Court is going beyond its powers.

PIL Petitioners and Amicus Curiae

A PIL petitioner is perceived by the Court as one who draws its attention to a grievance requiring remedial measures and having no personal stake in the matter. It expects her/him to be conscious of her/his obligation to the cause being espoused and conduct herself/himself accordingly. Thus persons bringing PILs to the Court cannot of their free will seek to withdraw the petition. The Court may take over the conduct of the matter if it feels that in the interests of justice that issue should be decided irrespective of the wishes of the petitioner. This is what happened in a case concerning children in jails brought to the Supreme Court by a letter petition from Sheela Barse, a journalist. Frustrated with the slow progress of the case, primarily due to the repeated adjournments sought and obtained by the state governments, she sought to withdraw the case. The Court, however, declined saying:[59]

The third ground is that the proceedings are brought as a 'voluntary action' and that the applicant is entitled to sustain her right to be the 'petitioner in person' in a public interest litigation and that the proceedings cannot be proceeded with after delinking her from the proceedings. This again proceeds on certain fallacies as to the rights of a person who brings a pubic interest litigation. Any recognition of any such vested right in the persons who initiate such proceedings is to introduce a new and potentially harmful element in the judicial administration of this form of public law remedy. That apart, what is implicit in the assertion of the applicant is the appropriation to herself of the right and wisdom to determine the course the proceedings are to or should take and its pattern. This cannot be recognized... the Court has ... already initiated an elaborate exercise. ... The petition cannot be permitted to be abandoned at this stage. Only a private litigant can abandon his claims.

PIL petitioners (who often appear in person) may be inarticulate in the presentation of the case or may so identify with the cause that they may not be able to maintain the necessary detachment. The Court may be better assisted by a lawyer who understands the legal dimensions of the issue and is objective in her/his approach to the cause. The Courts have, in PIL cases, sought the assistance of lawyers as amicus curiae. In order to ensure that the process of the Court is not misused, the Court may require that the information supplied to it by the petitioner or the state be verified by the amicus curiae.[60] Senior advocates of the Supreme Court have assisted it as amicus curiae in several cases, including those relating to bonded labour,[61] police excesses,[62] forests,[63] and public accountability.[64] It is a moot point whether the appointment of an amicus curiae shuts out the petitioner from being heard by the Court and being made dependent on the amicus curiae for the effective presentation of her/his point of view. None the less, the role of the amicus curiae has thus far been significant in the prosecution of PILs. Chief Justice J.S. Verma, speaking at a public function, eulogized the lawyer's role in PILs in these words:

It must be said to the credit of the Bar, and this I say from personal experience over the years, the most busy lawyers who charge large fees which I often openly criticize, if called upon to appear as amicus curiae in any such matter, leave every other work and without charging a single rupee put in their best effort in a PIL matter. That credit is due to the Bar. That is the beauty of the justice delivery system and that goes to show that the legal profession has not yet become wholly mercenary. Professionalism remains and professionalism is the essential trait of any such service-oriented enterprise.[65]

Non-adversarial

In the traditional adversarial system, the lawyers of each party are expected to present contending points of view to enable the judge to decide the issue for or against a party. In PIL there are no winners or losers and the mindset of both lawyers and judges can be different from that in ordinary litigation. The Court, the parties and their lawyers are expected to participate in resolution of a given public problem. This was explained by the Court in *Dr Upendra Baxi v State of UP*.[66]

It must be remembered that this is not a litigation of an adversary character undertaken for the purpose of holding the State Government or its officers responsible for making reparation but it is a public interest litigation which involves a collaborative and cooperative effort on the part of the State Government and its officers, the lawyers appearing in the case and the Bench for the purpose of making human rights meaningful for the weaker sections of the community.

PIL in Practice

The wide reach of PIL is best demonstrated by reference to some areas in which Courts have made particularly significant pronouncements. Although the Court has issued orders relating to a very wide range of PILs covering matters such as prisons and prisoners, the police, the armed forces, children, child labour, bonded labour, urban space, environment and resources, consumer issues, education, politics and elections, public policy and accountability, human rights and the judiciary, we confine ourselves to a detailed account of four broad areas as illustrative examples.[67]

Human Rights

Judicial activism in the area of human rights has been facilitated in considerable measure by PIL. This is exemplified by the Court's active concern with the rights of detenus and undertrials, police excesses including arbitrary arrests, custodial violence and extra-judicial killings, conditions in prisons and other custodial institutions like children's homes, women's homes, mental asylums, encounter killings in Punjab, and the rights of victims of crime.

In the early years of PIL, the Court focused on the rights of prisoners and the conditions of prisons. The Court acted upon postcards, letters, articles in newspapers, press reports, and petitions from a wide cross-section of citizens including lawyers and journalists to open the doors of the Courts to the millions of undertrials living in inhuman conditions in the country's prisons. First, the Court would convert the facts brought before it into a petition under Article 32. It would then issue directions to the state agency concerned to provide information, and if this was not forthcoming, it would appoint a commissioner to elicit the facts. Once convinced that the matter required its intervention, the Court would issue a mandamus to state agencies to carry out its directives within a specified time-frame. This would include release of persons unlawfully detained, ensuring the closure of their cases if found to be pending for an unduly long time, and even directing that the detenus be compensated and rehabilitated. The Court also took the opportunity to give directions to state agencies to minimize further violations of human rights.

In the first PIL on prisoners' rights, *Hussainara Khatoon v State of Bihar (I to VI)*,[68] the attention of the Court was drawn to the incredible situation of Bihar undertrials who had been detained pending trial for periods far in excess of the maximum sentence for the offences they were charged with. The Court not only proceeded to make the right to speedy trial the central issue of the case but passed an order of general release of undertrials who had undergone detention beyond such maximum period.

In a landmark judgement in *D.K. Basu v State of West Bengal*,[69] the Court acted upon a letter petition in August 1986 by the Chairman of the Legal Aid Services, West Bengal, which drew attention to the repeated instances of custodial deaths in West Bengal. In this case the Court laid down the procedure to be followed by the police on the arrest of a person. It said:

Police is, no doubt, under a legal duty and has a legitimate right to arrest a criminal and to interrogate him during the investigation of an offence but the law does not permit use of third degree methods or torture of the accused in custody during interrogation and investigation with a view to solve the crime. End cannot justify the means.... No society can permit it.[70]

The Court further mandated that a relative of the arrested must be promptly notified and that police stations must prominently display the basic rights available to a detainee. The Court made it clear that failure to comply with this direction would be punishable as contempt of Court.

The early PILs had witnessed the award of compensation by the Court to victims of human rights violations.[71] Later, in a custodial death case,[72] the Court explained the jurisprudential basis for the award of compensation in writ jurisdiction as a remedy for constitutional tort. These principles were authoritatively reiterated in *D.K. Basu's* case where the Court declared that:

Award of compensation for established infringement of the indefeasible rights guaranteed under Article 21 is a remedy available in public law since the purpose of public law is not only to civilize public power but also to assure the citizens that they live under a legal system wherein their rights and interests shall be protected and preserved.[73]

During the troubled years of militancy in the state of Punjab there were several instances of encounter killings, some of which came to be examined in the Supreme Court. In September 1991, it directed the investigation of the encounter killings in Pilibhit by the Central Bureau of Investigation.[74] The killing of lawyers practising in the Punjab and Haryana High Court during this period formed the subject matter of two PILs and resulted in the Supreme Court directing a CBI investigation and payment of compensation to the families of the victims.[75] In another PIL, on the basis of the CBI report which established that seventeen Punjab police personnel had been responsible for a custodial death, the Court awarded compensation of Rs 2 lakhs to the parents of a victim.[76]

The concern of the Court has also extended to the victims of crime. In *Delhi Domestic Working Women's Forum v Union of India*,[77] the Court was concerned with the rape of innocent tribal girls by Army *jawans* in a moving train between Ranchi and Delhi and ordered an ex-gratia payment of Rs 10,000 to each of the victims. The Court recognized the trauma of the rape victims and set out the parameters for providing legal assistance to them at various stages.

The Judiciary

Under the scheme of the Constitution, issues concerning appointment and transfer of judges, their terms and conditions of service and their removal were initially thought to be predominantly within the domain of Parliament and the executive. In a series of PILs, the Supreme Court has, however, articulated a dominant role for the judiciary in this area. *S.P. Gupta v Union of India*[78] was a PIL by a senior advocate practising in Allahabad. It challenged the transfer of judges from one high court to another. The Supreme Court declared that the executive had the final say in the matter of appointment of judges to the high courts and the Supreme Court. More than a decade later, pursuant to a PIL filed by another lawyer, the correctness of this declaration was referred to a larger Bench.[79] The resultant decision in *Supreme Court Advocates-on-Record Association (SCAORA) v Union of India*[80] saw a larger Bench of the Supreme Court reverse the view in *S.P. Gupta* and declare that the word 'consultation' occurring in Article 124(3) of the Constitution should be read to mean 'concurrence', thereby vesting the Chief Justice of India with the final say in the matter of appointments. The Court added that the power so vested in the judiciary would be exercised through a collegium consisting of the Chief Justice of India and his two most senior colleagues.[81] There is considerable controversy about whether the Court has not amended the language of the Article by purporting to interpret it. In yet another PIL, again by an advocate, the Court explained its ruling in *SCAORA* and held that the decision to transfer a judge was not justiciable except on the ground of procedural impropriety in the consultation process, and then again only at the instance of the affected judge.[82]

The events leading up to the unique impeachment motion for the removal of Justice V. Ramaswami of the Supreme Court witnessed a number of PILs. Pursuant to a notice given by 108 Members of Parliament, the Speaker of the Ninth Lok Sabha constituted a committee of three judges under the Judges (Inquiry) Act, 1968 to inquire into the allegations against the judge. With the dissolution of the Ninth Lok Sabha, the government did not constitute the committee on the ground that the motion for removal had lapsed. The Sub-Committee on Judicial Accountability, an association of lawyers, questioned this in a PIL. The Supreme Court held that the motion had not lapsed.[83] It clarified that the process of removal of a judge consisted of two stages. The stage of investigation and proof of misbehaviour was amenable to judicial review. It was the second stage, which began after the misbehaviour was proved, viz., the process of discussion and voting in Parliament, which was not amenable to judicial review.

Even while the inquiry was under way, two PILs were filed by advocates Raj Kanwar and Krishna Swami seeking to question the correctness of the judgement in *Sub-Committee on Judicial Accountability (supra)* and declaring the inquiry itself to be bad in law.[84] After the inquiry concluded and the report was submitted to Parliament, the wife of the judge, Sarojini Ramaswami, filed a petition asserting the right of the judge to be supplied with a copy of the report even before Parliament could debate the motion. The Constitution Bench disposed of the wife's petition,[85] declaring the law that the judge had to be given an opportunity at the stage of showing cause why a motion against him should not be accepted and supplied with a copy of the report. However, by a separate judgement delivered on the same day, the two other PILs were dismissed[86] on the ground that the judge was not impleaded as a party. The Court reiterated its traditional perception of standing, relying on the observations in *S.P. Gupta*, to the effect that '... if the person or specific class or group of persons who are primarily injured as a result of such act or omission, do not wish to claim any relief and accept such act or omission willingly and without protest, the member of the public who complains of a secondary public injury cannot maintain the action ...'.[87]

A PIL filed by the All India Judges' Association[88] provided the opportunity for the Supreme Court to give extensive directions to the state governments on various issues concerning the appointment and functioning of the subordinate judiciary. The Court's directions have included prescribing the minimum qualifications for appointment at various levels of the subordinate judiciary,[89] provision of residential accommodation to every judicial officer, libraries, vehicles for travel, and suggesting the setting up of an All India Judicial Service.[90]

Environment

The area in which PIL's contribution has been significant is environmental law. M.C. Mehta, as a petitioner in person, was a pioneer in bringing a large number of issues to the Court concerning environmental and ecological degradation. These included the issues arising out of the leak of oleum gas from a factory in Delhi,[91] pollution in Delhi,[92] the danger to the Taj Mahal from the Mathura refinery,[93] regulation of traffic in Delhi,[94] and the degradation of the Ridge area in Delhi.[95]

The Court's engagement with these matters has resulted in activating the statutory machinery established under various environmental laws. The Court's activism in this area has, however, also attracted criticism. For instance, when the Court ordered the closure of industries, it neither heard all the industries affected nor their workmen before passing the order. This has resulted in these parties approaching the Court with a series of interlocutory applications, taking up an inordinate amount of the Court's time, even while leaving the aggrieved parties dissatisfied.[96]

The Court has also been involved in the protection of the fragile Coastal Regulation Zone[97] and regulating the growth of shrimp farms dotting the coastline.[98] The dangers of unchecked industrialization has compelled the Court to come down heavily on industry and develop the 'polluter pays' principle. This principle has been applied in the cases concerning shrimp farms,[99] tanneries,[100] chemical industries in Rajasthan[101] and Andhra Pradesh,[102] and distillery units in Tamil Nadu,[103] each of which were found discharging untreated effluents into water bodies or the soil. The Court has adopted the practice of keeping these cases on its board to effectively monitor compliance with its directions.[104] By such monitoring, the Court has ensured that a polluting unit is reopened only after it has satisfactorily installed pollution control devices. The Court has also insisted on reparations at the cost of the pollutant and restoration of the damaged environment.

The other principle the Court has evolved is the 'precautionary principle' which enjoins the State to anticipate the dangers of the use of hazardous technology. In *Vellore Citizens Welfare Forum v Union of India*,[105] the Court was dealing with the problem of pollution caused by over 900 tanneries operating in five districts of Tamil Nadu. The Court noticed that the leather industry was a major foreign exchange earner and Tamil Nadu's export of finished leather accounted for 80 per cent of the country's export of that commodity. Nevertheless, the Court pointed out that the leather industry 'has no right to destroy the ecology, degrade the environment and pose a health hazard. It cannot be permitted to expand or even continue with the present production unless it tackles by itself the problem of pollution created by the said industry'.[106] The Court then drew on the concept of sustainable development, balancing ecology and development, which had become part of customary international law. Among the essential features of sustainable development are the 'Precautionary Principle' and the 'Polluter Pays Principle'. The Precautionary Principle meant that the environmental measures taken by the state authorities 'must anticipate, prevent and attack the causes of environmental degradation'.[107] Where there are threats of serious and irreversible damage, lack of scientific certainty should not be used as a reason for postponing measures to prevent environmental degradation. The onus of proof was on the actor or industrialist to show that this action was environmentally sound. The Court pointed out that these principles had been accepted as part of the environmental law of the country.[108] The Court gave extensive directions, including a direction to the central government to constitute an authority under section 3(3) of the Environment (Protection) Act, 1986. Each polluting industry was asked to pay a 'Pollution Fine' of Rs 10,000, which was to be kept under a separate 'Environment Protection Fund', to be utilized to compensate the affected persons as identified by the authorities and also for restoration of the damaged environment. The units which were shut down by the Court would be permitted to reopen only after they had set up effluent treatment plants to the satisfaction of the Pollution Control Board after obtaining its consent. The Court further directed that the matter be dealt with by the Madras High Court by a special Bench, to be known as *The Green Bench*.[109]

The Court undertook a similar exercise in relation to the pollution caused to the soil and ground water in a village in Jodhpur by five chemical industries which had been discharging untreated effluents into the soil.[110] The Court in this case resurrected the rule of strict liability earlier laid down in the *Oleum Gas Leak* case[111] and declared that once an activity was found to be hazardous, the person engaged in it was liable to make good the loss caused irrespective of whether or not he had taken reasonable care when engaged in it.[112] The Court through a series of orders has also sought to ensure the supply of lead-free petrol through retail outlets in four major cities[113] or deregistering old cars and compelling car manufacturers to switch over to higher internationally approved standards of manufacture.[114]

While the courts have enforced pollution standards and sometimes even improved on them in PILs, their orders have given rise to issues involving workers' rights. Whenever a polluting industry is shut down the people dependent on the industry, like the workmen and their families, are directly affected and are very often not heard before the closure is ordered. In Delhi alone, this has happened in the closure of the Idgah slaughterhouse,[115] the relocation of polluting industrial units in Delhi,[116] and removal of encroachments on the Ridge area of Delhi.[117] Similarly, in seeking to strictly implement the Forest Act and the Wildlife Protection Act,[118] the interest of the tribal population affected by such orders may not have been taken into account.

In this area, the Court may not so much be laying down new policy as prodding the government into implementing environmentally safe measures in order to curb pollution.

Public Accountability

Another area of abiding public concern which the Supreme Court has dealt with in PILs is good governance and the accountability of public officials. The trust reposed in persons holding public positions and exercising public power is belied when discretion is exercised irregularly and sometimes even for collateral considerations. These acts of misdemeanour get exposed through what have now been termed as 'scams'. The Supreme Court has played a major role in not only unearthing scams but also carrying the discovery of such facts to their logical conclusion. The Court has ensured that persons exercising discretion in the distribution of public largesse, whether it is petrol pumps or government accommodation, are accountable for their actions.

The problem of the discretionary quota vested in the minister concerned for allotment of petrol pumps and oil and gas dealerships first surfaced in a PIL filed by the Centre for Public Interest Litigation.[119] The Supreme Court requested the Attorney-General to submit draft guidelines and then set them down in its judgement as norms that would govern all future allotments of dealerships under the discretionary quota on compassionate grounds. The issue again surfaced in the Supreme Court in a PIL filed by Common Cause. Here the Court, on examining the records with the government, found many officials in the office of Captain Satish Sharma, the then Minister of State for Petroleum and Gas, or their relatives had been allotted petrol pump and gas agencies out of his discretionary quota. The Court found that

all the 15 allotments have been made by the Minister in a stereotyped manner. The applications have not been officially received by the Petroleum Ministry ... The applicants seem to have approached the Minister directly ... There is no indication in the allotment orders or anywhere in the record to show that the Minister kept any guidelines in view while making these allotments.... the allotments of petrol pumps were made in an arbitrary and discriminatory manner.[120]

The Court quashed the fifteen allotments. After issuing a show cause notice to Satish Sharma and hearing him, the Court directed that he pay a sum of fifty lakh rupees as exemplary damages to the exchequer. Further, the police was asked to register a case and initiate prosecution against him for criminal breach of trust.

The aftermath of this decision must also be noticed. The cancellation of allotments by the Supreme Court has been followed by a series of cancellations of similar allotments by the Delhi High Court. However, two years later, the other directions were reviewed by a different Bench of three judges.[121] The Court found that although the conduct of Captain Satish Sharma in making allotments of petrol outlets was 'atrocious'[122] and reflected 'a wanton exercise of power by the petitioner',[123] it fell short of 'misfeasance in public office' and therefore 'there was no occasion to award exemplary damages'.[124]

In the matter of out-of-turn allotment of government accommodation, the Court, in a PIL by an advocate, found that Sheila Kaul while serving as a Union Minister for Urban Development had allotted two shops to her grandsons, one to the maidservant of her son, one to the handloom manager of the firm owned by her son-in-law, another to a close friend, and one to the nephew of the minister of state in the same ministry. Likewise, using her discretionary power, she had allotted stalls to relatives and friends of her personal staff and officials of the Directorate of Estates. Here again, the Court quashed the allotments[125] and eventually directed her to pay a sum of sixty lakh rupees as exemplary damages to the government exchequer.[126]

Another PIL was filed by a journalist, Vineet Narain and three others, including two advocates, seeking directions to the Central Bureau of Investigation (CBI) to investigate allegations of bribe given by the Jain brothers to several high-ranking politicians and bureaucrats in return for favours in the award of government contracts. The petition, filed in 1993, pointed out that although the CBI had gathered evidence in 1991, it was not proceeding with the case since the persons involved held high positions in public life. The seizure of the diaries from the Jain brothers had led to the discovery of financial support to them by clandestine and illegal means, by use of tainted funds obtained through *hawala* transactions. This in turn disclosed a nexus between politicians, bureaucrats, and criminals who were all recipients of money from unlawful sources given for unlawful consideration.

After satisfying itself that the matter merited examination, the Court gave a series of directions to ensure that the investigation by the CBI proceeded to its logical conclusion. The Court declared that

it is of utmost public importance that this matter is examined thoroughly by this Court to ensure that all government agencies, entrusted with the duty to discharge their functions and obligations in accordance with law, do so, bearing in mind constantly the concept of equality enshrined in the Constitution and the basic tenet of rule of law: 'Be you ever so high, the law is above you'. Investigation into every accusation made against each and every person on a reasonable basis, irrespective of the position and status of that person, must be conducted and completed expeditiously. This is imperative to retain public confidence in the impartial working of the government agencies.[127]

The continuous monitoring of the case through a series of orders[128] resulted in thirty-four charge sheets being filed against fifty-four persons. Although the purpose of the proceedings came to an end with the filing of these charge-sheets, the Court issued a detailed order concerning the constitution and control of the investigating agencies. The Court felt that 'no doubt, the overall control of the agencies and responsibility of their functioning has to be in the executive, but then a scheme giving the needed insulation from extraneous influences even of the controlling executive, is imperative'.[129] The Court examined the validity of a 'single directive' under which there had to be prior sanction of the designated authority in the government before the CBI could even commence any proceeding against higher-ranking officers of the government, public sector undertakings, and nationalized banks. The Court struck down the 'single directive' as interfering with the independent functioning of the CBI. The Court also issued directions under which the Central Vigilance Commission (CVC) would be given statutory status and would be responsible for the efficient functioning of the CBI. Similar directions were issued in respect of the Enforcement Directorate, the nodal prosecution agency.[130]

Issues and Controversies

The Law and Policy Divide: Where do we draw the line?

The framers of the Indian Constitution did not incorporate a strict doctrine of separation of powers but envisaged a system of checks and balances. Policy-making and implementation of policy are conventionally regarded as the exclusive domain of the executive and the legislature, with judiciary enforcing the law. The Supreme Court has itself recognized that 'the Indian Constitution has not indeed recognized the doctrine of separation of powers in its absolute rigidity but the functions of the different parts or branches of the government have been sufficiently differentiated and consequently it can very well be said that our Constitution does not contemplate assumption, by one organ or part of the State, of functions that essentially belong to another'.[131] The power of judicial review cannot be used by the Court to 'usurp or abdicate the powers of other organs'.[132]

In the development of our writ jurisdiction, derived from the English Common Law and the principles of judicial review, the Court is primarily concerned with the decision-making process and not the decision itself. The Court has reiterated that matters of policy would be a bar to the Court's interference. PIL in practice, however, tends to narrow the divide between the role of the various organs of government, and has invited controversy principally for this reason. The Court has sometimes even obliterated the distinction between law and policy. The approach of the Court in policy matters is to ask whether the implementation or non-implementation of the policy results in a violation of fundamental rights. Where it does, the Court may interdict the violation, and issue orders accordingly. In *M.C. Mehta v Union of India*,[133] the Court explained how, despite the enactment of the Environment (Protection) Act, 1986, there had been a considerable decline in the quality of the environment. The Court noted that despite several PILs 'the required attention does not appear to have been paid by the authorities concerned to take the steps necessary for the discharge of duty imposed on the State ... Any further delay in the performance of duty by the Central Government cannot, therefore, be permitted. Suitable directions by the Court to require performance of its duty by the Central Government are mandated by the law and have, therefore, now to be given.'[134] The Court, however, required the central government to indicate what steps it had taken thus far and also place before it the national policy, if any, drawn up for the protection of the environment.

In the matter relating to forests, in *T.N. Godavarman Tirumulkpad v Union of India*,[135] the Court constituted an expert committee to examine the issue of depletion of forest cover, and to consider questions such as who could be permitted to use forest produce and in what circumstances this was permissible. The Court imposed restrictions on the felling of trees and the sale of timber. In an exercise of 'continuing mandamus' it closely monitored the implementation of its orders.[136]

A writ petition in 1985 filed by M.C. Mehta related to proper management and control of vehicular traffic in Delhi. It was suddenly activated on 20 November 1997[137] by the Supreme Court after a large number of children died when a school bus plunged into the river Yamuna. The Court justified its directions to the government to prescribe speed limits and mandate the installation of speed control devices on the ground of executive inaction when it found that although the provisions of the Motor Vehicles Act, 1988 were adequate, they had not been exercised.

The law and policy divide was obliterated in *Vishaka v State of Rajasthan*,[138] which was a PIL concerning sexual harassment of women at the workplace. A significant feature of this decision was the Court's readiness to step in where the legislature had not. The Court declared that till the legislature enacted a law consistent with the Convention on the Elimination of All Forms of Discrimination against Women, which India was obliged to do as a signatory, the guidelines set out by the Court in *Vishaka*, adopting the Convention, would be enforceable.

However, in the *Delhi Science Forum v Union of India*,[139] where the Government of India's telecommunication policy was challenged by a PIL, the Court refused to interfere with the matter on the ground that it concerned a question of policy. Likewise, PILs that have sought prohibition of the sale of liquor,[140] or for the recognition of a particular language as a national language,[141] or for the introduction of a uniform civil code[142] have been rejected on the ground that these were matters of policy.

The Court may refuse to entertain a PIL if it finds that the issues raised are not within the judicial ambit or capacity. Thus, a petition seeking directions to the central government to preserve and protect the Gyanvapi Masjid and the Vishwanath temple at Varanasi as well as the Krishna temple and Idgah at Mathura was rejected. The Court said: 'the matter is eminently one for appropriate evaluation and action by the executive, and may not have an adjucative disposition or judicially manageable standards as the pleadings now stand'.[143]

In the *Tehri Bandh Virodhi Sangarsh Samiti* case[144] the Court stated that it did

not possess the requisite expertise to render any final opinion on the rival contentions of the experts. In our opinion the Court can only investigate and adjudicate the question as to whether the Government was conscious to the inherent danger as pointed out by the petitioners and applied its mind to the safety of the dam. We have already given facts in detail, which show that the Government has considered the question on several occasions in the light of the opinions expressed by the experts. The Government was satisfied with the report of the experts and only thereafter clearance has been given to the project.

Despite such observations, the Court has not adopted a uniform and consistent approach in dealing with its emerging role as a policy-maker. While in some cases, the Court has expressed its reluctance to step into the legislative field, in others it has laid down detailed guidelines and explicitly formulated policy. The former approach was taken by the Court when dealing with the question of ragging of students in medical colleges. The Court overturned the high court's direction to the state government to introduce anti-ragging legislation. The Supreme Court held:[145]

The direction given by the Division Bench was really nothing short of an indirect attempt to compel the State Government to initiate legislation with a view to curbing the evil of ragging. ... It is entirely a matter for the executive branch of the Government to decide whether or not to introduce any particular legislation. If the executive is not carrying out any duty laid upon it by the Constitution or the law, the Court can certainly require the executive to carry out such duty and this is precisely what the Court does when it entertains public interest litigation.... But at the same time the Court cannot usurp the functions assigned to the executive and the legislature under the Constitution and it cannot even indirectly require the executive to introduce a particular legislation or the legislature to pass it or assume to itself a supervisory role over the law making activities of the executive and the legislature.

This view notwithstanding, the more recent trend, however, is for the Court to assert its new role as policy-maker, as the decision in *Vishaka*[146] demonstrates.

In the case of adoption of children by foreign nationals[147] and custodial torture,[148] similar guidelines were laid down. In a case dealing with vehicular pollution too, the Court stipulated the time-frame for enforcement of international pollution norms.[149] In the *Hawala* case,[150] the Court concerned itself with establishing a mechanism for the supervision of the CBI and the grant of statutory status to the office of the Central Vigilance Commissioner.

Problems of Procedure

The flexibility of procedure that is a characteristic of PIL has given rise to another set of problems. The Court, which operates in an adversarial framework, bound as it is by rules and by the pleadings of the parties concerned before it, requires delineation of issues in a legally manageable form. One method by which the Court has tackled this is to require the amicus curiae appointed by it to file, on the basis of a letter petition, a properly constituted writ petition.[151] This gives an opportunity to the opposite parties to ascertain the precise allegation and to respond to specific issues. The PIL relating to the depletion of forest cover is a case in point.[152] The petition, as originally drafted and presented, pertained to the arbitrary felling of Khair trees in Jammu & Kashmir. The PIL has now been enlarged by the Court to encompass all forests throughout India. Individual states, therefore, will not be able to respond to the original pleadings as such, since it may not concern them at all.

The reports given by court-appointed commissioners raise problems regarding their evidentiary value. No court can found its decisions on facts unless they are proved according to law. This implies the right of an adversary to test them by cross-examination or at least counter affidavits. Generally, even the reports of judges given under the Commission of Inquiry Act, 1952 are not proof of their contents.[153] Indeed, in at least one instance, the Court did not permit even counter affidavits to be filed in response to NEERI's report, making it difficult for individual parties affected to set out their own case.[154] In such instances the affected parties may have misgivings about the role of the Court, however well meaning, in championing a particular cause.

Some procedural questions about the epistolary jurisdiction are the subject matter of a pending PIL, *Sudipt Majumdar v State of Madhya Pradesh*.[155] Even while these questions remain to be answered, the Court has been attentive to the issues they raise. In 1996–7, Chief Justice J.S. Verma constituted a committee to prepare draft rules on PIL for general guidance and for maintenance of uniformity.[156]

It is a basic postulate of the rule of law that the law must be certain and not become vulnerable to the predilections of individual judges, however well meaning. In the area of PIL, the differences in the perceptions of individual judges of the Supreme Court are clearly discernible. The opinion of Justice Pathak, as he then was, in *Bandhua Mukti Morcha*[157] underscored the importance of treating the Court as a single institution with one voice rather than an assemblage of individual judges.

The Resistance of Legislators

In the political arena too, the debate over the limits of judicial activism, particularly in the area of PIL, has been vigorous. The attempt by the judiciary through PILs to enter the area of policy-making and policy implementation has caused concern in political circles. A private member's bill, entitled 'Public Interest Litigation (Regulation) Bill, 1996', was tabled in the Rajya Sabha. The Statement of Objects and Reasons stated that while the objective of PIL, particularly those intended to benefit the poorer sections of society was laudable, it was being misused. Moreover, PIL cases were being given priority over other cases, which had remained pending in the courts for years. It was urged that if a PIL petition failed or was shown to be mala fide, the petitioner should be 'put behind bars and pay the damages'.[158] Although the Bill lapsed, the debate in Parliament revealed some of the criticism and suspicion that PIL had begun to attract.

The Problem of Unpredictability: Judicial introspection

The emergence of PIL over the last twenty years has been a salutary development towards providing the vast majority of citizens with access to justice and effective protection of their fundamental rights. PIL has emerged as a powerful tool capable of fulfilling the promises that the Constitution held out. In the words of Chief Justice A.M. Ahmadi, PIL 'is a case of citizens finding new ways of expressing their concern for events occurring at the national level and exerting their involvement in the democratic process'.[159]

However, the credibility of the PIL process is now adversely affected by the criticism that the judiciary is overstepping the boundaries of its jurisdiction and that it is unable to supervise the effective implementation of its orders. It has also been increasingly felt that PIL is being misused by people agitating for private grievances in the garb of public interest and seeking publicity rather than espousing public causes.

The judiciary has itself recognized and articulated these concerns periodically. Many of the issues that have come up before the Court by way of PIL are highly technical, involving complex questions of policy-making, financial support for development projects, and industrial development. In addition to the perception of the judiciary as an institution that does not enjoy a democratic mandate, this criticism also focuses on the lack of expertise in the judiciary to deal with such complex and technical policy issues.

Judges have recognized that they have to act with circumspection. The concern was voiced by Pathak J (as he then was) as follows:[160]

Where the Court embarks upon affirmative action in the attempt to remedy a constitutional imbalance within the social order, few critics will find fault with it so long as it confines itself to the scope of its legitimate authority. But there is always the possibility, in public interest litigation, of succumbing to the temptation of crossing into territory which properly pertains to the Legislature or to the executive Government ... In the process of correcting executive error or removing legislative omission the Court can so easily find itself involved in policy making of a quality and to a degree characteristic of political authority, and indeed run the risk of being mistaken for one.

The judge particularly emphasized the need for predictability in the following words:[161]

There is great merit in the Court proceeding to decide an issue on the basis of strict legal principle and avoiding carefully the influence of purely emotional appeal. For that alone gives the decision of the Court a direction which is certain, and unfaltering, and that especial permanence in legal jurisprudence which makes it a base for the next step forward in the further progress of the law. Indeed, both certainty of substance and certainty of direction are indispensable requirements in the development of the law, and invest it with the credibility which commands public confidence in its legitimacy. This warning is of especial significance in these times, during a phase of judicial history when a few social action groups tend to show evidence of presuming that in every case the Court must bend and mould its decision to popular notions of which way a case should be decided.

The present Chief Justice, Dr A.S. Anand, has cautioned against what he termed 'judicial adventurism':[162]

With a view to see that judicial activism does not become 'judicial adventurism' and lead a Judge going in pursuit of his own notions of justice and beauty, ignoring the limits of law, the bounds of his jurisdiction and the binding precedents, it is necessary and essential that 'public interest litigation' which is taken recourse to for reaching justice to those who are for a variety of reasons unable to approach the Court to protect their fundamental rights should develop on a consistent and firm path. The Courts must be careful to see that by their overzealousness they do not cause any uncertainty or confusion either through their observations during the hearing of a case or through their written verdicts. ... The Courts have the duty of implementing the constitutional safeguards that protect individual rights but they cannot push back the limits of the Constitution to accommodate the challenged violation. All it means is that Judges are expected to be circumspect and self-disciplined in the discharge of their judicial functions.

A further concern is that as the judiciary enters into the policy-making arena it will have to fashion new remedies and mechanisms for ensuring effective compliance with its orders. A judicial system can suffer no greater lack of credibility than a perception that its order can be flouted with impunity. Justice S.P. Bharucha of the Supreme Court has expressed this concern as follows:[163]

This Court must refrain from passing orders that cannot be enforced, whatever the fundamental right may be and however good the cause. It serves no purpose to issue some high profile mandamus or declaration that can remain only on paper. It is counter productive to have people say, 'The Supreme Court has not been able to do anything' or worse. It is of cardinal importance to the confidence that people have in the Court that its orders are implicitly and promptly obeyed and it is, therefore, of cardinal importance that orders that are incapable of obedience and enforcement are not made.

Problem of Abuse of Process
Responding to the general criticism that PIL is being misused, the Court has in several decisions expressed its concern and suggested a possible corrective mechanism. In *Sachidanand Pandey v State of West Bengal*,[164] Khalid J observed;

If courts do not restrict the free flow of such cases in the name of public interest litigation, the traditional litigation will suffer and the courts of law, instead of dispensing justice, will have to take upon themselves administrative and executive functions.

Likewise, in *Raunaq International Ltd v I.V.R. Construction Ltd*,[165] which incidentally was not a PIL, it was observed:

When a petition is filed as a public litigation ... the Court must satisfy itself that the party which has brought the litigation is litigating bona fide for public good. The public interest litigation should not be merely a cloak for attaining private ends of a third party or of the party bringing the petition. ... Even when a public interest litigation is entertained the Court must be careful to weigh conflicting public interest before intervening. Intervention by the Court may ultimately result in delay in the execution of the project.

In a recent case,[166] the Court, while dismissing an ostensible PIL against the sale of a plot of land through public auction, held that the matter had not been raised in public interest at all, but to ventilate a private grievance. It observed:[167]

The directions and commands issued by the courts of law in a public interest litigation are for the betterment of the society at large and not for benefiting any individual. But if the Court finds that in the garb of a public interest litigation actually an individual's interest is sought to be carried out or protected it would be the bounden duty of the Court not to entertain such petition as otherwise the very purpose of innovation of public interest litigation will be frustrated.

Conclusion

While traditional lawyers have been critical about departure from the mould of adversarial litigation with its precise pleadings and procedure, and while politicians have been uneasy about judicial encroachment into the area of policy-making, the public by and large have welcomed the intercession of the Court through PIL. This is because of a general perception that the legislature is unwilling to take prompt remedial measures and the executive is unwilling even to enforce the existing law. Despite the problems of judicial predictability and the feeling that the constitutional balance may be affected, it has to be acknowledged that the far-reaching judgements in cases like the Bhagalpur blindings,[168] the Bihar undertrial case,[169] and the mentally ill in jail[170] have provided desperately needed relief and exposed executive failings. PIL has also helped in the development of legal principles such as the 'polluter pays' principle,[171] the 'precautionary' principle,[172] and the principle of award of compensation for constitutional wrongs.[173]

Bearing in mind the power and importance of PIL in making the Constitution a living reality for a large number of citizens, it is important to view these criticisms as indicators of the safeguards and checks that the Court must now build into its PIL jurisprudence. To allow public perception against PIL to fester would erode its credibility and that of the judiciary itself. In the words of Chief Justice J.S. Verma:[174]

The need is to prevent misuse of PIL and not to criticise the process. And this is what the Courts will have to do so that misuse of PIL is prevented and proper use of it has not to be blunted. Every innovation takes time to get into proper shape. Any attempt to curb it would be to throw the baby with the bath water. It is primarily for the Courts who devised this procedure to practise self-restraint and to also devise proper checks and balances to ensure that even persons who want to misuse it are not able to do so.

In many ways PIL imposes a burden on as well as poses a temptation for the judge. On the one hand there is the desire to resolve the problems of a society where laws are not seen to be enforced, particularly where the petitioner before the Court is espousing a public and not a private cause. On the other hand, there is the temptation for a well-meaning judge to extend the law, if necessary, by a policy decision, departing ever so slightly from the trodden path. Thus, there is an interplay of enforcing the law, moulding it by equity while also responding to the perception of 'an imperial judiciary' making history. The future of PIL will depend much on where the Court strikes the balance between the law, and its sense of history.

Notes

* We wish to thank Anuradha Bindra and Prateek Jalan, advocates, for their assistance.
[1] *Bandhu Mukti Morcha v Union of India* (1984) 3 SCC 161 at 188.
[2] Granville Austin, *The Indian Constitution: The Conerstone of a Nation*, Oxford University Press, New Delhi, 1999, p. 50.
[3] *A.K. Gopalan v State of Madras* (1950) SCR 88 at 286–7.
[4] *Golak Nath v State of Punjab* (1967) 2 SCR 762.
[5] *Kesavananda Bharati v State of Kerala* (1973) 4 SCC 225.
[6] 'No person shall be deprived of his life or personal liberty except according to procedure established by law.'
[7] In *A.K. Gopalan* Justice Das illustrated the point of procedural due process by citing the type of statute which could be passed by the English Parliament, namely that the Bishop of Rochester's cook be boiled to death (*supra* n. 3 at 320).
[8] *Maneka Gandhi v Union of India* (1978) 2 SCC 248.
[9] Delcared by the President under Article 352 of the Constitution on the advice of the Prime Minister Indira Gandhi and in force between 26 June 1975 and 21 March 1977 (see Basu's *Commentary on the Constitution of India*, Vol. N., 1988, 198 and 202).

[10] (1976) 2 SCC 521.

[11] C.K. Allen, *Law and Orders*, 3rd edn, 256, while commenting on *Liversidge v Anderson* 1942 AC 206.

[12] Then in the Gujarat High Court.

[13] Reproduced in Jagga Kapur (ed.), *Supreme Gourt on Public Interest Litigation*, Vol. I, SCALE, A-43 at A-53.

[14] Then in the Kerala High Court.

[15] *Report of the Expert Committee on Legal Aid: Processual Justice to the People*, May 1973, 208–10. Thereafter Justice Krishna Iyer developed this theme in *Mumbai Kamgar Sabha v Abdulbhai* were he said: 'Test litigation, representative actions, pro bono publico and like broadened form of legal proceedings are in keeping with the current accent on justice to the common man.' ((1976) 3 SCC 832 at 857)

[16] *Report on National Judicare: Equal Justice–Social Justice*, August 1977, 128. Also see *People's Union for Democratic Rights v Union of India* (1982) 3 SCC 235 at 240.

[17] Ibid.

[18] *M.C. Mehta v Union of India* (1987) 1 SCC 395 at 405.

[19] This is brought out in the film *Aakrosh* by Govind Nihalani, in which the accused is too afraid to speak to even the well-meaning lawyer provided to him.

[20] *Charanjit Lal v Union of India* (1950) SCR 869; *D. Nagaraj v State of Karnataka* (1977) 2 SCC 148.

[21] (1980) 4 SCC 162 at 163. Incidentally, this was a unique instance of section 166 of the Criminal Procedure Code, 1973 being invoked by public-spirited persons to seek redress against an apathetic municipality remiss in providing civic amentites.

[22] H.M. Seervai, *Constitutional Law of India*, 4th edn, Vol. I, 1381–2, N.M. Tripathi, Bombay, 1991. One of the co-authors who appeared for the petitioner recalls that even though the first petitioner was an architect, a politician, and an MP, yet he had to make a bid for purchase of the land being offered for sale to be assured of his standing.

[23] *S.P. Gupta v Union of India* 1981 Supp. SCC 87 at 210. See also *People's Union for Democratic Rights Case*, *supra* n. 16; *Forward Construction Co. v Prabhat Mandal* (1986) 1 SCC 100.

[24] *Bandhua Mukti Morcha v Union of India* (1984) 3 SCC 161 at 186.

[25] *R.K. Garg v Unior. of India* (1981) 4 SCC 675.

[26] *Dr Shiva Rao Shantaram Ram Wagle v Union of India* (1988) 2 SCC 115.

[27] *Sheela Barse v Union of India* (1983) 2 SCC 96.

[28] *Janata Dal v H.S. Chowdhary* (1992) 4 SCC 305.

[29] *Janata Dal v H.S. Chowdhary* (1991) 3 SCC 756 at 768. This was followed in *Simranjit Singh Mann v Union of India* (1992) 4 SCC 653 and *Karamjeet Singh v Union of India* (1992) 4 SCC 666.

[30] *Panchhi v State of U.P.* (1988) 1 SCC 177.

[31] Ibid. at 180.

[32] *R.K. Jain v Union of India* (1993) 4 SCC 119.

[33] *Bandhua Mukti Morcha case*, *supra* n. 2 at 186.

[34] *Janata Dal case*, *supra* n. 28 at 349.

[35] In *Subhash Kumar v State of Bihar* (1991) 1 SCC 598 at 598–605, the Supreme Court observed that a person to satisfy a personal grudge or enmity could not invoke PIL. See also *Ramsharan Autyanuprashi v Union of India* (1989) Supp 1 SCC 251 and *Chhetriya Pardushan Mukti Sangharsh Samiti v State of UP* (1990) 4 SCC 449.

[36] (1963) 372 U.S. 335.

[37] *Supra* n. 23.

[38] As in *Ram Kumar Misra v State of Bihar* (1984) 2 SCC 451. This case related to minimum wages not being paid to labourers employed in two ferries.

[39] As in *Paramjit Kaur v State of Punjab* (1996) 7 SCC 20, where the CBI at the instance of the Supreme Court unearthed the facts of the mass cremation of thousands of persons by the Punjab Police by labelling them 'unidentified'. The proceedings began with a telegram being sent to the residence of Kuldip Singh J.

[40] *Supra* n. 1 at 229.

[41] (1980) 3 SCC 488. This was a PIL concerning the rights of prisoners to humane treatment within prison walls.

[42] (1983) 2 SCC 308. This was a PIL concerning the functioning of the Agra Protective Home, constituted under the Immoral Traffic (Prevention) Act, 1956, to shelter and rehabilitate women rescued from prostitution.

[43] (1982) 2 SCC 583. This concerned the plight of mentally ill locked away in the jails of Bihar.

[44] (1982) SCC 253. This concerned the payment of minimum wages to construction labour engaged in building stadia and flyovers for the Asian Games in Delhi in 1982.

[45] The full text of this notification is set out in Sangeeta Ahuja, *People, Law and Justice: Cases and Materials on PIL,* Orient Longman, Delhi, 1996, Vol. II, 860.

[46] A mention must be made of the Official Secrets Act 1923 under which it may not be possible for any member of the public to access information which the government regards as being a secret for various reasons. However, barring an exceptional situation where the government may claim privilege, the Courts can always require the former to provide the necessary information either to it directly or to its Commissioners.

[47] A district judge was appointed in *Kamaladevi Chattopadhyay v State of Punjab* (1985) 1 SCC 41 to report on the women and children detained in Ludhiana jails.

[48] Krishan Mahajan of the *Indian Express* was appointed Commissioner along with Upendra Baxi, Law Professor in *Gulshan v Zila Parishad* (1987) Supp SCC 619.

[49] V.C. Mahajan and R.K. Jain were appointed Commissioners in *Gaurav Jain v Union of India* (1990) Supp. SCC 709. R.K. Jain and Indira Jaising were appointed as Commissioners in *M.C. Mehta v State of Tamil Nadu* (child labour case) (1996) 6 SCC 756. Gopal Subramanium was appointed Commissioner in *Sheela Barse v Union of India* 1994 (4) SCALE 493, to visit Assam and carry out the orders of the Court in regard to the release of the mentally ill held in the jails there.

[50] Dr Srinivasa Murthy, Professor of Psychiatry and Dr Amita Dhandha, Assistant Professor of Law were appointed Commissioners to visit jails in West Bengal and report on the mentally ill held there in *Sheela Barse v Union of India* (1993) 4 SCC 204 at 215.

[51] Dr L. Misra Joint Secretary, Government of India, was appointed Commissioner in *Bandhua Mukti Morcha* case, *supra* n. 1.

[52] In *Sheela Barse v State of Maharashtra* (1983) 2 SCC 96, the Director of Social Work, Nirmala Niketan, Bombay was appointed to investigate the ill-treatment of women prisoners. See also the committee appointed in *Rural Litigation and Entitlement Kendra v State of UP* (1985) 2 SCC 431.

[53] The Central Pollution Control Board. See *M.C. Mehta v Union of India* 1999 (4) SCALE 196.

[54] National Environmental Engineering Research Institute, Nagpur. See *S. Jagannath v Union of India* (1997) 2 SCC 87 and *In re Bhavani River–Shakti Sugars Ltd.* (1998) 6 SCC 335.

[55] (1996) 3 SCC 212. In the *Ram Kumar Misra* Case, *supra* n. 38, the Court directed the appropriate authority under the labour department of the government of Bihar to

hear the workmen and the employees and find out whether minimum wages had been paid. The authority was further empowered to direct arrears to be paid if they were due.

56 *Olga Tellis v Bombay Municipal Corporation* (1985) 3 SCC 545.

57 *Supra* n. 26.

58 *Tehri Bandh Virodhi Sangharsh Samiti v State of UP* (1992) Supp 1 SCC 44. The issue has been brought back to the Court in *N.D. Jayal v Union of India* 1999 (1) SCALE 463, and is pending.

59 *Sheela Barse v Union of India* (1988) 4 SCC 226 at 246. See also *S.P. Anand v H.D. Deve Gowda* (1996) 6 SCC 734 at 744 where the Court observed: 'In PIL cases, the Petitioner is not entitled to withdraw his petition at his sweet will unless the Court sees reasons to permit withdrawal. In granting the permission the Court would be guided by considerations of public interest and would also ensure that it does not result in abuse of processes of the law.'

60 See *State of West Bengal v Sampat Lal* (1985) 1 SCC 317. In the *Sheela Barse* case, where the Court disallowed the petitioner's prayer to withdraw the PIL, the Supreme Court Legal Aid Committee was asked to provide a lawyer to handle the petition thereafter.

61 A.K. Ganguly was the amicus curiae in *Peoples' Union for Civil Liberties v State of Tamil Nadu* 1997 (7) SCALE SP-17.

62 Dr A.M. Singhvi has been assisting the Court in *D.K. Basu v Union of India* (1997) 1 SCC 416.

63 In *T.N. Godavarman Tirumulkpad v Union of India* (1997) 2 SCC 267, the amicus curiae Harish Salve has been requested by the Court to screen all applications for intervention and it has further been directed that only he and the counsel for the Central and State Governments would be heard in the matter.

64 Kapil Sibal assisted the Court in the cases concerning out-of-turn allotments of government accommodation: *Shiv Sagar Tiwari v Union of India* (1996) 6 SCC 599. Anil B. Divan performed a similar role in *Vineet Narain v Union of India* (1998) 1 SCC 226. F.S. Nariman was amicus curiae to the Court in *Vishaka v State of Rajasthan* (1997) 6 SCC 241. K.K. Venugopal assisted the Court in one aspect of the case concerning the Narmada Dam: *Narmada Bachao Andolan v Union of India* 1999 (5) SCALE 437; 1999 (6) SCALE 571.

65 Justice J.S. Verma, 'The Constitutional Obligation of the Judiciary', R.C. Ghiya Memorial Lecture (1997) 7 SCC (Jrl.) 1 at 7.

66 (1986) 4 SCC 106 at 117.

67 For a detailed treatise on PIL cases in the High Courts and Supreme Court up to December, 1996 see Sangeeta Ahuja, *People Law and Justice*, *supra* n. 45. Also see Jagga Kapur (ed.), *Supreme Court on Public Interest Litigation*, *supra* n. 13.

68 (1980) 1 SCC 81. *Kadra Pahadiya v State of Bihar* (1981) 3 SCC 671 was another case that dealt with the issue of speedy trial. The conditions of life convicts in Tihar jail attracted the Court's concern in a petition sent to it by a prisoner. The Court introduced humaneness into the penitentiary system by requiring exceptional circumstances and adequate precautions for solitary confinement: *Sunil Batra v Delhi Admn.* (1980) 3 SCC 488. The horrific blinding of prisoners in Bhagalpur Jail in Bihar formed the subject matter of another PIL: *Anil Yadav v State of Bihar* (1981) 1 SCC 622; *Khatri(I) v State of Bihar* (1981) 1 SCC 623. In *Veena Sethi v State of Bihar* (1982) 2 SCC 583 the Court found that prisons were being used to house the mentally ill for thirty and forty years at a stretch. Corrective and preventive steps were put in motion. In *Supreme Court Legal Aid Committee Representing Undertrial Prisoners v Union of India* (1994) 6 SCC 731 the Supreme Court gave directions regarding release on bail of undertrials facing charges

under the Narcotic Drugs and Psychotropic Substances Act, 1985. The issue of handcuffing and fettering of undertrials was brought before the Supreme Court by jounalist Kuldip Nayyar. The Court reiterated its earlier directions and declared that without the prior permission of the magistrate, the authorities would not force handcuffs or other fetters on a prisoner while lodged in a jail or in transit from one jail to another or to the Court: *Citizens for Democracy v State of Assam* (1995) 3 SCC 743.

[69] *Supra* n. 62.

[70] Ibid. at 439.

[71] See *Sebastian M. Hongray v Union of India* (1984) 1 SCC 339 and *Bhim Singh v State of J&K* (1985) 4 SCC 677.

[72] *Nilabati Behera v State of Orissa* (1993) 2 SCC 746,

[73] *Supra* n. 62 at 439. The Court has been monitoring the implementation of the directions given by it in the case: see the orders in (1997) 6 SCC 642; (1998) 6 SCC 320; (1998) 7 SCC 507; 1999 (1) SCALE 465.

[74] *R.S. Sodhi v State of UP* (1994) Supp 1 SCC 143.

[75] *Punjab & Haryana High Court Bar Assn v State of Punjab* (1994) 1 SCC 616; *Navkiran Singh v State of Punjab* (1995) 4 SCC 591. The question of payment of compensation to claimants in the case of mass cremations by the Punjab police, *Paramjit Kaur, supra* n. 39 has, the Court directed, to be determined by the National Human Rights Commission.

[76] *Ranjeet Kumar v Secretary, Home, State of Punjab* 1996 (2) SCALE SP-51.

[77] 1994 (4) SCALE 608.

[78] *Supra* n. 23.

[79] *Subhash Sharma v Union of India* (1991) Supp 1 SCC 574.

[80] (1993) 4 SCC 441. The other issue in *SCAORA* was that by keeping unfilled a large number of vacancies in judges' posts the right to judicial review was being violated even while the independence of the judiciary was being challenged.

[81] This has now been expanded to include the four next senior most judges after the Chief Justice. See: *In Re Special Reference No. 1 of 1998* (1998) 7 SCC 739.

[82] *Ashok Reddy v Government of India* (1994) 2 SCC 303.

[83] *Sub-Committee on Judicial Accountability v Union of India* (1991) 4 SCC 699.

[84] *Krishna Swami v Union of India* (1992) 4 SCC 605. Krishna Swami was also an MP.

[85] *Sarojini Ramaswami v Union of India* (1992) 4 SCC 506.

[86] *Krishna Swami v Union of India, supra* n. 84. The PILs challenging the defeat of the impeachment motion in Parliament, on account of abstention by the largest party, the Congress (I), were also dismissed: *Virendra Kumar v Shivraj Patil* (1993) 4 SCC 97 and *Lily Thomas v The Speaker* (1993) 4 SCC 234.

[87] *Supra* n. 23 at 219–20.

[88] *All India Judges Association v Union of India* (1992) 1 SCC 119 and (1993) 4 SCC 288.

[89] *All India Judges' Association v Union of India* 1994 (4) SCALE 5; 1995 (2) SCALE 374; 1995 (6) SCALE 581.

[90] *All India Judges' Association v Union of India* 1995 (5) SCALE 634. The Court continues to monitor the implementation of its directions in this PIL: see Order in 1999 (2) SCALE 663.

[91] *M.C. Mehta v Union of India* (1987) 1 SCC 395.

[92] Ibid. (1996) 4 SCC 750.

[93] Ibid. (1996) 4 SCC 351 and 750.

[94] Ibid. (1997) 8 SCC 770.

[95] 1996 (1) SCALE SP-22. Mehta, who is an Advocate, has brought to the Court the issue of child labour. See *M.C. Mehta v State of Tamil Nadu* (1996) 6 SCC 756. Mehta also appears as counsel for PIL petitioners. See cases at *infra* n. 97 and 100.

[96] See the Orders in *M.C. Mehta v Union of India* (1997) 11 SCC 227, 312 and 327.

[97] *Indian Council for Enviro-Legal Action v Union of India* (1996) 5 SCC 281.

[98] *S. Jagannath v Union of India* (1997) 2 SCC 87.

[99] Ibid.

[100] *Vellore Citizens' Welfare Forum v Union of India* (1996) 5 SCC 647.

[101] *Indian Council for Enviro-Legal Action v Union of India* (1996) 3 SCC 212.

[102] Ibid. 1995 (6) SCALE 578.

[103] In Re *Bhavani River-Shakti Sugars Limited* (1998) 6 SCC 335.

[104] E.g. the PIL concerning vehicular pollution in Delhi has been listed for hearing on more than 50 occasions so far.

[105] *Supra* n. 100.

[106] Ibid. at 657.

[107] Ibid. at 658.

[108] Ibid. at 660.

[109] Similar directions were issued by the Court in relation to the pollution caused to the Nakkavagu river in Andhra Pradesh by 56 industries operating in the Patancheru Bolaram districts. The Court directed a compensation amount of Rs 1.39 crores to be paid initially by the state government which was then free to recover it from the industries. See *Indian Council for Envioro-Legal Action v Union of India* 1996 (5) SCALE 412. For a comprehensive and lucid restatement of the law on the subject, see: *AP Pollution Control Board v Prof M.V. Nayadu* 1999 (1) SCALE 140. The Court in this case requested the National Environment Appellate Authority to enquire into the factual aspects of a complaint of water and air pollution caused by an industry in Andhra Pradesh.

[110] *Indian Council for Enviro-Legal Action v Union of India, supra* n. 101.

[111] *M.C. Mehta v Union of India, supra* n. 18. Again the Court invoked the 'Polluter Pays' principle.

[112] See also: *Re Bhavani River–Sakthi Sugars Ltd.* (1998) 6 SCC 335. For orders on the closure of Shrimp farms, see *S. Jagannath v Union of India* 1996 (9) SCALE 167.

[113] *M.C. Mehta v Union of India* 1996 (2) SCALE SP-92; 1996 (4) SCALE SP-70.

[114] Ibid., 1999 (3) SCALE 6, 166, 501. The Court set deadlines for car manufacturers to switch over to Euro I and II standards.

[115] *Buffalo Traders Welfare Association v Maneka Gandhi* (1994) Supp 3 SCC 448. Here the Court required a seven-member expert committee to address, among the other things, the adverse impact the closure would have on the thousands of workers who would be rendered unemployed.

[116] See *supra* n. 96. For Order Concerning the closure of polluting chemical factories in Bombay, see *F.B. Taraporawala v Bayer India Ltd.* (1996) 6 SCC 58.

[117] *M.C. Mehta v Union of India, supra* n. 95.

[118] *Pradeep Krishen v Union of India* (1996) 8 SCC 599 and *Animal & Environmental Legal Defence Fund v Union of India* (1997) 3 SCC 549.

[119] *Centre for Public Interest Litigation v Union of India* (1995) Supp. 3 SCC 382.

[120] *Common Cause v Union of India* (1996) 6 SCC 530 at 552, 553.

[121] *Common Cause v Union of India* 1999 (4) SCALE 354 at 413.

[122] Ibid. at 401.

[123] Ibid.

[124] Ibid. The direction by the Court for investigation by the CBI also could not be sustained since it was violative of Satish Sharma's right to life under Article 21. The Court said: 'He cannot be hounded out by the police or CBI merely to find out whether he has committed any offence or is living as a law abiding citizen. Even under Article 142 of the Constitution, such a direction cannot be issued' (at 412).

[125] *Shiv Sagar Tiwari v Union of India* (1996) 6 SCC 558.

[126] *Shiv Sagar Tiwari v Union of India* (1996) 6 SCC 599. When Court in the same case directed eviction of out-of-turn allottees of accommodation in Type IV quarters, 1996 (9) SCALE 680, the government promptly reversed the judgement by issuing an Ordinance regularizing all the out-of-turn allotments.

[127] *Vineet Narain v Union of India* (1996) 2 SCC 199 at 200–1.

[128] 1996 (2) SCALE SP-84; 1996 (3) SCALE SP-12, 15; 1996 (4) SCALE SP-3, 21, 56; 1996 (5) SCALE SP-24 and 1996 (6) SCALE SP-24. Likewise, the Court also monitored the investigations into the 3 criminal cases involving the former Prime Minister, P.V. Narsimha Rao: See *Anukul Chandra Pradhan v Union of India* 1996 (3) SCALE SP-27, 35; 1996 (4) SCALE SP-13, 71; 1996 (6) SCALE SP-23 and 1996 6 SCC 354.

[129] *Vineet Narain v Union of India* (1998) 1 SCC 226 at 243.

[130] Although the CVC has, by an Ordinance, been granted statutory status, the government is yet to implement the judgement in its totality. Further, it should be noted here that many of the persons charge-sheeted as a result of CBI's inquiry in the *Hawala* case have been discharged principally on account of a judgement by another Bench holding that the diaries seized did not constitute admissible evidence: see *Central Bureau of Investigation v V.C. Shukla* (1998) 3 SCC 410. Also see the orders of the Supreme Court in PILs concerning the investigation into the Bihar Fodder Scam: *State of Bihar v Ranchi Zila Samata Party* (1996) 3 SCC 682; *Union of India v Sushil Kumar Modi* (1996) 6 SCC 500. The Supreme Court has overseen the investigation into the scam arising out of allotment of LPG dealerships through a private company and has taken matters to a logical conclusion, including the registration of criminal cases: See *Jagriti Upbhokta Parishad Samiti v State of UP* (1998) 5 SCC 640 and (1998) 9 SCC 68.

[131] *Ram Jawaya Kapur v State of Punjab* (1955) 2 SCR 225 at 235–6.

[132] *Fertilizer Corporation Kamgar Union v Union of India* (1981) 1 SCC 568 at 584.

[133] (1998) 9 SCC 589.

[134] Ibid. at 590.

[135] (1997) 3 SCC 312.

[136] For an explanation of the concept of 'continuing mandamus' see *Vineet Narain's* case *supra* n. 129 and 237.

[137] *M.C. Mehta v Union of India* (1997) 8 SCC 770.

[138] (1997) 6 SCC 241.

[139] (1996) 2 SCC 405.

[140] *Krishna Bhat v Union of India* (1990) 3 SCC 65.

[141] *Kanhya Lal Sethia v Union of India* (1997) 6 SCC 573. But see *Santosh Kumar v Secretary, Ministry of Human Resources Development* (1994) 6 SCC 579, where the Supreme Court, in a PIL, issued a mandamus to the government for an amendment of the syllabus for secondary schools to include Sanskrit as an elective subject.

[142] *Ahmedabad Women's Action Group v Union of India* (1997) 3 SCC 573. See also *Maharishi Avdesh v Union of India* (1994) Supp 1 SCC 713 to the same effect. However, a voluntary organization providing succour to women in distress was successful in persuading the Supreme Court to hold in a PIL that a Hindu husband married under Hindu law cannot by converting to Islam solemnise a second marriage. Although in this

case the Court directed the central government to file an affidavit to indicate the steps it has taken to enact a uniform civil code, it later clarified that this direction was not mandatory: *Sarla Mudgal v Union of India* (1995) 3 SCC 635.

[143] *Mohd. Aslum v Union of India* (1994) 2 SCC 48.

[144] *Supra* n. 58. See also *Sachidanand Pandey v State of West Bengal* (1987) 2 SCC 295 at 331.

[145] *State of HP v A Parent of a Student of Medical College* (1985) 3 SCC 169 at 174–5. In this case a parent of a student addressed a letter to the Chief Justice of the high court complaining about ragging of freshers by senior students of the college.

[146] *Supra* n. 138.

[147] *Lakshmi Kant Pandey v Union of India* (1985) Supp SCC 701.

[148] *D.K. Basu's* case, *supra* n. 62.

[149] *Supra* n. 114.

[150] *Vineet Narain's* case, *supra* n. 129.

[151] This happened in *Baljit Malik v Delhi Golf Club* (1998) 4 SCC 524, where one of the co-authors who assisted the Court as amicus curiae drew up a petition on the basis of the letter sent by the petitioner.

[152] *T.N. Godavarman Tirumulkpad's* case, *supra* n. 63. Another example of this is the writ petition of Common Cause raising the issue of the appointment of ombudsmen—Lokpals and Lokayukts—which provided the Court with an opportunity to deal with a specific instance of abuse of discretionary powers in relation to allotment of petrol pumps by a minister. The petition itself contained no pleadings to this effect. The Court's action proceeded entirely on the basis of a newspaper clipping: *Common Cause v Union of India*, *supra* n. 120.

[153] *Kehar Singh v State* (1988) 3 SCC 609.

[154] *S. Jagannath v Union of India*, *supra* n. 98. See also the grievance of workmen and their families in cases cited at *supra* n. 96 and 115.

[155] (1983) 2 SCC 258. The ten questions include the following:

1. Should this Court take notice of such letters addressed by individuals by post enclosing some paper cuttings and take action on them *suo moto* except where the complaint refers to deprivation of liberty of any individual?

2. Can this Court take action on letters addressed to it where the facts disclosed are not sufficient to take action? Should these letters be treated differently from other regular petitions filed in this Court in this regard and should the District Magistrate or the District Judge be asked to enquire and make a report to this Court to ascertain whether there is any case for further action?

3. Would such informality not lead to greater identification of the Court with the cause than would be when a case involving the same type of cause is filed in the normal way?

These were later resurrected by the Court by an order dated 5.12.94. These questions are still pending consideration by a Constitution Bench.

[156] Justice J.S. Verma, 'The Constitutional Obligation of the Judiciary', R.S. Ghiya Memorial Lecture (1997) 7 SCC (Journal) 1 at 7. The proposed amendments to the Supreme Court Rules include the addition of an entire chapter (Order XLIV) regarding PIL.

[157] See *supra* n. 1.

[158] The full text of the Bill introduced by Suresh Pachouri can be found in Jagga Kapur (ed.), *Supreme Court on Public Interest Litigation*, Vol. I, A-145.

[159] Justice A.M. Ahmadi, Dr Zakir Hussain Memorial Lecture, (1996) 2 SCC (Journal) 1 at 11.

[160] *Bandhua Mukti Morcha* case, *supra* n. 1 at 232.

[161] Ibid. at 234.

[162] Justice A.S. Anand, 'Protection of Human Rights—Judicial Obligation or Judicial Activism', Krishan Rao Memorial Lecture, (1997) 7 SCC (Journal) 11 at 23.

[163] Justice S.P. Bharucha, 'Inaugural Lecture of Supreme Court Bar Association's Golden Jubilee' lecture series, reproduced in Jagga Kapur (ed.), *Supreme Court on Public Interest Litigation*, Vol. IV, VI at VIII.

[164] (1987) 2 SCC 295 at 334. See also *Chhetriya Pardushan Mukti Sangharsh Samiti* and *Ramsharan Autyanuprasi, supra* n. 35.

[165] (1999) 1 SCC 492 at 501.

[166] *Malik Brothers v Narendra Dadhich* 1999 (5) SCALE 212.

[167] Ibid. at 214.

[168] See *Khatri, supra* n. 68.

[169] See *Hussainara Khatoon, supra* n. 68.

[170] *Sheela Barse v Union of India, supra* n. 50.

[171] See section on 'Environment' *supra*.

[172] Ibid.

[173] See section on 'Human Rights', *supra*.

[174] Justice J.S. Verma; 'The Constitutional Obligation of the Judiciary', R.C. Ghiya Memorial Lecture, (1997) 7 SCC (Journal) 1 at 7.

Eleven

The Evolution of Due Process of Law by the Supreme Court

T.R. Andhyarujina

Introduction

The Constitution of India does not mention the familiar US constitutional expression of 'due process of law' in any part of it. Due process of law is a concept found in the Fourth and Fifth Amendments to the Constitution of the United States. It is trite to say that this concept has given vast and undefined powers to the American judiciary over federal and state legislatures and their actions. Despite its deliberate omission by the makers of the Indian Constitution and its conspicuous absence in the Indian Constitution, the Supreme Court of India by a proces of interpretation of two Articles of the Constitution, namely Articles 14 (Right to Equality) and 21 (Protection of Life and Personal Liberty) has for all practical purposes introduced the concept of due process of law in the constitutional law of India. The judiciary in India has thereby acquired vast power to supervise and invalidate any union or state action, whether legislative or executive or of any public authority perceived by the Court to be 'arbitrary' or 'unreasonable'. The power so acquired, coupled with the abolition of the requirement of standing in public interest litigation (PIL), which has lent enormous vitality and widespread control to the Indian judiciary over the other branches of government and over all public authorities, has been loosely described as judicial activism.

In 1950, in *A.K. Gopalan v Madras*[1] the Supreme Court refused to read the concept of due process of law into the words 'procedure established by law' in Article 21. In 1957, in the context of Article 14, the Court observed 'it is extremely doubtful whether due process clause can have application under our Constitution.[2] In 1975 Ray CJ said, 'Our Constitution has not adopted the due process clause of the American Constitution. Reasonableness of legislative measures is unknown to the Constitution. The Constitution has denied due process as test of invalidity of law.[3] Twenty-eight years after the Constitution was promulgated, in 1978 the Supreme Court in *Maneka Gandhi v Union of India*[4] overruled these views. The Supreme Court held that the 'procedure established by law' in Article 21 means a just, reasonable, and fair law. Simultaneously, in a separate concurring judgement, Bhagwati J laid the foundations of a guarantee of non-arbitrariness or reasonableness in Article 14. The theme of this paper is that this reinterpretation of Articles 14 and 21, and consequent acquisition of a vast new power by the Court, has introduced due process of law provisions in the Indian Constitution.

Due Process in the US Constitution

Before examining this development in India, it would be useful to briefly refer to the history of due process in the USA as it has relevance to the making of the Indian constitution. The Fourth and Fourteenth Amendments to the US Constitution employ the due process clause. The relevant part of the Fourth Amendment states, 'No person shall ... be deprived of life, liberty, or property, without due process of law'. The relevant part of the Fourteenth Amendment couples due process of law with the equal protection of law and states, 'nor shall any State deprive any person of life, liberty or property without due process of law, nor deny to any person within its jurisdiction the equal protection of the laws'.

In consequence of the doctrine of due process of law as 'reasonable law', judicial review ceased to have definite and stable limits and depended on the Court's own discretion and on nothing else. During the period 1900 to 1937 this clause was frequently employed to challenge the substantive content of the legislation, or in other words to require Congress to exercise its powers 'reasonably', that is to say reasonably in the judgement of the Court. During this period the Court invalidated several legislative projects, state and federal, that curtailed business. After 'the Constitution Revolution of 1937, however, the Court stopped the use of substantive due process as a check on economic and social regulation. In 1955 the Court said, 'The day is gone when the Court uses the due process clause of the 14th Amendment to strike down State laws, regulatory of business and industrial conditions because they may be unwise, improvident or out of harmony with a particular school of thought'.[5] In *Ferguson v Skrupa*[6] Justice Black, speaking of the demise of due process in substantive matters of economic regulation, said:

The doctrine that prevailed in *Lochner, Coppage, Adkins, Burns,* and like cases—that due process authorizes courts to hold laws unconstitutional when they believe the legislature has acted unwisely—has long since been discarded. We have returned to the original constitutional proposition that courts do not substitute their social and economic beliefs for the judgement of legislative bodies, who are elected to pass laws. As this Court stated in a unanimous opinion in 1941 'We are not concerned ... with the wisdom, need, or appropriateness of the legislation

...

We refuse to sit as a 'superlegislature to weigh the wisdom of legislation', and we emphatically refuse to go back to the time when courts used the Due Process Clause to strike down state laws, regulatory of business and industrial conditions, because they may be unwise, improvident, or out of harmony with a particular school of thought.

Today, in the USA, the use of substantive due process in economic and social matters is dead but it has much vitality in relation to civil liberties and civil rights and as means of controlling arbitrary procedures.

Due Process Rejected by the Constituent Assembly

The framers of the Indian Constitution, after deep deliberation extending over several years, rejected the US concept of due process in the Indian Constitution. The debates in the Constituent Assembly, and the deliberations of the Drafting Committee and the Advisory Committee, show that the makers of the Constitution were deeply concerned with the possibility of interference and nullification by the judiciary of laws of social reform and of security of the state if the due process clause was introduced in the vigorous form it observed in United States Constitution in relation to the fundamental rights of property and personal liberty.[7] It took the Constituent Assembly members nearly three years to decide how to treat these matters in the Constitution. On the one hand it was recognized, in the words of K.M. Munshi, that the due process provision would prevent legislative extravagance and executive excesses. On the other hand, B.N. Rao, the Constitutional Advisor to the Constituent Assembly, believed it would provide excessive powers to the courts. He stated: 'The Courts, manned by an irremovable judiciary not so sensitive to public needs in the social or economic sphere as the representatives of a periodically elected legislature, will, in effect, have a veto on legislation exercisable at any time and at the instance of any litigant'. B.N. Rao warned that 40 per cent of the litigation before the

US Supreme Court during the past fifty years had centred around due process and due process meant only that which the Courts said it meant. 'It must be admitted', he stated, 'that the clauses are a safeguard against predatory legislation, but they may also stand in the way of beneficial social legislation'. It is remarkable that B.N. Rao did not emphasize the change in the US Supreme Court's view after 1937 of abandoning substantive due process in economic and social legislation.

Due Process in Property

In relation to the fundamental right to property, at an early stage of the making of the Constitution, it was decided that the due process provisions should not apply to the right to property. The Advisory Committee in its Interim Report to the Constituent Assembly confined due process to the deprivation of life and liberty, and the Constituent Assembly accepted this deletion without debate. Considerable debate ensued on the justiciability of the right to compensation in the Article on the fundamental right to property which was later to be Article 31. The anxiety of the members was that the provisions for compensation should not be justiciable. In the final round of the debate, Munshi explained to the Assembly that Parliament would be the sole judge of the propriety of the principles for compensation and the courts would not judge the adequacy of compensation on the basis of market value so long as the underlying principles of compensation were sound. As the Assembly had deleted the expression 'just compensation' from the Article, Nehru informed the Assembly that 'eminent lawyers have told us that on a proper construction of the property clause normally speaking the judiciary should not and does not come in'. He added that 'no Supreme Court and no judiciary can stand in judgement over the sovereign will of Parliament representing the will of the community.'[8]

The intention of the Constituent Assembly to keep the judiciary out of the compensation provisions in Article 31(2) of the Constitution was belied by a series of decisions of the Supreme Court in 1950 to 1970 in which the Court interpreted the Article in precisely the opposite way. Despite two amendments to Article 31, namely the Constitution (Fourth Amendment) Act, 1955 and the Constitution (Twenty-fifth Amendment) Act, 1971 to eliminate justiciability of compensation or the amount payable on acquisition in successive cases,[9] the Court sat in judgement over the relevance of the principles of awarding compensation or 'the amount'. Due process in the acquisition of property seemed difficult to exclude as the Court was not willing to give up justiciability altogether and leave the matter to the legislatures.

Eventually Parliament's will prevailed over the Court's quite dispro-portionately. Interference by the Supreme Court in social reforms in-volving property despite constitutional amendments to keep it out gave critics of the Court the convenient handle that it was anti-majoritarian and reactionary. Apparently to avoid such criticism of the judiciary, a new government coming into power in 1978 deleted the right to prop-erty in Article 19(1)(g) and Article 31 altogether by the Forty-fourth Constitution Amendment Act, 1978. Instead, it introduced Article 300A which simply stated, 'No person shall be deprived of his property save by authority of law'. This was the expression the Constitution-makers had used to eliminate due process of law in the fundamental right to life and personal liberty. This drastic measure by a constitutional amend-ment to eliminate the Court's interference was unnecessary, as after the Twenty-fifth Constitution Amendment to the Constitution in 1971, as interpreted in *Kesavananda Bharati v State of Kerala*[10] the Court's interference in the matter of awarding an 'amount' was minimal, being restricted in cases of what could be described as an illusory amount or no amount. No one seriously challenged this amendment as the right to property was held to not form part of the 'basic structure of the Consti-tution' in *Kesavananda Bharati* case. With the removal of the right to property as a fundamental right from the chapter on fundamental rights, the reading of the reasonableness in any 'law' of property with reference to other Articles concerning fundamental rights was eliminated by Par-liament. This spelt the demise of the right to property as a fundamental right and with it the demise of due process in property matters.

Due Process in Life and Personal Liberty

Members of the Constituent Assembly showed greater anxiety in ensur-ing the due process of law in the protection of life and personal liberty than in the right to property. Even here, the intention to retain the due process of law provision as a safeguard for personal liberty clashed with the belief that it was necessary to provide for preventive detention of persons liable to disturb the peace and stability of society. The Con-stituent Assembly had favoured due process of law in personal liberty, and it had been included in the draft Constitution published in Octo-ber 1947. However, it was strongly opposed by B.N. Rao. Rao had met Justice Felix Frankfurter of the US Supreme Court for advice in the drafting of the Indian Constitution. Frankfurter told him that he con-sidered the power of judicial review implied in the due process clause both undemocratic—because a few judges could negate legislation en-acted by the representatives of a nation—and also burdensome to the judiciary. As pointed out earlier, this view was highly exaggerated, as after 1937 the US Supreme Court had ceased to obstruct social and economic legislation through the use of substantive due process. Rao proposed an amendment to the draft Constitution to eliminate the due process of law clause, in favour of the expression 'according to the procedure established by law'.

The matter was keenly debated in the Drafting Committee. Eventually, in a close voting, it was decided that the provision of due process of law in the Article for deprivation of life and personal liberty should be deleted and the expression 'according to procedure established by law' be substituted. As it finally emerged in Article 21 of the Constitution, the Drafting Committee merely said that the latter expression was 'more specific' and the Committee cited in support Article XXXI of the Japanese Constitution of 1946. Despite further consideration by the Assembly, in which a number of members of the House favoured retention of due process in personal liberty, the Article was retained without it. However, as a mitigation of the members' fear that 'the procedure established by law' would allow the legislature to prescribe any procedure it deemed fit to deprive a person of his life or liberty, a new Article, the present Article 22, was adopted which provided for guaranteed safeguards in arrest and detention. Introducing the new Article 22, Dr Ambedkar said that the Article 'compensated' for what had been done in passing Article 21. He said the new Article 'certainly saves a great deal which had been lost by the non-introduction of the words "due process of law"'.[11] Apparently, the Constituent Assembly was satisfied that the provisions of Article 22 would serve as a sufficient safeguard in the absence of a due process of law provision in Article 21.

Concept of Reasonableness in the Constitution

Whilst due process of law was expressly negatived as a concept by the makers of the Indian Constitution, two concepts of reasonableness were implicit in the Constitution. First, Article 19 of the Constitution confers on citizens specific freedoms, but the Constitution permitted the imposition of *reasonable restrictions* on the exercise of the several rights conferred on citizens in that Article. A law which was not a reasonable restriction would be declared void by a court. This requirement of reasonableness of the restrictions is not to be considered in the abstract as reasonable or not by the court but with reference to the specific considerations stated in sub-articles (3) to (6) of Article 19. For example, the freedom of speech and expression in Article 19(1)(a) can be restricted only by a law that imposes reasonable restrictions in the interest of the sovereignty and integrity of India, the security of the State, friendly relations with foreign States, public order, decency, or morality, or in relation to contempt of court, defamation or incitement to an offence. This is very different from a general and undefined unreasonableness arising from the 'vague contours' of the concept of due process as in the Fourth and Fourteenth Amendment of the US Constitution. As the Court observed in a 1962 case:

Though the tests of reasonableness laid down by cls. (2) to (6) of Art. 19 might in great part coincide with that for judging of 'due process', it must not be assumed that these are identical, for it has to be borne in mind that the Constitution framers deliberately avoided in this context the use of the expression 'due process' with its comprehensiveness, flexibility and attendant vagueness, in favour of a somewhat more definite word 'reasonable', and caution has, therefore, to be exercised before the literal application of American decisions.[12]

Mathews J, in *Kesavananda Bharati v Kerala*[13] thought differently. He observed:

The concept of 'due process' enters into the meaning of reasonableness of restrictions in cls. 2 to 6 of the Art. 19. I am unable to understand how the word 'reasonable' is more definite than the words 'due process'. As the concept of 'due process' draws its nourishment from natural or higher law so also the concepts of 'reason' and 'reasonableness' draw the juice for their life from the law of reason, which for the common law lawyer is nothing but natural law.

The second way, in which a limited concept of reasonableness enters into consideration of the constitutionality of a law is in a permissible classification of objects and things implicit in the right to equal protection of laws. Article 14 of the Constitution states that the State shall not deny to any person equality before the law or the equal protection of the laws within the territory of India. A reasonable classification of objects and things with an intelligible differentia distinguishing them and maintaining a national relationship with the object of the law is not inconsistent with the requirement of equality. The requirement of the differentia being intelligible and a proper relationship with the law that is not arbitrary does impart a sense of reasonableness. As Fazl Ali J put it in *Kathi Raning Rawat v The State of Saurashtra*,[14] 'a distinction is to be drawn between discrimination without reason and discrimination with reason'. Similarly, the principle of equality is adjudged to be violated when unequals are treated equally for the want of a rational differentiation between unequals.[15] However, this judgement of a court on the validity of classification permissible or want of a classification under

Article 15 is quite distinct from the power of adjudging the general reasonableness of the law under the due process of law itself.

In a passage that has become a *locus classicus*, Patanjali Shastri J in *State of Madras v V.G. Row*[16] cautioned against the introduction of an abstract standard of resonableness and the introduction of the judge's view of reasonableness:

It is important in this context to bear in mind that the test of reasonableness, wherever prescribed, should be applied to each individual statute impugned, and no abstract standard, or general pattern, of reasonableness can be laid down as applicable to all cases. The nature of the right alleged to have been infringed, the underlying purpose of the restrictions imposed, the extent and urgency of the evil sought to be remedied thereby, the disproportion of the imposition, the prevailing conditions at the time, should all enter into the judicial verdict. In evaluating such elusive factors and forming their own conception of what is reasonable, in all the circumstances of a given case, it is inevitable that the social philosophy and the scale of values of the judges participating in the decision should play an important part, and the limit to their interference with legislative judgement in such cases can only be dictated by their sense of responsibility and self-restraint and the sobering reflection that the Constitution is meant not only for people of their way of thinking but for all, and that the majority of the elected representatives of the people have, in authorizing the imposition of the restrictions, considered them to be reasonable.

Due Process Rejected by Court from 1958 to 1978

In *Gopalan v Madras*[17] which was decided on 19 May 1950, within a few months of the promulgation of the Constitution, a majority of the judges held that in Article 21 the word 'law' had been used in the sense of state-made 'law' and not as an equivalent to 'law' in the abstract or general sense embodying the principles of natural justice, and 'procedure established by law' meant procedure established by laws made by Parliament or the state legislatures. The majority held that it was not proper to consider this expression in the light of the meaning given to the expression 'due process of law' in the American Constitution by the Supreme Court of America. This was the view held by Kania CJ, Mukherjee and Das JJ. Patanjali Shastri J struck a different note. Whilst he also held that 'law' in Article 21 does not mean *jus naturale* of the civil law but means positive, or state-made law, according to him 'procedure established by law' does not mean any procedure that may be prescribed by the legislature but the ordinary well-established criminal procedure, i.e. those settled usages and norms of procedure sanctioned by the Criminal Procedure Code which is the general law of criminal procedure in the country. Fazal Ali J alone, as a dissenting judge, held that the words 'procedure established by law' included the four principles of elementary justice that inhere in and are at the root of all civilized systems of law and which have been stated by the American Courts as consisting of notice, the opportunity to be heard, an impartial tribunal, and an orderly course of procedure.

In *Gopalan's* case the Court noted the constitutional history of enacting Article 21 and the rejection by the drafting committee of the American concept of due process of law in favour of the expression 'procedure established by law', an expression which was stated to be borrowed from the Japanese Constitution. However, as Seervai points out, the majority of the judges in *Gopalan's* case failed to note that Article 22 was enacted by the Constituent Assembly to mitigate the fear of any arbitrary procedure prescribed by the legislature. If Article 21 and 22 had been enacted at the same time in the Constituent Assembly and if they were read together, the safeguards in Article 22 for arrest and detention could have been considered as the requirements of the due process of law, as Ambedkar had stated to the Constituent Assembly.[18] In the absence of any constraints on the definition of 'procedure established by law' except state-made law, the logical extreme of the proposition was carried through by Das J. In a remarkable passage in his judgement, which is remarkable not only for the most abiding good faith in the legislatures but also the helplessness of courts, he said:[19]

Subject to the limitations I have mentioned which are certainly justiciable, our Constitution has accepted the supremacy of the legislative authority and, that being so, we must be prepared to face occasional vagaries of that body and to put up with enactments of the nature of the atrocious English statute to which learned counsel for the petitioner has repeatedly referred, namely, that the Bishop of Rochester's cook be boiled to death. If Parliament may take away life by providing for hanging by the neck, logically there can be no objection if it provides a sentence of death by shooting by a firing squad or by guillotine or in the electric chair or even by boiling in oil. A procedure laid down by the legislature may offend against the Court's sense of justice and fair play and a sentence provided by the legislature may outrage the Court's notions of penology, but that is a wholly irrelevant consideration. The court may construe and interpret the Constitution and ascertain its true meaning but once that is done the Court cannot question its wisdom or policy. The Constitution is supreme. The court must take the Constitution as it finds it, even if it does not accord with its preconceived notions of what an ideal Constitution should be. Our protection against legislative tyranny, if any, lies in ultimate analysis in a free and intelligent public opinion which must eventually assert itself.

The Court was adopting a higly positivistic legalism to the Constitution. Positivism is a result of black letter law learning and has been defined by Dworkin as a theory which holds that the truth of legal propositions consists in facts about rules that have been adopted by specific social institutions, and of nothing else. Considering the close proximity in time of that decision to the making of the Constitution and that faith in representative government in India had not been shaken by political events at that time, the Court would have been adventurous if any interpretation other than a positivistic one had been adopted on an assumption of possible abuse of legislative power.

Due Process Introduced in the Constitution by the Supreme Court

Gopalan's case stood unshaken and governed the scope of the fundamental right to life and personal liberty until 1978 when the *Maneka Gandhi* case was decided in 1978. Much water had flowed under the bridge since *Gopalan's* case was decided twenty-eight years earlier. For one thing, India had lived through the traumatic experience of the emergency in which fundamental rights to life had been suspended. The Supreme Court was perceived to have left the citizen unprotected in *ADM Jabalpur v Shiv Kant Shukla*[20] by giving a carte blanche to the executive to detain persons with no relief from the courts. After the emergency was lifted, the Supreme Court in *Maneka Gandhi v Union of India*, in essence a minor case involving the impounding of a passport without compliance with the provisions of the Passport Act, 1967, and one which could have been decided by avoiding wider constitutional issues, breathed life into Article 21 by introducing the concept of due process in it. At the same time, one of the judges, Bhagwati J, propounded a new theory of non-arbitrariness or reasonableness in the context of Article 14.

Fortunately for the Court in *Maneka Gandhi's* case, previously a full court of eleven judges in *R.C. Cooper v Union of India*,[21] had undermined the foundations of *Gopalan's* case in a case relating to the right to property. *Gopalan's* case had propounded the theory of exclusivity of Article 21 from Article 19 of the Constitution. It had held that a law for deprivation of life and personal liberty could not be examined for its reasonableness under Article 19 of the Constitution, as a person deprived of his life had of no freedoms outstanding under Article 19. The principle had been extended in relation to acquisition of property under Article 31(2) of the Constitution, and it was held that if property was acquired by the state there was no question of testing the law for its reasonableness under Article 19(1)(f) of the Constitution.[22] This view was overruled in the *R.C. Cooper* case by a majority of the full Court.

In *Maneka Gandhi's* case[23] the majority judges of the Court, relying upon the *R.C. Cooper* case, held that:

The law must, therefore, now be taken to be well settled that Article 21 does not exclude Article 19, and that even if there is a law prescribing a procedure for depriving a person of personal liberty and there is consequently no infringement of the fundamental right conferred by Article 21, such law, in so far as it abridges or takes away any fundamental right under Article 19, would have to meet the challenge of that article.

The Court also held as axiomatic that a law prescribing a procedure for deprivation of life and personal liberty in Article 21 could not be any sort of procedure but it had to be one that was neither arbitrary nor unfair nor unreasonable.[24] Curiously, in *Maneka Gandhi's* case no reference was made by the Court to the original intention of the makers of the Constitution whilst adopting Article 21 of the Constitution and the deliberate exclusion of the concept of due process of law from Article 21 of the Constitution which had been elaborately considered in *Gopalan's* case.

The combined result of these two lines of approach to Article 21 in *Maneka Gandhi* was that not only had a law depriving a person of life and liberty to be fair and reasonable but it had also to meet a possible challenge from the other provisions of the Constitution such as Articles 14 and 19. Legal positivism and the theory of 'original intent' of the makers of the Constitution propounded in *Gopalan's* case was abandoned in favour of an interpretation that would ensure just and fair laws under the Constitution. Justice O.W. Holmes said of constitutional interpretation restricted to the original intention of the makers:

When we are dealing with words that also are a constituent act like the Constitution of the United States we must realize that they have called into life a being, the development of which could not have been foreseen completely by the most gifted of its begetters. It was enough for them to realize or to hope that they had created an organism ... The case before us must be considered in the light of our whole experience and not merely what was said a hundred years ago.[25]

The Supreme Court in *Maneka Gandhi's* case did precisely that in the light of the recent experience of the emergency.

The Result of Maneka Gandhi's Case on the Scope of Article 21

As a result of *Maneka Gandhi's* case, every law which deprived a person of his life and liberty had to satisfy the test of being just, reasonable, and fair. In effect, the Court had introduced the concept of due process of law in the field of personal liberty. In *Sunil Batra v Delhi Administration*[26] Krishna Iyer J conceded this position when he stated

true our Constitution has no 'due process' clause or the VIII Amendment, but in this branch of law, after *Cooper* and *Maneka Gandhi,* the consequence is the same.

In *Bachhan Singh v State of Punjab,*[27] a constitutional Bench, through Sarkaria J stated that after *Maneka Gandhi's* case Article 21 must read as:

No person shall be deprived of his life or personal liberty except according to fair, just and reasonable procedure established by valid law.

In *Ranjan Dwivedi v Union of India,*[28] the Court said that 'It is difficult to hold that the substance of the American doctrine of due process has not been introduced in the conservative text of Article 21 of the Constitution.'

There can be no doubt that the Court's interpretation of Article 21 in *Maneka Gandhi's* case has saved the 'cook of the Bishop of Rochester' situation of a brutal law and a helpless court which Das J referred to so graphically in *Gopalan's* case. As Chinnappa Reddy J later said, the Court's interpretation of Article 21 in *Maneka Gandhi's* case made it the focal point around which revolved to advantage all claims of right touching life and liberty.[29] The words 'procedure established by law', released from the shackles of positive state-made law acquired a meaning which Patanjali Shastri J had broadly given in *Gopalan's* case as a more or less institutionalized well accepted canon of fair procedure. Patanjali Shastri J had applied these procedures to the deprivation of a person's life, but after *Maneka Gandhi's* case the Court began to apply the fair and reasonable requirements of law not only to deprivation of life but also to the well-ordered concept of human dignity and life.

The Court held that a person was entitled to a speedy trial and therefore his/her long detention as an undertrial prisoner was violative of the procedure established by law.[30] The state was obliged to provide free legal aid as an essential prerequisite of the procedure established by law.[31] Handcuffing of prisoners was held to be violative of procedure established by law.[32] The constitutionality of death penalty in India was considered in the context of the larger concept of a fair procedure for deprivation of life, even though the Constitution does not embody the US Eighth Amendment prohibition of cruel and unusual punishment.[33] The concept of 'personal liberty' in Article 21 was itself given a broad and expansive interpretation to include various human rights, including the right of women not to be subjected to sexual harassment in their workplaces.[34]

At the same time, the Court enlarged the concept of 'life' in Article 21 to include the dignity of the individual and the worth of the human person.[35] The Court has said that life does not mean merely animal existence or continued drudgery through life but the finer graces of human civilization which makes life worth living.[36] The right to life has been held to include right to privacy,[37] to development of urban area,[38] to fresh water or air,[39] to protection against environmental degradation,[40] to food and clothing and shelter,[41] to shelter,[42] to health,[43] to education,[44] and even a right to roads in hilly regions for access roads there are said to be access to life itself,[45] and rights to conservation of the physical environment[46] and protection against import of injurious insecticides.[47]

Indeed, there is no end to aspects of the protection or advancement of human life which cannot be brought into the ambit of 'life' in Article 21. That Article has become the most widely invoked provision for the Court's intervention in matters affecting the lives of persons, without any question of the state 'depriving' any person of his life or personal liberty. Truly, Article 21 has been metamorphosed from its original form and content beyond recognition. A large part of the Indian judiciary's present-day activism is a result of this wider interpretation.

Due Process in Article 14: Its 'New Dimension'

Whilst the majority of judges in *Maneka Gandhi*'s case held that the procedure of law in Article 21 must also answer the requirement of Article 14 without stating the contents of Article 14 for this purpose, Bhagwati J alone took the opportunity to find the content of reasonableness from the principle of equality in Article 14 itself. The same learned judge in three later judgements of his, which are noted below, dilated upon the meaning of equality in Article 14 and imported a general requirement of non-arbitrariness or reasonableness of every action of the state and public authorities, whether legislative or executive, the absence of which would in his view immediately invalidate the action. This highly controversial[48] interpretation of Article 14 of the Constitution has been heralded as the 'new dimension of Article 14'. Today, it is commonplace amongst judges and advocates to refer to 'the requirement of Article 14', not necessarily meaning equality of treatment but more generally in the sense of a state action requiring to conform to the standards of non-arbitrariness or reasonableness: the two concepts being considered synonymous for this purpose. It is the correctness of this view that is examined below.

In *Maneka Gandhi's* case Bhagwati J observed that 'even on principle the concept of reasonableness must be projected in the procedure contemplated by Article 21 having regard to the impact of Article 14 on Article 21'. How does the concept of reasonableness project from Article 14? As the entire jurisprudence of this new dimension of Article 14 is founded on this one passage of Bhagvati J's opinion in *Maneka Gandhi's* case it is necessary to set it out *in extenso.* Bhagwati J observed:[49]

Now the question immediately arises as to what is the requirment of Article 14. What is the content and reach of the great equalizing principle enunciated in this article? There can be no doubt that it is a founding faith of the Constitution. It is indeed the pillar on which rests securely the foundation of our democratic republic. And, therefore, it must not be subjected to a narrow, pedantic or lexicographic approach. No attempt should be made to truncate its all-embracing scope and meaning for, to do so would be to violate its activist magnitude. Equality is a dynamic concept with many aspects and dimensions and it cannot be imprisoned within traditional and doctrinaire limits. We must reiterate here what was pointed out by the majority in *E.P. Royappa v State of Tamil Nadu & Another*,[50] namely, that 'from a positivistic point of view, equality is an antithetic to arbtrariness. In fact, equality and arbitrariness are sworn enemies; one belongs to the rule of law in republic while the other, to the whim and caprice of an absolute monarch. Where an act is arbitrary, it is implicit in it that it is that it is unequal both according to political logic and constitutional law and is therefore violative of Article 14'. Article 14 strikes at arbitrariness in State action and ensures fairness and equality of treatment. The principle of reasonableness, which legally as well as philosophically, is an essential element of equality or non-arbitrariness pervades Article 14 like a brooding omnipresence and the procedure contemplated by Article 21 must answer the test of reasonableness in order to be in conformity with Article 14. It must be 'right and just and fair' and not arbitrary, fanciful or oppressive; otherwise, it would be no procedure at all and the requirements of Article 21 would not be satisfied.

Criticism of the 'New Dimension' of Article 14

Analysing this passage from *Maneka Gandhi's* case it will be observed that it is in the main rhetorical praise of the concept of equality which by itself does not elucidate the legal content of Article 14. Expressions such as 'great equalizing principle' in Article 14, 'founding faith of the Constitution', 'pillar on which rests securely the foundation of our democratic republic' do not explain the content of equality. That equality must not be subjected to a narrow, pedantic, and lexicographic approach or be truncated of its all-embracing scope and meaning, and that it has an 'activist magnitude' begs the question of its scope. Devoid of the rhetoric, the only propositions that emerge are (1) where a state action is arbitrary it is necessarily violative of Article 14, and (2) that the principle of reasonableness is an essential element of equality.

Though the learned judge says that this is a principle of constitutional law, no principle of constitutional law is adumbrated for the first proposition, and with respect, the proposition involves a logical fallacy. No doubt some arbitrary actions are unequal but not all arbitrary actions are unequal. When all persons in a 'universe of discourse' are arbitrarily treated alike the arbitrary action has no necessary relationship to any unequal treatment as all are treated arbitrarily alike. For example, if only red-haired students in a school are expelled from school without any cause, the action is arbitrary as well as unequal *vis-à-vis* other non-red haired students. If however all students in the school, whatever the colour of their hair, are expelled without any cause the action is simply arbitrary without any question of inequality. It is simply incorrect to say that arbitrariness necessarily results in inequality.

In *Bolling v Sharpe*[51] the US Supreme Court held that whilst the concept of equal protection and due process both stem from the ideal of fairness and are not mutually exclusive, nevertheless, the equal protection of laws is a more explicit sagfeguard against prohibited unfairness than due process of law and therefore the two concepts are not interchangeable phrases. It has however been recognized that discrimination may be so unjustifiable in certain cases as to be arbitrary and violative of due process. This essential distinction between the scope of the equality provision and the concept of reasonableness is lost sight of in Bhagvati J's formulation of 'arbitrariness = inequality'. Correctly stated, the proposition should be that some actions of the State which are arbitrary may violate the principle of equality but not all arbitrary actions do so. Hence, arbitrariness is not synonymous with a violation of the concept of equality in constitutional law though it would be unlawful in administrative law.

Nor is the next statement, i.e. 'the principle of reasonableness is an essential element of equality' legally sound. It has been shown earlier that there is an aspect of reasonableness in classifying objects and things, but that is very different from it being an essential element of equality which in the words of the learned Judge pervades Article 14 like a 'brooding omnipresence'. Incidentally, the expression 'brooding omnipresence' is most inappropriate. Justice O.W. Holmes had used the expression 'brooding omnipresence' in a pejorative sense. In a famous statement deploring an argument of general invalidity from the concept of common law he said, 'The Common Law is *not* a brooding omnipresence in the sky ...'.[52]

In subsequent judgements Bhagwati J dilates on this concept. In *Ramana Shetty v Airport Authority of India*[53] the learned judge, relying upon his previous judgements in the *Royappa* and *Maneka Gandhi* cases expands the principle thus:

Article 14 strikes at arbitrariness in State action and ensures fairness and equality of treatment. It requires that State action must not be arbitrary but must be based on some rational and relevant principle which is non-discriminatory: It must not be guided by any extraneous or irrelevant considerations, because that would be denial of equality. The principle of reasonableness and rationality which is legally as well as philosophically an essential element of equality or non-arbitrariness is protected by Article 14 and it must characterise every State action, whether it be under authority of law or in exercise of executive power without making of law.

In *Kasturilal v State of J&K*[54] the learned judge returned to the theme:

The government action must not be arbitrary or capricious, but must be based on some principle which meets the test of reason and relevance. This rule was enunciated by the Court as a rule of administrative law and it was also validated by the Court as an emanation flowing directly from the doctrine of equality embodied in Article 14.

It will be seen that in these passages the learned judge first brings in familiar concepts in administrative law of extraneous or irrelevant considerations which vitiate the actions of a deciding authority. By themselves these considerations in an administrative action or inaction are wrong and illegal in administrative law. No principle of equality necessarily arises by an authority taking into account such extraneous or irrelevant considerations. Secondly, the principle of reasonableness which is stated to be implicit in Article 14 is now applied to 'every State action whether it be under authority of law or in exercise of executive power'. This would mean that even a law enacted by a legislature would be struck down by the Court for its general unreasonableness: a power similar to substantive due process of law.

Finally, in *Ajay Hasia v Khalid Mujib Sehravardi*[55] the learned judge gives the denouement of the development:

Wherever therefore there is arbitrariness in State action whether it be of the legislature or of the executive or of an 'authority' under Article 12, Article 14 immediately springs into action and strikes down such State action. In fact, the concept of reasonableness and non-arbitrariness pervades the entire constitutional scheme and is a golden thread which runs through the whole of the fabric of the Constitution.

The last part of the observation suggests that Article 14 is not the only repository of non-arbitrariness and reasonableness but the entire Constitution is. This overarching of reasonableness in the Constitution makes it unnecessary to find a requirement of reasonableness in any Article of the Constitution. Any legislative or executive action of any authority in India can be determined to be unreasonable without the application of any specific principle for judging it from the Constitution of India.

The concept of 'brooding omnipresent' reasonableness inhering in the Constitution which invalidates every action of the state for unreasonableness is a variant of Coke's ancient but repudiated dictum in *Dr Bonham's* case.[56] Coke had said, 'when an Act of Parliament is against common right and reason or repugnant or impossible to be performed the common law will control it and adjudge such Act to be void'. The supremacy of common law over the actions of Parliament was established for a short time by the *Dr Bonham* case but disavowed in England in the case of *Lee v Bude*.[57] Coke's dictum was used in the early US Supreme Court cases such as *Loan Association v Topeka*[58] to invalidate laws on the ground that there were limitations on power that grow out of the essential nature of all free government.

Sir William Wade has observed that the interpretation given by the Indian Supreme Court to Article 14 is

a highly imaginative interpretation worthy to rank with the feats of the American Supreme Court. ... It means that the Supreme Court of India may now apply the test of reasonableness not only to administrative actions but also to legislation, both Central and State, and may invalidate laws which it finds to be arbitrary and unreasonable. This is a very big claim for even a Supreme Court to make, and it suggests comparison with discredited policy of the American Supreme Court in the nineteen-thirties when it invented the doctrine of substantive due process ... the same result in *Maneka Gandhi's* case could have been reached simply by applying the common law doctrine of reasonableness instead of by way of elaborate reasoning based on Article 14, 19 and 21 of the Constitution which opens such a wide door to judicial review of legislation as well as administration.[59]

Subsequent Developments in 'Article 14 Unreasonableness'

Bhagwati J's formulation of Article 14 has been cited and followed in innumerable cases subsequently. However, in two cases, counsel for the state questioned the premises on the basis of which Article 14 unreasonableness was deduced but with no success. The Court said it was too late to question the 'correctness of the landmark decision in *Maneka Gandhi's* case and innovative construction placed by Bhagwati J on Article 14 which had evolved new dimensions in judicial process'.[60]

As a corollary to Article 14 being the guarantee of reasonableness, the rules of natural justice were held to be part of the right to equality. The Court argued in a syllogism thus:

> violation of a rule of natural justice results in arbitrariness which is the same as discrimination; where discrimination is the result of State action, it is a violation of Article 14: therefore, a violation of a principle of natural justice by a State action is a violation of Article 14. Article 14, however, is not the sole repository of the principles of natural justice. What it does is to guarantee that any law or State action violating them will be struck down.[61]

Next, the Court extended the test of resonableness even in contractual relations of the State or instrumentalities of the State. The Court held that 'If a Government policy or action even in contractual matters fails to satisfy the question of reasonableness it would be unconstitutional'[62] and that unconscionable contracts by the State with its employees would be set aside as they would not conform to 'the mandate of the great equality clause in Article 14'.[63]

Apart from these extensions, the elevation of Article 14 to the status of a provision for general reasonableness, as unfolded by the Court in *Maneka Gandhi,* has generally not gone beyond the usual standards of invalidity of administrative or executive actions for irrationality such as the Wednesbury unreasonableness.[64] The Court has not at any time set aside economic and business regulations by recourse to substantive due process as was done at one time in the USA by the US Supreme Court. On the other hand, it has shown great deference to legislative wisdom in such matters.[65] No primary legislation has been invalidated merely on the ground of unreasonableness or arbitrariness. Indeed, the Court has said that no legislation can be struck down merely for arbitrariness or unreasonableness.[66] The farthest the Court appears to have gone is in a case where the Court condemned legislation as having become over the passage of time 'arbitrary and unreasonable' but avoided declaring it void.[67] Even the concept of 'proportionality' has not yet found firm roots in India.[68] Despite the apparent introduction of substantive due process in Article 14 at present, it appears that the concept is only theoretical in its application to legislation in the way substantive due process was at one time applied in the USA.

One unfortunate result of the introduction of the due process in the Indian Constitution is the indiscriminate use of the word 'arbitrary', almost as a talismanic word to invoke the Court's jurisdiction of violation of a fundamental right. 'Arbitrary' has become a favourite cliché in the vocabulary of the lawyers and the Courts in India and is used to describe many sins. Its lazy use has encouraged loose thinking and imprecise concepts in law and has retarded the development of public and constitutional law in India.

Conclusion

The reinterpretation of Article 21 and Article 14 by the Court after 1978 marks a watershed in the development of Indian constitutional law. The vast extent of public law and public interest litigation and the Court's routine intervention in administration which is seen in Indian courts today is the result of the reinterpretation of Articles 21 and 14 which has introduced the concept of due process of law in the Indian Constitution. It has been aptly said that judicial review is always a function, so to speak, of the viable constitutional law of a particular period.[69] The viable constitutional law of India since 1978 has been the concept of due process of law in the Constitution. It is time to recognize that.

Notes

[1] (1950) SCR 88.
[2] *A.S. Krishnan v Madras* (1957) SCR 399–412.
[3] *Indira Gandhi v Raj Narain* (1976) 2 SCR 347.
[4] (1978) 2 SCR 621.
[5] *Williamson v Lee Optical* (1955) 348 US 483.
[6] (1963) 372 US 726, 10 L Ed. 2d 93.
[7] CAD, Vol. III, 3, 468.
[8] CAD, Vol. IX, 31, 1192–5.
[9] *WB v Subodh Gopal Bose* (1954) SCR 587; *Dwarkadas Shrinivas of Bombay v Sholapur Spinning & Weaving Co. Ltd.* (1954) SCR 674; *State of WB v Mrs Bela Banerjee* (1954) SCR 558; *P. Vajravelu v Sp. Dy. Collector* (1965) 1 SCR 614; *R.C. Cooper v Union* (1970) 3 SCR 530.
[10] (1973) Supp SCR 1.
[11] CAD, Vol. IX, 35, 1497–8.
[12] *Collector of Customs Madras v Nathalu Chetty* (1962) 3 SCR 786, 816.
[13] (1973) Supp SCR 1.
[14] (1952) SCR 435.
[15] *K.T. Moopil Nair v Kerala* (1961) 3 SCR 77.
[16] (1952) SCR 597.

[17] (1950) SCR 88.

[18] Seervai, *Constitutional Law of India*, 4th edn, vol. II, pp. 971–2.

[19] (1950) SCR 88, 320.

[20] (1974) Supp SCR 172.

[21] (1970) 3 SCR 530.

[22] *The State of Bombay v Bhanji Munji* (1955) 1 SCR 777.

[23] (1978) 2 SCR 621, 673.

[24] Ibid. at 658, 671.

[25] *Missouri v Holland* (1920) 416 US 433.

[26] (1979) 1 SCR 392 at 428.

[27] (1983) 1 SCR 145, 222. See also *Mithu Singh v Punjab* (1983) 2 SCR 690, 697–8, 712.

[28] (1983) 2 SCR 982.

[29] *Mithu Singh v Punjab* (1983) 2 SCR 690, 712, 713.

[30] *Hussainara Khatoon v Bihar* (1979) 3 SCR 393.

[31] *H. Hoskot v Maharashtra* (1979) 1 SCR 192.

[32] *Prem Shankar Shukla v Delhi Administration* (1980) 3 SCR 855.

[33] *Bachan Singh v Punjab* (1983) 1 SCR 145. See also *Mithu Singh v Punjab* (1983) 2 SCR 690.

[34] *Vishaka v Rajasthan* (1997) 6 SCC 241.

[35] *Francis Coralie Mullin v Administrator, Union Territory of Delhi* (1981) 2 SCR 516.

[36] *Board of Trustees of the Bombay Port Trust v Nadkarni* (1983) 1 SCR 828.

[37] *Kharak Singh v UP* (1964) 1 SCR 332; *Neera Mathur v LIC* (1992) 1 SCC 286.

[38] *Ratlam Municipality v Vardichand* (1981) 1 SCR 97.

[39] *M.C. Mehta v Union of India* (1988) 1 SCR 279.

[40] *M/s ARC Cements Ltd. v UP* (1993) Supp 1 SCC 426.

[41] *Shantistar Builders v Narayan K. Totame* (1990) 1 SCC 520.

[42] *Olga Tellis v Bombay M.C.* (1985) Supp 2 SCR 51.

[43] *Vincent v India* (1987) 2 SCR 468.

[44] *Mohini Jain v Karnataka* (1992) 3 SCR 658; *Unnikishnan v AP* (1993) 1 SCC 645.

[45] *HP V Umed Ram Sharma* (1986) 1 SCR 251.

[46] *M.C. Mehta v Kamal Nath* (1997) 1 SCC 388, (1997) 2 SCC 411, (1997) 11 SCC 327; *T.N. Godavarman Thirumulpad v Union of India* (1997) 2 SCC 267, (1997) 2 SCC 353, (1997) 3 SCC 312, (1997) 5 SCC 760; *S. Jagannath v Union of India* (1997) 2 SCC 87.

[47] *Dr Ashok v Union* (1997) 5 SCC 10.

[48] See for example, criticism by Seervai (4th edn, Vol. I, p. 438); *Basu Commentary on the Constitution of India*, 7th ed., Vol. B, p. 8.

[49] (1978) 2 SCR 621, 671.

[50] (1974) 4 SCC 3.

[51] (1954) 347 US 497, 499–500.

[52] *Southern Pacific Co. v Jensen* (1917) 244 US 205–22.

[53] (1979) 3 SCR 1014–42.

[54] (1980) 3 SCR 1338, 1358.

[55] (1981) 2 SCR 79, 102.

[56] (1610) 8 Co. Rep 113 to 118.

[57] (1871) LR 6 CP 576, 582.

[58] (1875) 20 Wall 655, 622.

[59] Professor Sir William Wade, *Public Law in Britain and India*, N.M. Tripathi Pvt. Ltd., 1992, pp. 41–2.

[60] *A.C. Kalra v Project Equipment Corporation* (1984) 3 SCR 646, 663; *Express Newspapers v Union* (1985) Supp 3 SCR 382, 471, 472.

[61] *Union of India v Tulsiram* (1985) Supp 2 SCR 131, 233.

[62] *Dwarkadas Marfatia v Board of Trustees* (1989) 2 SCR 751, 764; *Tata Cellular v Union* (1994) 6 SCC 651–75.

[63] *Central Inland Water Transport Corporation Ltd. v Brojo Nath Ganguly* (1986) 2 SCR 278, 370.

[64] *G.B. Mahajan v Jalgaon Municipality* (1991) 3 SCC 91.

[65] *R.K. Garg v Union of India* (1982) 1 SCR 947.

[66] *AP v McDowel & Co.* (1996) 3 SCC 709; *State of Bihar v Bihar Distilleries Ltd.* (1997) 2 SCC 453.

[67] *Malpe Acharya v Maharashtra* (1998) 2 SCC 1.

[68] *Union v Ganayathim* (1997) 7 SCC 463.

[69] Corwin, Introduction to the *Congressional Edition of the US Constitution*, p. xxii.

Twelve

Human Rights: A Worldwide Dialogue*

Claire L'Heureux-Dubé

It is a great honour indeed to have been invited to contribute to this volume marking the golden anniversary of the Supreme Court of India. This anniversary is an important milestone in the Court's history. The Court's work over the past fifty years, especially in giving substantive content to the many human rights protections contained in the Constitution of India, has played a very significant role in shaping modern Indian society. It has been a leader in the protection of human rights in general, and especially those of women and children, the disadvantaged and marginalized. It has also led the world in promoting the rights of all citizens in myriad ways, including the right to a clean environment. The ethic of tolerance and peace that underlies the protection of all human rights is one that has been central in Indian society for centuries. In the eloquent words of the Honourable Justice A.M. Ahmadi, former Chief Justice of India:

India is one of the world's ancient civilizations and legitimately takes pride in its rich heritage. It is the land of Mahavir, saints and sufis and is one country where peoples of all religious faiths the world knows of live in harmony. It can also take pride in the fact that it could bring about a political change through a bloodless revolution which forced the colonial masters to concede freedom to India. India is one country which has firmly believed in peace and unity. Tolerance has been the *ethos* of this country which has enabled peoples of all faiths to live in harmony with each other. Peace and harmony are vital for coexistence and that is why the world over the emphasis is on peace and coexistence. They are vital to the cause of human beings.[1]

This anniversary of the Supreme Court of India deserves special celebration.

*I would like to thank my law clerks, David Wright and Eric Marcoux, for their excellent research and contributions to the preparation of this paper.

Despite the inevitable differences between Indian society and Canadian society, both derive their own democratic parliamentary and judicial institutions from the British tradition and the common law. Most importantly, perhaps, the Constitutions of both countries guarantee fundamental human rights, and our respective courts have given those rights real meaning and significance at the turn of the twenty-first century.

Many of the same difficult issues confront our courts and those around the world: from defining the right to equality to issues such as assisted suicide. For this reason and others, the judicial world is becoming a global one, where judges in different jurisdictions are increasingly looking to a wide variety of sources to interpret their own human rights provisions.[2] As courts look all over the world for authority, the process of international influence is changing from reception to dialogue. Judges no longer simply receive the cases of other jurisdictions and then apply them or modify them for their own jurisdiction. Rather, cross-pollination and dialogue between jurisdictions occurs more and more frequently. Judgements in different countries increasingly build on each other, and mutual respect and dialogue between appellate courts is fostered. No longer are some jurisdictions 'givers' of law while others, 'receivers'. Reception is turning to dialogue.

Reception of other courts' decisions, in a broad sense, is what has been most prominent for judges in Canada and India, as in other former colonies, throughout our history.[3] The Canadian Supreme Court was bound by the decisions of the British Judicial Committee of the Privy Council until the abolition of appeals to that body in 1949. For the common law provinces, as for other British colonies, the principle of the uniformity of the common law ensured that the solutions adopted in Britain would be those that applied elsewhere. The common law was as it was declared in Britain by the House of Lords and the Privy Council, and their cases were applied by colonial courts throughout the world.[4] Even as the formal bonds of colonialism were loosened and adherence to these decisions was no longer necessary, the influence of British jurisprudence on Canadian courts was very strong. In the province of Quebec, which has a civil law system, a similar one-way process occurred. Though there was no colonial link with France, French authors and decisions were examined far more frequently in Quebec than Quebec authors or decisions were examined in France.[5] In addition, the common law was examined, discussed, and sometimes followed far more often in civil law cases than Quebec decisions were considered elsewhere.[6] In general, until recently, influence always went one way: the reasoning of some jurisdictions was applied by others. American decisions, though they did not have binding authority in the sense that British decisions did, were also sometimes considered, certainly with much greater frequency than Canadian decisions were examined by American courts. The use of American precedents in Canada increased as our country developed.[7]

The same heritage of reception has affected Indian jurisprudence. In India, the courts applied common law in many fields during British rule. Even after Independence, Article 372 (1) of the Indian Constitution provides for the continuation of 'all the law in force in the territory of India immediately before the commencement of this Constitution ... until altered or repeated or amended by a competent Legislature or other competent authority'.

As the bonds of colonialism loosened, the prominence of American jurisprudence grew throughout the world. This is particularly true in the field of constitutionalism and human rights. The very concept of judicial review of legislation to ensure its conformity with the Constitution originated in the United States Supreme Court, in the classic case of *Marbury v Madison*.[8] India has adopted the doctrine of judicial review (in Article 13 of its Constitution), as has Canada.

As one of the first human rights instruments in the world to be interpreted and given meaning by the judiciary, the American Bill of Rights had a long history that made it natural for other countries to look to its text and interpretation when drafting and interpreting their own constitutions and human rights protections.[9] Canada and India are no exception. The language of the Indian Constitution borrowed heavily from the American document, to the point where, according to Professor P.K. Tripathi, 'almost every fundamental right which was included in these drafts and which finally became a part of the Constitution of India has its counterpart in the United States'.[10] This process took into account not only the textual wording of American provisions, but also their interpretation by American courts. In some instances, where the drafters of the Indian constitutional provisions believed that modifying the wording would better reflect the interpretation of the Constitution by the US Supreme Court, the language was changed to better reflect the approach of the Supreme Court.[11] The Constitution of India also established a Supreme Court more akin to its American counterpart than the British House of Lords and adopted a federal system that drew upon the experience of other federations such as the United States, Canada, Switzerland, and Australia.[12]

Canada has also been influenced by the American Constitution in the development of its own human rights-protections. Although the wording of the *Canadian Charter of Rights and Freedoms*[13] is arguably less rooted in the American Bill of Rights than in international human rights instruments, particularly the European Convention on Human Rights, the American influence can be particularly seen in the wording of certain sections of the *Charter*.[14] Even before the courts developed extensive *Charter* jurisprudence, Canadians looked southward for inspiration on its meaning and interpretation. Immediately after the passage of the *Charter* in 1982, that influence was scrutinized. Scholars compared and contrasted the language of the two documents for indications of how the *Charter* should be interpreted, focusing both on the similarities and differences in the two documents.[15] It was not long, however, before Canadian courts developed a jurisprudence of their own while being sensitive to other worldwide influences.

The influence of American law on Indian jurisprudence was also significant after the adoption of its Constitution. Many areas of Indian law, since 1950, have been inspired by United States Supreme Court decisions. There are several examples of the close intellectual connection between American and Indian Supreme Court decisions. In *Griffin v Illinois*,[16] *Douglas v California*,[17] and *Gideon v Wainwright*,[18] the US Supreme Court interpreted the due process and equal protection clauses of the Fourteenth Amendment to give indigent defendants the right to free copies of trial transcripts, and the right to counsel in criminal trials and appeals as of right. These three decisions from the US Supreme Court are frequently referred to in Indian Supreme Court decisions. For instance, they were important in *Madhav v Maharashtra*,[19] where the Court held that a right to counsel for indigent defendants and a right to receive a transcript of their trial were contained under the equal protection guarantees of the Indian Constitution.[20]

A more recent example which also illustrates this close connection is the Indian Supreme Court's decision in *Rajagopal and another v State of Tamil Nadu*.[21] Central to the case were issues of balancing freedom of expression and of the right to privacy. The court devoted several pages to the cases of *New York Times Co. v Sullivan*,[22] *Cox Broadcasting Corp. v Cohn*,[23] *Griswold v Connecticut*,[24] and *Roe v Wade*,[25] all classic Warren and Burger court decisions.

The Canadian Supreme Court's constitutional *Charter* jurisprudence similarly owes much to the US influence,[26] particularly in areas of freedom of religion, due process guarantees, and free speech.[27] American solutions to particular problems, be they the constitutionality of restrictions on abortion,[28] hate speech,[29] or publication of court proceedings,[30] to name just a few, have been considered, although not necessarily followed. To note just two examples among many, Canada's Supreme Court explicitly rejected the American approach in the areas of hate speech and mandatory contributions to unions for political purposes.[31] However, examining and considering this jurisprudence allowed us to benefit from the expertise built over two hundred years of interpretation of constitutional rights in a democratic society with many similarities to our own. When we rejected American approaches, we were able to identify the differences that led to this rejection. The same is true for India. In *Rangarajan v Jagjivan Ram*,[32] for example, the Supreme Court referred to US cases dealing with the right to freedom of expression, but warned against their use beyond general principles.

There were other reasons, of course, for the strong influence of countries like the United States and Britain. Until recently, only certain countries' law reports were widely available around the world. Accordingly, these were the only foreign sources to which it was possible to turn. Academic writing focused on the larger and most important jurisdictions, and this literature was also more easily accessible abroad. Judges and litigants naturally looked where they could most easily find materials.

Another especially influential factor is education. Judges, lawyers, and academics who pursue their studies abroad usually attend universities in Britain, France, and the United States, and are, therefore, more exposed to their jurisprudence and legal culture. When the time comes to look for solutions to similar problems, they naturally turn to those jurisdictions for inspiration and comparison. For example, American scholarship was brought to India by those who studied in American universities in the 1950s and 1960s, and American approaches dominated Indian law teaching.[33] Similarly, in Canada, legal educational backgrounds have clearly contributed to the influence of certain jurisdictions on our law. Supreme Court justices educated in the United States, it has been shown, have referred to the United States jurisprudence with greater frequency than others.[34] A shift in postgraduate legal education caused a similar shift in the focus of judicial thinking. As McWhinney remarked:

Legal education before World War I was essentially Anglocentric in character. British schools were the locus of such postgraduate education in law as was then undertaken by Canadian lawyers and law professors; and English legal traditions and English judicial attitudes were widely admired and imitated within Canada. Between the two World Wars, the emphasis shifted to the United

States. The lessons from American constitutional experience were then taught in the Canadian law schools.[35]

As lawyers and future judges from around the world pursued their studies in countries that were the centres of legal thinking, these countries' influence increased even more. This is as true for Canada as it is for India.

Current trends, however, show how dramatically this picture is changing.[36] Rather than comparative law being a one-way transmission of existing law from some jurisdictions to others, the development of human rights jurisprudence, in particular, is now becoming, to a greater extent, a dialogue. Judges look to a broad spectrum of sources in human rights law, in particular when deciding how to interpret their constitutions and deal with new problems. To a greater and greater extent, they are mutually reading and discussing each other's jurisprudence. Rather than each looking to the United States and Britain, countries like Canada and India are looking to each other, and our courts' words are being quoted and considered by judges in countries around the world.

There are several examples of the developing dialogue between Canada and India. In *Keegstra*,[37] Chief Justice Dickson of the Supreme Court of Canada referred to the Penal Codes of India, Netherlands and Sweden and the England and Wales *Public Order Act, 1986* (UK), to observe that many countries possessed laws suppressing hate propaganda similar to that found in Canada. In *McKinney v University of Guelph*,[38] one of the questions examined by the Court was whether citizens can contract out of their equality rights under Section 15 of the *Charter* or whether public policy prevents this. In addressing this issue, Wilson J dissenting, noted that 'the Supreme Court of India has held that if the right is in the nature of prohibition addressed to government and inserted in the Constitution on grounds of public policy, it cannot be waived by an individual even though he or she may be primarily benefited by it'.[39] Recently, in a case involving sexual assault and the defence of honest but mistaken belief in consent,[40] I was inspired by Anand CJ's opinion in *State of Punjab v Singh*.[41] I also referred to the words of wisdom of Thomas J of the Supreme Court of India in regard to the danger of basing conclusions on biased or stereotypical assumptions rather than on the evidence:

It is an irony that while we are celebrating women's rights in all spheres, we show little or no concern for her honour. It is a sad reflection and we must emphasize that the courts must deal with rape cases in particular with utmost sensitivity and appreciate the evidence in the totality of the background of the entire case and not in isolation.[42]

The Supreme Court of India has also frequently cited Canadian precedents. For instance, in a judgement which upheld the constitutionality of the criminalization of assisted suicide,[43] the Supreme Court considered American and British decisions and the opinion of the majority in *Rodriguez v British Columbia (Attorney General)*.[44] Another recent example can be found in *Sanjay Dutt v State*,[45] where the Court referred to a judgement of our Court[46] in support of the principle that 'mere conscious possession of a forbidden substance is sufficient to constitute an offence' and that the offence created under the *Terrorist and Disruptive Activities (Prevention) Act*, 1987 was 'not extraordinary or conceptually impermissible'.

Canadian and Indian jurisprudence are frequently referred to in a number of countries around the world, along with cases from many other countries. Take, as just one example among many, the recent Namibian case of *Mwellie v Ministry of Works*.[47] In that case, the High Court had to determine an appropriate interpretation of the guarantee of equality in the country's new constitution. In so doing, the Court looked to judgements from High Courts of India, Canada, the United States, England, Malaysia, and South Africa, as well as to decisions of the European Court of Human Rights. In the South African case of *State v Makwanyane*,[48] the Constitutional Court, in determining the constitutionality of the death penalty, examined in considerable detail decisions from India, Zimbabwe, Jamaica, Germany, Canada, the United States, the European Court of Human Rights, Hungary, the United Nations Committee on Human Rights, Botswana, Hong Kong, and Tanzania. A recent Privy Council decision dealing with the Constitution of Antigua and Barbuda, reviewed cases from Canada, India, the European Court of Human Rights, the European Commission on Human Rights, the United States, South Africa, and Zimbabwe. There are numerous other exmaples of similar approaches from, among others, England, Canada, South Africa, Zimbabwe, Australia, India, and New Zealand.[49] Judges in many countries are speaking and listening to each other through their judgements.

Another interesting example of cross-pollination is seen in the New Zealand Court of Appeal's *Police v Smith* and *Police v Herewini*[50] judgement. In that case, the issue was whether a person whose blood sample was taken in a hospital following a motor vehicle accident was entitled to a right to counsel warning under section 23(1) of the *New Zealand Bill of Rights Act 1990*.[51] Canadian courts had previously decided that there was a right to counsel in an equivalent situation under the Canadian *Charter*. The New Zealand judgement gave extensive consideration to Canadian jurisprudence, and affidavits of the Chief Coroner of Ontario and an Ontario Crown counsel were filed with the New Zealand court about the effects of the right to counsel requirement in Canadian hospitals. This evidence was useful to the High Court, since one of the arguments raised was that granting a right to counsel would be unworkable in practice. Although the majority of the New Zealand Court did not follow the Canadian approach, an examination of the Canadian process of reasoning and at least two people's views of its effects enabled the court to make a more informed decision about the proper rule for New Zealand.

There are a number of reasons why the legal world is becoming a global one, and this increasing dialogue is taking place. They include some of the same factors that are leading to change and globalization in the world at large as well as other developments internal to the legal community.

First, perhaps more than ever, the same issues are facing many courts throughout the world. Issues such as assisted suicide, abortion, hate speech, gay and lesbian rights, environmental protection, privacy, and the nature of democracy, to name just a few, are being placed before judges in different jurisdictions at approximately the same time. As social debates and discussions around the world become more and more similar, so of course do the equivalent legal debates. Again, the growing similarity of social debates and conflicts can be partially attirbuted to the advances in global communications and contacts. In addition, with this increasing transmission of news and information acrosss borders, potential litigants are made more aware of the results of litigation in a certain jurisdiction, and may see it as encouragement to pursue a similar course of action in their country.

A second factor leading to the globalization of the judicial world in the field of human rights is the global nature of human rights and human rights guarantees themselves. Since the Second World War, there has been a global emphasis on human rights, which led to the passage of the Universal Declaration of Human Rights, and the signing of the International Covenants on Civil and Political Rights and on Economic, Social, and Cultural Rights. These have been reflected in regional human rights treaties and in human rights guarantees in national constitutions. There are numerous genealogical 'links' between national human rights guarantees and international rights documents, as well as between various national and regional human rights provisions. For example, the 'founding fathers' of the Indian Constitution incorporated most of the rights enumerated in the Universal Declaration of Rights.[52]

Similarly, the drafters of the Canadian *Charter* drew extensively on international human rights treaties.[53] Such links are reflected in the similar language, organization, and principles of many human rights guarantees, and it may, therefore, be useful to refer to decisions of other courts because of the similar links to international law. In addition, national courts may often gain insights through reference to international human rights documents themselves and to decisions of other courts which apply their principles in relation to domestic law. In the words of P.N. Bhagwati, former Chief Justice of India, now Chairman of the CIJL Advisory Board:

The judiciary is not on an uncharted sea in this exercise of judicial interpretational lawmaking. The constitutional values and the international human rights instruments serve as a beacon light, a lodestar to guide and provide direction to the judge, and he must follow the dictates contained in these documents, since these documents represent the will of the people and the aspirations of the world community.[54]

The prolific use by the Supreme Court of India of international human rights instruments emphasizes their importance and that of India's international obligations. Today, many rights that exist in India, such as the right to privacy,[55] the right to freedom from torture, or cruel, inhuman, or degrading treatment or punishment,[56] the right to a speedy trial,[57] the right to free legal services,[58] freedom from imprisonment for an inability to fulfil contractual obligation,[59] the right to compensation for unlawful arrest or detention,[60] and the right to education[61] have all become part of India's constitutional heritage principally on account of their interpretation by the Supreme Court, influenced by international instruments.[62] The Supreme Court of India has emphasized that it may consider international conventions and norms in construing domestic law when there is no inconsistency and there is a void in domestic law.[63]

Recently, the Supreme Court of India examined the *Convention on the Elimination of All forms of Discrimination against Women* (hereinafter CEDAW) and the recommendations of the UN *Committee on the Elimination of Discrimination against Women* for the purpose of construing the scope of the constitutional guarantee of gender equality.[64] The Court concluded that 'the content of the fundamental rights guaranteed in the Constitution are of sufficient amplitude to encompass all the facets of gender equality including prevention of sexual harassment or abuse.'[65] Chief Justice Anand, for the majority in *Hariharan & Anr. v Reserve Bank of India & Anr.*,[66] also referred to international conventions. He held:

The message of international instruments—Convention on the Elimination of all Forms of Discrimination against Women, 1979 (CEDAW) and the Beijing Declaration, which directs all State parties to take appropriate measures to prevent discrimination of all forms against women is quite clear. India is a signatory to CEDAW having accepted and ratified it in June, 1993. The interpretation that we have placed on section 6(a) [of the Hindu, Minority and Guardianship Act, 1956] gives effect to the principles contained in these instruments.[67]

In the field of environmental law, the Supreme Court of India is a world leader and the subject of admiration by courts around the world for its reception of international environmental norms and its use of such norms as a tool for interpretation of constitutional provisions. International norms such as the declaration adopted by the United Nations Conference on the Human Environment at the Stockholm Conference in 1972 and the 1984 UN Resolution embodying the right to an environment adequate for health and well-being are frequently referred to.[68] The Court has recognized that Article 21 of the Indian Constitution includes the right to a clean and wholesome environment and, therefore, that 'any action that would cause environmental, ecological, air, water pollution, etc., should be regarded as amounting to a violation of Article 21'.[69] Recently, the Supreme Court had no hesitation in recognizing the 'polluter pays principle' as part of customary international law resulting from international deliberations culminating in the Earth Summit at Rio in 1992, and in importing that principle into Indian domestic law.[70]

International norms and treaties are also extensively referred to in Canadian jurisprudence. Our Court has stated on numerous occasions that international human rights documents and conventions should be ascribed a high degree of importance and should inform the interpretation of the rights guaranteed by the *Canadian Charter of Rights and Freedoms*.[71] In a recent judgement of our Court, I outlined, in concurring reasons, that CEDAW and the recommendations of the Committee on the Elimination of Discrimination against Women were a response to the pervasive violence against women around the world and that:

Violence against women is as much a matter of equality as it is an offence against human dignity and a violation of human rights.[72]

That larger framework was important to understand the context in which Canada revamped its sexual assault provisions. In the same fashion, the Supreme Court in *R. v Butler*[73] determined that the *Criminal Code* provision prohibiting obscene material was consistent with Canada's international obligations.

In *Keegstra*,[74] Canada's Supreme Court discussed at length the stance taken toward hate propaganda in international law. At issue was the constitutional validity of the *Criminal Code* provision prohibiting wilful promotion of hatred against identifiable groups. The Court considered the international community's position which condemns hate propaganda, and obliges state parties to the *International Convention on the Elimination of All Forms of Racial Discrimination* and *International Covenant on Civil and Political Rights* to prohibit such expression, to emphasize the purpose of the contested legislation and, in the words of Dickson CJ:

[T]he principles of equality and the inherent dignity of all persons that infuse both international human rights and the *Charter*.[75]

As these examples illustrate, links to international human rights law help form a kind of 'common denominator' of understanding between judges in the interpretation of national human rights documents. However, as the President of the Bar Association of India and senior advocate to the Supreme Court of India, Fali S. Nariman, wisely commented:

Declarations and written constitutions are not magic potions: they have to be applied and interpreted. They require independent advocates and brave judges.[76]

The Bar of India as well as the Supreme Court of India have been a model and an inspiration for the world in leading the way with leadership, courage, erudition and distinction in giving meaning to these rights.

In summary, the standards of international law are used by many countries as interpretative aids for domestic constitutional law,[77] and this contributes to globalization. The remarks of the former Chief Justice of India, P.N. Bhagwati are most apropos:

When the judiciary interprets the words of the charter of human rights embodied in the Constitution in a creative and goal-oriented manner, it is not defying the words used in the Constitution nor is it going contrary to the constitutional mandate but it is merely interpreting the Constitution—giving meaning to it—which is its legitimate function. The judiciary therefore, can and must internalize human rights norms embodied in the various international instruments adopted by the United Nations and its allied organs such as ILO. Even if the judiciary finds that a particular human rights instrument has not been ratified by its country, it must have regard to the human rights embodied in such instrument because these human rights represent norms accepted by the entire international community.[78]

Reference to international law and human rights instruments by courts in discharging their constitutional mandate can only strengthen our understanding of these instruments, and help develop a common language of human rights that permeates the jurisprudence of countries around the world.

A third factor leading to the growing internationalization of the judiciary is the advancement of communication technology.[79] With the existence of computers and electronic databases, access to decisions in a broad range of jurisdictions is possible. For example, anyone with a connection to the World Wide Web can obtain recent decisions of Canada's Supreme Court, free of charge, as soon as they are released.[80] Decisions of other courts around the world are also diffused electronically, and there are numerous Internet sites which consolidate access to banks of case law, statutes, and other materials from vaious jurisdictions.[81] The International Commission of Jurists has committed itself to facilitate this international communication of decisions relating to the independence of the judiciary. These developments make it much easier to consult comparative constitutional sources in argument and in judgements. It also means that the fact that law libraries may not subscribe to law reports from individual jurisdictions need not mean that there is no access to their decisions. In this age where so much legal research is done through computer searches, it is particularly important to be aware of all international decisions on a given topic for appropriate principles or citations. The increased access to information brought by changes in technology has had a particularly strong impact in the legal field, since the work of an advocate is, in large part, about managing and gathering information to support one's position. Lawyers and judges benefit from this increase in opportunities for access to other courts' decisions but ultimately, this exchange ensures better justice for all.

A fourth contributor to the increasing internationalization of the judicial world is the growing personal contact between members of the judiciary from different countries. Judges from various countries often discuss common problems at international judges' conferences, by e-mail, and over the telephone. While, until recently, it was uncommon for judges working in different continents to have opportunities to get to know each other, let alone communicate regularly about issues of mutual concern, close interactions are now becoming commonplace. I know that the friendships I have developed with judges from countries like the United States, Zimbabwe, South Africa, Morocco, Sri Lanka, Pakistan, Israel, and India, among others, have enabled me to discuss and exchange ideas with them about decisions of our respective courts, and about issues that cross national boundaries. In India, in particular, it has been a very great privilege during my visits to meet a number of judges and lawyers and interact on subjects of mutual interests for which I am extremely grateful. It has given me the opportunity to develop my interest in the jurisprudence of your courts and to deepen my knowledge of your great Constitution. All this has been to my immense benefit and hopefully to the benefit of our Canadian jurisprudence.

I believe that participating in such a worldwide dialogue helps improve the decisions we make, as well as our reasons, through contact with the ideas and insights of colleagues from all over the world. Speaking and communicating with those from outside our own country gives perspectives on the issues facing courts that would otherwise remain unknown. Meeting face to face, building relationships, and sharing ideas between judges from different jurisdictions is bound to improve and refine the process of judicial globalization, while also letting us identify the pitfalls to which we must be attentive when using the decisions of other countries.

A caveat is necessary here. Indeed, despite these positive aspects of increasing globalization, there are dangers that we must also recognize. Though the solutions of the international community are useful and important considerations, we must ensure that foreign reasoning is not imported without sufficient consideration of the context in which it is being applied. There are important reasons why the solutions developed in one jurisdiction may be inappropriate elsewhere. Political and social realities, values, and traditions differ across borders, regions, and levels of development.

This is particularly true of Canada and India. Though we have much in common, our societies face distinct social problems and issues, our economies are very different, and the make up of our societies is different in many ways. When reading and comparing each other's jurisprudence, therefore, jurists must be attentive to these differences. We should not assume without question that legal analysis which is appropriate in India is also appropriate in Canada, or vice versa. Especially in the area of human rights, the social context in which a decision is made may significantly affect its outcome, and an understanding of those contexts, their similarities and differences is crucial.

I should also emphasize that the legal community should be encouraged to continue to look elsewhere even after jurisprudence on constitutional human rights has been developed. We should not be global jurists only when constitutions are new, and then turn inward once jurisprudential principles have been developed. Because jurisprudence is constantly evolving, and solutions to new problems must always be found, foreign decisions are useful tools whether there is one case interpreting a human rights provision or one hundred. Dialogue must continue long after the rights themselves are articulated and tests for their interpretation have developed. Though India has fifty years of constitutional interpretation behind it, and Canada is approaching twenty, this does not mean that we can no longer benefit from the insights, ideas, or solutions of others elsewhere.

Perhaps most important, this should be a process of dialogue, and jurists in all countries must be careful not to slip into the familiar pattern of giving and receiving law. Though the Canadian Supreme Court, for example, is willing to look elsewhere, and does so frequently, it is cited by courts in places other than the United States more often than it refers to cases from countries like India, Zimbabwe, South Africa, or Israel. In part, litigants do not refer to such jurisprudence as much as they should, and more reference in argument would help courts like Canada's take a greater part in this international dialogue. Even though we have a head start on some other developing human rights jurisprudence, we have much to learn from them through consideration of their judgements and their addressal in our own decisions. If, in turn, we examine and reflect upon them, our thinking and knowledge will be strengthened.

In conclusion, judging at the turn of the millennium is undergoing fundamental changes. Among these is the fact that consideration of foreign decisions is becoming standard practice for more and more courts throughout the world. What has been called by Professor Tushnet 'the globalization of constitutional law'[82] is now a fundamental reality of decision making. No longer is it appropriate to speak of the impact or influence of certain courts on other countries, but rather of the place of all courts in the global dialogue on human rights and other common legal issues.

Courts in Canada and India may learn much from each other in the years to come, particularly in the field of human rights. Greater dialogue can only assist us both in the task which is at the heart of the work of all judges: serving the cause of justice. In emphasizing the importance of that task and the role of aggressively protecting human rights when achieving it, I can do no better than to quote the words of someone who has been a great friend and inspiration to me: Soli J. Sorabjee, your present Attorney-General and jurist par excellence:

Ultimately freedom cannot be preserved for an inert people by the Constitution or Courts. Civil liberties do not defend themselves. They are not sustained by the chanting of mantras or by any brooding omnipresence in the sky. Yet, without independent Courts manned by judges possessed with courage and vision, and above all, a vibrant sensitivity for human rights, civil liberties become cruel shibboleths. Above all else, the reality of their existence lies in their constant assertion by the people and their judicious judicial protection ...[83]

The Supreme Court of India can be proud of its achievements and commitment to human rights. Its influence through the dialogue it pursues with the legal community throughout the world will continue to inspire us. This is cause for celebration on this golden anniversary of its creation.

Notes

(Editors' note: SCR referred to in notes 26–31, 38, 40, 44, 73 refer to the *Canadian Supreme Court Reports* which are also cited as SCR.)

[1] 'Inaugural Address by the Honourable Shri A.M. Ahmadi' (1995) 55 *Int'l Comm. Jur. Rev.*, 17 at 18.

[2] Parts of this article have been adapted from : C. L'Heureux-Dubé, 'The Importance of Dialogue: Globalization and the International Impact of the Rehnquist Court' (1998) 34, *Tulsa L. J.*, 15.

[3] On the use of foreign decisions by Canadian common law courts, see H.P. Glenn, 'The Use of Comparative Law by Common Law Courts in Canada', in International Congress of Comparative Law, *Contemporary Law/Droit Contemporain*, Yvon Blais, Cowansville, 1994, 85.

[4] P.W. Hogg, *Constitutional Law of Canada*, Carswell, Toronto, 3rd edn, 1992 at 30–1.

[5] On the influence of French doctrine in Quebec, see P.G. Jobin, 'L'influence de la doctrine française sur le droit civil québécois: le rapprochement et l'eloignement de deux continents', 1992, RIDC, 381.

[6] See, e.g. Jobin, ibid., J.E.C. Brierley, 'Bijuralism in Canada', in International Congress of Comparative Law, *Contemporary Law/Droit contemporain,* Yvon Blais, Cowansville, Quebec, 1990, 22 at 39–43. On the increasing use of civil law decisions in common law courts, see Glenn, *supra* note 3.

[7] See G.V. La Forest, 'The Use of American Precedents in Canadian Courts' (1994) 46, *Maine L. Rev.,* 211 at 212–13.

[8] US (1803) (1 Cranch) 137, 2 L. Ed. 60.

[9] On the influence of the American constitution on drafters and interpreters of other constitutions, see Lester, *supra* note 1; W.J. Brennan, 'The Worldwide Influence of the United States Constitution as a Charter of Human Rights' (1991) 15 *Nova L. Rev.* E.A. Rapaczynski. 'Bibliographical Essay: The Influence of US Constitutionalism Abroad', in L. Henken and A.J. Rosenthal (eds), *Constitutionalism and Rights: The Influence of the American Constitution Abroad,* Columbia University Press, New York 1990, p. 405; and the essays on specific places collected in Henken and Rosenthal (eds), ibid.; L.W. Beer (ed.), *Constitutionalism in Asia: Asian Views of the American Influence,* University of California Press, Berkeley, 1979; G.A. Billias (ed.), *American Constitutionalism Abroad,* Greenwood Press, New York, 1990.

[10] P.K. Tripathi, 'Perspectives on the American Constitutional Influence on the Constitution of India', in Beer (ed.), ibid., 59 at 80.

[11] Ibid.

[12] R. Dhavan, 'Borrowed Ideas: On the Impact of American Scholarship on Indian Law' (1985) 33 *Am. J. Comp. L.*, 505 at 511; M. Kachwaha, *The Judiciary in India: Determinant of its Independence and Impartiality*, Centre for the Independence of Judges and Lawyers (CIJL), Geneva 1998, at 14.

[13] *Canadian Charter of Rights and Freedoms*, Part I of the *Constitution Act, 1982*, being Schedule B to the *Canada Act 1982* (UK), 1982, c. 11 (hereinafter *Charter*).

[14] *Charter*, ibid., Section 7, 10–14. See P.W. Hogg, 'Canada's New Charter of Rights' (1984) 32 *Am. J. Comp. L.*, 283

[15] See, e.g., W.S. Tarnopolsky, 'The New Canadian Charter of Rights and Freedoms as Compared and Contrasted with the American Bill of Rights' (1983) 5, *Hum. Rts. Q.* 227; P. Bender, 'The Canadian Charter of Rights and Freedoms and the United States Bill of Rights: A Comparison' (1983) 28, *McGill L.J.*, 811; Hogg, ibid.

[16] (1956) 351 US 12.

[17] (1963) 372 US 353.

[18] (1963) 372 US 335.

[19] (1979) 1 SCR 192.

[20] R.B. Charles, 'American Influence on the Indian Constitution: Focus on the Equal Protection of the Law' (1986) 17, *Columbia Human Rights L. Rev.*, 193 at 213.

[21] (1995) 3 LRC 566.

[22] (1967) 376 US 254.

[23] (1975) 420 US 469.

[24] (1965) 381 US 479.

[25] (1973) 410 US 113.

[26] C.P. Manfredi, 'The Canadian Supreme Court and American Judicial Review: United States Constitutional Jurisprudence and the Canadian Charter of Rights and Freedoms' (1992), 40, *Am. J. Comp. L.*, 213 at 214–18. See, e.g., *Hunter v Southam*, (1984) 2 SCR 145 at 156.

[27] See, e.g., *R. v Big M Drug Mart* (1985) 1 SCR 295; *Ford v Quebec* (1988) 2 SCR 712; *R. v Oakes* (1986) 1 SCR 103.

[28] *R. v Morgentaler* (1988)1 SCR 30.

[29] *R. v Keegstra* (1990) 3 SCR 697 (hereinafter *Keegstra*).

[30] *Edmonton Journal v Alberta (A.–G.)*, (1989) 3 SCR 1326.

[31] *Keegstra*, *supra* note 29; *Lavigne v OPSEU* (1991) 2 SCR 211.

[32] (1990) LRC 412 at 416–17.

[33] Dhavan, *supra* note 12 at 516–17.

[34] S.I. Bushnell, 'The Use of American Cases' 1986 35, UNBIJ, 157 at 169.

[35] E. McWhinney, 'The Constitutional Patriation Project, 1980–82' (1984) 32, *Am. J. Comp. L.*, 241 at 262.

[36] See, for example, B. Ackerman, 'The Rise of World Constitutionalism' (1997), 83, *Va. L. Rev.*, 771.

[37] *Supra* note 29 at 770.

[38] (1990) 3 SCR 229.

[39] Ibid. at 406, referring to *Behram Khurshid v State of Bombay* 1995 AIR SC 123 and *Basheshar Nath v Commissioner of Income Tax* (1959) Supp 1 SCR 528.

[40] *R. v Esau*, (1997) 2 SCR 777 at 797.

[41] (1996) 2 SCC 384.

[42] *State of AP v Murthy* (1997) 1 SCC 272 at 279–80.

[43] *Gian Kaur (Smt) v State of Punjab* (1996) 2 LRC 264 at 277–8.

[44] (1993) 3 SCR 519.

[45] (1996) 1 LRC 467 at 488.

[46] *Beaver v The Queen* (1957) SCR 531.

[47] (1995) 4 LRC 184.

[48] (1995) 2 SA 391.

[49] See, for example, *McGinty v State of Western Australia* 1996 1 LRC 599 Austl; *Re Chikweche*, (1995) 2 LRC 93 Zimb.; *M'Membe & Another v The People* (1996) 2 LRC 280 Zambia.

[50] (1994) 1 LRC 252.

[51] The taking of the blood samples was authorized by the *Transport Act, 1982*, section 58D.

[52] See, principally, the Fundamental Rights (Part III) and the Directive Principles (Part IV) of the Constitution of India, Kachwaha, *supra* note 12 at 109; A.M. Ahmadi (former Chief Justice of India), *Thoughts and Reflections of Sri Justice*, Judicial Academy, Andhra Pradesh, 1997, at 140.

[53] A. Bayefsky, 'International Human Rights Law in Canadian Courts', in B. Conforti and F. Francioni (eds) *Enforcing International Human Rights in Domestic Courts*, Martinus Nijhoff, The Hague, 1997, 295 at 310; J. Claydon, 'International Human Rights Law and the Interpretation of the Canadian Charter of Rights and Freedoms' (1982) 4, Supreme Court LR 287 at 287.

[54] P.N. Bhagwati, 'Judicial Independence vs Judicial Accountability: A Debate' (1999) 7, *CIJL Yearbook* 85 at 88.

[55] *Kharak Singh v State of Uttar Pradesh* (1964) 1 SCR 332 (Ayyangar J) and recently *State of Maharashtra v M.N. Mardikar* (1991) 1 SCC 57.

[56] *Sunil Batra v Delhi Adminstration* (1979) 1 SCR 392; *Prem Shanker (II) v Delhi Adminstration* (1980) 3 SCR 855; *Francis Coralie Mullin v Union Territory of Delhi* (1981) 2 SCR 516.

[57] *Hussainara Khatoon v State of Bihar* (1979) 3 SCR 169.

[58] *Khatri v State of Bihar* (1981) 1 SCC 635.

[59] *Jolly George Varghese v Bank of Cochin* (1980) 2 SCR 913.

[60] *Rudul Shah v State of Bihar* (1983) 3 SCR 508, where the Court awarded compensation to the petitioner, who was tortured while in police custody.

[61] *Mohini Jain v State of Karnataka* (1992) 3 SCC 666. See also *Ajay Hasia v Khalid Mujib* (1981) 2 SCR 79; *Unnikrishan v State of AP* (1993) 1 SCC 645.

[62] V. Sripati, 'Human Rights in India—Fifty Years after Independence' (1997) 26 *J. In'l L. & Pol'y*, Denvor, 93 at 118.

[63] *Vishaka v Rajasthan* (1997) 3 LRC 361 at 367 [hereinafter *Vishaka*], where the Court cites in support the decision of the High Court of Australia in *Minister for Immigration and Ethnic Affairs v Teoh* (1995) 3 LRC 1. See also *Hariharan & Anr. v Reserve Bank of India & Anr.*, at 532 (Anand CJ).

[64] *Vishaka*, op. cit., at 366–7.

[65] Ibid. at 367.

[66] *Supra* note 63. See also the decision of Anand CJ in *Apparel Export Promotion Council v A.K. Chopra*, Civil Appeal Nos. 226–7 of 1999 decided on 20 January 1999.

[67] Ibid.

[68] Sripati, *supra* note 62 at 128, referring to *M.C. Mehta v Union of India* (1987) 4 SCC 467; *Law Society of India v Fertilizers and Chemicals, Travancore Ltd.*

[69] *Subhas Kumar v State of Uttar Pradesh* JT 1991 (1) SC 531, at 538, quoted by Sripati, op. cit., at 21.

[70] *Vellore Citizens Welfare Forum v Union of India* JT 1996 (7) SC 375, discussed in D. Shanmuganathan and L.M. Warren, 'Status of Sustainable Development as a Principle of National and International Law: The Indian Approach' (1997) 9, *Journal of Env. L.,* 387 at 399–400.

[71] *Keegstra, supra* note 29; *Slaight Communications Inc. v Davidson,* (1989) 1 SCR 1038.

[72] *R. v Ewanchuk* 25 February 1999 at para. 69.

[73] (1992) 1 SCR 452.

[74] *Supra* note 29.

[75] Ibid. at 754–5.

[76] F.S. Nariman, 'The Universality of Human Rights' (1993) 50, *Int'l Comm. Jur. Rev.* 8 at 17.

[77] See, e.g., Bagyefsky, *supra* note 53.

[78] P.N. Bhagwati, 'Domestic Application of Human Rights Norms', in *Developing Human Rights Jurisprudence,* Vol. 4, Commonwealth Secretariat Interights, London, 1992, 23 at 28.

[79] See S.S. Abrahamson, 'All the World's a Courtroom: Judging in the New Millennium' (1997) 26, *Hofstra L. Rev.* 273 at 291.

[80] At www.droit,umontreal.ca/doc/csc-scc/

[81] In this respect, I would note that the High Court of Australia is at the forefront of the judicial use of the Internet. Michael Kirby, Justice of the High Court of Australia in M. Kirby, 'The Courts of the Future' (1991) 7, *CIJL Yearbook,* 51 at 53–4, explains that judgements are available within minutes of their delivery, transcripts of oral arguments and summaries of cases pending are also available as will soon also be the submissions of the parties. Furthermore, decisions are now given in medium neutral form which facilitates citation.

[82] Quoted in L. Greenhouse, 'Appealing to the Law's Brooding Spirit', *New York Times,* 6 July 1997, 4 at 4.

[83] S.J. Sorabjee, *The Law of Press Censorship in India,* Tripathi, Bombay, 1976, at 25–6, quoted by Lord Lester of Herne Hill QC in 'Private Lives and Public Figures: Freedom of Political Speech in a Democratic Society', *Times of India,* 17 December 1998.

Thirteen

The Supreme Court on Human Rights and Social Justice: Changing Perspectives

Atul M. Setalvad

Human Rights

The field of human rights and social justice is vast, and any useful discussion must, therefore, begin with an attempt to delimit the concepts being discussed.

The Universal Declaration of Human Rights, adopted in 1948, before our Constitution was adopted, embraces within its field both the right to personal liberty in the narrower sense, i.e. freedom from arbitrary arrest, a fair criminal trial, etc., as also wider concepts of social justice such as equality, equal pay for equal work, the right to work, the right to an adequate livelihood, and the right to education. This shows that the concepts of human rights and social justice overlap to a very considerable extent or, to put it differently, the right to social justice is as much a part of human rights as the more traditional rights such as the right to personal liberty.

Constitutional Provisions

Those who drafted our Constitution were people who had spent years fighting colonial rule, and opposing numerous laws which curtailed personal liberty. They were, therefore, keen to incorporate into the Constitution safeguards which would ensure that no government of independent India could deprive its people of the basic rights they had fought the British for. They were equally conscious of the need to give our people meaningful social and economic rights. They faced, however, two constraints. First, the last few years of British rule, and the partition of the country had resulted in grave breaches of law and order in many parts of India, with numerous instances of savage inter-communal strife. Amongst the administrators, and many political figures there was, therefore, the perception, right or wrong, that the provisions in the Constitution should not prevent the administration from dealing with what were called anti-national and fissiparous elements. Second, whilst there was near unanimity on enacting provisions designed to bring about an egalitarian society with social justice, it was realized that the country was just too poor to enshrine rights such as the right to work as enforceable rights.

The first constraint led to the qualification or curtailment of all the basic freedoms by enacting, at the same time, provisions permitting the curtailment of the rights in given situations, and, in a curious set of provisions, enacting in the chapter on fundamental rights, a charter to the executive to *preventively detain* persons. The second constraint led to the division of these provisions into two chapters, the enforceable rights being called fundamental *rights*, and the desirable objectives being called directive *principles*.

In the field of equality, our constitutional provisions broadly conform to the Universal Declaration:[1] Article 14 guarantees equality before the law and the equal protection of laws, and Article 16 guarantees equality in public employment. Article 15 prohibits any discrimination on the ground of religion, race, caste or place of birth, and considering our specific social problems, also prohibits discrimination or disability in access to shops, public restaurants, hotels, etc., or to wells, tanks and bathing places open to the general public on the ground of race, religion, caste, or place of birth. The latter part of Article 15 is a corollary to Article 17 which abolishes untouchability and provides that the enforcement of any disability arising out of untouchability shall be a criminal offence. The permitted exceptions to equality are provisions permitting positive discrimination[2] in the interests of women and children, socially and educationally backward classes or persons belonging to the scheduled castes or tribes. In the field of personal liberty, Article 20 provides against ex post facto laws and against self-incrimination and embodies, in part, the principle of *autre fois acquit*.[3] Article 21 provides that no person can be deprived of life or personal liberty except in accordance with a procedure established by law.[4] The words 'procedure established by law' were deliberately chosen in preference to the well-known 'due process of law', as there was a conscious desire to avoid the consequences of the phrase 'due process' which had been interpreted in the United States to signify a requirement that the law must be reasonable and fair. Article 22(1) and (2) provides that any person who is arrested must be produced promptly before a magistrate, informed of the grounds of his arrest, and would have a right to consult, and be defended, by a legal practitioner of his choice.[5]

Article 22(3) to (7), though part of the chapter on fundamental rights, curtails basic freedoms. These provisions permit persons to be arrested and detained for months, if not years, at the will of the executive, subject to the nominal safeguard that, at some time or the other, the case of the person detained will be considered by an advisory board, which need not even give a reasoned order. These provisions are directly contrary to Article 9 of the Universal Declaration which provides that there cannot be any arbitrary arrest, and Article 9 of the International Covenant on Civil and Political Rights, 1976, which requires that the continued detention of a person would only be permissible if a judicial authority has had an opportunity to review the detention.

It is noteworthy that the attempts to curtail the powers of the executive in the field of preventive detention, inserted in Article 22 by the Constitution (44th Amendment) Act, 1976, have been frustrated by the executive itself by failing to bring the provision into force though over twenty years have elapsed. Under the amendment, the advisory boards were made truly independent, and it was provided that the case of a detenu had to be reviewed by the Board within a maximum period of three months.

Article 19 of the Constitution guarantees to every citizen freedom of speech, freedom of assembly, freedom of association, freedom of movement, freedom to reside and settle anywhere in the country, and the right to carry on any trade or business. Each of these freedoms can, however, be curtailed by reasonable restrictions to the extent specified in sub-Article 19(2) to (6). These freedoms, as enacted, substantially correspond with the Universal Declaration and the International Convention on Civil and Political Rights. In the fields of freedom of religion, and minority rights, our constitutional provisions are exemplary, and in full accord with both the Universal Declaration, and the International Convention on Civil and Political Rights. Article 25 guarantees freedom to profess, preach and propagate the religion of one's choice and Article 26 provides that persons will have the right to establish and manage religious institutions. The only limitations on these rights are to save the right of the State to enact measures of social reform and to ensure against the practice of untouchability in Hindu religious institutions.[6] Similarly, Article 29 provides that every linguistic minority will have a right to conserve its language, script, or culture, and under Article 30, religious and linguistic minorities have the right to establish their own educational institutions.

Certain vital aspects of social justice are enshrined in the chapter on fundamental rights. Article 17 abolishes untouchability. Article 23 prohibits *begar* or forced or bonded labour, and Article 24 prohibits the employment of children under fourteen in factories or mines or any other hazardous employment.

It is, however, the chapter on Directive Principles which embodies the other requirements of social justice. Article 37 of the Constitution describes these principles as fundamental in the governance of the country and provides that it shall be the *duty* of the State to apply them in making laws; they cannot, however, be enforced by courts.[7]

The more important of these principles are:

1. Men and women shall have the right to an adequate means of livelihood.

2. There is to be equal pay for men and women in work.[8]

3. Subject to resources being available, there would be a right to work, right to education, and assistance in the case of sickness, unemployment, and old age.[9]

4. Workers are to receive a living wage, and enjoy proper conditions of work.[10]

5. Within ten years from the Constitution, the State is to endeavour to provide free and compulsory education to children up to the age of fourteen.[11]

The Decisions of the Supreme Court

Under the Constitution, it is the duty of the Supreme Court to enforce fundamental rights, the right to approach the Supreme Court being itself a fundamental right.[12] Beginning soon after its inauguration in 1950, it has decided some thousands of cases which involved a consideration of human rights. As the subject is too vast to be covered comprehensively in a paper, it is proposed to briefly consider here a few decisions on *some* human rights.

Preventive Detention

As the Constitution itself permits preventive detention, the Supreme Court had to uphold the Preventive Detention Act, 1950, which it did in *Gopalan v State of Madras,*[13] whilst describing it as a 'most unwholesome encroachment upon the liberties of the people'.[14] The Court, however, went much further, holding that the freedoms granted under Article 19 were not available to a person detained, thus denying itself the right to adjudge the reasonableness of the laws of preventive detention; it further held that the order of detention could be based on the subjective satisfaction of the detaining authority so that the courts could not go into the adequacy of the reasons that led to the order being passed.[15]

Over the years, the Court has upheld the conferment on the executive of wide powers under detention laws and avoided striking down detention orders even where the provisions of the law have not been complied with. It has, for example, upheld an order when the grounds were not supplied for sixteen days, observing that the delay was understandable as a large number of cases of detention had to be dealt with,[16] and where the representation of the detenu was not considered for two months.[17] The delay of sixteen days and two months has to be seen in the light of the constitutional requirement to produce an arrested person before a magistrate within twenty-four *hours*.

What is difficult to understand, or to justify, is the refusal of the Supreme Court to extend to the field of preventive detention principles it has uniformly applied in other branches of administrative law. For instance, though in numerous other fields of administrative law, non-speaking orders have been struck down, it is settled law that the advisory board need not give reasons! Similarly, it has refused to extend to detention orders the test laid down in *Barium Chemicals v Company Law Board*,[18] that though the formation of the opinion could not be gone into, the Court could scrutinize whether the conditions precedent for the exercise of the power existed.

Preventive detention was introduced in the Constitution to deal with persons whose acts threatened the very fabric of society.[19] The Court has, however, upheld detention orders for petty hoarding, smuggling, and even for the trivial 'crime' of trampling the national flag.[20] In *Attorney-General of India v Amratlal Pranjivandas*,[21] the question before a Full Bench of the Court was whether the Conservation of Foreign Exchange Act, which permitted preventive detention in cases of smuggling, was within the legislative competence of the Union Parliament. The question of the reasonableness of the law was not gone into as the Act was in the Ninth Schedule of the Constitution. The Court held that the security of the State could be threatened even by economic problems created by organized smuggling, thus justifying preventive detention for acts of smuggling. The Court asked the question as to whether the security of India included economic security. Surely, the question it could, instead, have asked was whether smuggling, however reprehensible and damaging, could not be curbed without resort to the draconian power of preventive detention? Had it posed that question, the answer may well have been different.

This approach of the Court has justified a proliferation of laws, both central and state, authorizing detention for alleged black-marketing, dealing in illicit liquor, 'land grabbing', and other activities described as being anti-social. The Court has permitted a person to be preventively detained though he was arrested for the same act under the ordinary criminal law, observing that a person can be preventively detained if there are 'cogent reasons' falling short of the proof required in a criminal court;[22] this decimation of the first principle of liberty is to be found in a decision of the Supreme Court!

Even when it was held that Article 19 was available to a person preventively detained, the Court, scrutinizing the Maintenance of Internal Security Act, 1971, found it reasonable as it provided for natural justice to the extent that the principles of natural justice are compatible with detention laws![23] In a recent decision,[24] the Court has gone even further, observing that the principles of natural justice are incorporated in Article 22(5), the hearing being granted after the order of detention was made but before it was confirmed. One could have understood it if the Court had upheld detention, followed by a post-decisional hearing which was effective; this is what the Court has often done when urgent action is required. The hearing granted under Article 22(5) is hardly an effective hearing as the detenu is not entitled to legal representation and no personal hearing is held. What the Courts have held, results in making a mockery of the very rules of natural justice which have been described by it in other judgements as essential to the rule of law and the very foundation of reasonableness. Perhaps the grossest failure of the Supreme Court in the field of preventive detention was its decision, by a majority, not to issue a mandamus to the executive to bring into force the constitutional amendment to Article 22, which, as noted above, curtailed the duration of time during which a person could be detained before referring his case to the advisory board.[25]

Underlying these decisions of the Court are two assumptions, each of which is contrary to the first principles of the rule of law. First, it is assumed that the executive can properly detain a person because *it* believes him guilty of an offence: this destroys the presumption of innocence which is the foundation of personal liberty,[26] and eliminates the need for an independent *judicial* scrutiny before the liberty of a person is interfered with. Second, it assumes that if a person has once been guilty of a crime he is, for that reason and for that reason alone, a person prone to commit crime again. This approach is reminiscent of the British practice of stigmatizing certain tribes as criminal tribes, which was rightly condemned as outrageous, and is wholly contrary to the underlying principles of our criminal jurisprudence, under which evidence of a previous conviction is not even admissible in a trial for a later offence. Further, by upholding detention orders in cases of acts which are ordinary crimes, the Court has given a licence to the executive to detain persons without trial rather than prosecute them in a criminal court which it ought to do. Preventive detention ought to be resorted to, if at all, in the rarest of cases to protect society against persons such as saboteurs, traitors and terrorists; it has now become the rule, not the exception.

I have discussed this approach of the Court because it is not confined to cases of preventive detention alone but has been adopted wherever the executive has sought to interfere with the liberty of the citizen.

Externment

We inherited from the British extraordinary laws empowering the police, albeit after a hearing, to remove from certain areas persons with a previous criminal record said to be engaged in terrorizing people if it was found that witnesses were too afraid to give evidence. Such laws clearly infringed Article 19(1)(d) and Article 21; and are also contrary to Article 9 of the Universal Declaration of Human Rights which provides *inter alia* that no one shall be subject to arbitrary exile.

The Court has, however, upheld the laws as they imposed reasonable restrictions in the interests of the general public and protected the public from dangerous and bad characters.[27] They are dangerous and bad because the police say so. Compare the cryptic comment of Krishna Iyer: '"Desperate character" is who?'[28] No doubt the persons being externed have had a previous conviction but surely 'there should be a desire and eagerness to rehabilitate in the world of industry those who have paid their due in the hard coinage of punishment'.[29] That the object of all punishment is to reform and rehabilitate the criminal has been reiterated by the Court in 1998 in *State of Gujarat v Hon'ble High Court of Gujarat*.[30] What an order of externment does is to further punish them.

In *State of MP v Bharat Singh*,[31] the Court did, however, strike down a provision which required an externee to reside in a particular area designated in the externment order. This was held to be unreasonable as he would have no means of supporting himself in such an area; but in every order of externment, where the externee is required to leave his normal area of residence, he would suffer the same difficulty—the laws, however, have been upheld!

Domiciliary Visits

Several police regulations provide for personnel of the police to keep track of ex-convicts, entailing visits to their homes at all times, whether day or night, and carrying out surveillance, i.e. ascertaining what they do and whom they meet, and requiring them to report to the police when they leave their home town or village.

In *Kharak Singh v State of UP*,[32] it was conceded that the regulations had no statutory authority. The Court was split 4:2. The majority held that Article 21 conferred on persons a right to be secure from intrusion into their homes, and as there was no statutory basis for the regulations it struck down the provisions regarding domiciliary visits. It, however, upheld the executive power to carry out surveillance. Even with regard to domiciliary visits it observed that had these rules been backed by law, it would have been inclined to uphold them as they were reasonable and meant to protect society. The minority held that the right to privacy also extended to surveillance and, therefore, struck down that regulation too.

In *Govind v State of MP*,[33] similar rules enacted under a statutory power were upheld as being reasonable restrictions in the public interest with an admonition that they should only be applied against persons who were determined to lead a 'life of crime'.[34] Finally, following a pattern followed in dozens of judgements, the Court, having upheld the regulations, concluded with an exhortation that such regulations did not accord with the essence of personal freedoms and that the State should revise them! If the regulations did not accord with the essence of personal freedom, how could they have been upheld? That they did not is clear from Article 12 of the Universal Declaration of Human Rights which provides that no one shall be subjected to an arbitrary interference with his privacy.

Recently, the Court has emphatically asserted that Article 21 includes the right to privacy.[35] It is to be hoped that these judgements will now be reconsidered.

Article 20: General

Article 20(1) provides that no person shall be convicted of an offence except for the violation of a law in force when he committed the act or subjected to a penalty not in force when the act was committed.[36] Article

20(2) provides that no person shall be prosecuted and punished for the same offence more than once. Article 20(3) provides that no person accused of an offence shall be compelled to be a witness against himself.

In construing Article 20(2) and (3), the Court has chosen to adopt a strict and somewhat linguistic construction, confining them to ordinary criminal proceedings under regular criminal law. A more liberal approach has, curiously, been adopted in construing Article 20(1) even though all the three sub-Articles are couched in similar language using the words 'convicted', 'offence', etc.

Ex Post Facto Laws

Applying Article 20(1), the Court has held that a person could not be prosecuted under section 304B of the Penal Code for causing a dowry death as the provision was not in force when the act was committed.[37] It has also been held that the sub-Article has no application to civil obligations, as when the obligation on an employer to pay compensation was retrospectively enhanced,[38] or where the charges payable for the unauthorized use of canal water were retrospectively increased even though the amount due could be recovered by adopting coercive process.[39]

In *Union of India v Sukumar*,[40] and *P.V. Mohammad Barmay Sons v Director of Enforcement*,[41] the Court has, however, held that higher penalties cannot be retrospectively imposed in an administrative adjudication under the Foreign Exchange Regulation Act; it found, as a fact, in both cases that the penalties sought to be imposed were not higher than those in force when the act was committed.

In *J.K. Cotton Spg. & Wvg. Mills v Union of India*,[42] the Court was considering the effect of the Finance Act, 1982, which retrospectively amended certain Excise Rules. It was specifically provided that no act could be punished as an offence by reason of the retrospective amendment if it was not an offence when committed. The Court construed this specific provision to apply also to administrative penalties. It observed: 'It will be against all principles of legal jurisprudence to impose a penalty on a person or to confiscate his goods for an act or omission which was lawful at the time when such act was performed ....'[43]

The judgement does not even refer to Article 20(1). It would, however, appear from the judgement that Article 20(1) is not confined to criminal prosecutions and extends to administrative adjudications.

Double Jeopardy

Article 20(2) provides that a person must not be prosecuted and punished more than once for the same act. In *Venkataraman v Union of*

India,[44] it was held that this did not preclude a domestic inquiry being held against a government servant resulting in his dismissal, and a subsequent prosecution. The Court arrived at this conclusion interpreting the words 'prosecuted and punished' as meaning a prosecution and conviction under the ordinary criminal law. In *Maqbool Hussein v State of Bombay*,[45] the same principle was extended to permit proceedings *in rem* under the Sea Customs Act resulting in an order of confiscation, followed by a prosecution. The same principle was, however, applied in 1959 by a majority judgement, when the proceedings under the Customs Act resulted in the imposition of an administrative penalty of the huge amount of Rs 25 lakhs, followed by a prosecution.[46] In a judgement delivered in 1996 these princples have been followed.[47] If the protection against ex post facto laws extends to administrative adjudications, it is difficult to appreciate why the rule against double jeopardy should not.

This approach has, however, to a considerable extent, nullified the constitutional protection as administrative agencies tend to prefer administrative adjudications in which very heavy monetary penalties can be imposed. No question of double jeopardy arises if the previous proceedings are without jurisdiction because the requisite sanction which was a condition precedent to the launching of a prosecution had not been obtained.[48]

Protection Against Self-incrimination

In *M.P. Sharma v Satish Chandra*,[49] a First Information Report was first lodged, and this was followed by an investigation under the Companies Act. It was held by a full Bench that the protection against self-incrimination was available to questions put during the investigation. In *Mohd. Dastagir v State of Madras*[50] and *Narayanlal v M.P. Mistry*,[51] this case was distinguished as no FIR had been lodged at the time and the petitioner could not, therefore, be said to be an accused. It was, the Court observed, irrelevant that a prosecution could be launched later. The distinction between the two situations is somewhat technical.

In *Ramesh Chandra v State of West Bengal*,[52] these decisions were followed and it was, therefore, held that the protection against self-incrimination did not apply to a statement before a customs officer. It was further held that as a customs officer was not a police officer, such a statement was admissible in evidence in a subsequent criminal prosecution. This judgement was followed in 1994.[53] This shows how a narrow reading of the words 'accused of any offence' in Article 20(3) has denuded it of much of its content, and permits it to be easily circumvented.

Life and Liberty: General

Article 21 provides that no person shall be deprived of life and liberty except in accordance with procedure established by law. This Article was virtually denuded of all content in the *Gopalan* case[54] as the Court held (1) that the words 'procedure established by law' meant merely enacted law, and that the law so enacted could not be tested before the courts to ascertain whether it was reasonable; and (2) that the right was only available to a person who was free. This decision was held not to be good law in *R. C. Cooper v Union of India*.[55] Since then, in many decisions, a wide meaning has been given to the words 'life and liberty' in Article 21.

Enlarging the ambit of the words by itself, however, does little to enlarge the effective scope of Article 21 as it only results in a wider range of laws being open to scrutiny to ascertain whether they are reasonable or fair. The real scope of Article 21 depends on the approach of the Court in determining what is meant by reasonable and fair in this context, and on the actual order passed and the direction given.

An analysis of some of the very many judgements on Article 21 in recent years shows several interesting features. The scope of Article 21 has been widened repeatedly, relying on general principles, international conventions and, interestingly, the Directive Principles of State Policy, thus making some of them enforceable. In some cases, the actual order passed or direction given has fallen short of the wide and sweeping enunciation of the content of the right to life. The Court has contented itself either with just the enunciation of the principle or merely recommending a course of action. The enunciation has, however, been far from idle rhetoric as it has been used in later cases to give effective directions. Many of these decisions are recent, and their precise impact can only be ascertained after the cases are followed or, perhaps, distinguished or overruled.

A cognate development that has given real and practical meaning to the enlarged meaning to the right to life has been the encouragement given by the Court to public interest litigation. The Constitution enacted Article 32 as a fundamental right and permitted persons to approach it under Article 32, and the high courts under Article 226, to enforce fundamental rights. This was wholly satisfactory in the case of people with the means or ability to secure legal assistance and move a Court. It, however, did little to help the millions of people too poor to do so. Permitting public interest litigation, and even entertaining postcards and letters as 'petitions' enabled hundreds of thousands of helpless persons, undertrials, bonded labourers, etc. to obtain justice and enforce their fundamental rights. Few of the cases discussed below would ever have come to the Court but for the efforts of many individuals and non-governmental organizations, and they could only do so because of the encouragement of public interest litigation.

It is proposed to discuss some of the more significant judgements in the field.

Protection of Arrested Persons

In *Joginder Kumar v State of UP*,[56] the Court held that it was inherent in Articles 21 and 22 that the police must, if they arrest a person, inform a relative or friend of the fact of his arrest and also inform them of the place where he was being detained. That this was done must be recorded in the Station Diary. The Court further directed that when the person arrested was produced before the magistrate, the magistrate must satisfy himself that this duty had been properly discharged.

Oppressed by many cases of custodial deaths which were coming before it, the Court has laid down detailed guidelines to be followed by all authorities empowered to effect arrests; that is, the police and revenue authorities, the Director of Enforcement, and officers of paramilitary forces.[57] The Court has, also, in several cases, relying on Article 21, directed the payment of compensation when a person died in police custody.[58] Compensation has also been awarded when a person under arrest for alleged theft was tortured whilst in custody,[59] and when a person injured when in custody was not given prompt medical treatment.[60]

In *People's Union of Civil Liberties v Union of India*,[61] the Court was dealing with a case where the police shot dead certain villagers who were in custody. The Court directed compensation to be paid. What makes the case particularly interesting is that the Court relied on the International Covenant on Civil and Political Rights and observed that the provisions of the Convention were 'facets of fundamental rights and enforceable as such'.[62] This approach, if followed in all fields, would have momentous consequences.

Speedy Trials

In *Hussainara Khatoon v State of Bihar*,[63] the Court laid down that a system of criminal procedure which did not prescribe a speedy trial could not be said to be either fair or reasonable. It ordered the immediate release of persons who had been detained longer than the maximum sentence they could have suffered had they been convicted. Whilst this judgement was truly laudable it only did the least the Court could have done. The order can be regarded as having made effective a right to a speedy trial only if it is assumed, first, that all the persons charged were, in fact, guilty, and second, that their conduct deserved the imposition of the maximum sentence. As a significant proportion of the undertials were likely to have been acquitted, and as many of even those convicted were not likely to be awarded the maximum sentence, the actual order of the Court merely ended their ordeal.

It was, however, only the first step. In *Common Cause v Union of India*,[64] the Court observed that it was necessary to give directions to all states and union territories to ensure that criminal proceedings did not operate as engines of oppression. Under the elaborate directions given, persons were ordered to be released on bail on only a personal bond if they had remained in custody a certain time, the time being laid down with reference to the maximum sentence that could be imposed under the offence with which they were charged. In the case of less serious offences such as traffic offences, or compoundable offences or non-cognizable offences, the accused were to be discharged if they had been under detention for specified periods of time. The directions were not to apply to certain graver offences.

These directions were clarified in a later case principally to exclude cases where the delay in the trial was attributable to the dilatory tactics adopted by the accused.[65] Where offences under the Narcotic and Psychotropic Substances Act were not being tried for an inordinate length of time as judges had not been appointed, the Court ordered the release on bail of persons accused of the less grave offences who had been in custody for half the period of the maximum sentence that could be imposed.[66]

Bail

Under our law, to obtain bail a person has, generally, to produce as a surety a person who is a person of some means. This is impossible for the thousands of persons who are poor or indigent. The Court has held that bail cannot be refused to indigent persons who are unable to procure a solvent surety.[67]

Handcuffing

In *Prem Shankar v State of Delhi*,[68] the Court laid down strict guidelines on when an undertrial or prisoner being taken to a Court could be handcuffed. This could only be done if there was a risk of the prisoner escaping or being violent, and if it was not practicable to secure his safety by other means such as having more guards. When a person was handcuffed, reasons for doing so should be contemporaneously recorded and submitted to the Court concerned for its approval.

The Supreme Court has also held to be illegal the handcuffing of TADA detenus in a hospital, observing that if there was any apprehension of their escaping, additional guards should have been provided.[69] Where a person accused of an offence was handcuffed and paraded through a public street, the Court has confirmed a high court order directing that compensation be paid to him.[70]

Prison Conditions

Even in a prison, a prisoner could not be kept in solitary confinement as this amounted to the imposition of a second punishment for the same offence; even keeping a prisoner in fetters should only be done if it is necessary for his safety.[71] Directions have also been given to segregate undertrials from convicts in prisons, and keep young persons separately; further, the prison authorities cannot impose prison punishments without judicial scrutiny.[72]

Right to Legal Representation

Article 22(1) only provides that any person who is arrested and detained in custody shall not be denied the right to consult, and be defended, by a legal practitioner of his choice. The Court has held that an accused person was entitled to free legal aid as a part of the right *guaranteed by Article 21*. The Court relied in this connection on Article 39A, a directive principle enjoining free legal aid being made available. It is noteworthy that the Court did not even refer to Article 22(1) which merely confers on an accused person a right to consult, and be defended by, a legal practitioner of his choice.[73] It has been held that the right conferred by Article 22(1) extends to proceedings before a panchayat at court where the maximum sentence that can be imposed is a sentence of a fine.[74]

In *Sheela Barse v State of Maharashtra*,[75] it was held that the necessary funds must be made available by the state. It was also incumbent on the authorities to inform the accused of the availability of legal aid, and if this was not done, the conviction would be set aside; the Court held, reversing the high court decision, that it was not necessary that a request should have been made by the accused for legal aid.[76] Curiously, however, the Court has, in cases relating to persons preventively detained, held that a detenu does not even have the right to be *represented* by a legal practitioner before the advisory board even though an order of detention has deprived him of his liberty, the reasoning being that Article 22(3) specifically exludes Article 22(1).[77] A detenu is, however, entitled to *consult* a legal pratitioner.[78] It has also been held that a right to file one appeal is an inherent part of a fair and reasonable law, and a person convicted must be promptly served with a copy of the judgement to enable him to appeal.[79]

Mandatory Death Sentence

The mandatory death sentence required under section 303 of the Indian Penal Code to be imposed on a life convict who was convicted of murder has been held to violate both Article 14 and Article 21.[80] The Court observed that taking away judicial discretion in sentencing was arbitrary.

Detention of Lunatics

It has been held that the detention of non-criminal lunatics in jail is illegal.[81]

Failure to Protect life

Though Article 21 is couched in negative terms, in several decisions the Court has given it a positive content reading into Article 21 an obligation to protect and save life. Applying this princple, the State has been directed to pay compensation for the killing of a convict in jail by another convict.[82] In an even more far-reaching decision, compensation was ordered to be paid to the victims of a hutment colony fire caused due to a short circuit which was found to be caused by illegal electricity connections given by employees of the Delhi Electricity Supply Undertaking, a public sector body.[83] Similarly, compensation has been awarded where the victim of an accident did not receive prompt medical treatment in a public hospital.[84] These decisions are likely to lead to a flood of litigation by victims of acts of malfeasance or nonfeasance by public authorities who would prefer to approach the Supreme Court or the high court rather than file a civil suit or pursue a remedy before the consumer forum.

In *National Human Rights Commission v State of Arunachal Pradesh*,[85] the Court was dealing with the threats to Chakma and Hajong tribals who were facing threats of being driven out of the state by the Arunachal Pradesh Students Union. The Court directed the state to ensure that they were protected, and also directed the Union of India to make available to the state the necessary paramilitary personnel.

Right to Die

In *P. Rathinam v Union of India*,[86] it had been held that Article 21 included a right to die. A larger Bench of the Court has reversed this decision and upheld the validity of section 309 of the Penal Code which makes an attempt to commit suicide an offence.[87]

Right to Livelihood

It had been held that the right to life under Article 21 did not include a right to receive a livelihood.[88] In *Olga Tellis v Bombay Municipal Corporation*,[89] the Court held that the right to life conferred by Article 21 included the right to a livelihood; the Court, therefore, restrained the Bombay Municipal Corporation from evicting slum and pavement dwellers without providing alternate accommodation within a reasonable distance.[90] That case did not, however, result in an order to anyone to pay an amount; this direction was given in 1993 when Wakf Boards were directed, relying on the right to live with dignity conferred by Article 21, to pay Imams a salary.[91]

Right to Privacy

In *Kharak Singh v State of UP*,[92] the Supreme Court had held that Article 21 included the right to privacy, though there are observations in a later decision doubting this.[93] In *People's Union for Civil Liberties v Union of India*,[94] the Court, dealing with the question of telephone tapping, has held that the right to privacy is included in the right to life, and extends to having a telephone conversation. As there were no statutory rules prescribing when telephones could be tapped, though there was power to make such rules, the Court laid down guidelines to how the power should be exercised.

Right to Travel Abroad

In *Satwant Singh v APO, New Delhi*,[95] it was held that the right to travel abroad was a part of the right guaranteed by Article 21, and that such right could only be curtailed by a valid law. This led to the enactment of the Passport Act, 1967. The Act set up a machinery requiring that an order impounding a passport could only be made after a hearing, to be granted before or after the order was passed, and that the order should contain reasons. The Act empowered the government to impound a passport *inter alia* in the interests of the general public. In *Maneka Gandhi v Union of India*,[96] the Court reiterated that the right to travel abroad was a part of the right to life guaranteed by Article 21. Laws empowering the seizure of passports had, therefore, to be procedurally reasonable, providing for a hearing and imposing an obligation to give reasons. The Court, however, upheld the provisions of the Act even though they gave very wide powers to the executive to impound the passport of a citizen 'in the interests of the general public', a power which it itself described as 'a rather drastic power to interfere with a basic human right' and contented itself with yet another exhortation to the government: 'we have no doubt that it [this drastic power] will be sparingly used and that too with great care and circumspection ...'.[97]

Right to Education

Article 41 provides that the State shall endeavour within the limits of its economic capacity to secure the right to education; and Article 45 enjoins on the State to provide, within ten years, free and compulsory education to children till they attain the age of fourteen. The effect of these two directive principles, and the interrelationship between them and the right to life guaranteed by Article 21, were exhaustively discussed in two cases where the actual issue before the Court was quite different.

In *Mohini Jain v State of Karnataka*,[98] the only question before the two-judge Bench was whether a notification permitting private colleges to charge a fee of Rs 60,000 was valid having regard to the provisions of the Karnataka Educational Institutions (Prohibition of Capitation Fees) Act, 1984, under which it had been issued. The Court held that the notification was illegal. The conclusion was reached after exhaustive discussion of Article 21 and other provisions of the Constitution. The Court observed that the fundamental rights guaranteed under Part III could not be appreciated and fully enjoyed unless citizens were educated and further observed: 'The "right to education", is concomitant to the fundamental rights enshrined under Part III of the Constitution. The State is under a constitutional mandate to provide educational institutions *at all levels* for the benefit of the citizens.'[99]

The question was placed before a five-judge Bench in *Unni Krishnan J.P. v State of Andhra Pradesh*[100] as *Mohini Jain* appeared to hold that there was a fundamental right to higher education. In the actual case before the Bench, the question of primary education was not directly in issue. Two learned judges[101] did not go into the question as they held that it was not before the Court in *Mohini Jain*. In two separate judgements, the other three learned judges[102] distinguished between the right to education till the age of fourteen, and the right to higher education. In both judgements it was held that it was permissible to read the constitutional mandate to provide education till the age of fourteen into the right to life guaranteed by Article 21; there was, therefore, such a right as a part of the right guaranteed by Article 21. It is difficult to assess the effect of this judgement as no directions to provide such education were issued. Merely holding that Article 21 includes the right has little practical effect till such directions are issued. Few states, in fact, offer free education till the age of fourteen to all children.

Right to a Clean Environment
The Court has held that the right to clean air and water is a part of the right to life. In several cases, the directions given by the Court have been to enforce existing anti-pollution laws effectively. Directions have been given, for instance, to curb or stop pollution of the Ganga, or prevent quarrying in Mussoorie, or close industries damaging the Taj. In some cases the Court has gone further and set up committees[103] or made recommendatios itself to the State to amend existing laws.[104]

Miscellaneous
The right to life under Article 21 also requires the State to provide roads in inaccessible hilly areas.[105]

Begar or Forced Labour
Article 23(1) of the Constitution provides that traffic in human beings and *begar* and similar forms of forced labour are prohibited and that any contravention of this prohibition would be punishable in accordance with law. The matter came up before the Court in a public interest litigation, *Peoples' Union of Democratic Rights v Union of India*[106] in connection with the employment of thousands of workers employed by labour contractors building the numerous projects being executed in connection with the Asiad games.

The Court held that *begar* described forced labour where a person was compelled to work without any remuneration. As Article 23 prohibited not only *begar* but other similar forms of forced labour, it covered cases where persons were *compelled to work* with or without remuneration as also cases where a person was compelled to work for a remuneration lower than the statutory minimum wage. The Court further held that Article 23(1), like Articles 17 and 24, was directed not only against the State but also against private individuals, and the Constitution imposed on the State a duty to prevent contravention of Article 23. The Court gave directions to ensure that such acts would stop. In later decisions, the Court has ordered the immediate release of all such persons from their compelled employment even if they still owed moneys to the employer.[107]

Following a drought in Rajasthan, the state announced a famine relief programme which consisted, as is usual, in providing employment in famine relief works. The state also enacted an Act exempting such employment from the operation of labour laws. The constitutional validity of this Act was considered by a two-judge Bench of the Supreme Court in *Sanjit Roy v State of Rajasthan*.[108] Bhagwati J (as he then was) struck down the Act as violative of Article 23. He observed that persons in famine relief work must be regarded as being compelled to work as they were economically in no position not to. Pathak J (as he then was) also struck down the Act, but for violating Article 14, not Article 23.

Acts such as the Minimum Wages Act are laws that empower, but do not compel, the state to fix minimum wages. Such Acts apply to select groups of workers and are not comprehensive. In *Mukesh Advani v State of MP*,[109] a two-judge Bench gave a direction to the Union of India to issue a notification under the Minimum Wages Act and prescribe minimum wages to workers in flagstone mines. Whether the Court can give such a direction does not, appear to have been seriously contested in that case. If the judgement is followed, it will have a pervasive effect as it would compel the State to make the Minimum Wages Act and other labour laws comprehensive.

It has been held that Article 23 applied to persons required to do labour in jails; this was illegal in the case of undertrials or persons sentenced to simple imprisonment but persons sentenced to rigorous imprisonment could be made to work provided they were paid statutory minimum wages.[110]

Article 23(1) also covers cases of women forced into prostitution.[111] It has also been held that it is the duty of the state to rehabilitate all bonded or forced labour after it is released.[112]

Children and Hazardous Employment

Article 24 prohibits the employment of children under fourteen years in factories and mines and other hazardous employment. It was held that the prohibition was not confined to industries listed in the Employment of Children Act, 1938, and covered employment on construction sites which was also hazardous.[113]

When children under fourteen were found to be employed in the Sivakasi match industry, the Court ordered that the employer should employ an adult in place of each child so that the parents who were dependent on the income of the child got relief, and also directed the employers to provide education to the children.[114]

Directive Principles

The directive principles enunciate the human rights which India was economically unable to guarantee in 1950. Article 37, therefore, provided that the directive principles could not be enforced in a Court but were fundamental in the governance of the country and that it was the duty of the State to apply them enacting legislation.[115] In *State of Madras v Champakam Dorairajan*[116] the Court held that where there was a direct conflict between a directive principle to provide for the advancement of the scheduled castes and the scheduled tribes,[117] and the fundamental right guaranteed under Article 29(2), which prohibited discrimination on the ground of caste in educational institutions, the latter prevailed.[118]

In numerous cases thereafter, the Court has relied on directive principles to uphold the reasonableness of legislation which, it was contended, violated a fundamental right. To take only a few examples: this has been done in upholding legislation banning the slaughter of cattle,[119] in upholding the Kerala Agriculturists (Debt Relief) Act,[120] in giving preferential promotion to persons belonging to scheduled castes and tribes,[121] and in upholding the prohibition of alcoholic liquor.[122] In *Bandhua Mukti Morcha v Union of India*,[123] the Court observed that it could not relieve the plight of quarry workers by directing the State to enact legislation to implement Article 39(b) and (c) and Articles 41 and 42 as the directive principles could not be enforced by a Court; it did, however, direct the State to implement existing labour and social welfare laws.

There is, however, a clear trend towards the implementation of directive principles. In the discussion above on the Right to Education, the result has been achieved indirectly by reading a directive principle into the right to life guaranteed under Article 21. In two decisions,[124] Article 39(d) was relied upon to issue directions to the state to pay equal remuneration to employees doing equal work. No doubt the same result could have been achieved by relying on Article 16, but the actual decisions are indicative of the trend I have mentioned. In *Comptroller & Auditor General v K.S. Jagannathan*,[125] the Court directed the authorities to exercise a discretion conferred on them to relax examination standards for candidates belonging to the scheduled castes and tribes in a departmental examination. In *State of Haryana v Darshan Devi*,[126] the Court, referring to Article 39A, upheld a high court direction to the state to extend the pauper provisions of the Code of Civil Procedure to proceedings before the Motor Accidents Tribunal. In *M.H. Hoskote v State of Maharashtra*,[127] the Court has described Article 39A as an 'interpretative tool' for Article 21.

These decisions may not be followed as they are contrary to the specific language of Article 37 and earlier decisions of the Court; if, however, they are, they will have the effect of enlarging the ambit of human rights to a very considerable degree.

Conclusion

This brief, and very selective, analysis shows a pronounced change in the perspective of the Court towards some human rights. Articles 21, 23, and 24 have been given a very wide construction. The Court has adopted innovative techniques of interpretation, referring to general principles, international conventions and, most imaginatively, the Directive Principles whilst interpreting these Articles and virtually incorporating them into Article 21 in particular. This has resulted in some rules of social justice, which were to be found in the Directive Principles, becoming enforceable.

In these fields, the leaden, mechanistic, approach of the early years has given way to a dynamic constructive approach. Puzzlingly, however, there has so far been no discernible change in the approach of the Court to the most basic human right: the right to personal liberty. The State, and the police and other agencies, continue to exercise powers to detain certain persons at will without judicial scrutiny.

If the Court applies in the field of personal liberty, the innovative techniques to which I have referred, it will have wide repercussions and may, perhaps, lead the Court to rethink its approach to the whole subject of preventive detention. If it could do that, it would be a vital contribution to human rights jurisprudence.

Notes

[1] See Article 2 which prohibits discrimination on the ground of race, colour, sex, language or religion, and Article 6 which provides for equality before the law.

[2] The exception in Article 15 was inserted by an amendment in 1951. These features were embodied in our Constitution long before the concept was evolved, or named, in the United States.

[3] Cf. Article 11 of the Universal Declaration.

[4] Cf. Article 3 of the Universal Declaration.

[5] Cf. Article 9 of the Universal Declaration.

[6] Cf. Article 18 of the International Covenant on Civil and Political Rights.

[7] Article 37.

[8] Article 39(d).

[9] Article 41.

[10] Article 42 and 43.

[11] Article 45.

[12] Article 32.

[13] AIR 1950 SC 27.

[14] Ibid. at p. 92 by Mukherjea J, as he then was.

[15] It could, however, strike down an order if the grounds were vague or extraneous.

[16] *Tarapada De v State of West Bengal* AIR 1951 SC 174.

[17] *B. Alamelu v State of Tamil Nadu* AIR 1995 SC 539.

[18] AIR 1967 SC 295.

[19] Cf. the distinction drawn in the context of Article 19(2) between grave acts and local breaches: *Romesh Thapar v State of Punjab* AIR 1950 SC 124.

[20] Hoarding matchboxes and soap: *Kamla Prasad v District Magistrate* AIR 1975 SC 726; smuggling two pieces of gold: *Shiv Ratan Makim v Union of India* AIR 1986 SC 610; trampling the national flag: *State of West Bengal v Ashok Dey* AIR 1972 SC 1660.

[21] AIR 1997 SC 2179.

[22] *Borjahan v State of West Bengal* AIR 1972 SC 2256.

[23] *H. Saha v State of West Bengal* AIR 1974 SC 2154, 2159.

[24] *State of Tamil Nadu v Senthil Kumar* (1999) 3 SCC 646.

[25] *A.K. Roy v Union of India* AIR 1982 SC 710.

[26] And embodied in Article 11 of the Universal Declaration of Human Rights.

[27] *N.B.Khare v State of Delhi* AIR 1950 SC 211; the order can be passed even if the witnesses said to be too afraid to give evidence are officers of the police or customs service whose duty it is to preserve the law: *Bhagubhai v District Magistrate* AIR 1956 SC 585.

[28] *Prem Shankar v Delhi Administration* AIR 1980 SC 1535, 1544.

[29] Per Sir Winston Churchill; quoted with approval by Krishna Iyer J, in *Sunil Batra v Delhi Administration* AIR 1980 SC 1579, 1583.

[30] (1998) 7 SCC 392.

[31] AIR 1967 SC 1170.

[32] AIR 1963 SC 1295.

[33] AIR 1975 SC 1373.

[34] It was, of course, the police who would decide this!

[35] See under 'Right to Privacy'.

[36] This corresponds to Article 11(2) of the Universal Declaration of Human Rights.

[37] *Soni Devrajbhai Babubhai v State of Gujarat* AIR 1991 SC 2173.

[38] *Hathising Mfg. Co. v Union of India* AIR 1960 SC 923.

[39] *Jawala Ram v State of Pepsu* AIR 1962 SC 1246.

[40] AIR 1966 SC 1206.

[41] AIR 1993 SC 1188.

[42] AIR 1988 SC 191.

[43] Ibid. at p. 199.

[44] AIR 1954 SC 375.

[45] AIR 1953 SC 325.

[46] *Thomas Dana v State of Punjab* AIR 1959 SC 375.

[47] *Director of Enforcement v M/s MCTM Corporation Pvt. Ltd.* AIR 1996 SC 1100.

[48] *Baij Nath Prasad v State of Bhopal* AIR 1957 SC 494.

[49] AIR 1954 SC 300.

[50] AIR 1960 SC 756.

[51] AIR 1961 SC 29.

[52] AIR 1970 SC 940.

[53] *Bhanabhai Khalpabhai v Collector of Customs* (1994) Supp 2 SCC 143.

[54] AIR 1950 SC 27.

[55] AIR 1970 SC 564.

[56] (1994) 4 SCC 260.

[57] *D.K. Basu v State of West Bengal* AIR 1997 SC 610.

[58] *Nilabat Behara v State of Orissa* (1993) 2 SCC 746; *Inder Singh v State of Punjab*

(1995) 3 SCC 702. In the latter case, directions were also given to effectively prosecute the police personnel concerned.

[59] *T.C. Pathak v State of UP* (1995) 6 SCC 357.

[60] *Gulabbai v Nalini Narsi Vohra* (1991) 3 SCC 482.

[61] AIR 1997 SC 1203.

[62] At pages 1207–8.

[63] AIR 1979 SC 1360.

[64] AIR 1996 SC 1619.

[65] *Common Cause, a Registered Society v Union of India* AIR 1997 SC 1539.

[66] *S.C. Legal Aid Committee v Union of India* (1994) 6 SCC 731.

[67] *Hussainara Khatoon v State of Bihar* AIR 1979 SC 1360.

[68] AIR 1980 SC 1535.

[69] *President, Citizens for Democracy v State of Assam* AIR 1996 SC 2193.

[70] *State of Maharashtra v Ravikant S. Patil* (1991) 2 SCC 373.

[71] *Sunil Batra v Delhi Administration* AIR 1978 SC 1675.

[72] Ibid. AIR 1980 SC 1579.

[73] *Khatri v State of Bihar* AIR 1981 SC 928.

[74] *State of M.P. v Shobharam* AIR 1966 SC 1910 (by a majority).

[75] AIR 1983 SC 378.

[76] *Suk Das v Union Territory of Arunachal Pradesh* AIR 1986 SC 991.

[77] *A.K. Roy v Union of India* AIR 1982 SC 710.

[78] *Francis Coralic v Union Territory of Delhi* AIR 1981 SC 746; and also to receive visits from members of the family.

[79] *M.H. Hoscot v State of Maharashtra* AIR 1978 SC 1548.

[80] *Mithu v State of Punjab* AIR 1983 SC 473.

[81] *Sheela Barse v Union of India* (1993) 4 SCC 204.

[82] *Kewal Pati v State of UP* (1995) 3 SCC 600.

[83] *Harvinder Chaudhary Srivastava v Union of India* (1996) 8 SCC 80.

[84] *P.B. Khet Mazdoor Samity v State of West Bengal* AIR 1996 SC 2426.

[85] AIR 1996 SC 1234.

[86] (1994) 3 SCC 394.

[87] *Gian Kaur v State of Punjab* AIR 1996 SC 946.

[88] *In rè Sant Ram* AIR 1960 SC 932; *Nachane v Union of India* AIR 1982 SC 1126.

[89] AIR 1986 SC 180.

[90] This case has been followed in *Ahmedabad Municipal Corporation v Khan Gulab Khan* (1997) 11 SCC 121; it was clarified that there was no absolute obligation to provide alternative accommodation.

[91] *All India Imam Organization v Union of India* AIR 1993 SC 2086.

[92] AIR 1963 SC 1295.

[93] *Govind v State of MP* AIR 1975 SC 1378.

[94] AIR 1997 SC 568.

[95] AIR 1967 SC 1836.

[96] AIR 1978 SC 597.

[97] Per Bhagwati J (as he then was), at page 650.

[98] AIR 1992 SC 1858.

[99] At pages 1864–5; emphasis mine.

[100] AIR 1993 SC 2178.

[101] Sharma, CJ, and Bharucha J.

[102] Mohan J and Jeevan Reddy J, with whom Pandyan J agreed.

[103] *M.C. Mehta v Union of India* (1991) 2 SCC 353; a monitoring committee to check vehicular pollution was set up.

[104] *AP Pollution Control Board v M.V. Nayudu* AIR 1999 SC 812.

[105] *State of HP v Umed Ram* AIR 1986 SC 847; the Court would not, however, direct the legislature to make funds available.

[106] AIR 1982 SC 1473.

[107] *Ram Pal v Maishi Lal Raj Kumar* (1982) 2 SCC 349; *Chhatisgarh Krishak Mazdoor Sangh v State of MP* (1987) Supp SCC 198.

[108] AIR 1983 SC 328.

[109] AIR 1985 SC 1363. The Court referred to Articles 36, 41, 42, and 43.

[110] *State of Gujarat v Hon'ble High Court of Gujarat* (1998) 7 SCC 392.

[111] *Vishal Jeet v Union of India* AIR 1990 SC 1412.

[112] *Neeraja Choudhary v State of MP* (1984) 3 SCC 243; *Balram v State of MP* AIR 1990 SC 44.

[113] *Peoples' Union for Democratic Rights v Union of India* AIR 1982 SC 1473; the Court also directed the government to notify such employment under the Act.

[114] *M.C. Mehta v State of Tamil Nadu* AIR 1997 SC 699.

[115] Article 37.

[116] AIR 1951 SC 226.

[117] Article 46.

[118] This led to the insertion of Article 15(4).

[119] But only to the extent Article 48 was applicable, i.e. only to cattle which were still productive and useful: *M.H. Qureshi v State of Bihar* AIR 1958 SC 731; followed in *Hasmattullah v State of MP* AIR 1996 SC 2076.

[120] The Court relied on Article 38 and 39(b): *Pathumma v State of Kerala* AIR 1978 SC 771.

[121] *A.B.S.K. Sangh (Rly) v Union of India* AIR 1981 SC 298. The Court relied on Article 46.

[122] *State of Andhra Pradesh v McDowell & Co.* AIR 1996 SC 1627.

[123] AIR 1984 SC 802.

[124] *Randhir Singh v Union of India* AIR 1982 SC 879; *P.K. Ramachandra Iyer v Union of India* AIR 1984 SC 541.

[125] AIR 1987 SC 537.

[126] AIR 1979 SC 855.

[127] AIR 1978 SC 1548, 1556.

Fourteen

The Supreme Court and Group Life: Religious Freedom, Minority Groups, and Disadvantaged Communities

Rajeeev Dhavan and Fali S. Nariman

India's Diversity: Interpreting a Constitution for a Complex Civilization

During the debates of the Constituent Assembly, the architect of India's Constitution—the indomitable B.R. Ambedkar—emphatically declared that the 'individual' and not the 'group' was the basis on which India's Constitution was designed.[1] As an 'untouchable' *dalit*, Ambedkar had suffered greatly at the hands of 'caste' communities and was fearful of the oppression that India's caste-based group life was capable of unleashing. Yet, the Indian Constitution itself recognized the importance of group life in India and sought to enhance India's rich plural diversity within a framework of social reform and change.

No country in the world has a greater diversity of group life. India's near billion people sustain a bewildering variety of religions, languages, cultures, social life, life styles, food and dress habits, music, colour, traditions, practices, attitudes, and beliefs. Its people speak in many distinct languages: each with a distinct script and innumerable dialects.[2] Virtually every major, and many lesser known faiths, continue to find creative self-expression in the sub-continent. Within the religions themselves, have grown innumerable sects, beliefs, practices, and philosophies. If demography were to tell its story, each faith has millions of adherents—making, for example, India demographically amongst the largest Muslim countries in the world, with over 100 million followers.[3] New faiths continue to emerge,—some rooted in Indian life and some which have been commoditized for the *'karma cola'* of spiritual export.[4] Inevitably, politics has caught up with suborned and appropriated religion for dubious and opportunistic reasons to claim the spoils of political power and economic development. The destruction of the centuries old Babri Masjid by politically driven fanatics in 1992 is a reminder of what can go wrong.[5] Yet, India's amazing diversity of group life defines India and symbolizes what it has stood for through the ages. Neither Europe, nor the Middle East, nor the Americas, nor Africa or the rest of Asia brings together such plurality. Riddled with poverty and inequitous disparities, fuelled by innumerable just claims and greedy demands, and caught within the throes of millennial change, India is not just a country or nation, but a veritable civilization constantly struggling for redefinition. India's Constitution and laws, no less those relating to group life as any other, face the unique task of confronting the demands of a complex living civilization.[6]

India's Constitution was drafted under uneasy cirumstances. The British had left an untidy legacy. The subcontinent was partitioned amidst chaos. The 572 odd Princely states were left free to balkanize India. Group life had been politicized along communal lines to create expectations of separate electorates and even separate homelands. According to the British themselves, this kind of politicization '... perpetrated class divisions ... stereotyped existing relations ... (and) constituted a serious hindrance to the development of the self-governance principle'.[7] We are concerned here with some groups, not all of them. Like everything else, group life manifests itself in many changing forms that are transformed over time.[8] The Constitution had little difficulty in granting associational freedom to all, including new associations, societies, unions, business groups, political parties, clubs, and many others. A special solicitude was however earmarked for traditional, religious, minority, and disadvantaged groups.

Faced with an array of demands from various groups, the Constituent Assembly articulated what could be summed up as a fourfold response to define its secular credentials. The *first* response was to depoliticize the insidious effect of religious and other minority group life on democratic governance by abolishing communal representation and separate electorates, rapidly assimilating the Princely states into the federation and strongly prohibiting group discrimination on grounds of group association or affiliation including caste, place of birth, residence or religion.[9] However, while denying religion a role in electoral processes and political life, the incipient possibility of politicization along caste lines was kept alive on the basis of special electoral representation for the backward classes (BC) consisting of the scheduled castes (SC) and scheduled tribes (ST), and extending affirmative action to include them and yet to be defined. Other backward classes·(OBC) who have steadily increased over the years to dominate and unsettle Indian politics—especially in the 1990s.[10] However, the *first* response to depoliticize religion was not intended to undermine the importance of the *second* objective of protecting, nurturing, and advancing the claims of traditional group life, especially those founded on religious beliefs and practices, social and cultural life, and language. The *third* response enunciated the countervailing idea that group life must yield to the reasonable public interest demands of public order, health, and morality, accept a general regulatory regime over its activities and coexist with India's somewhat open-ended commitment to social welfare and reform.[11] The *fourth* residuary response counselled a pragmatic, even if ad hoc, 'problem-solving' approach implicit in the text of the Constitution, when seeking to resolve the peculiar problems of opening 'temples' and public places to 'untouchables', cow slaughter, creating a gender-just uniform civil code of personal laws for all communities, and guaranteeing Sikhs the fundamental right to wear a *kirpan* (dagger) as part of their faith![12] These four responses—namely, depoliticizing group demands, maximizing the celebration of group life, confronting this celebration with an agenda of regulation and reform, and evolving ad hoc solutions to 'problem solve' emerging controversies were potentially much too complex and contradictory to be self-fulfilling. Amongst others, the Supreme Court was called upon to elucidate them.

Religious Freedom

The Supreme Court's life began with controversy. Provoked by judicial decisions on agrarian reform and censorship, an irate Nehru effected 'corrective' amendments to the Constitution and accused the judges of being reactionary and 'purloining the Constitution'.[13] This cast a shadow over the relationship between the judiciary and executive. Although sharply divided on issues of civil liberties and governance, the Supreme Court bore this attack with a collective fortitude, protesting its innocence but reinforcing its status as the undisputed institutional conscience of the Constitution.[14]

Eclipsed by these great political controversies, the Supreme Court was drawn into the vicissitudes of group life less dramatically. In the *Communal Representation* cases(1951)[15] the Court evinced little difficulty in striking down a distribution of affirmative action benefits and schemes as general 'largesse' along religious or caste lines. Its later forays were however more tentative and cautiously exploratory. In the *Religious Endowment* cases (1954)[16] the Court was called upon to pronounce upon the validity of comprehensive regulatory control of religious endowments which was far more extensive than the framework of oversight and accountability over these institutions introduced by the British since 1853 if not earlier.[17] Elaborating on the constitutional text, and seeking juristic inspiration from Australia and America, the Court permitted extensive regulation of the 'economic, political and ... other secular activities ... associated with religious practice', but refused to allow intrusive restrictions on the essential practices of the faith.[18] Though creatively invented by Justice B.K. Mukerjee to protect religious freedom, the 'essential practices' test has proved to be double-edged. Created as a principle of inclusion to make some practices more sacral than others, it was interpreted in later cases as a threshold principle of exclusion to deprive supposedly non-essential practices of constitutional protection altogether.[19] However, even after having crossed the first step, 'essential practises' are not immune from scrutiny, but confronted with the other public interest and social reform restraints permitted by the Constitution. Called upon to elaborate and give effect to and implement these principles, the role of the judges has become truly extraordinary. The judges are unequipped to deal with such issues, relying as they do on limited material in the form of selective affidavits presented to the courts in adversarial litigation, amidst the chaos of overcrowded dockets and congested court calendars. With a power greater than that of a high priest, *maulvi* or *dharmasastri*, judges have virtually assumed the theological authority to determine which tenets of a faith are 'essential' to any faith and emphatically underscored their constitutional power to strike down those essential tenets of a faith that conflict with the dispensation of the Constitution. Few religious pontiffs possess this kind of power and authority.

Having blessed an over-regulatory regime over religious endowments, the judges gradually abandoned their caution to rush in where angels would fear to tread. In 1958,[20] the Supreme Court was called upon to pronounce on the rights of Muslim butchers to slaughter cows; an activity claimed to be part of the Islamic faith. The Constitution-makers had consciously strayed away from this issue.[21] Speaking for a unanimous Court, S.R. Das CJ struck a balance to prohibit the indiscriminate slaughter of cows so that 'sentiment was respected and Muslim butchers retained a large part of their trade',[22] but rejected the claim that cow slaughter was an 'essential practice' of Islam by relying on his own interpretation of the Koran, Hamilton's translation of the Hedaya and the testimony of a Hindu pandit in the absence of an 'affidavit by a [Muslim] Maulana explaining the implications of these verses'.[23] Even if the result was unexceptional, this is an undesirably unsafe way of examining and pronouncing on a faith. Judges become theologians and are forced to make roving inquiries about all or any religious texts, beliefs, or practices. Once this door is opened, there is no limit to which the Court cannot go. While some judges have been cautious, their 'reformist' counterparts have felt free to deconstruct meaning at will and reconstruct events to suit their reformist or other agenda. Indeed, in the *Excommunication* case (1962),[24] a sharply divided Court upheld the right of the leaders of faith to excommunicate 'fallen' believers for religious reasons—no doubt leaving it to the courts to determine whether an excommunicatory reason was religious or not. Judges are now endowed with a *three step inquiry* to determine, in tandem, whether a claim was religious at all, whether it was essential for the faith and, perforce, whether, even if essential, it complied with the public interest and reformist requirements of the Constitution.

The advent of Justice P.B. Gajendragadkar,[25] a self-professedly reformist judge, found the courts making ample use of the multiple inquiries available for determination of questions relating to religious freedom. What followed was a veritable *tour de force*. By a skilful, even if not wholly convincing, interpretation of historical events, text and folklore, the Khadims of the Durgah Committee of Ajmer were denied constitutional protection to continue their long-standing association of the shrine as a matter of right.[26] A similar result followed for those intimately connected with the Nathdwara temple in Rajasthan.[27] In time, other Courts and judges followed this temple. A Jain sect was told that they had lost the right to manage their temple because of an obscure legislation of the Raja of Udaipur.[28] The role and functions of *archakas* (traditional helpers) in a temple were held to be secular in nature and susceptible to statutory abolition.[29] The *pandas* of the famous Kashinath temple suffered a similar fate.[30] Cow slaughter was decreed not to be an 'essential practice' of the Muslim faith.[31] Anand Margis were astonished to learn from the Supreme Court that the *tandava* dance was not part of their faith.[32] It took a very brave decision of the Calcutta High Court to tell the Supreme Court that the latter was wrong and had not examined all the facts.[33] The religious distinctness of some sects was recognized,[34] those of others was not.[35] The disciples of sage Ramakrishna who had created separate *maths* (religious endowments) and 'missions' throughout the world were denied their legitimate status of being recognized as a separate sect within Hinduism.[36] The Swaminarayans were told that on a true interpretation of Hinduism, they were Hindus, even if they protested they were not.[37] The followers of Sri Aurobindo were denied the status of a religion altogether.[38] The ceremonies of *shradh* and *pinda* were declared integral to the Hindu faith;[39] but, in a dramatic sidelight of the *Babri Masjid* case, praying in a mosque was pronounced not to be crucial to the Islamic faith becuase, according to the judge, Muslims could pray anywhere, 'even in the open'.[40] The dead fared no better, with the courts taking the view that nothing in the Holy Koran injuncted the shifting of graves and burial grounds.[41] Even though religions need generous endowments to survive, an invocation of the 'essentiality' test rendered property not strictly required for essential ceremonies vulnerable to regulatory control or acquisition.[42] The Gowda Saraswats were permitted to exclude non-caste Hindus from certain ceremonies,[43] but Muslims from one sect could not preclude followers from other sects in the shrines of the former.[44] In a dramatic decision, the Supreme Court held that children of the Jehovah's Witnesses faith need not stand up to sing the national anthem at school assemblies, but eventually decided the case on the narrower ground that the executive order in relation to the compulsory singing of the national anthem did not have the authority of law required to 'infringe a fundamental right'.[45]

This catalogue of cases is, perhaps, best understood in the specific situation in which each decision arose. That by itself would not, however, dispose of the more fundamental critique of the 'essential' practices test, the invocation of ambiguous history to disentitle legitimate claims, the overt reliance on intuition, and the Court cutting loose to play judge, jury, prince, and high priest to the extent that it has. Judges in India who delve into sacral facts and ancient texts and scripts acquire a further exalted status as ersatz *dharmasastris* (sages)—ostensibly being the wisest amongst the wise. An insightful sociologist reminds us that in India 'westernization' and 'sanskritization' are two well-recognized avenues to improve one's social status.[46] Supreme Court judges have used both these avenues to consolidate their social and self esteem. At one level, many judicial decisions, such as those relating to cow slaughter, the shifting of graves or the dispute over the Babri Masjid and many other uncomfortable claims, are 'problem solving' in nature. Rather than confront these issues with the full plenitude of constitutional courage, the judges have chosen to make threshold rejections to many claims by a skilful use of evidence, interpretation, and use of the 'essential practices' test. Although these decisions may be consequentially satisfying, they cut deeply into the secular framework of the Constitution and do not always constitute principled decision making.[47]

Quite apart from the travails of problem solving, Indian judges have been sensitive towards, but not very energetic in their support for, religious freedom against the onslaught of state regulation and control. Regulation has become almost in-built into the psyche of Indian governance. Indian courts have had little hesitation in approving the apparatus of law and order control put in place by the British.[48] In a remarkable decision based on a dubious distinction, the Supreme Court defended the constitutional right to propagate faith, but refused to accept that this included the right to persuade others to convert to the propagator's faith.[49] Faced with drastic use of the President's Rule provision whereby four states were placed under the Emergency Rule of the Union after the destruction of the Babri Masjid in 1992, the majority of judges in the celebrated *Bommai* case (1994),[50] approved such anti-democratic impositions in the name of 'secularism' which was declared to be part of the basic structure of the Constitution—almost as if democracy was not part of the Constitution's basic structure—whilst the minority refrained from expressing a view and denied judicial review on the grounds that such matters were not judicially manageable.

However, beyond the occasionally overwritten script on public order, both the executive and the judiciary have also indulged in excessive regulation of religious and related institutions. Since 1853, colonial legislation was content to tackle corruption in religious institutions with the help of 'weak' regulatory oversight of religious endowments, with the power to 'temporarily' take over errant institutions.[51] From 1950, and greatly emboldened by the Supreme Court's decision in the *Religious Endowments* case (1954), various governments have virtually wholly taken over the managements of many religious endowments, permanently placed them under the control of statutory boards (which include some believers) and forced them to be run by bureaucrats. The most celebrated and widely approved example of such a takeover was that of the Vaishno Devi shrine in the state of Jammu and Kashmir by Governor Jagmohan. Yet, the Vaishno Devi model[52] 'trades' state efficiency (for what it is worth!) in exchange for religious freedom, which under the Indian Constitution includes the right to manage one's own religious institutions. In this process both the government and judiciary tend to overlook the simple fact that *under the guise of regulatory control, religious endowments are, and have been, nationalized on a massive scale.* Vaishno Devi is one amongst many shrines which has suffered this nationalization. If the regulatory impetus provided by Justice B.K. Mukerjea in the fifties was enlarged by Justice Gajendragadkar in the sixties, the latest judgements of Justice K. Ramaswami in 1996–7[53] have enthusiastically supported the 'nationalization' of some of India's greatest shrines. *The nationalization of religious endowments, temples and places of learning sits uneasily with both the guarantee of religious freedom and secularism.* To check corruption in religious institutions is one thing, to pave the way for nationalizing them quite another. Religious faiths have to be run by their followers and not by bureaucrats. The followers have to emerge from the faith and not be appointed by the State or statute. In dealing with these situations, the Court seems to have missed the wood for the trees.

The Supreme Court needs to review its jurisprudence on religious freedom. The Court must take religions as it finds them, even if the claims made are unusual. Obvious cases of fraud can be easily detected. It does not lie with the judiciary to tell people what constitutes the faith, or whether they are Hindus or which particular tenet or practice is an 'essential practice' exclusively entitled to constitutional protection. The 'essential practices' test was originally designed to enhance those aspects of faith which called for rigorous scrutiny and not to deprive non-essential practices of constitutional protection altogether. If any particular practice is found to be invidious, it can always be restrained by way of the extensive range of permissible restrictions rather than be controversially rejected by judges playing high priests of each and every faith. Some restrictions will be upheld because they are *de-minimus* intrusions into the practice of a faith. Others would need to be more carefully balanced against public interest. Restrictions should be interpreted bearing in mind a dissenting judge's salutary advice that it is the rights that are fundamental and not the restrictions.[54] The fact that many faiths need to reform and suffer regulatory oversight to prevent fraud and corruption does not mean that courts can reform them out of existence or disentitle traditional custodians of such faiths from further custodial association with them. The nationalization of India's most famous Hindu shrines to arrest incipient corruption is an overkill. These are difficult times. To borrow a phrase, if taken at its ebb, the political tide in the affairs of Indian religions could well lead to misfortune. The Supreme Court-led judiciary needs to be careful to avoid joining this tide by permitting excessive regulation and supporting dubious intimations of social reform. Its jurisprudence needs to go beyond a 'problem solving' peacekeeping, sustain a discerning support for religious freedom and evolve a greater sensitivity towards the variety of group life to ensure that the social robustness of a complex civilization endures with vitality.

Minorities and their Institutions

The judiciary has been ineluctably drawn into controversies over the cultural and educational rights of minorities. Although the Constitution-makers defined these rights generously, major interpretative controversies have erupted in relation to them, especially in relation to the rights of minority educational institutions to manage their own affairs.

Since long before Independence, the private sector, especially denominational schools of the Christian faith, have provided the rich aspiring middle classes with quality school and college education.[55] This has continued after 1950 even though the Constitution enjoins that the state shall provide free and compulsory education for children under fourteen years; a duty declared to be mandatory by the Supreme Court in an otherwise controversial decision of 1993.[56] Aware of the criticism that these denominational schools provide an elite western-based cosmopolitan education and were linked to a proselytizing Christian faith, the Constituent Assembly devised a compromise formula to give minorities a broad right to preserve their language, script, and culture and 'establish and administer educational institutions of their choice'.[57] Assured the right of autonomous self-management, such institutions were also not to be discriminated against in the matter of funding and other support from the State. In return, such aided institutions did not force compulsory religious education on those who did not want it and could not discriminate between applicants who wanted education in these schools on grounds only of their religion, caste, or language.[58] This compromise leaned heavily in favour of the minorities but left open unanswered questions: What exactly was a minority? Were minority schools and colleges just for their respective communities or also for others? Was the Constitution's protection confined only to institutions dispensing primary, secondary, or religious education? Did 'self-management' rule out general regulatory control? Many of these and other questions remain incompletely or unsatisfactorily resolved to this day.

After 1950, several governments came up with an endless stream of schemes to undermine these rights to bring minority institutions within the ever increasing control of state regulation. Till about 1975 or so, the Supreme Court stood firmly against these over assimilative schemes. In the *Bombay Educational Society* case (1955),[59] the Court invalidated the then state of Bombay's attempt to restrict admissions to English medium schools to those children whose mother tongue was English as violative of the Constitution's injunction that aided schools could not discriminate in matters of admission on grounds of language, caste, and religion of the applicants. Close on the heels of this decision followed the *Kerala* case (1958).[60] In 1957, the newly elected 'communist' government of Kerala devised a much more elaborate plan to assimilate minority schools within a strict regulatory framework for all schools. A constitutional crisis ensued. The President invited the Supreme Court to 'problem-solve' the situation. Avoiding the question as to whether Christians were a 'minority' in local areas where they were in a majority and reserving the right to refuse to answer presidential references, the Court emphasized the rights of minorities to create 'institutions of their choice', and refused to deny the right of these institutions to admit 'outsiders' (even though its reference to a 'sprinkling of outsiders' created controversy for the future). The Court perceptively pointed out that 'no educational institution can in modern times, afford to subsist and efficiently function without state aid', and accepted that the price of aid was not the surrender of constitutional rights. At the same time, the Court safeguarded the State's regulatory power to vouchsafe proper safeguards against 'maladministration' in minority schools and to maintain such conditions connected with grants-in-aid and the recognition of the school which did not impinge on the minority's rights to manage their institutions. On this basis, several provisions of the Bill (including those dealing with the threat of 'State takeover' and the insistence on free tuition by these schools) were struck down, and honour was satisfied all round. However, crucial questions remained unanswered.

The state of Gujarat was not far behind the state of Kerala. In 1962,[61] the Supreme Court declared the state's attempt to impose a Hindi medium of instruction on university colleges to be legislatively incompetent. Then came *Sidhajbhai's* case (1963)[62] where grants were denied to Church Mission teachers' training schools which resisted the government's scheme to appropriate 80 per cent of the available seats in such schools for government nominees. Invalidating this scheme, and aware that broad appeals to public interest would destroy minority rights, Shah J refused to accept that all regulatory measures which were not wholly destructive or annihilative of minority rights were valid so long as they subserved the public interest. Emphatically propounding a new, but delicately balanced, approach, he insisted that any

... regulation must satisfy a *dual test* —the test of reasonableness and the test that it is regulative of the educational character of the institution and *is conducive to making the institution an effective vehicle of education for the minority community and others who resort to it* [emphasis added].[63]

If this salutary decision had been followed in letter and spirit, the later jurisprudence of the Court in this area would have been much clearer and more palatable to the cause of protecting minority rights.

For some time the Supreme Court stood by minority institutions against an over-regulatory onslaught by state governments and universities, be they those of Kerala, Bihar or Punjab. The Court was emphatic that state agencies could not foist their representatives or nominees on to minority institution management boards and committees.[64] Nor could they dictate who should be disciplined or exercise a right of appeal, veto, or approval over staff and other appointments or dismissals.[65] Apart from some controversial decisions like the *Aligarh University* and other cases over the definition of a 'minority institution',[66] there was one apparently contrary nuance. Hidayatullah CJ's decision in the *Second Kerala* case (1971)[67] contained an authoritative contrapuntal murmur which softened Shah J's second 'self betterment-of-the-minority' requirement and favoured a more open-ended public interest test. Wrongly overemphasizing that minority institutions generally served the public and existed not just for minorities but also others who resorted to this, this judgement exhorted that 'minority institutions not be allowed to fall below the standards of excellence of educational institutions ... [so that] whilst management must be left open to them, they may be compelled to keep in step with others [because] ... [t]he Constitution speaks of [their right to self-administration] and no more'. Taken to its illogical limits, if Shah J's 'self-betterment' test was abandoned in favour of a general public interest test, nothing would be left of the minority rights of educational institutions. They would be denuded of their special constitutional protection other than the mere right to do business.

The *St Xaviers* case (1975)[68] represents a watershed in the Court's thinking. Pronouncing on yet another challenge from Gujarat where the legislature had done all the wrong things, by planting people on minority boards, interfering with teaching, curricula, and examinations, forcing minority colleges to be constituent colleges of the University and requiring approval from the Vice-Chancellor for disciplinary action against staff. Broadly agreed on all, but some, aspects of the ultimate result, the nine-judge bench of the Court divided sharply along ideological lines. The assimilationist judges built on Hidayatullah CJ's enlarged emphasis on 'excellence' in the public interest to exhort minority institutions to become so excellent that they shed their minority character! The pluralist judges protested that whatever the government's 'spiritual mission' to promote secularism, the State cannot override 'its primary duty of providing justice and ensuring equality of differences'. The fact that amidst differences both sides broadly agreed on the end result and broadly relied on the same precedents added to the confusion This confusion was later exploited by other assimilationist judges to advance and increase regulatory control over minority institutions. Almost immediately after *St Xaviers* case, the Court split (2:1) in the *Agra University* case (1975)[69] to permit 'principal and staff' representation on the management board of a college on the basis that such inclusions were as *de minimus* as they were beneficial. Even though the Constitution Bench in the *Third Kerala (Lily Kurien)* case (1979)[70] made clear that disciplinary action by a minority institution could not be subject to the Vice-Chancellor's approval, in the *All Saints* case (1980)[71] the Supreme Court turned a blind eye to settled precedents to decide, in yet another split decision (2:1), that due process requirements for staff (including the requirement of prior approval of external authorities before suspending a teacher) could be impo d on minority institutions. Both the *Agra* and the *All Saints* decisions were contrary to earlier decisions of the Court even though sustenance was sought to be drawn from these earlier precedents! This was a prelude to yet another multiple judgement decision in a *Bihar* case (1994)[72] where the Court divided on whether the decision to deny statutory recognition to a college on spurious grounds was simply wrong because it was a bad decision or because it transgressed the minority's special rights. The tide was clearly turning. The rights of minority institutions were becoming no greater than the rights of any business enterprise.

This is precisely what was emphasized by a two-judge bench in the *Delhi (Frank Anthony School)* case (1986)[73] to make the emotional appeal that *all* schools and colleges simply had to be fair to their staff and employees. *Giving the minority institutions no leeway to devise their own system of fairness*, in the *Delhi* case, the Court validated the application of the entire gamut of regulatory control on minority institutions which it had refrained from fully imposing on minority institutions for thirty-five years, subject to the solitary exception that the 'external' executive authorities could not sit in approval over the dismissal of staff by the management of minority schools. The *Delhi (Frank Anthony School)* case completed the triumph of regulation over minority rights. Refusing to recognize the contradictions in its own decisions, a series of decisions flowed from the Supreme Court which permitted the requirement of prior approval by executive authorities for suspending employees,[74] the application of the general labour law,[75] employment related disciplinary rules and tribunals to such institutions,[76] the imposition of a regime requiring minority institutions to frame certain kinds of by-laws,[77] the takeover of the management of such institutions under some circumstances,[78] sustaining the requirement of 'concurrence' of state school boards for appointment of teachers,[79] leaving the state free to devise a 'language policy' as a general medium of instruction,[80] imposing syllabi, courses of study, and 'allied' matters,[81] increasing the basis on which recognition and affiliation could be denied to minority schools[82] and interposing an unprecedented and fantastic argument that aided minority insitutions could only reserve 50 per cent of their seats for their own community.[83]

Some of the Court's anxieties have stemmed from its concern that bogus claims for minority status have been made by bogus institutions.[84] However, throwing out 'fraud' cases does not require approval for such a heavy apparatus of regulatory control. A penchant for 'assimilating' differences into a new modernisitc Indian melting pot, ideological support for regulatory control, and a 'left wing' support for employees have provoked some judges to sustain the Court's near annhilation of minority rights. Yet, there are many loose ends which were brought to the fore in the aftermath of the *Technical Education* (Unnikrishnan) case (1993)[85] where the Court virtually nationalized admissions to technical educational institutions by giving detailed directions allocating admissions to, and the fees to be charged by, all such institutions. A question arose: did this scheme apply to 'minority colleges and universities'? The Supreme Court is yet to decide this and other questions relating to minority institutions. However, the worst fear of the minorities is that, in the present milieu, such a fresh *de novo* examination by a larger eleven-judge bench may not just approve the existing stranglehold of regulatory control, but deprive minority institutions which also provide technical, professional, university, and other forms of tertiary education of virtually any special constitutional protection altogether. Echoes of this possibility came from some judges in the abandoned hearings of 1997–8!

Minority institutions have not just been under pressure from excessive state regulation but also in the establishment of their credential as minority institutions. The most celebrated example of this was the *Aligarh University* case (1968)[86] in which the Aligarh University had universally acknowledged continuing association with Muslim culture and traditions. However, in a baffling pro-state decision, the Supreme Court refused to accept that this famous Muslim university had the status of a constitutionally protected minority institution for the unconvincing technical reason that the University had been reconstituted on a statutory basis in 1919 and had, therefore, become a public institution even though its strong Muslim associations continued before and after that date. At the root of the problem is the Court's over-legalized interpretation of the Constitution which empowers minorities with the right 'to establish and administer' institutions of their choice. However, the terms 'establish and administer' create rights, not disempowering impediments to make it more difficult for minority institutions to be recognized as such. The right of minorities to 'establish and administer' institutions of their choice has been converted into a test requiring minorities to show that they established, and have always continued to administer, the minority institution. This is a tall order for the many minority institutions which were established decades, if not centuries, ago. Nor is such excursus required by the Constitution.

The correct approach is to examine the broad community association and character of the institution rather than insist on legal technicalities or exact extensive historical proof of continuing past and present minority association with the institution especially in situations where no such requirement is practical or necessary. The policy of the Court has been as exacting as it has been inexact. The Christians of Bhagalpur,[87] Jesuits of Ranchi,[88] and Protestants of Delhi[89] were required to produce considerable proof to show that they and not non-resident aliens, truly established and administered these institutions during British rule. Denied the status of a religious sect, the Arya Samajis were treated as a distinct numerical minority in Punjab because they used the Hindi Devanagari script which, it happens, is also the national language.[90] Also, if the numerical test is applicable, since 1958 the Court has still not decided whether it should be applied on a local, regional, state, or national basis.[91] Apart from patent 'frauds', the widest possible claims to minority status on an all-India basis (including those of distinct minorities within majorities) should be accepted instead of dealing with these issues like the proverbial blind men and the elephant to seize on only one characteristic of a minority to the exclusion of others.

The Supreme Court's approach to minority rights and institutions has been far from consistent. Beginning with a far greater sensitivity in favour of these rights in the early years, it has gradually permitted extensive regulatory ingresses into the working of minority institutions by protecting only the rights of minorities to have their own people (amongst others) on the Boards of these institutions and invalidating mandatory external approvals of dismissals from employees, whilst making it harder for minority institutions to be recognized as such. This ingress has been spurred on for ideological reasons and a somewhat myopic view that minority institutions should play a less autonomous role in matters of education; that all persons must join a particular assimilationist version of the mainstream of Indian life. What however is Indian life, if it is not crowded in by the sheer variety that makes India what it is?

Social Reform, Affirmative Action, and Personal Laws

The Constitution looked to the future with a commitment to social reform and change. Specific provisions dealt with the abolition of untouchability and opening up public temples to all believers irrespective of caste.[92] Ameliorative provisions for women and children and affirmative action for BCs and OBCs were specifically permitted.[93] Aware that many personal laws were caste-ridden and gender unjust, a general 'directive principle' was accepted that there was a need for a uniform civil code of personal laws.[94] Contrary to political and academic assertions, traditional religious and other groups rights were not intended to be swallowed by an overriding modernist secularism to dissolve India's diversity into nothingness.[95] It was for governments to enable a consensus to set the pace of change; and for courts to control the permissible texture and speed of this change. There have been few problems in proposing and enacting measures in areas of 'high' formal consensus such as untouchability, temple entry, dowry abolition, prevention of child marriage, and the like.[96] These measures have not always proved to be effective and have even been toned down by courts. In more controversial areas such as affirmative action and the uniform civil code, the Court has been more circumspect in its enthusiasm for sustaining social change.

The issue of affirmative action to enable BCs and OBCs to receive better technical or professional education and government jobs has excited violent controversy. Till 1990, regimes at the Centre were reluctant to extend affirmative action for government jobs to extend beyond the BCs to include OBCs. Meanwhile, various state governments had drawn political mileage by quantitatively extending their affirmative action patronage beyond 50 per cent of the total seats or posts available and qualitatively increasing the range of persons and groups who would benefit from this benediction.[97] Since most beneficiary groups were defined on a caste basis, these programmes have been criticized as entrenching a group life based on caste even though the end result of such schemes is directed towards sustaining ameliorative social justice for the historically discriminated against and endemically disadvantaged.[98] In the earlier *Mysore* (Balaji) case[99] the Court refused to allow reservations to cross the limit of 50 per cent of the posts available and adroitly evolved an eclectic criterion of 'backwardness' which included caste as an important but not determinant element. Juristic wrangles continued on whether the criteria should be based on pure socio-economic criteria excluding caste.[100] In the meanwhile, the Supreme Court invented the novel 'doctrine-of-source', whereby candidates for posts and seats for jobs and opportunities could be exlusively drawn from any reasonably classifiable source so as to grant special benefits to particular groups such as families of freedom fighters, children of diplomats or (with some difference of opinion) students of particular universities for admissions to higher education.[101] All this was 'reservation' of posts, seats, and advantages for particular classes of people, and nothing else. The Supreme Court however refused to treat these benedictions as reservations. Reservations based on the 'doctrine-of-source' do not count towards the 50 per cent ceiling on the extent of permissible reservations. Implicitly realizing this, the Court refused reservation of seats under the 'doctrine-of-source' for the 'rectification of regional imbalances'[102] or as a welfare provision for 'wards of employees',[103] but permitted such reservation for the impoverished rural region of Uttarakhand in the state of Uttar Pradesh.[104] The 'doctrine-of-source', with its 'not-so-rigorous' and intuitively applied criteria to justify ad hoc classifications creates a third category of beneficiaries who were not specifically identified by the Constitution for preferential treatment. Anxious to help the BCs and OBCs to get into the mainstream, the Supreme Court has also permitted a reasonable relaxation of minimal criteria for those candidates unable to meet the normal eligibility requirements.[105] Some feel that the only really disadvantaged are the BC (i.e. SCs and STs). That is why, Krishna Iyer J referred to them as a 'super-classification' in the celebrated *Thomas* case (1976);[106] a case of relaxation of criteria in which a split decision inconclusively left open the doctrinaire question as to whether affirmative action was part of the doctrine of equality or a constitutionally devised exception to it. Concern about the 'caste' basis of reservations had been powerfully articulated as early as 1964 in which one judge counselled against 'the dubious obsession with caste', refused to allow '[t]he politics of power [to] ... sabotage the principles of one man, one value', and asserted that '[c]aste, *ipso facto* is not "class" in a secular State'.[107]

Such an untidy situation would have continued but for the famous *Mandal* controversy (1990–2).[108] Riots erupted as a response to Prime Minister V.P. Singh's introducing OBC reservations in the Central Services on the basis of the *Mandal Commission* Report of 1980. The Supreme Court was called to 'problem-solve' the crisis. As a matter of principle, the Court, in a split decision (6:3), of 1992[109] affirmed that reservations for BCs and OBCs were part of the doctrine of equality and not an exception to it, and that access to government jobs was a salutary form of empowerment for disadvantaged people and those discriminated against with no access to such power. Since caste plays an important role in determining which groups are disadvantaged or discriminated against, caste was accepted, amidst dissent, as part of the criteria for determining who was entitled to affirmative action and support. The *Mandal* case affirmed that reservations could not exceed 50 per cent of the posts or jobs available but excluded beneficiaries under the 'doctrine-of-source'. Relaxations of eligibility criteria was permissible, but 'reservations' could not be indiscriminately 'carried over' from one year to another beyond prescribed time limits and quotas. Aware that 'reservations' had become a form of largesse to politically grateful groups, the Court made it mandatory to devise a 'creamy layer' test (but only for OBCs and not the BCs) so that those who were no longer disadvantaged were excluded from entitlement to the benefits of affirmative action. Aware, too, that reservations had clogged up the higher echelons of the civil services, the Court declared that 'reservations' for promotional posts were unconstitutional even though this issue was not before the Court for decision in the *Mandal* case. The application of this embargo on reservation for promotional posts was deferred for five years. Parliament immediately responded by amending the Constitution to enable reservations for promotions, but only for SCs and STs. Not wholly satisfied with the *Mandal* decision, subsequent Benches of the Court struck down dubious creamy layer tests,[110] devised new methods to ensure that reservations remained within allocated quotas,[111] refused to allow 'reserved' candidates not selected on the basis of merit to gain further 'accelerated seniority' over their colleagues,[112] and limited the scope of relaxations in favour of these beneficiaries.[113]

The *Mandal* decision itself was received with a sigh of relief. The Court had 'problem-solved' an explosive situation after tidying up previous juristic controversies and striking a balance between justice and politics. However, by virtue of the fact that the *Mandal* case affirmed that caste could form the basis for selecting beneficiaries for affirmative action, schemes and programmes, a new caste-based politics was unleashed, of a kind that India has never witnessed. A new electoral nexus emerged between the new beneficiaries and their political patrons. From the 1980s, electoral 'reservations' had been made for OBCs for local government panchayats and boards. Extensive benefits and opportunities were extended to OBC caste-based groups. The very texture of politics was changed. The number and categories of OBCs have kept expanding, covering over a third of the population. OBC issues dominate the ballot. Even without OBC reservations in state assemblies and Parliament, OBC-dominated constituencies rule the roost to return OBC candidates. The entire balance of electoral power has altered. Instability stalks parliamentary governance. Caste is a fact of Indian social life, but it has been rejuvenated by politics to acquire a new and somewhat dangerous reincarnation.

In contrast to its interventions on affirmative action, the courts have attempted to steer clear of controversies over the Uniform Civil Code of Personal Laws (UCC).[114] If the 'social reform' provisions of the Constitution were taken to their logical limit, many of the personal laws of various communities would be cleansed of their social inequities. It is a moot point whether such equitable cleansing can take place by judicial action without creating a legislatively enacted statutory UCC. The Constitution-makers dealt with this in a Directive Principle suggesting that the legislature could devise a statutory solution to this problem by creating a UCC *(the Article 44 legislative solution)*. This did not however preclude judges from deciding that 'personal laws', like any other customary or other unwritten laws, were 'laws' within the meaning of Article 13 and would be invalidated as unconstitutional if they did not meet the equality, due process, and the social reform mandates of the Fundamental Rights chapter of the Constitution (the *Article 13 judicial solution*). Logically, if other customary laws were 'laws' within the meaning of Article 13 of the Constitution, so were personal laws. If judges struck down constitutionally invidious customary laws,[115] 'personal laws' had to be treated similarly. However, for wholly inexplicable and unacceptable reasons, the high courts rejected the 'Article 13-solution', refusing to test personal laws on the touchstone of fundamental rights.[116] The Supreme Court affirmed this in *obiter dicta* in 1980[117] and more comprehensively in 1997.[118] The ball was back with the legislatures. Enacting a UCC requires a high degree of unachievable consensus. Though supported by many liberals and feminists as a necessary ingredient for advancing gender justice,[119] the UCC has become a weapon in the hands of fundamentalist Hindus to exhort the Muslims to change their polygamist laws and agree to codify their laws just as the Hindus had done in 1955–6. The reform of Hindu law had not, however, come easily. After a gestation period of two decades, the full codification of the Hindu law was abandoned ... no less because of controversies between President Prasad and Prime Minister Nehru![120]

Radical judges cannot however resist being reformers. Inevitably, controversies have continued, especially in relation to the universal application of the 'maintenance' provisions of the Criminal Procedure Code[121] which, according to one Supreme Court judge, provided a 'scheme of relief for driftwood and destitute wives and divorcees by heartless husbands'.[122] Did these provisions apply to Muslims? In the celebrated *Shah Bano* case (1985),[123] the courts applied the maintenance provision of the Criminal Code to Muslims, to invite tumultuous controversy and cause Prime Minister Rajiv Gandhi's government in 1985 to enact a special compromise legislation for the maintenance for Muslim wives.[124] Even though in some respects this special legislation gives better protection to Muslim women than the general law, both the *Shah Bano* case and the legislation that followed have become *causes célèbres*. The legislation has been fiercely criticized for its unequal and overtly favourable anti-secular and differentiated treatment of Muslims.[125] These controversies have acquired both ideological and communal hues and colours. Extremist postures by all sides can only lead to attrition, a paralysis of mutual understanding, and a stagnation of the possibility of justly desired results. Despite its many brave words and its otherwise strong pitch for gender justice,[126] by resisting the Article 13 or 'fundamental rights' solution, the Supreme Court has wavered to avoid being mired in controversies over the much needed reform of personal laws which clearly fall within its fundamental rights remit. Such reticence ill becomes a Court so widely renowned for its activist reformism.

The Supreme Court has been a very powerful actor in its public interest decisions in favour of disadvantaged groups, workers, bonded labour, children, and others, and to contain corruption or defend the environment.[127] However, in the controversial area of traditional group rights, affirmative action, personal laws, and gender justice, the Court has been high sounding whilst adroitly avoiding a too courageous pursuit of the ends of egalitarian social justice. No doubt 'problem solving' is part of the pragmatism of the law,[128] but the Court needs to pay heed to the reminder of one of its reformist judges that 'in the inevitable chemistry of social change, judges are certainly not anti-catalysts'.[129]

Secularism and Electoral Politics

Spurred on by the specific inclusion of 'secularism' and 'socialism' in the Preamble to the Constitution in 1976, the Supreme Court has declared 'secularism' to be part of the 'basic structure' of the Indian Constitution and invoked it to be a relevant 'factor' in imposing President's Rule on the four BJP state governments after the Babri Masjid was destroyed in 1992.[130] However, there is an amazing lack of consistency and clarity about the meaning of Indian 'secularism'. Indian secularism does not post a strict separation between church and state, and articulates a strong commitment to social reform. Evolved in wholly different circumstances, it is very different from its American and other counterparts.[131] Some have criticized it for being too committed to an over-rationalized modernity.[132] Others argue that modern rationalist discourse is the true secular way forward.[133] Still others accept the ideal of diversity, but press for the need for social reform and gender justice.[134] Prime Minister Nehru, whose fondness for India's social diversity was as strong as his overriding commitment to social reform and modernity, is wrongly vilified as personifying a new modern India directed towards reforming its traditional life out of existence.[135] A balanced 'secularism' is hostile to both invidious, unjust, and discriminatory social practices as well as the politicized appropriation of religion in order to effect a 'fundamentalist' take-over by the State. It has been suggested that Indian secularism is founded on three constituent elements: (i) the *principle of religious freedom* which expansively protects all aspects of a religion including its beliefs, rituals, practices, thoughts, ideas and philosophies, and injuncts discrimination on grounds religion, race, caste, place of birth or gender; (ii) the *principles of depoliticization and celebratory neutrality* which prevent the state from being taken over by any one community but permits it to assist all faiths in their endeavours and celebrate their existence as part of the pageantry of India; and (iii) the *principle of social welfare and reform* which requires religions to yield to regulatory and reformative regulation and cleanse their inegalitarian, gender-unjust, and other constitutionally unacceptable prescriptions.[136] Consistent with these principles, the courts have extended religious freedom to protect both beliefs and practices, rejected challenges that the State cannot celebrate the 2500th birthday of the founder of Jainism Lord Mahavira[137] as not being violative of the state's secular neutrality, and correctly interpreted the constitutional text as permitting giving non-discriminate financial assistance to religious groups and institutions so long as taxes were not specifically appropriated for this purpose.[138] Yet, a clear judicial statement on what constitutes secularism continues to elude us. The issue of the depoliticization of religion has become important in recent times because Hindu political parties have appropriated religion to politics and excited a 'lumpen' fundamentalism to provoke social violence, of which the destruction of the Babri Masjid in 1992 and the attacks on Christians in 1998–9 are a shameful part.

All political parties indulge in some form of religious electioneering. Indeed, the Congress Party's statutory reversal of the Supreme Court's decision is criticized precisely because this initiative was to woo the Muslim vote.[139] India's election law specifically forbids invoking *threats* of social ostracism, excommunication, or expulsion from religious groups or castes, divine displeasure or special censure, making *appeals* to religion, race, caste, community, or language or religious symbols, or *attempts* to promote feelings of enmity amongst such groups or the propagation or glorification of *sati* as part of the election process.[140] Politicians pander to religious sentiments—both when they are in power and at the hustings. While considering whether elections should be set aside for violations of these injunctions, the Court has been more pragmatic than principled in its approach. After entering the usual caveat that the entire time, place, and context has to be taken into account and strict proof is required to show that any impugned anti-secular communal statement was made by the candidate or someone authorized by him, the Supreme Court has held that electoral appeals that there should be at least one Brahmin Minister,[141] or to a Rajput identity,[142] or that Muslims not voting for a candidate would be treated as renegades or heretics,[143] or that the candidate was akin to Lord Krishna or votes be cast in terms of a Sikh Hukamnama[144] (religious proclamation), or to Hindus to vote to teach Muslims a lesson[145] were clearly violative of the law and impermissible. More controversially, however, it has also decided that votes to defend the honour of the Sikh *panth*,[146] the use of the Hindu symbol 'Om'[147] or reference to the religiously significant *dhruv* star,[148] or an appeal in the name of 'Hindutva'[149] were not appeals to religion. Some inconsistencies abound which can, perhaps, be explained in the factual context of the case, but not always.

The 'Hindutva' decision (1995)[150] equating that term with 'Indianness' has been sharply criticized as supporting a majoritarian fundamentalism.[151] It is well known that the term 'Hindutva' has fundamentalist connotations and has been invoked electorally in recent years to excite Hindu fervour to masquerade as political passion. In the *Hindutva* case, the Supreme Court relied on the no less controversial elaboration of the Hindu faith in the *Swami Narayan* temple entry case[152] to pronounce that 'Hinduism' had an elastic, all-embracing meaning, and incorrectly drew support for a neutral interpretation of Hindutva by misconstruing writings of a Muslim scholar. Its view that such terms contribute to 'the development of a uniform culture by obliterating the differences between all the cultures coexisting in the country' have been rightly criticized as fundamentalist and inconsistent with a plural secularism. Although the opportunity to clarify its stance presented itself, the Court declined to do so.[153]

More generally, the Supreme Court's vacillation on these matters stems from an unclear judicial policy on the principle of the depoliticization of religion as an essential ingredient of Indian secularism. Even though some countries of the world permit reference to religion in elections, and India permits appeals to many non-religious ideologies, *a full interplay* in elections, there are good historical reasons for India to prohibit invocations to religion, caste, or language in Indian elections. Otherwise, a fragile nation which has already undergone a painful 'partition' may hurtle towards a new political fundamentalism contrary to the spirit of this unique civilization which is striving towards political unity amidst social diversity to provide justice to all.

Conclusion: If it Contradicts Itself, Well, then, it Does

It is easy to criticize a judiciary which has seen a turnover of 140-odd judges over a tumultuous period of fifty years. It is ahistorical not to place each judge and judicial decision in both its specific and historical context. Indian judges have reacted to specific challenges with a robust and intricate response. No doubt, akin to Gandhi's inimitable description of the Indian endeavours of the British Judicial Committee of the Privy Council, the Supreme Court too, has often committed 'egregious blunders',[154] but that should not detract from its undoubted and creative contribution to the ongoing discourse of Indian law and the 'argument without end' of which it is a significant part. When the Supreme Court was nearing its Silver Jubilee, one of us described the attitude of the Supreme Court judges as typical of the decision-making habits of middle-class metropolitan Indians:

technically unpredictable, not uninfluenced by imitative cosmopolitan habits, conditioned by native instinct to a depth not yet predictable by the psychologist or documented even by the novelist, the dramatist or the fiction-writer, and suffering from an over-sensitive opinion of their lonely and unparalleled position.[155]

Although the next twenty-five years of the Supreme Court saw the intervention of an emergency (1975–7), the flowering of an elaborate public interest law to address its social justice concerns and an unparalleled increase in the volume and range of its work, this past comment on the Supreme Court at the end of its Silver Jubilee continues as a valid verdict on the Court at the end of its Golden Jubilee. The Supreme Court does so much that it may feel, in Walt Whitman's phrase, that 'if it contradicts itself, well, then, it contradicts itself ... for it is large and can contain multitudes'.[156] However, as we transit into the next millennium, the Supreme Court has a lot to reflect upon, and not least on how to protect the minorities and their ilk from the onslaught of majoritarianism.

Notes

[1] B.R. Ambedkar, Speech to the Constituent Assembly, (1948), VII, *CAD*, 38–9.

[2] The Constitution of India devoted a whole part, XVII (Articles 343–9, 351) to 'Official Language'; and now lists eighteen official languages in its Eighth schedule. On Nehru's discomfiture with linguistic states being unfounded, see S.K. Agarwal's 'Jawaharlal Nehru and the Language Problem', in R. Dhavan et al. (ed.), *Nehru and the Constitution*, *infra* n. 13, 134–60.

[3] For the latest demographic distribution of persons according to religion, see Government of India *Census of India 1991: Religion*, paper 1 of 1995: New Delhi: Government of India, 1997.

[4] The term 'karma cola' is taken from Geeta Mehta, *Karma Cola: Marketing the Mystic East*, Simon & Schuster, New York, 1979. In 1986, UNESCO sponsored an anthology by James A. Beckford (ed.), *New Religious Movements and Rapid Social Change*, Sage, Delhi, 1986, surveying the contemporary growth of new faiths, sect, and cults throughout the world.

[5] On the demolition of the Babri Masjid, see S. Srivastava, *The Disputed Mosque: A Historical Inquiry*, Vikas Publications, Delhi, 1991; S. Gopal (ed.), *Anatomy of a Confrontation: The Babri Masjid Controversy*, Viking, Delhi, 1991; A.A. Engineer (ed.), *Babri Masjid: Ram Janma Bhoomi Controversy*, Ajanta Publications, Delhi, 1990; R. Thapar, et al., *The Political Abuse of History: Babri Masjid: Ram Janma bhoomi Disputes*, Centre for Historical Studies, Jawaharlal Nehru University, New Delhi, 1989: contrast the view of K. Elshd, *Ram Janma Bhoomi v Babri Masjid*, Voice of India, New Delhi, 1990.

[6] An analysis simultaneously explored in R. Dhavan's lecture in Sri Lanka in July 1998 entitled: 'A Constitution for a Civilization: India–2000' (mimeo, 1998) and Fali S. Nariman, 'The Indian Constitution: An Experiment amid Diversity', in Robert Goldwin, Art Kaufman and Wiliam Schumbra, *Forging Unity out of Diversity*, American Enterprise for Public Policy Research, Washington DC, 1985, 7–37.

[7] *Indian Statutory Commission* (known as the Simon Commission) (1930) Cmnd 3568, vol. I, pr. 147, p. 137 quoting from the Montague–Chelmsford Report (1919)at prs. 227–32.

[8] For an overwritten account of the adapatability and resilience of Indian groups, see S. Rudolph and L. Rudolph, *The Modernity of Tradition: Political Development in India*, University of Chicago Press, Chicago, 1967.

[9] On data on the Princely States, see S.S. Dhavan, *What are the Princely States*, Allahabad, 1946. The balkanization of India was prevented by a timely assimilation of states into the successor states. A solution to Kashmir is overdue. The complexities of the legal and political relationship between the Princely states and the British Raj created an awkward situation (see Copland, *The British Raj and the Indian Princes: Paramountcy in Western India*, Orient Longman, Bombay, 1982; I. Copland, *The Princes of India in the*

Endgame of Empire, 1917–47, Cambridge University Press, Cambridge, 1997. The Supreme Court did not find it easy to fully resolve constitutional controversies over the promises made to the Indian princes in the *Privy Purses* case (*Madhav Rao Scindia v Union of India* (1917) 3 SCR 745). Universal electorates were agreed by the Assembly on 16 June 1949 and are now in Article 325 of the Constitution of India (see, VIII, CAD, 1949, 930). More generally, on the distribution of seats to disadvantaged communities, see B. Shiva Rao, *The Framing of India's Constitution,* N.M. Tripathi, Bombay, 1968, 459–79, 741–80. Note the constitutional provisions on special electoral representation of disadvantaged groups in Parliament and the state of legislation (Article 330–2) and panchayats and local government (Article 243 D and 243 T). The constitutional injunction against anti-discrimination is written into many provisions (see Articles 14, 15(1)(2), 16(2), 16(5), 17, 2, 28(3), 29(2), 30(2), 325 of the Constitution of India).

[10] The Constitution contains specific provisions for affirmative action for the BCs (Backward Classes) and OBCs (Other Backward Classes), women and children (Articles 15(3) on women and children), 15(4), 16(4) and 16(4A) on BCs and OBCs read with Article 335 on BCs and more generally Articles 337, 338, 339, 340, 341 on Anglo-Indians, BCs, and OBCs). There is also a family of articles that deal with the special requirements of various states and regions—such as Article 370 on Kashmir and Articles 244–224A, 371 to 371 I on various states; and the proviso to Article 164(1) in relation to the BCs and OBCs of Bihar, Madhya Pradesh, and Orissa.

[11] Constitution of India, Article 25(2) generally.

[12] Constitution of India, Article 17 (on untouchability), Article 18 (abolition of titles), Article 25(2)(b) (on opening public temples for all and social reform in relation to religious rights) and, amongst other Directive Principles, Article 44 (on the uniform civil code) and Article 48 (on cow slaughter).

[13] In a well-known speech in Parliament J. Nehru said: 'Somehow we have found that this magnificent constitution that we have framed was later kidnapped and purloined by the lawyers'. See 1951, XII–XIII, Parliamentary Debates (PD) (Pt II), Col 8832 (17 May 1951). For an account of the controversies between the judges and the executive on agrarian reform, see H.C.L. Merrilat, *Land and the Constitution,* N.M. Tripathi, Bombay, 1970; and, more generally, R. Dhavan, Introduction to R. Dhavan et al. (ed.), *Nehru and the Constitution,* N.M. Tripathi, Bombay, 1992, (i) to (xcii).

[14] See R. Dhavan, *The Supreme Court of India: A Socio–Legal Analysis of its Juristic Techniques,* Bombay, 1977, Ch. III. Note Chief Justice Patanjali Shastri's post-retirement speech, reported in AIR 1955 SC 25, that the Court had been misunderstood.

[15] *State of Madras v Champakam Dorairajan* (1951) SCR 525; *Venkataramana v State of Madras* AIR 1951 SC 229. Stray observations provoked a constitutional amendment to obviate impediments to the affirmative action programme.

[16] *Commissioner, Hindu Religious Endowments v Sri Lakshmindra* (1954) SCR 1005 (the *Srirur Math* case); *Mahant Sri Jaganath v State of Orissa* (1954) SCR 1946; *Rati Lal v State of Bombay* (1954) SCR 1055. The author of these rulings had delivered the Tagore Law Lectures on this subject (see B.K. Mukherjea, *Hindu Law of Religious Endowments,* Eastern Law House, Calcutta, 1952).

[17] R. Dhavan, 'The Supreme Court and Hindu Religious Endowments: 1950–1975', 1978, 20, *Journal of the Indian Law Institute,* 52–102.

[18] See the *Srirur Math* case, *supra* n. 16, at 1024–5, 1028–9 which show that the 'essential practices' was never intended as a threshold rejection test. More strongly, note the unequivocal statement in *Rati Lal, supra* n. 16 at p. 1065: 'No outside authority has

any right to say that they are not essential parts of religion and it is not open to the secular authority of the state to restrict or prohibit them in any manner they like under the guise of administering the trust estate.'

[19] *Venkataramanna*, infra n. 43 at 909; *Durgah Committee* (*infra* n. 26 at 411–2; *Saifuddin*, *infra* n. 24), 529–30; *S.P. Mittal*, *infra* n.38 at 741–2, 745–7, 750–1, 773–4; *Bijoe Emmanuel v State of Kerala* (1986) 3 SCR 518 at 533.

[20] *Mohd. Hanif Qureshi* (1959) SCR 629; *A.H. Qureshi v State of Bihar* (1961) 2 SCR 610.

[21] Constitution of India, Article 48. This Directive Principle was suggested after the 'Draft Constitution' was circulated (see B. Shiva Rao, *The Framing of India's Constitution Select Documents*, N.M. Tripathi, Bombay, 1968, IV, 556, and debated on 24 Nov 1948 (see (1948) VII Constituent Assembly Debates (CAD), 568–81.

[22] A comment by J.D.M. Derrett, Case Comment (1959) 8 *ICLQ* 221 at 224.

[23] *Mohd. Hanif Qureshi* (*supra* n. 20) at 647 (on the 'Hindu' pandit submissions), 650–1 (on the absence of material on Muslim practice).

[24] *Saifuddin Sahab v State of Bombay* (1962) Supp 1 SCR 496; and note the comments of J.D.M. Derrett, (1960) 12 ICLQ 693.

[25] On Justice P.B. Gajendragadkar's distinctive approach to these questions see P.K. Tripathi: 'Mr Justice Gajendragadkar and Constitutional Interpretation 1966, 8 *Journal of the Indian Law Institute (JILI)*, 479. Justice Gajendragadkar is also known for his strong view that law should be used as an instrument of social change (see P.B. Gajendragadkar, *Law, Liberty and Justice*, Asia Publishing House, Bombay, 1965, and especially his *Secularism and the Constitution of India*, N.M. Tripathi, Bombay, 1972).

[26] *Durgah Committee Ajmer v Syed Hussain* (1962) 1 SCR 383.

[27] *Tilkayat Sri Govindlalji Maharaj v State of Rajasthan* (1964) 1 SCR 561.

[28] *State of Rajasthan v Sujjanmal* (1974) 2 SCR 741.

[29] *E.R.J. Swami v State of Tamil Nadu* (1972) 3 SCR 815. The *adya sewaks* of Jaganatha Temple at Puri suffered an only slightly better fate when the Supreme Court (in *Bira Kishore* case, *infra* n. 35 at 43–5) permitted a withdrawal of their sole right of management of the religious endowment in Puri.

[30] *Sri Adi Visheswaran of Kashi Nath v State of UP* (1997) 4 SCC 606.

[31] *Supra* n. 20.

[32] *Jagdishwaranand v Police Commissioner, Calcutta* (1984) 1 SCR 447.

[33] *Commissioner v Jagdishwaranand* AIR 1991 Cal 263.

[34] Thus, the Gowda Saraswats (see *Venkataramana* case (*infra* n. 43)), the followers of Madhavacharya (see *Srirur Math* case, *supra* n. 16) or *Vallabha* (see *Tilkayat* case, *supra* n. 27) were treated as sects. Similar decisions were made for the Swetambar Jains and Parsis (see *Ratilal's* case, *supra* n. 16); Chistia Soofies (see *Durgah Committee* case, *supra* n. 26), and the *Dawoodi Bohras* (see *Saifuddin*, *supra* n. 24).

[35] The term 'religious denomination' seems to have an elastic meaning (see *Bira Kishore Deb v State of Orissa* (1964) 7 SCR 32 at 48 leaving the question of an all-encompassing Hinduism open (cf. *Ramachandra v State of Orissa* AIR 1959 Orissa 5). Over-assimilationist in their approach to Hinduism, the court has been unable to accept the more recent claims of the Swami Narayans not to be treated as Hindus (see *Yagnapurushdasji*, *infra* n. 37), or the followers of Aurobindo (see S.P. Mittal, *infra* n. 38), or Ramakrishna (see *Brahmchari* case, *infra* n. 36) to be treated as distinct Hindu sects. *Quaere:* who is the Supreme Court to tell new faiths that they do not constitute a religion when the sects genuinely feel that they do? It is this kind of approach that led the Pakistan courts to declare that Ahmadis are not Muslims.

[36] *Brahmchari Sidheshwar v State of West Bengal* (1995) 4 SCC 646.

[37] *Swami Yagnapurushdasji v Muldas* (1966) 3 SCR 242, and note the comments of M. Galanter, *Law and Society in Modern India*, Delhi, 1989, 237–58; J.D.M. Derrett, 'The Definition of a Hindu' (1996) 2 *SCJ Jnl* 67; J.D.M. Derret, 'The Definition of a Hindu' 70 (1968) *Zeitschrift Vergleischende Rechtswissenschaft*, 110.

[38] *S.P. Mittal v Union of India* (1983) 1 SCR 729.

[39] See *R.M. Singh v State* AIR 1976 Patna 198. Does it however follow that those who do not perform these 'rites' are not Hindus?

[40] *M. Ishmail Faruqui v Union of India* (1994) 6 SCC 360; see further R. Dhavan, 'The Ayodhya Judgment: Encoding Secularism in the Law' 29 *Economic and Political Weekly (EPW)* (1994) 3034–40.

[41] *Ghulam Abbas v State of UP* (1984) 1 *SCR* 64; *Abdul Jalil v State of UP* (1984) 2 SCC 138.

[42] See *Acharya Maharaj v State of Gujarat* (1975) 2 SCR 317 at pr. 327–8; *Khajamian Wakf Estates v State of Madras* (1971) 2 SCR 790 at 777; *Mahant Ram Kishan Das v State of Punjab* (1983) 1 SCC 377 at 378–9; *M. Ishmail Faruqui v Union of India supra* n. 40 at 416 that properties can only not be acquired if they do not *'destroy or completely negative* its right ... [or threaten] the survival of a religious institution ...' (emphasis added).

[43] *Sri Venkataramma v State of Mysore* (1958) SCR 895. There is a conflict between the freedom of religious practice and belief clauses of the Constitution which implicitly allows only some persons or castes to perform ceremonies (see also *Seshammal v State of Tamil Nadu* (1972) 2 SCC 11 at 12) and its 'opening of temples to untouchables' clauses which permit untouchables to pray in a temple but not perform sacral ceremonies! Outsiders are allowed inside, but remain outsiders.

[44] Note the interesting decision of the Allahabad High Court in *Sarwar Hussain v Additional Line Judge* AIR 1983 All 252.

[45] *Bijoe Emmanuel v State of Kerala, supra* n. 19.

[46] See M.N. Srinivas' essay 'A note on Sanskritization and Westernisation' in his *Caste in Modern India*, Asia Publishing House, Bombay, 1962, 42–62.

[47] There is room for the alternative view put forward by F.S. Nariman (*supra* n. 6 at 31) that 'ambiguity' and 'vacillation' are also a part of the judicial process. The term 'principled decision making' is taken from H. Wechsler, 'Towards Neutral Principles of Constitutional Law, (1959) 73 *Harvard LR* 1.

[48] See *Ramjilal Modi v State of UP* (1957) SCR 860 on the reinforcement of the 'law and order' framework in the context of religious strife; and, more generally, R. Dhavan, *Only the Good News: On the Law of the Press in India*, Manohar, Delhi, 1987, 274–339.

[49] *Stanislaus v State of Madhya Pradesh* (1977) 2 SCR 611.

[50] *S.R. Bommai v Union of India* (1994) 3 SCC 1 (7:2).

[51] See R. Dhavan, *supra* n. 17.

[52] See *Bhumi Nath v State of J&K* (1977) 2 SCC 745.

[53] See *Sri Adi Visheshwaran ..., supra* n. 30; *Sri Sri Lakshmana v State of AP* (1996) 2 SCC 498; *A.S. Narayana v State of AP* (1996) 9 SCC 548 (1997), and also (1997) 5 SCC 383 and (1997) 5 SCC 376; *Pannalal v State of AP* (1996) 2 SCC 498; *Shri Jaganath Puri Management Committee v Chaintamani Khuntia* (1997) 8 SCC 422. Once state control is established, religious functionaries can even be suspended (see *Digyadarsan v State of AP* (1970) 1 SCR 703; cf. *Rati Lal supra* n. 16 at 1063–4). The rationale for the takeover of religious endowments and temples is that mismanagement must yield to state control (*Mahant Moti Das v S.P. Sahi* (1959) Supp 2 SCR 563) which in its prac-

tical working gives no greater protection to a religious endowment than that given to a trade or business.

[54] Bose J in *Ram Singh v State of Delhi* (1951) SCR 451.

[55] The privileged and middle classes have benefited greatly from the quality education provided by English medium schools available exclusively for those who can afford it.

[56] *Unnikrishnan v State of AP* 1993 virtually nationalized admissions to tertiary professional colleges and left behind a debris of problems which the Supreme Court is yet to resolve six years later.

[57] *Constitution of India*, Articles 29–30. For the discussion on these articles in the Constituent Assembly, see B. Shiva Rao, *supra* n. 9, pp. 272–81.

[58] Constitution of India, Article 28(1) read with 29(2).

[59] *State of Bombay v Bombay Educational Society* (1955) 1 SCR 568.

[60] *In Re Kerala Educational Bill* (1959) SCR 995.

[61] *Gujarat University v Sri Krishna* (1963) Supp 1 SCR 112.

[62] *Sidhajbhai v State of Bombay* (1963) 3 SCR 837.

[63] Ibid. at 857.

[64] E.g. *D.A.V. College, Jullundur, infra* n. 90, on the non-applicability of provisions of the Guru Nanak University Act 1969 and the statutory of the University; see also *State of Kerala v Mother Provincial, infra* n. 67.

[65] *D.A.V. College v State of Punjab, infra* n. 90.

[66] *Azeez Basha v Union of India* (1968) 1 SCR 833. For the historical background on the Muslim antecedents of Aligarh Muslim University, see G. Minault and D. Lelyveld, 'The Campaign for a Muslim University', 1974, 8, *Modern Asian Studies*, 145 and D. Lelyveld, *Aligarh, The First Generation: Muslim Solidarity in British India*, Princeton: Princeton University Press NJ, 1978. A.G. Noorani in his *President Zakir Hussain: A Quest for Excellence* (Bombay: Popular Prakashan 1967), quotes a statement of September 1923 made by Mohamed Ali of the Pakistan movement on the importance of Aligarh University to the Muslims which he hoped 'some day we will conquer'.

[67] *State of Kerala v Mother Provincial* (1970) 2 SCC 417.

[68] *St Xaviers College v State of Gujarat* (1975) 1 SCR 173.

[69] *Gandhi Faiz-e-Azam College v Shah Jahanpur* (1975) 1 SCC 283.

[70] *Lily Kurian v Sister Lewina and Others* (1979) 2 SCC 124.

[71] *All Saints High School v State of Andhra Pradesh* (1980) 2 SCC 478.

[72] *Milli Talimi Mission School v State of Bihar* (1984) 4 SCC 500.

[73] *Frank Anthony Public School Employees Association v Union of India* (1986) 4 SCC 707.

[74] Note, *Y. Theclamma v Union of India* (1987) 2 SCC 516 coming to the somewhat astounding conclusion that the decision in this case was not in conflict with *Lily Kurian's* case, *supra* n. 70. The distinction between approvals for 'suspension' as opposed to the 'dismissal' of employees in this case is thin when considering constitutional rights of the magnitude contained in minority education cases.

[75] *Christian Medical College Hospital Employees Union v CMC Vellore Association* (1987) 4 SCC 691; *Frank Anthony's* case, *supra* n. 73; *All Bihar Christian Schools Association v State of Bihar* (1998) 1 SCC 206; Note the earlier case of *DAV College v State of Punjab, infra* n. 90, on qualifications of teachers for various subjects.

[76] E.g. *Manohar Harries Walters v Basel Mission Higher Education Centre* 1992 Supp 2 SCC 301; *Frank Anthony's* case, *supra* n. 73, also permits appeals from decisions by the management of schools to a judicial tribunal but not to one constituted by an executive authority.

[77] All this is predicated on the broad argument in *St Johns Teachers Training Institute for Women v State of Tamil Nadu* (1993) 3 SCC 595 that even unaided institutions are not immune from the law of the land. Indeed, the purpose of the Constitution's solicitude for the protection of the minorities was to make their institutions immune to constitutionally intrusive provisions of the general law as any other. The generality of the law cannot defeat the specific constitutional protection.

[78] For this view that takeover of management is possible where there is a maladministration of the institution see *The Bihar Madrasa* case, *infra* n. 82.

[79] Note, however *Education Board of Secondary and Teacher Training v Director of Public Instructors Sagar* (1998) 8 SCC 555; *N. Ammad v Enjoy High School* (1998) 6 SCC 674 safeguarding the ultimate selection made by the school or college management; see also *Shaminda Hasan v State of UP* (1990) 3 SCC 48.

[80] Although arising in markedly different circumstances, the Supreme Court's approach has varied from case to case. Contrast the *Bombay Educational Society* (*supra* n. 59) and the *Gujarat University* (*supra* n. 61) cases with the *Kannada* (see *English Medium* (*infra* n. 81) and *Punjabi* (see *DAV College Bhatinda v State of Punjab* (1971) 2 SCC 261, *infra* n. 90) cases. Thus, now promotion of Punjabi or Kannada is not per se bad though it may not be imposed as a medium of instruction at higher levels of education. Appeals to preserve a 'language' is not a 'politicization' impermissible to electoral politics (see *Jagdev Singh v Pratap Singh* (1964) 6 SCR 750 at 769–70) and consistent with the broad protection to linguistic minorities. However, the imposition of a language as a medium of instruction on linguistic minority institutions is inherently problematic—an issue not properly explored by the courts.

[81] See *English Medium Students Association v State of Karnataka* (1994) 1 SCC 550; note the wide comments on syllabi and such matters in *Virindra Nath Gupta v Delhi Administration* (1990) 2 SCC 307 at 312 (even though the right to specially recruit a person who knew the Malayalam language was recognized; see also *The Bihar State Madrassa* case, *infra* n. 82.

[82] No doubt the Supreme Court has repeatedly said that constitutional rights cannot be surrendered as a condition for obtaining recognition or affiliation (see the *Frank Anthony* case, *supra* n. 73) but it is the constitutional rights that have been whittled down in recent years. Equally, the right to 'recognition' and 'affiliation' was implicitly agreed in the *Kerala Education Bill* case (*supra* n. 60) in the light of the fact that V. Ayyar J specifically dissented on this aspect in this case. After the *St Xaviers* case (*supra* n. 68), however, this issue does not appear to have been finally decided (see *Bihar State Madrasa Education Board v Madrasa Hanifia Arabic College* (1990) 1 SCC 428 or 433; *State of Tamil Nadu v St Joseph Teachers Training Institute* (1991) 3 SCC 87).

[83] *St Stephens College v University of Delhi* (1992) 1 SCC 558.

[84] *AP Christian Medical Educational Society v Government of AP* (1986) 2 SCC 667.

[85] *Supra* n. 62.

[86] *Supra* n. 66.

[87] *S.K. Patro v State of Bihar* (1970) 1 SCR 172.

[88] *W. Proost v State of Bihar* (1969) 2 SCR 73.

[89] *St Stephens* case, *supra* n. 83.

[90] *DAV College, Jullundur v State of Punjab* (1971) 2 SCC 269.

[91] The *Kerala Education Bill* case, *supra* n. 60, at 1050 left this issue open. That minorities can be computed in the context of a state was conceded in the *DAV College* case, *supra* n. 90 at 275.

[92] *Supra* n. 11–12. For the view that little has been done for women, see R. Kapur and B. Cossman, *Subversive Sites: Feminist Engagement with Law in India*, Delhi: Sage, 1996.

[93] *Supra* n. 10.

[94] Constitution of India, Article 44. The best review of the UCC controversy is Archana Parashar, *Women and Family Law Reform in India*, Delhi, 1992.

[95] *Infra* n. 132.

[96] All these laws, especially those related to gender justice, have an unfinished air about them (see Ratna Kapur and B. Cossman, *supra* n. 92).

[97] The criteria to define OBCs can be as elastic as any government wants them to be (see M. Galanter, 'Who are the Backward Classes: An Introduction to a Constitutional Puzzle' (1978) 13 *EPW*, 1812–28). The (Kalelkar) Report of the Backward Classes Commission (Delhi, 1955) identified almost a third of India's population to be backward. The Mandal Report (*infra* n. 104) estimated 52 per cent of the population to be OBCs. The 50 per cent rule to which reservations are constitutionally permissible was enunciated in the *Balaji* case (*infra* n. 99) and affirmed in the *Indra Sawhney* case (*infra* n. 108). However, Tamil Nadu wants a 69 per cent reservation for BCs and OBCs, a matter pending in the Supreme Court.

[98] This was the basis on which the petitioners argued the *Indra Sawhney* case, *infra* n. 108. For the view that the Supreme Court has 'problem-solved' most of the 'reservation' cases rather than evolved a clear 'principled decision', see R. Dhavan, 'The Supreme Court as Problem Solver: The Mandal Controversy', in V.A. Pai Panandikar (ed.), *infra* n. 108, 262–332.

[99] *M.R. Balaji v State of Mysore* (1963) Supp 1 SCR 439 at 455.

[100] Contrast the eclectic criterion in *Balaji* (*supra* n. 94) with the plea in *Chitralekha v State of Mysore* (1964) 6 SCR 368 at 386–9 that the term 'class' cannot be equated with 'caste' which is not the compelling criterion (see generally M. Galanter, *Competing Equalities: Law and the Backward Classes*, Delhi: Oxford University Press, 1984, 188–204, 290–305. After *Indra Sawhney* (*infra* n. 108), caste can be an identifying factor in an overall inquiry into social and economic backwardness. This does not wholly clarify the issue, leaving too much to the exigencies of government patronage.

[101] See *Chitra Ghosh v Union of India* (1970) 1 SCR 413; *Vasundra v State of Mysore* (1971) Supp SCR 381; *D.N. Chanchala v State of Mysore* (1971) Supp SCR 608; cf. *Deepak Sibal v Punjab University* (1989) 2 SCC 145. Some appeals to the doctrine of source that a classification can be made on the basis of 'administrative' units (*A. Periakaruppan v State of Tamil Nadu* (1971) 2 SCR 430), or districts (*Rajindram v State of Madras*) (1968) 2 SCR 786), or constituent colleges (*Jagdish v Union of India* (1980) 2 SCC 768) have been rejected. However, justification for particular sources on the basis of the doctrine of equality was *ad hoc* rather than systematic. In *Nidamarati v State of Maharashtra* (1986) 2 SCC 534 at pr. 4, pp. 539–40, the Court indicated that two considerations were important to assess a departure from merit: 'One is what may be called the State interest and the other is what may be claimed as a region's backwardness'. Both tests are far too broad.

[102] *Nishi Maghu v State of JK* (1980) 3 SCR 1253; *Arti Sapru v State of JK* (1981) 3 SCR 34.

[103] Note the decision of the Bombay High Court in *Prasanna v Director-in-charge, LIT Nagpur* AIR 1982 Bom 176. However, provision for children of defence personnel or political sufferers (*Chanchala, supra* n. 101) or government employees (*Chitra Ghosh, supra* n. 101) are valid.

[104] *State of UP v Pradip Tandon* (1975) 2 SCR 761 at 766; cf. *Janki Prasad v State of JK* (1973) 3 SCR 236 not extending benefits to 'artificial' groups such as 'small cultivators' or 'low paid pensioners'.

[105] See *State of MP v Nivedita Jain* (1982) 1 SCR 759; *Indra Sawhney (infra* n. 108) at pr. 837, pp. 751–2.

[106] *State of Kerala v N.M. Thomas* (1976) 1 SCR 906 at 998 (per Krishna Iyer J).

[107] *ABSK Sangh v Union of India* (1981) 2 SCR 185 at 203 (per Krishna Iyer J).

[108] *Indra Sawhney v Union of India* (1992) Supp 3 SCC 217; see generally the (Mandal) *Report of the Backward Classes Commission,* Delhi, 1980. On the general controversy over the Mandal Commission's recommendations, see generally V.A. Pai Panandikar: *The Politics of Backwardness,* Konark Publications, Delhi, 1997.

[109] The concept of a 'creamy layer' took root on a suggestion in *K.C. Vasanth Kumar v State of Karnataka* 1985 Supp SCC 714, which was approved in *Indra Sawhney, infra* n. 108, at para 521–2, p. 554; para 629 p. 626; para 792–3, pp. 744–5) and applied in *Ashok Kumar v State of Bihar* (1995) 5 SCC 403. The Supreme Court has given specific directions to states to formulate 'creamy layer' criterion in *Indra Sawhney* 1996 6 SCC 506.

[110] *R.K. Sabharwal v State of Punjab* (1995) 2 SCC 745.

[111] *Ajit Singh v State of Punjab* (1996) 2 SCC 715; *Union of India v Virpal Singh Chauhan* (1996) 6 SCC 684; owing to comments in *Jagdish v State of Haryana* (1997) 6 SCC 538; *Sube Singh v State of Haryana* (1997) 10 SCC 765; and *Chander Pal v State of Haryana* (1997) 10 SCC 474. The issue is now resolved by a constitution bench in *Ajit Singh v State of Punjab* (1999) 7 SCC 209 and *Sube Singh v State of Haryana* (1999) 8 SCC 213.

[112] See *Dr Sadhana Devi v State of UP* (1997) 3 SCC 90. Now see *Preeti Srivastava v State of MP* (1999) 7 SCC 120.

[113] Constitution of India, Article 293 D (panchayats), 243 T (municipalities). The full impact of this reservation of electoral seats for OBCs and women awaits assessment.

[114] Thus, in various cases *Maharishi Awadesh v Union of India* 1994 Supp 1 SCC 713 at 714; *Reynolds Rajamani v Union of India* (1982) 2 SCC 474 at 478–9; *Pannalal v State of AP* (1996) 2 SCC 498; *Madhu Kishwar v State of Bihar* (1996) 5 SCC 125, *Ahmedabad Women's Action Group* 1997, *infra* n. 118) at 575–801 the Court was reluctant to pronounce on these matters which were declared to be within the exclusive domain of the legislature (cf. *Sarla Mudgal v Union of India* (1995) 3 SCC 635 at 649–50 in which a plea was made for a Uniform Civil Code by Kuldip Singh J which was publicly accepted as an injunction to the government to change the law). In this vein, also see *Mathew v Union of India* (1999) 1 *Kerala Law Journal,* 824). Note the books of Justice A.M. Bhattacharjee, *Hindu Law and the Constitution,* Eastern Law House, Calcutta, 1994 edn, and *Muslim Law and the Constitution,* Eastern Law House, Calcutta, 1994 edn, criticizing the approach of the high courts and the Supreme Court.

[115] Article 13 of the Constitution includes 'custom' in the catalogue of 'Laws' which are subject to fundamental rights (see *Sant Ram v Labh Singh* (1964) 7 SCR 756; *Bhau Ram v B. Baijnath* (1962) Supp 3 SCR 724.

[116] *State of Bombay v Narasu Appa Mali* AIR 1952 Bom 84; *Srinivasa Aiyar v Saraswathi Ammal* AIR 1952 Mad 193.

[117] *Krishna Singh v Mathura Ahir* (1981) 3 SCC 689 (cf. *In Re Amina* AIR 1992 Bom 214).

[118] *Ahmedabad Women's Action Group v Union of India* (1997) 3 SCC 573.

[119] A. Parashar, *supra* n. 90, 201–63.

[120] See generally, A. Parashar, 1990, *supra* n. 94, 77–143. In 1999, the Law Commission has started an inquiry into gender biases in the uncodified law relating to the Hindu joint family.

[121] See section 125, Criminal Procedure Code, 1973 which replaced section 488 of the Criminal Procedure Code 1989.

[122] K. Iyer J in *Fuzlumbi* (*infra* this note) at 1131 *Shah Bano*'s case *(infra)* was preceded by judgements in *Bai Tahira v Ali Hussain* (1979) 2 SCR 75; and *Fazlumbi v K. Khader* (1990) 3 SCR 1127 and merely affirmed them.

[123] *Mohd. Ahmed Khan v Shah Bano* (1985) 3 SCR 844.

[124] The Muslim Women (Protection of Rights on Divorce) Act 1986.

[125] For an interesting analysis of the debates in Parliament on this Act, see N.G. Jayal, 'Secularism, Identities and Representative Democracy', in Mushirul Hasan (ed.), *Islam: Communities and the Nation: Muslim Identities in South and Beyond*, Manohar, Delhi, 1998, 159–78; see also Peter J. Awn, 'Indian Islam: The Shah Bano Affair' in J.S. Hawley (ed.), *Fundamentalism and Gender*, Oxford University Press, New York, 1994, 63–78 and more generally in Zoya Hasan, *Forging Identities: Gender Communities and the State in India*, Delhi, 1994.

[126] E.g. *Vishaka v State of Rajasthan* (1997) 6 SCC 241 (on sexual harassment and the importance of international human rights conventions); *Githa Hariharan v Reserve Bank of India* (1999) 2 SCC 228 (on Hindu woman's right to be a guardian).

[127] For an introductory analysis and critique of public interest law in India, see R. Dhavan, 'Law as Struggle: Public Interest Law Movement in India' (1991) 36 *Journal of the Indian Law Institute* 302–38.

[128] See F.S. Nariman (*supra* n. 6) and P.S. Atiyah, *Pragmatism and Theory in English Law*, Stevens, London, 1987.

[129] Krishna Iyer J in *Kunhu Mohammed v J.K. Ummayithi* (1969) KLR 629.

[130] *Bommai, supra* n. 50.

[131] For a misleading comparison, see V.P. Luthera, *The Concept of Secularism in India*, Oxford, 1964, and D.E. Smith, *India as a Secular State*, Princeton University Press, Princeton, 1963.

[132] See, especially, T.N. Madan, 'Secularism in its Place', (1987) 46 *Journal of Asian Studies*, 747–59; Ashis Nandy: 'The Politics of Secularism and the Recovery of Religious Tolerance', in Veena Das (ed.), *The Mirror of Violence*, Oxford University Press, Delhi, 1990, 69–93; see also M. Juergensmeyer, *New Cold War: Religious Nationalism Confronts the Secular State*, University of California Press, Berkeley, 1993; P. Van den Veer, *Religion and Nationalism: Hindus and Muslims in India*, Oxford University Press, Delhi, 1998.

[133] A. Vinayak, *Communalism Contested: Religion, Modernity and Secularism*, New Delhi, 1997.

[134] Flavia Agnes, *Law and Gender Inequality: The Politics of Rights in India*, Delhi: Oxford University Press, Delhi, 1999, and note the interesting views of Kumkum Sangari, 'Politics of Diversity: Religious Communities and Multiple Patriarchies', 1995, 30, *EPW*, 3287–310; 3381–9. Madhu Kishwar, *Religion at the Service of Nationalism*, Delhi, 1998, 225–47, combines a passion for social reform with a zest to preserve India's social diversity.

[135] On the complexity of Nehru's views on tradition, law, and social change, see R. Dhavan, 'Introduction', in R. Dhavan, *supra* n. 13.

[136] Taken from R. Dhavan, 'The Road to Xanadu: India's Quest for Secularism' in K.M. Pannikar (ed.), *The Concerned Indian's Guide to Communalism*, Viking, Delhi, 1999, 34–72.

[137] See *Suresh Chandra v Union of India* AIR 1975 Del 168.

[138] This flows from the constitutional text (see Article 27 and also 28). Thus, grants to renovate the water tank at Lord Jagannath's Temple (*Bira Kishore v State* AIR 1975 Orissa 8), restoring riot damage to religious buildings (*K. Raghunath v Kerala* AIR 1974 Ker 48), or celebrating Lord Mahavira's birthday (*supra* n. 137) are all valid and, presumably not inimical to Indian secularism. With respect, the Supreme Court overstated the 'secular' case in the *Srirur Math* case (*supra* n. 16) where, after acknowledging that the embargo in the Constitution was levying taxes specifically earmarked for a religion, the Court went on to observe (at p. 145): 'Ours being a secular State ... it is against the policy of the Constitution *to pay out* of public *funds, any money* for the *renovation and maintenance* of any particular religion or denomination' (at p. 1045, emphasis added). This is contrary to the constitutional text, the practice of the Indian state, and the principle of celebratory neutrality enunciated in this essay.

[139] *Supra* n. 123, 124.

[140] See Representation of Peoples Act, 1951 injuncting appeals section 123 (3) *inter alia* on grounds of religion, race, community, or language (section 123 (3)), provoking enmity, on similar grounds (Article 123 (3A), or propagating or glorifying sati (section 123 (3B)).

[141] *Kanti Prasad v Purshottamdas* (1969) 1 SCC 455. Note Hegde J's dissent (at 463, 466).

[142] *Ambica Saran Singh v Hemant Mahadeva* (1969) 3 SCC 492.

[143] *Ziauddin v Brij Mohan* (1976) 2 SCC 17 at 28–30 on a dilutionary emphasis on time, place and context in cases concerning appeals to Islam; see also *Abdul Hussain v Shamsul Huda* (1975) 4 SCC 533; and *Rahim Khan v Khurshid Ahmad* (1974) 2 SCC 660 at 674–6.

[144] *Komireddy Ramuloo v Chennemaneni* (1990) 3 SCC 612; *Mullapudi Venkata Krishna Rao v Vedula Suryanarayan* 1983 Supp 3 SCC 504; *S. Harcharan Singh v S. Sujjan Singh* (1985) 1 SCC 370.

[145] *Das Rao Deshmukh v Kamal Kishore* (1995) 5 SCC 123.

[146] *Kultar Singh v Mukhtiar Singh* (1964) 7 SCR 790 at 795–8.

[147] *Jagdev Singh v Pratap Singh* (1964) 6 SCR 650.

[148] *Ramanbhai v Dabhi* (1965) 1 SCR 712.

[149] *Manohar Joshi v Nitin Bhaurao* (1996) 1 SCC 169; *Dr Ramesh Yeshward Prabhu v Prabhakar* (1996) 1 SCC 130; *Ramakant Mayekar v Celine D'Silva* (1996) 1 SCC 399. The Court has also taken the view that, depending on certain circumstances, an appeal to 'Hindutva' could be an appeal to religion (see *Suryakant Venkatarao v Suraj* (1996) 1 SCC 384.

[150] *Supra* n. 149.

[151] See Ratna Kapur and B. Cossman, 'Secularism Benchmarked by Hindu Right', 31, no. 38, *EPW*, 26 September 1996, 2613–28.

[152] *Supra* n. 37.

[153] The Supreme Court failed to avail of an opportunity to clarify its stance in *Mohd. Aslam v Union of India* (1996) 2 SCC 749.

[154] See *Hindustan Times*, 7 August 1926.

[155] R. Dhavan, *supra* n. 14, 461.

[156] Taken from Walt Whitman's *Leaves of Grass*.

Fifteen

Gender Justice and the Supreme Court

Indira Jaising

Introduction

Our Supreme Court was an institution created by the Constitution; yet, it was heir to the Federal Court set up under colonial rule. Neither the Constitution itself nor the decisions of the Court can be understood without understanding the history of colonial rule and imperialism the world over. Colonial systems of governance were not based on democratic norms and the relationship between the rulers and the ruled was that between the monarch and subject. These were 'law and order' regimes; a framework within which 'rights' could be very easily reduced to the liberties allowed by a policing power. For India particularly, this meant that its legal personnel were trained in the British mould, accustomed to functioning under an unwritten Constitution with no guarantees of fundamental rights. The achievement of equality, much less gender equality, was not one of the political objectives of colonial rule.

Trade and commerce were the driving forces of change, if any, during that period. The legal categories with which judges of independent India have worked have been no different from those they inherited from the British, and as we shall see, many a constitutional issue has been reduced to an issue of semantics. As Justice Krishna Iyer points out, Maxwell and the *Oxford English Dictionary* have been the Bibles of the Court, rather than Mahatma Gandhi.

Although it would seem that the Court at one level is unaware of its constituent power, this is strictly not true. When it came to defence of vested rights to property, the Court was willing to rewrite the Constitution and evolve the theory of unamendable 'basic features'. At the other end of the spectrum, there is not a single known case of the Supreme

Court using its constituent power to evolve any doctrine of gender justice or to strike down legislation palpably discriminatory against women.

No institution functions in an ideological and political vacuum. We shall therefore examine how almost every one of the major decisions of the Supreme Court has been deivered in a given political context. The Supreme Court is but one of the many players on the journey to gender justice. The context of the framing of the Constitution, the mechanics of our political society and the interplay between constitutional philosophy and practice also require careful scrutiny as they breathe life and meaning into the 'judgements' of our apex court.

The Backdrop

The demand for a self-made Constitution by the Indian people arose in the context of the conclusion of the Second World War. The horrors of the holocaust had just shaken the world conscience. In quick succession, sovereign states adopted the United Nations Charter,[1] and the Universal Declaration of Human Rights and Fundamental Freedoms (UDHR).[2] It is against this backdrop that the Constituent Assembly sat to its task.[3] Equality, which had until then been politically and legally unattainable under colonial rule, now became an important national goal.

It is said that Eire, the United States, and the United Kingdom formed our Holy Trinity of Influence. This Trinity was however far from perfect. The suffragettes had just succeeded in securing the right of women to vote in a society where till recently, women and property were not very different in the eyes of law.[4] Equality, albeit enshrined in the Bill of Rights, was yet to evolve as a fundamental norm. Eire too was grappling with equality, and how to contextualize 'equality' in its Catholic ethos.[5] While the Rau–Frankfurter discourse contributed greatly to the making of our Constitution, one cannot escape from the reality that even in the United States 'equality' under the Fourteenth Amendment ironically accommodated 'segregation'.[6]

Reverting to the post-war cry for rights, it is interesting that the atrocities of the Third Reich led nations to focus on rights of individuals and 'communities' against the 'State'. Further, the 'rights' recognized were politico–civil in nature.[7] The world became obsessed with human rights and the role of the State in protecting them.

Therefore, the 'State actor'-centric rights jurisprudence deeply influenced the new States of the twentieth century.

The Political Context

Independence and republicanism represented a total break in political terms from colonial rule and the end of imperialism. True to political theory, the Indian Constitution reflects this break in setting up a sovereign nation-state which is federal in character. It carried the birthmarks of an emerging post-Second World War Nation-State and was richly laced with post-war-rights. Citizenship was a necessary construct of this political regime and henceforth all law-making function became the sole prerogative of the State. Rights were conceived of as a limitation of the law-making function of the State. These rights were guaranteed as fundamental rights.[8] Certain problems such as *untouchability*[9] and *begar*,[10] unique to our society, were addressed in terms different from the private–public distinction of the then existing rights jurisprudence. Rights against caste discrimination and forced labour were now rights *in rem*. However, the right to equality was *qua* the State, and it would seem that the private realm was left unaddressed. Strictly speaking it would be incorrect to say that the private realm was left unaddressed, for as we have seen, by virtue of citizenship, the State had the power to bind by coercive laws the realm of the public and the private. While neither was out of bounds for legislative activity, such a law would have to stand the scrutiny of fundamental rights. Whether our lawmakers exercised such powers, and if not, why not, is not a matter within the purview of this paper. Suffice it to say that the failure of the State to enter the 'private domain' cannot be laid at the doors of the Supreme Court. The question that will still have to be examined is whether the Supreme Court did in fact recognize this break with political theory and practice, especially as it impacts women.

As the review of the Court's performance indicates, it had several opportunities to test laws from the colonial period, especially in the realm of personal laws, but it failed to strike them down giving meaning to 'equal protection of laws' in Article 14. Though perhaps motivated by the desire to maintain a hands-off approach, much as the British did, the Court's halting interventions led to more political discontent than it resolved. The Supreme Court has displayed a pattern of behaviour that appeared politically correct at a given point of time rather than constitutionally correct. Tracking the approach to women's issues over the past fifty years, one cannot help observing that answers to hard constitutional questions have either been avoided or subsumed in a larger politics of pragmatism. One will have to examine not only what the Court decided but also what it did not decide at given points of time in our political history. Brief though the period of fifty years may appear, they represent the years in which the people of this country played out their aspirations for freedom not only from their political masters, but also from economic want and social deprivation. The history of the Court will therefore have to be assessed with reference to certain political benchmarks that had a decisive impact on the people of the country.

The Judges

It is pointless to evaluate a court without mentioning the manner in which the institution itself is constituted. Judges of the Supreme Court are appointed by the President after consultation with such of the judges of the Supreme Court and the high courts as the President may deem proper.[11] Since the President acts on the advice of the Council of Ministers, for all practical purposes, this means that it is the executive that is to make the appointment in consultation with the judges of the Court. For the past several decades, the executive has been appointing judges of its own choice. In 1992, this situation was reversed, when in the *Supreme Court Advocates of Record Association Case*,[12] the Supreme Court held that the Court would have primacy in the matter of appointments. This would mean that the Court could appoint judges of its choice. Feminists have never chosen to question the non-egalitarian nature of this method, or to demand greater representation for women on the Bench. If equality is to mean anything at all, it must mean equal representation for women on the Bench. The key therefore to ensuring that women are represented on the Bench would be the criteria for selection. In an amazing decision, appearing to be on the face of it neutral, and so representative of its formal understanding of 'equality', the Supreme Court decided that '*inter se* seniority among judges in their High Courts and their combined seniority' should be given due weight.

This formula sounded the death knell of equitable appointment of women judges as it is well known that they are low in the seniority list and far fewer in number than men in the high courts. By this apparently egalitarian formula, women will have to wait for generations before they make it to the Supreme Court. Merit is ostensibly the criterion for appointment. Persons of 'outstanding merit' may supersede persons with merit. Among those with equal merit, a high court which is not represented on the Supreme Court may be preferred. There is no reference in this discourse to women and the need for the Supreme Court to reflect the diverse composition of the nation. Quite apart from the fact that no basis for the assessment of merit is spelt out, for women to be serious contenders, they must be of 'outstanding merit' to be equal to men. While 'regions' need to be represented, gender need not to be so represented? There is no reference to Article 15(3) in the judgement and that it could be a source of empowerment binding not only on the State but also on the Supreme Court of India. The first woman judge to the Supreme Court was appointed only four decades after the apex court had been in existence, and till today in a Court of twenty-six, there is only one woman judge (since retired). During the several decades that the Court was grappling with the concept of equality, in its initial years there was no woman judge on the Bench.

The Politics of the Equality Guarantee

The constitutional discourse in the Constituent Assembly betrays very little of the framers' concern for gender equality. Scarred by the traumatic events of the time, they seem to have expended most of their efforts at preserving the political union. Interestingly, the notion of fundamental rights, albeit individual and civil in nature, fitted in perfectly with the framers' scheme of protecting the 'political union'. After all, to preserve a diverse and extremely sensitive nation of peoples, it was vital to provide for individual guarantees, including the guarantee of equality, against the State. Yet another major concern of the Constitution-makers, was the need to ensure the rights of the minorities in the context of Partition, which took place principally along religious lines. The nation had just witnessed some of the bloodiest communal riots ever resulting in the loss of thousands of lives on both sides of the newly created border. The guarantee of freedom of religion must be viewed not just as a right to freedom of religious belief, but as an attempt to secure the rights of minorities to self-preservation. This factor was to have a very significant and devastating impact on women and the debates on the uniform civil code that took place during and immediately following the period of Partition. On this one issue of religious freedom, two of the women members of the Constituent Assembly, Rajkumari Amrit Kaur and Mrs Hansa Mehta, displayed incredible foresight almost forecasting the nature of the challenges that were to come in the post-Independence period. Referring to the formulation of draft Article 19, now Article 25 of the Constitution, they wanted the Article to be rephrased so as to avoid any possible challenge to law reform for women on the ground that it would be an interference with the freedom of religion. In a letter to B.N. Rau dated 31 March 1947, Rajkumari Amrit Kaur on her own behalf and of Hansa Mehta wrote:

We still feel considerable hesitation in accepting clause 16 as worded, even with Explanation II. As we are all aware there are several customs and practices in the name of religion, e.g. purdah, child marriage, polygamy, unequal laws of inheritance, prevention of inter-caste marrieages, dedication of girls to temples. We are naturally anxious that no clause in any fundamental rights shall make impossible future legislation for the purpose of wiping out these evils....

Indeed we have a further fear that validity of existing laws such as the Sharda Act and the Widow Remarriage Act may even be questioned.

In the light of the above objections we would like to amend the clause as follows:
Freedom of conscience, freedom of religious worship and the free profession of religion subject to 'public order, morality or health and to the other provisions of the chapter are guaranteed to every citizen'.

In other words, we would like 'freedom of religious worship' to replace 'free practice of religion'.

The potential mischief of Article 25, when it comes to women, will be tested in the challenge to the Sati Prevention Act, now pending in the Supreme Court, where temple trustees of the Jhunjunur temple have claimed that the provisions of the Act, which prohibit the 'glorification' of Sati are unconstitutional as violative of Article 25.

Doctrine of Equality

The equality doctrine in our Constitution and its evolution through judgements of the Supreme Court is integral to our 'gendered' appraisal of the apex court. It is therefore necessary to articulate the conceptual basis on which judgements of the Court will be evaluated. Given that the right to non-discrimination based on sex is not negotiable, at the very least, the Constitution and the Supreme Court are both expected to ensure formal equality between the sexes. Since discrimination is often invidious and linked to the social construct of gender, it is not enough to define equality in formal terms. It is still necessary to conceptualize equality in a manner that will result in the eradication of historical disadvantage. The formal equality model, in which the law relies on sameness or similarity as an aid for classification, mandates equality for equals; dissimilar classes need not be similarly treated. Then there is the substantive equality model. In this paradigm, it is not the form but the substance or the effect which serves as an aid for classification. If equal treatment of subjects, classified and treated as similar on the basis of sameness, results in divergent impacts, the substantive equality model rings the alarm.[13]

The principal equality clause of our Constitution is a replication of the American guarantee.[14] The guarantee is against the State and it is in the negative, i.e. 'the State shall not deny'. It relates to *equality before the law* and *equal protection of the laws*. Its brevity enhances its omnipotence, enabling creative judges to read within it equality of results.

It needs once again to be emphasized that the Constitution left it to the courts to give life to the equality code. It did not elaborate on how, in a given situation, the equality code was to be applied. While the equality clause protects all persons, citizens are specifically protected by a supplementary provision (henceforth 'supplementary provision').[15] Again couched in the negative, the supplementary provision injuncts the State from discriminating against any citizen on grounds *only* of religion, race, caste, sex, place of birth or any of them. There cannot be a greater negation of the prohibition on sexual discrimination, than to restrict it only to biological discrimination. Discrimination is always on the basis of sex in its gendered state. The use of the word 'only' in this Article has enabled courts to segregate sex from gender and uphold blatantly discriminatory legislation. A classical example is a case decided in 1981[16] where airhostesses (AH) were seeking parity with male Assistant Flight Purses (AFP). While the Court held the rule terminating employment of the AH on first pregnancy as patently unconstitutional, it had no hesitation in validating discrimination between the AH and AFP on the basis of methods of recruitment, falling back on the logic that the discrimination was on the basis of recruitment and sex (females were not eligible for recruitment as AFP) and not sex alone.

In yet another departure from the then prevailing human rights norm, the second clause of the supplementary provision proceeds to confer rights *in rem* against any disability from accessing public places, wells, restaurants, etc.,[17] another example of our framers' keen desire to eliminate existing caste practices. It is arguable that neither during the framing of the Constitution, nor during the fifty years that have followed, or indeed even in the jurisprudence of the Supreme Court, have women enjoyed the preferential treatment that caste has at the hands of lawmakers. The reason for this, perhaps, is that there has been no clear political articulation of their interests. It is only in the post-Beijing period that we begin to see the Supreme Court view discrimination against women as an issue of the power relationship that sustains a system requiring legal redress.[18]

The third clause to the supplementary provision states: 'Nothing in this article shall prevent the State from making any special provision for women and children' (henceforth special provisions clause).[19] It is an altogether different matter that not many post-Independence laws or judicial decisions can trace their origins to this special provision. The seventy-third and seventy-fourth constitutional amendments making reservations for women in panchayats and municipalities form part of the Constitution itself and cannot be attributed to the special provisions clause. A challenge to the two amendments is pending in the Supreme Court on the ground of denial of equality, which is said to be a basic feature of the Constitution. The Supreme Court will no doubt be called upon to articulate its concept of equality and spell out more clearly the interrelation between the equality clause, the supplementary provision, and the special provisions clause. Case law indicates that the special provisions clause has been used to justify the regulation of female sexuality based on the *weaker sex* approach to gender issues. An example of this approach may be seen in the cases where the provisions dealing with adultery have been challenged in the Supreme Court.[20]

Clearly negating the ideology of spoils, the Constitution proceeds to guarantee equality in matters of public employment to all citizens (henceforth 'employment provision').[21] Sex is a prohibited marker for ineligibility for employment and pubilc office. The employment provision includes a clause (henceforth 'reservations clause') which reserves for the State, power to 'make provision for the reservation in matters of employment' for certain backward classes.[22]

Against this background, let us evaluate the decisions of our apex court, which have breathed life into the sanitary provisions of the Constitution in the crucible of contentions and real life disputes.

The Early Years

Land reforms were conceived of as one of the primary vehicles through which the social revolution would take place in a predominantly agrarian society. The early years of the Supreme Court witnessed battles over land reforms. The Court was unable to rid itself of the conservative Anglo-Saxon colonial jurisprudence in which most of the judges were trained. *Champakam Dorairajan*[23] questioned a government order which disqualified her in preference to a low caste candidate. The apex court struck down the order on the doctrine of formal 'equality'. Parliament stung back with the First Amendment to the Constitution reaffirming its understanding of equality.

The land reforms were integral to the Nehruvian understanding of empowerment and equality. The apex court clearly had quite a different perception of equality and ways of arriving at it. While most states had passed land reform Acts, almost all excluded the married daughter from the definition of 'family' unit, and much of this litigation was therefore of no relevance to women. While *Champakam* and *Bela Bannerjee*[24] were both women, and while they both obtained justice from the Supreme Court and on both occasions the Court had occasion to consider the empowerment model of equality, in none was gender justice the issue. It was a telling comment on the times. Yet, gender, the silent half of the population would be very greatly affected by the model of equality being adopted by the courts. The question was to remain unresolved for many years into the future.

The Evolution of Equality Jurisprudence

The Court tended to prefer a classificatory approach to equality as more and more challenges to state action were brought under the equality clause. This premium on classification was frowned upon by some judges. In *A.S. Iyer v Balasubramanyam*[25] Justice Krishna Iyer quoted the observation in *Lachman Das v State of Punjab*[26] that:

the doctrine of classification is only a subsidiary rule evolved by courts to give a practical content to the said doctrine. Overemphasis on the doctrine of classification or an anxious and sustained attempt to discover some basis for classification may gradually and imperceptibly deprive the article of its glorious content. That process would inevitably end in substituting the doctrine of classification for the doctrine of equality; the fundamental right to equality before the law and the equal protection of the laws may be replaced by the doctrine of classification.

The Iyer Court was at pains to emphasize that 'judges may interpret, even make viable, but not whittle down or undo the essence of the Article'. However, while working out the 'equality code', the Court found itself entrapped in the discourse of 'reasonable classification'. If the classification was based on *intelligible differentia* and if it had a *rational nexus* with the object of the state action, the Court would negative any challenge founded on the equality clause.[27] In the late 1970s, the apex court gave a new look to this doctrine. Arbitrariness, the new doctrine propounded, offended equality. Anything that was arbitrary was antithetical to the constitutional guarantee of equality.[28]

Before an analysis of judicial decisions on women, it would be useful to look into the approach of the Court to the employment provision and the reservations clause. Was the reservations clause an exception or an integral facet of the equality rule in the employment provision? The apex court has affirmed in two key decisions (in 1976[29] and 1992[30]) that the reservations clause is not an exception to the employment provision but is a component of the dynamic equality embodied in it. It embodies protective equality and merely clarifies the substantive equality of the employment provision.

The jurisprudence that has evolved through decisional law views the equality code in the Constitution as embodied in the equality clause, the supplementary provision and the employment provision. The three must be harmoniously construed. The supplementary provision and the employment provision do not qualify or restrict the equality clause, but merely illuminate the equality code by listing the various facets of the proactive, corrective, and substantive equality we gave ourselves. The apex court has drawn from this integrationist model to sustain reservations for women made under the special provisions clause.[31] It must however be said that, by and large, in matters of employment courts have been vigilant in protecting women's right to equality, be it in terms of a restriction on the continued employment of married women[32] or refusal of promotion in the Indian Foreign Service on grounds of marriage,[33] the courts have zealously safeguarded equality rights whenever they related to the public domain.

The discourse on *on grounds of sex only* must be positioned between the formalistic and substantive model of equality. The supplementary provision and the employment provision prohibit discrimination *on grounds of sex only*. However, sex is intrinsically gendered and socially conditioned. For example, in 1977 a high court negatived a challenge to a land reforms legislation which excluded an adult daughter from the definition of family members who could claim separate land relying on her disability to be a coparcener (which itself was a custom founded on gender).[34] The discrimination was based on sex plus property (no note was made of the fact that property itself was related to sexual status, as inheritance laws favoured men).[35] Substantive equality takes cognizance of this reality and would strike at discrimination based on sex plus gendered dimensions of sex, though, strictly speaking, such discrimination is not on grounds of sex alone. Conversely, substantive equality would sustain discrimination based on the sex plus gendered aspect of sex if the object of such action is to minimize the sex inequality.

Special Provisions Clause

As stated, the apex court has interpreted the special provisions clause as a facet of our dynamic 'equality code'. The approach has ranged from protectionism to correctivism.[36] In a similar protectionist vein, the apex court has validated the criminal provision on adultery, which does not permit the wife to initiate a prosecution against the husband or against the 'adulteress'.[37] These decisions also gave a new form to the special provisions clause; one which not only empowered the State to take positive measures for the alleviation of women but also validated provisions discriminatory towards men.

The Supreme Court and Personal Laws

As women faced the greatest rights violation in the private sphere, and these were more socio-economic and familial than politco-civil, the most significant branch of law which begs scrutiny is the realm of personal laws.

In India each community was governed by its own customary law. With the advent of the British, the colonial state secularized laws (or rather, introduced uniform Anglo-centric regimes) in areas of direct economic-political concern such as commercial and contract law, the laws of evidence, and criminal law. Again, the private domain was spared, as it simply did not impede imperial objectives. Most of these familial laws were discriminatory towards women and reinforced the oppression of women within their family.[38]

By the time the provincial legislature came into being, the dominant community, i.e. Hindus, and the minority community, i.e. Muslims, were divided along communal lines and both put in place legislation that they perceived as being in the interest of their communities.[39] These were all stated to have been based on the religion and applied only to members of that religious community.

The Constitution included a provision to recognize pre-constitutional laws only if they conformed to the fundamental rights (henceforth 'recognition clause').[40] All such laws thereafter stood recognized and continued after the Constitution came into force. Did the recognition clause hit discriminatory personal laws? Was there a conflict between the right to equality and the right to religion? The Bombay High Court has held in the negative, and immunized personal laws from judicial scrutiny of whether they violated any fundamental rights. While the recognition clause, though inclusive, specifically addresses *customs or usage* having the force of law, the court has proceeded on semantic considerations such as the omission of the term 'personal laws' in the recognition clause in contrast to its specific citation in the schedule to the Constitution.[41] Further, reference was made to the salutary principle in the Constitution exhorting the State to strive for a uniform civil code to infer a tacit approval for the perpetuation of personal laws. Another patently unsound justification proffered, was that personal laws were based on scriptural texts and not customs and usage.[42]

While the decision of the high court was clothed in 'reason', the Supreme Court, when it had its opportunity to address the recognition clause, immunized personal laws without recording any reason at all.[43] Curiously, both courts were motivated by public concern. The high court in ensuring that a bigamist did not escape the net, and the apex court, in preventing usurpation of property by raising the defence of caste disability.

The apex court revisited the recognition clause in another case in 1996.[44] While the case could have been disposed of by an interpretation of a testament, the Court made forays into the dangerous territories of the recognition clause and observed:

The basic structure permeates equality of status and opportunity. The personal laws conferring inferior status on women are anathema to equality. Personal laws are derived not from the Constitution but from the religious scriptures. The laws thus derived must be consistent with the Constitution lest they become void [under the recognition clause] if they violate fundamental rights.

While noble motives inform such words, empowerment goals still remain as distant, as the observations are mere *obiter*. However, notwithstanding that in constitutional jurisprudence no law is derived from the Constitution, it is merely recognized or validated if the decision is interpreted as a definitive pronouncement that personal laws must bow down to the equality clause; then it is indeed a leap towards empowerment. The Supreme Court has not however spoken in one voice, and at almost the same time another bench of the Supreme Court has categorically stated that personal laws were beyond the reach of fundamental rights.[45]

The Supreme Court, in refusing to give full effect to the recognition clause, has not made a break with the political legacy of the past. It has continued to allow women to be governed by the law of religion without subjecting such laws to test in the crucible of constitutionality.

The Story of a Wife, a Daughter, and a Mother

The unresolved relationship between the right to equality and the right to freedom of religion surfaced dramatically in the *Shah Bano* case.[46] It comes as no surprise that the battle was fought over the terrain of the rights of women. What was at stake was the right of a divorced Muslim woman to claim maintenance from her former husband under section 125 of the Criminal Procedure Code (CrPC). In response to her claim, her husband squarely stated that to compel him to pay maintenance would be in conflict with his personal laws. The Supreme Court was presented with an opportunity to discuss the recognition clause and decide the issue as an equality issue. It failed to do so. Instead, it launched into a debate on the content of the Koran and was at pains to explain that the Code was not in conflict with the Koran. The Supreme Court went to great lengths to avoid the constitutional question, namely, would a personal law, which discriminated against women, be recognized after the Constitution had come into force? In the aftermath of the protest by the conservative sections of the community, Parliament enacted the Musim Women's (Protection of Rights on Divorce) Act, 1986, which basically disabled Muslim women from availing of the provisions of section 125 of the CrPC and effectively denied them maintenance after divorce. The protest over the *Shah Bano* case thus ended up being a protest over the authority of the Court to pronounce on the interpretation of the Koran, rather than a straightforward protest over the right of women to equality. The debate had overtones of those that had taken place in 1937 over the Muslim Personal Laws Application Act, 1937, passed at a time when the British, through the Regulation Acts, had accepted the fact that laws applied by virtue of religion and not citizenship or territoriality. If, on the other hand, the Court had decided the question of equality for women, the debate would have focused on the rights of women and the legislature would at least have had a constitutional prescription to go by. The Court's desire to reach a particular result in favour of Shah Bano proved counterproductive, as it was not founded on the constitutional philosophy of our times. This avoidance of the constitutional question has been evident not only in the realm of Muslim Personal Law, but also in the realm of Christian law and Hindu law.

In 1982 Mary Roy had challenged the Travancore Christian Succession Act (TCSA) on the ground that it put an upper limit of Rs 5000 for the inheritance of the daughter, leaving the entire estate to the son.[47] The Supreme Court held that with the coming into force of the Indian Succession Act, the TCSA stood repealed and hence it was not necessary to decide the issue. Since the Indian Succession Act gave equal inheritance rights to daughters, in effect women governed by the TCSA succeeded in getting equal rights. Yet the efforts made by the Christian community to set aside that judgement by introducing bills in the Assembly, only indicate that it might have been better for the Court to decide the core issue of equality as the legislature is bound by the limitation of fundamental rights.

In the case of *Madhu Kishwar v State of Bihar*[48] the constitutionality of certain provisions of the Chota Nagpur Tenancy Act, 1908, disentitling tribal women from inheritance rights fell for consideration. The Court, while upholding the discriminatory provisions, read down the impugned provisions to preserve their constitutionality. The Court ruled that destitute women *could* assert a right of occupation against the male inheritors. It was unwilling in this case to declare that the custom of inheritance which disinherited the daughter offends Articles 14, 15, and 21 on the basis that customs differ from tribe to tribe and region to region. It is noteworthy that by the time the case came up for decision in the Supreme Court, the tribal woman petitioner had died and even the minimal relief granted by the Court was incapable of enjoyment. While she was alive, she faced constant harassment from the community for having taken the matter to the Supreme Court. Madhu Kishwar, one of the petitioners who had gone to great lengths to support the tribal women affected, was disappointed with the process which resulted in great delay, defeating justice even before judgement could be pronounced. Justice K. Ramaswamy, in a dissenting judgement struck down the provision and the case will be remembered in future years more for the dissent it aroused rather than for what it decided. As the recent ruling in the *Geetha Hariharan* case[49] indicates, even today the Court has preferred to move around the constitutional question when addressing the issue of gender justice. Geetha Hariharan had challenged the Hindu Minority and Guradianship Act, 1955. The law was blatantly discriminatory, yet the Court chose to avoid giving a finding of unconstitutionality and instead, used the interpretative tool of 'reading down' the law to include the mother as also the 'natural' guardian of a child.[50]

These cases indicate that the reluctance of the Court is not confined to entering the realm of minority rights alone. It is therefore not possible to say that the Court avoids getting into the politics of the minority community alone. Rather, the Court has been reluctant to work out the interrelationship between Article 14 and Article 25 in a meaningful way, at least when it comes to women's issues. It also proves the point that the Court has steered clear of the recognition clause and avoided articulating a clear jurisprudential basis within which the demand for equality for women can be articulated. The result has been that although in the *Shah Bano* case the woman appeared to have won the battle for a pittance of maintenance, the larger war was lost. The opposition to the *Shah Bano* case must be seen less as a dispute over the substantive rights of women, than a battle over the question of who has the authority and jurisdiction to determine rights, Parliament, and the courts, or the religious heads of the community? The answer in a democratic polity should have been obvious. As stated earlier, the adoption of a secular-democratic Constitution should have resolved the question in favour of Parliament and the courts. In this case, the Supreme Court was not ready for the challenge and it continues to pay homage to religion in many different hidden ways, at least when it comes to women. The Muslim Women (Protection of Rights on Divorce) Act, 1986, passed as a measure of political expediency soon after the judgement has been challenged in the Supreme Court. The petitions however have been kept in cold storage over the years. It will no doubt raise issues of the recognition clause and the 'sex only' debate. Nor would it be entirely correct to say that the Court is generally reluctant to touch the question of religion or of religious minorities. Witness the hyper activity over the rights of minority educational institutions. The Christian community owns the large majority of these, and has been zealously able to safeguard its rights.[51] Women within the community however have not found the same sanctuary in the Supreme Court which continues to recognize discriminatory personal laws, leaving it to the legislature to make appropriate changes. Rather, Muslim, Christian, Hindu and tribal women have received a 'hands off' approach. The truth is that the history of law relating to women is also the history of property law and to disturb the status quo would be to seriously question the existing property ownership patterns in a society based on male lines.

The only case in which the Supreme Court tangentially dealt with the misuse of the continued existence of separate personal laws was *Sarla Mudgal v Union of India*.[52] The Court was faced with a situation in which a Hindu husband was prosecuted for bigamy for having married a second time after converting to Islam. The Court held that a Hindu marriage could only be dissolved according to the Hindu Marriages Act, 1955. The judgement is significant not only because it enabled a woman to prosecute a dishonest spouse for bigamy, but also because it held that the dispute would not be decided by Muslim Personal Law but that it had to be decided according to 'justice, equity and good conscience'. This was a heroic attempt by the Court to resolve issues of conflict of laws so that 'Hindu law on the one hand and Muslim law on the other hand could operate in their respective fields'. A review-petition has been filed and is still pending. The prosecution has been stayed.

Emergency Days—The Turning Point

While remaining largely absent from the consciousness of the Court in the early years, women were also absent from legal discourse. Women's issues were put on the national agenda in December 1974 with the submission of the report 'Towards Equality'.[53] The report has been a benchmark for the women's movement in the country and has become a part of the movement's engagement with the law. It was the first concrete step in post-independence India to state that equality for women was not negotiable and was indeed a constitutional promise awaiting fulfilment. If women were to participate in national development the promise of equality must be redeemed. These were times perilously close to the internal emergency that was declared in June 1975. The political situation in the country changed dramatically. The repression of civil liberties, and the suspension of the right to life under Article 21 affected all the institutions of society. The Supreme Court held that no writ of habeas corpus would lie during an emergency even if an order of detention was mala fide.[54] When the right to life itself was suspended, where was the question of rights of women being agitated? The protection of the courts having been exhausted, the scene of struggle shifted and the engagement of civil society was with politics. The primary concern of all movements, including the women's movement, was the restoration of civil liberties.

The struggle for restoration of civil liberties resulted in the defeat of Prime Minister Indira Gandhi and the Janata Party formed the government at the centre. The media concentrated on questions of denial of civil liberties such as conditions in jails (where many of the rulers spent months as jailed opposition leaders), police torture, undertrials, and atrocities such as the Bhagalpur blindings. A series of important cases that focused on the rights of individuals against the State arose from this phase. Much of the public interest litigation of this period was based on news reports of which the judges took judicial notice.[55] There was little or no litigation for and on behalf of women.

The post-emergency period saw the apex court battle to reclaim much of its lost legitimacy. It is no coincidence that this period was one of increased judicial activism, witnessing the most spectacular contribution of the Supreme Court to the jurisprudence of public interest litigation. Internationally, this was a period that saw the development of various second-generation rights such as economic and social rights, right to development, etc. reflecting to some extent the development of community rights. The question of women's rights, however, was still not in the forefront.

It was in the cradle of the civil liberties consciousness, that the Supreme Court's decision in *Mathura* case[56] ignited the first indigenous legal battle for gender justice. Mathura, a 16-year-old tribal girl was raped by two policemen within the premises of a police station. The sessions court acquitted the policemen on the ground that since Mathura had eloped with her boyfriend she was 'habituated to sexual intercourse' and hence she could not be raped. The court further held that Mathura was of 'loose morals' and that the sexual intercourse was with her consent. The high court convicted the policemen and held that mere passive or helpless surrender induced by threats or fear cannot be equated with desire or will and hence cannot be deemed as consent. The Supreme Court stepped in to set aside the conviction and exonerate the police stating that since Mathura had not raised any alarm and since there were no visible marks of injury on her body, allegations of rape were untrue. As such, the basis was that there was insufficient evidence that the prosecutrix resisted the sexual intercourse. Four law teachers, Lotika Sarkar, Upendra Baxi, Raghunath Kelkar, and Vasudha Dhagamvar wrote a letter to the Chief Justice of India protesting against the judgement. The review petition that was filed was dismissed and the judgement remains to this day as testimony to the insensitivity to the rights of women. In a period of heightened awareness of civil liberties, one would have expected the Court to correct the bias that was so obvious in the decision. In the years that followed, some women's groups had occasion to approach the Court demanding a proper investigation of what had by then come to be known as 'dowry deaths'.[57] Though the subjects to these cases were women, the issues they raised were of minimal 'due process'. These cannot, therefore, be said to reflect an emerging consciousness on women's rights in the courts.

The potential of the Court having been exhausted, the women's movement took to law reform. The campaign for changes in rape laws that followed the verdict led the women's movement to attempt to challenge the prevailing legal and social understanding of rape and 'consent'. It is no coincidence that the *Mathura* case became the symbol of protest of the women's movement over issues of violence. Mathura was raped in a police station by two policemen. Those were days in which police brutality was under judicial scrutiny in a variety of contexts. The case stands at the intersection of gender and the repressive power of the State. It was the combination of these two factors that had brought legal activism to the forefront. The Supreme Court would never be the same again and every one of its judgements on women's issues would come under increasing scrutiny by the women's movement.

The immediate outcome of the movement was the amendment of the laws in relation to rape. The context of the case overwhelmed all else. Although the movement demanded that the law be changed so as not to permit the character of the prosecutrix to be brought in evidence, sadly this was not to be. The amendment pertained mainly to rape by persons in fiduciary capacity or in custodial situations. The emphasis on the character of the rape victim was to continue in the years that followed. Perhaps the fact that the *Mathura* case arose in the context of police brutality led to the movement focusing its energy on criminal law rather than civil law reform.

Violence and Dignity

Violence Issues

The right to life includes the right to dignity. Through its five decades of existence, the Supreme Court has had occasion to address this important issue. We shall pause in our odyssey for a moment and take a quick look at how the apex court has dealt with violence and dignity issues affecting women.

Unfortunately the Court has on many occasions approached rape as man's uncontrollable lust rather than as an act of sexual violence against women. In one such case[58] the sentence for the rape of a young girl by her cousin was reduced on the basis that:

Youth overpowered by sex stress in excess. Hyper sexed Homo sapiens cannot be rehabilitated by humiliating or harsh treatment. As part of [the] curative course for the prisoner should be designed to rid his aphrodisiac overflow and restore him into safe citizenship. [The] accused is barely 22 years. He has a young wife and farm to look after. Given correctional course his erotic aberrations may wither away. Taking an overall view of the criminal and familial factors involved, the societal proneness to sex and people's abhorrence of released prisoners, sentence is reduced.

Similarly, in another case, the Supreme Court held with regard to uncorroborated evidence that it is essential to consider human psychology and behavioural probability when assessing the credibility of the victim's version.[59]

However, despite such obstacles, post-Mathura the Court has gradually begun to demonstrate remarkable sensitivity to issues of sexual violence against women. A case in point was *Bharwada Bhogibhai Hrijibhai v State of Gujarat*,[60] where the Court held that in the Indian context, refusal to act on the testimony of the victim of sexual assault in the absence of corroboration is 'adding insult to injury'. The Court went on to ask: 'Why should the evidence of the girls or a woman who complains of rape or sexual molestation be viewed with the aid of spectacles tinged with doubt or disbelief? To do so is to justify the charge of male chauvinism in a male dominated society.'

There have also been setbacks such as the controversial *Suman Rani Rape* case[61] where the Supreme Court reduced the mandatory minimum sentence of ten years imposed on two police officers found guilty of raping a young woman on the basis of the 'peculiar facts and circumstances of the case coupled with the conduct of the victim girl...'. These 'peculiar facts' referred to the argument of the accused that the victim was a woman of questionable character and easy virtue with lewd and lascivious behaviour.[62]

To the apex court's credit, the march of the law of rape in the past two decades has been spectacular. The Court has gradually come around to the view that corroboration of the evidence of the victim of rape was not essential[63] and a conviction could rest even on the sole testimony of the victim, if credible.[64] Delay in the registration of an FIR has also been addressed in several judgements and the Court has ruled that mere delay in lodging the FIR does not raise the inference that the complaint was false.

The Court has also come down heavily on judgements that have cast a stigma on the character of the victim.[65] It has ruled that the Court must use self-restraint in recording such finding, even if the girl is found to be habituated to sexual intercourse. Past promiscuous behaviour of the prosecutrix is no ground to condone rape. Minor contradictions or insignificant discrepancies in the statement of the prosecutrix should not be a ground for throwing out an otherwise good prosecution case. The occasional contradictory judgements of the Court can perhaps be explained by differences in approach and the world-views of individual judges. This is something that is built into the nature of judicial functioning and is unavoidable. One cannot, however, help getting the impression that different Benches of the Court talk in different voices over very crucial issues. As a result, vital issues of 'consent' and 'character' have been left to the individual conscience of judges rather than forming part of a well worked out policy of the Court. Similarly, no clear sentencing policy emerges in rape cases, making legislative reform difficult. Indeed, Home Minister L.K. Advani has seriously suggested mandatory death sentence for rape. This must be attributed in part to the inability of the courts to evolve a sentencing policy on such vital issues. Women's groups largely rejected the suggestion and pointed out that the major problem with the law was that it allowed evidence regarding the character of the prosecutrix to be brought into the trial.[66] The state of Maharashtra has taken a decision to delete this provision and has submitted a proposal regarding this to the President.

The Court has sometimes taken a practical and pragmatic view of the complex issues that arise in the context of rape, such as 'penetration'. In *Madan Gopal Kakad Naval Dubey & Another*[67] it held that even slightest penetration without rupturing the vagina would constitute rape. This judgement has gone a long way in convicting in cases of child rape. Prior to this judgement, all such cases were being dealt with as a relatively minor offence under section 354 of the Indian Penal Code.[68] Yet, in another case,[69] the Court showed extreme insensitivity in a case of child sexual abuse, quashing a prosecution by the State against the father on the mother's complaint that the father had sexually abused his daughter. The Supreme Court quashed the FIR and did not allow the prosecution to proceed, completely immunizing the father from judicial scrutiny. The allegations were described as 'eerie' and 'incredulous ex facie', the inference being that a father could never sexually abuse his own child. The Court displayed scant respect for social reality and even less for the mother and the child. The Court fell into the usual stereotyping of women who dare to bring a charge against their husbands by giving credence to the theory that she had made the charge to 'wreak vengeance' on her husband. The learned judges went to the extent of entertaining a suggestion by the father that the mother may have mutilated the child's genitals, presumably to extract money from the father. The case will act as a major deterrent to women bringing charges of child sexual abuse. One might almost argue that the Court let down the interest of the child and was blinded by a matrimonial dispute which had arisen in the first place over the child and her right to a safe home. Perhaps this time the Court did not want the entry of criminal law into the matrimonial home, because it would be like a 'bull in a China shop'.

In the case of *State of West Bengal v Orilal Jaiswal*[70] where a woman had allegedly committed suicide, the Court partly reversed the high court decision acquitting the accused husband and his mother of charges under sections 498A and 306 of the IPC. The Supreme Court convicted the accused under section 498A of the IPC. This case is an outstanding vindication of the law under section 498A for it states very clearly, that 'cruelty' can, not only be physical, but also, and principally mental. The Court held that repeatedly telling a woman that she was an *'alakshmi'* (woman of evil luck) at a time when she had lost a child was an act of mental cruelty. This is perhaps one of the few cases where the Court has emphasized not physical cruelty but the emotional aspects of ill-treatment.

There have been very few cases, whether in the sphere of criminal law or in that of civil law, that have dealt with the economic aspects of the breakdown of marriage and of violence. One of the path-breaking judgements in criminal law was *Pratibha Rani v Suraj Kumar*.[71] The Supreme Court made very creative use of sections 405 and 406 of the IPC and introduced the concept of criminal breach of trust into matrimonial law. The Court reiterated that *stridhan* is a woman's separate property and is held in trust for her by her husband or in-laws. It is repayable on demand and if the husband or the in-laws fail to return it they can be prosecuted for breach of trust. There was, however, a dissenting judgement in that case. When an occasion arose later, in the case of *Rashmi Kumar v Mahesh Kumar Bhadra*[72] a Bench of three judges of the Court confirmed the majority view of the *Pratibha Rani* Court. These two cases have established an expeditious remedy for many women who are thrown out of the matrimonial home without their *stridhan* and have made its recovery possible.

In *Kundula Bala Subrahmaniyam & Another v State of AP*[73] the apex court, addressing a dowry death case, stated that the role of courts assumes great importance and it is expected that they will deal with such cases more realistically and not allow the criminals to escape on account of procedural technicalities or insignificant lacunae in the evidence. In short, the courts are expected to be sensitive in cases involving crimes against women.

This 'sensitivity' approach is echoed in the decision of *Delhi Domestic Working Women's Forum v Union of India*[74] in which the Court laid down guidelines for assisting rape victims. The facts brought before the Court in this case related to the rape of six women by army *jawans* on a train. The Court suggested, broadly, legal assistance at the police station, information on the rights of representation available to the woman, preservation of the anonymity of the victim, keeping in the police station a list of advocates willing to act in these cases, authorizing the advocate to act within the police station with respect to questioning of the victims without delay, and the setting up of a Criminal Injuries Compensation Board which would provide for compensation to the victim, whether or not a conviction had taken place. The Court also ordered that the scheme for compensation and rehabilitation of the victims be focused on by the National Commission for Women and a time period of six months for the scheme was set.

The case of *Bodhisattva Gautam v Chakraborthy*[75] is one in which the Supreme Court yet again used provisions of criminal law to deal with a difficult situation. The appellant, a Bodhisattva Gautam (the irony of the name can hardly be missed), had persuaded a woman to have sexual intercourse with him on the promise of marriage. He then went through a fake form of marriage with her. She was twice pregnant and on each occasion he compelled her to undertake an abortion. He then abandoned her on the plea that he was never lawfully married to her. In these circumstances, she lodged a complaint against him under sections 312, 420, 493, 496 and 498A of the Indian Penal Code. He applied to the high court to quash the prosecution which it refused to do. The appeal to the Supreme Court resulted in a historic judgement where the Court took *suo motu* notice of the facts in the complaint, and issued a notice to him to show cause why he should not be compelled to pay maintenance to the woman he had cheated. The Court held that offences like rape were crimes against the person's most basic cherished human rights, namely the right to life. The Court held that under Article 32 it could take *suo motu* notice of the facts and directed the appellant to pay interim maintenance of Rs 1000 per month to the woman pending the prosecution.

One of the rare occasions in which the Court had to address economics of gender discrimination was in a case relating to maintenance.[76] Though the case relates to the rights of widows, it could be of assistance to wives as well. The Court held that the word 'maintenance' in section 14 of the Hindu Succession Act, 1956, must necessarily encompass a provision for residence, in addition to food and clothing, and that a woman was entitled to live in a manner to which she was accustomed.

What emerges from a review of the case law is that while litigative strategies have been adopted in the field of criminal law, civil law has hardly witnessed any activity. One possible explanation for this is that criminal law is put in motion by the State and not the individual concerned, making access easier. Women are often absent from the court as 'access to justice' is expensive.

Dignity Issues

The remedy of Restitution of Conjugal Rights that compels a wife to reside with her spouse is an archaic provision of law which is most offensive to the dignity of women. The substantive test was applied by one high court to invalidate the matrimonial remedy for restitution of conjugal rights: a remedy which on paper was available to either spouse but would operate more to significantly alter the status of women in India.[77] Another high court frowned upon the challenge[78] and eventually the challenge was negatived by the Supreme Court,[79] which endorsed the high court's veiw that:

Introduction of Constitutional Law in the home is most inappropriate. It is like introducing a bull in a china shop. In the privacy of the home and the married life, neither Article 21 nor Article 14 have any place. In a sensitive sphere which is at once most intimate and delicate, the introduction of the cold principles of Constitutional Law will have the effect of weakening the marriage bond.

These cases exhibit the dual nature of the attitude of the Supreme Court towards issues affecting women directly. In some cases the Court treats the family as private and beyond the reach of law (for example the cases relating to restitution of conjugal rights). At other times the Court sees the family as private and in need of protection (for example the cases relating to adultery). These cases further show how the public/private divide has been used flexibly and usually to the detriment of women.

Interestingly, in this case the Supreme Court discussed the reasoning of the Andhra Pradesh High Court[80] in holding the provision unconstitutional. The high court had examined the issues in detail and come to the conclusion that the provision for restitution of conjugal rights was a savage and barbarous remedy violating the right of privacy and human dignity. The high court, in what is a commendable judgement, held that the provision denied the woman her free choice whether, when, and how her body was to become a vehicle for the procreation of another human being. Further, the court recognized that a decree for restitution of conjugal rights would deprive a woman of her choice as when and by whom her body should be allowed to be sensed and lose control over her most intimate decisions.

The high court showed an appreciable degree of sensitivity in considering the predicament of a woman keeping away from a relationship and probably contemplating divorce proceedings. A pregnancy as a result of such cohabitation would alter her position irretrievably and affect her decision to an extent that she lost control over it. Using the right to life approach, the court held that even though the provision on a plain reading fulfils the test of equality, considering the inequality of realities such an equal treatment was unjust. From a gender justice perspective this judgement reflects a high level of sensitivity inasmuch as it subverts the hitherto all-important familial leaning that had been a dominant aspect of the perspectives of courts and instead focuses on the experience of the woman. Also noteworthy is the court's express recognition of the importance of the right to dignity and privacy.

The Supreme Court, however, chose to endorse the reasoning of the Delhi High Court,[81] which had rejected similar arguments before it. In this case the high court has held that the object behind the provision for restitution was to bring about cohabitation in amity and that sexual relations were just an element of the concept of cohabitation and not the only aspect. It went on to state that the restitution decree does not enforce sexual intercourse and thus that the restitution of conjugal rights is not an invasion of marital privacy. The Court seems to have disregarded the right of privacy of the woman as an entity different from the marriage itself. The Supreme Court reasoned that conjugal rights in the Indian context were not creations of the statute but were rights inherent in the institution of marriage itself. While indulging itself in rhetoric about the beauty of living together in a marriage filled with love and sharing, the Supreme Court failed to take note of the many reasons why women may want a separation, including the prevalence of domestic violence. While rape is an issue that has attracted judicial attention domestic violence has not. Presumably rape happens among strangers and is therefore addressed as a crime, whereas domestic violence happens within the family and to introduce constitutional law would be like the much-mentioned 'bull in a china shop'.

The case of *Rupan Deol Bajaj v K.P. Singh Gill,*[82] widely covered by the press, is one that in many ways reflects the increasing sensitivity of the Supreme Court to feminist concerns. In a case where a male high-level police officer had, among a series of actions, slapped the posterior of a woman IAS officer in public view, the Supreme Court directed the Chief Judicial Magistrate to take cognizance of offence under sections 354 and 509 of the IPC, i.e. assault or use of criminal force on a woman with the intent to outrage her modesty and insulting the modesty of a woman by words, acts or gestures. The Supreme Court in this case held that the order of the high court quashing FIR was unjustified in view of the offences being made out prima facie. The Court, in the course of this decision was required to interpret the term 'modesty'. It held in this case that the ultimate test for ascertaining whether modesty has been outraged is whether the action of the offender could be perceived as one that is capable of shocking the sense of decency of a woman. The interesting point that the Court made was that in doing so, the test would have to be on an understanding of the contemporary societal standards, thereby setting a precedent of subjectivity. The Court held that the alleged actions of the officer amounted to outraging of the modesty of a woman as it was an affront to the normal sense of 'feminine decency' and also an affront to her *dignity*. It is important to note that the Supreme Court clearly stated that the presence of 'sexual overtones' was not necessary for an outrage to be established. The attendant circumstances, consisting of overtures, were sufficient indicators of intention required under the provision.

The other important aspect of this case is rejection of the argument that the injury should not be perceived as a wrong, as the injury caused was so slight that no reasonable person would complain of it.[83] The Court considered the principle that whether an act is trivial would depend on the nature of the injury, the position of the parties, the knowledge or intention with which the act is committed, and other related circumstances. Emphasis was laid on the fact that there can be no absolute standard or degree of harm that may be regarded as so slight that a person of ordinary sense and temper would not complain of the harm. On this basis, the Court held that section 95, IPC could not in the circumstances apply, as the ignominy and trauma of having to suffer the outrage of a slap on her posterior and continued behaviour of that kind despite her objections could not in any circumstances be considered as trivial. This is perhaps the first of the cases of sexual harassment that the Court recognized as such and dealt with squarely as an issue concerning the dignity of women in public spaces.

There has been a trend towards recognizing the importance of 'dignity' issues over the past decade and a half. The case of *Goutam Kundu v State of West Bengal* [84] is another interesting example of the trend towards treating matters of right to dignity with seriousness, although the Court did not explicitly state that it was considering a matter concerning dignity. In this case the appellant, in an attempt to avoid the obligation to provide maintenance under section 125 of the CrPC, had questioned the legitimacy of the child born to the woman married to him. The question before the Court was whether to rebut the presumption regarding the legitimacy of the child, a blood-grouping test could be permitted. The Court held that no person could be compelled to give a blood sample for analysis against her will and that no adverse inference could be drawn against her for such refusal. The Supreme Court held that in the normal course this test would not be ordered and that a strong case of non-access had to be made out by the person attempting to rebut the presumption. The Court held that a strong preponderance of probabilities and not merely a balance of probabilities would be required to displace the presumption. The Court also held that the terms access and non-access meant the existence or non-existence of opportunities for sexual intercourse and do not refer to actual 'cohabitation'. The Court went on to state that in considering whether such a test may be permitted the effect of such a test on the character of the woman and the status of the child was to be seriously considered.

This judgement is of significance first, because it addresses a mischief that already may be considered an oft-utilized way of harassing women in the domestic sphere. Challenges to paternity and legitimacy are made in various circumstances giving rise to societal sanction without reason. Secondly, this judgement should be appreciated for its concern for the impact of such a test on the reputation and dignity of the woman.

The most articulate case demonstrating the growing concern on issues of dignity is undoubtedly that of *Vishaka v State of Rajasthan*.[85] Although the immediate cause for filing of the PIL was the gang rape of a social activist in a village of Rajasthan, this case is the first comprehensive attempt at analysis of the issue of rights of working women against sexual harassment in workplaces. This PIL was brought to the Court with the aim of assisting in finding suitable methods for the realization of gender equality in the work place and to bring about change in the realities of the politics at these through judicial processes in the absence of legislation to this effect.

The Supreme Court held that women have rights to gender equality, to work with dignity and to a working environment safe and protected from sexual harassment or abuse. Significantly, the Court recognized that in the absence of a suitable legislation to enforce such rights, international conventions, so far as they are consistent with the constitutional spirit, can be relied upon. The Supreme Court considered the provisions in the Beijing Statement of Principles of the Independence of the Judiciary, 1995, the Convention on the Elimination of All Forms of Discrimination Against Women (CEDAW), and the Protection of Human Rights Act, 1993, in clarifying the issues as to judicial activism and legislation by the judiciary. The Supreme Court held that every incident of sexual harassment at the workplace results in the violation of the fundamental rights of gender equality and the right to life and liberty. Interestingly, the Court also considered that the effect of such a violation is also a violation of the woman's right of freedom to practise any profession, occupation, trade or business under Article 19(1)(g) of the Constitution.

An important aspect of the decision is that it states clearly that fundamental rights under the Constitution have an amplitude wide enough to cover all aspects of gender justice and that the international obligations are only a reflection of the common minimum requirement of gender justice. At the same time, the Court stated that the contents of international conventions may be used for the purpose of interpretation of the guarantees to gender justice within the Constitution, a standpoint that reflects the willingness to look beyond the bare words of the Constitution. This is a positive aspect, in that it provides for constant reconsideration of the content of the Constitution depending on the changing circumstances. There is no doubt that there are questions as to the consequence of opening local rights discourse to the international regime and its politics. Specifically, the questions of cultural specificity are of concern. The processes that go into the formulation of the specific principles of the human rights regime are, no doubt, focused on the developments of certain cultures and not of others. However, at this point in time, considering the absence of the political will to make changes in the realities of existence within our own polity, this is, no doubt a positive development.

To make the writ of mandamus effective, the Court drafted a set of guidelines for the enforcement of such rights. This combination was effectively supplemented by reference to the Beijing Statement of the Principles of Independence of the Judiciary.

The guidelines themselves place the onus of preventing or deterring the commission of sexual harassment and providing procedures for the resolution, settlement, or prosecution of acts of sexual harassment in the workplace on the employer. The guidelines go on to define sexual harassment broadly as sexually determined behaviour that is unwelcome as physical advances or contact, demands and requests for sexual favours, sexually coloured remarks, display of pornography and an open-ended provision covering any other unwelcome physical, verbal, or non-verbal conduct of a sexual nature. An important aspect of the judgement is that it does not limit the applicability of the guidelines to government offices but includes all private or public enterprises. Other guidelines deal with preventive steps such as notification and publicity of the rules framed, creation of procedures for providing appropriate penalties for actions of sexual harassment, and the creation of appropriate work conditions to ensure that there is no hostile environment at the workplace and to ensure that a woman employee does not have reasonable ground to believe that she is disadvantaged in relation to her employment. The guidelines also provide that the employer has the obligation to initiate criminal proceedings in cases where the action amounts to an offence and that disciplinary action should be initiated by the employer where the act amounts to misconduct under service rules. Where the act amounts to neither of these, the Court requires that a complaint mechanism be created. The guidelines also envisage situations of harassment by outsiders or third parties and provide that the employer shall take all steps reasonable and necessary in terms of support and prevention.

There is no doubt that this is, by any standards, a milestone in the development of the gender justice mechanism in our law. The issues and concerns are reasonably exhaustive and there are safeguards in the guidelines themselves to provide space for addressinig new issues that may come up or be recognized in the future. However, the judgement seems to lack the foresight that would be necessary for the effective implementation of the guidelines. One would like to believe that the judgement came out the way it did thanks to the presence of a woman judge on the Bench; a judge who herself had been to several international conferences on women including Beijing. The judgement in *Vishaka* was followed by *Apparel Export Promotion Council.*[86] This case brings to the forefront enforcement issues by clarifying that sexual harassment is a misconduct in service law making the accused person liable to dismissal.

In Conclusion

This brief survey indicates that the theoretical problematic of 'equality' enshrined in Article 14 has not been satisfactorily resolved by the Court. In particular, the interrelationship between Article 15 and 15(3) has never been addressed. Article 15(3) has been marginalized and almost relegated to the position of a non-justiciable directive principle. As against this, the Court has been very comfortable with Article 16 and as recently as 1992 has reiterated that Article 16(2) is not an exception to Article 14 but an aspect of it.

Although, in the initial years, women did not figure at all in legal discourse, in the later years, there has been a dynamic interaction between the Court and the women's movement. The Court is still all too 'male'. Women, especially on the Bench and at senior levels, are very poorly represented. If feminist jurisprudence is to move forward, this will have to change. The Court has come a long way from *Mathura* to *Vishaka*; from viewing women as sexual objects to active participants in the public life of the nation entitled to live and work with dignity. There has been a growing trend to raise the level of the rights debate and to recognize that statutory rights exist to breathe life and meaning into fundamental rights.

The importance of this era lies in the growing awareness of women's issues and of the women's movement. It was in this era again that the campaign for law reform in relation to dowry was undertaken by women's organizations, and the shift of focus from violence in the public sphere to violence within the home was attempted. The era also saw women's groups taking advantage of the liberalized *locus standi* rule, petitioning the courts more and more in the hope of vindicating injustices done to women. The development of the law by the Supreme Court has however remained uneven for a variety of reasons. There has been greater emphasis on criminal law remedies rather than civil. This is because in criminal law, the State has access to the justice system, making it easier for a person whose rights are violated to seek justice. The limited contribution of the Court has been to insist that due process issues are brought into the criminal justice system. As stated, the absence of women from the civil law jurisprudence of the Court indicates their poor access generally to courts. This has meant that the economic rights of women have remained unaddressed. Interestingly, the largest number of cases in the civil law regime have been under section 14 of the Hindu Succession Act which deals with the rights of widows in a dying regime. These cases belong to an era when Hindu widows did not inherit equally with their children from their husbands and are not likely to have any relevance beyond their times. Invariably they have been brought at the instance of the persons to whom the widow is alleged to have sold the property in which she is said to have had a limited estate. Very few have dealt with the rights of a wife within marriage; not even to something as basic as the right to a matrimonial home. The Court is still reluctant to enter the 'private' domain, the matrimonial home. The Court views crime against women by strangers as a violation of their fundamental rights but does not accord the same treatment to crime against women by a family member. It has failed to recognize that a woman and children face a greater threat of violence from family members than from strangers.

Organized Crime

In recent years one has seen the emergence of organized crime linked to commercial gain. This has been most evident in the case of crime against women. Prostitution rackets, sale and purchase of women, the sale and purchase of children for the purpose of prostitution are all issues that the Court has had to deal with. Obviously such cases cannot be dealt with in the same way as crimes of an individual nature, nor can male aggression be explained away as being the aberration of an individual person or as being crimes of 'passion' or of lust. There will have to be an obvious change of approach to these cases. In a recent case,[87] the judgement of the Kerala High Court, quashing a prosecution against a group of influential persons on charges of rape and abduction of minor girls for the purpose of prostitution was addressed by the Supreme Court. The Court, recognizing the importance of the case, reversed the judgement and allowed the prosecution to go ahead. This judgement marks the recognition of the existence of organized crime against women and children. In another pending case,[88] the Supreme Court has called for a report from the state government, the allegations being that an influential politician was involved in a sex racket in which minor girls were abducted and raped. Globalization and its attendant consumerism has brought with it crime of a high order, where women are viewed as purchasable commodities. One of the challenges before the Supreme Court in the coming days will be to deal with organized crime against women.

Issues of the Future

Sooner, if not later, the Court will be called upon to resolve the question of the constitutional validity of Personal laws. Reservations for women in panchayats will raise issues of substantive quality for decision. An increasing number of women on the Bench will hopefully change the perception of women from being passive recipients of rights and in need of protection to being fully autonomous in their decision-making and equal participants in public life. This millennium should belong to the woman. Let us hope this great institution will take the lead in ensuring that it does.

Notes

[1] Adopted in 1945, Article 55 states that the United Nations shall promote universal respect for and observance of human rights and fundamental freedoms for all without distinction as to race, sex, etc.

[2] Adopted on 10 December 1948.

[3] The Constitution of India was adopted on 26 November 1949 and came into operation from 26 January 1950.

[4] The Parliament (Qualification of Women) Act, 1918, which conferred voting rights on women, came into full effect in 1928. Full franchise was finally achieved in 1948 with The Representation of People Act, 1948. Equality for women was conferred as recently as in 1975, by the Sex Discrimination Act, 1975. However, under the European Economic Community Act, 1972, the Courts of the United Kingdom are obliged to recognize and give effect to the 'laws' of the European Community including the European Convention on Human Rights and Fundamental Freedoms even if national legislation is contrary to such 'law'.

[5] Articles 41.1, 41.2, 41.3.1 and 41.3.2 of the Constitution of Ireland reflect the Catholic bias of the Constitution, particularly in its approach to women, marriage, and family.

[6] The 'separate but equal' doctrine was finally overruled by the Warren Supreme Court in 1954 in *Brown v Board of Education* (1954) 347 US 483.

[7] For example, freedom from torture (Article 5, UDHR), freedom from arbitrary arrest and detention (Article 9, UDHR), right to fair trial (Article 10, UDHR), right to participate in government (Article 21, UDHR), and freedom of assembly (Article 20, UDHR).

[8] Part III of the Constitution of India lists the fundamental rights such as the right to equality (Articles 14, 15, 16, 17 and 18), the right to freedom (Articles 19, 20, 21 and 22), right against exploitation (Articles 23 and 24), right to freedom of religion (Articles 25, 26, 27 and 28), cultural and educational rights (Articles 29 and 30), and the right to constitutional remedy (Article 32).

[9] Article 17, Constitution of India.

[10] Article 23, Constitution of India.

[11] Article 134, Constitution of India.

[12] *Supreme Court Advocates-on-record Assn v Union of India* (1993) 4 SCC 441.

[13] Catherine MacKinnon, 'Difference and Dominance: On Sex Discrimination' [1984], *Feminist Legal Theory: Readings in Law and Gender,* ed. Katharine T. Bartlett and Rosanne Kennedy, Westview Press, Oxford, 1991, at p. 81.

[14] Article 14, Constitution of India.

[15] Article 15, Constitution of India.

[16] *Air India v Nargesh Meerza* (1981) 4 SCC 335. See also, *Miss Lena Khan v Union of India & Ors* (1987) 2 SCC 402.

[17] Article 15(2), Constitution of India.

[18] See *Vishaka v State of Rajasthan* (1997) 6 SCC 241, where the apex court addressed the issue of sexual harassment at the workplace.

[19] Article 15(3), Constitution of India.

[20] Section 497 of the Indian Penal Code, read with section 198(2) of the CrPC, which states that the only person who may be considered aggrieved in a case of adultery is the husband of the woman who has been party to adultery, confers upon a husband the right to prosecute the adulterer but does not confer such a right to the wife to prosecute the women with whom the husband who has committed adultery. As such, in practice, while a man has criminal action against an adulterous relationship involving the woman he is married to, a woman has no such action against an adulterous relationship that her husband is involved in. In the cases of *Sowmithri Vishnu v Union of India* (1985) Supp SCC 137 and *V. Revathi v Union of India* (1988) 2 SCC 72, the Supreme Court held that these provisions were not violative of Articles 14, 15, and 21. The reasoning of the Court was that the offence of adultery is an offence against the sanctity of the matrimonial home, and that the offence is generally committed by the man. The underlying emphasis in these cases was on the assumption that woman can never be the guilty party in adultery, and thus, that women are sexually passive, that women need to be protected. In taking a formal equality approach in these cases the Supreme Court has belittled the effect of the provision; that there is no criminal remedy to the woman where her husband is committing adultery or is sexually involved with another person.

[21] Article 16, Constitution of India.

[22] Article 16(4), Constitution of India.

[23] (1951) SCR 525.

[24] (1954) SCR 558.

[25] (1980) 1 SCC 634.

[26] (1963) 2 SCR 353 at 395.

[27] *Budan Choudhry v State of Bihar* (1955) 1 SCR 1045; *State of WB v Anwar Ali* (1952) SCR 284; *R.K. Dalmia v Justice Tendulkar* (1959) SCR 279.

[28] *Ajay Hasia v Khalid Mujib* (1981) 1 SCC 722; *E.P. Royappa v State of Tamil Nadu* (1974) 4 SCC 3, *Shetty v IAAI* (1979) 3 SCC 489; *Maneka Gandhi v Union of India* (1978) 1 SCC 248.

[29] *Kerala v N.M. Thomas* (1976) 2 SCC 310. See also *The Karmachari Sangh Case* (1981) 1 SCC 246 where Krishna Iyer J differs with his opinion in *Thomas* and concludes that Article 16(4) of the Constitution of India was an exception to Article 16(1).

[30] *Indra Sawhney v Union of India* (1992) Supp 3 SCC 217 (*Mandal Commission* case).

[31] *Government of AP v Vijayakumar* (1995) 4 SCC 520.

[32] *Bombay Labour Union v International Franchise* (1966) 2 SCR 493.

[33] *C.B. Muthamma v Union of India & Ors* (1979) 4 SCC 260.

[34] *Nalini Rnjan Singh v State* AIR 1977 Pat 171.

[35] *Mahadeb Jiew v B.B. Sen* AIR 1951 Cal 563.

[36] Ironically, neither protective nor corrective approaches have appealed to certain courts when the women before them did not meet the sex stereotypes. In *State of UP v Kaushaliya* (1964) 4 SCR 1002, the apex court negatived the challenge by a sex worker to the law on immoral traffic which conferred unfettered discretion on the magistrate to deal with prostituted women, including orders for their deportation. (Contra see: *Smt Sharma Bai v State of Uttar Pradesh* AIR 1959 All 57.)

[37] *Abdul Aziz v State of Bombay* (1954) SCR 930; *Sowmithri v Union of India* (1985) Supp SCC 137.

[38] Personal laws were either scriptural or codified. The Parsi Marriage and Divorce Act, 1936 and Christian Marriage Act, 1872 are examples of the latter.

[39] The Hindu Women's Right to Property Act, 1937, The Muslim Personal Laws (Shariat) Application Act, 1937, and Dissolution of Muslim Marriages Act, 1939.

[40] Article 13(1), Constitition of India. Also, Article 372 provides for recognition of laws in force prior to the commencement of the Constitution of India.

[41] *State v Narasu Appa Mali* AIR 1952 Bom 84, See also *Srinivasa Aiyar v Saraswati Ammal* AIR 1952 Bom 84.

[42] For a critique of the judgement, see A.M. Bhattacharjee, *Hindu Law and the Constitution*, Eastern Law House, Calcutta, 2nd edn., 1994 at p. 40.

[43] *Krishna Singh v Mathura Ahir* (1980) 2 SCR 660.

[44] *C. Masilamani Mudaliar v Idol of Sri S.S. Thirukoil* (1996) 8 SCC 525.

[45] *Ahmedabad Women's Group's* Case (1997) 3 SCC 573.

[46] (1985) 2 SCC 556.

[47] (1986) 2 SCC 209.

[48] (1996) 5 SCC 125.

[49] (1999) 2 SCC 228.

[50] The HMG Act states that this 'natural guardianship' vests in the father and after him, the mother. Prior to this judgement, the interpretation of this provision was that the mother would be the natural guardian only after the life time of the father. The Supreme Court in this case, however, rejected this interpretation and held that the 'after him' did not necessarily mean after the death of the father, but would include circumstances where the father was indisposed or incapable of being the natural guradian.

[51] See *St Stephen's College v University of Delhi* (1992) 1 SCC 558; *T.M.A. Pai Foundation v State of Karnataka* (1995) 5 SCC 220; *Ahmedabad St Xaviers College Society v State of Gujrat* (1974) 1 SCC 717; *Christian Medical College Hospital Employees' Union v CMC Vellore Association* (1987) 4 SCC 691; *Frank Anthony Public School Employees' Association v Union of India* (1986) 4 SCC 707.

[52] (1995) 3 SCC 635.

[53] Committee on the Status of Women appointed by the Government of India in 1971, of which Ms Vina Mazumdar was the member secretary.

[54] *Additional District Magistrate v Kant* (1976) Supp SCR 172.

[55] In *Batra v Delhi Administration* (1978) 4 SCC 494, the Court treated as a writ petition a mere letter of a prisoner alleging prison excesses by jail authorities against a fellow prisoner. It ruled that a writ of habeas corpus would be available against the actions of jail authorities that violated the Equality clause and the Right to Life. In the same breath, is recalled the *Hussainara Khatoon v Home Secretary* (1980) 1 SCC 81 series of petitions in which the Supreme Court has, relying upon the Right to Life, pronounced that an undertrial had a right to a speedy trial and that prolonged detention offended the Right to Life. The Court further ruled that such pre-trial detention must be based on reasonable, just and fair procedure.

[56] *Tukaram v State of Maharashtra* (1979) 2 SCC 143.

[57] See *Joint Women's Programme v State of Rajasthan* (1987) Supp SCC 707 where the Supreme Court directed that the investigation into dowry deaths be conducted by officers not below the rank of Superintendent of Police. The Supreme Court also directed the states of Rajasthan and Haryana to create special dowry cells at the state level to invesitgate into the dowry deaths through specialized investigative agencies. See also, the case of *Bhagwant Singh v Commissioner of Police* (1983) 3 SCC 344.

[58] *Phul Singh v State of Haryana* (1979) 4 SCC 413.

[59] *Krishnalal v State of Haryana* (1980) 3 SCC 159.

[60] (1983) 2 SCC 217.

[61] *Premchand v State of Haryana* (1989) Supp 1 SCC 286.

[62] Interestingly, the Supreme Court has never addressed the question of the constitutionality of section 155(4) of the Indian Evidence Act, 1872, which enables the previous sexual history of the prosecutrix to be brought in evidence to impeach her testimony.

[63] *State of Maharashtra v Chandraprakash Kewalchand Jain* (1990) 1 SCC 550.

[64] *Karnel Singh v State of Madhya Pradesh* (1995) 5 SCC 518.

[65] *The State of Punjab v Gurmit Singh & Ors* (1996) 2 SCC 384.

[66] Section 155 (4) of the Indian Evidence Act, 1872.

[67] (1992) 3 SCC 204.

[68] Section 354 of the IPC provides punishment for assault or use criminal force on a woman with the intent to outrage her modesty. The section provides a punishment where there is an intent or knowledge that such action would be likely to outrage the modesty of a woman, such punishment being limited to just two years imprisonment or fine or both.

[69] *Satish Mehra v Delhi Administration* (1996) 9 SCC 766.

[70] (1994) 1 SCC 73.

[71] (1985) 2 SCC 370.

[72] (1997) 2 SCC 397.

[73] (1993) 2 SCC 684.

[74] (1995) 1 SCC 14.

[75] (1996) 1 SCC 490.

[76] *Mangat Mal v Punni Devi* (1995) 6 SCC 88.

[77] *Sareetha v Venkata Subbaiah* AIR 1983 AP 356.

[78] *Harvinder Kaur v Harmander Singh Choudhary* AIR 1984 Del 66.

[79] *Saroj Rani v Sadarshan Kumar* (1984) 3 SCC 90.

[80] *Supra*, n. 77.

[81] *Supra*, n. 78.

[82] (1995) 5 SCC 194.

[83] Section 95 of the Indian Penal Code.

[84] (1993) 3 SCC 418.

[85] (1997) 6 SCC 241.

[86] (1999) 1 SCC 759.

[87] *State of Kerala v O.C. Kuttan* (1999) 2 SCC 651.

[88] *Anweshi Women's Counselling Centre v State of Kerala and Others,* Special Petition (Criminal) No. 3725 of 1998.

Sixteen

Detention Without Trial

Ram Jethmalani

One morning in September 1974 the nation awoke to screaming head-lines that top smugglers of the country had been arrested and detained. They were humiliated and marched in handcuffs along public streets and roughed up in jails. Their faces were prominently displayed on tele-vision with sarcastic comments. The government had struck at the root of our economic misery, so Akashwani claimed. The people applauded.

Naturally, any sober, long-range appraisal of injury to constitutional-ism and democracy became impossible. Such was the powerful propa-ganda machine unleashed by the government and its sycophantic ad-mirers. As the then Chairman of the Bar Council of India, I used to write the Chairman's page for a legal periodical published by the Coun-cil. In that, I recorded my protest and premonitions.

Senator Dirksen of the United States was once scheduled to make a speech on the unusual subject 'Frogs and Freedom'. A puzzled friend asked, 'What in the devil would frogs have to do with freedom?' The Senator explained:

You know if you take a frog with his delicate reflexes and drop him in a kettle of boiling water, and if the sides are not too high, he will pop right out of the water. But, put that frog in the same kettle and fill it with cold water, then turn on the gas; and that poor, unsuspecting frog will be boiled, because he did not have sense enough to climb out of that water before it got too hot.

The greatest danger to democracy and the rule of law comes not from a violent and manifest blow. It is by gradual erosion, a little precipi-tation, that freedom is usually and finally lost. I suspected that the govern-ment was about to strike a heavier blow against national freedom. This small one was only intended to acclimatize people to the horrible insti-tution of detention without trial. When an inherently evil law is put into service for an ostensibly beneficial purpose, that is the time when perceptive lovers of freedom must nip the threat in the bud. An evil law of preventive detention was today being used against notoriously bad people. After the people got used to it, the government would very soon start using it against good people whom it despised. My prophecy came true within a few months. The best that the nation could find or offer were put behind prison bars under the notorious Maintenance of Internal Security Act.

Mature democracies do not countenance detention without trial except in times of grave emergencies, such as war. The prestigious International Commission of Jurists in laying down minimum conditions of political freedom, has condemned the use of this instrument as a peace-time measure.

In the Draft Constitution of India, the Drafting Committee had introduced Article 15-A corresponding to the present Article 22 placing some curbs upon the power of preventive detention which had been introduced in the legislative lists like Entry 9 in List I and Entry 3 in List III. These are:

Entry 9, List I: Preventive detentions for reasons connected with Defence, Foreign Affairs or the Security of India; persons subjected to such detention.
Entry 3, List III: Preventive detention for reasons connected with the security of a State, the maintenance of public order, or the maintenance of supplies and services essential to the community, persons subjected to such detention.

The times were truly abnormal. Partition had rocked the nation. A war with Pakistan over Kashmir was on. States had not been integrated into a union and Hyderabad with its Razakars posed a grave threat. Dr Ambedkar had regretfully made up his mind that the government would need the power. Even so, the draft article was subjected to fierce criticism by some progressive members of the Constituent Assembly led by Jaspat Roy Kapoor and Mahavir Tyagi. The following excerpts from the Constituent Assembly Debates of 16 September make interesting reading:

Shri Mahavir Tyagi (UP General): 'Sir, Dr Ambedkar will please pardon me when I express my fond wish that he and other members of the Drafting Committee had the experience of detention in jail before they became members of the Drafting Committee.'

The Hon'ble Dr B.L. Ambedkar: 'I shall try hereafter to acquire that experience.'

Shri Mahavir Tyagi: 'I may assure Dr Ambedkar that although the British Government did not give him this privilege, the Constitution he is making with his own hands will give him that privilege in his lifetime. There will come a day when they will be detained under the provisions of the very same clauses which they are making *(Interruption)*. Then they will realize their mistake. It is all safe as long as the House is sitting and the Members are sitting on these benches. But then let us not make provisions which will be applied against us very soon. There might come a time when these very clauses which we are now considering will be used freely by a Government against its political opponents.

Sir, in this article we are required to grant rights and privileges to the people but along with them I am surprised to find that it has occurred to the Drafting Committee and their friends and advisers to provide therein penal clauses also. This is a charter of freedom that we are considering. But is this a proper place for providing for the curtailment of that very freedom and liberty? When freedom is being guaranteed, why does the Drafting Committee think it fit to introduce provisions for detaining people and curbing their freedom? This is the article which enables the future Government to detain people and deprive them of their liberty rather than guarantee it.

Shri Mahavir Tyagi: 'In Urdu, there is a couplet which says *"Kas rahe hain apni minqaron se hulqa jalka."* That is what really we are doing. We are making it easy and convenient and legal for the future Government to detain us. That is the meaning. Sir, I do not wish to say more on this point. I only wanted to warn the House that if we pass this article as it is we will simply be making a provision which will be used against us.'

There is no doubt, as Acting Chief Justice Shelat J pointed out in the *Sambhu Nath Sarkar* case[1] that: 'The Constitution-makers accepted preventive detentions as necessary evil to be tolerated in a constitutional scheme which otherwise guaranteed personal liberty in its well accepted form. Having accepted it, they proceeded to create in terms, clear and wide in their import, certain procedural safeguards.'

Procedure in this field is as important as substantive in others. It is at once the heart, the core, and the essence.

A smuggler of rice was detained by a district magistrate in exercise of his powers under the Maintenance of Internal Security Act on the evidence of some incidents of illegal transport of this essential commodity across state borders. One of the grounds lacked precise particulars and was, therefore, vague and indefinite. The Supreme Court proceeded to release him because the constitutional right of the detenu to make an effective representation had been infringed. The observations of Justice Mathew speaking for the majority of the Court have now become a part of the country's legal literature:

The facts of the case might induce mournful reflection on how an honest attempt by an authority charged with the duty of taking prophylactic measures to secure the maintenance of supplies and services essential to the community has been frustrated by what is popularly called *a technical error*. We say and we think it is necessary to repeat, that the gravity of the evil to the community resulting from anti-social activities can never furnish an adequate reason for invading the personal liberty of a citizen, except in accordance with the procedure established by the Constitution and the laws: "The history of personal liberty is largely the history of insistence on observance of procedure. And observance of procedure has been the bastion against wanton assaults on personal security over the years."

Under our Constitution, the only guarantee of personal liberty for a person is that he shall not be deprived of it except in accordance with the procedure established by law. The need today for maintenance of supplies and services to the community cannot be over-emphasized. There will be no social security without maintenance of adequate supplies and services essential to the community. But social security is not the only goal of a good society. There are other values in a society. Our country is taking singular pride in the democratic ideals enshrined in its Constitution and the most cherished of these ideals is personal liberty. It would indeed be ironic if in the name of social security, we would sanction the subversion of this liberty. We do not pause to consider whether social security is more precious than personal liberty in the scale of values, for, any judgement as regards that would be but a value judgement on which opinions might differ. But, whatever be the impact on the maintenance of supplies and services essential to the community, when a certain procedure is prescribed by the Constitution or the laws for depriving a citizen of his personal liberty, we think it our duty to see *that procedure is rigorously observed*, however strange this might sound to some ears. (See *Prabhu Dayal* case.[2])

The principle which Justice Mathew propounded in such felicitous prose was only a reiteration of what had been said earlier in many cases. Justice Sarkar, speaking for a Constitution Bench in *Ram Manohar Lohia v State of Bihar*[3] had held that where a man can be deprived of his liberty by the simple process of issuing a certain order under the Defence of India Rules 1962, he can only be so deprived if the order is in terms of the rules. He said: 'Strict compliance with the letter of the rule is the essence of the matter.' There are more cases that take the same view of the preventive detention law. In *S.K. Salim v State of WB*[4] Justice Chandrachud said:

Laws of preventive detention by which subjects are deprived of their personal liberty without the safeguards available in a judicial trial ought to be construed with the greatest strictness. Courts must therefore be vigilant to ensure that the detenu is not deprived of the modicum of rights and safeguards which the preventive law itself affords to him. The Maintenance of Internal Security Act contains what is evidently thought to be a scheme of checks and counter-checks by which the propriety or necessity of a detention order may at various stages be examined by various authorities.... This time schedule evolved in order obviously to provide an expeditious opportunity at different levels for reviewing the justification of the detention order has to be observed scrupulously and its rigour cannot be relaxed on any facile assumption that what is good, if done within 7, 12 or 30 days could as well be good if done, say, within 10, 15 or 35 days.

In *Sher Mohammed v State of WB*[5], a detenu had to be released because the state government did not report the detention within seven days which was the requirement under the statute. Justice Krishna Iyer explained:

In short, there has been an infringement of the procedural safeguard. This court has in several rulings held that the liberty of the citizen is a priceless freedom, sedulously secured by the Constitution. Even so, during times of emergency, in compliance with the provisions of the Constitution, the said freedom may be curtailed but only in strict compliance with statutory formalities which are the vigilant concern of the Courts to enforce.... We have pointed out how in the present case, there has been a failure on the part of the State Government to comply with section 3(4). Judicial engineering prevents breaches of Constitutional dykes protecting fundamental freedoms.

In *Wasi Uddin Ahmed v District Magistrate, Aligarh*[6], Justice A.P. Sen correctly observed:

The law insists upon the *literal performance* of a procedural requirement. The need for observance of procedural safeguards, particularly in cases of deprivation of life and liberty is of prime importance to the body politic.

In *Vijay Narain Singh v State of Bihar*[7] Justice Venkataramiah, with whom Justice Chinnappa Reddy fully concurred, observed:

The Court should examine the case without being overwhelmed by the gruesomeness of the incident involved in the criminal trial. It is well settled that the law of preventive detention is a hard law and, therefore, it should be strictly construed. Care should be taken that the liberty of a person is not jeopardized unless his case falls squarely within the four corners of the relevant law. The law of preventive detention should not be used merely to clip the wings of an accused who is involved in a criminal prosecution. It is not intended for the purpose of keeping a man under detention when under ordinary criminal law, it may not be possible to resist the issue of orders of bail, unless the material available is such as would satisfy the requirements of the legal provisions authorizing such detention. When a person is enlarged on bail by a competent criminal Court, great caution should be exercised in scrutinizing the validity of an order of preventive detention which is based on the very same charge which is to be tried by the criminal Court.

In *State of Punjab v Jagdev Singh*[8], Chief Justice Y.V. Chandrachud, speaking for the Constitution Bench, made the following pertinent remarks:

This Court has observed in numerous cases that while passing the orders of detention, great care must be brought to bear on their task by the detaining authorities. Preventive detention is a necessary evil but essentially an evil. Therefore, deprivation of personal liberty, if at all, *has to be on the strict terms of the Constitution, nothing less.* We will utter the oft-given warning yet once more in the hope that the voice of reason will be heard.

Strict compliance with procedural safeguards does often puzzle the layman. He does not usually distinguish between someone found guilty by the courts after a careful trial and one who is merely suspected by an executive officer usually acting on the recommendation of some inferior investigating agency. His common sense is offended when he hears of a notorious criminal released not because the court found him innocent but because of what strikes him as a trivial technicality. He does not appreciate that the courts are serving manifold higher public purposes, mitigating the rigours of an essentially evil law, ensuring meticulous application of mind to relevant facts by those who seek to rob a citizen of his liberty and upholding the majesty of law. Judges would not be judges if their only qualification was the common sense of the layman. Chief Justice Chandrachud's reference in *Jagdev Singh Talwandi* case clarifies that the 'voice of reason' was the reason of enlightened liberty-prone judges, not the common sense of the legal illiterates.

A discordant note was however struck by a decision given by Mr Justice Sabyasachi Mukharji sitting with two other judges in *Prakash Chandra Mehta v Government of Kerala & Others*.[9] A room in a hotel in Ernakulam was searched and a large quantity of illicit gold was recovered. The occupants of the room were one Venilal Mehta and his daughter Pragna Mehta. Both were arrested on 2 May 1984 and, while in custody of the Customs officers, made confessions. On 20 June 1984, both father and daughter were detained under an order of detention issued the earlier day. The grounds of detention were served upon them in English. The Hindi translation of these on 30 June 1984. Some of the documents relied upon which served as a part of these were in Malayalam and no translation of these either in English or Hindi was supplied. Eventually, a habeas corpus petition was filed. The first ground of attack on behalf of detenu Venilal was non-communication of the grounds for detention in violation of Article 22 of the Constitution.

Two binding decisions of the Supreme Court, *Hari Kishan v State of Maharashtra*[10] and *Harbandhu Das v District Magistrate, Cuttack*[11] had indisputably laid down that communication of grounds of detention required by the constitutional Article must be in a language and script that the detenu understood. The detenu claimed that he only knew Gujarati and, admittedly, a Gujarati translation of the grounds of detention in the Malayalam documents had never been supplied. The Court could have disposed of the detenu's contention by finding that the detenu Venilal Mehta knew English and that his denial of knowing was pretence. The Court however, dealt with this contention in a way that not only creates confusion but is apt to dilute one of the major constitutional safeguards of a detenu. The learned judge made the following observations:

The facts revealed that the detenu Venilal was constantly accompanied and was in the company of his daughter as well as son—both of them knew English very well. The father signed a document in Gujarati which was written in English which is his mercy petition in which he completely accepted the guilt of the involvement in smuggling. That document dated 30.6.1984 contained, *inter alia,* the statement: 'I myself am surprised to understand what prompted me to involve in such activity as dealing in imported gold.' He further asked for mercy. *There is no rule of law that common sense should be put in cold storage while considering constitutional provisions for safeguards against misuse of powers by authorities though these constitutional provisions should be strictly construed.*[12]

To say the least, this paragraph is unfortunate. The prayer for mercy made by the detenu in his application of 30 June 1984 disclosing consciousness of guilt was totally irrelevant. Observance of constitutional safeguards has nothing to do with the merits of the case or the conclusive nature of the evidence of guilt. Hundreds of detenus have been released because some comparatively unimportant safeguard was not followed, notwithstanding the fact that there was almost conclusive evidence of guilt.

Moreover, it is difficult to understand the learned judge's injunction against common sense being consigned to the cold storage. No one had argued before him that common sense should be put in cold storage while considering constitutional provisions, compelling His Lordship to repudiate it. One cannot but suspect that he was unconsciously influenced by the supposedly technical nature of the legal safeguards. He appears to have entertained the notion that common sense requires that no one should get away by reason of failure to comply with technical provisions, and particularly a person who has confessed his guilt and pleaded for mercy. It is reasonable to assume that the learned judge was making a sarcastic reference to authorities who have attached the highest importance to the observance of the technical requirements of procedure. He thus indulged in a veiled attack on the common sense of other judges. It is patently clear that even the detaining authority realized that the detenu did not understand English and that was why it proceeded to serve a Hindi translation of the grounds of detention. The learned judge was wholly wrong in the last paragraph of his observations that such constitutional provisions should be strictly construed. The law is that they should be liberally construed in favour of the detenu and be strictly applied by the detaining authority. To suggest that the applicable rules of procedure are to be strictly construed is to subvert the entire preventive detention jurisprudence.

If the learned judge, rightly or wrongly, concluded that the detenu knew English, these observations were totally unnecessary. They are calculated to cause confusion in administering this branch of law. The finding of fact itself appears to have been based upon unfortunate reasoning. The learned judge observed:

The principle is well settled. But in this case it has to be borne in mind that the grounds given on 25.6.1984 following search and seizure of gold biscuits from his room in the hotel in his presence and in the background of the mercy petition as we have indicated and he was in constant touch with his daughter and son and there is no evidence that these people did not know Hindi or English. Indeed, they knew English as well as Hindi. It is difficult to accept the position that in the peculiar facts of this case, the grounds were not communicated to the detenu Venilal. Whether grounds were communicated or not depends upon the facts and circumstances of each case.

The learned judge infers that the detenu is feigning ignorance of English from the act of being in constant touch with his daughter and son who knew English. With respect to him, many illiterate parents have literate children. The Constitution requires the grounds to be communicated to the person detained and not his children. The detenu is not bound to take the help of others to make the grounds of detention intelligible to him. This is the rule established by the authorities cited by the learned judge with approval. Indeed, these authorities were binding on him.

Still more untenable is the manner in which the learned judge rejected the detenu's second contention. The grounds of detention had relied upon his confessional statements but the retraction of the confession had not been made known to the detaining authority. There was thus non-application of mind to a relevant circumstance, the effect of which on the subjective satisfaction of the detaining authority cannot be determined by the Court by any objective appreciation of evidence. Scores of authorities which were binding upon the learned judge have so held. Naturally, cited before him was the decision in the *Ashadevi* case.[13] The detenu there was travelling in a car which, when intercepted and searched, yielded a large amount of illicit gold. The detenu in his confession had not only admitted his involvement in the transaction in question but to continual smuggling activity during the preceding six to eight months. Before the High Court of Gujarat, the detenu had argued that the detaining authority had not applied his mind to the fact that the confessional statement had been retracted. The high court considered the evidence for itself and came to the conclusion that the retraction of the confession was false and the confession was true and voluntary. The Supreme Court reversed the high court's decision. Mr Justice Tulzapurkar speaking for the Court, said:

It is well-settled that the subjective satisfaction requisite on the part of the detaining authority, the formation of which is a condition precedent to the passing of the detention order, will get vitiated if material or vital facts which would have a bearing on the issue and would influence the mind of the detaining authority one way or the other, are ignored or not considered by the detaining authority before issuing the detention order... The principle that could be clearly deduced from the above observation is that if material or vital facts which would influence the mind of the detaining authority one way or the other on the question whether or not to make the detention order, are not placed before or are not considered by the detaining authority, it would vitiate its subjective satisfaction rendering the detention order illegal. After all, the detaining authority must execute due care and caution and act fairly and justly in exercising the power of detention if taking into account matters extraneous to the scope and purpose of the statute vitiate the subjective satisfaction and renders the detention order invalid then failure to take into consideration the most material or vital facts likely to influence the mind of the authority one way or the other would equally vitiate the subjective satisfaction and invalidate the detention order.

The learned judge then proceeded to disapprove what the Gujarat High Court had done, namely, to examine the evidence and come to a conclusion for itself whether or not the confessions were voluntary. It accepted the submission that in so doing the high court clearly acted in excess of its jurisdiction and contrary to the well-established principles applicable to the issue of Habeas Corpus in preventive detention cases. The detention order was accordingly set aside and the detenu released.

It is impossible to distinguish the *Ashadevi* case from the case before Mr Justice Sabyasachi Mukharji. It was open to the learned judge to take one of two courses. He could have followed that case. If he strongly disapproved of the *ratio decidendi* of the case, he could have persuaded his brother judges to refer the matter to a larger Bench for determination of the correctness of the case. The learned judge could also have taken the view that section 5-A of COFEPOSA had not been considered in the *Ashadevi* case and that he would proceed to decide the case before him by invoking section 5-A. It is unfortunate, however, that the learned judge chose to disregard *Ashadevi* on the following grounds:

But in this case, the confessional statement was not the only fact upon which the detaining authority had passed an order. In the premises, even if the confessional statements which were retracted as such could not be taken into consideration, there are other facts independent of the confessional statement as mentioned herein before which can reasonably lead to the satisfaction that the authorities have come to.

With respect, this is an extraordinary way of distinguishing a case. Anyone reading the *Ashadevi* case should have no difficulty in discovering that the confessional statement was not the only fact relied upon by the detaining authority in that case. Both in the *Ashadevi* case as well as in that before Mr Justice Sabyasachi Mukharji, there was a telltale fact of the recovery of contraband from the car in one case and the hotel room in the other. To seize upon a non-existing fact to bypass a binding authority is pregnant with public mischief and sets an evil precedent for high courts and other subordinate courts to follow. No wonder then that when a few days later another Bench, with Mr Justice Tulzapukar on it, dealt with similar facts, the Bench reiterated the *Ashadevi* case, acted upon it, and released the detenu, totally ignoring Mr Justice Sabyasachi Mukharji's decision. Three more cases have quietly ignored the authority of Mr Justice Sabyasachi Mukharji's decision. These are:

1. *Kurjibhai Dhanjibhai Patel v State of Gujarat & Others* decided by Mr Justice V.D. Tulzapurkar on 16 April 1985.[14]

2. *Smt. Jayadevi Shantilal Jain v Union of India & Others* decided by Mr Justice V.D. Tulzapurkar and Mr Justice R.B. Misra on 5 February 1986.[15]

3. *Sitaram v State of Rajasthan.*[16]

The law of detention under the COFEPOSA was amended by the addition of section 5-A which reads:

5-A. Grounds of detention severable—Where a person has been detained in pursuance of an order of detention under sub-sec. (1) of section 3 which has been made on two or more grounds, such order of detention shall be deemed to have been made separately on each of such grounds and accordingly:

(a) such order shall not be deemed to be invalid or inoperative merely because one or some of the grounds is or are

(i) vague
(ii) non-existent,
(iii) not relevant,
(iv) not connected or not proximately connected with such person, or
(v) invalid for any other reason whatsoever, and it is not therefore possible to hold that the Government or officer making such order world have been satisfied as provided in Sub-sec (1) of section 3 with reference to the remaining ground or grounds and made the order of detentions;
(b) the Government or officer making the order of detention shall be deemed to have made the order of detention under the said sub-sec (1) after being satisfied as provided in that sub-section with reference to the remaining ground or some other grounds.

The validity of this section had been challenged periodically in many writ petitions but never decided until recently. In the *Shakeel Wahid* case[17] the point was squarely raised but the Court declined to go into the question because it released the detenu on the ground of non-application of mind. It was assumed that section 5-A cannot be invoked where the invalidity arises out of non-application of mind to some vital facts which could, though need not necessarily, have affected the mind of the detaining authority in favour of not ordering detention.

It is clear from the section that it refers to the invalidity of the 'grounds' of detention. 5-A(a)(v) must necessarily be construed *ejusdem generis* with the preceding clauses. Non-application of mind to vital facts will invalidate every ground and none will survive to leave room for 5-A to be invoked or applied. The section does not cure a defect in the mind of the detaining authority arising out of a gap in his knowledge of some relevant facts; it only cures defects in the grounds of detention, i.e. their text and contents.

The rule that invalidity of one ground of detention vitiates the entire detention order is a rule of constitutional law derived from Article 22. This rule cannot be nullified by any parliamentary legislation.

A recent nine-judge Bench of the Supreme Court[18] has however unanimously upheld the constitutional validity of this section. This decision is unfortunate. It expressly proceeds on the assumption that the constitutional amendments placing COFEPOSA in the Ninth Schedule and immunized from constitutional challenge were and are valid. This assumption is itself wrong. It is now settled law that non-agricultural legislation put into the Ninth Schedule after the *Kesavananda Bharati* judgement of 1973[19] is not immune from judicial review and can be declared invalid as being repugnant to Articles 19, 21, and 22 of the Constitution.

If the detaining authority is not prepared to issue a detention order separately on one ground the legislature cannot by legal fiction produce that result. The creation of this fiction is repugnant to Article 22. That Article requires the communication of the grounds of detention which in fact were the basis of the order, nothing more nothing less. The Court did not disapprove of the pre-Constitution judgement of the Andhra Pradesh High Court in *K.Y. Reddy* case.[20] The case was distinguished on the ground that the Andhra Pradesh provision under challenge contai ned only the second part of section 5-A and did not create the legal fiction created by the first part. The Court failed to realize that the entire mischief of section 5-A arises from the second part and not the first. As pointed out above, the first itself is repugnant to Article 22. Nobody challenges the right of Parliament to create legal fictions in some situations, but that is very far from arguing that every legal fiction created by Parliament is constitutionally valid. A legal fiction may be so unreasonable as to call for annulment under Article 21. The one in hand is plainly repugnant to both Articles 21 and 22. With respect, the decision needs to be reviewed on some suitable occasion.

The record of the Supreme Court in dealing with detention cases is one of which any court should be proud. Apart from some sporadic decisions, the Court has steadily frowned upon detention orders and made 'detention without trial' extremely difficult and not too oppressive. The major transformation in the Court's attitude and philosophy may be traced to its revulsion against the outrageous Jabalpur judgement delivered during the emergency. The *Maneka Gandhi* case[21] was a complete turnabout through 180 degrees. It was indeed a revolutionary trend setter. It banished the *Gopalan*[22] jurisprudence that had held sway from 1950 and smuggled 'Due Process' into our jurisprudence.

Notes

[1] *Sambhu Nath Sarkar v State of West Bengal* AIR 1973 SC 1425.
[2] *Prabhu Dayal Deorah v District Magistrate* AIR 1974 SC 183.
[3] AIR 1966 SC 740.
[4] AIR 1975 SC 602.
[5] AIR 1975 SC 2049.
[6] AIR 1981 SC 2166.
[7] AIR 1984 SC 1334.
[8] AIR 1984 SC 444.
[9] AIR 1986 SC 687.
[10] AIR 1962 SC 911.
[11] AIR 1969 SC 43.

[12] *Supra* n. 9, pr. 62, p. 696.

[13] *Ashadevi v K. Shiveraj* AIR 1979 SC 447.

[14] Crl. Appeal No. 332/85 with W.P. No. 1923/84 decided by Mr Justice V.D. Tulzapurkar on 16 April 1985.

[15] Crl. Appeal No. 115/86 decided by Mr Justice V.D. Tulzapurkar and Mr Justice R.B. Misra on 5 February 1986.

[16] AIR 1986 SC 1072.

[17] *Mohd. Shakeel Wahid Ahmed v State of Maharashtra* AIR 1983 SC 541.

[18] *Attorney-General for India v Amritlal Prajivandas* AIR 1994 SC 2179.

[19] *Holiness Kesavananda Bharati Sripadagalvaru v State of Kerala* AIR 1973 SC 1461.

[20] *K. Yadigiri Reddy v Commissioner of Police* ILR 1972 AP 1025.

[21] *Maneka Gandhi v Union of India* AIR 1978 SC 597.

[22] *A.K. Gopalan v State of Madras* AIR 1950 SC 27.

Seventeen

Constitution, Courts, and Freedom of the Press and the Media

Soli J. Sorabjee

The Chapter on fundamental rights, Part III in the Indian Constitution, was not incorporated as a popular concession to international sentiment and thinking on human rights in vogue after the conclusion of the Second World War. The demand for constitutional guarantees of human rights for Indians was made as far back as in 1895 in the Constitution of India Bill, popularly called the Swaraj Bill, which was inspired by Lokmanya Tilak, a lawyer and great freedom fighter. This Bill envisaged for India a Constitution guaranteeing to every one of its citizens, amongst other freedoms, the freedom of the press.

Freedom of the press was also one of the constitutional guarantees demanded in Mrs Annie Besant's Commonwealth of India Bill, finalized by the National Convention of Political Parties in 1925, on the recommendations of the Motilal Nehru Committee 1928, the 1932 Karachi Resolution of the Indian National Congress, and the Constitutional Proposals of the Sapru Committee, 1945.

The Founding Fathers of the Indian Constitution attached great importance to freedom of speech and expression and the freedom of the press. Their experience of waves of repressive measures during British rule, when the nationalist press was bludgeoned by sedition trials and forfeiture of security deposits, convinced them of the immense value of this right in the sovereign democratic republic which India was to be under its Constitution. They believed that freedom of expression and the freedom of the press are indispensable to the operation of a democratic system. They knew that when avenues of expression are closed, government by the consent of the governed would soon be foreclosed. The Founding Fathers believed that central to the concept of a free press is freedom of political opinion and at the core of that freedom lies the right to criticize the Government. They endorsed the thinking of Jawaharlal Nehru who said, 'I would rather have a completely free press with all the dangers involved in the wrong use of that freedom than a suppressed or regulated press.'[1]

Members of the Constituent Assembly hailed the guarantee of freedom of speech and expression as a fundamental right. However, some Founding Fathers were critical about the omission to guarantee freedom of the press as a distinct fundamental right. Professor K.T. Shah moved an amendment and made an impassioned plea for the inclusion of freedom of the press in the Chapter on Fundamental Rights. He declaimed:

the freedom of the press, as is very well known, is one of the items round which the greatest, the bitterest of constitutional struggles have been waged in all constitutions and in all countries where liberal constitutions prevail. ... I am amazed that in this Constitution a very glaring omission has taken place in the draft by leaving out the freedom of the press. I cannot imagine, why these draftsmen, so experienced and so seasoned, should have felt it desirable to leave out the freedom of the press, and leave it to the charity of the administrators of the Constitution when occasion arose to include it by convention or implication, and not by express provision. ... To omit it altogether, I repeat, and I repeat with all the earnestness that I can command, would be a great blemish.[2]

Dr Ambedkar in his brief reply to Professor Shah stated that 'the press has no special rights which are not to be given or which are not to be exercised by the citizen in his individual capacity. The editor of a press or the manager are all citizens and therefore when they choose to write in newspapers, they are merely exercising their right of expression, and in my judgement therefore no special mention is necessary of the freedom of the press at all'.[3] According to the constitutional adviser, Dr B.N. Rau, it was hardly necessary to provide for freedom of the press specifically, because freedom of expression would include freedom of the press.[4]

The views of Dr Ambedkar and Dr B.N. Rau have been vindicated by the Supreme Court. In a series of decisions from 1950 onwards the Supreme Court has ruled that freedom of the press is implicit in the guarantee of freedom of speech and expression. Consequently, freedom of the press by judicial interpretation is one of the fundamental rights guaranteed by the Constitution of India.[5]

The majority of the Founding Fathers did not accept the theory of absoluteness of any fundamental rights, including freedom of speech and expression. They firmly believed that no freedom could be absolute and it had to be subject to reasonable regulations. There was however considerable controversy as regards the extent and area of restrictions that might be imposed upon the exercise of fundamental rights.

One of the heads of restrictions on the freedom of speech and expression in the draft Constitution was 'sedition', aptly described by Gandhiji as the Prince of the Indian Penal Code. Sedition was frequently invoked to crush the freedom movement and incarcerate freedom fighters, including prominent nationalist leaders like Tilak, Gandhiji, Nehru and several others. In the heyday of British colonialism sedition was construed by the Privy Council in the cases of *Tilak*,[6] *Wallace-Johnson*[7] and *Sadashiv Bhalerao*[8] to include any statement that was liable to cause 'disaffection', namely, exciting in others certain inimical feelings towards the government, even though there was no element of incitement to violence or rebellion. To restrict speech under the head of 'sedition' was galling to the framers of the Constitution.

K.M. Munshi assailed the inclusion of 'sedition' as a head of restriction on freedom of expression and moved an amendment for its deletion. In the course of the debate he pointed out:

Even holding an opinion against, which will bring ill-will towards government, was considered sedition once. Our notorious Section 124-A of Penal Code was sometimes construed so widely that I remember in a case a criticism of a District Magistrate was urged to be covered by Section 124-A. But the public opinion has changed considerably since and now that we have a democratic government a line must be drawn between criticism of government which should be welcome and incitement which would undermine the security or order on which civilized life is based, or which is calculated to overthrow the State ... As a matter of fact the essence of democracy is criticism of government. The party system which necessarily involves an advocacy of the replacement of one government by another is its only bulwark; the advocacy of a different system of government should be welcome because that gives vitality to a democracy. The object therefore of this amendment is to make a distinciton between the two positions.[9]

Almost all the members supported K.M. Munshi's amendment and sedition did not disfigure the Indian Constitution.

Article 19(1)(a) and Article 19(2) which finally emerged and were enacted in the Constitution were in these terms:

Article 19(1): All Citizens shall have the right—
    (a) to freedom of speech and expression;

(2) Nothing in sub-clause (a) of Clause (i) shall affect the operation of any existing law in so far as it relates to, or prevent the State from making any law relating to libel, slander, defamation, contempt of Court or any matter which offends against decency or morality or which undermines the security of, or tends to overthrow the State.

Public order and incitement to an offence were not specified as heads under which freedom of speech and expression could be restricted. The requirement of reasonableness of the restrictions that may be imposed was also absent.

Barely four months after India became an independent republic the Supreme Court had occasion to determine the constitutionality of state laws impinging on freedom of expression and freedom of the press. On the basis of the original Article 19(2) the Supreme Court ruled that Madras Maintenance of Public Order Act, 1949 and section 7(1)(9c) of the Punjab Public Safety Act, 1949 were unconstitutional.[10]

In the *Romesh Thapar* case the Court laid down an important principle:

So long as the possibility of the law being applied for purposes not sanctioned by the Constitution cannot be ruled out, it must be held to be wholly unconstitutional and void. In other words, Clause 2 of Article 19 having allowed the imposition of restrictions on the freedom of speech and expression only in cases where danger to public security is involved, an enactment, which is capable of being applied to cases where no such danger could arise, cannot be held to be constitutional and valid to any extent.[11]

On the same date and on essentially the same reasoning the Court also struck down the East Punjab Public Safety Act, 1949, which, by section 7(1)(c), provided for special measures to ensure public safety and the maintenance of public order.[12]

The high courts of Patna[13] and Punjab,[14] basing themselves on the said decisions of the Supreme Court, held that incitement to an offence was a head of restriction which was not covered by clause (2) of Article 19 and accordingly laws restricting the freedom of speech on that ground were declared unconstitutional.

Article 19(2) was subsequently amended by the Constitution (First Amendment) Act, 1951, which was enacted with retrospective effect on 18 June 1951. The substituted Article 19(2) was as follows:

(2) Nothing in sub-clause (a) Clause (1) shall affect the operation of any existing law, or prevent the State from making any law, in so far as such law imposes *reasonable* restrictions on the exercise of the right conferred by the said sub-clause in the interests of the security of the State, friendly relations with foreign States, public order, decency or morality, or in relation to contempt of court, defamation or incitement to an offence.

After the Constitution (First Amendment) Act, the decisions of the Punjab and Patna High Courts can no longer be regarded as good law in as much as the amendment expressly permits imposition of reasonable restrictions under the head of incitement to an offence. Moreover, the said Punjab and Patna decisions have been held by the Supreme Court to be erroneous and have been strongly criticized.[15]

The Supreme Court expressed its doubt in parentheses whether the Constitutional First Amendment could be enacted with retrospective effect but did not rule on the point.[16] Therefore the provisions of amended clause (2) of Article 19 must be taken to be available from 26 January 1950 without a break. The fiction when given full effect to leads to no other conclusion.[17] Accordingly the question about the validity or otherwise of laws enacted between 26 January 1950 and 18 June 1951 when the Constitution (First Amendment) Act was enacted and the further question whether such laws were *non est* to which the doctrine of eclipse cannot apply, do not arise for consideration.

The amendment of Article 19(2) by the Constitution (First Amendment) Act, 1951, was a further curtailment of the freedom of the press in so far as it enlarged the existing heads of permissible restrictions by adding 'friendly relations with foreign state, public order, and incitement to an offence'. However, the inclusion of the word 'reasonable' before 'restrictions' was a significant gain.

Article 19(2) was subsequently amended by the Constitution (Sixteenth Amendment) Act. By the said amendment another head of restriction, 'sovereignty and integrity of India', was added in clause (2) of Article 19 with prospective effect.

Article 19(2) in the Constitution is at present as follows:

(2) Nothing in sub-clause (a) of clause (1) shall affect the operation of any existing law, or prevent the State from making any law, in so far as such law imposes reasonable restrictions on the exercise of the right conferred by the said sub-clause in the interests of the sovereignty and integrity of India, the security of the State, friendly relations with foreign States, public order, decency or morality, or in relation to contempt of court, defamation or incitement to an offence.

The resultant position is that freedom of the press is not absolute. It can be restricted provided three distinct and independent prerequisites are satisfied.

(1) The restriction imposed must have the authority of law to support it. Freedom of the press cannot be curtailed by executive orders or administrative instructions which lack the sanction of law.

(2) The law must fall squarely within one or more heads of restrictions specified in Article 19(2), namely, (a) security of the state, (b) sovereignty and integrity of India, (c) friendly relations with foreign states, (d) public order, (e) decency or morality, (f) contempt of court, (g) defamation or

(h) incitement to an offence. Restriction on freedom of expression cannot be imposed on such omnibus grounds as 'in the interest of the general public'.[18]

(3) The restriction must be reasonable. In other words, it must not be excessive or disproportionate. The procedure and the manner of imposition of the restriction also must be just, fair, and reasonable.[19]

The validity of the restriction is justiciable. Courts in India exercising the power of judicial review can invalidate laws and measures which do not satisfy the above requirements, and have done so.[20]

Freedom of the press does not occupy a preferred position in the Indian Constitution which does not recognize a hierarchy of rights.[21] There are however dicta of the Supreme Court describing this freedom as 'the Ark of the Covenant of Democracy',[22] 'the most precious of all the freedoms guaranteed by our Constitution'.[23]

In its landmark judgement in the case of *Sakal Papers*, the Supreme Court ruled that Article 19(2) of our Constitution permits imposition of reasonable restrictions under the heads specified in Article 19(2) and on no other grounds. It is not open to the State to curtail the freedom of speech of one for the promoting of the general welfare of a section or a group of people unless its action can be justified by a law falling under clause 2 of Article 19. Freedom of the press cannot be curtailed, like the freedom to carry on business, in the interest of the general public. The only restrictions which may be imposed on the rights guaranteed under Article 19(1)(a) are those which clause (2) of Article 19 permits and no other.[24]

If legislation or executive action interferes with the freedom of the press, it is no answer that it is a regulation of the business aspect of a newspaper.[25] The object of giving some kind of protection to small or newly started newspapers may be good and desirable, but Article 19(2) does not permit the State on that ground to make inroads on the freedom guaranteed to other newspapers. Again carrying on unfair practices may be a matter for condemnation and monopolies may be assumed to be obnoxious and against public interest. Even so, restriction for the above purpose are beyond the scope of Article 19(2) and are unconstitutional.[26]

In another celebrated decision, *Bennett Coleman & Co. v Union of India*,[27] the Supreme Court again came to the rescue of the press. It held that freedom of the press entitles newspapers to achieve any volume of circulation and freedom lies both in circulation and in content. The Court ruled that the question about the quantity of newsprint to be imported is a matter of government policy. Courts cannot adjudicate on such policy measures unless the policy is alleged to be mala fide.[28]

However, a newsprint policy under the Import and Export Control Act under the garb of distribution of newsprint cannot control the growth and circulation of newspapers. A newsprint policy cannot impose restrictions which constrict the newspapers in adjusting their page number and circulation.[29] The Court recognized that the principal source of income for the newspapers is from advertisements which are not only a source of revenue but also one of the factors for circulation. If the area for advertisement is curtailed the price of the newspapers will be forced up. If that happens the circulation will inevitably drop and earnings would decline, and that would directly interfere with the freedom of the press. The Court ruled that loss of advertisements seriously affects the circulation of a newspaper and a restraint on advertisements would affect the fundamental right of the freedom of the press under Article 19(1)(a).[30]

An interesting case arose in the state of Andhra Pradesh. The proprietor of a Telugu daily, *Eenadu*, complained that government had withdrawn advertisements from its paper on account of extraneous reasons, and this had adversely affected the revenue and circulation of the paper. The action of the government was challenged. The high court did not accept the contention that a newspaper has a constitutional right to obtain advertisements from the government. It, however, ruled that the government cannot exercise this power or privilege

to favour one set of newspapers or to show its displeasure against another section of the press. It should not use the power over such large funds in its hands to muzzle the press, or as a weapon to punish newspapers which criticize its policies and actions. It has to use the funds in a reasonable manner consistently with the object of the advertisement, viz., to educate and inform the public about the activities of the government.[31]

The press is not immune from the ordinary forms of taxation for support of the government nor from the application of the general laws relating to industrial relations.[32] However, in another of its celebrated judgements in *Indian Express Newspapers v Union of India*,[33] in which a steep levy of customs duty on newsprint was challenged, the Court observed that whilst newspapers did not enjoy any immunity from payment of taxes and other fiscal burdens, the imposition of a tax such as customs duty on newsprint is an imposition on knowledge. The Court accepted the plea that a fiscal levy on newsprint would be subject to judicial review because

in the case of ordinary taxing statutes, the laws may be questioned only if they are openly confiscatory or a colourable device to confiscate. But in the cases before us the Court is called upon to reconcile the social interest involved in the freedom of speech and expression with the public interest involved in the fiscal levies imposed by the Government specially because newsprint constitutes the body, if expression happens to be the soul.

Therefore 'in the case of a tax on newsprint, it may be sufficient to show a distinct and noticeable burdensomeness clearly and directly attributable to the tax'.[34] The Court did not strike down the levy because all the relevant materials were not placed before it. The government was directed to reconsider the matter afresh and fix the import duty on newsprint in the light of the principles enunciated in the judgement.

The Indian judiciary has placed a generous construction on the ambit of freedom of the press and given it a capacious content.

Freedom of the press has been held to entitle a newspaper to the right to publish its own views or the views of its correspondents concerning what may be the burning topic of the day. This right is not confined to newspapers and periodicals but includes pamphlets, leaflets, handbills, and every sort of publication, affording a vehicle of information and opinion. Freedom of circulation is essential to the effective exercise of the freedom of the press. Indeed, without circulation publication would be of little value. Newspapers have the right to determine the extent of their pages, their circulation, and the new editions which they can bring out within the quota of newsprint allotted to them.[35] Freedom of the press includes freedom in the matter of employment of editorial staff.[36]

The Supreme Court in the case of *Hamdard Dawakhana*[37] dealt with advertisement of prohibited drugs as commodities. The Court came to the conclusion that the sale of prohibited drugs was not in the interest of the general public and as such 'could not be speech' within the meaning of freedom of speech and expression under Article 19(1)(a) of the Constitution. In reaching its conclusion the Court relied on the judgement of the American Supreme Court in the case of *Lewis J Valentine v F.J. Chrestensen*.[38]

In its subsequent judgement in *Indian Express Newspapers*[39] the Court noted that the view expressed by the US Supreme Court in *Chrestensen's* case had not been fully approved by the American Supreme Court itself in its subsequent decisions. The Court concluded that all commercial advertisements cannot be denied the protection of Article 19(1)(a) of the Constitution merely because they are issued by businessmen.

The question again arose in the case of *Tata Press Ltd. v Mahanagar Telephone Nigam Ltd.* Tata Press was engaged in the publication of the Tata Press Yellow Pages which would be appended to the Telephone

Directory. A suit was filed by the Union of India to restrain Tata Press from printing, publishing, and circulating the Yellow Pages. The main issue that arose was whether Tata Press had a fundamental right to publish and circulate the Yellow Pages which raised the wider issue of whether a commercial speech is protected under Article 19(1)(a). The Court, after an extensive review of the judgements of the US Supreme Court and the previous Supreme Court judgements, reached the conclusion that commercial speech is within the guarantee of Article 19(1)(a) and commercial advertisements are entitled to its protection.[40]

The test adopted by the Supreme Court for determining whether a particular piece of legislation infringes freedom of expression and freedom of the press is the effect and operation of the legislation upon these fundamental rights. It is not the object of the law or the form of executive action that determines the invasion of a fundamental right. The true test is whether the direct and inevitable effect of the impugned legislation or action is to abridge freedom of the press. The tests of the object of the legislation and pith and substance of the subject matter of the legislation are irrelevant to the question of infringement of fundamental rights.[41] Earlier Supreme Court decisions[42] adopting these tests can no longer be regarded as laying down good law.

Censorship

It is a paradox that humanity's yearning for freedom of expression, in times ancient and modern, is matched by the urge for its suppression. Plato was its respectable exponent. Milton, who thundered in his famous *Areopagitica*, 'Give me liberty to know, to utter and to argue freely according to conscience, above all liberties', became Cromwell's official censor.

There is no provision in the Indian Constitution permitting or proscribing censorship. The sting of censorship lies in prior restraint which affects the heart and soul of freedom of the press. Expression is snuffed out before its birth. The communication in question may never see the light of day. Suppression by a stroke of the pen is more likely to be applied by the censoring authorities than suppression through a criminal process, and thus there is far less scope for public appraisal and discussion of the matter. That is the real vice of prior restraint and its irresistible attraction to the censor.

There is a clear distinction between the requirement for a licence and the imposition of pre-censorship. When pre-censorship is imposed, it requires the citizen to submit his views to the authorities concerned as a condition precedent to its publication. When a citizen is required to obtain a licence, he is not required to submit his views to the authorities prior to publication. All that he is required to do is obtain a licence before exercising the right of free speech.[43]

Is prior restraint intrinsically evil? Is it per se unconstitutional? There is unending debate on this vexed question. In the Japanese Constitution (Article 21) and the German Constitution (Article 5) pre-censorship is prohibited. Again, the American Convention on Human Rights (San Jose) 1969 (ACHR) expressly states in Article 13(2) that freedom of expression 'shall not be subject to prior censorship'. There was strong American influence in the drafting of the Japanese and German Constitutions after the Second World War. Yet even in the land of the First Amendment, and despite the robust American tradition and the thrust of US judicial opinion against censorship, there is no absolute rule against prior restraint. Indeed, its necessity has been recognized, albeit in exceptional cases, by the United States Supreme Court in the celebrated case of *Near v Minnesota*,[44] the sheet anchor of the opponents of prior restraint. The Court observed that 'the protection even as to previous restraint is not absolutely unlimited'[45] and listed as exceptions obstructions to recruitment during war, publication of military movements, obscenity, 'incitements to acts of violence and the overthrow by force of orderly government', and words that 'may have all the effect of force'.

The Supreme Court of India in May 1950 had to resolve the tension between freedom of expression and censorship in *Brij Bhushan v State of Delhi*.[46] Section 7(1)(c) of the East Punjab Public Safety Act, 1949, provided for submission of material for scrutiny if the government was satisfied that such action was necessary for the purpose of preventing or combating any activity prejudicial to public safety or the maintenance of public order. The Court declared the statutory provision in question unconstitutional on the ground that the restrictions imposed were outside the purview of Article 19(2) as it then stood, which did not include public order as a permissible head of restriction. The Court did not rule that prior censorship is per se unconstitutional. Indeed, in 1957 the Court upheld censorship imposed under the Punjab Special Powers (Press) Act, 1956, for a temporary period, which provided for a right of representation to the government.[47] It is noteworthy that another statutory provision imposing censorship without any time limit and without providing any right of representation was struck down by the Court in a judgement delivered on the same day.[48]

India's worst brush with censorship occurred during the spurious emergency declared by the government of Prime Minister Indira Gandhi on 25 June 1975. Censorship of the press was imposed for the first time in independent India by the promulgation of a Central Censorship Order dated 26 June 1975. No censorship was imposed during two previous declarations of emergency, in 1962 and in 1971, when the nation was fighting a war. Under the Indian Constitution, during an emergency, fundamental rights, including freedom of speech and expression and the freedom of the press, stand suspended. Censorship, which in normal times would be struck down, becomes immune from constitutional challenge. Taking advantage of the emergency, numerous repressive measures were adopted in the form of executive non-statutory guidelines, and instructions were issued by the censor to the press. One of the instructions of the censor was the following: 'Nothing is to be published that is likely to convey the impression of a protest or disapproval of a government measure.'[49]

Consequently, anything that smacked of criticism of governmental measures or action was almost invariably banned, even if the criticism was sober and moderate. The censor's scissors were applied arbitrarily, and in a few cases its decisions bordered on the farcical. Quotations from Mahatma Gandhi, Tagore, and Nehru were banned. A statement by the Chairman of the Monopolies and Restrictive Trade Practices Commission criticizing the working of public sector undertakings was blacked out. Other ludicrous instances were the bans imposed on news about a member of a former royal family, Begum Vilayat Mahal, squatting at New Delhi railway station, a report about junior lawyers marching to the Delhi High Court, a London report of the arrest of a famous Indian actress for shoplifting; and the news about a meeting of the Wild Life Board, which considered the grant of a hunting licence to a certain Maharajah's brother.[50] These bans had nothing to do with the security of the state or preservation of public peace and order but reflected the capricious working of the censoring authorities.

Some of the censor's directives were sinister, like those prohibiting any reference to the transfer of state high court judges, banning publication of judgements of high courts which ruled against the censor, 'killing' news of the opposition of certain state governments to proposed constitutional amendments, banning reports of alleged payoffs made during the purchase of Boeing aircraft, and suppressing criticism of family planning programmes. The object was not merely withholding information but manipulation news and views to legitimize the emergency and make it acceptable. One tragic consequence was that inhuman practices like forcible sterilization of young men after disembarking them from buses and other excesses of overenthusiastic family planning officials came to light much after the events, by which time family planning had become anathema to the rural masses. An urgent and important programme suffered a serious setback thanks to suppression of freedom of the press by the censor.

The Indian judiciary, especially the state high courts, displayed commendable courage in striking down the censor's orders and upheld the right of dissent even during the emergency. The Bombay High Court in its landmark judgement in *Binod Rao v Masani*[51] delivered on 10 February 1976 declared:

It is not the function of the censor acting under the Censorship Order to make all newspapers and periodicals trim their sails to one wind or to tow along in a single file or to speak in chorus with one voice. It is not for him to exercise his statutory powers to force public opinion in a single mould or to turn the Press into an instrument for brainwashing the public. Under the Censorship Order the censor is appointed the nursemaid of democracy and not its gravedigger. ... Merely because dissent, disapproval or criticism is expressed in strong language is no ground for banning its publication. ...[52]

The Court, however, cautioned that the voice of dissent cannot take the form of incitement of revolutionary or subversive activities, for then instead of serving democracy it would subvert it.[53]

The Gujarat High Court in its judgement in *C. Vaidya v D'Penha* castigated the censorship directives for imposing upon the people 'a mask of suffocation and strangulation'. In construing the expression 'prejudicial report', the Court observed: 'To peacefully protest against any government action with the immediate object of educating public opinion and the ultimate object of getting the ruling party voted out of power at the next general elections is not a prejudicial report at all. Such a public education is the primary need of every democracy.'[54]

These judgements were delivered at a time when 'inconvenient' judges were transferred from one state to another in India. Notwithstanding this, the high courts rose to the occasion. Indeed, it was their finest hour.

The Gauhati High Court, in a path-breaking judgement dealing with a censorship order passed under the Assam Special Powers (Press) Act, 1960, laid down certain important principles. Section 2(1) of the Act provided that if the Governor was satisfied that a situation existed whereby the maintenance of communal harmony was threatened in the state and it was necessary to use the special powers under the Act for the purpose of preventing or combating any activity affecting or likely to affect public order, he might make a declaration to that effect. Section 2(2)(a) of the Act empowered the state government or an authorized officer to prohibit the printing or publication of any document in a newspaper or a periodical after a declaration under section 2(1) was made.

The high court upheld the validity of section 2(1). However, the high court held that section 2(2)(a) of the Act did not empower the censoring authority to require a press to submit all material relating to any subject it might choose. The subject matter had necessarily to be relatable to communal harmony, and it was further necessary that communal disharmony would affect public order. Secondly, before taking any action or step against a particular press, prior hearing should be given and the grounds of decision stated. Thirdly, there should be an independent forum before which the press could ask for redress in respect to an illegal or unjust order of the censoring authority. As the Act under challenge provided no such forum, the Court struck down section 2(2)(c) which required submission of all material to the Censor for prior scrutiny. The Court held that representation to the state government or to any governmental authority was not adequate because censorship was often invoked against government's own policies and programmes, and, in such a situation, a representation or an appeal to the government would be nothing short of an appeal from Caesar to Caesar and, as such, not meaningful and effective at all.[55]

Prior restraint has been upheld by the Supreme Court with regard to the exhibition of motion pictures in *K.A. Abbas v Union of India*. According to the Court 'it has been almost universally recognized that the treatment of motion pictures must be different from that of other forms of art and expression. This arises from the instant appeal of the motion picture ...'[56]

The Court, however, emphasized the necessity for a corrective machinery in the shape of an independent tribunal and also a reasonable time limit for the decision of the censoring authorities. In laying down certain guidelines for the censor, the Court was at pains to point out that the 'standards must be so framed that we are not reduced to a level where the protection of the least capable and the most depraved amongst us determines what the morally healthy cannot view or read. The standards that we set for our censors must make a substantial allowance in favour of freedom.'[57]

Courts have ruled that in adjudging the question of proscription of articles in the press or banning the exhibition of a movie or programmes on the TV channels, the standards to be employed must be of reasonable, strong-minded human beings and not those of weak and vacillating minds nor of those who scent danger in every hostile point of view.[58]

It is not permissible to stifle all free expression of opinion by imagining lurking dangers in every corner and discovering sharp curves and hair-pin bends when all that exists is a straight road.[59] Regard must be had to the theme of the article or the movie and its general tenor and drift. It is not right to pick up a strong expression here and there. The correct test is: what impression the article or movie as a whole would produce upon a man of ordinary common sense.[60]

In *R. Rajagopal v State of TN* the Supreme Court held that neither the government nor the officials who apprehend that they may be de-famed, had the right to impose a prior restraint upon the publication of the autobiography of Auto Shankar, a convict serving a sentence of death in jail, which was likely to reveal a nexus between criminals and high officials in the police. 'The remedy of public officials/public figures, if any, will arise only after the publication....'[61]

Onslaughts on freedom of expression can emanate also from groups or individuals who demand the banning of a book or a movie which appears offensive or hurtful to them. Recently a determined effort was made to ban the exhibition of a movie by a group of persons who re-garded its theme and its presentation as hostile to the policy of reserva-tion of jobs in public employment and seats in educational institutions in favour of scheduled castes and backward classes, for whose benefit special provisions by way of protective or compensatory discrimination are enacted in the Constitution of India. The Madras High Court[62] in an incredible judgement, revoked the certificate granted by the Board of Censors permitting exhibition of the film and restrained its exhibi-tion.

In a landmark decision, the Supreme Court promptly reversed the high court judgement and ruled: 'Our commitment to freedom of ex-pression demands that it cannot be suppressed, unless the situations created by allowing the freedom are pressing and the community inter-est is endangered. The anticipated danger should not be remote, con-jectural or far-fetched.'[63] The Court apparently applied the test of 'clear and present danger'. It approved the observations of the European Court of Human Rights that 'freedom of expression protects not merely ideas that are accepted but those that offend, shock or disturb the State or any sector of the population. Such are the demands of the pluralism, tolerance and broadmindedness without which there is no democratic society.'[64] The Court laid down a vital principle:

If the film is unobjectionable and cannot constitutionally be restricted under Article 19(2), freedom of expression cannot be suppressed on account of threats of demonstrations and processions or threats of violence. That would be tantamount to negation of the rule of law and surrender to blackmail and intimidation. Freedom of expression which is legitimate and constitutionally protected cannot be held to ransom by an intolerant group of people.[65]

This judgement has far-reaching implications. Its wholesome effect and timeliness cannot be overemphasized in view of the rising intolerance of late witnessed in India. Tranquillity ought to be maintained in all cases by sacrifice of liberty. In order to prevent a threat to law and order, the State should not suppress freedom of expression, which it is the duty of every democratic state to uphold.

Another instance of a judicial gag order was the injunction issued by the Aurangabad Bench of the Bombay High Court temporarily injuncting the telecast of episodes 12 and 13 of a serial entitled *Honi Anhoni*. The Supreme Court reversed the order of the High Court. It observed that 'freedom of expression is a preferred right which is always very zealously guarded by this Court' and 'in the absence of any prima facie evidence of grave prejudice that was likely to be caused to the public generally by the exhibition of the serial it was not just and proper to issue an order of temporary injunction'.[66] The Supreme Court left open the question whether a citizen has a fundamental right to establish a private broadcasting station or television centre.

One of the heads on which freedom of the media can be restricted under the Indian Constitution is 'decency or morality'. In matters of morality and obscenity courts do not always reflect contemporary standards and perceptions though they purport to do so. 'Obscenity', 'indecency', 'immorality' are equivocal and relative concepts. Sin, as Pascal reminds us, is geographical. Standards of morality and decency in the same society vary from time to time and from person to person, and there is no uniform test of community standards of acceptance.

Judges, despite valiant efforts, have failed to evolve a satisfactory definition of obscenity. The Federal Court of Appeal in Canada[67] concluded that the expressions 'immoral' and 'indecent' are highly subjective and emotive, and freedom of expression cannot be restricted on these grounds because uncertainty and vagueness are unconstitutional vices when they are used to restrict guaranteed rights and freedoms. The judicial predicament is vividly summed up in the lament of Justice Stewart of the US Supreme Court who confessed that he could not define obscenity but recognized it when he saw it.[68] Apparently, obscenity, like beauty, lies in the eyes of the beholder.

The least unsatisfactory position would be to restrict obscenity and indecency laws only to publications and movies which are patently offensive and in which exploitation of the prurient interest in sex is the sole motive and object without the slightest redeeming feature in terms of art, literature, or any other discipline.

D.H. Lawrence's novel, *Lady Chatterley's Lover* was held to be obscene by the Supreme Court in the case of *Ranjit Udeshi* decided on 19 August 1964. The Court came to the surprising conclusion that the book was obscene judged 'from our community standards and there is no social gain to us which can be said to preponderate'.[69]

Two decades later, in 1985, the Supreme Court adopted a less illiberal approach in *Samaresh v Amal Mitra*[70] and held that the Bengali novel, *Prajapati*, was not obscene 'merely because slang and unconventional words have been used in the book in which there has been emphasis on sex and description of female bodies'.[71] The Court emphasized that vulgarity was not synonymous with obscenity.

In India vulgarity and strong erotic language are often treated as interchangeable with obscenity. In its recent judgement concerning the movie, *The Bandit Queen*,[72] the Court ruled that neither nudity nor vulgarity can necessarily be equated with obscenity. It endorsed the observations in its previous decision in *Samaresh Bose v Amal Mitra*,[73] in the context of a novel that, 'If a reference to sex by itself in any novel is considered to be obscene and not fit to be read by adolescents, adolescents will not be in a position to read any novel and will have to read books which are purely religious'. With reference to the objected brief scene of frontal nudity of Phoolan Devi, the bandit, the Court observed:

Nakedness does not always arouse the baser instinct. The reference by the Tribunal to the film *Schindler's List* was apt. There is a scene in it of rows of naked men and women, shown frontally, being led into the gas chambers of a Nazi concentration camp. Not only are they about to die but they have been stripped in their last moments of the basic dignity of human beings. Tears are a likely reaction; pity, horror and a fellow feeling of shame are certain, except in the pervert who might be aroused. We do not censor to protect the pervert or to assuage the susceptibilities of the over-sensitive.[74]

Defamation is one of the heads of restrictions specified in the Constitution. Libel laws can have a chilling effect on freedom of the press. The United States Supreme Court in its landmark decision in *New York Times v Sullivan*[75] ruled that every inaccurate statement should not be actionable unless it is made with malice, i.e. with actual knowledge of the falsity of the statement or with reckless and utter disregard of the true state of affairs. This is because erroneous statements are unavoidable in free debate in a democracy and must be tolerated if freedom of expression is to have 'the breathing space it needs to survive'. These principles have been approved by the House of Lords in the *Derbyshire*

County Council case. The Lords recognized that threat of a civil action for defamation must inevitably have an inhibiting effect on freedom of speech. It enunciated a very salutary principle, namely, that 'it would be contrary to public interest to permit institutions of government to sue for libel because that would place an undesirable fetter on freedom of speech'.[76]

The Supreme Court of India in its path-breaking judgement in *R. Rajagopal v State of TN*[77] approved of the *Sullivan* and *Derbyshire County Council* cases and *inter alia* laid down that

... even where the publication is based upon facts and statements which are not true, unless the official establishes that the publication was made [by the defendant] with reckless disregard for truth. In such a case, it would be enough for the defendant [member of the press or media] to prove that he acted after a reasonable verification of the facts; it is not necessary for him to prove that what he has written is true. Of course, where the publication is proved to be false and actuated by malice or personal animosity, the defendant would have no defence and would be liable for damages.[78]

Contempt is another head of restriction on freedom of expression and freedom of the Press. The Supreme Court has upheld the constitutionality of the Contempt of Courts Act, 1952 on the ground that the Act did not impose unreasonable restrictions on the right of freedom of speech and is saved under Article 19(2).[79] The High Courts of Patna and Delhi have held that the expression 'contempt of court' has a set meaning given to it by judicial pronouncements. The fact that the Contempt of Courts Act, 1952 did not define the expression 'contempt of court' did not render the statute so vague and indefinite as to make it unconstitutional.[80] It is submitted that the same reasoning would apply to the Contempt of Court Act, 1971, which is not substantially different.

Courts have frowned upon comments made in the press upon pending cases. The Punjab High Court ruled that 'liberty of the press is subordinate to the proper administration of justice. The plain duty of a journalist is the reporting and not the adjudication of cases.'[81] In the view of the Orissa High Court, 'the responsibility of the press is greater than the responsibility of an individual because the press has a larger audience. The freedom of the press should not degenerate into a licence to attack litigants and close the door of justice nor can it include any unrestricted liberty to damage the reputation of respectable persons.'[82]

The judiciary has provided generous protection to freedom of the press in several cases. One should have thought that the judiciary and the press are natural allies. Both the press and the judiciary perform in their own way the function of checking and controlling abuse of governmental authority. This function is performed by the press by exposing deception and secrecy in the working of the government, be it Watergate or Bofors, or the housing or fodder scam. The courts perform their role by enforcing accountability of the holders of power. Unfortunately they appear like natural adversaries in cases where the court punishes journalists in exercise of its contempt jurisdiction. In practice the law of contempt in India is an instance of the paradox of the love–hate relationship between the press and the judiciary.

Any person, including the press, is free to criticize a judgement, to comment on it pungently, severely, because justice is not a cloistered virtue and can suffer the outbursts of even the wrongheaded. However, it is an altogether different matter to impute motives to the judges who have delivered the judgement: to accuse them of dishonesty or having been swayed by extraneous considerations.

But what then is the position if the charge happens to be true and the journalist is prepared to establish it to the hilt by unimpeachable documentary evidence? That is the vexed question. Today under the law of contempt as it stands and has been interpreted in India, the country which proclaims *satyameva jayate*, truth is no defence to an action for contempt.[83] If a person attempts to establish his allegations of misconduct against a judicial officer that will be regarded as an aggravation of contempt.

This is a serious anomaly. Indeed, it is highly arguable that rejection of the plea at the threshold for establishment of the truth of the allegations operates as an unreasonable restriction on the freedom of the press. It prevents exposure of corruption in the judiciary which, regrettably, is to some extent prevalent. Consequently many journalists and media persons succumb to self-censorship and are deterred from exposing the misconduct of some errant judges. It is a mistaken notion that an enforced silence by the threatened use of the contempt power leads to enhancement of the public image of the judiciary when corruption within some of its ranks is the talk of the town. A corrupt judge should not get away under the shield of the law of contempt and thereby successfully suppress disclosure of his misdeeds. Our contempt law should be amended to provide the defence of truth coupled with public interest. It should also provide for imposition of stiff civil and criminal penalties upon a person who fails to substantiate his allegations. This would discourage frivolous and baseless allegations being levelled by disgruntled litigants or persons motivated by ill will.

An important question regarding use and control of the electronic media and airwaves and frequencies was decided by the Supreme Court in *Secretary, Ministry of I&B v Cricket Association of Bengal.*[84] The Court ruled that 'the right to communicate includes right to communicate through any media that is available whether print or electronic or audio-visual such as advertisement, movie, article, speech etc. ... This freedom includes the freedom to communicate or circulate one's opinion without interference to as large a population in the country, as well as abroad, as is possible to reach.'[85] At the same time, the Court recognized that 'since the airwaves/frequencies are public property and are also limited, they have to be used in the best interest of the society and this can be done either by a central authority by establishing its own broadcasting network or regulating the grant of licences to other agencies, including the private agencies.'[86] It directed that 'the central government shall take immediate steps to establish an independent autonomous public authority representatives of all sections and interests in the society to control and regulate the use of the airwaves.'[87]

The Supreme Court of India recently had to deal with the issue of the right of reply. Professor Manubhai Shah published a study paper which was strongly critical of the working of the Life Insurance Corporation (LIC). A reply to Professor Shah's article was published in *Yogakshema,* a magazine of the LIC. Shah's request that his article should also be published in the same magazine was refused. The Supreme Court applied the fairness doctrine and held that LIC's refusal was 'unfair because fairness demanded that both viewpoints were placed before the readers'.[88] The attention of the Supreme Court was not drawn to the advisory opinion of the Inter-American Court of Human Rights delivered on 29 August 1986 and consequently the Supreme Court had no occasion to consider the social dimension of the right to reply based on the important premise that 'the formation of public opinion based on true information is indispensable to the existence of a vital democratic society'.[89]

On the basis of the recommendation of the First Press Commission, Parliament passed the Parliamentary Proceedings (Protection of Publication) Act, 1956. The object of this Act was to define the privilege available to publications made in good faith of reports of proceedings of either House of Parliament whether in a newspaper or by wireless telegraphy. Under the Act, except in cases where the publication of report of any proceedings of Parliament was not for the public good, no person was liable to any proceedings, civil or criminal, in any court in respect of the publication in a newspaper of a substantially true report of any proceedings of either House of Parliament, unless the publication was proved to have been made with malice.

The Act was repealed by Parliament in 1976 during the emergency and the privilege which was being enjoyed by the press for nearly twenty years was lost. The next year, however, the privilege was restored by re-enacting the law on the subject, namely the Parliamentary Proceedings (Protection of Publication) Act, 1977. The law on the subject was also accorded constitutional protection by the Constitution (Forty-fourth Amendment) Act, 1978 whereby a new article 361A was introduced in the Constitution making impossible for Parliament to deprive the privilege by passing an ordinary law by a simple majority. The Article which came into force on 20 June 1979 reads as under;

361A. Protection of publication of proceedings of Parliament and State Legislatures.
(1) No person shall be liable to any proceedings, civil or criminal, in any court in respect of the publication in a newspaper of a substantially true report of any proceedings of either House of Parliament or the Legislative Assembly, or, as the case may be, either House of the Legislature of a State, unless the publication is proved to have been made with malice.
Provided that nothing in this clause shall apply to the publication of any report of the proceedings of a secret sitting of either House of Parliament or the Legislative Assembly, or, as the case may be, either House of the Legislature of a State.
(2) Clause (1) shall apply in relation to reports or matters broadcast by means of wireless telegraphy as part of any programme or service provided by means of a broadcasting station as it applies in relation to reports or matters published in a newspaper.
Explanation: In this article, 'newspaper' includes a news agency report containing material for publication in a newspaper.

The provisions of Article 361A extend to proceedings of state legislatures as well. Hence, separate legislation by the states would no longer be necessary. The immunity conferred by Article 361A would be available equally to reports of union and state legislatures, and it makes no difference between civil and criminal proceedings or liability.

The Privy Council in the case of *Arnold v Emperor* opined that 'it is a time-worn fallacy that some kind of special privilege attaches to the profession of the Press and the position of a journalist. His privilege is no other and no higher than that of a member of the public'.[90] Our Supreme Court has endorsed that position in the *Sharma* case.[91] None the less, decisions of the Supreme Court on the whole reveal a judicial soft spot for freedom of the press.

What could be the reason? A close analysis would indicate that one of the main considerations for this judicial solicitude is that freedom of the press embraces a variety of rights. The right guaranteed is not merely the individual right of the proprietor of the newspaper, or the editor, or the journalist. It includes within its capacious content the collective right of the community; the right of citizens to read and to be informed. In substance, it is right of the public to know. The Right to Know has been spelled out by the Supreme Court from the guarantee of free speech in Article 19(1)(a) in its path-breaking judgement in *S.P. Gupta*.[92]

The Right to Know is not meant for gratifying idle curiosity or mere inquisitiveness but is essential for the effective functioning of democracy. Transparency and accountability are *sine qua non* in a genuine democracy. In the memorable words of Justice Mathew: 'The people of this country have a right to know every public act, everything that is done in a public way, by their public functionaries. They are entitled to know the particulars of every public transaction in all its bearing.'[93] This enables citizens to make intelligent and informed decisions amongst a variety of choices and thus play their part in controlling the government and enforcing the accountability of the holders of power. As recent events have shown informed public opinion is a potent check on maladministration. 'The purpose of the press is to advance the public interest by publishing facts and opinions without which a democratic electorate cannot make responsible judgements.'[94]

The ground realities are that a citizen is largely dependent on the press for the quality, proportion, and the extent of news. He can seldom obtain for himself the information necessary for the intelligent discharge of his political duties and responsibilities. In disseminating news, the press therefore acts as the representative or, more appropriately, as the custodian of the public. It serves public interest in a pluralistic democracy by permitting expression of opinions and views of all persons, parties and interests and projecting a broad spectrum of views. Hence freedom of the press has a dimension and range that is vastly different from the ambit and content of other individual freedoms. Press freedom embodies the principle of accountability and thus enables the press to be an instrument of democratic control. Protection and promotion of freedom of the press in substance subserves and strengthens democracy, an essential feature of our Constitution.

If we have not grasped the true rationale for judicial solicitude for freedom of the press and the true rationale of press freedom then freedom of the press is a hollow slogan, a narrow self-serving concept, and the judicial encomiums showered on it are undeserved rhetorical flourishes.

We rightly prize press freedom and should be vigilant in repelling encroachments, direct or indirect, on the exercise of this precious freedom. Freedom of the press is undoubtedly one of the basic freedoms in a democratic society based on the Rule of Law. None the less, freedom of the press is not an end in itself. It is the means to the attainment of a democratic society in which law and order prevail, there is good governance, transparency in administration, enforcement of accountability of the wielders of power, and where human dignity and other human rights are respected. Whilst we must vigorously defend this freedom against onslaughts from fanatics, one should not be fanatical about it and forget that freedom of the press entails social responsibility. The public function which belongs to the press makes it an obligation of honour to exercise this function with the fullest sense of responsibility.

Thomas Jefferson, who had more than a normal amount of tolerance for the frailties of the press, said in 1802: 'It is a melancholy truth that a suppression of the press could not more completely deprive the nation of its benefits, than is done by its abandoned prostitution to falsehood. Nothing can now be believed which is seen in a newspaper. Truth itself becomes suspicious by being put into that polluted vehicle.'[95]

Joseph Pulitzer pointed out that 'commercialism has a legitimate place in a newspater, namely, in the business office ... But commercialism, which is proper in the business office, becomes a degradation and a danger when it invades the editorial rooms. Once let the publisher come to regard the press as exclusively a commercial business and there is an end of its moral power.'[96] According to him, 'without high ethical ideals a newspaper not only is stripped of its splendid possibilities for public service, but may become a positive danger to the community.'[97]

Our Supreme Court has observed that the press is a mighty institution wielding enormous powers which are expected to be exercised for the protection and the good of the people. The press must observe self-imposed restrictions. Otherwise there is the risk of public interest being jeopardized. Liberty of the press is not to be confused with its licentiousness.[98]

Should the press fail to play its true societal role, can it legitimately or morally invoke the benefit and protection of the constitutional guarantee of freedom of the press? A newspaper that systematically and intentionally suppresses or manipulates information, restricts the content of information, and denies its accessibility to the public who are its readers betrays its true role and forfeits its trust as the trustee of a vital public resource. It is no longer the educator of the public, it has ceased to be its watchdog and sentinel and it no longer guards the Ark of the Covenant of democracy. It is arguable that a press which has persistently failed to perform its proper role cannot legitimately lay claim to its strict protection under Article 19(2). Such a newspaper may yet claim the fundamental right to carry on trade and business in which case the scope for imposition of restrictions is wider than in the case of freedom of expression or freedom of the press.

The vexed problem however is who will determine whether the newspaper in question has so disentitled itself. The insidious entry of censorship in such situations poses a greater danger. Therefore rather than indulge further in such subversive thoughts, on balance we may console ourselves with the regret of Madison, 'that it is better to leave a few of its noxious branches to their luxuriant growth, than, by pruning them away, injure the vigour of those yielding the proper fruits'.[99]

Press freedom will depend not on the state of the laws or the provisions of the Constitution but on the integrity and independence of the press. 'Over the years, Governments in different parts of the world have used diverse methods to keep press under control. They have followed carrot-and-stick methods.'[100] Lippman has rightly warned that the real danger to the press springs not so much from the pressures and intimidation to which it may be subject but from the sad fact that journalists can be captured and captivated by the company they keep, their constant exposure to the subtleties of power. Judicial protection is certainly helpful but that is not the sovereign remedy. It is trite that civil liberties do not defend themselves. Freedoms cannot be preserved for an inert people by the Constitution or the courts. That is true of presss freedom too. That lesson was bitterly brought home during the spurious June 1975 emergency. With few honourable exceptions, the press chose to crawl when it was required to bend. Editors were keen to retain their jobs, and printers did not want to risk forfeiture of their presses.

In the ultimate analysis, the reality of press freedom will be realized by the will and determination of its champions and defenders to assert their rights and to defend this cherished freedom, remembering at all times the spirit of Benjamin Franklin's admonition to his compatriots: 'They who would give up essential liberty to purchase a little temporary safety deserve neither liberty nor safety.'[101]

Notes

[1] Nehru's speech on 20 June 1916 in protest against the Press Act, 1910.

[2] *Constituent Assembly Debates*, Vol. VII, pp. 714–16.

[3] Ibid., at p. 780.

[4] B. Shiva Rao, *The Framing of India's Constitution: A Study*, pp. 219–20.

[5] *Brij Bhushan v State of Delhi* AIR 1950 SC 129; *Express Newspapers Ltd v Union of India* AIR 1958 SC 578; *Sakal Papers Ltd v Union of India* AIR 1962 SC 305; *Bennett Coleman Co. v Union of India* AIR 1973 SC 106.

[6] 25 IA 1.

[7] 1940 AC 231.

[8] AIR 1947 PC 82.

[9] *Supra* n. 2, p. 731.

[10] *Romesh Thapar* AIR 1950 SC 124; *Brij Bhushan* AIR 1950 SC 129.

[11] *Romesh Thapar* AIR 1950 SC 124.

[12] *Brij Bhushan* AIR 1950 SC 129.

[13] In *re: Bharati Press* AIR 1951 Pat (SB) 12 (per Sarjoo Prasad and Ramaswamy JJ) Shearer J dissenting.

[14] *Amar Nath v State* AIR 1951 Punj (SB) 18.

[15] *State of Bihar v Shailabala Devi* AIR 1952 SC 329.

[16] *Madhu Limaye v Sub-Divisional Magistrate* AIR 1971 SC 2486 at 2491.

[17] Ibid., at 2491 (para 5).

[18] *Sakal Papers (P) Ltd v Union of India* AIR 1962 SC 305.

[19] *Chintaman Rao v State of Madhya Pradesh* AIR 1951 SC 118 at 119; *State of Madras v V.G. Rao* AIR 1952 SC 196 at 199, 200; *Tikaramji v State of Uttar Pradesh* AIR 1956 SC 676 at 711; *Express Newspapers* AIR 1958 SC 578 at 621; *State of Bihar v R.N. Mishra* AIR 1971 SC 1667.

[20] *Supra* n. 18, *Sakal Papers; Bennett Coleman & Co. v Union of India* AIR 1973 SC 106.

[21] *Supra* n. 16, *Madhu Limaye*, at 2493.

[22] *Bennett Coleman & Co. v Union of India* AIR 1973 SC 106.

[23] *Supra* n. 18, *Sakal Papers*.

[24] Ibid., at 315.

[25] Ibid.

[26] Ibid.

[27] *Supra* n. 22, *Bennett Coleman*.

[28] Ibid., at 117, para 29.

[29] Ibid., at 130.

[30] Ibid., at 126.

[31] *Ushodaya Publications (P) Ltd. v Govt. of Andhra Pradesh* AIR 1981 AP 109.

[32] *Express Newspapers Ltd v Union of India* AIR 1958 SC 578.

[33] *Indian Express Newspapers v Union of India* AIR 1986 SC 515.

[34] Ibid., at 540.

[35] *Supra* notes 18, 22.

[36] *Supra* n. 32.

[37] *Hamdard Dawakhana (Wakf) Lal Kuan v Union of India* (1960) 2 SCR 671.

[38] *Lewis J. Valentine v F.J. Chrestensen* 316 US 52.

[39] *Supra* n. 33, *Indian Express Newspapers*.

[40] *Tata Press Ltd v Mahanagar Telephone Nigam Ltd.* (1995) 5 SCC 139 at 154.

[41] *Supra* n. 27, *Bennett Coleman*, at 199; *Maneka Gandhi* AIR 1978 SC 597 at 635.

[42] *A.K. Gopalan v State of Madras* AIR 1950 SC 27; *Ram Singh v State of Delhi* AIR 1951 SC 270; *Hamdard Dawakhana* AIR 1960 SC 554; *Naresh v State of Maharashtra* AIR 1967 SC 1.

[43] *Indulal Yagnik v State* AIR 1963 Guj 259.

[44] 1931 283 US 697.

[45] Ibid., at 716.

[46] *Supra* n. 12, *Brij Bhushan*.

[47] *Virendra Kumar v State of Punjab* AIR 1957 SC 896.

[48] Ibid., at 903.

[49] Soli J. Sorabjee, *The Emergency Censorship and the Press in India 1975–77*, 1977 p. 13.

[50] Ibid., at 31, 27, 29.

[51] 1976 78 Bom. L.R. 125.

[52] Ibid., at 169.

[53] Ibid.

[54] *C. Vaidya v H.D'Penha* in Sp.CA 141/1976, 22 March 1976 (unreported).

[55] *T.G. Barua & Ors. v State of Assam* CR No.4/81 1983 1 GLR (NOC) 12 decided on 6 May 1981.

[56] AIR 1971 SC 481 at 489.

[57] Ibid., at 498.

[58] *Bhagwati Charan v Provincial Government* AIR 1947 Nag 1; *Ramesh v Union of India* (1988) 1 SCC 668 at 675.

[59] *Supra* n. 51.

[60] *Shailabala Devi* AIR 1952 SC 329; *Badri Narayan v Chief Secretary, Bihar Government* AIR 1941 Pat 132 (SB).

[61] (1994) 6 SCC 632 at 649.

[62] Judgement dated 29 April 1988 in WR 469/488 of 1988.

[63] *S. Rangarajan v P.J. Ram* (1989) 2 SCR 204.

[64] Ibid., at 229, citing *Handyside v United Kingdom* (1976) 1 EHRR 737.

[65] Ibid., at 230.

[66] *Odyssey Communication Pvt. Ltd v Lokvidayan Sanghatana* AIR 1988 SC 1642 at 1645.

[67] *Re Luscher and Deputy Minister, Revenue Canada* 17 DLR (4th) 503.

[68] *Jacobellis v Ohio* 12 L 2d 793 at 804 (per Justice Stewart).

[69] AIR 1965 SC 881 at 891.

[70] AIR 1986 SC 967.

[71] Ibid., at 983.

[72] *Bobby Art International v Om Pal Singh Hoon* (1996) 4 SCC 1.

[73] *Supra* n. 69.

[74] *Supra* n. 72, *Bobby Art Internatinal* at 15.

[75] 376 US 254.

[76] *Derbyshire County Council v Times Newspapers Ltd* (1993) AC 534.

[77] *Supra* n. 61.

[78] Ibid., at 650.

[79] *C.K. Daphtary v O.P. Gupta* AIR 1971 SC 1132.

[80] *Legal Remembrancer v Bibhuti Bhushan* AIR 1954 Pat 203; *E.T. Sen v E. Narayanan* AIR 1969 Del 201 (F.B.). The Contempt of Courts Act, 1971 defines contempt vide sections 2(a) and (b) of the Act.

[81] *Rao Harnarain v Gumori Ram* AIR 1958 Punj 273.

[82] *Bijoyananda v Bala Krishna* AIR 1953 Ori 249.

[83] *Supra* n. 79, *C.K. Daphtary* at 1146–7.

[84] (1995) 2 SCC 161.

[85] Ibid., at 213.

[86] Ibid., at 226.

[87] Ibid., at 252.

[88] *Life Insurance Corporation of India v Manubhai Shah* (1992) 3 SCC 637.

[89] *Enforceability of the Right of Reply or Correction,* Advisory Opn. OC-7/85 of 29 August 1986.

[90] AIR 1914 PC 116.

[91] *M.S.M. Sharma v Sri Krishna Sinha* AIR 1959 SC 395.

[92] AIR 1982 SC 149.

[93] *State of UP v Raj Narain* AIR 1975 SC 865 at 884.

[94] *Supra* n. 33, *Indian Express Newspapers* at 527.

[95] Gerald Gross (ed.), *The Responsibility of the Press,* Clarion Books, New York, 1966, pp. 39–40.

[96] Ibid., at 42.

[97] Ibid.

[98] *Virendra v State of Punjab* AIR 1957 SC 896; *Santokh Singh v Delhi Administration* AIR 1973 SC 1091 at 1094.

[99] Referred to in *Near v Minnesota, supra* n. 44, at 718; see also *Romesh Thapar,* supra n. 11, at 29.

[100] *Supra* n. 33, *Indian Express Newspapers* at 527.

[101] Referred to in Soli J. Sorabjee, *supra* n. 50 at p. 25.

Eighteen

Justice Between Generations: Environment and Social Justice

Harish Salve

Introduction

And the Lord God formed man of the dust of the ground, and breathed into his nostrils the breath of life; and man became a living soul.

And the Lord God planted a garden eastward in Eden; and there he put the man whom he had formed.

And the Lord God took the man, and put him into the garden of Eden to dress it and to keep it.

And the Lord God commanded the man, saying, Of every tree of the garden thou mayest freely eat:

And Man's appetite not satiated by the fruits, he used his knowlege to create more and more for himself, and in the process ravaged the garden by felling its trees, contaminating its waters, and polluting its air. The history of mankind is a story of violation of God's commands and an abuse of everything that God nature has given us.

That the earth and its environ are God's munificence and should be treated with sanctity is a common thread that runs through all faiths. An old Hindu prayer runs as follows:

the earth is our mother, and we are all her children. Supreme Lord, let there be peace in the sky and in the atmosphere, peace in the plant world and in the forests; let the cosmic powers be peaceful; let Brahma be peaceful; let there be undiluted and fulfilling peace everywhere.[1]

The Christians are baptized in water; a sign of purification. In the Lotus Sutra, the Buddha is presented metaphorically as a rain cloud, covering, permeating, fertilizing, and enriching all parched living beings,[2] yet, having discovered the means of mass production and concomitant wealth untold, man forgot the sanctity of mother nature, of the generations to come, his fellow man, himself! The production of wealth for the aggrandizement of those who had secured for themselves access to the means of production was the only end in sight. It was the era of 'sweatshops'—whither social justice!

Tracing the history of the law in Europe Richard Burnett-Hall, in his reputed treatise *Environment Law* says: 'Historically, water, air and (to a degree) land have been treated as free resources that industry has been able to pollute at little or no cost to itself, and thereby pass on to the community, directly or indirectly, costs attributable to its own operations'. This attitude reflects the thinking of the times. Property rights had primacy in that what a person did on his property was his business; its deleterious effects on the life of others was of little significance.

History has proved that nature, if defied, teaches a vicious lesson. The unabated molestation of nature took a predictable toll: pollution of the air and water resulted in hitherto unknown diseases manifesting themselves, first amongst the workers immediately exposed to the hazardous activity, and then amongst those living in the vicinity of such industries.

The United Kingdom represents an interesting example of the hesitant recognition accorded to the significance of the environment. The remarkable growth of the English industry in the nineteenth century was largely unchecked by pollution controls despite its acute adverse effect on the health of the people; and all in the name of national prosperity. The first attempt at legislative control of air pollution was the Alkali Act of 1863 provoked by the illnesses manifested by workers employed in those industries. The smog of December 1952 (allegedly the cause of 4000 deaths in London alone) led to the passage of the Clean Air Act of 1956, which was updated periodically and finally replaced by the Clean Air Act of 1993.

In the fullness of time, political upheavals brought home the realization that freedom can only survive if it honours basic human rights and is founded on principles of social justice: the emergence of the socialist bloc of countries post Second World War has had a cathartic effect on the free world. Indeed, there is no area of social justice as important as the environment. Every activity that impinges upon the environment affects not just the actor but his immediate neighbours, distant neighbours, and eventually humanity as a whole. When it comes to the environment, the world is a global village. The principles of environmental law that have evolved—nationally and internationally—have to be viewed against this backdrop.

Evolution of Environmental Laws

There is now, the world over, a proliferation of environmental laws operating at various levels: in the states (in a federal system), at the national level, and also at the international level. Perceptions differ; for the legal profession it is the new sunrise industry! For the manufacturing industry it is the new roadblock standing between it and prosperity. Interestingly, that and the succeeding Alkali Acts, form the basis of air pollution control in the UK.

Environmental laws are now almost fifty years old. (Emission control laws in California date back to 1955 as do the Clean Air laws in the UK.) The industrially developed nations have been experimenting with anti-pollution laws, with mixed success.

However, on the eve of the millennium, looking back, the most significant development has been *international recognition* of the need for the protection of the environment, and this as a facet of social justice—and not just between persons of the same generation but also between the present and the future. The Declaration of the United Nations Conference on the Human Environment, adopted at Stockholm on 16 June 1972, represents the first structured attempt by the influential nations of the world to acknowledge that environmental degradation was a global problem, and not just a series of isolated misadventures such as the pollution of the Thames river or the smog caused by too many cars in California. It recognized that development would have to be conditioned to the needs of the environment, and that in balancing the equities, justice between nations was vital. It also was perhaps the first multilateral attempt to define the parameters that would form the basis of controlling environmental degradation by human activity, although at that stage the primary focus was industrial activity.

The Declaration of Stockholm enunciates twenty-six principles. The first segment of the first principle illuminates the fundamental change in attitude. It says:

Man has the *fundamental right to freedom, equality and adequate conditions of life,* in an environment of a quality that permits a life of dignity and well-being, and he bears a solemn responsibility to protect and improve the environment for *present and future generations.*

It recognizes that 'in the developing countries most of the environmental problems are caused by under-development'. Millions continue to live far below the minimum levels required for a decent human existence, deprived of adequate food and clothing, shelter and education, health and sanitation. It calls upon the developing countries to '... direct their efforts to development, *bearing in mind* their priorities *and the need to safeguard and improve the environment'*. For the same purpose, the industrialized countries should make efforts to reduce the gap between themselves and the developing countries.

Principles 5 and 9 focus on social justice, mandating that 'The non-renewable resources of the earth must be employed in such a way as to guard against the danger of their future exhaustion and to ensure that benefits from such employment are *shard by all mankind....'*

Environmental deficiencies generated by the conditions of under-development and natural disasters pose grave problems and can best be remedied by accelerated development through the transfer of substantial quantities of financial and technological assistance as a supplement to the domestic efforts of the developing countries and such timely assistance as may be required.

The Stockholm Declaration was followed by a number of international conventions and treaties. Of particular significance is the Rio Declaration of 1992, which once again focused on issues of social justice in the context of protection of the environment. The two most significant contributions of this Declaration are the development of the concept of 'sustainable development' and recognition of 'inter-generational equities'.

The first principle declares that: 'Human beings are at the centre of concerns for sustainable development. They are entitled to a healthy and productive life in harmony with nature'. Principle 3 propounds that '... The right to development must be fulfilled as to equitably meet development and environmental needs of *present and future generations'*.

These two treaties have significantly influenced the development of law in India. In the realm of statutory law, the Indian response to the Stockholm Declaration was the enactment of the Water Act in 1974[3] followed by the Air Act in 1981[4]. Both these statutes sought to control pollution by proscribing discharges/emissions in excess of the prescribed parameters, created statutory authorities (the Pollution Control Boards) to monitor and secure compliance with the laws, and provided for imposition of penalites and fines and prosecution of transgressors of the law. Enforcement has never been a known strength of our system, yet there can scarcely have been any laws that have proved to be as ineffectual as the pollution control statutes. There may however be some comfort in the thought that other nations have had similar problems in the containment of their pollution problems through similar laws. An article published in the *Dickinson Journal of Environmental Law and Policy* states:

... air pollution has become a serious health problem across the entire [*152] United States. One hundred fifty million Americans continue to breathe air that fails to meet national health-based standards for ozone pollution.

Senator Lieberman went on to state that 'research conducted at Harvard University indicates that air pollution may be a contributing factor in one out of every 20 deaths in the United States...'

... the Employer Trip Reduction Program (hereinafter ETRP) mandated by the 1990 Clean Air Act ... requires employers of 100 employees or more to reduce the number of vehicles commuting to their workplaces.

The author notes that American citizens are unwilling to alter their driving habits without governmental intervention despite the severity of the automotive emission pollution problem.[5]

An article in the *UCLA Journal of Environment Law and Policy*, written as recently as 1992 (considering automobile pollution containment efforts date back to the mid-fifties) states:

The air pollution which hangs over many cities in the United States remains a serious environmental problem, caused in large part by our reliance on the automobile. Separating individual Americans from their automobiles continues to be a personally and politically unpopular, but necessary, element of efforts to reduce air pollution. These efforts, embodied in the federal Clean Air Act,... must succeed so that over one hundred million Americans can once again breathe clean air.[6]

The problem of enforcement of these laws is so piquant, that one view now propounded is the route of negotiations as a way to enforcement. In an article written in the *Harvard Environment Law Review* (1999),[7] the authors suggest that:

Negotiation—as an alternative or an adjunct to the adversarial process—increasingly is touted as the wave of the future. It is argued that negotiation is a more efficient use of societal resources, because it is more likely to produce a result that all sides can accept....

First, there is negotiated rulemaking, whereby negotiation is used to help set regulatory standards....

Second, negotiated implementation is used to determine how regulatory standards, once set, are to be applied to a particular firm or other members of the regulated community....

Third, negotiated compliance is used to determine the terms by which regulatory standards will be enforced against a particular firm or other regulated entity that is out of compliance with those standards. By its nature, of course, almost all enforcement involves some amount of negotiation between the enforcing agency (or, in the case of citizen enforcement suits, the enforcing citizen) and the alleged violator....

The degradation of Indian forests was sought to be contained by the enactment of the Forest Conservation Act in 1980; the forests continue to be depleted while the Forest Policy of 1988 emphasizes the need to increase forest cover.

Unfortunately, reports written in purple prose cannot mask the failure of the administration. State after state publishes reports about the great work achieved in the area of afforestation, some celebrating Van Mahotsavs to pat themselves on their back, and yet the *Forest Survey Reports* compiled through satellite imaging reveal incessant depletion of the forest cover in the significant areas covered by dense forests.

The proactive Supreme Court of the 1980s was surely not going to turn its face on executive apathy in an area so critical to human existence. This led to a step by step development of a body of environment law in Indian jurisprudence, the credit for which goes entirely to the Court.

Common Law Principles

In order to appreciate the true significance of the path-braking decisions of the Supreme Court in this branch of law, it is necessary to briefly trace the existing (or more appropriately, non-existent) state of the law, particularly in the field of common law.

The initial relief against what would by current definitions constitute environmental pollution was obtained through the device of the tort of nuisance, an ancient tort of medieval origin, the essence of which was an act or omission that would constitute an interference with, disturbance of, or annoyance to a person in the exercise or enjoyment of either his ownership of occupation of land of some easement, property, or other right used or enjoyed in connection with the land (private nuisance) or to a right belonging to him as a member of the public (public nuisance).

In 1610, William Aldred brought an action against his neighbour Thomas Benton for building a pigsty so near his house that the air within was corrupted. Benton argued that the pigsty was necessary for the sustenance of men and one ought not to have so delicate a nose as cannot bear the smell of hogs. Mercifully, the court found in favour of William Aldred: clean air (then considered necessary for wholesome habitation), ordinary comfort, and necessity being the criteria. Significantly, the extent of a plaintiff's injury was measured in accordance with the contemporary standards of comfort.

The development of the law, however, centred around comfort in populated areas, and thus on the test based on 'localities' in industrial areas; the business of industries could not be made to suffer at the behest of individual discomfort. The House of Lords held that 'if a man lives in a town, it is necessary that he should subject himself to the consequences of those operations of trade which may be carried on in his immediate localities, which are actually necessary for trade and commerce ... and for the benefit of the inhabitants of the town and the public at large ...'. The application of the tort of private nuisance, narrowed by the test of localities, made it ineffective where it came to containing industrial pollution.[8] The number of cases reported in the nineteenth century shows that public nuisance did not play any significant role in the containment of damage to the environment.

The common law in India follows its British counterpart, with the added disincentive of coping with the Indian justice delivery system which can sometimes make a snail's pace seem rushed. Added to this was the pronounced disapproval of the contingent fee system which is perhaps the single most important factor in the development of 'Mass Tort' jurisprudence in the United States.

The real growth in the field of environmental law took place in the exercise of the original jurisdiction of the Supreme Court of India under Article 32 of the Constitution by way of enforcement of the right to a clean environment as a facet of the right to life itself.

European Community Law

The history of the law in the European Community is also instructive in terms of how it is interwoven with notions of social justice. Although the original Treaty of Rome did not contain any mention of the environment whatsoever, in October 1972 a declaration was made by the six EC member states recognizing that economic expansion is not an end in itself, and that 'as befits the genius of Europe, particular attention will be given to intangible values and to protecting the environment, so that progress may really be put at the service of mankind...'.[9] The Single European Act, which came into effect on 1 July 1987, made a specific provision that the Commission's proposals concerning *inter alia* environment protection would '... take as a base *a high level of protection*'. Article 100A of the Maastricht Treaty incorporated both the precautionary principle as well as the polluter pays principle. The first paragarph of Article 130S(2) states:

Community policy on the environment shall aim at a high level of protection taking into account the diversity of situations in the various regions of the community. It shall be based on the precautionary principle and on the principles that preventive action should be taken, that environmental damage should as a priority be rectified at source and that the polluter should pay ....

Thus a radical change in the philosophy of the law on the subject is apparent even in Europe, the law now being based on broad principles of social justice.

The Supreme Court of India and the Law of the Environment

The 1980s saw a sea-change in the perception of the law of the environment. However, any discussion of this must notice the paradigm changes in the concept of standing *(locus standi)* as also of the role of the Court.

The initial development of administrative law along traditional Anglo-Saxon lines brought in its wake the well-known limitations of *locus standi*, judicial remedies being available only upon the infringement or assertion of a legal right. The 'can't helps' of the judges of the sixties and even the early seventies would have perhaps stood in the way of their entertaining a direct petition in the Supreme Court for a direction to a State Pollution Control Board to close down an industry because it was not complying with a law that regulated emissions, and that too a petition at the behest of a stranger who did not live anywhere near the noxious industry.

The initiation of Public Interest Litigation, the timely demise of the law of standing, and expansive interpretation of Article 21 of the Constitution[10] paved the way for the development of a body of environment law through judicial edict. A historical account of the evolution of the institution (rather than a critique of its functioning) would suggest that the shift was really in the perception of the role of the institution. The perception of a conventional role of a final court of appeal meant for adjudication of disputes in the adversarial format changed to that of an institution as a vehicle for the delivery of justice, particularly to those who need it most and get it least. In a sentence, it represented a shift in emphasis from legalistic justice to social justice. In this process, restrictive dogmas such as rules of pleadings, rules of evidence, rules regarding standing to sue, etc. fell by the wayside.

The Court also 'discovered' the potential of Article 142 of the Constitution which could be used as a battering ram wherever procedural justice (or rather injustice) sought to bar social justice. It was a fascinating sight to see lawyers firmly and solemnly telling some of the judges that

'... no you can't; it's against the settled law', and the judges responding '... of course we can; we are the Supreme Court'.

Another remarkable feature of this evolution was the shift from mere enforcement of the statutory provision of the Air Act and Water Act to founding restitutionary as well as injunctive relief on the basis of constitutional jurisprudence and weaving environmental law buzzwords such as 'sustainable development', 'polluter pays', 'precautionary principle', 'doctrine of trust', and 'intergenerational equity' into Article 21 of the Constitution.

The problems that the Court faced in the area of environmental law were not only those of executive apathy in terms of non-enforcement of the law, but of a complete lack of sensitivity to the problem. It would be no exaggeration to say that sometimes it was not just that the executive had failed to find a solution to the problem; they had not even realized that they had a problem or the slightest idea of the dimensions of the problem! The most telling example of this is the vehicular pollution problem in Delhi. The capital has grown from a secretarial town to a sprawling megapolis covering 1600 sq. km. It now has almost 3 million vehicles on its roads. The official figure of pollution-related deaths has crossed the 10,000 mark, though NGOs working in the field believe that this is a mere fraction of the truth. A photograph of a non-smoker's lungs produced in the Supreme Court left the judges shocked: they looked like the lungs of someone addicted to Lady Nicotine. This notwithstanding, when for the first time the pollution control authorities were asked about ozone levels they betrayed a childlike innocence! Ozone levels far below those ordinarily present in Delhi have caused certain countries to declare a state of emergency: vehicular traffic in Paris was shut down when ozone levels reached a point which was below Delhi's average. In this case, the Supreme Court eventually 'persuaded' the government to appoint an authority under the Environment Protection Act, 1986, on whose reports the Court issues appropriate directives to ensure compliance.[11]

The consciousness of the Court towards environmental problems can be traced to the early 1980s, much before the Rio Treaty and long before the Court started reaching out to international treaties to provide a jurisprudential basis for its decisions. Although the expressions 'sustainable development', 'precautionary principle', and 'polluter pays' h~ become common currency amongst environmental law lawyers post I some of the earlier decisions of the Supreme Court also echo a sim, sentiment: e.g. the *Ratlam Municipal Council* case.[12]

The problem that presented itself before the Court was in one sense no different from a daily spectacle in the overpopulated townships of India: the absence of a proper drainage system creating the nuisance of garbage accumulation on the streets. The response of the Court was however fascinatingly different: it reached out to section 133 of the Criminal Procedure Code which confers upon the magistracy summary powers to give directions for abatement of a public nuisance and elected the judicial magistrate to frame a scheme to provide a working drainage system of sufficient capacity to meet the needs of the people. It rejected the plea of lack of finances, holding that the defence of financial constraints had '... no juridical basis'. The Court also warned the elected representatives of the public that they would open themselves to action under the law of tort were they to leave this problem unattended.

Around this time, when the Court heard the *Ratlam* case, and also delivered a judgement for the first time liberalizing the concept of *locus* in public interest litigation,[13] M.C. Mehta, a young lawyer who had decided that it was time to wage war on the polluters of this country, brought to the Court the problem of the rapidly deteriorating quality of the water of the Ganges. The Court issued directions to the municipal authorities from time to time to take appropriate steps to provide facilities to the citizens living in the towns on the banks of the river, and also to contain the industries that were mercilessly discharging toxic effluents into the river. In the first instance, the Court founded its directions on the statutory duty imposed upon the municipal authorities by legislation: the Water Act, the Air Act, and the Environment Protection Act, 1986. The basis for finding *locus* in favour of the petitioner is interesting: the Court held that while in common law the municipal corporation, in an action brought by a riparian owner, could be restrained by an injunction from discharging into the river insufficiently treated sewage, the petitioner, who was a person interested in protecting the lives of the people who lived on the banks of the river and would use the water flowing in the river, had a right to maintain such a petition.[14]

In directing the closure of the tanneries, the Court noted that 'the financial capacity of the tanneries should be considered as irrelevant while requiring them to establish primary treatment plants. Just like an industry which cannot pay minimum wages towards workers cannot be allowed to exist, tanneries which cannot set up a primary treatment plant cannot be permitted to continue to be in existence for the immense adverse effect on the public at large ...'. The Court also held that although closure of the tanneries might create unemployment and mean a loss of revenue, life, health, and ecology are of greater importance to the people[15]—which is the essence of 'sustainable development'.

The approach of the Court also reflects a departure from the 'proof of injury' approach that dogged Common Law. Non-compliance with prescribed standards was considered sufficient to grant injunctive relief without proof of actual pollution. This is an approach which assumes injury where standards are transgressed and not very different from the precautionary principle. The legal basis of the injunction is the transgression of law.

The Ganges case was only the beginning. In a large number of cases, the Court classified the cases by state, zone, and activity (e.g. the Calcutta tanneries) or by resource (e.g. state-wise pollution of the Yamuna), and examined the case of each polluting industry that fell within the purview of its scrutiny, giving time to each to set up treatment plants, pass orders of closure, etc. These orders were criticized as being bereft of any legal basis or reasoning, but then in the face of incontrovertible proof of non-conforming behaviour, where was the need to spell out any legal principle to grant relief!

The other criticism of this methodology, and with some justification, was that the Court took upon itself a task it was ill-equipped to handle, and for which it had to rely on the mercies of the very administration whose abject failure had brought this awful situation to come to pass. Industries were shut down or permitted to function on the say of the Pollution Control Board: a distillery once complained that it was tipped off of the surprise visit, and had drained its effluents replacing them with fresh water, only to be branded as a polluting unit upon a sample of such water! These criticisms cannot however detract from the awakening that has followed this endeavour of the Court.

There are however significant judgements of the Supreme Court which wove into the domestic law, international principles recognized by most countries as a common minimum basis for survival.

The law on standing to sue was summed up in the *Bangalore Medical Trust* case.[16] A public-spirited gentleman filed a petition in the high court assailing the allotment of a public park for the construction of a hospital. The high court quashed the allotment, and this decision was upheld by the Supreme Court. The Supreme Court held that the protection of the environment, open spaces for recreation and fresh air, are matters of great public concern and of vital interest to be taken care of in a development scheme. The residents of the locality are persons intimately, widely, and adversely affected by any action which is destructive of the environment and as such have the necessary *locus* to challenge such decisions. Mr Justice Sahai's leading opinion brings out clearly and candidly the change in the approach of the Court as a response to failing administration. Once the Court recast its sights and considered it a part of its constitutional duty to administer not just justice, as it was traditionally understood, but also to administer, within the parameters of judicial review, social and constitutional justice, the classic principle of *locus standi* had to fall by the wayside.

Although a full dress discussion of the vicissitudes of the doctrine of *locus standi* is beyond the scope of this essay, it bears mention that while relaxing the standards of standing, the Court did create an avenue for the unscrupulous to blackmail under the garb of public interest litigation. This problem has now been addressed by the Court by evolving an innovative procedure by which, at the first hint of any possible ill-motive on the part of the petitioner, the Court removes the petitioner without sacrificing the cause. This is achieved by appointing an amicus curiae and even rechristening[17] the the the matter as '*In re ...* etc'.

There were three important decisions post Rio which laid down, in judgements that repay study, the cardinal principles that have now come to be accepted as the law of the environment in India.

The first of these is the decision in *Indian Council for Enviro-Legal Action v Union of India*[18] in which the Court enunciated three independent legal bases for the award of monetary damages in a petition on Article 32 of the Constitution. Firstly, it relied upon Article 48A and Article 51-A of the Constitution, the provisions of the Air Act, Water Act, and the Environment Protection Act. It held that section 3 of the Environment Protection Act empowers the central government to take 'all such measures as it deems necessary or expedient for the purpose of protecting and improving the quality of the environment' and thus the Supreme Court could always direct the central government to determine and recover the cost of remedial measures from the offending industry.

Burying once and for all the ghost of *Rylands v Fletcher* (noticing that the Australian High Court had also expressed its disinclination to follow the *Rylands* rule as an independent head for claiming damages) it held that the statement of the law in the *Oleum Gas Leak* case[19] was more appropriate in the Indian context, and was also binding.[20] The principle affirmed therefore was that hazardous activity 'can be tolerated only on the condition that the enterprise, which uses such hazardous, odd or inherently dangerous activity indemnifies all those who suffer on account of carrying on of such hazardous, odd, inherently dangerous activity regardless of whether it is carried on carefully or not ...'.

The third legal basis was the 'polluter pays' principle. The Court held that sections 3 and 5 of the Environment (Protection) Act, 1986, empower the central government to give directions 'for giving effect to this principle'.

The shift from *Rylands v Fletcher* to the absolute liability principle is a clear policy choice made by the Court, and is entirely consistent with its reappraised role of being a Court closely concerned with the issues of social justice while *Rylands v Fletcher* was a relic of an era when industrial activity was given primacy. Equally, transplanting the doctrine of 'polluter pays' from an international treaty into existing domestic law by the mechanism of purposive interpretation of an existing statute[21] reflects the approach of the Court to fill gaps in the law without waiting for legislative intervention.

This decision was followed by two more important decisions, once again dealing with pollution caused by tanneries (possibly just a coincidence) in two separate parts of India: West Bengal and Tamil Nadu. The significance of the *Tamil Nadu* case [22] is that the tanneries of that area are a major foreign exchange earner for the country as leaders in the export of leather goods. Thus the argument about balancing environmental protection with other needs such as that for foreign exchange, providing employment, etc arose. The terse answer of the Court to this was that notwithstanding all this, it is not right to destroy the ecology, degrade the environment, or cause a health hazard. Referring to the principle of sustainable development, the Court stated 'during the two decades from Stockholm to Rio, "sustainable development" has come to be accepted as a viable concept to eradicate poverty and improve the quality of human life while living within the carrying capacity of supporting ecosystems ...'. The Court then held that the precautionary principle and the polluter pays principle are essential features of 'sustainable development'. Delineating the contours of the precautionary principle in the context of municipal law, it held that environmental measures must anticipate and prevent by attacking the causes of environmental degradation, and 'the onus of proof is on the actor or the developer/industrialist to show that his action is environmentally benign'. The legal authority for these principles was found in the Constitution and the statutory provisions of the anti-pollution laws. The Court however went on to further hold that once these principles were accepted as a part of customary international law there would be no difficulty in accepting them as a part of the domestic law. 'It is almost an accepted proposition of law that the rules of customary international law which are not

contrary to the municipal law shall be deemed to have been incorporated in the domestic law and shall be followed by the courts of law ....'

The importance of this decision is that it squarely places the cardinal
environmental law principles in the secure lap of Article 21—it is now
doubtful whether even a constitutional amendment can dilute these
principles. Secondly, it paves the way for the courts to bring in, either
through the window of 'aid to statutory interpretation', or as an inherent principle flowing from the constitutional guarantee of a clean
environment, other environmental treaties without waiting for legislative action. In the forest matters, the Court has already made interim
orders, *inter alia* taking into account the Biosphere Treaty. It creates a
strong precedent for the Court to initiate measures of social justice in
the realm of environment law as a part of its constitutional jurisdiction.
Sustainable development is the balance between social justice and poverty eradication by way of creation of wealth. The Court has read into
the constitutional law, this canon of social justice.

The significance of environmental protection has permeated other
areas, even where the immediate issue is not pollution or environmental
degradation. The promotion of environmental conservation is viewed
as a strong public purpose which outweighs other private interests and
can be the basis of sustaining the validity of other statutes or executive
actions that have a nexus with it.

Apart from enforcing the laws against pollution, the Court has taken
stringent action to oversee the implementation of various laws, such as
the Wildlife Protection Law, the Forest Protection Law, the Town Planning Laws (in so far as they provide measures to decongest cities, provide parks, etc.). The Court, for example, is overseeing the implementation of the provisions of the Wild Life Protection Act, 1972, which
requires the establishment of centres for immunization of livestock, registration of persons in possession of arms, and most importantly, settlement of the rights of residents of areas falling within sanctuaries. The
last of these is a subject where the needs of the environment have to be
delicately balanced with the needs of the underprivileged. Most of the
people who live within the sanctuaries are those who have inhabited
those areas for centuries. They have a symbiotic relationship with the
environment. In the changed circumstances, however, the fragile state
of the flora and fauna cannot take the pressure of human habitation
and therefore it becomes necessary to settle the rights of the inhabitants. In the circumstances, the Court, being unable to itself accomplish
the task of finding the right balance, directs the executive to do its duty
under the law, while monitoring its implementation.[23] Similarly, in a

petition brought to secure the rights of Indian farmers in relation to plant varieties, etc., the Court is overseeing governmental action in relation to the preparation of a 'Biodiversity Act', a very important step in securing social justice in the field of environment law.[24]

The decision to establish an abattoir in the state of Andhra Pradesh was challenged on the ground that it would be prejudicial to the interest of conservation of cattle. In a country like India, preservation of cattle is not just a matter of preservation of flora and fauna, but is also a matter of protection of the interests of the large number of rural people for whom cattle is a vital resource, and yet who do not have the financial might to compete with a corporation. The Court responded to the challenge by asking the Government of India to re-examine the matter over a period of time, and in the interregnum imposed severe restraints on the functioning of the abattoir.[25] However, once the matter was cleared by experts, the restraints were removed. In this manner, the Court sought to balance the needs of industrialization and export earnings with social justice consistent with the needs of the environment.

The doctrine of 'public trust' was evolved under ancient Roman law, founded on the idea that certain common properties such as rivers, seashores, forests, and the air are held by the government in trust for free and unimpeded use by the general public. Drawing upon this, to strike down the grant of a lease in an eco-sensitive area, the Supreme Court held that 'our contemporary concern about the environment bears a close conceptual relationship to this legal doctrine ...'. It went on to hold that 'The public trust doctrine primarily rests on the principle that certain resources like air, sea, waters and the forests have such a great importance to the people as a whole that it would be wholly unjustified to make them a subject of private ownership ...'. The Court drew inspiration from the decisions of the American courts which had extended the public trust doctrine to protect ecologically lease-sensitive areas (for example, the decision of the Supreme Court of California in the *Mono Lake* case).

It cannot be gainsaid that perhaps the single most important element of Indian ecology are its forest resources. The Indian economy is, and will continue to be for some time, an agricultural economy. It was not without reason that the Father of the Nation always maintained that India lives in its villages and there can be no economic development and growth permeating down to the common man if the Indian farmer is ignored. Farming in India is substantially irrigated from the rainfall or from rivers and waterbodies which are rain fed, and it is now established beyond doubt that the forest cover has an immediate and direct impact upon the pattern of the monsoon.

The world's resource of forests is mind-boggling in its extent, complexity, and diversity. Forests and woodlands occupy 4000 million ha. of land,[26] yet the average forest area per person is now down to three-quarters of a hectare (an area roughly equal to a soccer pitch). In recognition of the need to protect our forests, the Forest Conservation Act was enacted in 1980 which wrested the control of the forests from the states in favour of the Union and mandated that no activity within a forest, which could be classified as a non-forest activity, could be permitted by a state government without the prior permission of the central government. The Forest Conservation Act, 1980, reflects a paradigm change, treating forests as a precious ecosystem and seeks to regulate it in that spirit rather than as a valuable resource to be harvested to yield the maximum possible revenue.

A profound policy was pronounced in 1988 whose avowed object was, amongst other things, to seek to increase the forest cover to at least 33 per cent of the landmass of India, to preserve in pristine condition the biospheres (in conformity with India's international obligations under the Biosphere Treaty) and to ensure that no development programme results in a depletion of the forests. Where the felling of trees is imperative for development activity, it suggests imposition of suitable terms of compensatory reafforestation so that not only is the system restored but some of the degraded areas are also brought under forest cover. Like most well-meaning policies, even this one has remained largely a parchment in a glass case.

In a public interest litigation, however, the Supreme Court has issued directions from time to time to ensure that all the states strictly comply with the Forest Conservation Act and that the central government strictly adheres to its policy wherever it is required to grant clearance for any non-forest activity. The Court, using the simple device of 'purposive interpretation', held that since the Forest Conservation Act was enacted with a view to checking further deforestation, which eventually results in ecological imbalance, the provisions of the law must apply to all forests irrespective of the nature of ownership or their classification. In these few sentences, the Court buried the notion that a person who owns a forest is free to destroy its resources in exercise of his proprietary rights. This proposition of law has far-reaching ramifications; as a proposition of constitutional law it clearly underscores the triumph of social justice over property rights. The development of Indian constitutional law has been marked by repeated confrontation between the legislature, bent upon recasting property rights in conformity with its notions of social justice, and the Court of the fifties and sixties insisting, in one way or another, upon handsome compensation for any curtailment of property rights. Contrast this with the manner in which the Supreme Court of the late nineties, without hesitation, readily interprets a statute in a way that seriously impairs vested rights so long as it is for the cause of the environment.

A Critique

In a strongly worded admonition to the administration, the Court, in the *Span Motel* case[27] says, 'The aesthetic use and the pristine glory of the natural resource, the environment and the ecosystems of our country cannot be permitted to be eroded for private, commercial or any other use unless the Courts find it necessary, in good faith, for the public good and in public interest to encroach upon the said resources ...'.

This formulation does appear to suggest that it is the Court alone that is the guardian of public properties. As against this, even the purists accept that environmental protection entails a delicate balance between protection of the environment and other competing equities. It cannot be gainsaid that the utilization of the environment and its natural resources has to be in a way that is consistent with principles of sustainable development and intergenerational equity, but balancing these equities may entail policy choices. In the ultimate analysis, the choice of the elected representatives of the people cannot be entirely supplanted by the wisdom of the Court. In areas of administrative decision-making, the Court has carved out its niche: it reviews the decision-making process and not the decision. In the circumstances, decisions relating to the utilization of natural resources for productive purposes have to be tested on the anvil of the well-recognized principles of judicial review: Have all the relevant factors been taken into account? Have any extraneous factors influenced the decision? Is the decision strictly in accordance with the legislative policy underlying the law (if any) that governs the field? Is the decision consistent with principles of sustainable development in the sense that has the decision-maker taken into account the said principle and, on the basis of the relevant considerations, arrived at a balanced decision? The applicability of the classical tests of judicial review, undoubtedly in the strict scrutiny mode, with all the doubts and grey areas being resolved in favour of the environment consistent with the *precautionary principle*, would perhaps better satisfy the constitutional duty of the Court to take appropriate steps to ensure that the citizen is not deprived of his constitutional right to a clean environment.

There have been occasions on which the Court has taken upon itself the task of deciding the matter of merits rather than reviewing the decision-making process, and on some such occasions the Court has faltered! One such instance is the decision by which the Court imposed a blanket ban, as it were, on prawn farming in India. Prawn exports are a major source of foreign exchange so desperately needed by the country for its infrastructural development. A petition was brought before the Court seeking an injunction against prawn farming on various ecological grounds. The Court sought the opinion of NEERI (a leading Government of India environmental research institution), and also sought to educate itself on the technical nuances of the various kinds of prawn farms (i.e. intensive farming, semi-intensive farming, and so on) and issued a mandamus to the government to demolish all existing prawn farms and not to permit any prawn farming in India. The decision of the Court clearly reflects the danger of the Court supplanting the decision-making authority. (The Court has allowed review petitions and recalled its judgement, and the matter is pending further consideration.) One option certainly available to the Court was to direct the government to obtain independent technical advice and then arrive at an informed decision. It surely cannot be suggested that prawn farming is per se a noxious activity more dangerous than industrial activities, particularly in the hazardous chemicals area—a distinction has to be drawn between the criticism of prawn farming on ethical grounds and on environmental concerns—the Court being clearly concerned only with the latter.

In the circumstances, absent judicially manageable standards for the Court taking on the task of deciding such matters on merits itself, it is perhaps advisable that the Court reviews the decision-making process to ensure that it is fair and fully informed, based on the correct principles, and free from any bias or restraint. Once this is ensured, then, in the absence of any statutory transgression, the Court must defer to the wisdom of the executive. The perspective would of course change entirely in cases in which the Court finds that the decisions of the executive are either ill-informed or based on extraneous considerations, contrary to legislative policy or otherwise so gross that no reasonable person could arrive at such decisions. The Court has itself on occasion expressed its limitations in trying to decide issues that are of a technical nature.[28] However, such occasions are few and far between and cannot tarnish the tremendous contribution of the Court to the development of environmental law in India.

The Court is now experimenting with a new methodology: in the *Yamuna Pollution* case, it has now directed the government to ensure that the discharge of industrial effluents into the drains that eventually reach the river is stopped by a given date; it is for the government to find ways and means of performing its statutory, indeed, constitutional duty.

Conclusion

The law to protect the environment is in itself a measure of social justice. The need for these laws arose not because of any criminality or aberration in behaviour from the accepted societal norms in an industrial society, but because of the need to redefine those very societal norms. Professor Henry J. Fletcher (Professor of Law and Associate Dean for Faculty Research and Development, University of Minnesota) says:

In a well-ordered society, presumably, the law on the books would generally correspond with observed conduct, apart from the inevitable shortfall due to human error or antisocial motivations. In environmental law, however, shortfalls are widespread at all levels of the system, for reasons that cannot simply be attributed to antisocial or deviant conduct.

The evolution of these laws is a step towards recognizing the rights of the common man, the ranker along with the ruler, and placing it on a higher pedestal than the right of the affluent to create more wealth. These laws are therefore a step in the direction of social justice. In the words of Professor Michael Anderson:

the creation of a reliable and effective system of environmental protection would help ensure the well-being of future generations as well as the survival of those persons, often including indigenous or economic league marginalized groups, who depend immediately upon natural resources for their livelihood ... the legal protection of human rights is an effective means to achieving the end of conservation and environmental protection. Thus the full realization of a broad spectrum of first and second generation rights would constitute a society and a political order in which claims for environmental protection are more likely to be respected ...

Yet protecting the environment sometimes itself throws up issues of balancing the interests of the weaker sections of society with the needs of the environment. It is at these times that our true commitment to the principle of sustainable development is put to the test.

India is a country with a hoary past, yet its experiments with democracy, as established under its great Constitution will undoubtedly be one of the most exciting chapters in its history, and as the other organs of state evolved into their present form and created the present political system, so has its apex court. The Supreme Court of India, perhaps the most powerful constitutional court in the world both in terms of the ambit of its jurisdiction as well as the fact that it is the protector of democracy in the second most populous country in the world, influencing the fortunes of one billion people in the nineties is very different from the Court of the fifties or even the sixties. It has always been true to its duty to protect the constitutional rights of the citizens of India, yet the perceptions of these rights have drastically changed over the past fifty years. From a Court committed to protecting rights recognized in the classical legal formats, and unfortunately those rights are predominantly property rights, it became a Court exercising its vast jurisdiction to redress the grievances of citizens as far as was possible within judicially manageable standards, keeping in view the chronic bureaucratic apathy and legislative sluggishness which marked the governance of this developing nation. Somewhere along the way it lost interest in merely protecting conventional rights; its attention now focused on the downtrodden, underprivileged Indian whose voice had hitherto usually been lost in the wilderness.

This approach has now become the signature of this Court, and as long as this holds sway, the Court will continue to be a haven for environmental activists. This approach needs a brave and innovative face, and those who seek new paths will undoubtedly sometimes lose themselves in the wilderness. One must however always remember what Sir Fredrick Pollock maintained, 'Those who make no mistakes will never make anything, and the judge who is afraid of committing himself may be called sound and safe in his own generation, but will leave no mark on the law.'

Notes

[1] Al Gore, *The Earth in the Balance: Ecology and the Human Spirit*, (New York, Plume 1993).

[2] Ibid.

[3] Water (Prevention and Control of Pollution) Act, 1974.

[4] Air (Prevention and Control of Pollution) Act, 1981.

[5] Anya C. Musto: 'Comment: California as a model for federal regulation of automobile emissions pollution: Replacing Title II of the Clean Air Act of 1990', (1996) 5 *Dickinson Journal of Environmental Law and Policy* 151.

[6] Philip E. Rothschild, 'Comment: The Clean Air Act and Indirect Source Review: 1970–1991', (1992) 10 UCLA, *Journal of Environmental Law and Policy* 337–354.

[7] Charles C. Caldart and Nicholas A. Ashford: 'Negotiation as a means of developing and implementing Health and Safety Policy', (1999) 23 *Harvard Environmental Law Review* 141–62.

[8] Richard Burnett-Hall, *Environmental Law*, Sweet & Maxwell, London, 1995.

[9] (1975) *OJC* 112 at para 5.

[10] *Maneka Gandhi v Union of India* (1978) 1 SCC 248—the 'procedure established by law' giving way to due process of law—the right to life being understood as more than just a right to animal existence.

[11] *M.C. Mehta v Union of India* (1998) 8 SCC 206; *M.C. Mehta v Union of India* (1999) 6 SCC 12: phasing out of old vehicles, permitting vehicles only conforming to Euro II norms.

[12] *Municipal Council Ratlam v Vardichan* (1980) 4 SCC 162.

[13] *Fertilizer Corporation Kamgar Union of India* (1981) 1 SCC 568—even prior to this, the Court had started entertaining petitions from public interest litigants, although there is no judgement on the subject.

[14] *M.C. Mehta v Union of India* (1988) 1 SCC 471.

[15] *M.C. Mehta v Union of India* (Kanpur Tanneries) (1987) 4 SCC 463.

[16] *Bangalore Medical Trust v B.S. Muddappa* (1991) 4 SCC 54.

[17] *In Re Bhawani river* (1998) 6 SCC 335.

[18] *Indian Council for Enviro-Legal Action v Union of India* (1996) 3 SCC 212.

[19] *M.C. Mehta v Union of India* (Shriram - Oleum Gas) (1987) 1 SCC 395.

[20] *Vellore Citizen's Welfare Forum v Union of India* (1996) 5 SCC 647.

[21] *M.C. Mehta v Kamal Nath* (1997) 1 SCC 388.

[22] *Centre for Environment Law WWF-I v Union of India* (1999) 1 SCC 263.

[23] *Research Foundation for Science, Technology, Ecology v Ministry of Agriculture* (1999) 1 SCC 655.

[24] *Akhil Bharat Goseva Sangh v State of AP* (1997) 3 SCC 707.

[25] Alexander S. Mather: *Global Forest Resources*, [London, Belhaven, 1990].

[26] *M.C. Mehta v Kamal Nath* (1997) 1 SCC 388.

[27] *Indian Council for Enviro-Legal Action v Union of India* (1996) 5 SCC 281.

[28] *AP Pollution Control Board v Professor M.V. Nayudu* (1999) 2 SCC 718.

Nineteen

The Supreme Court and the Employee

P.P. Rao

A significant proportion of litigation before the Supreme Court has been with regard to the employment and terms and conditions of service of employees of the government, public sector corporations, and public bodies. 'Service' cases are a post-Constitution phenomenon. Disputes with regard to seniority between various categories have frequently come up for consideration. Reservation of posts as part of affirmative action has also been the subject of contentious debate. The Court has frequently dealt with cases of dismissal from service, compulsory retirement, and termination of services of probationers. Employees who have continued for years together on an ad hoc basis without security of tenure have approached the Court for regularization, while those not selected for employment have questioned selection procedures. This is merely illustrative and not exhaustive of the types of cases in this area of law that are taken to Court. 'Service' cases have inevitably involved the application of principles of constitutional and administrative law, and have often required interpretation of the provisions of the Constitution, enacted law and subordinate legislation. The 'service jurisprudence' thus evolved by the Court forms a part of the constitutional and administrative law of the land. This survey focuses on some selected areas where the Court has laid down important principles.

Access to the Court

The Constitution of India contains more safeguards for employees than the Government of India Act, 1935. The fundamental right to equality (Articles 14, 16) is the sheet anchor of much of 'service' litigation. Article 32 guarantees the right to move the Supreme Court for the enforcement of any of the fundamental rights. The high courts have the power to issue writs for the enforcement of fundamental rights or for any other purpose. In *Randhir Singh v UOI*,[1] the Supreme Court spoke with pride and satisfaction about the glory of the Constitution which enabled a driver-constable in the Delhi Police force to directly approach the highest court in the land for redressal of his grievance of denial of equal pay for equal work. Subsequently, the Supreme Court found it difficult to cope with the volume of writ petitions filed by employees under Article 32. In *Kanubhai Brahmbhatt v State of Gujarat*,[2] the Court dissuaded persons from approaching the Supreme Court directly under Article 32 instead of moving the high courts under Article 226, comparing itself to a national hospital established especially for the performance of open heart surgery and the high courts to regional hospitals which could take care of all other patients' ailments. In *P.N. Kumar v Municipal Corporation of Delhi*,[3] the Court gave elaborate reasons for declining to entertain a petition under Article 32 while reserving liberty to the petitioners to approach the high court under Article 226 of the Constitution.

As the high courts were found to be overburdened with a heavy backlog of cases, on the recommendation of experts, Article 323A was inserted in the Constitution by the Forty-second Amendment providing for the constitution of administrative tribunals by law. Administrative tribunals were established under the Administrative Tribunals Act, 1985 to deal exclusively with service matters. An employee amenable to the jurisdiction of an administrative tribunal was required to move the tribunal in the first instance. The aggrieved party could thereafter approach the Supreme Court under Article 136 for grant of leave to appeal from the judgement of the tribunal. In *L. Chandrakumar v UOI*,[4] the Supreme Court, while reviving the jurisdiction of high courts under Articles 226 and 227, laid down that the tribunals would continue to function as courts of first instance, but after that stage the aggrieved party would be entitled to move the high court under Articles 226/227 of the Constitution. From the decision of a division Bench of the high court, the aggrieved party could move the Supreme Court under Article 136. This decision has restricted direct access to the high courts under Articles 226 and 227 in service matters. The journey from the tribunal to the Supreme Court has become longer now. The Supreme Court entertains petitions directly under Article 32 only in cases of exceptional importance. Article 32, the only guaranteed right in Part III, has become a discretionary remedy. Employees who are not subject to the jurisdiction of administrative tribunals can approach the high courts under Articles 226 and 227 for the enforcement of their fundamental or statutory rights. Workmen covered by the Industrial Disputes Act, 1947 have efficacious remedies under the Act, after exhausting which, they can move the high court and thereafter the Supreme Court. Although the Supreme Court has jurisdiction to entertain a special leave petition directly from the judgement or order of any court or tribunal, including the award of an industrial tribunal, the aggrieved party itself would ordinarily like to move the high court first. Persons in private employment other than in an industry have to approach the civil courts and move the Supreme Court only after the high court has decided the matter. Thus, barring a few writ petitions under Article 32, all other service matters come to the Supreme Court through high courts.

Public Interest Litigation (PIL)
The Supreme Court liberalized the concept of *locus standi* and paved the way for Public Interest Litigation in a case involving a trade union.[5] The Court accepted the *locus standi* of workmen in the winding up proceedings of a company[6] and also entertained PIL on behalf of labourers under Article 32.[7] In *S.P. Gupta v UOI*,[8] the Court entertained PIL involving appointment and transfer of judges. However, in *R.K. Jain v UOI*,[9] one of the judges observed that a non-appointee alone could assail the appointment of a person and a third party has no *locus standi*.

Fundamental Rights
(a) Article 12
From the outset, the Court has consistently shown its concern for fundamental rights and has not hesitated when enforcing them. The Court has been interpreting the provisions of Part III liberally so as to widen the scope of the rights. By enlarging the definition of 'State' in Article 12, the Court has extended the reach of fundamental rights to employees of public sector undertakings, statutory bodies, and government-owned or controlled institutions. The decisions in *Rajasthan State Electricity Board v Mohan Lal*,[10] *Sukhdev Singh v Bhagat Ram*,[11] *Ajay Hasia v Khalid Mujib*[12] are conspicuous landmarks in this direction. Once an institution is held to be 'State' within the meaning of Article 12, the employees acquire a status as they will be entitled to the fundamental rights which they can enforce by moving the administrative tribunals or superior courts, as the case may be.

(b) Right to equality
Article 14 mandates the State not to deny any person equality before the law or the equal protection of the laws. Article 16 provides for equality of opportunity in matters of public employment and prohibits discrimi-

nation amongst citizens on grounds only of religion, race, caste, sex, descent, place of birth, residence, or any of them. Clause (4) clarifies that the State has power to make any provision for the reservation of appointments or posts in favour of any backward class of citizens which in the opinion of the State is not adequately represented in the services under it. In the beginning the Supreme Court took the traditional view of the right to equality. Whenever a provision was challenged as violative of Article 14, the Court would consider whether the classification made by the State was permissible. For sustaining the classification, two conditions must be fulfilled: (1) the classification must be founded on an intelligible differentia, and (2), the differentia must have a rational relation to the object sought to be achieved by the impugned provision.[13] In *R.K. Dalmia v Justice S.R. Tendulkar*,[14] the Court summed up the case law on the subject. In *Jyoti Pershad v Administrator for the Union Territory of Delhi*,[15] the Court reiterated the scope of Article 14, noticing the case law to date. In *State of J&K v Thakur Ganga Singh*,[16] the Court observed 'that the interpretation of Article 14 in the context of classification has been finally settled in several decisions and there is no further scope for putting a new interpretation on the provisions of Article 14 of the Constitution vis-à-vis the doctrine of classification'. However, a new touchstone of arbitrariness was formulated in *Maneka Gandhi v UOI*.[17] In order to satisfy Article 14, the impugned provision must be 'right and just and fair' and not arbitrary, fanciful, or oppressive. In other words, state action must be reasonable, just, and fair. If not, it will be liable to be struck down on the anvil of Article 14. This new test has widened the scope of the right to equality. The judgement in *Union of India v Tulsiram Patel*[18] is yet another milestone in the expansive interpretation of the right to equality. Relying on *E.P. Royappa v State of Tamil Nadu*[19] and *Maneka Gandhi v UOI*, the Court declared that the principles of natural justice have come to be recognized as being a part of the guarantee contained in Article 14 because of the new and dynamic intepretation given by the Court to the concept of equality. In view of this development, employees of public sector undertakings are no longer at a disadvantage for not falling within the ambit of the safeguards contained in Article 311(2) available to civil servants in the matter of dismissal, removal, or reduction in rank.

(c) Interpretation of fundamental rights

In *Randhir Singh v UOI*,[20] the Court interpreted Articles 14 and 16 in the light of the Preamble and Article 39(d) which is a directive principle of state policy requiring the State to ensure that there is equal pay for equal work for both men and women. The principle aims at securing gender justice. Men and women who do equal work shall be entitled to equal pay. Implicit therein is the basic principle of equal pay for equal work. The Court enlarged the scope of Articles 14 and 16 by reading into them the principle of equal pay for equal work. However, since the decision in *State of UP v J.P. Chaurasia*[21] the Court has been taking the view that equation of posts must be determined by expert bodies like the Pay Commission and the Court should not interfere unless the determination is shown to be made with extraneous consideration. Subsequent to the decision of the Court in *Kesavananda Bharati v UOI*,[22] the Court has been adopting the technique of interpreting fundamental rights in the light of the directive principles of state policy and absorbing the principles in the fundamental rights. In *Olga Tellis v Bombay Municipal Corporation*,[23] the Court held that the directive principles contained in Articles 39(a) and 41 must be regarded as fundamental in the interpretation of fundamental rights. If there is an obligation upon the State to secure to the citizens an adequate means of livelihood and the right to work, it would be sheer pedantry to exclude the right to livelihood from the content of the right to life. The State may not, by affirmative action, be liable to be compelled to provide adequate means of livelihood or work to its citizens. However, any person who is deprived of his right to livelihood except according to just and fair procedure established by law, can challenge the deprivation as offending the right to life conferred by Article 21. Earlier, in *Bandhua Mukti Morcha v UOI*,[24] the Court had declared that the right to live with human dignity enshrined in Article 21 derives its life breath from the directive principles of state policy and particularly clauses (e) and (f) of Article 39 and Articles 41 and 42, and where legislation already exists providing the basic requirements of health to the workmen, the State can be obligated to ensure observance of such legislation. Inaction on the part of the State would amount to a denial of the right to life contained in Article 21. In *J.P. Unnikrishnan v State of Andhra Pradesh*,[25] S. Mohan J, in his separate judgement, noticed the cases in which the Court had enlarged the scope of Article 21 in the light of the directive principles of state policy.

(d) Reservation of posts under Article 16(4)

The limits of the power of the State to make reservation of appointments or posts in favour of backward classes repeatedly came up for consideration. In *General Manager, Southern Railway v Rangachari*,[26] a Constitution Bench took the view that Article 16(4) is an exception to

Article 16(1) and 16(2) and should, therefore, be strictly construed. The principal question in that case was whether reservation of selection posts in favour of the members of the scheduled castes and scheduled tribes was permissible. The Court, while declaring that Article 16(4) permitted such reservation in selection posts, pointed out that in excercising its powers under Article 16(4) the State has a duty to harmonize the claims of the backward classes and those of the other employees consistent with the maintenance of efficiency of administration as contemplated by Article 335 of the Constitution. In *M.R. Balaji v State of Mysore*,[27] another Constitution Bench interpreted Article 15(4), a provision similar to clause (4) of Article 16. The Court took the view that the extent of reservation in favour of backward classes, including scheduled castes/scheduled tribes should be less than 5 per cent. A larger Bench in *State of Kerala v N.M. Thomas*[28] by a majority held that Article 16(4) is not an exception to Article 16(1), but only an emphatic way of indicating the degree to which equality of opportunity could be carried, namely, even up to the point of making reservation. Article 16(1) itself permits classification of employees and clause (4) of Article 16 is an illustration of constitutionally sanctified classification. This view was reiterated by a Bench of nine judges in *Indra Sawhney v UOI*,[29] which incidentally overruled the *Rangachari* case decision by declaring that Article 16(4) did not permit reservations in the matter of promotion. Subsequently, Parliament inserted clause (4-A) in Article 16 permitting reservations in promotion by the Seventy-seventh Amendment in 1995. The validity of this amendment is an open question.

Is the word 'class' used in Articles 15(4) and 16(4) synonymous with 'caste'? In *M.R. Balaji v State of Mysore*, while interpreting Article 15(4), the Court held that 'class' does not mean 'caste' and a classification made solely on the basis of caste is not permissible under Article 15(4), though 'caste' is a relevant factor. In *R. Chitralekha v State of Mysore*,[30] the Court declared that caste is not a compelling circumstance affording a basis for ascertaining the backwardness of a class, and if in a given case, caste is excluded in ascertaining a backward class, it does not vitiate classification provided it satisfies other tests. In *K.C. Vasanth Kumar v State of Karnataka*[31] judges differed on the question of caste being a relevant factor. In *State of Kerala v N.M. Thomas*, V.R. Krishna Iyer J pointed out one of the consequences of reservation. 'Its benefits, by and large, are snatched away by the top creamy layer of the "backward" caste or class, thus keeping the weakest among the weak always weak and leaving the fortunate layers to consume the whole cake.' A nine-judge Bench in *Indira Sawhney's* case by a majority rejected the argument that secularism being a basic feature of the Constitution, 'caste' cannot be a relevant consideration for determining the backwardness of a class and held that a 'caste' can be and quite often is a social class in India and could be a backward class for the purposes of Article 16(4), but the creamy layer of a backward class must be excluded from the benefit of reservation. It must follow logically that a caste with a creamy layer cannot be regarded as a backward class. A better view more consistent with the concept of secularism, as expounded in *S.R. Bommai v Union of India*[32] appears to be that in a secular State 'caste' cannot be regarded as a relevant factor either for granting a benefit or denying a facility by the State. The Constitution aims at a classless and casteless society. Dr B.R. Ambedkar categorically declared in the Constituent Assembly that 'castes are anti-national'.[33]

In the *Indira Sawhney* case, the Court, while reiterating that the reservations contemplated in clause (4) of Article 16 should not exceed 50 per cent, permitted departure from this norm in extraordinary situations. The Court allowed 'carry-forward' of reservations, when the reserved vacancies were not filled for a period of three years. In *R.K. Sabharwal v State of Punjab*,[34] the Supreme Court held that a member of a backward class promoted to a higher post on the basis of reservation cannot gain seniority in the higher post by virtue of his promotion. The Court further held that computation of the percentage of posts reserved has to be done in relation to the number of posts comprising the cadre and not in relation to vacancies, and once representation is secured for the reserved categories to the extent provided in the rules or instructions, the operation of the roster should stop. Only when a vacancy in a reserved post arises subsequently can the benefit of promotion be again given on the basis of reservation. The Court clarified that members of backward classes could compete with the general category candidates and secure appointment on the basis of relative merit, and such appointments would be outside the reserved posts. The Court reiterated the same view in *UOI v Virpal Singh Chauhan*.[35] Going a step further in *Ajit Singh Juneja v State of Punjab*,[36] the Court held that a person who has been appointed or promoted against a reserved post cannot be considered first for the next promotion for filling up a general category post in preference to a general category candidate promoted later. He could, however, be considered for a reserved post. Another coordinate Bench to some extent unsettled the law in *Jadgish Lal v State of Haryana*.[37] A Constitution Bench has since resolved the conflict by overruling the latter decision.[38] The Bench declared that the roster point promotees (reserved category) cannot count their seniority in the promoted category from the date of their continual officiation in the promoted post, vis-à-vis the general candidates who were senior to them in the lower category and who were later promoted. In *Post Graduate Institute of Medical Education & Research v Faculty Association*[39] a Constitution Bench has categorically held that there cannot be reservation in a cadre consisting of a single post. In all these cases relating to reservation of posts under Article 16(4), the Court is required to balance the interests of the general category candidates and the candidates belonging to backward classes keeping in view the mandate of Article 335. The exercise is not easy.

(e) Hire and fire

In *Rattan Lal v State of Haryana*[40] the Court deprecated the practice of appointing ad hoc teachers for short periods and renewing the appointments after a break and denying the teachers the vacation salary. The Court held that the teachers were being unnecessarily subjected to an arbitrary 'hiring and firing' policy. In *West Bengal State Electricity Board v Deshbandhu Ghosh*,[41] the Supreme Court struck down regulation 34 of the Electricity Board, which permitted termination of services of a permanent employee by serving three months' notice or on payment of salary in lieu thereof, as violative of Article 14. The Court observed: 'It is a naked "hire and fire" rule, the time for banishing which altogether from employer–employee relationship is fast approaching.' In *Central Inland Water Transport Corporation Ltd v B.N. Ganguly*,[42] the Supreme Court struck down rule 9 which contained a similar provision for termination of services of a permanent employee and also incorporated an additional ground of 'services no longer required in the interest of the company', with liability to pay some compensation. The Court struck down the rule as arbitrary and violative of Article 14 of the Constitution. The Court found that even as a term of contract, it was unconscionable and contrary to public policy. The Court observed:

A clause such as Rule 9(i) in a contract of employment affecting large sections of the public is harmful and injurious to the public interest for it tends to create a sense of insecurity in the minds of those to whom it applies and consequently it is against public good. Such a clause, therefore, is opposed to public policy and being opposed to public policy, it is void under Section 23 of the Indian Contract Act.

In *Delhi Transport Corporation v DTC Mazdoor Congress*,[43] a Constitution Bench struck down regulation 9(b) which permitted termination of service of an employee on one month's notice or pay in lieu thereof. Appreciating that employees have no bargaining power and tend even to accept unfair terms given their dire need for employment, the Court has consistently refused to permit 'hire and fire' and insisted that termination of service of a permanent employee can be made only on the ground of misconduct after holding an inquiry consistent with the principles of natural justice. The State should behave like a model employer.

(f) Excess appointments

The validity of appointments made in excess of the number of posts advertised has been coming up frequently in recent years. In *Hoshiar Singh v State of Haryana*[44] the Supreme Court declared that the Public Service Commission cannot recommend more names than the number of vacancies advertised or mentioned in the requisition. Any appointments made in excess of the said number would be arbitrary as it would deprive candidates who were not eligible for appointment to the posts on the last date for submission of applications mentioned in the advertisement and who became eligible for appointment thereafter of the opportunity of being considered for appointment to the additional posts. If these additional posts were advertised subsequently, those who became eligible for appointment in the meanwhile would be entitled to apply for them. This decision has been followed by the Supreme Court, the high courts, and administrative tribunals mechanically and a large number of excess appointments made by various governments and public sector undertakings of candidates selected by the Public Service Commissions or other authorities in accordance with the rules have been struck down mostly at the instance of candidates who had not been selected. The appointing authorities had to issue fresh advertisements for the additional posts not covered by the earlier advertisements and make ad hoc arrangements till the additional posts were duly filled after going through the dilatory procedure prescribed for direct recruitment, which in most cases takes at least a year or two. Ad hoc appointments are a source of corruption and favouritism and not at all conducive to efficiency of administration. In *Prem Singh and Others v Haryana State Electricity Board and Others*,[45] the Supreme Court, while reiterating the law declared in the *Hoshiar Singh* case, softened the rigour of the law to some extent by holding:

the State could deviate from the advertisement and make appointments on posts falling vacant thereafter in exceptional circumstances only, or in an emergent situation and that too by taking a policy decision in that behalf. Even when filling up of more posts than advertised is challenged the Court may not, while exercising its extraordinary jurisdiction, invalidate the excess appointments and may mould the relief in such a manner as to strike a just balance between the interest of the State and the interest of persons seeking public employment.

In formulating the exception, the Court was obviously guided by overriding public interest. Recently, in *Virendra S. Hooda v State of Haryana*,[46] the Court held that if there are instructions requiring not only the vacancies advertised but also the vacancies available within a period of six months after the announcement of the previous selection to be filled up from the waiting list maintained by the Commission, this could be enforced at the instance of the selected candidates. The Court directed the government of Haryana to appoint the candidates on the waiting list of posts which became available within a period of six months after the selection was completed. This decision will facilitate manning of posts by duly selected candidates and obviate the need for ad hoc appointments pending fresh recruitment. The Court has taken a pragmatic view on this issue.

(g) Arbitrariness in Recruitment

The Court was conscious of the risk of allowing a viva-voce test to become the determining factor in the selection process. In *Liladhar v State of Rajasthan*,[47] the Court held that it was not for the Court to lay down whether an interview test should be held at all or how many marks should be allowed for it. For some posts the only proper method of selection might be by a viva-voce test. In *Ashok Kumar Yadav v State of Haryana*,[48] the Court prescribed a ceiling of 12.2 per cent marks for the viva-voce out of the total marks taken into account for the purpose of selection on the basis of a written test and the viva-voce. In *Anzar Ahamad v State of Bihar*,[49] the Court clarified that the question of the weight to be attached to the viva-voce would not arise where the selection was to be made on the basis of an interview.

Unfortunately, selections made by some of the State Public Service Commissions and Selection Boards have become suspect. The credibility of some of the members of these is very low. In *Krishan Yadav v State of Haryana*,[50] the Court ordered an investigation by the CBI into the alleged malpractices vitiating selection of Taxation Inspectors by the State Subordinate Selection Board. After considering the report of the CBI, the Court set aside the entire selection and directed prosecutions to be launched against all concerned on the basis of the report.

(h) Seniority

Inter se seniority of direct recruits and promotees has been a vexed question of law which has frequently arisen for consideration. Initially, the Court gave effect to the rules strictly, including the rules providing for separate quotas of intake from the two sources as well as the rule of rotation without any regard to the consequences. In *Mervyn Cutendo v Collector of Customs*,[51] the Court held that there was no inherent vice in the principle of fixing seniority by rotation in a case when a service is composed in fixed proportion of direct recruits and promotees. Subsequently, the Court realized that indiscriminate application of a rota based on quota was likely to cause injustice to the promotees and give an undue benefit to the direct recruits in cases where recruitment did not take place simultaneously from the two sources. Therefore, the Court permitted the filling up of vacancies from the two sources independently subject to the quota prescribed for each source.[52] In *A.K. Subraman v UOI*,[53] the Court pointed out that the existence of the quota and rotational rule, by itself, will not violate Article 14 or Article 16, but the unreasonable implementation of this may, in a given case, attract the frown of the equality clause. In *B.S. Yadav v State of Haryana*,[54] the Court declared that the rule of 'rota' cannot be read into the rule of quota. The quota shall have to be adhered to at the stage of recruitment. In *A. Janardhana v UOI*,[55] the Court took the view that if the quota rule is directly interrelated with the seniority rule, once the quota rule gave way, the seniority rule would become wholly otiose and ineffective. If the quota rule breaks down, the seniority rule, which is interlinked with the quota rule, cannot be given effect. In such cases, the principle of continuous officiation governs the seniority of persons appointed. In *G.S. Lamba v UOI*,[56] the Court held that once there is a power to relax the mandatory quota rule, the appointments made in excess of the quota from any given source would not be illegal. In *S.B. Patwardhan v State of Maharashtra*,[57] the Court declared that the date of confirmation could not be the basis for seniority. These decisions gave an advantage to the promotees whose promotions were not strictly in accordance with the rules. The entire question of *inter se* seniority of direct recruits and promotees was reconsidered by a Constitution Bench in *Direct Recruit Class II Engineering Officers Association v State of Maharashtra*.[58] The Court held that seniority has to be counted from the date of appointment according to the rules and not according to the date of confirmation. If the appointment is only ad hoc and not according to the rules, officiation in the post cannot be considered for seniority. Where the quota rule has broken down and appointments are made in excess of the quota after following the procedure prescribed by the rules, the appointees should not be pushed down below the appointees from the other source inducted in the service at a later date. These and other principles laid down in this case hold the field today with further clarifications given in subsequent judgements like *K.C. Joshi v UOI*[59] and *State of West Bengal v Aghore Nath Dey*.[60]

(i) Bias

Reasonable likelihood of bias vitiates administrative action. A candidate cannot be a member of the selection committee at all, as held in *A.K. Kraipak v UOI*.[61] When a relative of a member of the selection committee is a candidate, that member cannot participate in the selection of his relative. The practice generally followed in such cases is for the member to abstain from the selection committee meeting while the candidature of his relative is being considered. He can participate in the rest of the selection. This practice has been approved by the Court in *Nagaraja v State of Mysore*,[62] *Javed Rasool Bhat v State of J&K*[63] and *Ashok Kumar Yadav v State of Haryana*.[64]

(j) Selection by Public Service Commissions

The Constitution provides for Public Service Commissions for the Union and the states. These are expert bodies which are to be consulted by the respective governments in matters relating to appointments, promotions, disciplinary action, etc. The members enjoy a fixed tenure with certain safeguards intended to make them function independent of the government concerned. In *State of UP v M.L. Srivastava*,[65] the Court held that the requirement of consultation with the Commission does not extend to making the advice of the Commission on those matters binding on the government. In *Jatinder Kumar v State of Punjab*,[66] the Court held that although the selection made by the Commission is only a recommendation and the final authority for appointment is the government, if a vacancy is to be filled up, the government has to make appointment strictly adhering to the order of merit recommended by the Public Service Commission, not disturbing the order of merit except for good reasons such as bad conduct or character. It also cannot appoint a person whose name does not appear in the list. The endeavour of the Court has been to eliminate arbitrariness in appointments.

(k) Claims of ad hoc employees

Initially, the Court was inclined not only to grant equal pay for equal work for casual workers engaged on a daily basis performing the same duties as performed by regular Class IV employees against sanctioned posts, but also to direct regularization of their services.[67] Subsequently, the Court took notice that ad hoc appointments are made on various considerations, including money, and therefore, the employer cannot be directed to regularize the services of such employees. In *Delhi Development Horticulture Employees' Union v Delhi Administration*,[68] the Court permitted the administration to keep the ad hoc employees on a panel and if they are registered with the employment exchange and are qualified to be appointed to the relevant posts, give them preference in employment whenever a vacancy occurs in the regular posts. In *State of Haryana v Piara Singh*,[69] the Court laid down comprehensive guidelines with regard to regularization of ad hoc employees, work-charged employees, and casual workers/daily rated employees, who possessed the prescribed qualifications and put in a few years of service. Once again it has been an exercise in balancing the interests of the employees, on one hand, and the public interest, on the other.

(l) Contract labour

Section 10 of the Contract Labour (Abolition and Regulation) Act, 1970 empowers the central government to prohibit by notification of employment of contract labour in any work in any establishment after being satisfied about the existence of the relevant factors mentioned therein. In *Catering Cleaners of Southern Railway v UOI*,[70] the Court, after being satisfied prima facie that all the relevant factors mentioned in section 10(2) had been made out, directed the central government to take appropriate action under section 10 of the Act in the matter of prohibiting the employment of contract labour in the work of cleaning catering establishments and pantry cars in the Southern Railways within six months. In *Air India Statutory Corporation v United Labour Union*,[71] the Court held that on the abolition of the contract labour system, by necessary implication, the principal employer will be under a statutory obligation to absorb the contract labour. The Court endeavours to give full effect to the object of welfare legislation.

(m) Transfer

While the Court is sympathetic to employees who are subjected to arbitrary termination of services, it does not ordinarily interfere with orders of transfer. In *E.P. Royappa v State of Tamil Nadu*,[72] a Constitution Bench declined to interfere with the posting of the petitioner who was working as Chief Secretary, as Deputy Chairman in the State Planning Commission, a newly sanctioned post in the grade of Chief Secretary. The Court negatived the plea of arbitrariness and mala fides. The Court observed that the allegations of mala fides are often more easily made than proved and the very seriousness of such allegations demands proof of a high order of credibility. Mere suspicion cannot take the place of proof. In *N.K. Singh v UOI*,[73] the Court delcared that unless the decision is vitiated by mala fides or infraction of any professed norm or principle governing the transfer, which alone can be scrutinized judicially, there are no judicially manageable standards for scrutinizing all transfers and the courts lack the necessary expertise for personnel management of all government departments. In *State of MP v S.S. Kaurav*,[74] the Court held that courts or tribunals are not appellate forums to decide on transfers of officers on administrative grounds. The Court cannot go into the question of relative hardship. It would be for the administration to consider and mitigate the hardship, if any. In *Chief General Manager v Rajendra Bhattacharji*,[75] the Court pointed out that a government employee or any servant of a public undertaking, who holds a transferable post, has no legal right to insist on being posted to any particular place. In *Arvind Dattatraya Dhande v State of Maharashtra*,[76] the Court was convinced that the order of transfer of the appellant was not in public interest, but a case of victimization of an honest officer at the behest of liquor dealers. The transfer order was set aside.

(n) Administrative Instructions

In *Sant Ram Sharma v State of Rajasthan*,[77] the Court recognized the necessity to fill up gaps in statutory rules and to supplement the rules by administrative instructions by government, provided the instructions are not inconsistent with the rules already framed. In *A.S. Ahluwalia v State of Punjab*,[78] the Court declared that administrative insructions are binding and any departure from these by the government without reason will be arbitrary and violative of Articles 14 and 16. In *R.D. Shetty v International Airport Authority*,[79] the Court pointed out that apart from Article 14, it is a well-settled rule of administrative law that an executive authority must be rigorously held to the standards by which it professes its actions to be judged and it must scrupulously observe these on pain of invalidation of an act in violation of them. In *B.S. Minhas v Indian Statistical Institute & Others*,[80] the Court declared that non-statutory bye-laws laying down the procedure for appointment to a post are bound to be complied with as they have been framed to avoid arbitrariness.

(o) Retrospective Rules

In *B.S. Vadera v UOI*,[81] it was held that government had the power to make rules under the proviso to Article 309 both prospectively and retrospectively. In *B.S. Yadav v State of Haryana*,[82] the Court took the view that the date from which retrospective effect was given to the rules must be shown to bear nexus with the provisions contained in the rules. In *State of Gujarat v Ramanlal Keshavlal Soni*,[83] the Court declared that a legislature cannot legislate today with reference to a situation that obtained twenty years ago and ignore the constitutional rights accrued in the course of twenty years. Following this decision, in *T.R. Kapur v State of Haryana*,[84] the Court held that the benefits acquired under the existing rules cannot be taken away by an amendment with retrospective effect. In *S.S. Bola v B.D. Sardana*,[85] the Court reiterated the principle that a retrospective law cannot take away any accrued or vested rights of the employees, while upholding an Act passed by the Haryana State legislature in 1995 with effect from 1 November 1966 except part of section 25 which made the pre-existing rules applicable to persons who were members of the service prior to 1 November 1966.

Article 311(2)

P.L. Dhingra v UOI[86] is an important judgement in service law as it deals with the scope of the doctrine of pleasure embodied in Article 310 and the nature of safeguards to civil servants provided in Article 311. The Court declared that Article 310, according to which every member of a civil service and every holder of a civil post holds office during the pleasure of the President or of the Governor of the State, as the case may be, is subject to Article 311. Under Article 311, every member of a civil service and every holder of a civil post, either under the Union or of a state, cannot be dismissed or removed by an authority subordinate to that by which he was appointed and no such person shall be dismissed or removed or reduced in rank except after an inquiry in which he has been informed of the charges against him and given a reasonable opportunity of being heard in relation to those charges. Initially, Article 311 provided for a second opportunity after the inquiry to represent against the proposed penalty, but by an amendment to the Constitution this opportunity has been withdrawn. The second proviso to Article 311(2) mentions the categories of cases in which the requirement of reasonable opportunity need not be complied with. They are: (a) where the order of dismissal or removal or reduction in rank is based on the employee's conviction on a criminal charge; (b) where it is not reasonably practicable to hold an inquiry; and (c) where the President or the Governor, as the case may be, is satisfied that in the interest of the security of the state, it is not expedient to hold such inquiry. Article

311(2) will be attracted only in cases where a civil servant has a right to hold the post or he is sought to be dismissed, removed, or reduced in rank by way of punishment. A temporary employee or a probationer has no right to hold the post. His services can be terminated by an innocuous order in terms of the rules without casting any stigma. *UOI v Mohammed Ramzan Khan*[87] has widened the scope of 'reasonable opportunity' contemplated in Article 311(2). In *Managing Director, ECIL v B. Karunakar,*[88] the Court held that when the inquiry officer makes an inquiry into the charges framed against an employee and submits his findings to the disciplinary authority, the employee is entitled to receive a copy of the inquiry report and represent to the disciplinary authority against the adverse findings in the report. The Court further held that if not furnishing a copy of the inquiry report did not cause any prejudice to the employee, the Court/tribunal should not interfere with the order of punishment. Even if prejudice is shown and the order of punishment is set aside, the appropriate order to be passed will be to direct reinstatement of the employee with liberty to the authority/management to proceed with the inquiry by placing the employee under suspension and continuing the inquiry from the stage of furnishing him with the report. The question of back wages should be left to be decided by the authority concerned according to law depending on the final outcome.

Retirement in Public Interest

The Supreme Court upheld the rules permitting compulsory premature retirement of government servants in public interest after completion of a reasonable qualifying service.[89] In *Gurudev Sidhu v State of Punjab,*[90] the Supreme Court struck down a rule which permitted the government to retire any government servant after he had completed ten years of qualifying service in public interest on the ground that the said rule violated Article 311(2) as the period of qualifying service is not reasonably long. In *UOI v J.N. Sinha*[91] the Court declared that the order of compulsory premature retirement made in public interest did not involve civil consequences and therefore no opportunity need be given to the employee to show cause against the proposed retirement. In *Baikuntha Nath Das v Chief District Medical Officer*[92] the Court seems to have gone too far in holding that even uncommunicated adverse remarks could be relied upon in taking a decision to retire an employee prematurely. This proposition requires reconsideration as it would be irrational and unfair to take a decision to retire an employee on unverified material.

Interference with Disciplinary Action

(a) In *State of Orissa v Bidyabhushan Mohapatra*[93] a Constitution Bench declared that the high court had no jurisdiction to direct the Governor to review the penalty. The order of dismissal passed by a competent authority on a public servant, if the conditions of the constitutional protection have been complied with, was not justiciable. In *Ranjit Thakur v UOI*,[94] finding that the punishment was shockingly disproportionate, the Court interfered with the punishment. In *UOI v Parmananda*,[95] the Court reiterated its earlier view that if the penalty can be lawfully imposed and is imposed for proven misconduct, the tribunal has no power to substitute its own discretion for that of the authority. The only exception to this proposition is where a person is punished without an inquiry on the basis of conviction by a criminal court. The tribunal may examine the adequacy of penalty imposed in the light of the conviction and sentence inflicted on the person. In *UOI v G. Ganayutham*,[96] the Court considered in depth the doctrine of proportionality in the matter of punishment and eventually concluded that unless the court or tribunal gives a finding of irrationality, the punishment cannot be quashed. Even then, the matter has to be remitted back to the appropriate authority for reconsideration. Only in very rare cases may the court substitute its own view as to the punishment in lieu of that awarded by the competent authority.

(b) In *UOI v Upendra Singh*,[97] the Court declared that interference by the tribunal with a pending departmental inquiry was not justified unless there was patent lack of jurisdiction to proceed with the inquiry. The right to speedy departmental inquiry was recognized by the Court. In *State of Punjab v Chaman Lal Goyal*[98] the Court dealt with this aspect in detail and extended the principles governing the right to speedy trial of criminal cases set out by a constitution Bench in *A.R. Antulay v R.S. Nayak*[99] to disciplinary inquiries.

Judicial Officers

Judicial officers constitute a separate class of government employees. The Constitution contains express provisions dealing with subordinate courts, including appointments of district judges and judicial officers, their postings, promotions, etc. The Constitution mandates consultation with the high court concerned in these matters and provides for control of the high court over subordinate courts. This was intended to ensure independence of the judiciary. In *Shamsher Singh v State of Punjab*,[100] the Court found fault with the high court of Punjab & Haryana for

requesting the government to depute the Director of Vigilance to hold
an inquiry into allegations of misconduct of a subordinate judge. The
Court regarded this as self-abnegation by the high court, in total disregard
of Article 235. The high court should have entrusted the inquiry to a
district judge. The Court has ensured the independence of the judiciary
by declaring that the recommendations of the high court are binding
on the government in all matters relating to the conditions of service of
subordinate judiciary in view of the control vested in the high court by
Article 235.[101] In *All India Judges Association v UOI*,[102] the Court issued
a set of directions to the central and state governments to set up an All
India Judicial Services, to bring about uniformity in designation of
officers, to raise the retirement age of judicial officers to 60 years, etc.
Traditionally, courts do not issue binding directions to the State to
legislate; at the most suggestions are made for amendment of the law.
The question arises whether the Court exercised judicial power or legislative power? The Court has been monitoring the implementation of its
directions from time to time.

In *I.C. Jain v High Court of Punjab*,[103] the Court pointed out that
while exercising control over the subordinate judiciary, the high court
is under a constitutional obligation to guide and protect judicial officers, as an honest and strict judicial officer is likely to have adversaries in
the mofussil. If judicial officers are under contant threat of complaint
and inquiry over trifling matters the subordinate judiciary will not be
able to administer justice independently and honestly. Interference by
the Supreme Court with the decisions of high courts in matters of discipline of the subordinate judiciary is minimal, particularly in cases of
doubtful integrity of judicial officers.

Workmen

The Industrial Disputes Act, 1947 confers valuable rights on workmen,
i.e. persons employed in any industry, to perform certain types of work
at lower levels. The Act provides for conciliation. It encourages settlements that are made statutorily binding. It provides effective remedies
against unfair labour practices. Such remedies are not available under
the law of contract or the Specific Relief Act. It protects the conditions
of service of workmen. As held in *Executive Committee of Vaish Degree
College v Laxmi Narain*,[104] a contract of personal service cannot ordinarily be specifically enforced and a court would not normally give a
declaration that the contract subsists. Industrial law permits the grant
of such a declaration. In *Rajasthan State Road Transport Corporation v*

Krishnakant,[105] the Supreme Court pointed out that the policy of industrial law is to provide a speedy, inexpensive, and effective forum for resolution of disputes arising between workmen and their employers:

The idea has been to ensure that the workmen do not get caught in the labyrinth of civil courts with their layers upon layers of appeals and revisions and the elaborate procedural laws, which the workmen can ill afford. The procedures followed by civil courts, it was thought, would not facilitate a prompt and effective disposal of these disputes. As against this, the courts and tribunals created by the Industrial Disputes Act are not shackled by these procedural laws nor is their award subject to any appeals or revisions. Because of their informality the workmen and their representatives can themselves prosecute or defend their cases. These forums are empowered to grant such relief as they think just and appropriate. They can even substitute the punishment in many cases. They can make and remake the contracts, settlements, wage structures and what not. Their awards are no doubt amenable to jurisdiction of the High Court under Article 226 as also to the jurisdiction of this Court under Article 32, but they are extraordinary remedies subject to several self-imposed constraints. It is, therefore, always in the interest of the workmen that disputes concerning them are adjudicated in the forums created by the Act and not in a civil Court. That is the entire policy underlying the vast array of enactments concerning workmen.

By widening the scope of the definition of 'industry' given in section 2(j) of the Act, a Bench of seven judges in *Bangalore Water Supply & Sewerage Board v R. Rajappa*[106] has brought workmen engaged in most of the establishments under the umbrella of the Industrial Disputes Act. The Court laid down a threefold test where there is systematic activity organized through cooperation between employer and employee for the production and/or distribution of goods and services calculated to satisfy human wants and wishes. Prima facie, there is an industry in that enterprise. On the basis of this interpretation, professions, clubs, educational insitutions, cooperatives, research institutes, charitable projects, etc. have been brought under the definition of 'industry'. Although in *Coir Board v Indira Devi*,[107] a Bench of two judges doubted the correctness of the decision in *Bangalore Water Supply & Sewerage Board* and desired reconsideration, a Bench of three judges presided over by the Chief Justice of India has declined the reference.

Not only has the word 'industry' been given a wide meaning, but the word 'workman' has been liberally interpreted to cover even piece-rated workmen. The approach of the Court is consistent with the principles governing interpretation of welfare legislation.

Conclusion

Oliver Wendell Holmes very aptly said that the life of law has not been logic; it has been experience. It is fascinating to observe the evolution of law from decision to decision. The law of employment is one of the most complex branches of law. The law has been changing fast in this area. The Court had to balance competing interests; the interests of employees and employers. Bearing in view the parameters of the Constitution and, in particular, the fundamental rights and the directive principles of state policy, the Court has been readjusting employeremployee relations periodically in the light of experience and circumstance. The Court could not shut its eyes to the stark reality that employees, as a class, are vulnerable and have no bargaining capacity, particularly when the country is unable to solve the massive problem of unemployment. The Court has been enlarging the scope of fundamental rights and statutory safeguards. Sir Henry Maine observed in his celebrated work *Ancient Law* that the movement of the progressive societies has hitherto been a movement from status to contract. In the law of employment, as developed by the Supreme Court, it is just the reverse. The movement has been from contract to status. The Court's interpretation of the provisions of the Constitution and the laws has given status to most of the employees who were previously governed by the law of contract. As a result of the liberal intepretation of Article 12 and the dynamism imparted to the right to equality in particular, employees of public sector undertakings are able to enjoy security of tenure similar to that of civil servants. The Court has not hesitated to revise its interpretation on any aspect of service law to the extent necessary. There are no final answers or permanent solutions to the problems that arise in this area. The quest for permanent solutions is an endless one. The Court is doing its utmost.

Although it is not the function of the Court to promote a work culture, if it can incidentally promote proper work culture, that would be a most welcome step. Awareness of constitutional and statutory safeguards as well as judicial remedies tends to promote a confrontationist attitude in some sectors of employment. The leadership of trade unions is largely in the hands of politicians. They lay emphasis on the rights of workmen but rarely remind them of their duty to work. Litigation, particularly class litigation, sometimes generates hostility. Conciliation, as a method of resolution of disputes, has not been very successful. The absence of an in-house mechanism for redressal of employees' grievances gives rise to more and more litigation. Honest employees cannot afford litigation, and are therefore bereft of any remedy. Arbitrariness in administration is widespread. Political interference in appointments, promotions, transfers etc. is on the increase. State Public Service Commissions and Selection Boards have lost much of their credibility, with the result that selections become suspect and unsuccessful candidates instinctively turn to courts. All this adds to the burden of the courts. A clean, honest, transparent, and efficient administration alone can arrest this tendency.

Notes

[1] (1982) 3 SCR 298.
[2] (1987) 2 SCR 314.
[3] (1988) 1 SCR 732.
[4] (1997) 3 SCC 261.
[5] *Fertilizer Corporation Kangar Union v UOI* (1981) 2 SCR 52.
[6] (1983) 1 SCR 922. *National Textile Workers Union v P.R. Ramkrishnan* (1983) 1 SCR 922.
[7] (1984) 2 SCR 67. *BMM v Union of India.*
[8] (1982) 2 SCR 365.
[9] (1993) 3 SCR 802, 861 B C.
[10] (1967) 3 SCR 377.
[11] (1975) 3 SCR 619.
[12] (1981) 2 SCR 79.
[13] (1955) 1 SCR 1045. *Budhan Chaudhary v State of Bihar* (1955) 1 SCR 1045.
[14] (1959) 1 SCR 279.
[15] (1962) 2 SCR 125.
[16] (1960) 2 SCR 346, 354.
[17] (1978) 2 SCR 621, 674.
[18] (1985) Supp 2 SCR 131, 233.
[19] (1974) 2 SCR 348.
[20] (1982) 3 SCR 298.
[21] (1988) Supp 3 SCR 288.
[22] (1973) Supp SCR 1.
[23] (1985) Supp 2 SCR 51, 80.
[24] (1984) 2 SCR 67, 103.
[25] (1993) 1 SCR 594, 700–1.
[26] (1962) 2 SCR 586.
[27] (1963) Supp 1 SCR 439.
[28] (1976) 1 SCR 906.
[29] (1992) Supp 2 SCR 454.
[30] (1964) 6 SCR 368.
[31] (1985) Supp 1 SCR 352.
[32] (1994) 2 SCR 644.
[33] *Constituent Asembly Debates,* Vol. XI, p. 980.
[34] (1995) 2 SCC 745.

[35] (1995) 6 SCC 684.
[36] (1996) 2 SCC 715.
[37] (1997) 6 SCC 538.
[38] *Ajit Singh v State of Punjab* 1999 (5) SCALE 556.
[39] (1998) 4 SCC 1.
[40] (1985) Supp 2 SCR.
[41] (1985) 2 SCR 1014.
[42] (1986) 2 SCR 278.
[43] (1990) Supp 1 SCR 142.
[44] (1993) Supp 4 SCC 377.
[45] (1996) 4 SCC 319.
[46] (1999) 3 SCC 696.
[47] (1982) 1 SCR 320.
[48] (1985) Supp 1 SCR 657.
[49] (1994) 1 SCC 150.
[50] (1994) 4 SCC 165.
[51] (1966) 3 SCR 600.
[52] *B.S. Gupta v UOI* (1975) Supp SCR 491.
[53] (1975) 2 SCR 979.
[54] (1981) 1 SCR 1024.
[55] (1983) 2 SCR 936.
[56] (1985) 3 SCR 431.
[57] (1977) 3 SCR 775.
[58] (1990) 2 SCR 900.
[59] (1990) Supp 2 SCR 573.
[60] (1993) 2 SCR 919.
[61] (1970) 1 SCR 457.
[62] (1966) 3 SCR 682.
[63] (1984) 2 SCR 582, 596.
[64] (1985) Supp 1 SCR 657, 687.
[65] (1958) SCR 533.
[66] (1985) 1 SCR 899.
[67] *Dhirendra Chamouli v State of UP* (1986) 1 SCC 637; *Surinder Singh v Engineer-in-Chief* (1986) 1 SCC 639.
[68] (1992) 1 SCR 565.
[69] (1992) 3 SCR 826.
[70] (1987) 2 SCR 164.
[71] (1997) 9 SCC 377.
[72] (1974) 2 SCR 348.
[73] (1994) 6 SCC 98.
[74] (1995) 1 SCR 482.
[75] (1995) 1 SCR 360.
[76] (1997) 6 SCC 169.
[77] (1968) 1 SCR 111.
[78] (1975) 3 SCR 82.
[79] (1979) 3 SCR 1014.
[80] (1984) 1 SCR 395.
[81] (1968) 3 SCR 575.
[82] (1981) 1 SCR 1024.

[83] (1983) 2 SCR 287.

[84] (1987) 1 SCR 584.

[85] (1997) 8 SCC 522.

[86] (1958) SCR 828.

[87] (1990) Supp 3 SCR 248.

[88] (1993) 4 SCC 727.

[89] *Shyamlal v UP* (1955) 1 SCR 26; *Motiram Deka v GM, N.E. Railway* (1964) 5 SCR 683; *T.G. Shivacharan Singh v State of Mysore* AIR 1965 SC 280.

[90] (1964) 7 SCR 587.

[91] (1971) 1 SCR 791.

[92] (1992) 1 SCR 836.

[93] (1963) Supp 1 SCR 648.

[94] (1988) 1 SCR 512.

[95] (1989) 2 SCR 19.

[96] (1997) 7 SCC 463.

[97] (1994) 3 SCC 357.

[98] (1995) 1 SCR 695.

[99] (1992) 1 SCC 225.

[100] (1975) 1 SCR 814.

[101] *Chief Justice of AP v L.V.A. Dixitulu* (1979) 1 SCR 26.

[102] (1991) Supp 2 SCR 206.

[103] (1988) Supp 1 SCR 396.

[104] (1976) 2 SCR 1006.

[105] (1995) 3 SCR 1118.

[106] (1978) 3 SCR 207.

[107] (1998) 3 SCC 259.

Twenty

The Supreme Court and Tort Litigation

Anil Divan

Introduction

The law of torts deals with breaches of duty independent of contract giving rise to an action for unliquidated damages. Tort is increasingly concerned with the allocation or prevention of losses. Damage may be injury to person, damage to property, reputation, or financial interests.

Tort is a residuary category for redress and has sometimes been called the dustbin of the law of obligation. Tort law deals with situations where the law will grant redress (or the law will deny it), and the measure of liability and the principles on which damages are to be quantified.

In India, the English Common Law relating to torts was applied by the courts while administering justice 'according to justice and right', and 'according to justice, equity, and good conscience'. This meant the rules of English law were applicable if found appropriate for Indian society and circumstances.

In India a large part of personal injury litigation is now handled by the Motor Accident Claims Tribunals. Many claims go to the consumer fora functioning under the Consumer Protection Act, 1986. Civil suits claiming damages caused by torts are virtually non-existent. The trial of the suit together with appeals would take no less than twenty years or even more. Further, at the initial stage *ad valorem* court fees even before a suit is instituted stifle most claims for damages. In many states such fees are without a maximum limit. Again, similar court fees are payable for each appeal. Civil suits for damages are therefore non-starters. Action for preventive reliefs like injunctions is more frequent, particularly in cases of defamation or nuisance.

The areas discussed in this article are:
- Defamation: government and public officials.

- The rule of absolute liability: Beyond *Rylands v Fletcher* (the gas leak cases: *Shri Ram* and *Union Carbide*).
- The sovereign immunity of the State.
- Compensation/damages for breach of fundamental rights (tort, quasi tort, or not a tort).
- Misfeasance in public office: arbitrary, oppressive, and unconstitutional actions by the State and its officials. The article states the law as on May 1999.

These topics have been selected because in most of them there has been a quantum leap in the development of the law or some further modernization of the law is required. It will be noticed that most of these developments and improvements in the law have taken place where human rights jurisprudence is involved.

Defamation: Government and Public Officials

The tension between freedom of speech and the law of defamation is reflected in many cases all over the world. The problem has been to balance the interests of the individual whose reputation is harmed as against the cherished values of freedom of speech, criticism of persons occupying high public office, and the furthering of public interest in a democracy by fearless, unrestricted, and trenchant criticism of public officials on public issues.

The Constitution of India notices this tension and has balanced the two competing interests between protection of private reputation and freedom of speech. Article 19(1)(a) guarantees the right to freedom of speech and expression. Article 19(2) enables the state to impose reasonable restrictions on the right, *inter alia*, in relation to defamation.

The traditional defences of justification, fair comment, and qualified privilege place an enormous burden on the defendants. Indeed it was a widely shared view that the English law tilted the balance in favour of protecting reputation and consequently fettered the freedom of speech. This would be particularly true in matters of public interest where it would be impossible for the defendant either to prove truth or lay the basis for fair comment by proving the truth. A large claim of damages would ruin the defendant and would have a 'chilling effect' on media exposure of the misdeeds of public officials.

In a seminal and path-breaking judgement delivered by the Supreme Court in *R. Rajagopal v State of Tamil Nadu*[1] Jeevan Reddy and S.C. Sen JJ) the Indian Law of Defamation relating to government, local authorities, and public officials and their criticism was brought substantially in line with developments in England and the USA.

Before I discuss the case however it would be interesting to notice developments in other jurisdictions.

In the United States, under the umbrella of the First Amendment, a much more liberal interpretation was adopted in the famous case of *New York Times Co. v Sullivan*.[2] The law was further strengthened by several other judgements.

Meanwhile English law, under the influence of the European Convention on Human Rights, was also evolving new principles in the law of defamation. The seed of the new development was sown in the *Spycatcher Case*. The British government moved the courts for interim injunction to prevent publication of a book written by Peter Wright, a former member of the British Secret Service, which had already been published in the USA. Certain newspapers wanted to serialize it. This gave rise to an enormous controversy regarding prior restraints on publication and the freedom of expression. The Court of Appeal granted an injunction and issued a 'gag' order. The matter was carried to the House of Lords. Unfortunately the House of Lords upheld by a narrow majority of three against two the right of the government, to obtain an interim injunction and stop publication of the extracts. This decision in *Attorney General v Guardian Newspapers*[3] was widely and robustly criticized in the press.

The Times (London) in a blistering editorial said:

Yesterday morning the law looked simply to be an ass. Those who regretted this fact were waiting with quiet confidence for the law lords to do something about it. We hoped that they would accept the reality that the secrets of Mr Peter Wright's book *Spycatcher* were irretrievably in the public domain ... But yesterday afternoon the law was still an ass. But as a result of their Lordships' judgement it was no longer a cozy docile domestic creature whom a kick in the right place would restore to useful activity. In the hands of Lords Templeman, Ackner and Brandon [the majority who ruled for the Gag order] it had become unpredictable and wild, seemingly responsive only to autocratic whims.

The *Daily Mirror* went one better. It came out with a front-page caption 'You Fools' and published photographs of Lords Templeman, Ackner, and Brandon upside down. This front page has now been immortalized as the cover of a book by Simon Lee called *Judging Judges*. The final judgement after trial is reported in *Attorney-General v Guardian Newspapers* (No. 2)[4] where substantially the injunctions were not granted.

However the path-breaking decision of the House of Lords in England was the *Derbyshire County Council v Times Newspapers Ltd*[5] affirming the judgement of the Court of Appeals.[6] It was unanimously held that a local authority was not entitled to maintain an action in libel concerning its governmental and administrative functions. The House of Lords not only relied upon the American decision but also a decision of the Supreme Court of South Africa. Some of the observations of Lord Keith are worth noting.

After referring to *New York Times v Sullivan* he observed:

While these decisions were related most directly to the provisions of the American Constitution concerned with securing freedom of speech, the public interest considerations which underlay them are no less valid in this country. What has been described as the 'chilling effect' induced by the threat of civil actions for libel is very important. Quite often the facts which would justify a defamatory publication are known to be true, but admissible evidence capable of proving those facts is not available. This may prevent the publication of matters which it is very desirable to make public.[7]

The House of Lords also strongly relied on the observations in a South African judgement where the Supreme Court of South Africa observed:

Nevertheless it seems to me that considerations of fairness and convenience are, on balance, distinctly against the recognition of a right in the Crown to sue the subject in a defamation action to protect that reputation. The normal means by which the Crown protects itself against attacks upon its management of the country's affairs is political action and not litigation, and it would, I think be unfortunate if that practice were altered.

These influences from other common law jurisdictions led to a cross-fertilization of ideas and an advance in Indian legal thought.

On 17 October 1994 a seminal judgement was delivered by the Supreme Court in the famous case of *R. Rajagopal v State of TN*[8] Jeevan Reddy and S.C. Sen JJ). The facts are unusual. The petitioners were editors and printer and publishers of a Tamil weekly magazine called *Nakkheeran*. They wanted to serialize and publish the autobiography of a condemned prisoner called Auto Shankar alias Gauri Shankar alias Shankar. Auto Shankar was condemned to death on conviction but his mercy petition was pending. The editor and publisher presented a writ petition under Article 32 because the Inspector General of Prisons asked them not to publish the autobiography on the ground that it was not written by Auto Shankar. They apprehended adverse action by the state of Tamil Nadu. The autobiography related that the condemned prisoner and several public officials in the police, Indian adminstrative, and other services had a close nexus with his criminal activities. Several questions arose in the petition including the right of privacy.

The questions relating to defamation were whether the government of Tamil Nadu could maintain an action for defamation and whether the government and the public officials who apprehended that the publication would defame them could impose a prior restraint upon the press.

The Court considered the American and English cases, particularly the *Sullivan* case, the *Pentagon Papers* case, and the *Derbyshire* case, and substantially followed them with some reservations and modifications.

The Court answered the question relating to defamation by holding that the government, local authority, and other organs and institutions exercising governmental power cannot maintain a suit for damages for defamation. It also held that in the case of public officials the remedy of an action for damages is not available in relation to their acts and conduct relevant to the discharge of their official duties. Even where the publication is based upon facts and statements which are not true, to succeed, the official must establish that the publication was made with reckless disregard for truth. The press or the publisher had only to show that he had published after reasonable verification of facts. Of course, where actual malice or personal animosity is shown the defendant will not have the benefit of this rule. It was further held that neither the government nor the public officials have a right to impose a prior restraint upon the publication of such material. The Court observed:[9]

But what is called for today—in the present times—is a proper balancing of the freedom of press and laws consistent with the democratic way of life ordained by the Constitution. Over the last few decades press and electronic media have emerged as major factors in our nation's life. They are still expanding—and in the process becoming more inquisitive. Our system of Government demands—as do the systems of Government of the United States of America and United Kingdom—constant vigilance over exercise of governmental power by the press and the media among others. It is essential for good Government.

However, the Court framed principles modifying some of those emerging in the USA to suit our needs. The Court reaffirmed the right of the editor and publisher to publish what they had gathered from public records (including Court records) even without the consent of the citizen concerned, but made an exception in favour of a female victim of sexual assault, abduction, etc. or a like offence.

The Indian law of tort on defamation, as far as the right of public officials and government and other governmental authorities are concerned, is now marching in step with American, English, and other common law jurisdictions. The fundamental right of freedom of speech and expression has been suitably enlarged to embrace within its fold, the uninhibited right to discuss public issues on corruption, maladministration and dereliction of duty by politicians, public officials, and government; a quantum leap to secure a more transparent, a more accountable, and a more responsible government.

The Rule of Absolute Liability—Beyond *Rylands v Fletcher*: The Gas Leak Cases—*Shriram* and *Union Carbide*

The law of torts has been traditionally judge-made law. The common law adapting itself to changing circumstances with a view to seeing that wherever there is damage or injury the injured party should not be without legal redress. It has been said that law is not static and new torts emerge as the courts respond to new problems and developments in society. The categories of torts are never closed.

A new tort was boldly innovated by the Supreme Court in *M.C. Mehta v Union of India,* also known as the *Shriram Fertilizers* case or the *Oleum Gas Leak* case[10] hereinafter called the *Shriram* case). I would characterize the new tort as 'the rule of absolutely absolute liability' because it admits of no exception as formulated by the Supreme Court. The enterprise is liable even if there is an act of God (earthquake, floods, lightning strike) or an act of terrorism or enemy action.

A caveat is essential. I was conducting the case for the Shriram factory throughout, after the oleum gas leak. I was also briefed as counsel throughout for the American Union Carbide Corporation and have mentioned certain facts which are not widely known. My perception and views are to some extent influenced by my participation in these cases and this the reader should know.

The Background Facts

On the midnight between 2–3 December 1984 there was a massive escape of methyl isocyanate (MIC) from the Bhopal plant of Union Carbide India Ltd (UCIL), an Indian company which was a subsidiary of the Union Carbide Corporation, USA (UCC) which held 50.9 per cent of UCIL shares. This was the Bhopal gas tragedy which resulted in the estimated death of over 3000 persons and serious personal injuries to over 30,000.

Exactly a year and a day later, on 4 December 1985, there was a leak of oleum gas from a factory in Delhi of Shriram Foods and Fertilizer Industries (called Shriram) which enveloped parts of Delhi in yellow smoke causing considerable panic. There was already a pending writ petition *(M.C. Mehta v Union of India)* for closure and relocation of the Shriram factory. The gas leak occurred during the pendency of the petition and applications were made by public interest groups for compensation on account of damages suffered by individuals due to the oleum gas leak. Fortunately, oleum gas is non-toxic and is less harmful than 'tear gas' routinely used by the police to control mobs. In fact, Dr Varadarajan, Secretary, Department of Science and Technology (Government of India) was reported in the press as opining: 'The gas that leaked out ... was sulphur trioxide which was not toxic'.

Chief Justice Bhagwati was hearing the *Shriram* case and certain questions were referred to a Constitution Bench of five judges (where Bhagwati CJ presided) which delivered the judgement reported in *M.C. Mehta v Union of India*.[11]

One of the points raised on behalf of Shriram was that a private corporation like Shriram would not fall within the scope and ambit of Article 12 (State) and therefore the writ petition under Article 32 and the claim for compensation therein was not maintainable. The judgement notices the arguments on maintainability of the petition and the application of the American doctrine of state action and its applicability to India. Both questions remained unanswered.

The Court held:

But we do not propose to decide finally at the present stage whether a private Corporation like Shriram should fall within the scope and ambit of Article 12, because we have not had sufficient time to consider and reflect on this question in depth. The hearing of this case before us concluded only on 15 December 1986 and we are called upon to deliver our judgement within a period of four days on 19 December 1986. We are, therefore, of the view that this is not a question on which we must make any definite pronouncement at this stage.[12]

The judgement was actually delivered on Saturday, 20 December 1986, the last day of Bhagwati, CJ's tenure. His successor, Justice R.S. Pathak, was sworn in as Chief Justice on 21 December 1986.

The New Tort—The Principle of Absolute Liability for Hazardous Industries
Rylands v Fletcher[13]

The rule of strict liability was formulated in the classic English case. This rule makes the owner of land liable to damages caused by the escape of anything which the owner brings or collects on his own land. This rule applied only to what is known as non-natural use of land but does not apply to things naturally on the land. There is no liability if the escape is due to an act of God, the act of a stranger, or default or consent of a person injured or his consent or cases of statutory authority.

Bhagwati CJ after noticing *Rylands v Fletcher* observed:

We have to evolve new principles and lay down new norms which would adequately deal with the new problems which arise in a higly industrialized economy. We cannot allow our judicial thinking to be constricted by reference to the law as it prevails in England or for the matter of that in any other foreign country. We no longer need the crutches of a foreign legal order ... If the enterprise is permitted to carry on an hazardous or inherently dangerous activity for its profit, the law must presume that such permission is conditional on the enterprise absorbing the cost of any accident arising on account of such hazardous or inherently dangerous activity as an appropriate item of its overheads. Such hazardous or inherently dangerous activity for private profit can be tolerated only on conditions that the enterprise engaged in such hazardous or inherently dangerous activity indemnifies all those who suffer on account of the carrying on of such hazardous or inherently dangerous activity regardless of whether it is carried on carefully or not. This principle is also sustainable on the ground that the enterprise alone has the resource to discover and guard against hazards or dangers and to provide warning against potential hazards. We would therefore hold that where an enterprise is engaged in a hazardous or inherently dangerous activity and harm results to anyone on account of an accident in the operation of such hazardous or inherently dangerous activity resulting, for example in escape of toxic gas the enterprise is strictly and absolutely liable to compensate all those who were affected by the accident and such liability is not subject to any of the exceptions which operate vis-à-vis the tortious principle of strict liability under the rule in *Rylands v Fletcher*.[14]

The above observations when analysed yield the following propositions:

(1) The Court clearly observed that it was evolving a new principle of liability (p. 420) and laying down new norms. The Court constructed this new principle of liability to deal with the unusual situation that had arisen and was likely to arise in future on account of hazardous and inherently dangerous industries.

(2) The new liability was evolved on the presumption that permission to carry on such hazardous activity was conditional on the enterprise absorbing any cost of the accident as part of its overheads.

(3) The new liability was applied to working for private profit.

(4) Such liability to compensate was not subject to any exceptions which operate vis-à-vis the tortious principle of strict liability under the rule of *Rylands v Fletcher*.

(5) The industry was liable to indemnify all who suffered regardless of whether the operations were carried on carefully or not (i.e. No fault liability).

Then came a further quantum leap on the measure of damages. It was further held:

We should also like to point out that the measure of compensation in the kind of cases referred to in the preceding paragarph must be co-related to the magnitude and capacity of the enterprise *because such compensation should have a deterrent effect. The larger and more prosperous the enterprise, the greater must be the amount of compensation payable by it* for the harm caused on account of the accident in the carrying on of the hazardous or inherently dangerous activity by the enterprise.[15] (emphasis supplied)

To put it pithily, the liability was neither strict nor absolute, but absolutely absolute. It is not apposite in this article to trace in detail how, in what manner, and under what circumstances this principle was evolved even though there was no argument on the question of punitive or exemplary or deterrent damage and whether the Court was entitled to go into and lay down the principle of punitive damages when the Court itself had stopped counsel for Shriram from arguing the matter. The point was raised by Shriram in a new writ petition and also in an application for the constitution of a larger Bench. It was contended by Shriram that the observations in relation to deterrent compensation were made after counsel was directed not to argue the question of punitive and exemplary damages as recorded in the written submission given on 15 December 1986, and as a result the judgement was contrary to natural justice, a nullity and *per incuriam.* When the judgement was reserved, Shriram submitted written submission on 15 December 1986 in which it was stated:

during the course of the argument on behalf of SFFI [Shriram Food and Fertilizer Industries] Respondent No. 4, the Court indicated that it was not deciding:
  (i) the question of exemplary or punitive damages,
 (ii) the question of negligence of SFFI.

This issue was never debated as the oleum gas leak claims were settled.

This principle of absolutely absolute liability was relied upon in the *Bhopal gas leak* case which was then pending before the district court. It was utilized by the district judge to give interim damages in the sum of Rs 350 crores. When the matter was carried to the Madhya Pradesh High Court, Justice Sheth, again relying upon the principle of absolute liability formulated in the *Shriram* case, gave reduced interim damages in the sum of Rs 250 crores. The matter was carried both by the Union Carbide Corporation, USA and the Union of India to the Supreme Court where it gave rise to four reported decisions and orders.

The first decision was the compromise between UCC and the Union of India and the Settlement Order reported in *UCC v UOI*[16] dated 14/ 15 February 1989.

In view of the criticism in the media and from various sources, the Bench on 4 May 1989 delivered an order explaining the reasons and the basis on which the Court had approved the said settlement and compromise.[17]

Several social action groups challenged the Bhopal Act and the settlement and a Constitution Bench presided over by Chief Justice Mukharji heard the matter at great length and upheld the validity of the Act and did not set aside the settlement on certain conditions. The victims and the organizations representing the victims were directed to be heard on the question of the validity of the settlement in the then pending review petitions. These judgements were delivered on 22 December 1989.[18]

The sequel was the review hearing on which judgements were delivered on 3 October 1991 by another Constitution Bench.[19] The judgement on review upheld the settlement except in regard to the clauses which gave immunity from criminal proceedings to the company and its directors and officials. The clauses of the settlement which quashed the criminal proceedings were held to be not justified and the criminal proceedings were accordingly directed to be proceeded with.

The above narration of facts and events and the various judgements and orders delivered in the Bhopal gas leak litigation only serve as a background for the doubts expressed by several judges on the principle of exemplary or punitive damages.

One of the controversies that arose before the Bench and which was urged on behalf of the Union Carbide Corporation was that the application of the new principle of liability, as formulated in the *Shriram* case, should be reconsidered, and in any event if the decree of Rs 250 crores passed by the Madhya Pradesh High Court was to go for execution in the United States courts it would have to face the challenge of 'due process'. A discussion on this argument is not pertinent within the ambit of a short essay. What is pertinent are the observations and perceptions of several judges on the validity, applicability and correctness of this principle of absolute liability linked with exemplary or punitive damages. Before discussing this, it is important to highlight some of the infirmities in the line of reasoning adopted by the Constitution Bench in the *Shriram* case.

First, the absolutely absolute liability was *a fortiori* a no-fault liability. Second, there were no exceptions or defences against such liability. Even an act of God like an earthquake or lightning strike or floods would not absolve the enterprise. Further, an act of terrorism equally would not be a defence. If this be so, the Court without going into the question of fault or negligence or breach of statutory duties would straightaway hold the enterprise liable. Can such an absolutely absolute liability principle, where the escape of lethal gas may have been caused by outside agencies or an act of God, be regarded as rational, reasonable, or just? Third, the imposition of punitive or exemplary damages as a deterrent, which was co-related to the size and resources of the enterprise, again flew in the face of a no-fault liability principle. If the accident occurred because of an act of God, where was the question of punishment or deterrence qua the enterprise? If the accident occurred because of an act of terrorism where was the question of punishing the defendant enterprise? The linkage of punitive or exemplary damages to the resources and size of the enterprise was difficult to justify and uphold on grounds of rationality, reasonableness, or justice. Punitive or exemplary damages should be awarded as a punishment if there is an element of fault, negligence, wilful misconduct, or gross breach of statutory duties. Only after a finding of fact is arrived at could the principle of punitive or exemplary damages be invoked.

The core of the criticism of the *Shriram* judgement had its echoes in the observations of various judges in the group of *Union Carbide* cases which may now be discussed.

UCC v UOI[20] (4 May 1989) reflects this concern. The Court observed:

One aspect of this matter was dealt with by this Court in *M.C. Mehta v Union of India* [i.e. the *Shriram* case] which marked a significant stage in the development of the law. *But, at the hearing there was more than a mere hint in the submissions of the Union Carbide that in this case the law was altered with only the Union Carbide Corporation in mind, and was altered to its disadvantage even before the case had reached this Court.* The criticism of the *Mehta* principle, perhaps ignores the emerging postulates of tortious liability whose principal focus is the social limits on economic adventurism. There are certain things that a civilized society simply cannot permit to be done to its members, even if they are compensated for their resulting losses.[21] (emphasis supplied)

The Court further observed:

The tremendous suffering of thousands of persons compelled us to move into the direction of immediate relief which, we thought, should not be subordinated to the *uncertain promises of the law*, and when the assessment of fairness of the amount was based on certain factors and assumptions not disputed even by the plaintiff.[22] (emphasis supplied)

Again in *Charanlal Sahu*[23] Sabyasachi Mukharji CJ observed, when discussing the *Shriram* case and the principle of absolute liability:

The question of liability was highlighted by this Court in *M.C. Mehta* case [*Shriram* case] where a Constitution Bench of this Court had to deal with the rule of strict liability ... This Court noted that law has to grow in order to satisfy the needs of the fast-changing society and keep abreast with the economic developments taking place in the country. Law cannot afford to remain static. This court reiterated there that if it is found necessary to construct a new principle of liability to deal with an unusual situation which has arisen and which is likely to arise in future on account of hazardous or inherently dangerous industries which are concomitant to an industrial economy; the Court should not hesitate to evolve such principle of liability merely because it has not been so done in England.[24]

Further:

As in the instant adjudication, this Court is not concerned with the determination of the actual extent of liability, we will proceed on the basis that the law enunciated by this Court in *M.C. Mehta* case is the decision upon the basis of which damages will be payable to the victims in this case ... Perhaps, in this case, had the action proceeded, one would have realized that the fall out of this Gas disaster might have been the formulation of a concept of damages, blending both civil and criminal liabilites. *There are, however, serious difficulties in evolving such an actual concept of punitive damages in respect of a civil action which can be integrated and enforced by the judicial process. It would have raised serious problems of pleading, proof and discovery, and interesting and challenging as the task might have been, it is still very uncertain how far decision based on such a concept would have been a decision according to 'due process' of law acceptable by international standards. There were difficulties in that attempt.*[25] (emphasis supplied)

Justice K.N. Singh concurred with Chief Justice Mukharji. He referred to the *Shriram* case (p. 710) and characterized it as a judicial innovation in laying down principles with regard to liability of enterprises carrying on hazardous or inherently dangerous activity.

Justice Ranganathan (for himself and Ahmadi J) observed:

One of the contentions before us was that the UCC and UCIL are accountable to the public for the damages caused by their industrial activities not only on a basis of strict liability but also on the basis that the damages to be awarded against them should include an element of punitive liability and that this has been lost sight of while approving of the proposed settlement. Reference was made in this context to *M.C. Mehta* case [*Shriram* case]. *Whether the settlement could have taken into account this factor is, in the first place, a moot question. Mukharji CJ has pointed out—and we are inclined to agree—that this is an 'uncertain province of the law' and it is premature to say whether this yardstick has been, or will be, accepted in this country,* not to speak of its international acceptance which may be necessary should occasion arise for executing a decree based on such a yardstick in another country.[26] (emphasis supplied) (p. 722, para 156)

Further:

We, therefore, think it necessary to clarify, for our part, that we are not called upon to express any view on the observations in *Mehta* case (*Shriram* case) and should not be understood as having done so.[27] (p. 723, para 157)

The next decision was on the review petitions where the settlement judgement was to be reconsidered after hearing the viewpoints of the victims and various organizations supporting them. The judgement was delivered on 3 October 1991 and is reported in 1991.[28]

Chief Justice Misra referred to the *Shriram* case as well as *Rylands v Fletcher* and observed:[29]

In *M.C. Mehta* case (the *Shriram* case) no compensation was awarded as this Court could not reach the conclusion that *Shriram* (the delinquent Company) came within the meaning of 'State' in Article 12 so as to be liable to the discipline of Article 21 and to be subjected to a proceeding under Article 32 of the Constitution. *Thus what was said was essentially obiter.* (emphasis supplied)

We are not concerned in the present case as to whether the ratio of *M.C. Mehta* [*Shriram* case] should be applied to cases of the type referred to in it in India. We have to remain cognizant of the fact that the Indian assets of UCC through UCIL are around Rs 100 crores or so. For any decree in excess of that amount, execution has to be taken in the United States and one has to remember the observation of US Court of Appeals that the defence of due process would be available to be raised in the execution proceedings. The decree to be obtained in the Bhopal suit would have been a money decree and it would have been subject to the law referred to in the judgement of the US Court of Appeals. *If the compensation is determined on the basis of strict liability—a foundation different from the accepted basis in the United States—the decree would be open to attack and may not be executable.* (emphasis supplied)[30]

Chief Justice Misra was conscious of the minefield of due process and further observed:

In the event the US Courts would have been of the view that strict liability was foreign to the American jurisprudence and contrary to US Public Policy, the decree would not have been executed in the United States[31] ... this however is not an occasion when such an experiment would have been undertaken to formulate the *Mehta* principle of strict liability at the eventual risk of ultimately losing the legal battle.[32]

The leading judgement of Venkatachaliah J referred to *Rylands v Fletcher* and the *Shriram* case and noticed that:

Respondents [i.e. UCC] however raised several contentions as to the soundness of the Mehta principle and its applicability. It was also urged that *Mehta* principle even to the extent it goes, does not solve the issues of liability of the UCC as distinct from that of UCIL as *Mehta* case only spoke of the liability of the offending enterprise and did not deal with principles guiding the determination of a holding company for the torts of its subsidiaries. ... It is not necessary to go into this controversy. The settlement was arrived and is left undisturbed on an overall view. *The settlement cannot be assailed as violative of Mehta principle which might have arisen for consideration in a strict adjudication* ... There is, therefore, no substance in the point that *Mehta* principle should guide the quantification of compensation to the victim claimants.[33] (emphasis supplied)

Though there is a general acceptance of the new tort of 'absolute liability' in the case of a hazardous and inherently dangerous industry, many judges have expressed grave doubt about the measure of damages and the punitive principle of visiting the enterprise with exemplary damages co-related to its resources and size.
To sum up:

(1) The unanimous order of 4 May 1989 explaining the basis of the settlement, which has been extracted above, characterizes the *Shriram* principle as an uncertain premise of law.

(2) Again, Chief Justice Mukharji (with whom Saikia J concurred) expressed grave doubts about the principle of exemplary or deterrent damages and as to whether such a decision would be internationally acceptable. He in fact observed that he could not foresee any reasonable possibility of acceptance of this yardstick internationally.

(3) To the same effect is the observation of Justice Ranganathan who delivered the judgement for himself and Ahmadi J. He, while agreeing with Chief Justice Mukharji echoed doubts about the linkage of punitive damages with absolute liability. He even observed that it was premature to say whether this yardstick has been or would be accepted in this country not to speak of its international acceptance. It is reasonable to conclude that the *Shriram* case para 32 (exemplary damages) has raised doubts in the minds of several judges dealing with the Union Carbide case to which the *Shriram* case observations were apparently meant to apply.

The question whether the observations made in the *Shriram* case were *obiter dicta* or not was subsequently specifically canvassed in *Indian Council for Enviro-Legal Action v Union of India*[34] before a Bench of two judges, Jeevan Reddy and Kirpal JJ. It was held that these observations in the *Shriram* case and the law declared were not *obiter dicta*. It was held that it was not unnecessary for the purpose of that case as parties were directed to institute cases on the basis of the law so declared. The Bench also held that the law stated in the *Shriram* case was appropriate apart from the fact that it was binding upon them.[35]

It is therefore clear that the principle of absolute liability for hazardous enterprise is now firmly entrenched in Indian jurisprudence. It will therefore clearly apply to multinationals operating in India. It is however very doubtful whether a decree of punitive damages passed by Indian courts on the basis of the principle of absolute liability coupled with punitive damages could be executed against non-Indian assets of such multinationals.

Further, it is not clear whether a public sector enterprise would be subject to the principle of absolute liability and exemplary damages co-related to their assets. Take the case of a public sector oil refinery. This is clearly a hazardous and inherently dangerous enterprise. In case of an accident or mishap causing injury to individuals, could the principle of absolute liability coupled with punitive damages co-related to its assets be the correct rule to apply? Indeed, a close reading of para 31 of the *Shriram* judgement seems to confine the principle to enterprises set up for 'private profit', thereby making it inapplicable to public sector enterprises.

This again reinforces the criticism that the *Shriram* judgement was hurriedly delivered with the Union Carbide case in mind and a new tort was suddenly evolved to meet the claims of the victims of the Bhopal gas disaster. It is to be particularly noticed that the Court did not decide the question of maintainability under Article 12 against Shriram but left it open.

Further, barring the cryptic para 32, there is no discussion on the theory or basis of visiting punitive damages when there is absolute liability. In fact, once the enterprise is subject to a no-fault liability it becomes its own insurer for all risks and without a finding of negligence how could a deterrent award of punitive damages be made? Is the damage to be paid by an insurer to be measured by the assets of the insurer? Suppose the incident occurred due to an earthquake or lightning why should the enterprise be saddled with punitive damages in the absence of negligence?

In the future, when the passions and emotions generated by the Bhopal gas tragedy have subsided, the Supreme Court of India must have a fresh look at the validity of this principle of punitive damages linked to a no-fault liability.

The National Environment Tribunal Act, 1995 (which has not been brought into force) statutorily prescribes unlimited no-fault liability in relation to hazardous substances. It accepts the principle of absolute liability but is silent on the penal element. Earlier, under the Public Law Insurance Act, 1991, a no-fault liability up to Rs 25,000 per individual was imposed with an obligation on the industry to insure.

The Defence of Sovereign Immunity in a Tort Action

The defence of sovereign immunity is still available in Indian Law to state and government officials. This is an anachronism that needs to be overturned by the Supreme Court as soon as an opportunity arises.

In *State of Rajasthan v Vidhyavati*,[36] a Constitution Bench of five judges rejected the defence of sovereign immunity. A jeep owned by the government of Rajasthan knocked down one Jagdishlal who was walking on the footpath in Udaipur city. Jagdishlal died as a result and his widow and son sued for damages. The jeep was being used by the Collector. It was driven rashly and negligently and its driver was a temporary employee of the state who was driving it back from the workshop where it had been sent for repairs.

Two questions were raised: first that the state was not liable under Article 300 of the Constitution and second, the jeep was being maintained 'in exercise of sovereign functions'. Both defences were rejected. The Court held that the tortious act was committed in circumstances wholly dissociated from the exercise of sovereign powers. It was held, tracing the history of legislation from 1858, that the state of Rajasthan was liable to the same extent as the East India Company. The liability of the East India Company was discussed and the leading case of *The Peninsular and Oriental Steam Navigation Company v The Secretary of the State*[37] was considered. The Court held that the East India Company was not a sovereign and could not claim exemption as a sovereign. Viewing the case on first principles, the State was held to be as much liable for the tort of its servants as any other employer. The Court held that under a Republican Constitution, there was no justification in principle or in public interest why the State should not be held liable vicariously for the tortious act of its servant. The Court also noticed that this immunity is no longer available in England and that there is no warrant for holding that it has any validity in India after the Constitution.

This case established a healthy trend substantially restricting the defence of sovereign immunity.

Unfortunately, a very regressive judgement was delivered by the Supreme Court in *Kasturilal v State of Uttar Pradesh*[38] by a Constitution Bench of five judges. This case sought to draw a distinction between the liability of the State while it was discharging sovereign functions and non-sovereign functions. In consequence, plaintiff's suit was dismissed and no relief was given to him. The cause of action for damages was not returning the gold seized by a police officer, which had been lost while in police custody. The earlier case of *State of Rajasthan v Vidhyavati* was distinguished. The justification was that in the facts of the *Vidhyavati* case, the cause of action arose while the jeep was being driven at a time when the driver's functions did not fall within the ambit of discharging sovereign functions. Unfortunately, the *Kasturilal* case has never been directly reconsidered though there are several cases where it was ignored while similar facts were at issue. Even in the *Kasturilal* case, the Court recommended that the legislature should step in and rectify the situation.

Unfortunately, the Parliament has neither taken note of these observations nor implemented what was recommended by the Law Commission of India in its first report in 1956.

The Supreme Court in *Shyam Sunder v State of Rajasthan*,[39] with a Bench of two judges, namely Justice Mathew and Justice Alagiriswami, awarded damages to the plaintiff. The claim was made by the heirs of the deceased Navneetlal who was an employee of the state of Rajasthan. He was travelling in a truck belonging to the State in connection with famine relief work. The truck was not properly maintained and caught fire. The deceased Navneetlal jumped out of it and was hit by a stone lying by the road and died instantaneously. The heirs claimed damages against the state. In paragraph 20 and 21, the Court held that famine relief work was not a sovereign function and the plaintiff was entitled to succeed, but it made critical remarks about the *Kasturilal* case which are worth reproducing:

We do not pause to consider the question whether the immunity of the State for injuries on its citizens committed in the exercise of what are called sovereign functions has any moral justification today. Its historic and jurisprudential support lies in the oft-quoted words of Blackstone [*Blackstone's Commentaries*, 10th edn, 1887]: 'The king can do no wrong ...'

Today hardly anyone agrees that the stated ground for exempting the sovereign from suit is either logical or practical. We do not also think it necessary to consider whether there is any rational dividing line between the so-called sovereign and proprietary or commercial functions for determining the liability of the State.

In another case, *Smt Basavva Patil v State of Mysore* ,[40] a Bench of three judges (Justices Bhagwati, Sarkaria, and Fazal Ali) awarded the complainant the cash equivalent of property recovered from the possession of the accused but lost from the possession of the police officer. The high court and lower courts had rejected the claim of the complainant on the ground that the articles never reached the custody of the court. Without considering the ratio of the *Kasturilal* case the Court awarded a cash equivalent for the property lost. The Mysore High Court judgement was reversed. The Court ignored the *Kasturilal* case although it appears to have been referred to and relied upon by the high court of Mysore. In the *Kasturilal* case the gold was lost from police custody; a set of facts not very different from the *Smt Basavva Patil* case.

In another case, *State of Bombay v Memon Mohammad* ,[41] the *Vidhyavati* and *Kasturilal* cases were held inapplicable by a Bench consisting of Justices Bachawat, Shelat, and Bhargava. The facts were that two trucks and a station wagon belonging to the claimant/plaintiff were seized by the customs authorities. The plaintiff succeeded in revenue appeals and the seizure was set aside. When he applied for return of the vehicles, he was informed that they had been disposed of under the magistrate's orders. The plaintiff then filed a suit. The plaintiff succeeded, the reasoning being that there was a duty to preserve the property and also an obligation on the part of the government to take reasonable care of the seized goods until the validity of the seizure was finally determined. The liability of the government was founded on the ground that the principle of the liability of a bailor applied to a bailment which was not contractual. The Court also held that even if the government was not in a position of a bailee it was under a statutory obligation to return the goods.

The *Kasturilal* case has met with adverse criticism by various authors.[42] Apart from the above, in a series of cases the Supreme Court, over a period of many years, has awarded compensation (independent of damages in torts) for violation of Article 21 in cases of wrongful detention and custodial deaths. To a great extent, therefore, the tortious action for damages in such cases has become irrelevant even though, while ordering damages, the Supreme Court clearly preserves the independent right of damages arising out of a tort.

Compensation/Damages for Breach of Fundamental Rights (Tort, Quasi Tort, or not a Tort)

We have seen how the Supreme Court has treated the defence of sovereign immunity in tort litigation. The injured citizen had enormous difficulty in instituting an action for torts against government officials and government servants. These difficulties were virtually insuperable.

Ad valorem court fees for instituting the action and for each appeal, and the enormous delay before getting a final judgement coupled with the plea of sovereign immunity by which the state would claim that the damage was caused in the exercise of sovereign functions effectively rendered the citizen helpless.

The Supreme Court increasingly observed that persons were being deprived of personal liberty by wrongful and mala fide detentions, by police high-handedness, and on many occasions by custodial deaths. In view of these formidable difficulties it was impossible for citizens to get justice and compensation under our legal system against the state. The law of torts in the traditional sense was a mere paper tiger and did not subserve the cause of truth or justice.

It was in these circumstances that in a series of cases the Supreme Court of India, while exercising its jurisdiction under Article 32 read with Article 21 and other Articles relating to personal liberty, fashioned the doctrine of awarding compensation for breach of a fundamental right. This violation, if clearly established, would give rise to a cause of action in torts as now universally recognized, but an additional remedy was created which would be the right to compensation for violation of the constitutional right of personal liberty. The consequence was a swift, quick, rough and ready justice by way of compensation. The cases which are discussed below deal with that position, but the reason why they have been included in the discussion in the law of torts is that this remedy and redress is a practical substitute for damages for wrongful detention or custodial death. Further, a new tort, namely 'misfeasance in public office', has been developed. This is discussed in the next section.

Three cases need to be discussed. In *Rudul Shah v State of Bihar*,[43] the petition under Article 32 for habeas corpus complained of illegal detention. The illegal detention extended over a period of fourteen years. The petitioner also demanded compensation for this illegal detention which violated his right to life under Article 21. The state was ordered to pay damages and he was awarded a sum of Rs 30,000 in addition to Rs 5,000 already paid.

The Court, speaking through Chandrachud CJ, made important observations:

It is true that Article 32 cannot be used as a substitute for the enforcement of rights and obligations which can be enforced efficaciously through the ordinary processes of courts, civil and criminal. A money claim has therefore to be agitated in and adjudicated upon in a suit instituted in a Court of lowest grade competent to try it. But the important question for our consideration is whether in the exercise of its jurisdiction under Article 32, this Court can pass an order for the payment of money if such an order is in the nature of compensation consequential upon the deprivation of a fundamental right.[44]

The Court held that the detention after his acquittal was wholly unjustified and illegal. The Court observed:

In these circumstances, the refusal of this Court to pass an order of compensation in favour of the petitioner will be doing mere lip service to his fundamental right to liberty which the State Government has so grossly violated. Article 21 which guarantees the right to life and liberty will be denuded of its significant content if the power of this Court were limited to passing orders of release from illegal detention. One of the telling ways in which the violation of that right can reasonably be prevented and due compliance with the mandate of Article 21 secured, is to mulct its violators in the payment of monetary compensation ... *therefore the State must repair the damage done by its officers to the petitioner's rights. It may have recourse against those officers.*[45] (emphasis supplied)

In *Nilabati Behera v State of Orissa*[46] in a judgement delivered on 24 March 1993 (Verma, Dr Anand, and Venkatachaliah JJ) the point again arose for decision. A letter written by Smt Nilabati Behera, mother of one Suman Behera, claiming compensation for the death of her son Suman in police custody was treated as a writ petition under Article 32. The Court examined the facts in detail and arrived at a finding that there was custodial death and Suman Behera died as a result of injuries inflicted upon him while he was in police custody. The Court held, applying several cases after *Rudal Shah,* that the State was liable to pay compensation. The Court reiterated that contravention of fundamental rights gave rise to a strict liability for payment of compensation and the defence of sovereign immunity did not apply even though it might be available as a defence in private law in an action based on tort. The decision of the Court in *Kasturi Lal v State of UP*[47] was confined to the sphere of liability in tort which was held to be distinct from the state liability for contravention of a fundamental right and which was no defence against the award of compensation for contravention of a fundamental right. The leading case of *Maharaj v Attorney General of Trinidad and Tobago* (No. 2)[48] was relied upon where Lord Diplock observed:

The claim is not a claim in private law for damages for the tort of false imprisonment under which the damages recoverable are large and would include damages for loss of reputation. It is a claim in public law for compensation for deprivation of liberty alone.

The Court relied upon the principle that it should be prepared 'to forge new tools and devise new remedies' for doing complete justice and enforcing fundamental rights. The Court directed that a sum of Rs 1,50,000 be paid as compensation to the petitioner. It was however observed that the award of compensation would be taken into account for adjustment in the event of any other proceeding taken by the petitioner for recovery of compensation on the same ground to ensure that the petitioner was not compensated twice over.

Dr A.S. Anand J delivered a concurring opinion. It is significant that he characterized the relief of monetary compensation under Article 32 or Article 226 for established infringement of the right under Article 21 as a public law remedy, characterizing the compensation as being in the nature of 'exemplary damages'. He observed:

It is a sound policy to punish the wrongdoer and it is in that spirit that the courts have moulded the relief by granting compensation to the victims in exercise of their writ jurisdiction. In doing so the Courts take into account not only the interest of the applicant and the respondent but also the interests of the public as a whole with a view to ensure that public bodies or officials do not act unlawfully and do perform their public duties properly particularly where the fundamental right of a citizen under Article 21 is concerned. Law is in the process of development and the process necessitates developing separate public law procedures as also public law principles.[49]

The emphasis in the majority judgement of Verma J was to demonstrate that the compensation remedy under Article 32 was in addition to the ordinary remedy of damages in tort. It is to be noted that Verma J's judgement uses the word compensation and not exemplary damages. Dr A.S. Anand J's concurring judgement however introduces the concept of 'relief of monetary compensation in the nature of exemplary damages'. He also brings in the concept of punishment.

This law has been further developed in the case of *D.K. Basu v State of West Bengal* (Kuldip Singh and Dr A.S. Anand JJ).[50] A letter complaining about custodial deaths from a non-political organization in West Bengal was treated as a writ petition. The matter concerned custodial deaths while in police custody. The case raised important issues concerning police powers, including that of whether monetary compensation should be awarded for established infringement of the fundamental rights guaranteed by Articles 21 and 22 of the Constitution of India.[51] The Court characterized custodial deaths as perhaps one of the worst crimes in a civilized society governed by the rule of law.[52] The Court proceeded to give certain directions in the form of requirements to be followed in all cases of arrest or detention till legal provisions were made in that behalf as preventive measures.[53] The Court declared that failure to comply with those requirements would render the official liable for contempt of court. Relying upon the maxim that there is no wrong without a remedy *(ubi jus, ibi remedium)* the Court, referring to the earlier cases held that the Supreme Court has judicially evolved a right to compensation in cases of established unconstitutional deprivation of personal liberty or life.[54]

Summing up Dr A.S. Anand J observed that:

The claim of the citizen is based on the principle of strict liability to which the defence of sovereign immunity is not available and *the citizen must receive the amount of compensation from the State, which shall have the right to be indemnified by the wrongdoer.* In the assessment of compensation the emphasis has to be on the *compensatory and not on punitive element.* The objective is to apply balm to the wounds and not to punish the transgressor or the offender, as awarding appropriate punishment for the offence (irrespective of compensation) must be left to the criminal courts in which the offender is prosecuted, which the State, in law, is duty bound to do. This remedy and redress is in addition to the traditional remedies and not in derogation of them. (emphasis supplied)

The observations of Dr A.S. Anand J in the *Nilabati Behera* case in his concurring judgement talks of monetary compensation by way of exemplary damages. However, Dr A.S. Anand J's judgement in *D.K. Basu*[55] appears to strike a more conservative note when he holds that 'in the assessment of compensation the emphasis has to be on the compensatory and not on punitive element'.

It may be noticed that before delivery of this judgement on 18 December 1996 several judgements had been delivered by the Supreme Court where the principles of exemplary damages in relation to public servants were formulated where the conduct had been oppressive, arbitrary and unconstitutional. This was the new tort developed after the case of *Lucknow Development Authority* and referred to in *Common Cause*[56] and *Shiv Sagar Tiwari.*[57]

None of these judgements has been referred to in the *D.K. Basu* judgement, presumably because they may not have been delivered when the judgements were reserved. However, in future the theory of exemplary damages for oppressive, arbitrary and unconstitutional conduct of the State or its officials requires to be further developed in cases of established custodial torture and deaths.

Misfeasance in Public Office: Arbtirarty, Oppressive, Unconstitutional Action by State Officials

In 1996, through the medium of public interest litigation, the Supreme Court had to grapple with many issues relating to corruption and abuse of power. On 30 January 1996 the Supreme Court (Verma, Bharucha and Sen JJ) delivered its seminal order in the *Vineet Narain* case. Several prosecutions were launched against ministers and former ministers consequent to hearings in this case.

On 1 March 1996 the Supreme Court, speaking through the same Bench, delivered its order directing the Director of the CBI not to report to anyone involved or likely to be involved as a result of its investigation, however high he might be: in effect, not to report to Prime Minister Narasimha Rao who was in charge of the Ministry of Personnel under which the CBI functions.

It was against this backgroud that a new tort was developed by the Supreme Court and exemplary damages awarded against ministers occupying high offices. These judgements were delivered in quick succession and formed an integral whole.

These cases are (1) *Common Cause v UOI*,[58] judgement dated 25 September 1996 per Kuldip Singh and Faizan Uddin JJ; (2) *Common Cause v UOI*,[59] judgement delivered on 4 November 1996 by the same Bench; (3) *Shiv Sagar Tiwari v UOI*,[60] judgement delivered on 11 October 1996 by Kuldip Singh and Hansaria JJ; followed by (4) *Shiv Sagar Tiwari v UOI*,[61] judgement delivered on 8 November 1996.[62] Both Shiela Kaul and Captain Satish Sharma presented review petitions challenging the judgements against them. The review petition of Captain Satish Sharma was argued before a three-judge Bench and the judgement has been reserved. The law as stated is as of May 1999 when this essay was written. It is pertinent to note that the *Common Cause* judgement was altered in review (see *Common Cause, A Registered Society v Union of India*).[63]

The facts of the first case, *Common Cause v UOI*[64] arose from a public interest petition under Article 32 of the Constitution by H.D. Shourie, Director of Common Cause. The petition drew attention to the news item dated 11 August 1995 in the *Indian Express* under the caption 'In Satish Sharma's reign petrol and patronage flow together'. Captain Satish Sharma was Minister of State for Petroleum and Natural Gas in the central government. The news item mentioned that petrol pumps were allotted by the minister from his discretionary quota to diverse persons. The allottees were related to various officials working with the minister or were related to politicians or ministers and several were either members of the Oil Selection Boards or their relations.

The Court held that the allotments were largesse which was distributed by the State, a new form of wealth as held in *Ramana Dayaram Shetty v International Airport Authority*.[65] Thus it was held that public property had been given in a wholly arbitrary manner violative of Article 14 of the Constitution; a violation of the collective rights of Indian citizens.

The allotments were set aside and the Court observed per Kuldip Singh J):

The Government today—in a welfare State—provides large number of benefits to the citizens. It distributes wealth in the form of allotment of plots, houses, petrol pumps, gas agencies, mineral leases, contracts, quotas and licences etc. Government distributes largesses in various forms. A Minister who is the executive head of the Department concerned distributes these benefits and largesses. He is elected by the people and is elevated to a position where he holds a trust on behalf of the people. He has to deal with the people's property in a fair and just manner. He cannot commit breach of the trust reposed in him by the people. We have no hesitation in holding that Capt. Satish Sharma in his capacity as a Minister for Petroleum and Natural Gas deliberately acted in a wholly arbitrary and unjust manner. ... The allotments made by him were wholly mala fide and as such cannot be sustained.[66]

The Court went on to hold (per Kuldip Singh J):

Capt. Satish Sharma has betrayed the trust reposed in him by the people under the Constitution. *It is high time that the public servants should be held personally responsible for their mala fide acts in the discharge of their functions as public servants.* This Court in *Lucknow Development Authority v M.K. Gupta,*[67] approved *'misfeasance in public offices' as part of the Law of Tort.* Public servants may be liable in damages for malicious, deliberate or injurious wrong doings. According to Wade: 'There is, thus, a tort which has been called misfeasance in public office and which includes malicious abuse of power, deliberate maladministration, and perhaps also other unlawful acts causing injury' ... With the change in socio-economic outlook, the public servants are being entrusted with more and more discretionary powers even in the field of distribution of Government wealth in various forms. We take it to be perfectly clear, that if a public servant abuses his office either by an act of omission or commission, and the consequence of that is injury to an individual or loss of public property, an action may be maintained against such public servant. No public servant can say 'you may set aside an order on the ground of mala fide but you cannot hold me personally liable'. No public servant can arrogate to himself the power to act in a manner which is arbitrary.[68] (emphasis supplied)

Consequently the Court *inter alia* directed a show cause notice to Captain Satish Sharma as to why he should not be liable to pay damages for his mala fide action, as also why he should not be prosecuted for criminal breach of trust or any other offence.

It is pertinent to notice the *Lucknow Development Authority* case[69] (Kuldip Singh and R.M. Sahai JJ). The judgement was delivered in an appeal against the order passed by the National Consumer Disputes Redressal Commission. The question of law was whether statutory authorities in various states who were developing housing projects were subject to the jurisdiction of the Consumer Commission for delay or non-delivery of possession to allottees. The Court held that the Commission had jurisdiction. The further question was whether the Commission had jurisdiction to award compensation for harassment and agony caused to the consumer. The further important point which was considered was the liability for payment: namely, should the society or the taxpayer be burdened for oppressive and capricious acts of public officers or the burden be laid on those responsible for such acts or omissions. The Court posed the question: 'Today the issue thus is not only the award of compensation but who should bear the brunt.'[70] The Court cited several authorities where public servants were held liable in torts personally when damage and injury was caused to individuals by their oppressive, arbitrary, or unconstitutional actions.

A quantum jump was then taken by the Court. The Court affirmed the power of the National Commission to award compensation against the statutory authority and also empowered the Commission to further direct the authority concerned to pay the amount of compensation to the complainant from the public funds, but recover it from those officers found responsible proportionately from their salary after making a proper finding in that case. Thus, even though the complainant had not instituted an action against an individual public servant in tort, the Court protected the public funds administered by the statutory authorities and held that the delinquent officers must make good and reimburse public funds.

In the *Common Cause* case these observations were used as a springboard to create a new tort.

The departure from the traditional actions and the contours of the new tort are:

(1) The action is not by an individual or individuals suffering injury and damage but in the format of a PIL (public interest litigation).

(2) The action is not a civil suit or civil action for torts.

(3) The injury and damages are suffered by the State and the public exechequer by reason of a mala fide action of the minister.

(4) The Court in safeguarding fundamental rights, including the right under Article 14 of the public (a collective right of Indian citizens) directed the minister to show cause why he should not make good damages to the State.

(5) Most importantly, this rapid result was achieved in a direct writ petition instituted in the highest Court under its writ jurisdiction in the public interest: an enormous saving of time, energy, and resources, and a swift punishment by way of exemplary damages against the offending minister.

The sequel is reported in the next judgement *Common Cause v UOI*,[71] decided on 4 November 1996 by the same Bench. After hearing the minister Satish Sharma and recording the findings the Court awarded a large sum of Rs 50 lakhs (Rs 5 million) to be paid by the minister, Captain Satish Sharma, as exemplary damages because of his oppressive, arbitrary, and unconstitutional conduct. The Court pressed into service observations in *Rookes v Barnard*,[72] relying on Lord Devlin's observations, namely that exemplary damages can be awarded for oppressive, arbitrary, and unconstitutional actions by servants of the government. The Court also cited several English cases reiterating this principle. Finally the Court held:

We are of the view that the legal position that exemplary damages can be awarded in a case where the action of a public servant is oppressive, arbitrary or unconstitutional is unexceptionable.[73]

The Court further directed that:

Capt. Satish Sharma to pay a sum of Rs 50 lakhs as exemplary damages to the Govt. exchequer. Since the property with which Capt. Sharma was dealing was public property, the Government which is by the people has to be compensated.

The *Shiv Sagar Tiwari* cases reiterated the principle and two judgements were delivered. The first one on 11 October 1996[74] and the sequel[75] was decided on 8 November 1996. The bench consisted of Justices Kuldip Singh and Hansaria. The first judgement was delivered by Justice Hansaria. In this case, on the facts it was found that a former Minister of Urban Development Smt. Shiela Kaul had allotted shops to relatives, relations of her personal staff, and relations and friends of politicians and ministers. The Court cited various authorities from other jurisdictions and held that the law of tort all over the world recognizes a cause of action for arbitrary, oppressive, or unconstitutional actions by state officials as inviting exemplary damages. The Court observed:

the world of jurisprudence has thus accepted misfeasance in public office *as a species of tortious liability and, to prevent misuse, different courts across the sea have been awarding exemplary damages.*[76] (emphasis supplied)

Then follows the extension of the tort law in a public intrest litigation. The Court observed:

We are conscious that the aforesaid cases dealt with injury to a third party (following misuse of power) who had sought damages for the loss caused, whereas in the present case there is no injury as such to any third person. Even so, the aforesaid cases have been referred for two purposes. Firstly and primarily to bring home the position in law that misuse of power by a public official is actionable in tort. Secondly, to state that in such cases damages awarded are exemplary. *The fact that there is no injury to a third person in the present case is not enough to make the aforesaid principles non-applicable inasmuch as there was injury to the high principle in public law that a public functionary has to use its power for bona fide purpose only and in a transparent manner.* In so far as the aspect of loss is concerned, it deserves to be pointed out that there was loss in the present case also; and this was to the State Exchequer resultant upon giving of allotments without calling tenders as required by the policy. Needless to say that if tender would have been called, higher revenue would have been earned by the State on giving the allotments. *For these reasons, we are of the view that the mere fact that in the present case there is no injury to a third person and he has not come forward to claim damages, has no sequitur in so far as the tortious liability following misfeasance of public office is concerned.*[77] (emphasis supplied)

The Court then issued a show cause notice to Smt. Shiela Kaul regarding damages.

The sequel is reported in *Shiv Sagar Tiwari v Union of India*[78] where the same bench heard Smt. Shiela Kaul. The Court held that Smt. Sheila Kaul's action was wholly arbitrary, mala fide and unconstitutional and she was liable to pay exemplary damages. The Court further directed Smt. Sheila Kaul 'to pay a sum of Rs 60 lacs (on all counts) as exemplary damages to the Govt. exchequer. Since the property with which Smt. Sheila Kaul was dealing was public property, the Government which is "by the people" has to be compensated.'

It is gathered that the Review Petition in Satish Sharma's case has been argued and judgement is awaited. A fresh look may become necessary thereafter.

Notes

[1] (1994) 6 SCC 632.
[2] 376 US 254.
[3] (1987) 3 All ER 316 (HL).
[4] (1988) 3 All ER 545.
[5] (1993) 1 All ER 1011.
[6] (1992) 3 All ER 65.
[7] Ibid. at p. 1018.
[8] (1994) 6 SCC 632.
[9] Ibid. pr. 21, p. 648.
[10] (1987) 1 SCC 395.
[11] Ibid.
[12] Ibid. pr. 30, p. 419.
[13] 1868 L.R. (3) H.L. 330.
[14] *Supra* n. 10 at pr. 31, p. 420.
[15] Ibid. at pr. 32, p. 421.
[16] (1989) 1 SCC 674.
[17] *Union Carbide Corporation v Union of India* (1989) 3 SCC 38.
[18] *Charanlal Sahu v Union of India* (1990) 1 SCC 613.
[19] *Union Carbide Corporation v Union of India* (1991) 4 SCC 584.
[20] *Supra* n. 17 at prs 35–6, p. 50–1.
[21] Ibid. pr. 35, p. 50.
[22] Ibid. pr. 36, p. 51.
[23] *Supra* n. 18.
[24] Ibid. pr. 91, p. 684.
[25] Ibid. pr. 92, pp. 686–7.
[26] Ibid. pr. 156, p. 722.
[27] Ibid. pr. 157, p. 723.
[28] (1991) 4 SCC 584.
[29] Ibid. at pr. 13, pp. 605–6.
[30] Ibid. at pr. 16, p. 608.
[31] Ibid. pr. 17, pp. 608–9.
[32] Ibid. pr. 19, p. 609.
[33] Ibid. at prs 201–2, pp. 682–3.
[34] (1996) 3 SCC 212.
[35] Ibid. prs 65–6, p. 246–7.
[36] (1962) Supp 2 SCR 989.
[37] (1868–9) 5 Bom H.C.R. App. 1.
[38] (1965) 1 SCR 375.
[39] (1974) 1 SCC 690.
[40] (1977) 4 SCC 358.
[41] (1967) 3 SCR 938.
[42] See Seervai's *Constitutional Law* (4th edn, vol. 2, pp. 2131–2); Gandhi's *Law of Tort* (1987) edn, pp. 95–100); Thakker's *Administrative Law* (1992 edn, p. 502).
[43] (1983) 4 SCC 141.
[44] Ibid. pr. 9, p. 147.
[45] Ibid. pr. 10, p. 147.
[46] (1993) 2 SCC 746.

[47] *Supra* n. 38.

[48] (1978) 2 All ER 670.

[49] *Supra* n. 46 at p. 769.

[50] (1997) 1 SCC 416.

[51] Ibid. at pr. 9, p. 424.

[52] Ibid. at pr. 22, p. 428.

[53] Ibid. at pr. 35, pp. 435.

[54] Ibid. at pr. 42, p. 438.

[55] *Supra* n. 50 at pr. 54, p. 443.

[56] (1996) 6 SCC 530, (1996) 6 SCC 593.

[57] (1996) 6 SCC 558, (1996) 6 SCC 599.

[58] (1996) 6 SCC 530.

[59] (1996) 6 SCC 593.

[60] (1996) 6 SCC 558.

[61] (1996) 6 SCC 599.

[62] The judges concerned in these cases soon retired. Hansaria J retired on 25 December 1996, Kuldip Singh J retired on 1 January 1997 and Faizan Uddin J retired on 5 February 1997.

[63] (1999) 6 SCC 667.

[64] *Supra* n. 58.

[65] (1979) 3 SCC 489.

[66] *Supra* n. 58 at pr. 22, p. 553.

[67] (1994) 1 SCC 243.

[68] *Supra* n. 58 at pr. 26, p. 555.

[69] *Supra* n. 66.

[70] Ibid. at pr. 1, p. 263.

[71] *Supra* n. 59.

[72] (1964) 1 All ER 367.

[73] *Supra* n. 70 at para 12, p. 598.

[74] *Supra* n. 60.

[75] *Supra* n. 61.

[76] *Supra* n. 73 at para 15, p. 563.

[77] Ibid. at para 16, p. 563.

[78] *Supra* n. 74.

Twenty-one

The Supreme Court Bench and Bar: Reminiscences of the Formative Years

B. Sen

Halfway through the Michaelmas law term in 1949, I received an encouraging response from Mr C.K. Daphtary to the long letter I had written to him about the possibility of my coming to India and joining the Federal Court Bar. Daphtary's message, in his inimitable public school style of a sixth former writing to a prospective entrant, had concluded with the words 'keep your chin up: When in doubt, consult Murthy. You can't go wrong.'

I had met Mr Daphtary, who was then the Advocate General of Bombay in the summer of that year at a tea party given by Lord Porter for Sir Harilal Kania to enable the lawyers of Indian origin practising in England to meet the Chief Justice of India. Sir Harilal was very keen that the Indian lawyers in England should move to Delhi to form the nucleus of a resident Bar for the Supreme Court which was to come into being within the next few months. He had met individual members and urged them to do so, using his charm and power of persuasion.

P.N. Murthy was then the all-powerful Registrar of the Federal Court, having moved up to that position following upon the departure of both the Registrar and the Assistant Registrar at the time of Independence. I had corresponded with Murthy during the previous few months and he had proved to be extremely helpful in removing the first hurdle in my joining the Federal Court Bar by processing my application for enrolment as a special case although I had standing at the Bar of barely three years, rather than the requisite five, and that too not in an Indian high court.

Meeting him face to face for the first time, I was thrilled to find someone so friendly and ready to lend a helping hand. He was a mine of information and knew all the ropes for getting along in bureaucrat-dominated Delhi. The registry of the Court over which Murthy presided was then slowly waking up from its long slumber of pre-Independence Federal Court days and was about to gear itself to cope with the expected increase in the volume of work consequent upon the abolition of the Privy Council appeals.

Murthy soon became my mentor; a relationship that was to last until his untimely death. I began to spend quite a lot of time in his office, and that gave me the opportunity of being introduced to the leading Federal Court agents of the day who usually gathered around Murthy's table in mid-mornings seeking guidance on new procedures for the Supreme Court. That helped me to get a few briefs; so I could truly say that I had practised before the Federal Court during its last few days.

In a week or two I began to call on the judges—they were only five in number then. The appointment with the Chief Justice was fixed for a Sunday, and when I went to see him at his residence, 10 Tees January Marg, he had just returned from his game of golf. He was very informally dressed in a dhoti and a shirt, and extended a broad smile with the words of welcome, 'Oh, so you have come; I have already spoken to Setalvad about you. He will take over in January, but go and see him during his next visit to Delhi. He is expected here next week.' He then talked about a few things and the brief meeting was over. Sir Syed Fazl Ali, who was the senior judge, was soft spoken and an embodiment of grace and courtesy. He received me like an equal although he was older than my father. He talked about the days when he was reading for the Bar in England, the days of Birkenhead and Marshall Hall, and wondered whether the profession in England had retained the original standards. Justice Patanjali Sastri was very courteous and certainly believed in simple living. He talked about his days at the Bar and on the Bench, and wondered whether by the grace of God he had been worthy of his high office. Justice Mehar Chand Mahajan received me in his study. He was dressed in a three-piece suit and was looking over the briefs of cases that were to come before him the following day. He spoke softly, offering me a few hints about how to get along in India. 'Don't be shy. You must get to know people. You must not behave as if you are English. Come to dinner tomorrow night. You will meet a few friends.' That dinner proved not only to be extremely sumptuous but also rewarding in many ways. I continued to enjoy his hospitality periodically over the years, and he even hosted a lavish party for me at the time of my marriage some ten years later.

Justice Bijan Kumar Mukherjea greeted me with a sort of initial disapproval, 'Why have you come? This is not the place to begin your practice. I don't know why they have decided to locate the Supreme Court in Delhi? They should have chosen one of the traditional centres for legal learning like Allahabad. Here we are too close to the government. There is no Bar worth the name: the only lawyers we have are the District Court practitioners.' After this somewhat lukewarm initial greeting he mellowed and then he talked for over an hour about sundry matters like proper grounding in the law, about moral values, and a host of other subjects. He appeared to be a very lonely person, being a widower with his only son living in Calcutta. He was not a party-going man but provided a ready welcome to anyone who dropped in for a private chat. The visit ended with his suggestion that I should come to see him whenever I was free. This was easy because there were no security guards at the residences of judges in those days and a prior appointment was seldom necessary. One could just drop in if one knew the judge, and even if one did not, a member of the Bar was granted an appointment that very day.

A few days before Christmas, I received a message from Justice S.R. Das that he was in town staying at Western Court, and would like me to see him. Justice Das who was at that time Chief Justice of Punjab was on an inspection tour of the Delhi courts. I had known him from childhood and rushed to see him with great enthusiasm at the prospect of meeting him again. By the time I arrived at Western Court, a large number of visitors had already arrived, most of them from the Punjab Bar. He was extremely popular as the Chief Justice and made it a point to be present at each of the functions that the members of the Bar wanted to organize in his honour. A few days later it was announced that he was appointed the sixth judge of the Federal Court.

Soon after my meeting with Chief Justice Harilal Kania, I was looking for an opportunity to meet Mr M.C. Setalvad who, I was told, always stayed at the Imperial Hotel during his visits to Delhi. I did not know him by sight but one day in December someone in the hotel pointed out to me that the gentleman sitting in the lawn was Mr Setalvad himself. He had finished his lunch and was sitting in the sun reading the newspapers. I went forward and introduced myself. He looked up without a smile and said, 'You are the gentleman Kania spoke to me about?' Then he asked me to be seated and told me that he did not intend to remain in Delhi for more than a year and that G.N. Joshi, his junior in Bombay, would generally come to assist him in constitutional and tax cases, but if I still wanted to be in his chambers, he had no objection. I assured him that I welcomed the opportunity to assist him in any way I could.

During the last few days of the Federal Court I made it a point to watch the proceedings to get used to the way advocacy was practised in the highest court in India. Happily, there appeared to be no difference between the way cases were presented or the judges reacted to counsel's arguments from the way matters were conducted in England both before the Privy Council or the House of Lords. The six judges who adorned the bench of the Federal Court seemed to be as traditional as the judges in England and at least equal in stature and legal learning as their English counterparts. Four out of the six judges, namely Chief Justice Harilal Kania, Justices Patanjali Sastri, B.K. Mukherjea, and S.R. Das came from the chartered high courts and were steeped in the age-old traditions those institutions embodied. Sir Fazl Ali was an embodiment of courtesy, always smiling and ready to lend a helping hand to young juniors. Justice M.C. Mahajan, apart from being a seasoned judge, had also an insight into political life, having served as the Diwan of Kashmir. He would quickly get to the root of any matter and had a practical approach to delivering justice without too much concern about the niceties of law.

When the Constitution came into force on 26 January 1950, the six judges of the Federal Court became judges of the newly constituted Supreme Court of India. The inauguration of the Supreme Court was marked by a solemn ceremony, but without much fanfare, on 28 January 1950 in the Princes' Chamber of the Parliament building, the same chamber where the Federal Court had sat for twelve years and where the Supreme Court was to function for another eight years. The solemnity of the occasion was evident when Chief Justice Kania, wearing his purple Gujarati headgear, and the judges in their robes arrived and took their seats on the bench. Then Mr M.C. Setalvad, the Attorney General, rose like a Roman Senator to address the court in a manner akin to the opening of the Senate in bygone ages. With a voice that echoed through the Chamber, he outlined the extensive powers and the functions that were being entrusted to the Court under the Constitution. The Chief Justice responded, expressing the resolve of the Court to uphold the rule of law. The Attorney General rose again to convey on behalf of the Bar its greetings to the Bench, and the ceremony was over within three-quarters of an hour.

The opening of the Supreme Court, the third and the most powerful organ of the Republic, was undoubtedly a state occasion, and all arrangements were in the hands of the Protocol Department. The Prime Minister Pandit Nehru, the Deputy Prime Minister Sardar Patel, and other cabinet ministers as well as the diplomatic corps, the Chiefs of the armed forces, the Secretaries to the government, and other dignitaries were all present, yet there was scarcely any visible security arrangement. Invitees were quietly taken to their seats by Court officials without any necessity to screen them. A few days before the event there were rumours that lawyers, apart from the visiting Advocates General, might not be invited to the opening of the Court as there was insufficient space inside the Princes' Chamber to accommodate them. Later, we were informed that we might be accommodated in the galleries, but when we arrived that morning in our robes ready to observe the proceedings from the gallery it was a great surprise to find that an extra row of chairs had been placed in the chamber itself earmarked for advocates and agents enrolled in the Federal Court; and senior bureaucrats, including personalities like Mr V.P. Menon as well as the press had been seated in the galleries. This, we were informed, was done at the intervention of the judges who had also insisted on a group of lawyers being invited to every function connected with the inauguration of the Court. Such gestures on the part of the Court helped to forge a close bond between the Bench and the Bar which was to last over a decade.

The Supreme Court at its very inception was called upon to decide a number of questions relating to the interpretation of the Constitution which were of far-reaching importance to define the powers of the government and the rights of the citizens. The case I remember best was one that was heard in the very first months of the court—*A.K. Gopalan v Province of Madras*.[1] The question of detention without trial was at issue and that involved interpretation of Articles 14, 19, 21, and 22 of the Constitution. The constitutional questions raised were new, both to the judges and the lawyers, and when M.K. Nambyar appearing for the detenu expounded his arguments, day after day, citing case law from all over the globe with comparisons between the Indian, the Irish and American Constitutions, the entire courtroom seemed to be completely spellbound. There were no interruptions nor questions, the all-pervading silence broken only by Nambyar's voice and the rustling of the pages of the law reports.

The resident Bar in the initial years was very small in number. Amongst the seniors, apart from Mr Setalvad, there was only Mr N.C. Chatterjee until Mr C.K. Daphtary took over as the Solicitor-General in the later part of 1951. Consequently, persons of proven ability, though in semi-retirement, like Bakshi Sir Tek Chand or Sir Alladi Krishnaswamy Ayyar were often brought in to argue cases whenever the occasion arose. However, the vast majority of the leading counsel appearing before the Supreme Court were the leaders of the Provincial Bars who came over to assist the Court in individual cases. M.P. Amin from Bombay, V.K.T. Chari and Rajah Iyer from Madras appeared fairly frequently in the early days of the Court. P.R. Das, who was regarded as the doyen of the Indian Bar, Sir S.M. Bose, Advocate-General of West Bengal for over twenty-five years, Sachin Chaudhuri, later Finance Minister of India, G.S. Pathak who became the Vice President of India, H.M. Seervai, P.L. Banerjee, the then Advocate General of UP, Sir N.P. Engineer, Krishnaswamy Ayyar, Somnath Iyer, Advocate-General of Mysore, and K.M. Munshi were among the prominent personalities at the Bar who could be seen arguing cases in the Supreme Court. Even Fakhruddin Ali Ahmad, who later became the President of India and Sir Jamshedji Kanga, were among the luminaries to be seen amidst the distinguished gathering at the Bar of the Court. Jaigopal Sethi, A.S.R. Chari, and Nuruddin Ahmed often appeared in criminal cases. R.J. Kolah and N.A. Palkhivala, although not designated as seniors, came over to argue income tax cases.

The junior Bar was fortunately much larger. Apart from H.J. Umrigar and myself, there were over a dozen juniors practising exclusively before the Supreme Court. S.M. Sikri, who subsequently became Advocate-General of Punjab, would frequently appear in constitutional cases on behalf of the Union of India and later for Punjab. G.N. Joshi, who came over from Bombay to assist Mr Setalvad, spent almost half the year appearing before the Supreme Court. Amongst the others who readily come to my mind were G.C. Mathur, K.B. Asthana, Jindra Lal, S.N. Andley, Hardayal Hardy and S.K. Kapur, all of whom later became high court judges. J.B. Dadachanji, who came from Bombay in 1951, with his strong grounding in corporate law, soon made his mark. Some of the juniors who appeared frequently, included Rameshwar Nath, S.K. Aiyar, R. Ganpathi Iyer, S.N. Mukherjee, B. Banerjee, Danial Latifi, T.R. Bhasin, and P.S. Safeer. The presence of a resident junior Bar did away with the necessity of bringing junior counsel from the state high courts. Nevertheless, in many cases seniors preferred to be assisted by their juniors from their home states. The names that readily come to mind are C.R. Pattabhiraman from Madras, M.M. Desai, K.T. Desai, R.J. Joshi, and P.N. Bhagwati from Bombay, Asoke Sen and Ranadev Chowdhary from Calcutta.

Amongst the Federal Court agents who were transferred to the roll of Supreme Court, Rajinder Narain had the largest volume of work followed by S.P. Varma and I.N. Shroff. P.A. Mehta was the government agent whose name appears in almost half the reported cases in those initial years. The others who had a substantial number of cases, included R.S. Narula, later Chief Justice of Punjab High Court, P.K. Chatterjee, R.R. Biswas, Sukumar Ghosh, M.S.K. Shastri, Ganpat Rai, S. Subramaniam, Tarachand Brijmohan Lal, B.P. Maheshwari, R.C. Prasad, and Naunit Lal.

An important characteristic of the Bar in those early years, irrespective of whether they were resident at the seat of the Court or they came from the provincial capitals, was the conscious awareness on the part of members of their responsibilities in assisting the highest court of the land in the enunciation of legal principles or in the interpretation of the Constitution. Days would be spent in the preparation of arguments before their actual presentation. I remember senior counsel arriving in Delhi three or four days in advance, which they devoted to shaping and reshaping their notes of arguments. Another noticeable feature was the degree of cooperation that existed between counsel to ensure that the arguments were not repeated whilst all the points were put forward. Conferences would be arranged in the chambers or in the hotel suite of the senior counsel who was to lead the arguments. Every lawyer briefed in the case for a supporting party or an intervener would make it a point to be present and make whatever contribution he wished so that it could be included in the principal line of argument that was to be advanced.

Another factor which was no less important was the encouragement that the seniors provided to the juniors at the Bar. There were some instances that I vividly recall. A month or two after the inauguration of the Supreme Court, Mr K.P. Khaitan, who was then the standing counsel at Calcutta, came over to lead me in a tax matter. He had been in Delhi for two or three days for preparation and was due to return the morning after the case was over. That very day I was sent a brief in the *Bharat Bank* case[2] which involved an important constitutional issue relating to the scope of Article 136. I was reluctant to take on the brief as I considered myself unequal to the task of arguing a case of that magnitude. Mr Khaitan insisted on my accepting the brief and promised to stay on a day longer to prepare me for the case which he proceeded to do right away by dictating the notes of arguments which I would put forward before the Court. Another instance that comes to mind is when Sir S.M. Bose sat by my side and made me argue an important constitutional case in which he was leading me. The seniors were equally keen to ensure that their juniors were adequately remunerated. One particular instance comes to mind. Mr P.R. Das had come over to argue the Bihar and UP zamindari abolition cases.[3] He desired that I should be engaged in the case as his junior. We were having a conference with the representatives of the zamindars in his suite at the Imperial Hotel. I was seated by his side when Mr Das mentioned a particular sum as my fee. I was simply astounded at the figure he mentioned which was completely disproportionate to my standing at the Bar. I whispered to him that the fee was too high. He turned to me and said, 'No, that is your fee. You are from the Privy Council Bar.' That was true in a way because I still retained my tenancy in Chambers and spent a few months each year appearing in colonial appeals.

Most of the seniors were considerate to the juniors, and as in England, treated them in a manner befitting their status as members of the Bar. I recall once going for a conference with Sir Alladi. It was a hot summer afternoon in April. I had arrived at his small bungalow at Janpath a few minutes before the others. I knocked and knocked but there was no answer. Just as I was about to leave Sir Alladi opened the door to enquire what I wanted. When I told him about the conference, he profusely apologized for having fallen asleep. I said that I could wait but he pulled out his brief straightaway and sat down after tightening his dhoti, saying that he would not wish a member of the Bar to wait.

In the early fifties, the Supreme Court sat as a full court in all constitutional cases and in not more than two divisions where other matters were concerned. The judges also read out their opinions in open court, as was the case in the House of Lords, which at times could take the entire day. This invariably meant that whenever the Court was hearing an appeal or a petition of some importance, such as the *Delhi Laws Act* case[4] or *Gopalan's case*[5] there was hardly any work even for a small resident Bar. Petitions for special leave were few in number, perhaps not more than twenty in a whole week as most of the cases would come upon a certificate given by the high court concerned. The room allotted for the Bar in the Parliament house was comparatively small and the books in the library were few; this deficiency was redressed by the free access granted to the judges' library which was availed of frequently for research and preparation. There was hardly any room for Bar gossip, and those practising exclusively in the Supreme Court had no option other than to attend the hearings which undoubtedly proved to be of benefit to them. There you could observe the great advocates of the day making their submissions and the way judges would react to the points made. One could observe Chief Justice Kania get to the heart of the matter in a flash and then wait for the arguments to be completed. You could detect a faint smile on his face when he was not convinced by the point sought to be made. He was hardly ever ruffled, but could be visibly annoyed if a petition or a document placed before him was carelessly typed. Once I remember his addressing Mr Setalvad pointing to a document in his hand, 'Mr Attorney, look at this'. 'My Lord, this is Delhi', was the reply. 'I see', said the Chief Justice with a broad smile. Being used to the original side in the Bombay High Court he would occasionally express his disapproval of the slipshod way things were done here. 'What are the agents doing; only taking money?' Only once did I see him feel really out of form. That was when one Mr Shamdasani, a chronic litigant from Bombay, appeared in person. The Chief Justice would not even look up and the next senior judge had to take charge of the proceedings.

Justice Fazl Ali took very few notes during arguments. He would often sit back in his chair reflecting over what was being said by counsel. From his expression one could distinguish whether he was pondering over a point or rejecting it. Whenever he presided over a Bench hearing special leave petition, and was dismissing one he would apologetically smile and say, 'No, not this time', as if he was doing so with reluctance. Justice Patanjali Sastri would look up as if puzzled with a point and ask a question or two to clarify his thoughts. Justice Mukherjea would listen patiently, then ponder over the point that was being made before jotting it down in his notes. Justice Das would make his notes with a sphynx-like expression, not revealing the slightest hint of his reaction to an argument. Justice M.C. Mahajan was much more articulate and made no bones about saying what he thought of the counsel or his arguments. He had a very quick grasp and was in the habit of reading the briefs overnight even in regular appeals. I remember a case where the records ran into some forty volumes and the estimated time set apart for the hearing was the entire week of five days. Sir N.P. Engineer was appearing on one side and Mr Setalvad on the other. Engineer had opened the appeal and was expecting to continue for the next three days but immediately after the lunch break Justice Mahajan called upon Mr Setalvad and asked him to answer a point in relation to some document reproduced in the voluminous records. No one had anticipated the question put by the Bench, not even the appellant's counsel, and the whole case was over within the hour.

Justice Mahajan would at times show his impatience by reclining in his chair and pretending to doze off, but he was always alert as I once learnt to my cost. Whenever a junior argued, he would listen attentively for a few minutes and would continue do so with rapt attention if there was substance in the arguments. There are some instances which I can vividly recall.

Within a month of the inauguration of the Supreme Court, I was briefed in an appeal[6] where Mr Setalvad was on the opposite side. I had thought that I was on velvet, since the judgement under appeal was that of Chief Justice Harries and Justice Bijan Kumar Mukherjea. I had hoped that I would not be called upon, but when Mr Setalvad in his opening began to meticulously tear apart the reasonings in the judgement, piece by piece I knew that the game was lost and began to feel nervous. Chief Justice Kania with a faint smile called upon me and I began to struggle, distinguishing authority after authority cited by Mr Setalvad. Justice Mahajan was looking at me with a touch of amusement and then began helping me by pointing out the passages I should read. I knew I had lost but I had to give a good fight. A month or two later, the *Bharat Bank*[7] case came up for hearing before the full court. Bakshi Sir Tek Chand was appearing for the appellants and I for the respondent workmen. Sir Alladi was appearing for the intervener, the Union of India. I had done a lot of homework and had virtually written out what I had to say. Mahajan listened with rapt attention, perhaps wondering what I would say, but as I made my points, I could notice his encouraging smile leading me on. When I had finished and apologized to the Court for taking longer than expected, he turned to me and said: 'You need not apologize. You have done very well.' I won the case by a majority of three to two.

There was another occasion I remember when the attitude of the judge was not all that kindly. I was briefed to appear for the state in a case[8] regarding validity of the Saurashtra Special Court Ordinance. The matter was virtually covered by a seven-judge Bench decision in *Anwar Ali Sirkar*'s case[9] delivered a few days earlier holding the West Bengal Special Courts Act as violative of Articles 14, 19, and 21 of the Constitution. It was before the same bench that my appeal had come and I sought to distinguish the *Saurashtra* case on the basis of geographical classification relying upon certain observations in the judgements in the West Bengal case. When I was asked by the Bench as to which of the judgements I wished to rely upon, I mentioned the observations made in the judgements of Patanjali Sastri, Fazl Ali, and S.R. Das and then after a brief pause, believing that Mahajan was snoozing, I mentioned also the judgement of Justice Mahajan.

He promptly opened his eyes and looked at me with a chilling expression! 'You are making a mockery of my judgement', he shouted. 'Now, point out the passages where you say you found support.' I slowly began to read his judgement. He was getting impatient. 'Point out those passages and don't beat about the bush.' When I had placed the passages I was relying upon, he sat back in his chair without a smile and said, 'I am not convinced but you are free to persuade my brothers.' I could see a faint smile playing on the faces of some of the members of the Bench. Justice Chandrasekhara Aiyar interrupted, 'You say your case is better than the West Bengal case—in fact it is worse.' He looked at the other judges, tilted his turban, and scratched his head. By the end of my arguments, I was fairly certain about approval from three out of the seven judges but not at all sure about another judge deciding in my favour. On the morning of the day when the judgement was to be delivered, Justice Das rang me up to ask whether I had seen the cause list and then said, 'Be sure to be present in the Court'. Each of the judges began to deliver his separate opinion and I was still uncertain whether I was going to win or lose but when Justice Bijan Mukherjea's decision came in my favour, I knew that I had secured a majority.

In December 1950, D.N. Pritt, who was the most sought after lawyer in those days for Privy Council appeals, came over to argue the Special Leave Petition in the *Telengana Death Sentence* cases[10] where the point at issue was whether an appeal to the Supreme Court under Article 136 from a decision of the Hyderabad High Court before the Constitution had come into force would be competent. The matter was heard for a whole day, and at the end the decision had been announced dismissing the petition. I had known Pritt in England; in fact he was my leader in my very first case before the Privy Council and had gone out of his way to help me at the Bar. I had, therefore, thought it fit to invite him for dinner along with Setalvad. I enquired of Justice Das whether he could join. He readily agreed and suggested that I should ask the Chief Justice too. I left a message with his Private Secretary almost expecting a refusal but to our great delight, he also came over with Lady Kania and joined us at the club. Throughout the meal, I silently watched the great giants of the law from two different countries exchanging pleasantries and light hearted anecdotes. It made me feel that in the great profession of law there could be no barriers between countries and it mattered little whether one was at the Bar or on the Bench.

Justice Chandrasekhara Iyer joined the Supreme Court as the seventh judge in September 1950. Sitting amongst the great men of the law, he appeared to feel somewhat self-conscious. Every time he asked a question or made a remark, he would look at his brother judges and the members of the Bar as if to assure himself that the remark or the question was appropriate. In March 1951, Justice Vivian Bose was appointed a judge of the Court. He was a perfect gentleman, soft spoken and a firm believer in personal liberty and human rights as was evident from his judgements. He was a man of strong principles, reluctant to compromise his values. He would not hesitate to dissent even when he found himself in a minority of one. He was perhaps a little ahead of his time in his exposition of legal norms and standards on issues of fundamental rights. He looked more like a Christian missionary than a judge. In his personal life, he observed every norm of human dignity. He would never use his official staff for domestic purposes. He preferred to drive his own car and he could be seen quite often in the queue on Saturday mornings at the small post office outside Gymkhana Club waiting to buy postage stamps for his personal correspondence.

One common feature noticeable among the judges in the early days of the Supreme Court was their humility, their patience in hearing counsel in an unhurried manner, and their willingness to give themselves sufficient time for reflection and consultation which alone could find expression in those monumental judgements that have stood the test of time.

Mr Setalvad from those early days dominated the Bar. Just his stature and bearing arrested attention, and with this he combined moral, ethical, and professional standards which the Supreme Court Bar was to observe for years to come. He had fixed fees irrespective of the complexity of the matter. He took engagements only in one Court which he never left until the case was over. He was a man of very few words. A gesture or a nod was sufficient to convey his approval or diapproval of a particular act or omission which I learnt to recognize over the years when I worked in his chambers. He would never ask for any particular junior to be briefed with him, but whenever an instructing solicitor mentioned a name, a faint smile of approval would appear on his face if he felt that the choice was right. If however he was not particularly enthusiastic about the person, he would brusquely say 'alright then'. He was a giant in legal learning and was meticulous about accuracy in citation of authorities in support of his arguments. He made it a point that anyone seeking his professional services, however high, must come to his chambers. I well remember cabinet ministers like Mr C.D. Deshmukh or Krishna Menon coming for conferences at his residence where he would ask the junior to explain the case and permit the ministers to speak only after that was done. He was a stickler for punctuality, and conferences fixed were always held on time even though he might have important visitors paying him social visits at that time. I remember one evening arriving at his residence for a conference. Chief Justice Kania and his wife were sitting with the Setalvads in the front garden. I had anticipated that the conference would start a little later and had advised others accordingly, but at 7 o'clock on the dot, the time fixed for the conference, Mr Setalvad came into his study leaving the distinguished visitors in the care of his wife.

Setalvad was a man of high moral principles. He would stick to his view, however unpopular or unpalatable that might be to the political leaders of the day. He would never compromise. He was close to Pandit Nehru but one day, in the latter part of 1957, during our usual Friday night dinner, I noticed that he was very silent, and then a tear or two trickled down his face. He was visibly upset over some press reports or something said in Parliament. With great hesitation, I ventured to ask him whether anything was the matter. To this he responded: 'What saddens me is the deterioration in Jawaharlal's moral values: his tolerance of dishonest elements.' He was referring to the Mundra inquiry in which T.T. Krishnamachari was involved and the support Nehru lent to Kairon, the Chief Minister of Punjab.

Mr C.K. Daphtary was the finest advocate in the country, but his knowledge of law was not as profound as Setalvad's. He was a friendlier person, full of humour, always ready for a joke in Court or outside. He was extremely helpful to the juniors and his Court craft was superb. He was never tense and could not be easily ruffled; and if he was ever cornered by the Bench over a point he sought to argue he would overcome his predicament by relating an anecdote or two. He had a busy social life and thoroughly enjoyed it.

Mr N.C. Chatterjee was fond of having people around: both lawyers and clients. He was not overly meticulous about punctuality for his conferences, being involved in politics half the time. He had a tremendous memory for case law and knew the references almost by heart. His arguments in the Court were superb. Before going to Court, he would sometimes display a touch of nervousness about how his point would go down with the judges but once inside the courtroom he was in top form. In important cases, he would rehearse his arguments in his chambers and ask for comments from his juniors, reminding them that appearing before the highest court was no joke, entailing a great responsibility to the client as well as to the Court.

Mr P.R. Das, in his quiet way, was the most persuasive advocate of the day. He used to maintain a notebook for each case where he would write out his entire argument, even indicating the points he would emphasize. He commanded tremendous respect from the judges and was extremely generous to his juniors and all those around him. He entertained lavishly, and whenever he came to Delhi one could expect to see the entire 'Patna community', including judges, enjoying his hospitality.

Sir S.M. Bose was always very succinct in his arguments, never repeating himself. He was very supportive of his juniors, always giving them opportunities to argue cases.

In September 1951, Justice Fazl Ali was to retire from the Bench. Setalvad hosted a tea party at the poolside of Gymkhana Club. The guests were limited to fifty in number in accordance with the rationing laws that were then in force. Practically no food could be served with the exception of tea and nuts. Setalvad had selected his guests to include the judges, a few members of the Bar, both senior and junior, the Speaker of the Lok Sabha, and a couple of ministers. When the function was under way we saw Pandit Nehru getting down from his Cadillac and walking across the lawns to join us for tea. He appeared to be in good humour, exchanging jokes with the judges and of course, no Black Cat commandos or gun-toting jawans were in evidence in the vicinity for that culture had yet to become a status symbol for dignitaries and lesser mortals alike. A few days later, Fazl Ali rejoined the Bench as an ad hoc judge but retaining his seniority among the judges, and continued in that capacity for another year.

On 6 November 1951, a great calamity struck the Court in the sudden death of India's first Chief Justice Sir Harilal Kania. He had seemed to be in normal health and had presided over the Court only a couple of days earlier. He had hosted his usual Gujarati New Year party the day before, receiving guests at the entrance of his 10 Tees January Marg residence. The entire Diplomatic Corps was there even though he served no alcohol. No one had any inkling that night that his end was so near. The announcement brought a sense of gloom and grief that pervaded the entire legal community. As streams of visitors filed past his body, there was scarcely a pair of dry eyes, and as the body moved across to the cremation ground on a gun carriage with the members of the Bar marching behind en masse, there could be no doubt as to how widely respected the daparted Chief Justice had been. For me personally it was an irreparable loss. I had known him for barely two years but his magnanimity and the kindness that he had extended had drawn me to him. Justice Patanjali Sastri who took over as Acting Chief Justice, in a reference to his memory on the following day, echoed the sentiments of the entire judiciary and the Bar when he said, 'We miss his stately presence and benign smile. It is difficult to believe that he would no longer guide this Court with his vast legal learning and wide judicial experience. As a judge, he was always zealous in maintaining and guarding the prestige of this Court and was generous in dealing with his colleagues.' Mr Setalvad addressing the Court on the same occasion, said, 'The Supreme

Court, yet in its infancy, and the judiciary of the land undoubtedly needed at its helm his great talent and his unrivalled experience. I have not known a truer man and a more trusted friend.'

The Supreme Court Rules of 1954 brought in some significant changes of concern to the Bar. The institution of Supreme Court agents was abolished and replaced by what is known as 'Advocates on Record' who were also to have the right of audience. That in effect meant that they could appear on their own or brief a senior leaving very little scope for the engagement of another junior. The second change was that advocates needed to have seven years practice in a high court before being enrolled in the Supreme Court. That was meant to ensure that only those with a certain minimum experience in the high courts could practise in the Supreme Court. The most important change that was brought in by these rules was that a 'senior advocate' had henceforth to be designated by the full Court, doing away with the automatic enrolment as a senior after practice for ten years contemplated under the Federal Court rules. For well over two years, no one had mustered sufficient courage to apply for designation as a senior for fear of being turned down, but then the Court itself resorted to the practice of informally sounding those who, in its opinion, deserved that distinction, thereby enhancing the prestige associated with that status. However, the Advocates Act, 1961, brought in an anticlimax by empowering the high courts to designate 'Senior Advocates' and by abolishing altogether the requirement of a period of practice in a high court before enrolment in the Supreme Court. This was to prove to be a disaster in later years when with the increase in Court work, fresh law graduates with little or no training or grounding in tradition, began to flock around the Supreme Court Bar.

Until 1957, the strength of judges in the Supreme Court had not exceeded the number originally envisaged in the Constitution, i.e. a Chief Justice and not more than seven other judges. Justice Ghulam Hussain was appointed after the retirement of Sir Fazl Ali and Justice N.H. Bhagwati had filled the vacancy caused by the sudden demise of Sir Harilal Kania, and by 1954, three other judges had been sworn in to occupy the vacancies caused by the retirement of the existing incumbents, namely Justice Jagannadhadas, T.L. Venkatarama Ayar and B.P. Sinha followed by Justice Jafar Imam and S.K. Das in 1956.

Justice Ghulam Hussain had the aura of the old world aristocracy. He was soft spoken, patient, and courteous but his tenure was cut short by his untimely death after only two years in office. Justice Bhagwati was quick in his grasp, had a strong common sense, and an uncanny way of detecting when someone was trying to be smart. He was a typical original side judge in a chartered high court. We had heard rumours about his not being particularly pleasant as a judge and of making fun of certain juniors whilst in the Bombay High Court, but when he came to Delhi, he made it a point to show every courtesy to juniors and was extremely popular throughout his seven years on the Supreme Court Bench. This was not unlike what often happened in England where a judge known to be quick tempered and impatient whilst in a court of first instance, would undergo a complete transformation by the time he reached the court of appeal or the House of Lords. Justice Jagannadhadas was known for his simplicity and had no airs about him. As a judge, he could be firm, and I remember on one occasion, when sitting with four other judges, he prevailed in granting special leave even though the rest of his colleagues were opposed to it. The appeal was eventually allowed. He simply refused to be overawed.

Justice Venkatarama Aiyar was known for his scholarly approach. His monumental judgements over many difficult matters earned him a portrait from the Bar during his tenure as a sitting judge of the Court. Justice B.P. Sinha, who had a long stint of four and a half years as Chief Justice, was a very patient judge. He mixed freely with the members of the Bar and, like his predecessors, made it a point to attend any function arranged by a member of the Bar. His knowledge of land tenure and tenancy laws was second to none. He asked so few questions in the course of arguments that one would sometimes wonder whether he had grasped the point, but when the judgement came, it was evident that he had taken in all that was argued before him. He once told me that his one regret had been that he had not been able to go to England to read for the Bar and that was because his grandfather nurtured a superstition about crossing the black waters!

Justice Jafar Imam was a man with a great deal of tradition behind him. He was courteous, patient, and helpful to juniors. He was keen on maintaining a degree of decorum in court, insisted on citation of official reports, and could get quite upset if counsel used language he considered inappropriate for use in court. He was usually suspicious of the prosecution in criminal matters and was ready to extend the benefit of doubt to the accused person. He could never tolerate a counsel who, he thought, was being unfair. He was a bit too old fashioned for new labour legislations. He found it difficult to imagine that an employer could not sack his workmen if they misbehaved. I remember once appearing for the government in the *Journalists Wage Board* cases.[11] I wanted to cite a book by the renowned economist Barbara Wootton. 'Is she a living author?' asked Justice Imam. When I replied in the affirmative, the judge ruled, 'Then you cannot refer to the work, however eminent may be the author'.

Justice S.K. Das proved to be one of the most eminent judges who had adorned the Court, and was the first Civil Service judge to be appointed. Although he did not have a degree in law, and had learnt the law entirely during his long tenure on the Bench, his knowledge of virtually every branch of the law was profound. He seemed completely at ease hearing whatever matter was brought before him, whether it was a constitutional question or a criminal appeal or a tax reference or a labour dispute. He could be a little reserved but was always pleasant. He would look a bit suspicious about taking in facts if he was not familiar with the counsel, and if a proposition or a point of law was put forward that seemed to him to be without substance, he would reveal his mind by gazing towards the back of the Court or towards the ceiling, but would never cut short the arguments.

In August 1958, the Court shifted to its own premises on Mathura Road. The building seemed to be enormous at that time, with provision for five courtrooms, two huge rooms for the Bar and spacious offices for the Registry. The strength of the Court had increased to eleven in 1957 with the addition of three more judges, that was just sufficient to constitute three benches according to the norms observed at that time. Three more judges were added in 1960, thus providing a full complement of judges for four courts to function: a Constitution Bench and three Division Benches. This was necessary to cope with the growing number of appeals, including a large volume of industrial disputes and tax references. This development provided a new impetus to the growth of a resident Bar since the dates of hearing could no longer be fixed in advance.

In October 1959, S.R. Das retired as Chief Justice. With his retirement the first decade of the functioning of the Supreme Court came to a close and a new era was to commence. Over his three-year tenure, he had succeeded in keeping the judges together as a paterfamilias. He had kept the Bar happy, had his way in the appointment of judges, and had encountered little or no friction with the government notwithstanding the difficult days. Almost everyone had free access to him. He received them in his study or even at his bedside in the early evenings whilst reading the court papers for the following day. He managed to please almost every visitor; even aspirants for high court judgeship and chief ministers felt that their views had received full attention. Industrialists, like G.D. Birla or Sir Biren Mookerjee as well as union leaders could come to him freely, but this did not in any way alter his judicial functioning; his list would simply not include any matter of concern to industry. He was extremely fond of food, especially dishes that had been forbidden by his doctor like bacon and eggs for breakfast. Once in a while, he would break away from broiled fish and fruit, the daily fare at his home, and pop across next door to Gymkhana Club escaping his wife's strict eye. He would hurriedly devour the platter of bacon and eggs sitting in my cottage at the club. On those occasions I would feel seriously concerned about the possibility of incurring Mrs Das's displeasure but fortunately we were never caught and nothing ever happened that showed adverse effect on his health.

He was a very amiable and kindly person, and treated his personal staff like members of his family. No one had a harsh word to say about him. The Bar fully echoed this sentiment in bidding farewell to a great Chief Justice in the form of floral tributes when he left for Shantiniketan to take up his new responsibilities as Vice Chancellor.

The first ten years of the Supreme Court proved to be a fascinating experience. A small number of judges of outstanding calibre and an equally small number of men at the Bar, each trying to do his bit to build a great institution that would enhance the rule of law within the framework of the Constitution. Almost every judge made a conscious effort to get to know the lawyers who regularly appeared before the Court and to make them feel like an intrinsic part of the judicial process. Even when a judge appeared to be tough in resisting counsel's arguments, these could still be pursued provided there was a point to be made in the certain knowledge that the judge had an open mind.

Justice B.P. Sinha who took over as Chief Justice, though lacking the intellectual brilliance of his predecessor, was a pleasant judge. He had no strong views or preconceived notions on the newer branches of the law and could easily be persuaded to their viewpoints by the strong personality of brother judges like Gajendragadkar or J.C. Shah. He was not a good administrator, often allowing himself to be influenced by others and was ready to leave matters concerning the Registry to his Deputy Registrar Mr S.N. Sharma.

Gajendragadkar, who came to the Court in 1957, had a forceful personality. He was extremely intelligent and was quite at home with almost every branch of law apart from the highly specialized ones. His forte, however, was labour law, and he could mould his judgements in such a way as to meet the needs of what he called 'social justice'. He strongly believed in the rights of workmen and considered managements to be exploitative in the extreme. He virtually dominated the Bench wherever he sat except when N.H. Bhagwati was the presiding judge.

After B.P. Sinha became Chief Justice, he succeeded in having a Bench to himself even though he was not the seniormost judge, and had all labour appeals placed before it. There was always some kind of tension in his court: counsel were sometimes hassled when appearing for the management, and if a point was made, counsel would be confronted with the question why the Court should interfere in the grant of special leave. Gajendragadkar was a bit of a politician, a hangover perhaps from his younger days. He would pamper the press and allow a lot of latitude to counsel with political links who could be suffered to interrupt the arguments of the opposite side. He was quick in deciding cases and could be an excellent judge where the matter did not relate to labour law or had no political flavour. He was quite sociable and was keen on placating the Bar; at least the few whom he cultivated. He would sometimes drop in at my place for a cup of tea after his morning walk and relate anecdotes about his meetings with politically important persons both from India and abroad.

The more prominent among judges during the sixties were Subba Rao, M. Hidayatullah, J.C. Shah, S.M. Sikri, and K.S. Hegde. Subba Rao was a very patient and balanced judge. He would hardly ever interrupt counsel and allowed a full hearing even when the arguments might be far from convincing. He was very particular about the question of personal liberty and would want to look into every detail of preventive detention cases, much to the discomfiture of counsel appearing for the state. He was a firm believer in a true federal form of government for India and thought that the states should have greater autonomy and cease to be politically subservient to a strong central government. In interpreting the Constitution, he would always endeavour to strike a balance between the interests of the centre and the states and jealously guard against any encroachment by the centre over the powers of the state even though this might entail straining the language. He strongly believed in building up the image of the Court and considered a maximum strength of nine judges to be an appropriate number for a Supreme Court.

Justice Hidayatullah brought to the Court a great deal of learning and a fund of good humour. His knowledge of constitutional law could hardly be matched by anyone else, whether at the Bench or at the Bar; and that included not only an in-depth knowledge of the Constitution of India and the Government of India Act, but also the Canadian, US and Australian Constitutions and the entire gamut of case law that had developed around their interpretation. He was never known to have given a wrong reference when he wanted counsel to cite a case. He was

always courteous but occasionally enjoyed pulling the leg of some senior counsel. During tense moments in heated debates, a witty interjec-
tion by him could ease the situation. I remember once, during arguments in the presidential reference about the powers of the UP legislature and the courts, counsel was asserting that '*lex et consuetudino
parliamenti*' was the supreme law and kept repeating this over and over
again. Gajendragadkar, who was presiding, was getting impatient. He
curtly told the counsel, a very senior member, to be a bit serious. At
that tense moment, Hidayatullah interrupted with a smile, '... why don't
you just say "law and custom of Parliament" so that we all can understand you!' Hidayatullah was a scholar and familiar with many languages. He was very popular both with the Bar and his brother judges.
On another occasion, Sachin Chaudhuri was arguing a case involving
the design of a ship. Gajendragadkar appeared to be quite puzzled and
was about to start the usual 'Why should we interfere under Article
136?' Hidayatullah came to our rescue: 'Why don't you take us for an
inspection of the ship and educate us?' The Chief Justice got the message. He sat back in his chair and began jotting down points.

J.C. Shah was somewhat reserved and hardly ever smiled in Court.
He never had favourites, treating every member of the Bar equally,
whether senior or junior. He had no time for offensive advocacy, prefer-
ring to remain silent with the occasional remark like 'If this is the best
way to serve your client it is for you to judge'. He was quick to grasp a
point in a case and then apply his enormous fund of knowledge in deciding the matter. I remember tax reference cases when he would ask
counsel to read the statement of the case and by the time that was done,
he would make up his mind and then ask counsel whether a particular
case would cover the issue. He was quick in disposal, sometimes dealing
with eight to ten tax appeals a day without making anyone feel that he
had not been given a fair hearing.

S.M. Sikri, when he came to the Bench directly from the Bar, had
the distinct advantage of having practised before the Court from its
very inception. He was more familiar with the Bar than any other judge
and could often guess what it expected from the Bench. He was very
industrious and whenever he sat on the Constitution Bench, he would
continue with his own research whilst the arguments were in progress.
He had close friends in official and social circles, but when it came to
his judicial responsibilities he proved to be a completely independent
judge.

K.S. Hegde was a stern judge and would brook no nonsense in his
court, rather like Lord Thankerton or Lord Wright when they sat in the

Privy Council. He could be quite helpful if counsel was prepared and ready to come to the point, but could occasionally be impatient, especially if counsel were beating about the bush. I clearly remember an occasion when counsel had prepared a long list of propositions which he intended to read out and expected the judges to note down. Halfway through that exercise, Hegde stopped writing, put his pencil down, and looking straight at the person with a frown asked 'Just tell me what the point is'. The practice was never repeated in his court. He presided over the tax bench after the retirement of Justice Shah and he virtually adopted his style in dealing with tax references. He was certainly a great judge, whether or not one liked his style of functioning.

With the Supreme Court regularly functioning in four divisions during the sixties, the resident Bar continued to grow in numbers. At the senior level it largely comprised retired judges of the high courts and law officers but the junior Bar began attracting talent from various parts of the country. Amongst the seniors, A.V. Viswanatha Sastri was in great demand. In course of time, he virtually became a one-man institution and was quite a favourite with the Bench as well as the briefing advocates. His preparation was thorough, having read his briefs carefully in entirety, and he had an amazing memory for dates and events. His presentation in Court, which he did in a simple, matter of fact way, was always precise and based on facts and figures. He had no airs about him, and treated everyone equally and always with a smile. He lived very simply in a Nizamuddin flat and preferred to walk to the Court unless someone volunteered to give him a lift. There were practically no books in his study which was sparsely furnished with a small table and a few chairs. He did not appear to mind anyone enjoying a joke at his expense, and would in fact often join in with some amusing remark. Once we were arguing a case on opposite sides regarding Lipton's tea. One of the judges remarked that in his student days in England, Lipton was famous for its breakfast food shops and then he jocularly added, 'Of course Mr Sastri would not know anything about breakfast foods.' Sastri laughingly retorted, 'Why should I know anything about the breakfast that English people eat—I have my own breakfast.'

S.T. Desai, who also enjoyed a large practice, was a good lawyer but he could get quite excited if cornered over some point during his arguments. He could never understand how someone whom he considered a friend could forcefully argue against his views. M.C. Chagla returned to the bar after having served as a judge for over twenty years followed by important ambassadorial assignments and having served in the Cabinet. To begin with, he appeared to find it somewhat embarrassing to appear before judges whom he had helped to appoint, but very soon he picked up an enormous amount of work and fitted in comfortably in the informal atmosphere of the Bar. He would sip his lunchtime coffee in the small tea room exchanging notes with the junior members. The presence of a man of his stature among the resident Bar seemed to add a certain glamour to the profession. He was always courteous, never raised his voice in Court, and was very supportive of the junior Bar. Mr H.R. Gokhale, who came from Bombay after a short spell as a high court judge, made his mark in labour matters until he became a cabinet minister. Asoke Sen had a field day right from the time he returned to the Bar in 1966. He was an extremely able advocate, quick in his grasp, and could quite often pick up a new line of reasoning in the course of arguments. He could be seen hard at work well into the early morning hours pondering over briefs assisted by an enormous library of textbooks and law reports from different parts of the world. His style of functioning however was quite different from other seniors of the time. He would accept engagements in all the four courts at the same time and even outside, and one could never be certain whether he would actually turn up in the court to argue the case.

H.N. Sanyal came as a law officer in 1957. He had left behind an enormous practice in Calcutta High Court and was well known for his legal acumen. He could not get accustomed to the atmosphere in the Supreme Court at a time when one was expected to stick to one court and sit for days together listening to the arguments of the opposing side. He felt somewhat overshadowed by the towering personalities of the other two law officers, Setalvad and Daphtary. His ways were somewhat eccentric and he could be very generous to his juniors and the staff provided his vanity was pandered to. S.V. Gupte, who succeeded Sanyal, was a straightforward and industrious lawyer. He was a stickler for etiquette and traditions of the Bar and believed in maintaining the high stature of the office of a law officer. Like Setalvad, he also insisted that anyone coming for his professional advice, however high, must come to his chambers. Niren De, who became Attorney-General after Daphtary, was well versed in labour law but he felt somewhat ill at ease in handling the intricate questions of constitutional law that came up before the courts during his term of office. He was a powerful advocate and a gentleman in every sense. Fali Nariman who came as a law officer immediately after the end of the sixties, found himself completely at home handling important government briefs in the courts. A good deal of work began to come to him when his advocacy and his legal acumen were seen to produce results.

Soli Sorabjee, though still functioning from Bombay, could almost be counted as a member of the resident Bar in those days. He could be seen appearing on the opposing side in important cases argued by Chagla or Viswanatha Sastri. Amongst the other advocates who could frequently be seen in the courts during the sixties, whether appearing on their own or assisting seniors, were G.B. Pai, B.R.L. Iyengar, Seyid Muhammad, I.N. Shroff, R.K. Garg, Leila Seth, M.C .Bhandare, Dr L.M. Singhvi, G.L. Sanghi, Gobinda Mukhoty, Dilip Sinha, P.P. Rao, Suresh Agarwala, S.S. Javali, and a few others. G.B. Pai was the foremost in labour law whilst A.S.R. Chari scored in criminal law. Garg was aggressive in his advocacy but managed to get away with it. Suresh Agarwala was superb in his preparation and proved to be an asset to any senior he was to assist. Amongst the younger members at the Bar during that period, B.N. Kirpal was the most brilliant and simply outstanding in cases concerning tax law. He had an analytical mind and a quick grasp of factual details. Leila Seth was a very dependable advocate. She knew her brief very thoroughly and would not tolerate a client interfering in her preparation.

Towards the closing years of the sixties, the political manoeuvres that seemed to enmesh the higher echelons in the government of the day were seen to cast their shadow even over the functioning of the Court. Following upon Bank nationalization and abolition of Privy Purses, there were strong rumours of appointment of 'committed' judges and the decision of the Supreme Court in the *Kesavananda Bharati* case provided the signal for supersession of three senior judges in the appointment of the next Chief Justice. This visible affront to the independence of the judiciary was deeply resented and a sense of gloom seemed to descend on the entire legal community as well as the Court. Some sections of the Bar were vocal in their criticism of the newly appointed Chief Justice for no fault of his own other than that he had not refused the offer of the high office. Chief Justice A.N. Ray was an upright judge, quick in his decision-making, and an able administrator. During his tenure as Chief Justice, many of the prevailing malpractices concerning listing of cases were sought to be removed. As a man, he was humble, scrupulously honest, deeply religious, and a loyal friend. He was somewhat reserved and he made no effort to placate the vocal members of the Bar who were critical of him. Two years later, the Court had to withstand another shock in the form of the emergency. The powers of the Court were curtailed through constitutional amendments; the enforcement of fundamental rights was suspended, and the Court was burdened with the task of hearing special leave petitions directly from the decisions of all kinds of tribunals, be it in service matters or customs and excise. In the prevailing atmosphere, a sense of distance began to grow between the Bench and the Bar, and even the camaraderie among the members of the Bar seemed to be affected. No one was prepared to talk, or take someone into confidence, for fear of being reported. The Court functioned, arguments were advanced within the limited parameters available, but there seemed to be no particular zest or enthusiasm in the practice of the law.

The emergency was lifted, the enforcement of fundamental rights was restored but the shadow cast by the emergency continued to linger on. Soon thereafter I left the Bar in search of new avenues elsewhere, driven by the then confiscatory nature of taxation in our country. Some ten years later, when disillusioned by the vagaries of international politics, where the manoeuvring of nation states prevailed over individual attainment, I sought refuge once again in the profession. I found myself a stranger amidst novel surroundings. The Supreme Court building with its imposing dome looked the same; the courtrooms were just the same, but the atmosphere had changed beyond recognition. The open corridors in front of the courtrooms presented a scene that was so very different from the Supreme Court I had known. Here I saw masses of litigants jostling with men in robes, struggling to get across from court to court. Many of the judges could match their predecessors of the earlier days in intellect and learning and yet they were snowed under with the load of public interest litigation and applications for special leave, some with merit, others with no merit at all, allowing little or no time for reflection or leisure. I asked myself: 'Did the framers of the Constitution ever imagine the Supreme Court of this country to be anything but a final court of appeal that would enunciate the law for the guidance of the courts throughout the country?' Then the thought came to me that every institution of this great democracy had to gear itself to the needs of its people: the need for protection against executive excesses or inaction, and to be a balancing force to ensure that the organs of the federation, legislative and executive, kept within their constitutional bounds. Yes, the Constitution itself had guaranteed the right of every citizen to petition the highest court for the enforcement of his fundamental rights. Article 136 had empowered the Court to entertain petitions and correct errors against any judgement and order of any court or tribunal throughout the length and breadth of India. The Supreme Court at fifty is truly discharging this role. In the words of Winston Spencer Churchill 'Every age has its great men; if it lacks them, it produces them.' So it is with the Bench and the Bar of the Supreme Court.

Notes

[1] *A.K. Gopalan v State of Madras* (1950) SCR 88.

[2] *Bharat Bank Ltd v Bharat Bank Employees' Union* (1950) SCR 459.

[3] *State of Bihar v Maharajadhiraj Sir Kameshwar Singh* (1952) SCR 889; *Raja Suriyapal Singh v The State of UP* (1952) SCR 1056.

[4] *In re Delhi Laws Act* (1951) SCR 747.

[5] *Supra* n. 1.

[6] *Abdullah Ahmed v Animendra Kissen Mitter* (1950) SCR 30.

[7] *Supra* n. 2.

[8] *Kathi Raning Rawat v State of Saurashtra* (1952) SCR 435.

[9] *State of West Bengal v Anwar Ali Sarkar* (1952) SCR 284.

[10] *Janardan Reddy v State of Hyderabad* (1951) SCR 344.

[11] *Express Newspapers (P) Ltd v Union of India* (1959) SCR 12.

Twenty-two

From Kania to Anand and Setalvad to Soli
Memories of the Early Days of the Supreme Court

R.S. Narula

It seems like yesterday when I recall the inauguration of the Supreme Court of India in the then glittering Princes' Chamber in the present Parliament House, a little over forty-nine years ago, on 28 January 1950, consequent upon the adoption of the Constitution of the Republic of India on 26 November 1949.

Seated on the dais were Chief Justice Kania in his red turban along with his five companion judges of the Court in order of seniority (two of them wearing white turbans).

In the last eight decades of my life I have never seen assembled in one room, such a galaxy of the top representatives of the judiciary, executive, legislature, and diplomatic corps as on that august occasion. Besides the Chief Justice and Advocates-General of most high courts, we had with us in the hall, Prime Minister Jawaharlal Nehru, Deputy Prime Minister, Sardar Patel, other cabinet ministers, and leading members of the Bar of the entire country. I was one of the twenty-three agents of the erstwhile Federal Court of India (which had been inaugurated on 6 December 1937, in the same Chamber) who became from that day (28 Januray 1950) agents (equivalent to solicitors or the present advocates-on-record) of the Supreme Court of India. In front of each of our seats, we had two buttons, one for heating and the other for cooling, our individual cushioned seats, there being no central air-conditioning in those days.

Shri M.C. Setalvad, the first Attorney General of the Republic India, in the course of his long address to the Court, assuring it, on behalf of the legal fraternity of the country, of its 'loyal and whole-hearted cooperation', said *inter alia*:

We at the Bar have confidence that the Supreme Court of India, which is being inaugurated today, will in course of time, attain the same judicial eminence [as has been attained by their Lordships of the Privy Council], and that memorable and epoch-making judgements will illumine its records.

and added these prophetic words: 'We hope and trust that this Court will play a great and singular role and *establish itself in the consciousness of the Indian people.*' (emphasis supplied)

Today, when the faith of the majority of the people of India has been rudely shaken in the other two wings of the government, namely the executive and the legislative, and substantially eroded in respect of a section of the subordinate judiciary in some regions of the country, our citizens almost unanimously feel and justly boast that our Supreme Court has indeed 'established itself in the consciousness of the people'. That is why I characterized those words uttered by Setalvad as 'prophetic'. The Chief Justice and his companion judges, and most of their predecessors, can justly feel proud of their great achievement.

In the course of the Court's reply given by Chief Justice Kania, he emphasized that:

In democratic countries the Supreme Court should be quite untouchable by the legislature or the executive authority in the performance of its duties...

An independent Supreme Court ... will have far-reaching influence in the constitutional history and progress of the Union of India.

To maintain the high standard of the judiciary, recruitment from the Bar is the normal channel. Unless the leading members of the Bar accept Judgeships, it will be difficult to strengthen the Bench and the hope of producing great Judges may not be realized.

The Court stands to administer the law for the time being in force, has goodwill and sympathy for all, but is allied to none.

Once again Chief Justice Kania's prediction about the Court having 'far-reaching influence in the constitutional history and progress of the Union' appears to have substantially come true.

I still have with me a copy of the original photograph of the twenty-three agents of the Supreme Court taken immediately after the inauguration ceremony on 28 January 1950. Looking at their faces and names, I have been able to identify only three out of the twenty-three (namely Mr P.K. Chatterji, Mr S.L. Chibber, and myself) as the lone survivors. It may be of some interest that in that group photograph are the late Mr Sardar Bahadur, father of Justice Arun Bahadur Saharya, the present Chief Justice of the Punjab and Haryana High Court (lately judge, Delhi High Court) and the late Mr S.P. Varma, father of Mr M.L. Varma, senior advocate, Supreme Court of India, who was also briefly a judge of the Delhi High Court.

Three of the counsel appearing in the first two or three days of the commencement of the work of the Court on 26 January 1950, in special leave petitions to the Court (R.L. Kohli, Pritam Singh Safeer, and senior advocate Raghbir Singh) were instructed by me. Of course, so far as I remember, each of those petitions was dismissed after a brief hearing with a bewitching smile from Kania CJ.

The practice of grant of special leave in exercise of the discretionary powers of the Court under Article 136 in very rare cases, continued to be relaxed as time went on. So much so, that due to the different standards laid down for this by different judges at different times not only did the rate of admission improve, but sometimes made the result of a petition depend so much on the petitioner's stars and good fortune. So much so, that Setalvad once told the Bench somewhat light humouredly, in reply to the Court's query as to the difference between a 'wager' and 'lottery': 'What happens in this court every morning from 10.30 a.m. to about 11.30 a.m. is a lottery.' Still later, even the individual predilections of individual judges made a difference. For example, hardly any petition of a tenant against the order of his eviction was ever dismissed at the threshold by D.A. Desai J. He would at least grant reasonable time to the tenant to vacate. A few judges had a peculiarly socialistic approach in all matters involving money. I had an experience of such an approach in one case which I have never been able to erase from my memory. In *Balbir Singh v Union of India*, the only point on which the special leave petition for higher compensation for acquired property was pressed was fully covered in the petitioner's favour by an earlier judgement of the Court provided he had not already accepted the lesser amount. At the first hearing of the petition in or about 1979, instead of granting me special leave, the Bench of two judges rightly observed that the matter was so simple that it would not serve any purpose to grant leave and keep the appeal pending for years. The Bench accordingly ordered issuance of show cause notice to the respondent. On the date on which the notice was returnable, the law officer of the government orally represented to the Court that the petitioner had already accepted the amount. This factually incorrect statement was vehemently denied by me on the basis of the petitioner's affidavit on record but the Bench fairly adjourned further hearing to enable the law officer to produce some document to support his version. So far so good. At the next hearing, however, Justice O. Chinnapa Reddy happened to replace one of the judges on the Bench. Without hearing a word he observed that

Article 136 was not intended to provide landlords with more and more money as compensation for their property acquired for a public purpose. He refused to go into the question for the determination of which the case had been adjourned twice. Of course, the law officer had not produced any document to support his original contention. The other soft spoken judge remained a silent spectator. The petition was dismissed!

During the period 1950 to 1961, the senior advocates whom I instructed in various cases included Sarvashri M.C. Setalvad, C.K. Daphtary, N.C. Chatterji, Sir Jamshed G. Kanga, Sir Alladi Krishnaswami Ayyar, M.K. Nambyar, K.M. Munshi, and J.G. Sethi. I learnt much from each of them. Soon after that, I was myself designated as a Senior Advocate under the 1961 Act. The judges who have left an indelible mark on me included Vardhachariar, Bijan Kumar Mukherjea, S.R. Das, Gajendragadkar, Subba Rao, and Krishna Iyer.

Having graduated in law from Lahore in 1936, and after doing odd jobs for about two years, I was enrolled in 1938 as a pleader and as an advocate in 1940 or 1941, practising principally in the district courts of Delhi. I witnessed the glamour of the functioning of the Federal Court of India since 1939 (as law assistant of senior advocate Raghbir Singh, who appeared for one side or the other in most of the cases before that Court, carrying his papers). I got myself enrolled as an agent of the Federal Court in 1943. In those days work in the Court (set up in the hope of the formation of the Federation of Indian States) was so sparse that the Court enjoyed summer vacations for three and a half months and judges did not come to Court except when a particular case was fixed for hearing.

When Mr Storr, a handsome young European who was the first Registrar of the Court, sent me to Guru Datt, the then receipt clerk in the Registry, to file an appeal, (prepared by me on behalf of the ex-Maharani of Nabha against the judgement of the Madras High Court dismissing two suits filed by her) I was asked by Mr Guru Datt on perusal of the papers if I could split it into two appeals to increase the work of the Court. On my doing so, a few days later, the beaming officer rang up Chief Justice Sir Maurice Gwyer to inform him and to gladden him with the news that I had filed two appeals. He then handed over the receiver to me to greet the Chief Justice, who thanked me for getting more work for the Court.

Let me relate another anecdote about the relaxed atmosphere of the Federal Court before concluding. This was in April 1943 when, in the course of the hearing of *Venugopala Reddiar v Krishnaswami Reddiar* my senior advocate Raghbir Singh went on pressing a particular point for the third time in spite of the Bench having indicated that he should proceed to the next point. Mr Justice Mohammed Zafrulla, to the surprise of the Chief Justice and his fellow judge Varadhachariar, asked the counsel in Punjabi 'Kion kathi te kathi pai jannen' and then turned to his fellow judges to relieve them of their apparent bewilderment, and said, 'I have told him in his mother tongue: "Why are you saddling an already saddled horse?"'

The first chapter of my personal association with the working of the Supreme Court came to an end in March 1965 when I was raised to the Bench of the then East Punjab High Court after having had the singular honour of serving at that time as Chairman of the Delhi State Bar Council as well as President of the High Court Bar Association, Delhi.

From 1950 to 1974, the functioning of the Supreme Court of India could be the envy of any of the highest courts of the world at any given time. Everything went on smoothly and gracefully in accordance with the highest established traditions and standards. The Court heard and decided complicated matters and gave historic judgements without any interference from or special expectation from the executive or the legislature.

After the two-year era of judicial turmoil during 1975–6 and after the elections in March 1977, the Supreme Court not only regained its pre-1975 glory, but enhanced it during Chief Justice Venkatachaliah's time and ever thereafter. During this period, the doctrine of locus standi was relaxed for public interest litigation, and the court started intervening wherever the executive and/or the legislature had failed to perform its legal duty. Exercising such powers has been labelled by some as 'judicial activism'.

It was during this period that the law relating to the power of appointment and transfer of judges was settled step by step. The decision of 1982 in S.P. Gupta's case giving the final say to the Prime Minister was reversed by a Bench of nine judges by a majority of seven to two in 1993. The latest judgement on the subject given in 1998 on the President's Reference has merely resulted in 'sharing the responsibility' of the Chief Justice of India by a larger number of his Lordship's companion justices.

It is during the last decade that almost the entire law extending the scope of the right to life under Article 21; including the right to have a pollution free environment and the right to get ad hoc compensation for loss of life (extending Rudul Shah) was laid down. The law relating to the environment was not only explained, but even implemented under monitoring by the Court to a great extent. This gave Justice Kuldip Singh the name and distinction of a 'Green Judge'. Public interest litigation by Mr M.C. Mehta and by Common Cause led to shifting of stone crushers polluting the atmosphere and shifting of industries polluting the river under judicial fiats, to give a few important examples of exercise of this jurisdiction. Again in the current phase, the Court has had to step in where the executive failed to keep buses in the left lane, and even to implement its decision to weed out commercial vehicles which are more than fifteen years old.

The glory and glow of the Court left behind by illustrious Chief Justices Kania, Patanjali Sastri, Mehr Chand Mahajan, S.R. Das, P.B. Gajendragadkar and Subba Rao between January 1950 and April 1967, have been regained many times more by Chief Justice M.N. Venkatachaliah in February 1993. That glory and glow have been kept alive by Chief Justice Verma and now Chief Justice Dr Anand; may they ever continue to brighten the horizon of the Indian judicial system. The Court has come from Kania to Anand, with the able assistance of Attorneys General from Setalvad to Soli.

I cannot express the hope for the future in any words, better than those used by Chief Justice Anand:

Whatever we have learnt from experience of judicial administration in the past five decades will stand in good stead in the years to come, so that the judicial set up can appropriately deliver inexpensive and quick justice to the teeming millions—the consumers of justice—to maintain the faith of the common man in the judiciary.

Ladies and Genglemen, the future has hope. It is with this optimism that I wish you all good luck.

After the two-year era of judicial turmoil during 1975–76 and after the elections in March 1977, the Supreme Court not only regained its pre-1975 glory, but enhanced it during Chief Justice Venkatachaliah's time and ever thereafter. During this period the doctrine of locus standi was relaxed for Public Interest Litigation, and the court started intervening wherever the executive and/or the Legislature had failed to perform its legal duty. Exercising such powers has been labelled by some as 'Judicial Activism'.

It was during this period that the law relating to the power of appointment and transfer of judges was settled step by step. The decision of 1982 in S.P. Gupta's case giving the final say to the Prime Minister was reversed by a Bench of nine Judges by a majority of seven to two in 1993. The latest judgement on the subject given in 1998 on the President's Reference has merely resulted in 'sharing the responsibility' of the Chief Justice of India by a larger number of his Lordship's companion justices.

It is during the last decade almost the entire law extending the scope of the right to life under Article 21; including the right to have a pollution free environment and the right to get ad hoc compensation for loss of life (extending Rudal Shah) was laid down. The law relating to the environment was not only explained, but even implemented under monitoring by the Court to a great extent. This gave Justice Kuldip Singh the name and distinction of a 'Green Judge.' Public Interest.

Twenty-three

Landmarks

J.B. Dadachanji

In its early days the Supreme Court was located in the Chamber of Princes in Parliament House. There, in the Chief Justice's Court, each seat was separately air-conditioned both for winter and summer. There was a common restaurant where parliamentarians met and rubbed shoulders with members of the Bar.

Then, members of the Supreme Court Registry would refer to the newspapers each day to find out which high court had given a certificate under Article 133 of the Constitution or under section 110 of the Civil Procedure Code, and there was jubilation among them whenever such a certificate was granted. This was because it would mean work for the Registry in the Supreme Court as special leave was very restricted by the Court and special leave to appeal under Article 136 of the Constitution was rarely granted. Mr P.N. Moorthy, the first Registrar of the Supreme Court, had begun his career as a stenographer to the then Chief Justice of the Federal Court, and much later became the Registrar of the Federal Court, and subsequently the first Registrar of the Supreme Court. His daughter, Babu, later became a senior advocate.

On 26 January 1950, when the Supreme Court was inaugurated, Mr Setalvad, the then Attorney-General made a very brilliant speech and the then Chief Justice of the Supreme Court and Chief Justice of India, Mr Justice H.J. Kania, responded with an equally brilliant reply at the function to mark the occasion in the presence of Mr Jawaharlal Nehru, the first Prime Minister of India and Mr Vallabhbhai Patel, the then Home Minister. The inaugural function was attended by the Chief Justices of all the high courts in India.

Subsequently new premises on Mathura Road were inaugurated in 1957 when Mr Justice S.R. Das was the Chief Justice of India, at the opening ceremony of which Mr Jawaharlal Nehru was also present.

I was enrolled in the Supreme Court only on 13 October 1951 because there was a rule then that no advocate practising in a high court could be enrolled without having previously practised in a high court for ten years which I only completed that year. I had however appeared in a couple of cases there, such as the *Bharat Bank* case[1], when I worked as a junior to Mr C.K. Daphtary who had been nominated as the Solicitor-General of India when the new Supreme Court building was inaugurated.

Justice William O. Douglas, then sitting judge of the American Supreme Court, was asked to deliver the Tagore Law Lecture which, delivered in July 1955, was entitled 'From Marshall to Mukherjea: Studies in American and Indian Constitutional Law', because Justice Douglas was of the view that Marshall and Mukherjea were in the same tradition.

It was Chief Justice Marshall who wrote in *Marbury v Madison*[2], 'Certainly all those who have framed written constitutions contemplate them as forming the fundamental and paramount law of the nation, and consequently the theory of every such government, must be, that an act of the legislature, repugnant to the constitution, is void.'

It was Chief Justice Mukherjea who wrote in *Deo v Orissa*[3]:

If the Constitution of a State distributes the legislative powers amongst different bodies, which have to act within their respective spheres marked out by specific legislative entries, or if there are limitations on the legislative authority in the shape of fundamental rights, questions do arise as to whether the legislature in a particular case has or has not ... transgressed the limits of its constitutional powers. Such transgression may be patent, manifest or direct, but it may also be disguised, covert and indirect ... In other owrds, it is the substance of the Act that is material and not merely the form or outward appearance ... The legislature cannot violate the constitutional prohibitions by employing an indirect method.

Chief Justice Gwyer appointed his private secretary as the first Registrar of the Federal Court of India. Sir Maurice Gwyer, brought up in true British tradition, objected to Justice Varadachary walking barefoot in Connaught Place and doing his *japa* while doing so. Justice Varadhachary was one of the most eminent judges of the Federal Court and sadly did not live long enough to serve as a judge of the Supreme Court of India.

Later, when I was a junior to Mr C.K. Daphtary, then the Advocate General of Bombay, he asked me to work on the *Bharat Bank Award* case. The *Bank Award* was set aside on the ground that Justice Chandrasekara Iyer, then judge of the Supreme Court, did not attend the hearings of the tribunal as he had been appointed by Mr Nehru to sit on the tribunal set up to divide India and Pakistan.

There was an appeal from the Nagpur High Court by Sir Manekji Dadabhoy and others against Daga's family. Sir N.P. Engineer had appeared along Mr R.J. Joshi for Manekji Dadabhoy and Mr M.C. Setalvad and Mr C.K. Daphtary appeared for Daga's family. Justice Mahajan, who had read every page of the voluminous record, showed great judicial acumen in understanding the case and Sir N.P. Engineer had no alternative but to agree to a compromise. Chief Justice Patanjali Sastry presided over the Bench.

Bank Nationalization Award

On a Saturday, the Bank Nationalization Ordinance was issued and the following day, a Sunday, Mr Palkhivala flew to Delhi and came to my office to dictate the writ petition to be filed on behalf of R. Cavasjee Cooper and other Directors against the Union of India.

In a record time of three hours Mr Palkhivala dictated the writ petition under Article 32 which was ready to be filed the following day. It was filed early on Monday morning, cited in Court, and an interim stay of the Ordinance granted. The writ petition No. 222/69 was decided on 10 February 1970 by a Bench of eleven judges consisting of Hon'ble Justices J.C. Shah, S.M. Sikri, J.M. Shelat, V. Bhargava, G.K. Mitter, C.A. Vaidialingam, K.S. Hegde, A.N. Grover, P. Jaganmohan Reddy, and I.D. Dua. The Ordinance was struck down as invalid by the majority, the majority judgement being delivered by Justice J.C. Shah and the minority judgement by Justices A.N. Ray and G.K. Mitter. It was declared that the Banking Companies (Acquisition and Transfer of Undertakings) Act 22 of 1969 was invalid and the action taken or deemed to have been taken in exercise of the powers under the Act was declared unauthorized.[4]

Privy Purse

The next important case was the so-called *Privy Purse* case[5] filed by His Highness Maharajadhiraja Madhav Rao Jiwaji Rao Scindia Bahadur and Others. Mr Palkhivala argued brilliantly convincing a majority of the judges of the Supreme Court. It was decided by a Bench of eleven judges of the Supreme Court consisting of Justice M. Hidayatullah CJ, Justices J.C. Shah, S.M. Sikri, J.M. Shelat, V. Bhargava, G.K. Mitter, C.A. Vaidialingam, K.S. Hegde, A.N. Grover, A.N. Ray, and I.D. Dua.

On 2 September 1970 a Bill entitled the Constitution (Twenty Fourth Amendment) Bill, 1970 providing that Articles 291 and 362 of the

Constitution and clause (22) of Article 366 be omitted, was introduced in the Lok Sabha and passed. On 5 September 1970 the motion for consideration of the Bill in the Rajya Sabha did not receive the requisite majority of not less than two-thirds of the members present and voting as required by Article 368 of the Constitution and was declared lost. A few hours thereafter the President of India, purporting to exercise power under clause (22) of Article 366 of the Constitution, signed an instrument withdrawing recognition of all the rulers. A communication to this effect was sent to all the rulers in India who had been previously recognized under Article 366(22) of the Constitution. The petitioners moved this Court under Article 32 of the Constitution challenging the order of the President derecognizing them as unconstitutional, *ultra vires* and void. They contended that the President had no powers to withdraw recognition of a ruler once recognized; that the order of the President derecognizing all the rulers en masse amounted to arbitrary exercise of power for a collateral purpose; that the order being one without the authority of law infringed the guarantee of fundamental rights under Articles 19(1)(f), 21, and 31 of the Constitution.

The Supreme Court delivered an important judgement in the case *Kavalappara Kottarathil Kochunni v State of Madras*[6] concerning the scope of Article 32. C.J. Das (on behalf of N.H. Bhagwati, B.P. Sinha, K. Subba Rao JJ delivered the judgement. Justice K.N. Wanchoo gave a dissenting judgement but eventually agreed with the proposed order. This, a classical judgement by Chief Justice Das, lays down the scope of Article 32 of the Constitution. Most of the work was done by M.K. Nambyar, senior advocate, who assisted M.C. Setalvad, the then Attorney-General of India. Even if the judgement laid down that there were questions of fact, a petition under Article 32 was not barred. It further ruled that declaratory relief that was proper be given to the aggrieved party. It also ruled that in such a case the infringement of the fundamental right was complete *co instanti* the passing of the amendment and therefore there could be no reason why a person so prejudicially affected by the law should not be entitled to immediately avail himself of the constitutional remedy under Article 32 of the Constitution.

The three pivotal judgements of the Supreme Court were (i) *Bank Nationalization*; (ii) *Privy Purse*; and (iii) *Kesavananda Bharati v State of Kerala*. In the *Kesavananda Bharati* case[7] it was held by the full Bench that the Constitution Twenty-fourth Amendment Act, sections 2(a) and 2(b), the Twenty-fifth Amendment Act, and the Twenty-ninth Amendment Act are valid. In this case Chief Justice S.M. Sikri delivered the judgement of the full court with Justice K.S. Hegde delivering a separate concurring judgement. The most brilliant and outstanding arguments that I have ever heard were advanced by Mr N.A. Palkhivala in the case *Golak Nath*[8] and thereafter in the *Bank Nationalization, Privy Purse,* and *Kesavananda Bharati* cases. Mr Palkhivala displayed outstanding legal acumen in all of them and the ability with which he convinced the Court was to be witnessed to be believed. Mr H.M. Seervai, the then Advocate-General of Maharashtra responded with an equally brilliant reply replete with erudition and legal acumen.

In the course of his judgement Justice Khanna held:

The power of amendment under Article 368 does not include power to abrogate the Constitution nor does it include the power to alter the basic structure or framework of the Constitution. Subject to the retention of the basic structure or framework of the Constitution, the power of amendment is plenary and includes within itself the power to amend the various Articles of the Constitution, including those relating to Fundamental Rights as well as those which may be said to relate to essential features. No part of a Fundamental Right can claim immunity from amendatory process by being described as the essence or core of that right. The power of amendment would also include within itself the power to add, alter or repeal the various Articles.

Six judges, plus the Chief Justice held one way and the six other judges took the contrary view. Mr Justice Khanna's role was pivotal, inasmuch as his acceptance of the therory of basic structure, which caused him to agree with the six judges in favour of it, caused it to become the majority judgement.

Golak Nath's case[9]

The Bench consisted of: K. Subba Rao, CJ, K.N. Wanchoo, M. Hidayatullah, J.C. Shah, S.M. Sikri, R.S. Bachawat, V. Ramaswami, J.M. Shelat, C. Bhargava, G.K. Mitter, and C.A. Vaidialingam JJ.

Hidayatullah J however upheld the validity of section 2 of the Constitution Seventeenth Amendment Act, 1961 but declared section 3 was ultra vires the amending process.

Per majority (Subba Rao CJ, Sikri, Shah, Shelat, Vaidialingham and Hidayatullah JJ) (Wanchoo, Bhargava, Mitter, Bachawat and Ramaswamy JJ dissenting).

The majority judgement held that:

(1) The doctrine of prospective overruling can be invoked only in matters arising under the Constitution,

(2) It can be applied only by the highest court of the country, i.e., the Supreme Court as it has the constitutional jurisdiction to declare laws binding on all the Courts in India,

(3) The scope of the retroactive operation of the law declared by the Supreme Court superseding its earlier decisions was left to its discretion to be moulded in accordance with the justice of the cause or matter before it.

The majority of their Lordships held that the interpretation given in *Shankari Prasad* case[10] and *Sajjan Singh* case[11] was not correct and, therefore, applied the doctrine of prospective overruling.

Kesavananda Bharati's case[12]

The Bench consisted of: S.M. Sikri, CJ, J.M. Shelat, K.S. Hegde, A.N. Grover, A.N. Ray, P. Jaganmohan Reddy, D.G. Palekar, H.R. Khanna, K.K. Mathew, M.H. Beg, S.N. Dwivedi, A.K. Mukherjea, and Y.V. Chandrachud JJ.

Held (by full court): The Constitution Twenty-fourth Amendment Act, section 2(a) and 2(b) of the Constitution Twenty-fifth Amendment Act and the Constitution Twenty-ninth Amendment Act are valid.

By majority: Per Hegde, Ray Jaganmohan, Reddy, Palekar, Khanna, Mathew, Beg, Dwivedi, Mukherjea and Chandrachud JJ: The decision of the majority in *Golaknath* that the word 'law' in Article 13(2) included amendments to the Constitution and the article opearted as a limitation upon the power to amend the Constitution in Article 368 is erroneous and is overruled.

By majority: Per Ray, Palekar, Khanna, Mathew, Beg, Dwivedi and Chandrachud JJ: The power of amendment is plenary. It includes within itself the power to add, alter or repeal the various articles of the Constitution including those relating to fundamental rights.

By majority: Per Sikri, CJ and Shelat, Hegde, Grover, Khanna, Jaganmohan Reddy and Mukherjea, JJ. (Ray, Palekar, Mathew, Beg, Dwivedi and Chandrachud, JJ, dissenting): The power to amend does not include the power to alter the basic structure or framework of the Constitution so as to change its identity.

By majority: Per Ray, Palekar, Khanna, Mathew, Beg, Dwivedi and Chandrachud JJ: (Sikri, CJ and Shelat, Hegde, Grover, Mukherjea, JJ holding contra and Jaganmohan Reddy, J leaving the question open): There are no inherent or implied limitations on the power of amendment under Article 368.

By majority: The first part of Article 31C is valid. The second part of the article, viz., 'and no law containing a declaration that it is for giving effect to such policy shall be called in question in any court on the ground that it does not give effect to such policy' is invalid.

[Sikri CJ and Shelat, Hegde, Grover and Mukherjea JJ held both the parts of Article 31C invalid.

Ray, Palekar, Mathew, Beg, Dwivedi and Chandrachud JJ held both the parts of the article valid.

Jaganmohan Reddy J held the second part of the article invalid and the first part of the article valid subject to the severance of the words 'inconsistent with or takes away' and the words 'Article 14' therein.

Khanna J held the first part of the article valid and the second part invalid.]

There was a Review Petition filed in the *Kesavananda Bharati* case.

One of the judges told me that one of the best arguments he has ever heard in his lifetime was that by Mr Nani A. Palkhivala in defending the Review Petition which was eventually dismissed.

Original Research of Mr M.K. Nambyar, Senior Advocate

The most original research of Mr M.K. Nambyar, Senior Advocate, was made in the case of *A.K. Gopalan v State of Madras.*[13] Mr Nambyar had a creative bent of mind and his research in *Gopalan's* case was classic and though the arguments he advanced were rejected by the majority, these very arguments were later, after almost twenty years, accepted by the Hon'ble Supreme Court in the case of *Maneka Gandhi v Union of India*[14] by a Bench consisting of Hon'ble Mr Justice M.H. Beg CJ, Y.V. Chandrachud, P.N. Bhagwati, V.R. Krishna Iyer, N.L. Untwalia, Murtaza Fazal Ali, and P.S. Kailasam JJ. Even the earlier Supreme Court judgements accepted Mr Nambyar's arguments on Articles 14 and 21, and the Court held in the case of *Addl. District Magistrate, Jabalpur*[15] by reference to the decision that the ambit of the protection provided by Article 21 is wide and comprehensive. The question relating to either deprivation or restriction of personal liberty raised later fell outside the ambit of Article 22 and remains unanswered by the *Gopalan* case. It is one of the greatest achievements of Mr M.K. Nambyar that all his arguments advanced in the *Gopalan* case were subsequently accepted by the Hon'ble Supreme Court as valid, and as is evidenced by this he made a great contribution to constitutional history through his research and arguments in this case.

In the case of *Additional District Magistrate, Jabalpur v S.S. Shukla & Others*, it was held that the rules of law in relation to natural justice, being on the same footing as fundamental rights, do not override the express terms of the statute.

Basic Structure of the Constitution

The limitation on the power to amend the Constitution, i.e. of not changing its basic structure, was propounded by Messrs M.K. Nambyar and N.A. Palkhivala in the case of *Golak Nath v State of Punjab*. This issue was central in the case of *His Holiness Kesavananda Bharati v State of Kerala*. The basic structure argument tilted the balance in the Court, with as we have noted, six of the twelve judges deciding one way and Justice H.R. Khanna, basing his judgement on the acceptance of the basic structure theory, causing it to become the majority judgement.

In the celebrations of January 1950 a dinner party was held at the Cricket Club of India, at which the Advocate-General, Mr C.K. Daphtary raised a toast to the establishment of the Supreme Court and observed in the course of his speech that a 'Republic without a Pub was a Relic'. That caused a great deal of embarrassment to Mr Morarji Desai, then Chief Minister of Maharashtra, as the prohibition policy was at the time in operation in Maharashtra.

In recent times the Supreme Court has, through public interest litigation initiated and intervened in many matters of civic concern such as pollution, hygiene, etc., to ensure that executive functions are properly performed. Overall, over the past fifty years it has shown its independence and ensured that the legislative and executive branches remain within the framework of the Constitution. I believe that in the future too the Supreme Court will carry forward its great traditions of providing justice to all.

Notes

[1] *Bharat Bank Ltd v Bharat Bank Employees Union* (1950) SCR 459.
[2] (1803) 1 Cranch 137.
[3] *K.C. Gajapati Narayan Deo v State of Orissa* (1954) SCR 1.
[4] *Rustom Cowasjee Cooper v Union of India* (1970) 3 SCR 530.
[5] *H.H. Maharajadhiraja Madhav Rao Jiwaji Rao v Union of India* (1971) 3 SCR 9.
[6] (1959) Supp 2 SCR 316.
[7] (1973) Supp SCR 1.
[8] *I.C. Golak Nath v State of Punjab* (1967) 2 SCR 762.
[9] Ibid.
[10] *Sankari Prasad v Union of India* (1952) SCR 89.
[11] *Sajjan Singh v State of Rajasthan* (1965) 1 SCR 933.
[12] *Supra* n. 7.
[13] (1950) SCR 88.
[14] (1978) 2 SCR 621.
[15] *Additional District Magistrate, Jabalpur v S.S. Shukla* (1976) Supp SCR 172.

Twenty-four

Present at the Creation

Inder Malhotra

Call it destiny or a mere accident of a journalist's life. To me however it was a stroke of great good luck that I was able not only to be present at the inauguration of the Supreme Court but also to report it during the first few of its formative years that were, at times, historic.

I was then a very young and a very raw reporter, working for the United Press of India on whose ashes was later built the United News of India. My experience in the troubled trade, in which I have by now spent half a century, then barely exceeded a year. I had never been to a law college though, like every beginner, I had done my share of what is termed 'court–police reporting'. Here I might mention, parenthetically, that in that lovely, bygone era the Kafkaesque sprawl of Tis Hazari courts was not even a gleam in the bleary eye of a CPWD architect. There were only a handful of magistrates' courts in a two-floor barrack-like stone building at Kashmere Gate. Even this limited space was shared by the Inspector General of Police. The District and Sessions Judge functioned from a bungalow, within walking distance from Kashmere Gate on the appropriately named Court Road. However, between them, they generated enough news for us to earn our daily bread. What is more, in the process, I had picked up a smattering of the legal jargon such as 'culpable homicide not amounting to murder', the meaning and ramifications of section 120-B, and so on.

In view of all this, and even more because of the brash overconfi-dence, born of sheer youthfulness, I hadn't batted an eyelid when my boss, Charu Sarkar, whose birth centenary was celebrated the other day, told me that to 'cover' the Supreme Court would be my job. Indeed, I took it as a merited compliment to my skills and versatility. What he said next however was a surprise. 'Initially,' he told me, 'the Court will have little work. So you will have ample time to continue doing your other assignments as well.' Being well-versed in law (he had worked in undivided Bengal's legislative assembly) and as a man of the world Charu Babu evidently knew what he was talking about.

In the initial weeks we discovered that the apex court that met from 10 to 12 in the morning and then 2 to 4 in the afternoon, in the ornate, oak-panelled former 'Chamber of Princes' in Parliament House had very little on its plate. Some of the matters before it, though important, were so technical as to be of limited interest to us, the small bunch of Supreme Court reporters most of whom, unlike me, were trained, indeed practising, lawyers. I remember some of them—M.K. Ramamurthi of the *Hindu*, alas, no more, Verma of the *Statesman*, whose current whereabouts I am unaware of, and A. Balu of the PTI, still a dear friend and neighbour—with great warmth and gratitude. It was a wonderful, cooperative group. If one of us was late for an important hearing, others were always willing to help him out with their notes.

It did not take long for even a man of Charu Sarkar's sagacity to be proved wrong. All of a sudden, covering the Supreme Court became an absorbing, full-time task for us. This minor miracle was wrought by what every lawyer worth his salt and even the lay citizen knows as the *Gopalan* case. A.K. Gopalan was, as is well known, a prominent leader of the then undivided Communist Party of India and later of the Communist Party (Marxist). In a writ petition, listed as *A.K. Gopalan v State of Madras*, Gopalan, along with one of his comrades, M.K. Kalyanasundaram, had questioned the very validity of the Preventive Detention Act under which not just they but hordes of Communists were detained without trial.

Understandably, the *Gopalan* case became a legal cause célèbre almost at once. The underlying issue was intensely emotive. Politics accentuated the emotions. The Communists were not alone in decrying the PDA; the Liberals were opposed to it even more vehemently, considering detention without trial repugnant to the very concept of democracy. Even so, the mainstream view of the political class, vigorously pressed by Sardar Patel and quietly shared by Jawaharlal Nehru, was that in Indian conditions preventive detention was an unfortunate necessity if Indian democracy was to be saved from 'disruption, subversion and destruction', in Patel's words while introducing the PDA in the provisional Parliament.

The Supreme Court judges were deeply conscious of the task before them. They knew they had to interpret the Constitution, especially the precise ambit of fundamental rights and permissible restrictions and limitations on them, with a view to deciding whether the impugned law on preventive detention could be upheld or must be thrown out.

To me, and I am sure to my journalist colleagues, to report the *Gopalan* case, unquestionably the Indian Republic's first major legal landmark, was a rich, rewarding, exciting and educative experience. Both sides put forward their rival arguments with consummate skill and remarkable eloquence. Their presentations were an uplifting blend of deep erudition, strong feelings, and judicious restraint. The six judges constituting the Bench—Kania CJ, Sastri, Fazal Ali, Mukherjea, Mahajan, and S.R. Das JJ—showed every sign of treating the matter with the utmost seriousness. Their interjections and observations were both witty and weighty. There were occasional flashes of humour and a few interludes of tension. On the whole, however, the tenor of the prolonged proceedings, during which I remained glued to my seat day after day, was such as to lend them a touch of majesty.

The undoubted hero of the hearing was M.K. Nambyar, the learned counsel who had come from down south to plead for the petitioners. (Years later I was to learn that he was the father of the even more renowned K.K. Venugopal.) He had a slightly nasal voice but whatever he said had the clarity of crystal. There was a palpable frisson in the court when he opened his arguments with the proposition that there were certain 'immutable principles of justice' which, in a democracy that had just attained independence after centuries of colonial bondage, no man-made law could override. He then went on to contend that the PDA violated these immutable principles 'brazenly and flagrantly'.

Nambyar's next point was that the law on preventive detention contravened even the Constitution and must not be allowed to remain on the statute book. Preventive detention, he argued, might have been mentioned in Article 22, but this Article could not be considered in isolation. It has to be read together with other fundamental rights enunciated in Articles 19 and 21. If this was done the impugned Act did not have a leg to stand on.

Thereafter, a prolonged debate followed on the meaning of Article 21 that lays down that no person shall be deprived of 'life and personal liberty' save through 'procedure established by law'. Nambyar contended that these words meant exactly what the Americans called 'due process of law'. Some others, who had been allowed to intervene, supported him, but the Attorney-General, M.C. Setalvad, made short work of this elaborate plea.

Tall, handsome, attractively grey, and mathematically logical in his presentation, Setalvad asked: 'Why would the Constituent Assembly substitute the words "procedure established by law" for the expression "due process of law", contained in the original draft Article, if its intention was to follow the American pattern?' If memory serves, he did inform the Court that the change was made at the behest of Sir B.N. Rau, advisor to the Constituent Assembly. Rau had discussed the matter with the famous Supreme Court judge of the United States, Frankfurter J. The American jurist had told him that the expression 'due process of law' had caused many problems in his country, and India would be well-advised not to include it in its Constitution. As far as I remember, beyond this, there was no reference to the Constituent Assembly's debate on Article 22. Nambyar was however unfazed.

He said that no legislature could possibly enact a 'lawless law', as freedom fighters had aptly described the Rowlatt Act, for example. Every law had to respect and conform to basic principles of justice. At this point Das J remarked that the learned counsel was perhaps pleading for 'procedural due process'. 'That plus more,' was Nambyar's response. Setalvad said, however, that a legislature competent enough to pass a law had the competence also to lay down the procedure.

This was one of the few junctures when there was tension. 'What happens', demanded Nambyar, 'if the legislature lays down death as punishment for a crime and prescribes that it be carried out by beheading the convict?' 'Where is the problem?' retorted Setalvad, 'death is the penalty and decapitation the procedure'.

Shortly thereafter tension was replaced by amusement. Nambyar sought permission to counter Setalvad's arguments by quoting an 'authoritative book' by a 'respected author'. There was some fidgeting around the Attorney-General's seat. Apparently, Kania CJ had an inkling of what Nambyar wanted to cite. It was Setalvad's book on civil liberties, published some years earlier. 'Is it really necessary?' asked the Chief Justice of Nambyar. Before the counsel could reply, Mahajan J interjected: 'You, please, read. I want light from whatever source it might come.' To Setalvad's embarrassment and to the amusement of others, Nambyar proceeded to quote some telling passages from the Attorney-General's book that ran totally counter to his arguments so forcefully presented to the Court. This was nice drama but, needless to say, had no effect on the outcome of the case.

Eventually the hearings ended and the day of judgement arrived. By the time the judges entered, the court chamber was overflowing with an excited and expectant crowd. We of the press were able to occupy our allotted seats only by arriving an hour earlier. A hush fell as Kania CJ started reading his judgement. It also seemed that each of the six judges was going to deliver a separate verdict. To me it was a new and incomprehensible arrangement, but M.K. Ramamurthi knew it only too well.

'Old boy', he whispered to me, 'we will have to wait for hours before we know what the verdict is'. He could not have been more wrong, for, precisely at that moment the Chief Justice, wearing the multicoloured circular cap in vogue on the West Coast, interrupted himself to announce: 'The law is valid. We have held this by a majority of four to two. We have also held two sections of the Preventive Detention Act to be *ultra vires* of the Constitution, but these are severable.'

Balu and I, as representatives of the two competing news agencies and therefore anxious to be the first with the news, immediately left the chamber to look for the nearest telephone. I could find it only in the first-floor office of Guru Dutt, a charming and helpful man, and the Court's deputy registrar and later to be its registrar. By the time I returned to my seat, the court chamber had emptied more than a little. The judges went on delivering their respective judgements.

With all due respect I must add that it was rather dull going. There was some animation when Fazl Ali J read his dissenting judgement, though he did so in a measured tone, and positive excitement when Mahajan J, in his booming voice, started his judgement with the ringing words of the preamble to the Constitution. Though he did not actually say so his meaning was clear to his audience. The Act that he was about to hold invalid went against the grain of the promises that 'we, the people of India' had made unto ourselves.

Of the two sections of the PDA that the apex court had struck down, the more alarming had provided that, in public interest, the detaining authority could refuse to disclose the grounds of detention even to the detainee. The absurdity of this power, which revealed the strange state of mind of the law-makers, was manifest even to the meanest intelligence. However, with this provision gone, there was a spate of petitions in the apex court for the quashing of some detention order or the other on the plea that the grounds of detention were either mala fide, fictitious, flimsy or inadequate. A lot of my time was spent on covering these cases which farily frequently led to the release of detainees considered 'dangerous' by the executive.

Two memorable events concerning preventive detention remain fresh in my memory even today. On the first occasion, there was great excitement inside the court and out of it because a famous British lawyer, D.N. Pritt, himself a communist, had come all the way to appear in India's Supreme Court. His mission was to seek the release of several communist leaders of Andhra Pradesh who had been detained because of their role in the armed uprising in Telengana. The word had also gone round that Pritt had declined to accept any fees or even expenses from his clients. This had further enhanced the public's already intense interest in the case that had brought him to New Delhi. Once again there was standing room only in the court chamber. Pritt was heard with great courtesy, even respect, but his plea was dismissed.

The following morning I interviewed Pritt at the Imperial Hotel, where he was staying, for the UPI. After discussing the failure of his mission, the state of the world communist movement, the Korean war that was raging then and some other matters, I asked him how he was meeting the rather heavy cost of travel to India. 'Very simple', he said, 'I wouldn't dream of charging my comrades a penny. But from here I am going to Bombay to appear in the High Court for a big business house that has 55 cases of income-tax evasion against it. They are paying me handsomely.'

The second interlude focusing on preventive detention was both unforgettable and intensely moving. It occurred during the summer vacation. Mahajan J was the vacation judge. A large number of petitions against preventive detention had piled up. Justice Mahajan dispensed with the lunch interval and announced that he would sit for as long as necessary to hear all the cases in the course of the day. He lived up to his promise in a manner that was heartwarming. With exemplary patience he listened to what each of the detainees had to say, for most of them were arguing their own cases. One of them was a Sikh in his eighties. With his flowing white beard he looked like a biblical seer. He spoke only Punjabi, both his and Justice Mahajan's mother-tongue. In the best Punjabi tradition, he addressed the judge as *'Motianwalayo'*. Literally the expression means someone bedecked with pearls. Historically, this has been the standard mode for a supplicant to address the monarch or anyone else wielding authority on the monarch's behalf.

Notwithstanding his being unlettered, this petitioner was remarkably fluent. In his rustic style he ridiculed the main ground of his detention: that he was 'a danger to public safety and the security of the nation'. He beseeched Mahajan J to decide for himself whether a frail, virtually blind man of his age could be a danger to anyone. He then added that he was being accused of having gone 'well below the earth' (underground), and urged the judge to ask the police whether or not they had arrested him from outside his home when he was sitting on a cot under a tree. He was released instantly. So were quite a number of others.

Among them was Mohan Kumaramangalam, a British-trained barrister and son of a prominent Congress leader P. Subbaroyan. Though an active communist at that time, he was later a member of Indira Gandhi's cabinet. His son, Rangarajan Kumaramangalam, is now Minister of Power in the Vajpayee government. Among the high points of the elder Kumaramangalam's career as cabinet minister was his leading role in the first of a series of supersessions in the Supreme Court.

There was an amusing sideshow to Kumaramangalam's release that found its way into print a few days later. On being set free he took a tonga (now banished from Lutyens' New Delhi but then a major means of transport in the capital) and drove to 3 Race Course Road. Now a part of the complex housing the Prime Minister, it was then the residence of his elder brother Lieutenant-General (later General and Army Chief) P.P. Kumaramangalam. Since no visitor to that house had until then arrived in a tonga, the sentry was at first reluctant to let him in, but relented when told that the new arrival was the General's brother!

The *Gopalan* case defined the law on personal liberty for more than a decade, until subsequent Supreme Court judgements overruled some of its basic tenets. Shortly thereafter the apex court had to decide how far the Union and state governments could curb the freedom of the press. The issue arose from the state of Bombay's ban on *Crossroads*, a pro-Communist weekly published from Bombay and edited by Romesh Thapar. To the extent I can remember, the hearing of this case was brief because the Bombay government's ban was hardly sustainable. It was declared invalid. The issues of the freedom of speech and expression of both the individual and the press were thrashed out in later years when I was no longer reporting the Supreme Court.

Much greater excitement was generated, however, by the zamindari abolition case. The legendary P.R. Das came from Allahabad to appear on behalf of the landlords questioning the take-over of their lands though on payment of compensation. The *Pioneer*, then published only from Lucknow, and higly partisan in favour of the talukdars of UP sent a special legal correspondent to report Das's arguments at length. The arguments went on for days and were often lively. The famous counsel knew however that his was a losing case. Land reforms, aimed at distribution of agricultural lands to the tillers were among the core commitments of the freedom struggle. There was no escape for them. Setalvad's task of rebuting P.R. Das's submissions was therefore easy. At one stage Das argued passionately that taking lands away from absentee landlords to give them to tenants was a 'classic case of robbing Peter to pay Paul'. Instantly, Setalvad was on his feet. Das yielded, and the Attorney-General said: 'Peters are few; Pauls are many. Moreover, the Peters have been exploiting the Pauls.'

P.R. Das was unquestionably the dominant figure during the rather stretched zamindari hearings. There were however several other lawyers, representing hordes of petitioners, who also had a lengthy say. One of them, P.S. Bindra evoked roars of laughter by contending that all anti-zamindari laws be thrown out summarily because 'Johnnies who are not properly elected enacted them.'

The pièce de resistance came when, on a rather complex point of law, P.R. Das quoted from a judgement of S.K. Das, then Chief Justice of the Patna High Court, who later became a Supreme Court judge. To the surprise of S.R. Das J, who was on the Bench hearing the zamindari case, P.R. Das also cited what S.R. Das had observed as Chief Justice of the Punjab High Court and later, in another case in the Supreme Court. Thereupon, Mahajan J remarked: 'I need clarification. There is a complete confusion of Dases. P.R. Das quotes S.K. Das in one breath, he quotes my brother S.R. Das in another, and he might bring up some other Das, for all I know.' P.R. Das: 'My Lord, there is only one truly famous Mahajan. Is it my fault that every second eminent man turns out to be a Das?'

I was still reporting the Supreme Court, though by fits and starts because of other preoccupations, when the strength of the Court was raised and a second Bench started functioning in a first-floor room of Parliament House. Justice N.H. Bhagwati, father of a subsequent CJI, presided over this bench when some matter concerning the State Bank of India, formerly the Imperial Bank of India, was under discussion. I mention this only to be able to report that even then some obstreperous litigant or unduly loquacious lawyer was not beyond wasting the court's valuable time. P.D. Shamdasani, who owned a few shares of the State Bank filibustered the proceedings for several hours without saying anything besides hurling accusations at the bank's management. The judges found it hard to persuade him to resume his seat. For his part, he even tried to teach the Bench the correct pronunciation of some words. Their Lordships laughed away his effrontery.

All these are, of course, my recollections. May I conclude with just one reflection? With the utmost respect I would submit to the apex court that it should make its judgements much more concise and succinct than they are. To wade through over 250 typed pages of the six separate judgements in the *Gopalan* case was a tough task fifty years ago. Since then judgements have become even longer. I never attended the Court during the hearing of the epoch-making *Kesavananda Bharati* case, but, over a period of time, I did manage to read the thirteen judgements that laid down the doctrine of the 'basic structure' of the Constitution that cannot be amended by Parliament. It was a nerve-racking exercise. To reformulate an old cliché, let brevity be the soul of wit.